ADVANCE PRAISE FOR THE SECOND EDITION

"I welcome this second edition of *This Sacred Earth*, more comprehensive and inclusive than ever, probing the opportunities—and the pitfalls—in bringing religious experience to bear on caring for nature. Can Earth's marvelous religious diversity help to save Earth and its marvelous biodiversity? We can inherit the Earth only in justice and love. The promise of religion is splendidly and urgently documented here."

—Holmes Rolston, III, University Distinguished Professor, Colorado State University

"The updated edition of *This Sacred Earth* brings together an impressive selection of recent insights on Religion As If the Earth Mattered. We dare not settle for less."

—Charlene Spretnak, author of *The Resurgence of the Real*

"The second edition of *This Sacred Earth* documents the exponential acceleration of the greening of religion. Back in 1967, Lynn White, Jr. could plausibly claim that the "historical roots of our ecologic crisis" were the Abrahamic religions. Now those religions and practically all the others of the world are uniting to resist the real roots of our ecologic crisis, the worship of Mammon and the cult of Consumerism. Roger Gottlieb has done a masterful job in covering the diversity of the spiritual responses to this newest form of idolatry—from traditional world religions such as Judaism, Christianity, Islam, Hinduism, and Buddhism to new ecology-inspired spiritual movements such as Deep Ecology and Ecofeminism. It remains *the* textbook for college courses that focus on the link between religion and environment."

—J. Baird Callicott, Institute of Applied Sciences, University of North Texas

"A rich and valuable compendium assembled around the premise that Judeo-Christian belief is moving from belief to disbelief in the inherent value of earth and its creatures. Writings that support this premise in the central text are introduced with spiritual and nature writings and followed by writings from Islamic, Hindu, Buddhist, Animal Rights, Ecofeminist and Deep Ecology perspectives. A fine sourcebook for a wide range of religious and spiritual environmental writings."

—Calvin B. DeWitt, Professor of Environmental Studies, University of Wisconsin-Madison
and Director, Au Sable Institute of Environmental Studies

PRAISE FOR THE FIRST EDITION

"The most comprehensive anthology available on the convergence of ecology and religion, an essential link for our future on the planet. Every college should have a course on this topic, and they all should use this book."

—David Rothenberg, editor of *Terra Nova* and author of *Hands End*

"This collection, together with its excellent introductions, makes manifest the presence in our society of a new religious movement that crosses all traditional lines. For millions of people, now, a faith that does not celebrate the Earth is meaningless or worse. This book makes it clear that this faith exists. Perhaps it can rally the energies to change our collective behavior. It should be made widely available."

—Professor John B. Cobb, Claremont College

"There is no better single volume that covers all the essential facets of religious environmentalism. Highly recommended."

—*The Readers Review*

" . . . an ambitious and successful anthology . . . Gottlieb addresses religionists and secular humanists alike . . . after an initial section of selections from writers who link nature and spirit (from Thoreau and Emerson to Aldo Leopold and Annie Dillard), there is an especially useful survey of how traditional religions have viewed nature, with well-chosen excerpts from Hindu, Aztec, Greek, Jewish, Christian, Taoist, Islamic, and African sources."

—*Cross Currents*

" . . . an impressive chorus of thoughtful voices urging that our efforts to attain spiritual wisdom be grounded in ecological wisdom."

—*Whole Earth*

" . . . provocative, ecumenical, and immensely useful."

—*Sierra*

THIS
SACRED
EARTH

T H I S
SACRED
E A R T H

Religion, Nature, Environment

SECOND EDITION

EDITED BY
ROGER S. GOTTLIEB

Routledge

New York and London

Published in 2004 by
Routledge
29 West 35th Street
New York, NY 10001
www.routledge-ny.com

Published in Great Britain by
Routledge
11 New Fetter Lane
London EC4P 4EE
www.routledge.co.uk

Printed in the United States of America on acid-free paper.

10 9 8 7 6 5 4 3 2 1

Every effort has been made to contact all of the copyright holders, but if any have been omitted inadvertently, the publishers will be pleased to make the necessary arrangements at the earliest opportunity.

Library of Congress Cataloging in Publication Data

This sacred earth : religion, nature, environment / edited by Roger S. Gottlieb. — 2nd ed.
        p. cm.
Includes bibliographical references.
    ISBN 0-415-94359-0 (alk. paper) — ISBN 0-415-94360-4 (pbk. : alk. paper)
    1.   Human ecology—Religious aspects. 2.   Philosophy of nature. 3. Ecofeminism. 4.   Deep ecology—Religious aspects.   I. Gottlieb, Roger S.

GF80.T49 2003
304.2—dc22   2003016009

For all beings who have suffered needlessly because of human folly and injustice:
May we remember their pain and change our ways.

CONTENTS

PART III   *Ecotheology in an Age of Environmental Crisis Transforming Tradition*   189

PREFACE
AND
ACKNOWLEDGMENTS

This book surveys traditional religious perspectives on nature, and shows how contemporary theologians, spiritual teachers, and religious institutions are responding to humanity's devastation of the environment.

I have chosen particular selections for a number of reasons, including historical importance, depth of insight, and quality of writing or representation of a particular tradition. And I have tried to enable the reader of *This Sacred Earth* to gain both a comprehensive overview of the field and some quiet moments of spiritual illumination. While I am happy with what is here, I also regret that many fine authors were omitted.

There is perhaps a disproportionate amount of space given here to Judaism and Christianity relative to other religions. My reasoning is that these are the principal traditions of the overwhelming majority of the people who will read this book; and that the close relationship between the dominant Western traditions and the environmental effects of European industrialism and imperialism make it critically important for us to assess quite carefully the content and meaning of those traditions. There are also, however, extensive selections from non-Western religions, indigenous teachings, and nondenominational spiritual thinkers.

This book is organized into seven parts, each with a particular focus. This focus is outlined in the general introduction and in introductions to each part. Nevertheless, a number of pieces are hard to categorize, and some overlap exists. For instance, Stephanie Kaza's essay on Buddhist environmental activism is placed in Part III, "Transforming Tradition," but since the essay also presents material concerning Buddhist environmental social action, it is also relevant to Part VII, "Ecology, Religion, and Society." Clearly, some of the analyses of past views in Part II contain material relevant to contemporary ecotheology, in Part III.

One cannot help approaching the task of anthologizing such a vast range of material with a certain amount of fear and trembling—and, perhaps, a little chutzpah as well. Perhaps I would not have been so bold if I did not think that this book was needed; or if I were not confident, as I indeed am, that other books in this area will compensate for whatever deficiencies exist here.

As the preparation of a manuscript draws to a close, there is nothing more pleasurable than giving thanks to the many people who helped along the way.

To begin with, I am deeply indebted to Joanna Macy, Miriam Greenspan, and Bill McKibben; all three helped open my mind and heart to the spiritual dimensions of the environmental crisis.

Bettina Bergo and Miriam Greenspan provided extremely useful responses to my own contributions to this book.

Many colleagues took time from their own busy lives to give me very helpful feedback on proposed contents and to suggest resources: Carol Adams, William Beers, Ellen Bernstein, Eugene Bianchi, Marcia Falk, Ethan Fladd, Tamara Frankiel, Beverly Harrison, Stephanie Kaza, Belden Lane, Catherine Mchale, John Mabry, Wes Mott, Linda Nef, Kodzo Tita Pongo, Judith Scoville, Bron Taylor, Arthur Waskow, and Susan Zakin.

My very special appreciation goes to staff at Worcester Polytechnic Institute: Penny Rock from the Humanities Department and the Interlibrary Loan Services of Gordon Library.

Routledge has been a pleasure to work with in this process. Maura Burnett helped organize a response session at the American Academy of Religion. Maura and Mary Carol De Zuetter put in a great deal of work dealing with a seemingly endless list of permissions. Andrew Rubin has been close at hand for promotions and marketing.

Marlie Wasserman, my editor at Routledge, deserves a separate appreciation. Working with me from the beginning, she provided enthusiastic support and intelligent feedback, was always there to answer my anxious phone calls, and made a challenging project much easier.

Most importantly, this book is only possible because of the open-hearted and clear-minded writings of dozens of theologians, scholars and spiritual seekers.

Together with grassroots activists, environmental organizations, passionate neighborhood committees, international coalitions and lovers of life everywhere—and with the help of God, Goddess, and the Spirit of Trees, Rocks, and Water—may we find a way to rediscover the sacredness of the earth.

ACKNOWLEDGMENTS FOR THE SECOND EDITION

My gratitude and appreciation:

To all those who found the first edition useful enough to warrant a second edition.

To the supportive, helpful, and highly polished staff at Routledge, especially Tenessa Gemelke for her efforts on the near-endless permissions work.

To the many friends, colleagues, and perfect strangers who made suggestions for changes: Jim Ball, David Barnhill, Barbara Darling-Smith, Richard Foltz, Lorel Fox, Lois Lorentzen, Les Sponsel, Bron Taylor, Mary Evelyn Tucker, Mark Wallace, and Glenn Whelker.

To the members of the Religion and Ecology section of the American Academy of Religion: for your fellowship, intelligence, and passion.

And, most of all, to the brave and dedicated souls who are doing the work.

Introduction

RELIGION IN AN AGE OF ENVIRONMENTAL CRISIS

If we were not so single-minded
about keeping our lives moving,
and for once could do nothing,
perhaps a huge silence
might interrupt this sadness
of never understanding ourselves
and of threatening ourselves with
death.

—Pablo Neruda

The best remedy, for those who are afraid, lonely, or unhappy is to go outside, somewhere where they can be quite alone with the heavens, nature, and God. Because only then does one feel that all is as it should be and that God wishes to see people happy, amidst the simple beauty of nature. As long as this exists, and it certainly always will, I know that then there will always be comfort for every sorrow . . .

—Anne Frank

If a person kills a tree before its time, it is like having murdered a soul.

—Rebbe Nachman of Bratslav,
eighteenth century

RELIGION IN AN AGE OF ENVIRONMENTAL CRISIS

THE PROBLEM BEFORE THE PROBLEM

The problem is humanity's devastation of the natural world. The problem before the problem is that it is very difficult to face this devastation. Threats to the environment are so often threats to our own lives and the people—or parts of nature—that we love, threats about which we can often do virtually nothing. And the hazards involved are so enormous, so potentially irreversible, that it may seem easier to hide from the information than to take it in. As Joanna Macy observes, ". . . we are barraged by data that render questionable the survival of our culture, our species, and even our planet as a viable home for conscious life. Despair, in this context . . . is the loss of the assumption that the species will inevitably pull through."[1] Not surprisingly many of us skip over the environmental articles in the newspaper, pass up the magazines focusing on ecological issues, and do our best to ignore the lurking feelings of doom. Wouldn't we prefer to continue with "business as usual"?

On the first day of my environmental philosophy course I tell students of my own fear, grief, and anger about the ecological crisis. I then ask them to speak in turn about what they feel. They respond hesitantly, emboldened by my example but still unsure that a university classroom is the proper place for emotions. As the hour progresses, however, their statements become increasingly more revealing.

"I'm terribly angry," one will say, "because the field where I used to hunt for grasshoppers was turned into a parking lot for a mall; and they hardly even use it. What a waste."

"I'm scared," a young woman admits. "Every time I go out in the sun in the summer I think about skin cancer. My aunt died from it."

Several young men tell me they don't see much use in thinking about all these problems. I ask one: "What would happen if you *did* think about it?" "I don't know," he replies,

"I'm not sure I could go on with what I'm supposed to do in this life. If I started to cry, I might never stop."

It helps to begin not with a long list of environmental problems, but with the acknowledgment that our anguish over the fate of the earth is a real element in our everyday emotional lives. Bury these emotions as we may, they surface whenever we hear of another oil spill, another summer day in the city with "unhealthy air," another childhood forest or meadow turned into a parking lot. Before we can take in or effectively act in response to the environmental crisis we must admit just how deeply we feel for the earth. This admission helps us emerge from hidden despair, psychic numbing and the frantic attempts to fill our time with a "busyness" which distracts us from the problem. The alternative is to continue to mask the truth—or to pretend we feel nothing about it. This strategy takes a significant psychic toll. If we deny what we feel when we read of a species made extinct, or a leaking toxic dump, we may start to deaden ourselves, and come to suffer what Kierkegaard called "a disorder of feelings, the disorder consisting in not having any."

There is nothing shameful or "weak" in the pain we feel about the environment. Grief and fear are rational responses to our losses and perils. And sorrow over what we have done is a hopeful sign that despite everything we can still love and mourn.

THE PROBLEM

> Pesticides are used in agriculture in all parts of the world. While most cases of acute, high-exposure poisoning are related to occupational exposure (there are more than 200,000 deaths world-wide each year, mainly in this population, from acute pesticide poisoning), significant exposure can occur through ingestion of treated food. . . . With respect to low-level exposure to humans, the toxic outcomes of greatest concern are cancer, immunotoxicity, and the reproductive effects. . . .[2]

> Weedkiller found in high levels in US tap water.
>
> —*Boston Globe*, October 19, 1994

> In our conversations with Filipinos about their dreams and hopes and their children's prospects, they often raise on their own the topic that we have come to study: the future of the country's natural resources.

"What will your children be when they grow up?" we ask a poor fisherman in Bataan. He sighs. "My father was a fisherman and so I too am a fisherman. I was born a fisherman. But the fish are dying. So there will be no fish for my son to catch. . . . A peasant woman whose family grows rice on a small plot of land . . . gives a strikingly similar answer: "The forests are disappearing, and so the soil of our rice field is being washed to the sea. There will be no soil left by the time our children are grown. . . . How will they grow rice?"[3]

[In Central America] the widespread destruction of forests for cattle ranching is . . . resulting in regional climatic changes. A pristine rainforest canopy acts as a protective umbrella, breaking the force of torrential downpours and recycling the moisture throughout the ecosystem. But with the clearing of the forest, water-recycling systems are destroyed. Daytime temperatures rise on the converted savannas, decreasing relative humidity and precipitation levels while increasing the rate of transpiration. As a result the grasslands and surrounding forests suffer from increased drought stress. . . . When it does rain, the water rushes off the barren slopes to cause downstream flooding, soil erosion, and siltation of waterways.[4]

The U.S. government estimates that over sixteen thousand active landfills have been sopped with industrial and agricultural hazardous wastes. Most are located near small towns and farming communities—and the contents of all of them, according to the Environmental Protection Agency, will eventually breach their linings and penetrate the soil, as many already have done. Underground chemical and petroleum storage tanks scattered throughout cities, suburbs, and rural America number between three and five million; 30 percent already leak. . . . According to industry's own reports, 22 billion pounds of toxic chemicals are spewed into the air, water, and soil each year. . . . The Congressional Office of Technology Assessment estimates the real figure to be vastly higher.[5]

Con Ed Admits to Conspiracy to Cover Up Asbestos in Blast.

—*New York Times*, November 1, 1994

Which of the following animals is extinct; and which is endangered?

—Quiz on the back of a breakfast cereal box

Daddy, could a time come when there are no more trees?

—Anna Gottlieb, age 7

The above passages reveal some of the critical features of the environmental crisis. First, there is its sheer magnitude: the staggering amount of toxic chemicals in the U.S. alone; the fact that pesticides are used in "every part of the world." Second, the range of areas represented even in these few quotations reminds us that the environmental crisis is a global event.

Third, however, no matter how immense this crisis, its impact is immediate, personal, direct. The disappearance of fish from *this* river, the high incidence of leukemia on *this* street, *this* particular childhood Eden lost to a mall. Facile generalizations about "tree-huggers" or "environmental extremists" make little sense when we find out, for instance, that the Canadian Dermatological Society has advised that because of UV radiation coming through a weakened ozone layer, school playgrounds must be built in shaded areas and that recess should never be between 10 AM and 2 PM; or that due to environmental pollution average male sperm counts have dropped 50 percent over the last 50 years and testicular cancer has risen 300 to 400 percent.

A brief overview of the environmental crisis provides us with at least the following eight areas of acute concern:

1. *Global climate/atmospheric change.* Burning fossil fuels, releasing methane into the atmosphere, and destroying the rainforest threaten us with an unprecedentedly fast global warming. This climate change will alter the living conditions for the entire planet and lead to what Bill McKibben calls the "end of nature." That is, an earth in which *everything* bears the stamp of human acts, because *everything* is affected by the human-altered climate. Global warming will cause unforeseen damage to agriculture, wild lands, and animals; and the rise of the oceans from melting polar icecaps will submerge coastlines and threaten the lives of island peoples.

The reduction in the ozone layer, which shields the earth from UV rays, poses an immediate danger to human health because these rays damage the immune system, increase skin cancer and cataracts, and threaten the DNA molecules of all living things. Also vulnerable are the phytoplankton, the foundation of the oceanic food chain, which are weakened by UV exposure.[6]

2. *Toxic wastes.* Chemical, heavy metal, biological, and nuclear wastes have accumulated in staggering quantities. Concentrated in dumps and distributed throughout the atmosphere, water system, and land, they are found in every region, no matter how remote. The result is a plague of environmentally caused diseases; most obviously the dramatic increase in cancer, both in general and especially in areas closest to sources of toxic materials.

3. *Loss of land.* From overuse of chemical agriculture and the destruction of forests, the loss of land threatens the production of food throughout the developing nations and leads

to erosion and desertification. Massive erosion can also destroy ecosystem balance in rivers and coastal fishing areas.

4. *Loss of species*. This has become what some call a "crisis of biodiversity." With the decimation of a variety of habitats, as well as the killing of animals for sport, use, or food, current rates of extinction are reducing the number of species to the lowest since the end of the age of dinosaurs, 65 million years ago. The result is incalculable *human* loss. Potential medicines vanish, ecosystems are destabilized, and irreplaceable natural beauties are lost forever. There is also damage to our ethical faith in humanity's own worth. Those who believe that nature has its own value apart from people's interests see these mass, human-caused extinctions as a kind of mass murder.

5. *Loss of wilderness*. Ecosystems free to develop without human interference or intrusion have become increasingly rare. Besides the loss of biodiversity this entails, human beings face a strange and paradoxical loneliness. People are everywhere; yet we are haunted by the loss of that natural Other which has been our long-time companion for biological ages. As Edward Abbey observes, "We need wilderness, because we are wild animals."[7]

6. *Devastation of indigenous peoples*. These are the last examples of human communities integrated into nonhuman nature. As their environments are poisoned, native peoples lose their land and culture, and too often their lives.

> The discovery of anything which can be exploited is tantamount to the crack of doom for the Indians, who are pressured to abandon their lands or be slaughtered on them. And economic discoveries do not have to be exceptional for the Indians to be plundered.[8]

7. *Human patterns and quantities of consumption*. These patterns are unsustainable. The developed world's insatiable consumerism depletes natural resources and contributes to global warming and the accumulation of waste. In the underdeveloped world overpopulation relative to existing technological resources and political organization decimates the landscape. In particular, a widespread culture of meat-eating undermines ecosystem integrity through the overutilization of water, grazing land, chemicalized pesticides, and food additives; and constitutes a horribly inefficient drain on resources of vegetable food that might alleviate world hunger.

8. *Genetic engineering*. Such engineering seems to promise miracle cures for everything from food shortages to inherited diseases. Yet it also menaces us with the dismal prospects of engineered life forms and the potentially catastrophic invention of insufficiently tested organisms. Just as the nuclear industry developed before adequate thought was given to the disposal of nuclear wastes or the global effects of nuclear fallout, so genetic engineering has come into existence before we have, as a world society, given adequate consideration to what this magnitude of human control over evolution could possibly mean. Given

our track record with pesticides and toxic chemicals, and the level of maturity of our political and economic elites, it seems highly doubtful that we are ready to create new life forms.

And so we have an "environmental crisis." And this has created, in turn, an emotional crisis of despair over our planet's future, and a crisis of confidence in humanity's right to further develop industrial civilization. Past certitudes about humanity's special place in the world seem absurd when our species is poisoning that world.

In fact, *the environmental crisis is a crisis of our entire civilization.* It casts doubt on our political, economic, and technological systems, on theoretical science and Western philosophy, on how we consume or eat. Corporate greed, nationalistic aggression, obsessions with technological "development," philosophical attitudes privileging "man's" reason above the natural world, addictive consumerism . . . all these collaborate in the emerging ruin of the earth.

Yet from the early conservation efforts of the late nineteenth century to the wide range of organizations throughout the world today, a global environmental movement has resisted this ruin. Environmentalists recognize that despite the enormous accomplishments of our technological civilization, we have begun a process of environmental degradation not unlike a slow collective suicide. Accordingly, there are now a plethora of political, social, intellectual, and spiritual responses to the environmental crisis, responses which seek to keep people from further devastating humanity's own natural setting.

RELIGION IN AN AGE OF ENVIRONMENTAL CRISIS

By "religion" I mean those systems of belief, ritual, institutional life, spiritual aspiration, and ethical orientation which are premised on an understanding of human beings as *other* or *more than simply* their purely social or physical identities. Teachings can be marked as "religious" in the way they assert (as in Judaism, Christianity, and Islam) that people are essentially connected to a Supreme Being whose authority is distinct from worldly powers; or by the Buddhist belief that we can achieve a state of consciousness which transcends the attachments and passions of our ordinary social egos; or in the Wiccan celebration of human sexuality as an embodiment of the life-giving force of the Goddess rather than as the source of purely individual gratification. Religious attitudes thus turn on a sense of what theologian Paul Tillich called "ultimate significance." They seek to orient us to that which is of compelling importance beyond or within our day-to-day concerns.

At the same time, religions provide norms of conduct for the familiar interpersonal settings of family, community, and world. Religious moral teachings presuppose a spiritual foundation and are meant to root our everyday behavior in a spiritual truth about who we really are.

Finally, religions provide rituals—acts of prayer, meditation, collective contrition, or celebration—to awaken and reinforce a personal and communal sense of our connections to the Ultimate Truth(s). These practices aim to cultivate an impassioned clarity of vision in which the world and the self are, as Miriam Greenspan put it, "charged with the sacred."

This understanding of "religion" allows us to include here paradigm religions of both West and East, suppressed native traditions, and prepatriarchal goddess worship; as well as more individual, idiosyncratic, and eclectic spiritual visions. All such voices will be heard in this volume.

How has religion shaped our understanding of and our conduct towards nature? And how has the environmental crisis challenged and transformed modern theology and spiritual practice? As key components of every human civilization, religions are necessarily critical elements of the environmental crisis. Yet in recent years religious institutions have also tried to alter our current destructive patterns. In short, religions have been neither simple agents of environmental domination nor unmixed repositories of ecological wisdom. In complex and variable ways, they have been both.

Historically, religions have taught us to perceive and to act on nonhuman nature in terms of particular *human* interests, beliefs, and social structures. Through religious myths and laws we have socialized nature, framing it in human terms. And to a great extent we have done so to satisfy *our* needs, abilities, and power relations. Yet at the same time *religion has also represented the voice of nature to humanity*. Spiritual teachings have celebrated and consecrated our ties to the nonhuman world, reminding us of our delicate and inescapable partnership with air, land, water, and fellow living beings. To assess religion's view of nature—and to see how contemporary theology deals with the environmental crisis—we must therefore attend with care to the full range of writings and practices which religious traditions offer.

Consider, for instance, that many writers have found in biblical writings about "man's" right to "master the earth" (Genesis 1:28) an essential source for the havoc wreaked by Western societies upon the earth. Other religious environmentalists have discovered environmentally positive passages in classic texts, and claim that Judaism and Christianity are "really" more environmentally minded than they seemed at first glance. Yet whatever marginalized ecological voices or texts may be found now, it is also true that the Judeo-Christian tradition was taken by its leading authorities to have a predominant meaning over the centuries, and especially during the modern age. And this meaning was typically concerned (at best) with the "wise use" of the earth and its creatures, and not with any notion of their inherent value.[9]

> The social and moral traditions that have been dominant in the West . . . have not involved
> the idea that animals, trees, or the land in their own right, as distinct from their owners or
> their Creator, have moral standing. Only a few saints and reformers have taught that people
> have direct moral responsibilities to nonhuman creatures.[10]

In support of this observation, we need only reflect on how few and far between were the religious voices opposing the last century's juggernaut of technological development and environmental degradation.

In any case, the full answer to our dilemmas will not be found in identifying past views. The environmental agenda of religious is continually set and reset by their adherents, as they engage in the complex and controversial process of reinventing traditions to meet contemporary concerns.

Further, whatever of environmental value we may find in particular Biblical passages (e.g., the injunction to be kind to your enemy's animals) or writings of particular saints (e.g., the nature poetry of 12th-century Catholic Julian of Norwich), it is too much to expect ancient traditions to be fully adequate to the crisis of today. Despite the brilliance or revelatory quality of the founding teachings, or the way those teachings have been elaborated over the centuries, we now live in a very different world.

To begin with, ancient traditions could not have foreseen the scope of modern technological power. No past empire was able to threaten the earth's climate or so pollute the air and water that mothers' breast milk may not be fit for their babies to drink. Also, the spread of democracy and the critical intellectual tendencies embedded in Enlightenment philosophy and modern science cast heavy doubt on any particular religion's claims to absolute truth. This doubt leads some people to a complete rejection of religion. For many others, abandoning the claim to literal veracity of a particular theology allows adherents of very different traditions to recognize common ground and celebrate each other's spiritual gifts. This ecumenism is, I believe, quite beyond the imagination of earlier religious thinkers.[11]

Similarly, the recent feminist critique of religion has identified patriarchal biases in virtually all established traditions. Modern spiritual life therefore has the historically unprecedented task of respecting women as individuals and recognizing the social contributions and spiritual gifts entailed by women's experience.

This book—and the enormous literature from which it has been taken—demonstrates that there has already been an extensive range of religious responses to environmental problems. Within this range we can identify four general approaches, more than one of which may be found in any given writer.

Ecotheologians have sought to *reinterpret* old traditions: finding and stressing passages in classic texts that help us face the current crisis. Thus we are reminded that the *Talmud* instructs us not to live in a city without trees; or that St. Francis's love of animals makes him a kind of early, Christian, Deep Ecologist. Thinkers have also tried to *extend* more familiar religious beliefs, especially ethical ones concerning love and respect for other people, to non-human nature. Nature becomes the Body of God, or the "neighbor" whom we must treat as we would like to be treated. Creative ecotheologians *synthesize* elements of different traditions.[12] As part of the ecumenical tendency of contemporary spiritual life described above, we see some Christian thinkers unhesitatingly using Taoist images of humanity's integration into a natural setting, or Jews quoting Buddhist nature poetry. In particular, ideas from indigenous, or native peoples—communities whose relations to nature originated before the current mode of the domination of the earth—have been studied. Finally spiritual thinkers are *creating* new ideas, practices, and organizations.

Contemporary ecotheology voices the sorrow of a broken-hearted earth and expresses our despair over the past and fear for the future. Simultaneously, theoreticians of religion and the environment alike question whether and in what ways religious energies can be connected to secular environmental philosophy and ecological activism.

Yet why do we need religion at all? Why can't governments, corporations, and individuals just stop polluting and eliminating species—and let religion be an essentially private matter of personal faith?

The first answer is that for many people religious beliefs provide primary values concerning our place in the universe, our obligations to other people and other life forms, and what makes up a truly "good" life. All these are part of the religious world-view and part of what must be scrutinized and altered if we are to pull through. Further, we have historical examples, from the U.S. civil rights movement to the nonviolent campaigns of Indian independence from the British, of creative and successful mergings of religion and social action.

In fact, the significance of religion is heightened because several of the guiding lights of modernity have become increasingly suspect. Faith in science and materialist/liberal democracies has been undermined by the political violence, technological disasters and cultural bankruptcy of the late 20th century. Purely secular radical politics have been rendered doubtful by the economic failures and totalitarian political excesses of communism. Hence spiritual perspectives can be a source of social direction as well as personal inspiration. From Buddhist teachings about compassion for animals to Christian creation theology, from Native American images of the "sacred hoop" of life to indigenous people's political resistance to the environmental desecration of their sacred lands, religious teachings and practices are bound up in humanity's ongoing struggles to live in harmony with an increasingly threatened earth.

I want also to stress that the pain we feel over the environmental crisis is *not* solely a self-interested desire to lower cancer rates or retain some wilderness in which to hike. Our response is, in the broadest sense of the term, a *spiritual* one; that is, it involves our deepest concerns about what is truly of lasting importance in our lives. I remember reading McKibben's *The End of Nature*—with its thesis that human global climate alteration spells the "end of nature" as an autonomous presence—and feeling a deep sense of desolation. I also felt that an enormous and unrectifiable sacrilege had been committed, a sacrilege of which I, as a beneficiary of modern technological society, was partly guilty. My feelings were not simply a fear for my own health or recreational possibilities, but a concern for what I would like to call my soul.

Finally, spiritual resources can help us face the truth of the present without giving way to despair. Environmentally oriented prayer, meditation, celebration, and confession all seem particularly appropriate to our current plight.

ABOUT THE BOOK

This Sacred Earth provides representative historical and contemporary selections from traditional religions and contemporary ecotheology. Original sources, documents, and the writings of modern theologians and social activists are joined by scholarly reflections on theology, religious history, and religion's social role.

We begin with reflections by a variety of naturalist writers. Here we find that a spiritual encounter with nature may arise in the most casual and unexpected of ways; and that a brief moment of grace on this sacred earth may forever alter how we think and feel about our one and only home.

Part II surveys the views of traditional religions on nature. This survey will give the reader a sense of both the historic roots and the heterogeneity of religious attitudes in this area. By "nature" I mean that commonsense construct in which we view the universe, the geological earth and its life forms as a prehuman unity, separate and independent from humanity. We will see that religions provided the normative basis for respectful as well as domineering views of nature, for ecological sanity as well as unrestrained domination. It is this broad scope which allows some contemporary ecotheologians to recommend a "return to the sources" while others council a rejection of tradition altogether.

Parts III through V investigate "Ecotheology in an Age of Environmental Crisis." Here we realize that the concept of the "environment" has emerged alongside that of "nature" to express our awareness of how human society threatens the very conditions which make our lives possible. The "environment" we might say, is nonhuman nature considered as an object of human practice; especially, it is nonhuman nature considered as the victim of our cancerous models of economic growth, commodity worship, militarism, scientism, and patriarchal ideologies of domination. While past religious traditions focused their major attention on "nature" and paid little if any attention to "the environment," contemporary theology is now facing a natural world threatened by humanity.

Throughout Parts III, IV and V there are contrasts between "liberal" or "conservationist" outlooks, which seek to preserve "nature" because of human needs; and a more "deep ecological" approach which sees nature as having value in its own right. Similarly, some viewpoints tend to focus solely on the natural world; while others see integral connections between the domination of nature and the oppression of social groups.

Part III contains writings clearly identifiable by religious tradition; for example, new environmental theologies by self-identified Jews, Christians, and Buddhists. Part IV focuses on ecofeminist spirituality, which is based in the realization that patriarchal society dominates women and nature with parallel ideologies and practices. Spiritual deep ecology—which offers an ecological rethinking of human identity—is explored in Part V.

In Part VI, "Religious Practice for a Sacred Earth," we encounter a variety of religious observances devised in response to the environment in general and the ecological crisis in particular.

Part VII explores the complex relations between religions, society, and politics. There now exists a spiritually based sense that modern industrial practices are not just "polluting the environment," but are actually desecrating the earth. This sensibility has been embodied in political movements resisting the forces of ecological degradation; and joined that resistance to concerns structured around class, race, gender, or ethnic differences. This Part also explores some of the familiar but confusing aspects of trying to live a spiritual life while remaining closely in touch with one's social surroundings.

Simultaneously the voice of God and the product of human insight, folly, and hope, religious teachings are part of social struggles. Our study of religion and the environment, therefore, raises many questions. I will explore some of these in Introductions to each Part, but some deserve brief mention here.

Who has the right to appropriate—to write about, teach, and profit from—the environmental practices and ideas of the indigenous or native peoples who have been the victims of cultural and physical genocide?

When we talk of what "people" have done to the earth, will we recognize the ways in which the environmental crisis was created not just by a generalized "humanity" but by social structures determining decisive differences in power and wealth, differences mapped along lines of race and gender as well as class?

If we seek a truly "sustainable" social order who or what will we be sustaining? and whose voices will determine what is truly of value and what is unnecessary or oppressive?

How much of our environmental concern stems from our own desires for health or pleasure—and how much from a love of nature for its own integrity and value?

Can we harmonize our love of God's creation with our concern for social justice? Can either be truly fulfilled without the other?

❧

The task before us is very great and the outcome deeply uncertain. Yet if we devote ourselves to it, we will at least have the satisfaction of knowing that what we are doing with our lives is important. I hope that this text may fuel our awareness of what needs to be done—even as it also helps remind us of our simple joy in the divinity of the earth.

NOTES

1. Joanna Macy, *World as Lover, World as Self* (Berkeley, CA: Parallax Press, 1991), pp. 16–7.

2. Elizabeth Bowen and Howard Hu, "Food Contamination due to Environmental Pollution," in *Critical Condition: Human Health and the Environment*, eds. Eric Chivian, Michael McCally, Howard Hu and Andrew Haines (Cambridge: MIT Press, 1993), pp. 50–52.

3. Robin Broad, *Plundering Paradise: The Struggle for the Environment in the Philippines* (Berkeley: University of California Press, 1993), p. 17.

4. Daniel Faber, *Environment Under Fire: Imperialism and the Ecological Crisis in Central America* (New York: Monthly Review Press, 1993), p. 144.

5. Fred Setterberg and Lonny Shavelson, *Toxic Nation: The Fight to Save Our Communities from Chemical Contamination* (New York: John Wiley & Sons, 1993), p. 4.

6. Some scientists believe that the recent dramatic reduction in frog populations stems from exposure of their eggs to increased UV radiation.

7. Edward Abbey, *The Journey Home* (New York: Penguin, 1977), p. 229.

8. Darcy Ribeiro, Brazilian anthropologist, quoted in Al Gedicks, *The New Resource Wars* (Boston: South End Press, 1992), p. 13.

9. The complexity of the issues is revealed in the considerable debate over the precise meaning of this (and other) Biblical passages. Some commentators see the "mastery" as understood within a master/servant model which presumes reciprocal responsibility and care. By contrast, the critically important 11th century Talmudic scholar Moses Nachmanides (the Ramban) states that "mastery" means God "gave them power and dominion over the earth to do as they wish with the cattle, the reptiles, and all that crawl in the dust, and to build . . . and from its hills to dig copper, and other similar things." (Ramban, *Commentary on the Torah, Genesis* (New York: Shilo Publishing House, 1971), p. 55). A modern interpretation of *Genesis* claims:

> In a sense, the universe is like a machine that was built for a specific purpose. Every part of its design was dictated by a particular need, and the machine is maintained only so long as its purpose remains valid. . . . The universe was brought into existence as the means by which to carry out the Torah. Remove the Torah and there is no need for the universe.
>
> —*The Family Chumash: Bereishis,* Overviews by Rabbi Nosson Scherman (New York: Mesorah Publications, 1989), p. ix.

Yet the contrary view is expressed by Maimonides, perhaps the most influential medieval rabbinical authority:

> It should not be believed that all the beings exist for the sake of the existence of humanity. On the contrary, all the other beings too have been intended for their own sakes, and not for the sake of something else. . .
>
> —*Guide to the Perplexed,* Part III, Chapter 13, quoted in *Judaism and Ecology,* a Hadassah Study Guide (New York: Hadassah, 1993), p. 110.

The most complete study of Genesis 1:28 is Jeremy Cohen, *Be Fertile and Increase, Fill the Earth and Master It: The Ancient and Medieval Career of a Biblical Text* (Ithaca and London: Cornell University Press, 1989).

10.   Steven C. Rockefeller, "Faith and Community in an Ecological Age," in Steven C. Rockefeller and John C. Elder, eds. *Spirit and Nature: Why the Environment is a Religious Issue* (Boston: Beacon Press, 1992), p. 142.

11.   For a development of this theme see Roger S. Gottlieb, ed. *A New Creation: America's Contemporary Spiritual Voices* (New York: Crossroad, 1990).

12.   Some thinkers believe that only by uniting insights from virtually all established traditions can we possibly develop a theology adequate to the demands of our age. See Charlene Spretnak, *States of Grace* (San Francisco: HarperSanFrancisco, 1992).

GOOD NEWS/BAD NEWS

There is, as the saying goes, the good news and the bad news.

The bad news is that in the seven years since *This Sacred Earth* came out, the environmental crisis has for the most part been getting worse. In the several areas listed in the Introduction to the first edition—climate change, toxic wastes, loss of land, species, wilderness, indigenous peoples, overconsumption, and genetic engineering—the overwhelming worldwide trend has been at best inconsistent improvement, and at worst a continuing downward spiral. Even a few minutes' cursory examination of information from reliable environmental sources reveals the following:

- Carbon emissions from fossil fuel combustion increased 1.1 percent in 2001, to a new high of 6.55 billion tons. Annual emissions have more than quadrupled since 1950, contributing to global climate change.

- Freshwater fish species are being extinguished at an alarming rate by dams, river diversions, and pollution.

- Cultural and even physical genocide against indigenous peoples, typically as a result of habitat destruction through the pursuit of oil or mineral wealth, is the accepted policy of most of the world's governments.

- Pesticide sales have increased fifteen-fold since 1950. They cause three million severe poisonings and 220,000 deaths each year.[1]

- "Drought and desertification threaten the livelihood of over 1 billion people in more than 110 countries around the world."[2]

Such problems have been the depressing and challenging focus of environmentalists for decades.

It is true that over the years some real victories have been won: the Montreal Protocols leading toward the elimination of ozone-destroying CFCs; outlawing the export of toxic waste; the return of wolves to Yellowstone National Park; recognition of the importance of environmental racism; and international opposition to globalization. Yet the fundamental shape of industrial civilization has not been successfully challenged. We are still addicted to fossil fuels; we still allow new chemicals to be used before they are thoroughly tested (or tested at all); and where the money is present, we are still addicted to wasteful consumerism.

One reason for environmentalists' few victories and many setbacks is the frightening dimension of globalization, a phenomenon intimately linked to environmentalism for several reasons. First, the new global institutions—the World Bank, the International Monetary Fund, and the World Trade Organization—consistently engage in environmentally destructive programs. Preempting local efforts to control pollution or create sustainable economies, their tribunals have punished Canadian restrictions on toxic gasoline additives, international attempts to protect marine mammals, European rejection of hormone-injected beef, and efforts to favor indigenous organic farmers over Chiquita bananas.[3] Second, huge international corporations, often supported by pressure from powerful Western governments, are penetrating the rest of the world: they undertake disastrous dam projects in India and development schemes in Brazil that wipe out native tribes and rainforest; they develop an oil industry in Nigeria that leaves hundreds of square miles—and tens of thousands of people—in ruins. Third, the new U.S. intellectual property law enables corporations to claim as private property the results of generations of collective folk knowledge, cultivation, and resource management. Fourth, "privatization" of resources means that governments are encouraged to turn over the "commons" of land, air, or water to the control and profit-seeking of corporate power. Water and clean air become sellable items. Those who cannot afford to buy, of course, will simply have to do without. Fifth, there is the frightening specter of genetic engineering. Although this is similar in some ways to breeding programs dating back millennia, the enormous difference in scale—introducing fish genes to tomatoes or enabling plants to manufacture bacterial pesticides—threatens our collective environment with the possibility of disastrous and irreversible blunders. From the same social sources that brought us CFCs and the hole in the ozone layer, the "miracles" of DDT, and nuclear wastes, unrestrained genetic engineering holds, I believe, an unprecedented danger.

The stakes have never been higher. The future of humanity—and of virtually all the rest of the earth's community—continues to be at grave risk.

As disheartening as the daily environmental updates are, however, we can find some good news. Since the first edition of *This Sacred Earth*, there has been explosive growth in scholarship, institutional commitment, and public action embodying connections between religion and environmentalism.

In the intellectual realm, I must confess that while deciding among excellent selections for this book in the early 1990s was a daunting task, the range of material that exists now is just short of overwhelming. Harvard University has sponsored a comprehensive series of conferences and subsequent publications on the connections between ecology and virtually all of the world's religious traditions.[4] Academic and popular journals focus on the subject.[5] There will soon be a massive two-volume encyclopedia with more than a thousand entries and a rich on-line resource[6]; and the University of Florida now offers a Ph.D. concentration in religion and ecology.

These intellectual developments signal a continuing theological, cultural, and political shift. For example, the public commitment and action of faith communities has grown dramatically. Reminding us that "Every religion forbids theft—let us not steal from our children to support our addiction to fossil fuels. Every religion forbids idolatry. Let us not sacrifice Creation on the altar of consumption and profit," twenty-two religious leaders were arrested for nonviolent civil disobedience at the U.S. Energy Department while protesting the government's policies on global warming. The U.S. Conference of Catholic Bishops has committed resources to a special campaign linking children's health and environmental pollution. The Interfaith Coalition for Climate Change has groups in eighteen states. Dozens of single-religion and interfaith organizations, proclamations, letter-writing campaigns, and public demonstrations have focused on virtually every key environmental issue, from species extinction and urban sprawl to toxic wastes and the economics of sustainable development. In a proliferation of websites, seminary offerings, public statements, and internal education programs, all flavors of Christians and Jews, Muslims and Buddhists, indigenous peoples and freelance spiritual types have declared that industrial civilization's treatment of nature is incompatible with their own deepest religious commitments. Although such manifestations existed when this book first came out, they have multiplied exponentially since then.

But it is not just that there is more religious environmentalism; it is also that a good deal of what exists is better than it used to be. Like the environmental community as a whole, every stripe of religious environmentalism has understood the deep ties between humanity's treatment of nature and levels of justice or injustice within the human community itself. Concerns for ecosystems, biodiversity, or the web of creation are now, more often than not, joined to concerns with environmental racism, the human costs of globalization, and the way indigenous cultures, along with exotic species, are being made extinct. Ecotheology, in short, has given rise to ecojustice. In the words of a congregational commitment proposed by the National Council of Churches: "In our community, the nation and the world, our congregation will witness to and participate in God's redemption of creation by supporting public efforts and policies which support vulnerable people and protect and restore the degraded earth."[7]

With this crucial development, adherents of religious environmentalism are now learning from and using the entire tradition of progressive political theory and activism. Dialogues on how traditional religions viewed nature, and how these views should be reinterpreted or altered in light of the environmental crisis, now join criticisms of economics, technology, energy policies, science, transportation, agriculture, taxation, and education—for a start! Ecotheologians seek a comprehensive way to think about the sacredness of the earth and the fairness of our social relationships, about the fate of our oceans and the living conditions of the poor, about the world we want for our grandchildren and the destructive consequences of domination and exploitation.

In society as a whole, the overlap between religion and ecological struggle is becoming clearer. In May 2002 *Detroit News* columnist Thomas Bray criticized environmentalists for waging a "jihad" with "grim religious determination" in defending the Arctic National Wildlife Refuge from oil development. The compulsion to pursue more fossil fuel while our roads are teeming with gas-guzzling SUVs and conservation measures are ignored, of course, struck Brady not as "religious," but as "rational capitalism."[8] Similarly, in a rather bizarre legal action, two timber companies sued the National Forest Service for being influenced by environmentalists' (including the well-known Julia Butterfly Hill's) "religious" motives in the protection of old-growth forests. The director of one of the groups mentioned in the suit was disturbed to learn that he was thought to be practicing Wicca and Gaia worship. "I realized that they were trying to make us look like witches or something—I'm a practicing Methodist, for goodness sake."[9] What the suit refused to even consider, of course, is that in the timber companies' compulsive pursuit of profits capitalism is waging its own jihad: one against biodiversity, old-growth forests, and human health.

These critics of the "religion of environmentalism" are right about one thing: nonreligious environmental groups now realize that they can make common cause with communities of faith. This powerful alliance—one so vital that it sometimes blurs all distinctions between the secular and the religious—arises partly because environmental politics are inescapably "spiritual." Environmentalists are necessarily concerned with the meaning of life, the destiny of our species, and the value of the universe—or at least life—as a whole. More than political movements for gender or racial equality or workers' rights, environmentalism therefore often has to be both "political" and (in a very broad sense) "spiritual." Its concerns are as close and familiar as the emissions from our cars, as global as the World Trade Organization's refusal to allow countries to restrict the importation of carcinogenic pesticides, and as cosmic as our deepest questionings about our proper place in a world lushly peopled by the "more-than-human." It is both important and heartening, I believe, that the Sierra Club and the National Council of Churches cosponsored a TV ad about the need to resist oil drilling in the Arctic National Wildlife Refuge. Or that when the leading progressive magazine, *The Nation,* published a story about how George W. Bush's policies were arousing resistance among environmentalists, it included religious groups with secular ones.[10]

The convergence of religion and political action in the environmental movements is based in the realization of the full interconnection of all that lives. This interconnection is as real as the acid rain from smokestacks that may be thousands of miles away; as encompassing as the alteration of the earth's climate; or as heartening as the fact that environmentalists, no less than corporations, now have ties across continents and can work on coordinated campaigns throughout the world. While the specter of globalization should frighten us, we should also be encouraged by our victories: the Brazilian metropolis of Ciutuba, which combines community and ecology, human services and respect for the earth; Nayakrishi Andolan, the sixty-thousand-member organic farming organization of Bangladesh, which rejects pesticides, genetically altered seeds, and chemical fertilizer; the "Green nuns" who work to save wetlands in Ohio; the countless barely recorded victories which remind us that while there is life, there should still be hope.

If the perils of our time are unprecedented, so are our opportunities. The messages of compassion and love, humility and the pursuit of justice, which animate world religion are needed now as never before. If we do not heed those calls, things will go from bad to much, much worse. In spreading the religious messages contained in this book—and trying to live them ourselves—those of us who believe that the earth is sacred can find out if our faiths are true and if holiness is really to be found in lives of love and care. When one species is saved from extinction, one inner city neighborhood protected from a toxic waste dump, one indigenous tribe has its land and culture defended, then we will know that God's Spirit continues to move among us.

NOTES TO INTRODUCTION TO THE SECOND EDITION

1. Sources: www.worldwatch.org; www.culturalsurvival.org.

2. United Nations head Kofi Annan. http://www.unccd.int/main.php.

3. The antiglobalization literature is now very large. For informative recent treatments, see Jerry Mander, "Economic Globalization and the Environment," *Tikkun* (September–October 2001); Mark Weisbrot, "Tricks of Free Trade," *Sierra*, September-October 2001; the International Foundation on Globalization, www.ifg.org; and Global Exchange, www.globalexchange.org.

4. The Harvard Forum on Religion and Ecology, http://environment.harvard.edu/religion.

5. The academic journal *Worldviews: Religion, Culture, Environment*, http://www.brill.nl; and the more popular *Earthlight: The Magazine of Spiritual Ecology*, http://www.earthlight.org.

6. *Encyclopedia of Religion and Nature*: http://www.religionandnature.com.

7. The Environmental Justice Congregational Covenant Program, www.ncc.org.

8. Thomas J. Bray, "Ardor Day: Environmentalism has become a religion," OpinionJournal.com, May 7, 2002.

9. Laura Barandes, Court TV website, Dec. 23, 1999.

10. "Bush Unites the Enviros," May 7, 2001.

Part I

THE
MOMENT
OF SEEING

*Selections from
Nature Writers
Linking Nature and Spirit*

this earth is in our hands
let it fly, a bird of earth and light
All that moves will rejoice . . .

—Meridel Le Sueuer

The indescribable innocence and beneficence of Nature—of sun and wind and rain, of summer and winter—such health, such cheer, they afford forever! . . . Shall I not have intelligence with the earth? Am I not partly leaves and vegetable mold myself?

—Henry David Thoreau

The plants give off the fragrance of their flowers. The precious stones reflect their brilliance to others. Every creature yearns for a loving embrace. The whole of nature serves humanity, and in this service offers all her bounty.

—Hildegard of Bingen

No more cars in national parks. Let the people walk. Or ride horses, bicycles, mules, wild pigs—anything—but keep the automobiles and the motorcycles and all their motorized relatives out. We have agreed not to drive our automobiles into cathedrals, concert halls, art museums, legislative assemblies, private bedrooms and the other sanctums of our culture; and we should treat our national parks with the same deference, for they, too, are holy places. An increasingly pagan and hedonistic people (thank God!) we are learning that the forests and mountains and desert canyons are holier than our churches. Therefore let us behave accordingly.

—Edward Abbey

The worship of God, Gods, or Goddesses, prayers for forgiveness or bounty, ethical imperatives to love our neighbors—or at least have compassion on them—all these are familiar and essential elements of religious life. Perhaps less familiar, but certainly as essential, is that "moment of seeing" which occurs when some perfectly magical—and perhaps also perfectly ordinary—aspect of nature awakens our spirits.

This awakening can take many forms. We many find ourselves, as Thoreau understands it, discovering our true nature in wildness—a wildness of place matched, he believes, by our own potential wildness of spirit. Matsuo Bashō, William Hazlitt, Ralph Waldo Emerson, and Robert Finch find a mysterious and comforting presence in the perfectly ordinary.

This presence may affect some of our basic values. In a modern age of "human rights," obligations to social groups, and struggles of oppressed peoples, we may also ask: Of what value is nature? Can we speak of love or mutual respect for a particular tree, an endangered species, or an ecosystem? When Aldo Leopold describes humanity as simply a "plain citizen" of a complex natural setting, or John Muir challenges our presumption that the earth is made only for us, they are responding to the sacred quality of the earth and hoping to revise our view of humanity's place on that earth.

Luther Standing Bear reminds us that for some traditional cultures being a "naturalist" was not a distinct specialty, but an essential part of everyone's education. And Linda Hogan brings us back to the ties between love of nature and ethical concern for the human community.

SELECTIONS FROM THE *HAIBUN* OF MATSUO BASHŌ

Translated by David Landis Barnhill

ON MT. FUJI

Mt. Kunlun is said to be far away, and in Mt. Penglai and Mt. Fangzhang dwell Taoist immortals. But right here before my eyes: Mt. Fuji's great peak rises from the earth. It seems to hold up the blue heavens and open the cloud gate for the sun and moon. From wherever I gaze, there is a consummate vista as the beautiful scenery goes through a thousand changes. Even poets can't exhaust this scene in verse; those with great talent and men of letters give up their words; painters too abandon their brushes and flee. If the demigods of faraway Gushe mountain were to appear, I wonder if even they could succeed in putting this scene into a poem or a painting.

> with clouds and mist
>   in a brief moment a hundred scenes
>   brought to fulfillment
> *kumokiri no/zanji hyakkei o/tsukushikeri*

MATSUSHIMA

It's been said that Matsushima has the most splendid scenery in our land of beauty. Past and present, people with artistic minds have been enthralled with these islands, exhausting their hearts and setting their skill in motion. The sea here is about three leagues, with islands upon islands of various shapes and sizes, as if it were the wondrous carving of heaven's artistry, so fascinating and fresh. Each single pine is flourishing, all so lovely, gorgeous, beyond words.

> islands and islands–
>   shattered into a thousand pieces,
>   summer's sea
> *shimajima ya/chiji ni kudakete/natsu no umi*

Used by permission of the translator.

AN ACCOUNT OF EIGHTEEN VIEW TOWER

In Mino there is a stately mansion facing the Nagara River whose owner is named Kashima. Behind it tower the Inaba mountains and to the west a disturbance of mountains cluster together, neither close by nor far away. A temple in the rice fields is hidden by a stand of cryptomeria and bamboo surrounding the homes along the river bank is deep green. Here and there bleached cloth is stretched out to dry, and to the right a ferry boat floats by. The townsfolk busily go back and forth, the eaves of this fishing village are lined up close together, and fishermen are pulling in the nets and dangling fishing lines. All this seems to enhance for the viewer the enjoyment of the scene.

Enchanted, I forget the summer day, which seems to hold off the coming dark. The light of the setting sun changes into the moon; the light of the fishing fires, too, formed on the waves, slowly approaches. The cormorant fishing under the high railing is a truly striking spectacle. The eight views of the Xiao River and the ten sites of the Xiang River are experienced together in the one flavor of the cool wind. If I were to give a name to this mansion, I might call it the Eighteen View Manor.

in this area
  all that meets the eye
   is cool
kono atari/me ni miyuru mono wa/mina suzushi

"ON THE LURE OF THE COUNTRY"

William Hazlitt

I do not know that any one has ever explained satisfactorily the true source of our attachment to natural objects, or of that soothing emotion which the sight of the country hardly ever fails to infuse into the mind. Some persons have ascribed this feeling to the natural beauty of the objects themselves, others to the freedom from care, the silence and tranquillity which scenes of retirement afford—others to the healthy and innocent employments of a country life—others to the simplicity of country manners—and others to different causes; but none to the right one. All these causes may, I believe, have a share in producing this feeling; but there is another more general principle, which has been left untouched, and which I shall here explain, endeavouring to be as little sentimental as the subject will admit . . .

Were it not for the recollections habitually associated with them, natural objects could not interest the mind in the manner they do. No doubt, the sky is beautiful; the clouds sail majestically along its bosom; the sun is cheering; there is something exquisitely graceful in the manner in which a plant or tree puts forth its branches; the motion with which they bend and tremble in the evening breeze is soft and lovely; there is music in the babbling of a brook; the view from the top of a mountain is full of grandeur; nor can we behold the ocean with indifference . . .

It is not, however, the beautiful and magnificent alone that we admire in Nature; the most insignificant and rudest objects are often found connected with the strongest emotions; we become attached to the most common and familiar images as to the face of a friend whom we have long known, and from whom we have received many benefits. It is because natural objects have been associated with the sports of our childhood, with air and exercise, with our feelings in solitude, when the mind takes the strongest hold of things, and clings with the fondest interest to whatever strikes its attention; with change of place, the pursuit of new scenes, and thoughts of distant friends; it is because they have surrounded us in almost all situations, in joy and in sorrow, in pleasure and in pain; because they have been one chief source and nourishment of our feelings, and a part of our being, that we love them as we do ourselves.

"On the Lure of the Country" from *The Examiner*, November 1814.

There is, generally speaking, the same foundation for our love of Nature as for all our habitual attachments, namely, association of ideas. But this is not all. That which distinguishes this attachment from others is the transferable nature of our feelings with respect to physical objects; the associations connected with any one object extending to the whole class. My having been attached to any particular person does not make me feel the same attachment to the next person I may chance to meet; but, if I have once associated strong feelings of delight with the objects of natural scenery, the tie becomes indissoluble, and I shall ever after feel the same attachment to other objects of the same sort. I remember when I was abroad, the trees, and grass, and wet leaves, rustling in the walks of the Thuilleries, seemed to be as much English, to be as much the same trees and grass, that I had always been used to, as the sun shining over my head was the same sun which I saw in England; the faces only were foreign to me. Whence comes this difference? It arises from our always imperceptibly connecting the idea of the individual with man, and only the idea of the class with natural objects. In the one case, the external appearance or physical structure is the least thing to be attended to; in the other, it is every thing. The springs that move the human form, and make it friendly or adverse to me, lie hid within it. There is an infinity of motives, passions, and ideas, contained in that narrow compass, of which I know nothing, and in which I have no share. Each individual is a world to himself, governed by a thousand contradictory and wayward impulses. I can, therefore, make no inference from one individual to another; nor can my habitual sentiments, with respect to any individual, extend beyond himself to others. But it is otherwise with respect to Nature. There is neither hypocrisy, caprice, nor mental reservation in her favours. Our intercourse with her is not liable to accident or change, interruption or disappointment. She smiles on us still the same. Thus, to give an obvious instance, if I have once enjoyed the cool shade of a tree, and been lulled into a deep repose by the sound of a brook running at its feet, I am sure that wherever I can find a tree and a brook, I can enjoy the same pleasure again. Hence, when I imagine these objects, I can easily form a mystic personification of the friendly power that inhabits them, Dryad or Naiad, offering its cool fountain or its tempting shade. Hence the origin of the Grecian mythology. All objects of the same kind being the same, not only in their appearance, but in their practical uses, we habitually confound them together under the same general idea; and, whatever fondness we may have conceived for one, is immediately placed to the common account. The most opposite kinds and remote trains of feeling gradually go to enrich the same sentiment; and in our love of Nature, there is all the force of individual attachment, combined with the most airy abstraction. It is this circumstance which gives that refinement, expansion, and wild interest to feelings of this sort, when strongly excited, which every one must have experienced who is a true lover of Nature. The sight of the setting sun does not affect me so much from the beauty of the object itself, from the glory kindled through the glowing skies, the rich broken columns of light, or the dying streaks of day, as that it indistinctly recalls to me numberless thoughts and feelings with which, through many a year and season, I have watched his bright descent in the warm summer evenings, or beheld him struggling to cast a 'farewel sweet' through the thick clouds of winter. I love to see the trees first covered with leaves in the spring, the primroses peeping out from some sheltered bank, and the innocent lambs running races on the soft green turf; because, at that birth-time of Nature, I have always felt sweet hopes and happy wishes—which have not been fulfilled! The dry reeds rustling on the side of a stream,—the woods swept by the loud blast,—the dark massy foliage of autumn,—the grey trunks and naked branches of the trees in winter,—the sequestered copse and wide extended heath,—the warm sunny showers, and December snows,—have all charms for me; there is no object, however trifling or rude, that has not, in some mood or other, found the way to my heart . . . Thus Nature is a kind of universal home, and every object it presents to us an old acquaintance with unaltered looks. For there is that consent and mutual harmony among all her works, one undivided spirit pervading them throughout, that, if we have once knit ourselves in hearty fellowship to any of them, they will never afterwards appear as strangers to us, but, which ever way we turn, we shall find a secret power to have gone out before us, moulding them into such shapes as fancy loves, informing them with life and sympathy, bidding them put on their festive looks and gayest attire at our approach, and to pour all their sweets and choicest treasures at our feet. For him, then, who has well acquainted himself with Nature's works, she wears always one face, and speaks the same well-known language, striking on the heart, amidst unquiet thoughts and the tumult of the world, like the music of one's native tongue heard in some far-off country.

from "WALKING"

Henry David Thoreau

I wish to speak a word for Nature, for absolute freedom and wildness, as contrasted with a freedom and culture merely civil—to regard man as an inhabitant, or a part and parcel of Nature, rather than a member of society. I wish to make an extreme statement, if so I may make an emphatic one, for there are enough champions of civilization: the minister and the school committee and every one of you will take care of that . . .

The West of which I speak is but another name for the Wild; and what I have been preparing to say is, that in Wildness is the preservation of the World. Every tree sends its fibers forth in search of the Wild. The cities import it at any price. Men plow and sail for it. From the forest and wilderness come the tonics and barks which brace mankind. Our ancestors were savages. The story of Romulus and Remus being suckled by a wolf is not a meaningless fable. The founders of every state which has risen to eminence have drawn their nourishment and vigor from a similar wild source. It was because the children of the Empire were not suckled by the wolf that they were conquered and displaced by the children of the northern forests who were.

I believe in the forest, and in the meadow, and in the night in which the corn grows. We require an infusion of hemlock, spruce or arbor vitae in our tea. There is a difference between eating and drinking for strength and from mere gluttony. The Hottentots eagerly devour the marrow of the koodoo and other antelopes raw, as a matter of course. Some of our northern Indians eat raw the marrow of the Arctic reindeer, as well as various other parts, including the summits of the antlers, as long as they are soft. And herein, perchance, they have stolen a march on the cooks of Paris. They get what usually goes to feed the fire. This is probably better than stall-fed beef and slaughterhouse pork to make a man of. Give me a wildness whose glance no civilization can endure—as if we lived on the marrow of koodoos devoured raw . . .

Life consists with wildness. The most alive is the wildest. Not yet subdued to man, its presence refreshes him. One who pressed forward incessantly and never rested from his labors, who grew fast and made infinite demands on life, would always find himself in a new country or wilderness, and surrounded by the raw material of life. He would be climbing over the prostrate stems of primitive forest-trees.

Hope and the future for me are not in lawns and cultivated fields, not in towns and cities, but in the impervious and quaking swamps. When, formerly, I have analyzed my partiality for some farm which I had contemplated purchasing, I have frequently found that I was attracted solely by a few square rods of impermeable and unfathomable bog—a natural sink in one corner of it. That was the jewel which dazzled me. I derive more of my subsistence from the swamps which surround my native town than from the cultivated gardens in the village . . .

In literature it is only the wild that attracts us. Dullness is but another name for tameness. It is the uncivilized free and wild thinking in Hamlet and the Iliad, in all the scriptures and mythologies, not learned in the schools, that delights us. As the wild duck is more swift and beautiful than the tame, so is the wild—the mallard—thought, which 'mid falling dews wings its way above the fens. A truly good book is something as natural, and as unexpectedly and unaccountably fair and perfect, as a wild-flower discovered on the prairies of the West or in the jungles of the East. Genius is a light which makes the darkness visible, like the lightning's flash, which perchance shatters the temple of knowledge itself—and not a taper lighted at the hearthstone of the race, which pales before the light of common day . . .

In short, all good things are wild and free. There is something in a strain of music, whether produced by an instrument or by the human voice—take the sound of a bugle in a summer night, for instance—which by its wildness, to speak without satire, reminds me of the cries emitted by wild beasts in their native forests. It is so much of their wildness as I can understand. Give me for my friends and neighbors wild men, not tame ones. The wildness of the savage is but a faint symbol of the awful ferity with which good men and lovers meet.

I love even to see the domestic animals reassert their native rights—any evidence that they have not wholly lost their original wild habits and vigor; as when my neighbor's cow breaks out of her pasture early in the spring and boldly swims the river, a cold, gray tide, twenty-five or thirty rods wide, swollen by the melted snow. It is the buffalo crossing the Mississippi. This exploit confers some dignity on the herd in my eyes—already dignified. The seeds of instinct are preserved under the thick hides of cattle and horses, like seeds in the bowels of the earth, an indefinite period . . .

I rejoice that horses and steers have to be broken before they can be made the slaves of men, and that men themselves have some wild oats still left to sow before they become submissive members of society. Undoubtedly, all men are not equally fit subjects for civilization; and because the majority, like dogs and sheep, are tame by inherited disposition, this is no reason why the others should have their natures broken that they may be reduced to the same level. Men are in the main alike, but they were made several in order that they might be various. If a low use is to be served, one man will do nearly or quite as well as another; if a high one, individual excellence is to be regarded. Any man can stop a hole to keep the wind away, but no other man could serve so rare a use as the author of this illustration did. Confucius says, "The skins of the tiger and the leopard, when they are tanned, are as the skins of the dog and the sheep tanned." But it is not the part of a true culture to tame tigers, any more than it is to make sheep ferocious; and tanning their skins for shoes is not the best use to which they can be put . . .

Here is this vast, savage, howling mother of ours, Nature, lying all around, with such beauty, and such affection for her children, as the leopard; and yet we are so early weaned from her breast to society, to that culture which is exclusively an interaction of man on man—a sort of breeding in and in, which produces at most a merely English nobility, a civilization destined to have a speedy limit. . . .

I would not have every man nor every part of a man cultivated, any more than I would have every acre of earth cultivated: part will be tillage, but the greater part will be meadow and forest, not only serving an immediate use, but preparing a mould against a distant future, by the annual decay of the vegetation which it supports . . .

We had a remarkable sunset one day last November. I was walking in a meadow, the source of a small brook, when the sun at last, just before setting, after a cold, gray day, reached a clear stratum in the horizon, and the softest, brightest morning sunlight fell on the dry grass and on the stems of the trees in the opposite horizon and on the leaves of the shrub oaks on the hillside, while our shadows stretched long over the meadow east ward, as if we were the only motes in its beams. It was such a light as we could not have imagined a moment before, and the air also was so warm and serene that nothing was wanting to make a paradise of that meadow. When we reflected that this was not a solitary phenomenon, never to happen again, but that it would happen forever and ever, an infinite number of evenings, and cheer and reassure the latest child that walked there, it was more glorious still.

The sun sets on some retired meadow, where no house is visible, with all the glory and splendor that it lavishes on cities, and perchance as it has never set before—where there is but a solitary marsh hawk to have his wings gilded by it, or only a musquash looks out from his cabin, and there is some little black-veined brook in the midst of the marsh, just beginning to meander, winding slowly round a decaying stump. We walked in so pure and bright a light, gilding the withered grass and leaves, so softly and serenely bright, I thought I had never bathed in such a golden flood, without a ripple or a murmur to it. The west side of every wood and rising ground gleamed like the boundary of Elysium, and the sun on our backs seemed like a gentle herdsman driving us home at evening.

So we saunter toward the Holy Land, till one day the sun shall shine more brightly than ever he has done, shall perchance shine into our minds and hearts, and light up our whole lives with a great awakening light, as warm and serene and golden as on a bankside in autumn.

"NATURE"

Ralph Waldo Emerson

To go into solitude, a man needs to retire as much from his chamber as from society. I am not solitary whilst I read and write, though nobody is with me. But if a man would be alone, let him look at the stars. The rays that come from those heavenly worlds, will separate between him and what he touches. One might think the atmosphere was made transparent with this design, to give man, in the heavenly bodies, the perpetual presence of the sublime. Seen in the streets of cities, how great they are! If the stars should appear one night in a thousand years, how would men believe and adore; and preserve for many generations the remembrance of the city of God which had been shown! But every night come out these envoys of beauty, and light the universe with their admonishing smile.

The stars awaken a certain reverence, because though always present, they are inaccessible; but all natural objects make a kindred impression, when the mind is open to their influence. Nature never wears a mean appearance. Neither does the wisest man extort her secret, and lose his curiosity by finding out all her perfection. Nature never became a toy to a wise spirit. The flowers, the animals, the mountains, reflected the wisdom of his best hour, as much as they had delighted the simplicity of his childhood.

When we speak of nature in this manner, we have a distinct but most poetical sense in the mind. We mean the integrity of impression made by manifold natural objects. It is this which distinguishes the stick of timber of the wood-cutter, from the tree of the poet. The charming landscape which I saw this morning, is indubitably made up of some twenty or thirty farms. Miller owns this field, Locke that, and Manning the woodland beyond. But none of them owns the landscape. There is a property in the horizon which no man has but he whose eye can integrate all the parts, that is, the poet. This is the best part of these men's farms, yet to this their warranty-deeds give no title.

To speak truly, few adult persons can see nature. Most persons do not see the sun. At least they have a very superficial seeing. The sun illuminates only the eye of the man, but shines into the eye and the heart of the child. The lover of nature is he whose inward and outward senses are still truly adjusted to each other; who has retained the spirit of infancy even into the era of manhood. His intercourse with heaven and earth, becomes part of his daily food. In the presence of nature, a wild delight runs through the man, in spite of real sorrows. Nature says,—he is my creature, and maugre all his impertinent griefs, he shall be

---

From *Nature: Addresses and Lectures*, published in 1849.

glad with me. Not the sun or the summer alone, but every hour and season yields its tribute of delight; for every hour and change corresponds to and authorizes a different state of the mind, from breathless noon to grimmest midnight. Nature is a setting that fits equally well a comic or a mourning piece. In good health, the air is a cordial of incredible virtue. Crossing a bare common, in snow puddles, at twilight, under a clouded sky, without having in my thoughts any occurrence of special good fortune, I have enjoyed a perfect exhilaration. I am glad to the brink of fear. In the woods too, a man casts off his years, as the snake his slough, and at what period soever of life, is always a child. In the woods, is perpetual youth. Within these plantations of God, a decorum and sanctity reign, a perennial festival is dressed, and the guest sees not how he should tire of them in a thousand years. In the woods, we return to reason and faith. There I feel that nothing can befall me in life,—no disgrace, no calamity, (leaving me my eyes,) which nature cannot repair. Standing on the bare ground,—my head bathed by the blithe air, and uplifted into infinite space,—all mean egotism vanishes. I become a transparent eye-ball; I am nothing; I see all; the currents of the Universal Being circulate through me; I am part or particle of God. The name of the nearest friend sounds then foreign and accidental: to be brothers, to be acquaintances,—master or servant, is then a trifle and a disturbance. I am the lover of uncontained and immortal beauty. In the wilderness, I find something more dear and connate than in streets or villages. In the tranquil landscape, and especially in the distant line of the horizon, man beholds somewhat as beautiful as his own nature.

The greatest delight which the fields and woods minister, is the suggestion of an occult relation between man and the vegetable. I am not alone and unacknowledged. They nod to me, and I to them. The waving of the boughs in the storm, is new to me and old. It takes me by surprise, and yet is not unknown. Its effect is like that of a higher thought or a better emotion coming over me, when I deemed I was thinking justly or doing right.

Yet it is certain that the power to produce this delight, does not reside in nature, but in man, or in a harmony of both. It is necessary to use these pleasures with great temperance. For, nature is not always tricked in holiday attire, but the same scene which yesterday breathed perfume and glittered as for the frolic of the nymphs, is overspread with melancholy today. Nature always wears the colors of the spirit. To a man laboring under calamity, the heat of his own fire hath sadness in it. Then, there is a kind of contempt of the landscape felt by him who has just lost by death a dear friend. The sky is less grand as it shuts down over less worth in the population.

from *THOUSAND-MILE WALK TO THE GULF*

John Muir

A THOUSAND-MILE WALK

The world, we are told, was made especially for man—a presumption not supported by all the facts. A numerous class of men are painfully astonished whenever they find anything, living or dead, in all God's universe, which they cannot eat or render in some way what they call useful to themselves. They have precise dogmatic insight of the intentions of the Creator, and it is hardly possible to be guilty of irreverence in speaking of *their* God any more than of heathen idols. He is regarded as a civilized, law-abiding gentleman in favor either of a republican form of government or of a limited monarchy; believes in the literature and language of England; is a warm supporter of the English constitution and Sunday schools and missionary societies; and is as purely a manufactured article as any puppet of a half-penny theater.

With such views of the Creator it is, of course, not surprising that erroneous views should be entertained of the creation. To such properly trimmed people, the sheep, for example, is an easy problem—food and clothing "for us," eating grass and daisies white by divine appointment for this predestined purpose, on perceiving the demand for wool that would be occasioned by the eating of the apple in the Garden of Eden.

In the same pleasant plan, whales are storehouses of oil for us, to help out the stars in lighting our dark ways until the discovery of the Pennsylvania oil wells. Among plants, hemp, to say nothing of the cereals, is a case of evident destination for ships' rigging, wrapping packages, and hanging the wicked. Cotton is another plain case of clothing. Iron was made for hammers and ploughs, and lead for bullets; all intended for us. And so of other small handfuls of insignificant things.

But if we should ask these profound expositors of God's intentions, How about those man-eating animals—lions, tigers, alligators—which smack their lips over raw man? Or about those myriads of noxious insects that destroy labor and drink his blood? Doubtless man was intended for food and drink for all these? Oh, no! Not at all! These are unresolvable difficulties connected with Eden's apple and the Devil. Why does water drown its

---

Reprinted from *Thousand-Mile Walk to the Gulf* by John Muir, 1916.

lord? Why do so many minerals poison him? Why are so many plants and fishes deadly enemies? Why is the lord of creation subjected to the same laws of life as his subjects? Oh, all these things are satanic, or in some way connected with the first garden.

Now, it never seems to occur to these farseeing teachers that Nature's object in making animals and plants might possibly be first of all the happiness of each one of them, not the creation of all for the happiness of one. Why should man value himself as more than a small part of the one great unit of creation? And what creature of all that the Lord has taken the pains to make is not essential to the completeness of that unit—the cosmos? The universe would be incomplete without man; but it would also be incomplete without the smallest transmicroscopic creature that dwells beyond our conceitful eyes and knowledge.

from *A SAND COUNTY ALMANAC*

Aldo Leopold

WILDERNESS

Wilderness is the raw material out of which man has hammered the artifact called civilization.

Wilderness was never a homogeneous raw material. It was very diverse, and the resulting artifacts are very diverse. These differences in the end-product are known as cultures. The rich diversity of the world's cultures reflects a corresponding diversity in the wilds that gave them birth.

For the first time in the history of the human species, two changes are now impending. One is the exhaustion of wilderness in the more habitable portions of the globe. The other is the world-wide hybridization of cultures through modern transport and industrialization. Neither can be prevented, and perhaps should not be, but the question arises whether, by some slight amelioration of the impending changes, certain values can be preserved that would otherwise be lost.

To the laborer in the sweat of his labor, the raw stuff on his anvil is an adversary to be conquered. So was wilderness an adversary to the pioneer.

But to the laborer in repose, able for the moment to cast a philosophical eye on his world, that same raw stuff is something to be loved and cherished, because it gives definition and meaning to his life. This is a plea for the preservation of some tag-ends of wilderness, as museum pieces, for the edification of those who may one day wish to see, feel, or study the origins of their cultural inheritance.

THE ETHICAL SEQUENCE

This extension of ethics, so far studied only by philosophers, is actually a process in ecological evolution. Its sequences may be described in ecological as well as in philosophical terms. An ethic, ecologically, is a limitation on freedom of action in the struggle for existence. An ethic, philosophically, is a differentiation of social from anti-social conduct.

These are two definitions of one thing. The thing has its origin in the tendency of interdependent individuals or groups to evolve modes of co-operation. The ecologist calls these symbioses. Politics and economics are advanced symbioses in which the original free-for-all competition has been replaced, in part, by co-operative mechanisms with an ethical content.

The complexity of co-operative mechanisms has increased with population density, and with the efficiency of tools. It was simpler, for example, to define the anti-social uses of sticks and stones in the days of the mastodons than of bullets and billboards in the age of motors.

The first ethics dealt with the relation between individuals; the Mosaic Decalogue is an example. Later accretions dealt with the relation between the individual and society. The Golden Rule tries to integrate the individual to society; democracy to integrate social organization to the individual.

There is as yet no ethic dealing with man's relation to land and to the animals and plants which grow upon it. Land, like Odysseus' slave-girls, is still property. The land-relation is still strictly economic, entailing privileges but not obligations.

The extension of ethics to this third element in human environment is, if I read the evidence correctly, an evolutionary possibility and an ecological necessity. It is the third step in a sequence. The first two have already been taken. Individual thinkers since the days of Ezekiel and Isaiah have asserted that the despoliation of land is not only inexpedient but wrong. Society, however, has not yet affirmed their belief. I regard the present conservation movement as the embryo of such an affirmation.

An ethic may be regarded as a mode of guidance for meeting ecological situations so new or intricate, or involving such deferred reactions, that the path of social expediency is not discernible to the average individual. Animal instincts are modes of guidance for the individual in meeting such situations. Ethics are possibly a kind of community instinct in-the-making.

THE COMMUNITY CONCEPT

All ethics so far evolved rest upon a single premise: that the individual is a member of a community of interdependent parts. His instincts prompt him to compete for his place in that community, but his ethics prompt him also to co-operate (perhaps in order that there may be a place to compete for).

The land ethic simply enlarges the boundaries of the community to include soils, waters, plants, and animals, or collectively: the land.

This sounds simple: do we not already sing our love for and obligation to the land of the free and the home of the brave? Yes, but just what and whom do we love? Certainly not the soil, which we are sending helter-skelter downriver. Certainly not the waters, which we assume have no function except to turn turbines, float barges, and carry off sewage. Certainly not the plants, of which we exterminate whole communities without batting an eye. Certainly not the animals, of which we have already extirpated many of the largest and most beautiful species. A land ethic of course cannot prevent the alteration, management, and use of these 'resources,' but it does affirm their right to continued existence, and, at least in spots, their continued existence in a natural state.

In short, a land ethic changes the role of *Homo sapiens* from conqueror of the land-community to plain member and citizen of it. It implies respect for his fellow-members, and also respect for the community as such.

In human history, we have learned (I hope) that the conqueror role is eventually self-defeating. Why? Because it is implicit in such a role that the conqueror knows, *ex cathedra*, just what makes the community clock tick, and just what and who is valuable, and what and who is worthless, in community life. It always turns out that he knows neither, and this is why his conquests eventually defeat themselves.

In the biotic community, a parallel situation exists. Abraham knew exactly what the land was for: it was to drip milk and honey into Abraham's mouth. At the present moment, the assurance with which we regard this assumption is inverse to the degree of our education.

The ordinary citizen today assumes that science knows what makes the community clock tick; the scientist is equally sure that he does not. He knows that the biotic mechanism is so complex that its workings may never be fully understood.

Aldo Leopold

"NATURE"

Luther Standing Bear

The Lakota was a true naturist—a lover of Nature. He loved the earth and all things of the earth, the attachment growing with age. The old people came literally to love the soil and they sat or reclined on the ground with a feeling of being close to a mothering power. It was good for the skin to touch the earth and the old people liked to remove their moccasins and walk with bare feet on the sacred earth. Their tipis were built upon the earth and their altars were made of earth. The birds that flew in the air came to rest upon the earth and it was the final abiding place of all things that lived and grew. The soil was soothing, strengthening, cleansing, and healing.

This is why the old Indian still sits upon the earth instead of propping himself up and away from its life-giving forces. For him, to sit or lie upon the ground is to be able to think more deeply and to feel more keenly; he can see more clearly into the mysteries of life and come closer in kinship to other lives about him.

The earth was full of sounds which the old-time Indian could hear, sometimes putting his ear to it so as to hear more clearly. The forefathers of the Lakotas had done this for long ages until there had come to them real understanding of earth ways. It was almost as if the man were still a part of the earth as he was in the beginning, according to the legend of the tribe. This beautiful story of the genesis of the Lakota people furnished the foundation for the love they bore for earth and all things of the earth. Wherever the Lakota went, he was with Mother Earth. No matter where he roamed by day or slept by night, he was safe with her. This thought comforted and sustained the Lakota and he was eternally filled with gratitude.

From Wakan Tanka there came a great unifying life force that flowed in and through all things—the flowers of the plains, blowing winds, rocks, trees, birds, animals—and was the same force that had been breathed into the first man. Thus all things were kindred and brought together by the same Great Mystery.

Kinship with all creatures of the earth, sky, and water was a real and active principle. For the animal and bird world there existed a brotherly feeling that kept the Lakota safe among them. And so close did some of the Lakotas come to their feathered and furred friends that in true brotherhood they spoke a common tongue.

Reprinted from *Land of the Spotted Eagle* by Luther Standing Bear, by permission of the University of Nebraska Press. Copyright © 1933 by Luther Standing Bear. Renewal copyright © 1960 by May Jones.

The animal had rights—the right of man's protection, the right to live, the right to multiply, the right to freedom, and the right to man's indebtedness—and in recognition of these rights the Lakota never enslaved the animal, and spared all life that was not needed for food and clothing.

This concept of life and its relations was humanizing and gave to the Lakota an abiding love. It filled his being with the joy and mystery of living; it gave him reverence for all life; it made a place for all things in the scheme of existence with equal importance to all. The Lakota could despise no creature, for all were of one blood, made by the same hand, and filled with the essence of the Great Mystery. In spirit the Lakota was humble and meek. 'Blessed are the meek: for they shall inherit the earth,' was true for the Lakota, and from the earth he inherited secrets long since forgotten. His religion was sane, normal, and human.

Reflection upon life and its meaning, consideration of its wonders, and observation of the world of creatures, began with childhood. The earth, which was called *Maka*, and the sun, called *Anpetuwi*, represented two functions somewhat analogous to those of male and female. The earth brought forth life, but the warming, enticing rays of the sun coaxed it into being. The earth yielded, the sun engendered.

In talking to children, the old Lakota would place a hand on the ground and explain: 'We sit in the lap of our Mother. From her we, and all other living things, come. We shall soon pass, but the place where we now rest will last forever.' So we, too, learned to sit or lie on the ground and become conscious of life about us in its multitude of forms. Sometimes we boys would sit motionless and watch the swallow, the tiny ants, or perhaps some small animal at its work and ponder on its industry and ingenuity; or we lay on our backs and looked long at the sky and when the stars came out made shapes from the various groups. The morning and evening star always attracted attention, and the Milky Way was a path which was traveled by the ghosts. The old people told us to heed *wa maka skan*, which were the 'moving things of earth.' This meant, of course, the animals that lived and moved about, and the stories they told of *wa maka skan* increased our interest and delight. The wolf, duck, eagle, hawk, spider, bear, and other creatures, had marvelous powers, and each one was useful and helpful to us. Then there were the warriors who lived in the sky and dashed about on their spirited horses during a thunder storm, their lances clashing with the thunder and glittering with the lightning. There was *wiwila*, the living spirit of the spring, and the stones that flew like a bird and talked like a man. Everything was possessed of personality, only differing with us in form. Knowledge was inherent in all things. The world was a library and its books were the stones, leaves, grass, brooks, and the birds and animals that shared, alike with us, the storms and blessings of earth. We learned to do what only the student of nature ever learns, and that was to feel beauty. We never railed at the storms, the furious winds, and the biting frosts and snows. To do so intensified human futility, so whatever came we adjusted ourselves, by more effort and energy if necessary, but without complaint. Even the lightning did us no harm, for whenever it came too close, mothers and grandmothers in every tipi put cedar leaves on the coals and their magic kept danger away. Bright days and dark days were both expressions of the Great Mystery, and the Indian reveled in being close to the Big Holy. His worship was unalloyed, free from the fears of civilization.

I have come to know that the white mind does not feel toward nature as does the Indian mind, and it is because, I believe, of the difference in childhood instruction. I have often noticed white boys gathered in a city by-street or alley jostling and pushing one another in a foolish manner. They spend much time in this aimless fashion, their natural faculties neither seeing, hearing, nor feeling the varied life that surrounds them. There is about them no awareness, no acuteness, and it is this dullness that gives ugly mannerisms full play; it takes from them natural poise and stimulation. In contrast, Indian boys, who are naturally reared, are alert to their surroundings; their senses are not narrowed to observing only one another, and they cannot spend hours seeing nothing, hearing nothing, and thinking nothing in particular. Observation was certain in its rewards; interest, wonder, admiration grew, and the fact was appreciated that life was more than mere human manifestation; that it was expressed in a multitude of forms. This appreciation enriched Lakota existence. Life was vivid and pulsing; nothing was casual and commonplace. The Indian lived—lived in every sense of the word—from his first to his last breath.

The character of the Indian's emotion left little room in his heart for antagonism toward his fellow creatures, this attitude giving him what is sometimes referred to as 'the Indian point of view.' Every true student, every lover of nature has 'the Indian point of view,' but there are few such students, for few white men approach nature in the Indian manner. The Indian and the white man sense things differently because the white man has put distance between himself and nature; and assuming a lofty place in the scheme of order of things has lost for him both reverence and understanding. Consequently the white man finds Indian philosophy obscure—wrapped, as he says, in a maze of ideas and symbols which he does not understand. A writer friend, a white man whose knowledge of 'Injuns' is far more profound and sympathetic than the average, once said that he had been privileged, on two occasions, to see the contents of an Indian medicine-man's bag in which were bits of earth, feathers, stones, and various other articles of symbolic nature; that a 'collector' showed him one and laughed, but a great and world-famous archeologist showed him the other with admiration and wonder. Many times the Indian is embarrassed and baffled by the white man's allusions to nature in such terms as crude, primitive, wild, rude, untamed, and savage. For the Lakota, mountains, lakes, rivers, springs, valleys, and woods were all finished beauty; winds, rain, snow, sunshine, day, night, and change of seasons brought interest; birds, insects, and animals filled the world with knowledge that defied the discernment of man.

But nothing the Great Mystery placed in the land of the Indian pleased the white man, and nothing escaped his transforming hand. Wherever forests have not been mowed down; wherever the animal is recessed in their quiet protection; wherever the earth is not bereft of four-footed life—that to him is an 'unbroken wilderness.' But since for the Lakota there was no wilderness; since nature was not dangerous but hospitable; not forbidding but friendly, Lakota philosophy was healthy—free from fear and dogmatism. And here I find the great distinction between the faith of the Indian and the white man. Indian faith sought the harmony of man with his surroundings; the other sought the dominance of surroundings. In sharing, in loving all and everything, one people naturally found a measure of the thing they sought; while, in fearing, the other found need of conquest. For one man the world was full of beauty; for the other it was a place of sin and ugliness to be endured until he went to another world, there to become a creature of wings, half-man and half-bird. Forever one man directed his Mystery to change the world He had made; forever this man pleaded with Him to chastise His wicked ones; and forever he implored his Wakan Tanka to send His light to earth. Small wonder this man could not understand the other.

But the old Lakota was wise. He knew that man's heart, away from nature, becomes hard; he knew that lack of respect for growing, living things soon led to lack of respect for humans too. So he kept his youth close to its softening influence.

"SEEING THE LIGHT"

Robert Finch

On Wednesday—a cold, clear winter's day—I finished work at three and went for a walk with my dog along the Herring River. The tall grass by the river's edge is blanched and sere now, the path along the bank padded down by the hunters of autumn, the river itself full and black, swollen by winter rains, drowning thin birches beside the lower bank, its deep current indicated only by little whirlpools and kinetic wrinkles in its otherwise smooth skin. It seems to run like a highway, gently curving, slick black, and about the width of a newly paved road.

To my left is the rising, wooded slope of Merrick Island, like a forested version of the eroding ocean bluffs; to my right, the river, a constant waterway, like the sea, ever changing, from stretch to stretch, season to season. At this season, and this time of day, Ollie and I walk directly into the lowering sun, so that my vision of things is occluded, fragmented, blinded, and double-sunned by reflections in the water. It is like walking through a visual bramble, or maze, with my hand held in front of my eyes for protection. All is back-lit and glaring, so that I can get no hold on the landscape. The elements are all familiar: overhanging, twisted oak limbs, the worn path, the black ribbon of water, but everything is splintered and incohesive to my sight, and so to the mind.

This doesn't bother Ollie, of course, for whom sight is at best a peripheral sense. He snorts and sniffs, pees and poops, shoots his blond shaggy body along the path, lags behind to investigate a novel smell, then bounds ahead to wait, like a small lion in the path, ready to pounce.

There is little life on the river today—only a single small duck, which through my glasses I make out to be a female bufflehead: dove grey with a dark band on her back, white smudge of a cheek patch on each side of her head. She skitters and shoots down the river ahead of us for a hundred yards or so, then comes to rest again. I know this will happen again and again as we continue along the river-course, like the bird in Robert Frost's poem "The Woodpile" that similarly flies on ahead of him, refusing to undeceive himself about the poet's intentions, "like one who takes/Everything said as personal to himself."

As the river bends and heads south toward the bay, the hills of Merrick Island seem to veer away to the east, leaving a wide plain of brown wet meadows studded with patches of

From *Death of a Hornet and Other Cape Cod Essays* by Robert Finch. Reprinted by permission of PublicAffairs, a member of Perseus Books, L.L.C.

shrubs, willows, and chokecherries. Then, across the river, the larger bulk of Griffin Island begins to slide nearer, moving in from the west. The bufflehead, who has disturbed herself several times fleeing ahead at our approach, finally tires of the game and flies overhead back up the river, unaware that we are about to turn back ourselves and thus unintentionally putting herself in a position that will only increase her paranoia. But it is a mind that is used to being thought of as prey and so is probably comfortable with its fear.

When we do turn back, the fragmented, Cubist landscape I walked through coming out is transformed—as I knew it would be, counted on it being—into a sudden unity of form. What was broken is now whole, what was obscured is now revealed. Cacophony has become harmony. The hillsides are bathed in a golden flood of light. The grey tree trunks stand out with breathtaking clarity. Their stark and twisted forms take on a comeliness—no, more than that: an idealization of form that belongs to Greek statues. The warped, scaly trunks are redeemed. They vibrate and sing with incandescence. The whole island, bristling with its head of tough, twisted oaks, now stretches before me like some kind of revelation, like an idealized form. But of what?

Of a bare hillside with leafless oaks in late sunlight on a winter's afternoon.

In other words, like a perfection of itself, a thing come into its own. And all because of a simple change in the angle of light. And at the same time I feel as if some great clarification has taken place within myself, as if my own life, as Frost says elsewhere, had been "too much like a pathless woods," but that now I saw things clear.

Now this is the curious thing: for several minutes after turning back, I felt as if some profound illumination had taken place within my own life, as if I had come out of some brambly, dark passage and emerged into clarity, had come through and into my own. But even as I experienced this sense of revelation I knew that no such thing had happened. I had not walked out here under any personal cloud, deeply troubled or lost in any way I was aware of. Nor had any question I carried with me been answered. There *was* no question. I was simply on a walk with my dog.

But the emotion—the sense of things unexpectedly opening up, the rush of suddenly pushing through, beyond confusion, into knowing and seeing without obstruction—that was real. And what was more, it was identical to the feeling at those times when I really *had* experienced such a clarification in my life. The scene, in other words, provided me with a *pattern* for such revelation, an external template for internal emotions, a way of recognizing, giving shape to, an inner process.

I had had these experiences of outer weather triggering inner weather before—on the beach, inside watching spiders in my study, in a pine woods—but rarely had there been such a clear separation and wide gulf between the emotional experience and my actual psychological state. It seemed to suggest strongly that the physical natural world might in fact be the source of our emotional, psychological, and even spiritual lives.

The earliest civilizations interpreted natural events—floods or good hunting—as signs of divine favor or retribution. The ancient Greeks, Plato in particular, gave us the notion of natural objects as imperfect incarnations of Ideal Forms. Christianity, especially the Puritans who settled this narrow peninsula, took up this idea and saw the natural world in terms of "signs" or "types," reading God's will and intent in astronomical portents and the suggestive shapes of plants, finding the Devil's abode and his minions in wilderness and its "wild men." More recently, Romanticism and Transcendentalism conceived of nature as a storehouse of images, metaphors, and symbols reflecting and illuminating the inner life of man: Wordsworth's cloud, Blake's tyger, Shelly's west wind, Keats's nightingale, Emerson's rhodora, and Thoreau's beloved pond ("Walden, is it you?").

But my walk that afternoon seemed to suggest that the main historical thrust of understanding the "meaning" of nature might be misdirected—might in fact be 180 degrees wrong. Nature, rather than being seen as an imperfect manifestation of ideal truth, or a symbolic system of divine intent, or even a set of correspondences to psychological states or aspects of the human mind, might be more accurately regarded as the source, the very building blocks, of human identity.

A bird, say, or a duck, fleeing ahead of us, allows us to understand a type of human behavior by giving it a physical image. A moldering, abandoned woodpile, or a light-fractured landscape and its subsequent restoration to visual wholeness, provides us a moment of self-revelation—or if not actual revelation, at least the pattern for it, part of a multifarious guide we have constructed from its materials for being human in this world where we must live both within and without nature.

Whether such experiences in nature are firsthand, or are culturally learned, or whether they actually relate to our immediate state of mind, does not matter. The psychological reality of the experience is true and reflects an evolutionary heritage and connection with our natural surroundings that go far beyond biological, behavioral, and perceptual links. It suggests that we are directly dependent on nature for the raw materials of our inner lives, and for the cultures they generate. Put another way, our souls may be created both individually and as a species by what we experience through our senses. If this is so, then when a society increasingly lives without direct access to natural experience, does it run the risk of literally becoming soulless?

None of this, of course, matters in the least to Ollie, who barrels ahead, bounding through the bleached white fire of winter's grass, into spring.

"THE KILL HOLE"

Linda Hogan

In New Mexico there were an ancient people called the Mimbres. They were skilled potters. What they made was far superior to the work of later potters in the Southwest. The Mimbres formed bowls out of rich, red clay that held generations of life, and they painted that shaped clay with animals, people, plants, and even the dusty wind that still inhabits the dry New Mexico land.

Like the Anasazi and other ancient nations, these were people of the mystery, having abandoned their place and vanished into a dimension that has remained unknown to those of us who have come later. But before they disappeared into the secret, the Mimbres "killed" their pots by breaking a hole in the center of each one. It is thought that the hole served to release the spirit of the pot from the clay, allowing it to travel with them over land and to join them in their burial grounds. It is called a "kill hole."

At the third death I attended, I thought of these earlier people, and wondered about the kill hole, how life escapes the broken clay of ourselves, travels away from the center of our living. It's said that at death, the fontanelle in the top of the skull opens, the way it is open when we are born into the world. Before her spirit escaped through the crown, I wanted to ask that dying woman what she could tell me about life. But dying is hard work and it leaves little time for questions. That afternoon, there was time only for human comfort as the woman balanced those last hours between the worlds of life and raspy death.

That woman died in California, not far from the place where Ishi, the last Yana Indian, was found in 1911. Ishi came from a small group of Indians who lived undiscovered for over fifty years in the Mill Creek area, concealed by forest. They knew the secret of invisibility. Not even a cloud of smoke had revealed their whereabouts. But as the settling of the continent expanded to the West, and as the logging of the forests continued, Ishi was found, finally, by surveyors who must have believed he was not a man in the way they were men, for they carried away his few possessions as souvenirs for their families.

For the next four years Ishi lived in a museum as a living exhibit. He offered scholars his tools, his crafts, and his language. His was a tremendous gift to the people who were near him, but during that time he was transformed from a healthy man into a wasted skeleton. He died from tuberculosis, one of the diseases of civilization. But sometimes

Reprinted with permission of the author. This essay appeared in *Parabola: The Magazine of Myth and Tradition*, Volume 13:2, May 1988, pp. 50–53.

death has such a strange way of turning things inside out, so that what is gone becomes as important as what remains. Such an absence defines our world as surely as a Mimbres pot contains a bowl of air, or as a woman's dying body holds a memory and history of life. This is especially true in the case of Ishi; his story illuminates the world of civilization and its flaws. It tells us what kind of people we are, with our double natures. It speaks of loss and of emptiness that will never again be filled, of whole cultures disappeared, of species made extinct, all of these losses falling as if through a hole, like a spirit leaving earth's broken clay.

In our own time, there have been events as striking as the discovery of Ishi, events that, in their passing, not only raise the question of what kind of people we are, but give us reason to ask what is our rightful place within the circle of life, we beautiful ones who are as adept at creation as we are at destruction?

One of these events, one that haunts us like a shadow from the dark periphery of our lives, is the recent research where apes were taught American sign language. Through that language of the hands, a dialogue began between signing chimpanzees and human beings, a dialogue that bridged the species barrier for perhaps the first time. Within a relatively short time, the chimps learned to communicate with humans and with one another. They asked questions, expressed abstract thought, and combined signs and symbols to create new words they had not been taught by their human teachers. With their hands, they spoke a world of emotion, of feelings similar to our own. One angry chimp called his handler, "dirty." Another one, Ally, developed hysterical paralysis when separated from his mother. Later, one of the subjects had to be tranquilized as he was taken away, distraught and protesting, and sold into scientific research.

From these studies, we learned that primates have a capacity for love and resistance, that they not only have a rich emotional life, but that they are able to express their pain and anguish. This is an event whose repercussions astonish us with their meaning, whose presence throws us into an identity crisis equal to that in Galileo's time when the fabric of belief was split wide open to reveal that earth was not the center of the universe. This event bespeaks our responsibility to treat with care and tenderness all the other lives who share our small world. Yet the significance of this research has gone largely unheeded. Many members of the scientific community played down the similarities between apes and humans, ignoring the comfort of such connections. They searched instead for new definitions of language and intelligence, ones that would exclude apes from our own ways of speaking and thinking. They searched for a new division, another wall between life and life. In itself, this search sheds light on us, and in that light, we seem to have had a failure of heart.

But perhaps this armor of defence comes from another failure, from the downfall of our beliefs about who and what we are as human beings. One by one, in our lifetimes, our convictions about ourselves and our place within the world have been overturned. Once the use of tools was considered to be strictly a human ability. Then it was found that primates and other species make use of tools. Then altruism was said to be what distinguished us from other species, until it was learned that elephants try to help their sick, staying the long hours beside their own dying ones, caressing and comforting them. And we can't even say that art is an activity that sets us apart, since those same compassionate elephants also make art. In fact, when the artist de Kooning was shown anonymous paintings by elephants, he thought the artist to be a most talented individual, one who knew how to "finish" and compose a drawing. On hearing that the artist was an elephant, he said, "That's a damned talented elephant." Jane Goodall, also on the subject of art, says that not only do chimpanzees make and name paintings, but that when shown their artwork as much as a year later, they remember the title they originally gave it.

Even humor is not entirely limited to humans. Recently Jane Goodall also related an exchange between the signing gorilla Koko and trainer Penny Patterson. A researcher was visiting them, and Penny wanted Koko to exhibit her intelligence.

Penny held up a piece of white cloth.

"Koko, what color is this?"

Koko signed, "Red."

Because the gorilla made an error, the woman asked again. "Koko, what color is this?"

Koko again replied, "Red."

Exasperated, the trainer said, "Koko, if you want to eat supper, you'd better answer the question. What color is this?"

Koko leaned forward and picked a tiny piece of red lint off the white cloth, looked her caretaker in the eye, showed her the lint, and laughed. "Red, red, red, red!"

Still wanting a place of our own, a place set aside from the rest of the creation, now it is being ventured that maybe our ability to make fire separates us, or perhaps the desire to seek revenge. But no matter what direction the quest for separation might take, there has been a narrowing down of the difference between species, and we are forced to ask ourselves once again: what is our rightful place in the world, our responsibility to the other lives on the planet? It's a question of crucial importance as we live in this strange and confusing time, when so many of our scientists prefer to meddle with the creation of new life forms rather than to maintain and care for those, even human lives, who are already in our presence. Oren Lyons, Iroquois traditionalist, has said, "We forget and we consider ourselves superior, but we are after all a mere part of this creation. And we must consider to understand where we are. And we stand somewhere between the mountain and the ant, somewhere and only there as part and parcel of the creation."

We are of the animal world. We are part of the cycles of growth and decay. Even having tried so hard to see ourselves apart, and so often without a love for even our own biology, we are in relationship with the rest of the planet, and that connectedness tells us we must reconsider the way we see ourselves and the rest of nature.

A change is required of us, a healing of the betrayed trust between humans and earth. Caretaking is the utmost spiritual and physical responsibility of our time, and perhaps that stewardship is finally our place in the web of life, our work, the solution to the mystery of what we are. There are already so many holes in the universe that will never again be filled, and each of them forces us to question why we permitted such loss, such tearing away at the fabric of life, and how we will live with our planet in the future.

Ishi is just one of those losses. Ishi was what he called himself, and the word meant only "man." Ishi kept his real name to himself. It was his only possession, all that remained for him of a lost way of life. He was the last of a kind of human being. His absence left us wondering about these lives of ours that unfold in the center of a tragic technology. When we wake up in the night, full of fear, we know the hole is all around us, pulling at even our dreams. We learn from what has fallen through before us. It's why we study history. It's why I wished a dying woman would balance between the worlds a moment, teetering there, and gaze backward in time to tell me any wise secret of survival. The kill hole where everything falls out is not just found in earth's or the body's clay. It is a dusky space between us and others, the place where our compassion has fallen away, our capacity for love failed. It is the time between times, a breached realm where apes inform us of a truth we fear to face. It is a broken mirror that reveals to us our own shady and dualistic natures and lays bare our human history of cruelty as well as love. What we are lives in that abyss. But we have also to ask if this research is not a great step in creating a bridge across that broken world, if these first explorations between humans and apes are not hands held out in welcome. Some of us have reached out across the solitude of our lives with care and mercy, have touched away the space between us all.

There is a Mandan story that tells how the killed buffalo left through a hole in the sky. From that hole, it's said, the grandmother still looks down at earth, watching over her children.

Today in San Diego, a young California condor is breaking a hole in an egg, pecking its way through to life. There are only twenty-eight California condors left in the world, all of them in captivity. They've been dwelling on the brink of extinction. But how amazing it is, this time a new life coming in, turning another way through that hole. A mending is taking place, a life emerging like the thread out of the labyrinth, the thread leading out of a Navajo rug's pattern of loss. The old woman in the sky is looking down on us, keeping watch.

Part II

HOW HAVE TRADITIONAL RELIGIONS VIEWED NATURE?

I, the fiery life of divine essence, am aflame beyond the beauty of the meadows, I gleam in the waters, and I burn in the sun, moon, and stars . . . I awaken everything to life.

—Hildegard of Bingen

Pleasant it looked,
this newly created world.
Along the entire length and breadth
of the earth, our grandmother,
extended the green reflection
of her covering and the escaping odors
were pleasant to inhale.

—Winnebago/Native American

Apprehend God in all things,
for God is in all things.
Every single creature is full of God
and is a book about God.
Every creature is a word of God.
If I spent enough time with the tiniest creature—
even a caterpillar—
I would never have to prepare a sermon. So full of God
is every creature.

—Meister Eckhart

Assuredly the creation
of the heavens
And the earth
Is greater
Than the creation of humankind;
Yet most people understand not.

—*Qur'an*

We sit in the lap of our Mother . . . We shall soon pass, but the place where we now rest will last forever.

—Lakota saying

Of all that the Holy One created in His world, He did not create a single thing that is useless.

—Talmud

When a tree that bears fruit is cut down, its moan goes from one end of the world to the other, yet no sound is heard.

—Midrash

Religions help situate human beings in both the natural and the social worlds. The latter function is served by their moral teachings, the former by a combination of creation myths, narrative accounts of the origin of particular phenomenon (for example, death), and norms governing our relation with our natural surroundings. To find out how "traditional" (that is, predating the modern age) religions viewed nature, we must consult a broad range of stories, philosophical accounts, and moral teachings. What follows in Part II is a representative sampling from that range, one that supports three tentative generalizations.

First, we see that human beings have taken nature to be something which requires an explanation. The Bible's account of creation, no less than Greek mythology's story of how the change of the seasons began, shows that people have wanted to put the multiplicity, variability, and sheer scope of their natural surroundings into a humanly comprehensible framework.

Second, we see that these accounts, for all their diversity, share a common bond: nature is to be made sense of in a way that directly connects it to the fundamental values of human existence. The contrast between the religious view of nature and that of modern (post-sixteenth century) science is thus revealed. For science, the natural world serves as a neutral backdrop to human activities, to be studied, manipulated, and mastered at will. It is, as Albert Camus put it, a setting of "benign indifference." To the religious sensibility, the universe is "enchanted": the gift of a loving God, a land destined for a holy people, the cosmic analog of our own mothers, a setting filled with spirit forces who are to be our guardians, or, perhaps, even a temptation to be overcome.

Yet, third, traditional religions represent nature in very different ways. These differences hold within as well as between religions, hardly surprising when we remember for how long and in how many different settings some of these traditions have existed. The notion that people are to "master the earth" (Genesis 1:28), even if interpreted as defining a relation which includes responsibility and care, is different from a view that sees nature as a model for human virtue (as it is at times portrayed in Taoism); or in which animals or parts of the landscape can serve as guides of spiritual development (as in Australian Aboriginal or certain Native American traditions). When in the ancient Sumerian epic, *Gilgamesh,* the hero seeks immortality by destroying the forest (see Harrison's retelling below), we see a bitter anticipation of the contemporary devastation of the rain forest. The teachings of Native Hawaiian religion, by contrast, contain values which may help us achieve a more sane and modest relation to nature.

Selections from original texts and commentary by scholars in Part II reflect the central point that we now read religious traditions in a fundamentally new way: we need to know in what ways they support or obstruct our desperate task of recovering some ecological sanity. The complex nature of our traditions leads to considerable controversy here. Thus some people claim that the view of nature in the Hebrew Bible is supportive of unrestrained domination of nature. Others argue that the Talmudic tradition of Rabbinical Judaism is actually conducive to a restrained and nature-respecting (if not worshipping) form of life. Daniel Swartz's reading of the full historic range of Jewish teachings, and Ginzberg's brief selection from Jewish poetic textual interpretation and biblical retelling (Midrash) reveal a rich and multifaceted tradition—one not easily summarized as having any single attitude toward nature.

A number of critics have suggested that the environmental destruction flowing from European science, industrial capitalism, and colonialism is particularly compatible with Europe's dominant religion. And some writers have suggested that there is a more nature respecting view in Chinese, Indian, African or indigenous religions. Overall, assessing the environmental viability of different religious traditions is a central task of this book. In this section, alongside the examination of Judaism and Christianity, there are writings from or discussions of Native American, Malaysian, Hindu, African, Islamic, Buddhist, Hawaiian, and Chinese ways of imagining and understanding the natural world.

To make matters more complicated still: the enormous variability of religious attitudes towards nature may lead us to wonder if the conduct of religious institutions towards the environment at any particular time is as much a product of the general culture, politics, and economic structure of the wider society as it is of the religions themselves.

"THE CREATION"

Fanetorens (Ray Fadden)

Many Winters in the past (arrow going backward)

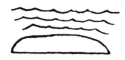

the Earth was entirely covered by a great blanket of water. There was no sun, moon, or stars and so there was no light. All was darkness.

At that time, the only living creatures of the world were water animals such as the beaver, muskrat, duck and loon.

Far above earth was the Land of Happy Spirits where lived Rawennio, the Great Ruler. In the center of this upper world was a giant tree.

This great tree was an apple tree whose roots sank deep into the ground.

One day, Rawennio pulled this giant tree up by its roots.

The Great Spirit called his daughter who lived in the Upper World and commanded her to look into the pit caused by the uprooted tree.

Reprinted with permission from *Akwesasne Notes* (1972 and 1992).

This woman, who was to be the mother of the Good and Evil Spirits, came and looked into the hole by the uprooted tree.

She saw far below her the Lower World covered with water and surrounded by heavy clouds.

"You are to go to this world of darkness," said the Great Spirit. Gently lifting her, he dropped her into the hole.

She floated downward.

Far below on the dark water floated the water animals. Looking upward, they saw a great light, which was the Sky Woman, slowly falling toward them.

Because her body shone as a great light they were at first frightened.

Fear filled their hearts and they dove beneath the deep waters.

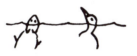

But upon coming to the surface again, they lost their fear. They began to plan what they would do for the woman when she reached the water.

"We must find a dry place for her to rest on," said the beaver, and he plunged beneath the water in search of some earth. After a long time, the beaver's dead body floated to the top of the water.

The loon tried next, but his body never came to the surface of the water. Many of the other water creatures dived, but all failed to secure any earth.

Finally, the muskrat went below and after a long time, his dead body floated to the surface of the water. His little claws were closed tight. Upon opening them, a little earth was found.

The water creatures took this earth, and calling a great turtle, they patted the earth firmly on her broad back. Immediately, the turtle started to grow larger. The earth also increased.

This earth became North America, a great island. Sometimes the earth cracks and shakes, and waves beat hard against the seashore. White people say, "Earthquake." The Mohawk say, "Turtle is stretching."

The Sky Woman had now almost reached the earth. "We must fly up and let her rest upon our backs so as to make her landing easy," said the chief of the white swans. Flying upward, a great flock of white swans allowed the Sky Woman to rest upon their backs. Gently, they bore her to earth.

After a time, the Sky Woman gave birth to twins. One who became the Good Spirit was born first. The other, the Evil Spirit, while being born, caused his mother so much pain that she died during his birth.

The Good Spirit immediately took his mother's head and hung it in the sky. It became the sun. The Good Spirit, from his mother's body, fashioned the moon and stars and placed them in the sky.

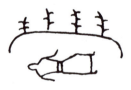

The rest of his mother's body he buried under the earth. That is why living things find nourishment from the soil. They spring from Mother Earth.

The Evil Spirit put darkness in the west sky to drive the sun before it.

The Good Spirit created many things which he placed upon the earth. The Evil Spirit tried to undo the work of his brother by creating evil. The Good Spirit made tall and beautiful trees such as the pine and hemlock.

The Evil Spirit stunted some trees. In others, he put knots and gnarls. He covered some with thorns, and placed poison fruit on them.

The Good Spirit made animals such as the deer and the bear.

The Evil Spirit made poisonous animals, lizards, and serpents to destroy the animals of the Good Spirit's creation.

The Good Spirit made springs and streams of good, pure water.

The Evil Spirit breathed poison into many of the springs. He put snakes into others.

The Good Spirit made beautiful rivers protected by high hills.

The Evil Spirit pushed rocks and dirt into the rivers causing the current to become swift and dangerous. Everything that the Good Spirit made, his wicked brother tried to destroy.

Finally, when the earth was completed, the Good Spirit fashioned man out of some red clay. He placed man upon the earth, and told him how he should live. The Evil Spirit, not to be outdone, fashioned a creature out of the white foam of the sea. What he made was the monkey.

After mankind and the other creatures of the world were created, the Good Spirit bestowed a protecting spirit upon each of his creations.

Fanetorens (Ray Fadden)

He then called the Evil Spirit, and told him that he must cease making trouble upon the earth. This the Evil Spirit refused to do. The Good Spirit became very angry with his wicked brother. He challenged his brother to combat, the victor to become ruler of the earth. They used the thorns of a giant apple tree as weapons.

They fought for many suns (days).

Finally, the Evil Spirit was overcome.

The Good Spirit now became ruler over the earth. He banished his wicked brother to a dark cave under the earth. There he must always remain.

But the Evil Spirit has wicked servants who roam the earth. These wicked spirits can take the shape of any creature that the Evil Spirit desires them to take. They are constantly influencing the minds of men, thus causing men to do evil things.

That is why every person has both a bad heart and a good heart. No matter how good a man seems, he has some evil. No matter how bad a man seems, there is some good about him. No man is perfect.

The Good Spirit continues to create and protect mankind. He controls the spirits of good men after death. The Evil Spirit takes charge of the souls of wicked men after death.

Fanetorens (Ray Fadden)

"DEATH AND REBIRTH OF THE UNIVERSE" (*Hindu*);

"THE PARADE OF ANTS" (*Hindu*);

"THE FIVE SUNS" (*Aztec*);

"PERSEPHONE" (*Greek*)

Joseph L. Henderson and Maud Oakes

"DEATH AND REBIRTH OF THE UNIVERSE" (HINDU)[1]

The cosmic unit of time, according to Hindu mythical astronomy, is the Kalpa, or a day of Brahma the creator. Brahma creates in the morning, and at night the three worlds, . . . Earth, Heaven and Hell, are reduced to chaos, every being that has not obtained liberation retaining its essence which takes form according to its Karma, when Brahma wakes up in the morning. Thus the eventful days and nights pass on, till Brahma reaches the hundredth year of his life when "not only the three worlds but all planes and all beings, Brahma himself, Devas, Rishis, Asuras, men, creatures and matter" are all resolved into Mahapralaya (the great cataclysm). After a hundred years of chaos, another Brahma is born. . . . A Kalpa or day of Brahma is equivalent to 4,320,000,000 earth years . . . .

The manner of destruction of the world at the end of the Kaliyuga[2] is differently described in the Puranas. In one account it is related that Vishnu will appear as Kalki, "an armed warrior, mounted on a white horse, furnished with wings and adorned with jewels, waving over his head with one hand the sword of destruction and holding in the other a disc.

The horse is represented as holding up the right fore-leg; and when he stamps on the earth with that, the tortoise supporting the serpent Shesha on whose hood the world rests, shall fall into the deep, and so rid himself of the load; and by that means all the wicked inhabitants of the world will be destroyed."

In the Bhagbata we are told that the "age of destruction is so horrible that during it the clouds never fall on the earth as drops of rain for one hundred years. The people then find no food to eat . . . and are compelled to eat one another. Being thus overpowered by what is wrought by time, the men gradually lead themselves to utter destruction."

Elsewhere the universal cataclysm is predicted in vivid detail. "After a drought lasting many years, seven blazing suns will appear in the firmament; they will drink up all the waters. Then the wind-driven fire will sweep over the earth, consuming all things; penetrating to the netherworld it will destroy what is there in a moment; it will burn up the universe. Afterwards many coloured and brilliant clouds will collect in the sky looking like herds of elephants decked with wreaths of lightning. Suddenly they will burst asunder, and rain will fall incessantly for twelve years until the whole world . . . is covered with water. The clouds will vanish. Then the self-created lord, the first cause of everything, will absorb the winds and go to sleep. The universe will become one dread expanse of water."

"THE PARADE OF ANTS" (HINDU)[3]

During the period of the supremacy of the dragon, the majestic mansions of the lofty city of the gods had cracked and crumbled. The first act of Indra was to rebuild them. All the divinities of the heavens were acclaiming him their savior. Greatly elated in his triumph [over the dragon] and in the knowledge of his strength, he summoned Vishvakarman, the god of arts and crafts, and commanded him to erect such a palace as should befit the unequaled splendor of the king of the gods.

The miraculous genius, Vishvakarman, succeeded in constructing in a single year a shining residence, marvelous with palaces and gardens, lakes and towers. But as the work progressed, the demands of Indra became even more exacting and his unfolding visions vaster. He required additional terraces and pavilions, more ponds, groves, and pleasure grounds. Whenever Indra arrived to appraise the work, he developed vision beyond vision of marvels remaining to be contrived. Presently the divine craftsman, brought to despair, decided to seek succor from above. He would turn to the demiurgic creator, Brahma, the pristine embodiment of the Universal Spirit, who abides far above the troubled Olympian sphere of ambition, strife, and glory.

When Vishvakarman secretly resorted to the higher throne and presented his case, Brahma comforted the petitioner. "You will soon be relieved of your burden," he said. "Go home in peace." Then, while Vishvakarman was hurrying down again to the city of Indra, Brahma himself ascended to a still higher sphere. He came before Vishnu, the Supreme Being, of whom he himself, the Creator, was but an agent. In beatific silence Vishnu gave ear, and by a mere nod of the head let it be known that the request of Vishvakarman would be fulfilled.

Early next morning a brahmin boy, carrying the staff of a pilgrim, made his appearance at the gate of Indra, bidding the porter announce his visit to the king. The gate-man hurried to the master, and the master hastened to the entrance to welcome in person the auspicious guest. The boy was slender, some ten years old, radiant with the luster of wisdom. Indra discovered him amidst a cluster of enraptured, staring children. The boy greeted the host with a gentle glance of his dark and brilliant eyes. The king bowed to the holy child and the boy cheerfully gave his blessing. The two retired to the hall of Indra, where the god ceremoniously proffered welcome to his guest with oblations of honey, milk, and fruits, then said: "O Venerable Boy, tell me of the purpose of your coming."

The beautiful child replied with a voice that was as deep and soft as the slow thundering of auspicious rain clouds. "O King of Gods, I have heard of the mighty palace you are building, and have come to refer to you the questions in my mind. How many years will it require to complete this rich and extensive residence? What further feats of engineering will Vishvakarman be expected to accomplish? O Highest of Gods,"—the boy's luminous features moved with a gentle, scarcely perceptible smile—"no Indra before you has ever succeeded in completing such a palace as yours is to be."

Full of the wine of triumph, the king of the gods was entertained by this mere boy's pretension to a knowledge of Indras earlier than himself. With a fatherly smile he put the question: "Tell me, Child! Are they then so very many, the Indras and Vishvakarmans whom you have seen—or at least whom you have heard of?"

The wonderful guest calmly nodded. "Yes, indeed, many have I seen." The voice was as warm and sweet as milk fresh from the cow, but the words sent a slow chill through Indra's veins. "My dear child," the boy continued, "I knew your father, Kashyapa, the Old Tortoise Man, lord and progenitor of all the creatures of the earth. And I knew your grandfather, Marichi, Beam of Celestial Light, who was the son of Brahma. Marichi was begotten of the god Brahma's pure spirit; his only wealth and glory were his sanctity and devotion. Also, I know Brahma, brought forth by Vishnu from the lotus calix growing from Vishnu's navel. And Vishnu himself—the Supreme Being, supporting Brahma in his creative endeavor—him too I know."

"O King of Gods, I have known the dreadful dissolution of the universe. I have seen all perish, again and again, at the end of every cycle. At that terrible time, every single atom dissolves into the primal, pure waters of eternity, whence originally all arose. Everything then goes back into the fathomless, wild infinity of the ocean, which is covered with utter darkness and is empty of every sign of animate being. Ah, who will count the universes that have passed away, or the creations that have risen afresh, again and again, from the formless abyss of the vast waters? Who will number the passing ages of the world, as they follow each other endlessly? And who will search through the wide infinities of space to count the universes side by side, each containing its Brahma, its Vishnu, and its Shiva? Who will count the Indras in them all—those Indras side by side, who reign at once in all the innumerable worlds; those others who passed away before them; or even the Indras who succeed each other in any given line, ascending to godly kingship, one by one, and, one by one, passing away? King of Gods, there are among your servants certain who maintain that it may be possible to number the grains of sand on earth and the drops of rain that fall from the sky, but no one will ever number all those Indras. This is what the Knowers know.

"The life and kingship of an Indra endure seventy-one eons, and when twenty-eight Indras have expired, one Day and Night of Brahma has elapsed. But the existence of one Brahma, measured in such Brahma Days and Nights, is only one hundred and eight years. Brahma follows Brahma; one sinks, the next arises; the endless series cannot be told. There is no end to the number of those Brahmas—to say nothing of Indras.

"But the universes side by side at any given moment, each harboring a Brahma and an Indra: who will estimate the number of these? Beyond the farthest vision, crowding outer space, the universes come and go, an innumerable host. Like delicate boats they float on the fathomless, pure waters that form the body of Vishnu. Out of every hair-pore of that body a universe bubbles and breaks. Will you presume to count them? Will you number the gods in all those worlds—the worlds present and the worlds past?"

A procession of ants had made its appearance in the hall during the discourse of the boy. In military array, in a column four yards wide, the tribe paraded across the floor. The boy noted them, paused, and stared, then suddenly laughed with an astonishing peal, but immediately subsided into a profoundly indrawn and thoughtful silence.

"Why do you laugh?" stammered Indra. "Who are you, mysterious being, under this deceiving guise of a boy?" The proud king's throat and lips had gone dry, and his voice continually broke. "Who are you, Ocean of Virtues, enshrouded in deluding mist?"

The magnificent boy resumed: "I laughed because of the ants. The reason is not to be told. Do not ask me to disclose it. The seed of woe and the fruit of wisdom are enclosed within this secret. It is the secret that smites with an ax the tree of worldly vanity, hews away its roots, and scatters its crown. This secret is a lamp to those groping in ignorance. This secret lies buried in the wisdom of the ages, and is rarely revealed even to saints. This secret is the living air of those ascetics who renounce and transcend mortal existence; but worldlings, deluded by desire and pride, it destroys."

The boy smiled and sank into silence. Indra regarded him, unable to move. "O Son of a brahmin," the king pleaded presently, with a new and visible humility, "I do not know who you are. You would seem to be Wisdom Incarnate. Reveal to me this secret of the ages, this light that dispels the dark."

Thus requested to teach, the boy opened to the god the hidden wisdom. "I saw the ants, O Indra, filing in long parade. Each was once an Indra. Like you, each by virtue of pious deeds once ascended to the rank of a king of gods. But now, through many rebirths, each has become again an ant. This army is an army of former Indras."

"Piety and high deeds elevate the inhabitants of the world to the glorious realm of the celestial mansions, or to the higher domains of Brahma and Shiva and to the highest sphere of Vishnu; but wicked acts sink them into the worlds beneath, into pits of pain and sorrow, involving reincarnation among birds and vermin, or out of the wombs of pigs and animals of the wild, or among trees, or among insects. It is by deeds that one merits happiness or anguish, and becomes a master or a serf. It is by deeds that one attains to the rank of a king or brahmin, or of some god, or of an Indra or a Brahma. And through deeds again, one contracts disease, acquires beauty and deformity, or is reborn in the condition of a monster.

"This is the whole substance of the secret. This wisdom is the ferry to beatitude across the ocean of hell.

"Life in the cycle of the countless rebirths is like a vision in a dream. The gods on high, the mute trees and the stones, are alike apparitions in this phantasy. But Death administers the law of time. Ordained by time, Death is the master of all. Perishable as bubbles are the good and evil of the beings of the dream. In unending cycles the good and evil alternate. Hence, the wise are attached to neither, neither the evil nor the good. The wise are not attached to anything at all."

The boy concluded the appalling lesson and quietly regarded his host. The king of gods, for all his celestial splendor, had been reduced in his own regard to insignificance. . . . [Then] the brahmin boy, who had been Vishnu, disappeared. . . . The king was alone, baffled and amazed.

"THE FIVE SUNS" (AZTEC)[4]

The Aztec gods were givers of the laws of nature. In this tale, their struggles give rise to the death and rebirth of the universe. The well-known Aztec Calendar Stone called "Eagle Bowl" is an image of a cosmic cycle (Plate 3). On it are carved the symbols of the five suns.

The nocturnal Tezcatlipoca,[5] whose *nahual* or disguise is the jaguar, its spotted skin resembling the heavens with their myriad stars, was the first to become a sun, and with him began the first era of the world. The first men created by the gods were giants; they neither sowed grain nor tilled the soil, but lived by eating acorns and other fruits and wild roots. Tezcatlipoca was also the constellation of Ursa Major, whom the Aztecs pictured as a jaguar. While he was ruling the world as the sun, his enemy, Quetzalcoatl, struck him a blow with his staff. Tezcatlipoca fell into the water, changing into a jaguar. He devoured the giants, and the earth was depopulated and the universe was without a sun. This occurred on the day called "Jaguar."

Then Quetzalcoatl became the sun, until the jaguar struck him down with a blow of his paw. Then a great wind arose, and all the trees were uprooted, and the greater part of mankind perished. Those men who survived were transformed into monkeys, that is, into subhuman creatures. This took place on the day "Wind." Men at that time ate only pine nuts or *acocentli*. The creator gods then chose Tlaloc, the god of rain and celestial fire, as the sun, but Quetzalcoatl made the fire rain down, and men either perished or were changed into birds. This happened on the day "4 Rain." The sustenance of men during this age was a seed called *acecentli*, or "water corn."

Then Quetzalcoatl selected Tlaloc's sister as the sun. She was the goddess Chalchiuhtlicue, "the lady of the jade skirts," goddess of water. But no doubt it was Tezcatlipoca who caused it to rain so hard that the earth was flooded and men either perished or were transformed into fish. This occurred on the day called "4 Water." During this age men ate . . . *teocentli*, the ancestor of corn.[6]

Laurette Sejourne believes that there were five suns. The face in the centre of the Calendar Stone is the face of Quetzalcoatl, our present sun.

That is why the Fifth Sun (five is the number of the centre), is the Sun of Movement [earthquake], . . . "The name of this Sun is Naollin (Four Movements), now is ours, by which today we live. . . . It was also the Sun of Quetzalcoatl . . ."

This sun, whose emblem is a human face, not only represents the central region, but also what is above and what is below, that is, heaven and earth. The symbol of the world is thus brought together in a cross.

"PERSEPHONE" (GREEK)[7]

Persephone, . . . was in the Nysian plain with the Ocean nymphs gathering flowers. She plucked the rose, the violet, . . . when she beheld a narcissus of surprising size and beauty, an object of amazement . . . for one hundred flowers grew from one root; unconscious of danger the maiden stretched forth her hand to seize the wondrous flower, when suddenly the wide earth gaped, Hades in his gold chariot rose, and catching the terrified goddess carried her off in it shrieking to her father for aid, unheard and unseen by gods or mortals, save only Hecate, . . . who heard her as she sat in her cave, and by king Helios, whose eye nothing on earth escapes.

So long as the goddess beheld the earth and starry heavens, the fishy sea and the beams of the sun, so long she hoped to see her mother and the tribes of the gods; and the tops of the mountains and the depth of the sea resounded with her divine voice. At length her mother heard: she tore her head-attire with grief, cast a dark robe around her, and like a bird hurried "over moist and dry." Of all she inquired tidings of her lost daughter, but neither gods nor men nor birds could give her intelligence. Nine days she wandered over the earth, with flaming torches in her hands; she tasted not of nectar or ambrosia, and never once entered the bath. On the tenth morning Hecate met her. . . . Together they proceed to Helios: . . . and Demeter entreats that he will say who the ravisher is. The god of the sun, . . . tells her that it was Hades, who by permission of her sire had carried her [Persephone] away to be his queen; . . .

. . . the goddess, incensed at the conduct of Zeus, abandoned the society of the gods, and came down among men. But now she was heedless of her person, and no one recognized her. Under the disguise of an old woman, . . . she came to Eleusis, and sat . . . by a well, beneath the shade of an olive tree . . .

The Princess Kallidike [who had come to the well to draw water] tells the goddess . . . to wait till she had consulted her mother, Metaneira, who had a young son in the cradle, of whom, if the stranger could obtain the nursing her fortune would be made; . . . [Metaneira] agreed to hire the nurse at large wages; . . . As she entered the house a divine splendor shone all around. . . . She undertook the rearing of the babe, . . . beneath her care "he throve like a god." . . .

It was the design of Demeter to make him immortal, but the curiosity and folly of Metaneira deprived him of the intended gift. . . . Demeter tells who she is, and directs that the people of Eleusis should raise an altar and temple to her . . . and the temple was speedily raised. The mourning goddess took up her abode in it, but a dismal year came upon mankind; the earth yielded no produce, . . . in vain was the seed of barley cast into the ground; "well-garlanded Demeter" would suffer no increase. The whole race of man ran risk of perishing, the dwellers of Olympos of losing gifts and sacrifices, had not Zeus discerned the danger and thought on a remedy. He . . . invites Demeter back to Olympos, but the disconsolate goddess will not comply with the call . . . she will not ascend to Olympos, or suffer the earth to bring forth, till she has seen her daughter. (*Plate* 14.)

. . . Zeus sends . . . [Hermes] to Erebos, to endeavor to prevail on Hades to suffer Persephone to return to the light . . . he [Hermes] quickly reached the "secret places of earth," and found the king at home . . . with his wife, who was mourning for her mother. On making known to Hades the wish of Zeus, "the king of the Subterraneans smiled with his brows" and yielded compliances. He kindly addressed Persephone, granting her permission to return to her mother. The goddess instantly sprang up with joy, and heedlessly swallowed a grain of pomegranate which he presented to her.

Hermes conducted his fair charge safe to Eleusis . . . and Persephone sprang from the car to meet and embrace her mother . . .

Demeter anxiously inquired if her daughter had tasted anything while below; . . . if but one morsel had passed her lips, nothing could save her from spending one-third of the year with her husband; she should however pass the other two with her and the gods.

Persephone ingenuously confesses the swallowing of the grain of pomegranate, and then relates to her mother the whole story. . . . Zeus sends Rhea to invite them back to heaven. Demeter now complies.

NOTES

1.   P. Thomas, *Epics, Myths and Legends of India* (8th ed.; Bombay: D.B. Taraporevala Sons & Co., Ltd., n.d.), p. 4–6.

2.   The day of Brahma is divided into 1,000 Mahayugas (great ages) of equal length, each consisting of four Yugas; namely, Krita, Threta, Dwapara, and Kali. Kaliyuga is the present age of degeneration (and consists of 432,000 years).

3.   Heinrich Zimmer, *Myths and Symbols in Indian Art and Civilization* (Princeton: Princeton University Press, 1971), pp. 3–10.

4.   Alfonso Caso, *The Aztecs*, tr. Lowell Dunham (Norman, Oklahoma: University of Oklahoma Press, 1958), pp. 14–15.

5.   Tezcatlipoca . . . signified the noctural cycle and was connected with the moon and all stellar gods, hence he brought misfortune, death, and destruction, and war associated with witchcraft.

6.   Another legend reverses the order of the suns.

7.   L. Schmitz, *Keightley's Classical Mythology* (London: G. Bell & Sons, 1896), pp. 152–56.

from FORESTS: THE SHADOW OF CIVILIZATION

Robert Pogue Harrison

Gilgamesh was the legendary but real king of Uruk, a Sumerian city born under the auspices of Anu—god of the sky. He lived during the Early Dynastic II period, around 2700 B.C., some six hundred years before the composition of the first Sumerian epics that commemorate him. In the Sumerian and Babylonian literature Gilgamesh is commonly referred to as the "builder of the walls of Uruk." The epitaph effectively summarizes his civic heroism. Walls, no less than writing, define civilization. They are monuments of resistance against time, like writing itself, and Gilgamesh is remembered by them. Walls protect, divide, distinguish; above all, they *abstract*. The basic activities that sustain life—agriculture and stock breeding, for instance—take place beyond the walls. Within the walls one is within an emporium; one is within the jurisdiction of a bureaucracy; one is within the abstract identity of race, city, and institutionalized religion; in short, one is within the lonely enclosure of history. Gilgamesh is the builder of such walls that divide history from prehistory, culture from nature, sky from earth, life from death, memory from oblivion.

But the same walls that individuate the city, as well its hero, are precisely what oppress Gilgamesh, at least insofar as the epic cycle portrays him. Within his walls Gilgamesh finds himself exposed to insidious reminders of the fatality of personal death—the linear finality of human existence. It is in direct response to his aggravated sense of transience that Gilgamesh decides to undertake his forest journey. In the following passage from Samuel Noah Kramer's translation of "Gilgamesh and the Land of the Living," we hear Gilgamesh declaring to his friend Enkidu that he would perform some glorious deed by which he may inscribe himself within the annals of historical memory:

> O Enkidu, not (yet) have brick and stamp brought forth the fated end,
> I would enter the "land," I would set up my name,
> In its places where the names have been raised up, I would raise up my name,
> In its places where the names have not been raised up, I would raise up the names of the gods.
> (4–7)

Harrison, Robert Pogue, *Forests: The Shadow of Civilization*, 1992, The University of Chicago Press. Reprinted with permission of the author and the University of Chicago Press.

The "land" where Gilgamesh would go and set up his name is the forested Cedar Mountain. Because he has not yet achieved a lasting fame, because he has not yet *stamped his name in brick* (or in the tablets of the scribes), Gilgamesh must go to the "land" and slay the forest demon, Huwawa. This is the deed that will monumentalize him in stone or brick—preserve his memory after death.

But again, why precisely a forest journey? Before we can answer the question we should listen to Gilgamesh's plea to Utu, the Sumerian Sun god. Utu is the god who must grant Gilgamesh the permission to undertake the journey, for the land is in Utu's charge. The god does not understand Gilgamesh's irrational desire to go to the land, nor does he initially approve of the idea. Huwawa, whom Gilgamesh would slay, is after all a sacred forest demon. Utu does not understand why Gilgamesh wishes to challenge the demon. To convince the god of his desperate need to undertake the journey, Gilgamesh offers a pathetic confession:

> "O Utu, I would enter the 'land,' be thou my ally,
> I would enter the land *of the cut-down* cedar, be thou my ally."
> Utu of heaven answers him:
> ". . . verily thou art, but what art thou to the 'land'?"
> "O Utu, a word I would speak to thee, to my word thy ear,
> *I would have it reach thee*, give ear to it.
> In my city man dies, oppressed is the heart,
> Man perishes, heavy is the heart,
> I *peered over* the wall,
> Saw the dead bodies . . . *floating on* the river;
> As for me, I too will be served thus; verily 'tis so.
> Man, the tallest, cannot stretch to heaven,
> Man the widest, cannot *cover* the earth.
> Not *(yet)* have brick and stamp brought forth *the fated end*,
> I would enter the 'land,' I would set up my name." (17–31)

In ancient Sumerian funeral rites, the bodies of the dead were floated down the river in ceremonious processions. Gilgamesh has peered over the walls of his city and has seen the bodies floating on the river. In other words he has seen beyond life to the inanimate corpse—the mere object drifting toward decomposition and reintegration with the earth. He has peered over the wall of history and seen the remorseless transcendence of nature. With despair in his heart he has looked at the outlying earth: dumb, inert, insurmountable, revolving her relentless cycles, turning kings into cadavers, waiting impassively to draw all things into her oblivion. Is this not intolerable for someone who is a builder of walls, someone who is devoted to the memorial transcendence of history? Must Gilgamesh not react to the scene of dead bodies floating on the river by challenging such oblivion with the might of memory?

We come closer to accounting psychologically for Gilgamesh's desire to undertake the forest journey. He wants the glory of his deed to spare him from such oblivion. But what glory is there in slaying the forest demon? When Gilgamesh obtains the necessary permission from Utu for his journey, he arrives at the sacred cedar forests and engages Huwawa in battle, cutting off the demon's head. The cutting off of Huwawa's head represents, in its poetic image, the cutting down of the cedar forest. The "glory" of this exploit can be understood only against the historical background. We know from the written records that certain Sumerian individuals actually achieved considerable fame by undertaking expeditions to the cedar forests and seizing huge quantities of timber. Timber was a precious commodity for the Sumerians, since the alluvial plains of Mesopotamia were by that time devoid of forests. In the Early Dynastic periods the Sumerians apparently got their timber from the east, in nearby Elam, but after the deforestation of these regions they had to travel much further to the Amanus mountains in the north. To obtain wood they had to undertake dangerous expeditions to the mountains, cut down the cedars and pines, and ferry the logs back to the cities down the rivers. Such exploits were fraught with peril, especially since the forests were often defended by fierce forest tribes, but a leader could derive considerable fame from a successful expedition.

We can understand, therefore, why Gilgamesh's desire for monumental fame might lead him to conceive of a forest expedition. But the epic probes the hero's psychological motivations much deeper than this. There is more to Gilgamesh's inspiration than mere childish heroism and desire for fame through adventure. If Gilgamesh resolves to kill the forest demon, or to deforest the Cedar Mountain, it is because forests represent the quintessence of what lies beyond the walls of the city, namely the earth in its enduring transcendence. Forests embody another, more ancient law than the law of civilization. When Gilgamesh declares to Utu, "Man, the tallest, cannot stretch to heaven," he avows that human beings, however great, cannot become gods, or attain immortality. And when he declares: "Man the widest, cannot *cover* the earth," he avows that neither can they be like forests, which cover the earth and endure through the millennia according to their own self-regenerating cycles. Gilgamesh, in other words, is trapped within walls that close him off from two dimensions of transcendence, the one vertical and the other horizontal.

Gilgamesh journeys toward the forest as toward the veritable frontier of civilization. The forest is the counterpart of his city. He imagines perhaps that he could transcend the walls that enclose him through an act of massive deforestation. But to understand the hero's deeper psychological motivations we must try to imagine what really goes on in his mind when he peers over the walls of Uruk.

Gilgamesh peers over the walls and sees human bodies floating down the river in funeral processions. The sight of these bodies inspires in him the idea of a forest expedition. It is a visionary moment for Gilgamesh. In revolt against the scene of finitude, Gilgamesh has a vision: he will go to the forests, cut down the trees, and send the logs down the river to the city. In other words, he will make the trees share the fate of those who live within the walls. *Logs will become the cadavers.* The hero who dies within the city will project his own personal fate onto the forests. This is no doubt what Gilgamesh means when he says that he would enter the land and raise up his name. For if he is not wide enough to "cover the earth," yet may he still uncover it.

It is a sorry fact of history that human beings have never ceased reenacting the gesture of Gilgamesh. The destructive impulse with respect to nature all too often has psychological causes that go beyond the greed for material resource or the need to domesticate an environment. There is too often a deliberate rage and vengefulness at work in the assault on nature and its species, as if one would project onto the natural world the intolerable anxieties of finitude which hold humanity hostage to death. There is a kind of childish furor that needs to create victims without in order to exorcise the pathos of victimage within. The epic of *Gilgamesh* tells the story of such furor; but while Gilgamesh ends up as the ultimate victim of his own despair, the logs meanwhile float down the river like bodies of the dead.

From the epic cycle as a whole in its Sumerian and Akkadian versions, we gather that Gilgamesh's expedition to the Cedar Mountain was in fact a vain attempt to overcome the source of his afflictions. To begin with, the slaying of Huwawa angers the gods. It was a sacrilege, for Huwawa had the dignity of a sacred being. In some versions of the story, Gilgamesh's beloved friend, Enkidu, must pay for the crime of killing Huwawa with his own life. Upon the death of his friend Gilgamesh falls into an exacerbated state of melancholy, consuming himself with thoughts about death. Fame and the monuments of memory no longer console him for the fact of dying. That is why Gilgamesh sets out on another journey, this time in search of everlasting life. Yet the long and desperate quest for personal immortality only leads him to the knowledge that death is the ineluctable and nonnegotiable condition of life—that the cadaverous logs he sent down to the city from the Cedar Mountain cannot spare him his last journey of all down the very same river. And this, at the dawn of civilization, is called "wisdom."

from THE *TAO TE CHING*

Lao Tzu

ONE

Tao, the path of subtle truth,
cannot be conveyed with words.
That which can be conveyed with words
is merely a relative conception.
Although names have been applied to it,
the subtle truth is indescribable.
One may designate Nothingness as the origin of the universe,
And Beingness as the mother of the myriad things.
From the perspective of Nothingness,
one may perceive the gentle operation of the universe.
From the perspective of Beingness,
one may distinguish individual things.
Although differently named,
Nothingness and Beingness are one indivisible whole.
The truth is so subtle.
As the ultimate subtlety, it is the Gate of All Wonders.

FOUR

The gentle Way of the universe appears to be empty,
yet its usefulness is inexhaustible.
Fathomless, it could be the origin of all things.
It has no sharpness,
yet it rounds off all sharp edges.
It has no form,
yet it unties all tangles.
It has no glare,
yet it merges all lights.

Reprinted from *The Complete Works of Lao Tzu: Tao Te Ching and Hua Hu Ching* translated by Hua-Ching Ni, 1979, with permission of Seven Star Communications.

It harmonizes all things
and unites them as one integral whole.
It seems so obscure,
yet it is the Ultimate Clarity.
Whose offspring it is can never be known.
It is that which existed before any divinity.

FIVE

The virtue of the universe is wholeness.
It regards all things as equal.
The virtue of the sage is wholeness.
He too regards all things as equal.
The universe may be compared to a bellows.
It is empty,
yet it never fails to generate.
The more it moves,
the more it brings forth.
Many words lead one nowhere.
Many pursuits in different directions
only bring about exhaustion.
Rather, embrace the profound emptiness
and silence within.

SIX

The subtle essence of the universe is eternal.
It is like an unfailing fountain of life which
flows forever in a vast and profound valley.
It is called the Primal Female, the Mysterious Origin.
The operation of the opening and closing
of the subtle Gate of the Origin performs
the Mystical Intercourse of the universe.
The Mystical Intercourse brings forth all things
from the unseen sphere into the realm of the manifest.
The Mystical Intercourse of yin and yang
is the root of universal life.
Its creativity and effectiveness are boundless.

Lao Tzu

TEN

Can you always embrace Oneness
without the slightest separation of body and mind?
Can you maintain undivided concentration
until your vital force is as supple as a newborn baby's?
Can you clarify your inner vision to be flawless?
Can you love your people and serve your state
with no self-exaltation?
As Life's Gate opens and closes
in the performance of birth and death,
Can you maintain the receptive, feminine principle?
After achieving the crystal clear mind,
can you remain detached and innocent?
Give birth to and nourish all things
without desiring to possess them.
Give of yourself,
without expecting something in return.
Assist people, but do not attempt to control them.
This is to realize the integral virtue of the universe.

ELEVEN

Thirty spokes together make a wheel for a cart.
It is the empty space in the center
of the wheel which enables it to be used.
Mold clay into a vessel;
it is the emptiness within
that creates the usefulness of the vessel.
Cut out doors and windows in a house;
it is the empty space inside
that creates the usefulness of the house.
Thus, what we have may be something substantial,
But its usefulness lies in the unoccupied, empty space.
The substance of your body is enlivened
by maintaining the part of you that is unoccupied.

THIRTY-FOUR

Tao, the subtle energy of the universe,
is omnipresent.
It may go to the left or the right.
All things derive their life from it,
and it holds nothing back from them,
Yet it takes possession of nothing.
It accomplishes its purpose,
but it claims no merit.
It clothes and feeds all,
but has no ambition to be master over anyone.
Thus it may be regarded as 'the Small.'
All things return to it, and it contains them,
Yet it claims no authority over them.
Thus it may be recognized as 'the Great.'
The wise one who never attempts
to be emotionally great
And who accomplishes each small task with full devotion,
as if it were the greatest of tasks
Is naturally recognized as great.

SEVENTY-TWO

When people lack a sense of pure spiritual piety
toward natural life,
then awful things happen in their life.
Therefore, respect where you dwell.
Love your life and livelihood.
Because you do not disparage
your life and livelihood,
You will never become tired of life.
Thus, one of whole virtue respects his own life,
But is not egotistical.
He loves his life, but does not exalt himself.
He holds a sense of spiritual serenity for all things,
and disparages nothing.
Hence, he does what is right
and gives up what is not right.

from THE HEBREW BIBLE

GENESIS

1 ¹When God began to create heaven and earth—²the earth being unformed and void, with darkness over the surface of the deep and a wind from God sweeping over the water—³God said, "Let there be light"; and there was light. ⁴God saw that the light was good, and God separated the light from the darkness. ⁵God called the light Day, and the darkness He called Night. And there was evening and there was morning, a first day.

⁶God said, "Let there be an expanse in the midst of the water, that it may separate water from water." ⁷God made the expanse, and it separated the water which was below the expanse from the water which was above the expanse. And it was so. ⁸God called the expanse Sky. And there was evening and there was morning, a second day.

⁹God said, "Let the water below the sky be gathered into one area, that the dry land may appear." And it was so. ¹⁰God called the dry land Earth, and the gathering of waters He called Seas. And God saw that this was good. ¹¹And God said, "Let the earth sprout vegetation: seed-bearing plants, fruit trees of every kind on earth that bear fruit with the seed in it." And it was so. ¹²The earth brought forth vegetation: seed-bearing plants of every kind, and trees of every kind bearing fruit with the seed in it. And God saw that this was good. ¹³And there was evening and there was morning, a third day.

¹⁴God said, "Let there be lights in the expanse of the sky to separate day from night; they shall serve as signs for the set times—the days and the years; ¹⁵and they shall serve as lights in the expanse of the sky to shine upon the earth." And it was so. ¹⁶God made the two great lights, the greater light to dominate the day and the lesser light to dominate the night, and the stars. ¹⁷And God set them in the expanse of the sky to shine upon the earth, ¹⁸to dominate the day and the night, and to separate light from darkness. And God saw that this was good. ¹⁹And there was evening and there was morning, a fourth day.

²⁰God said, "Let the waters bring forth swarms of living creatures, and birds that fly above the earth across the expanse of the sky." ²¹God created the great sea monsters, and all the living creatures of every kind that creep, which the waters brought forth in swarms, and all the winged birds of every kind. And God saw that this was good. ²²God blessed them, saying, "Be fertile and increase, fill the waters in the seas, and let the birds increase on the earth." ²³And there was evening and there was morning, a fifth day.

---

²⁴God said, "Let the earth bring forth every kind of living creature: cattle, creeping things, and wild beasts of every kind." And it was so. ²⁵God made wild beasts of every kind and cattle of every kind, and all kinds of creeping things of the earth. And God saw that this was good. ²⁶And God said, "Let us make man in our image, after our likeness. They shall rule the fish of the sea, the birds of the sky, the cattle, the whole earth, and all the creeping things that creep on earth." ²⁷And God created man in His image, in the image of God He created him; male and female He created them. ²⁸God blessed them and God said to them, "Be fertile and increase, fill the earth and master it; and rule the fish of the sea, the birds of the sky, and all the living things that creep on earth."

²⁹God said, "See, I give you every seed-bearing plant that is upon all the earth, and every tree that has seed-bearing fruit; they shall be yours for food. ³⁰And to all the animals on land, to all the birds of the sky, and to everything that creeps on earth, in which there is the breath of life, [I give] all the green plants for food." And it was so. ³¹And God saw all that He had made, and found it very good. And there was evening and there was morning, the sixth day.

2 ¹The heaven and the earth were finished, and all their array. ²On the seventh day God finished the work that He had been doing, and He ceased on the seventh day from all the work that He had done. ³And God blessed the seventh day and declared it holy, because on it God ceased from all the work of creation that He had done. ⁴Such is the story of heaven and earth when they were created.

When the LORD God made earth and heaven—⁵when no shrub of the field was yet on earth and no grasses of the field had yet sprouted, because the LORD God had not sent rain upon the earth and there was no man to till the soil, ⁶but a flow would well up from the ground and water the whole surface of the earth—⁷the LORD God formed man from the dust of the earth. He blew into his nostrils the breath of life, and man became a living being.

⁸The LORD God planted a garden in Eden, in the east, and placed there the man whom He had formed. ⁹And from the ground the LORD God caused to grow every tree that was pleasing to the sight and good for food, with the tree of life in the middle of the garden, and the tree of knowledge of good and bad.

¹⁵The LORD God took the man and placed him in the garden of Eden, to till it and tend it. ¹⁶And the LORD God commanded the man, saying, "Of every tree of the garden you are free to eat; ¹⁷but as for the tree of knowledge of good and bad, you must not eat of it; for as soon as you eat of it, you shall die."

¹⁸The LORD God said, "It is not good for man to be alone; I will make a fitting helper for him." ¹⁹And the LORD God formed out of the earth all the wild beasts and all the birds of the sky, and brought them to the man to see what he would call them; and whatever the man called each living creature, that would be its name. ²⁰And the man gave names to all

the cattle and to the birds of the sky and to all the wild beasts; but for Adam no fitting helper was found. ²¹So the Lord God cast a deep sleep upon the man; and, while he slept, He took one of his ribs and closed up the flesh at that spot. ²²And the Lord God fashioned the rib that He had taken from the man into a woman; and He brought her to the man. ²³Then the man said,

> "This one at last
> Is bone of my bones
> And flesh of my flesh.
> This one shall be called Woman,
> For from man was she taken."

²⁴Hence a man leaves his father and mother and clings to his wife, so that they become one flesh.

²⁵The two of them were naked, the man and his wife, yet they felt no shame.

3 ¹Now the serpent was the shrewdest of all the wild beasts that the Lord God had made. He said to the woman, "Did God really say: You shall not eat of any tree of the garden?" ²The Woman replied to the serpent, "We may eat of the fruit of the other trees of the garden. ³It is only about fruit of the tree in the middle of the garden that God said: 'You shall not eat of it or touch it, lest you die.'" ⁴And the serpent said to the woman, "You are not going to die, ⁵but God knows that as soon as you eat of it your eyes will be opened and you will be like divine beings who know good and bad." ⁶When the woman saw that the tree was good for eating and a delight to the eyes, and that the tree was desirable as a source of wisdom, she took of its fruit and ate. She also gave some to her husband, and he ate. ⁷Then the eyes of both of them were opened and they perceived that they were naked; and they sewed together fig leaves and made themselves loincloths.

⁸They heard the sound of the Lord God moving about in the garden at the breezy time of day; and the man and his wife hid from the Lord God among the trees of the garden. ⁹The Lord God called out to the man and said to him, "Where are you?" ¹⁰He replied, "I heard the sound of You in the garden, and I was afraid because I was naked, so I hid." ¹¹Then He asked, "Who told you that you were naked? Did you eat of the tree from which I had forbidden you to eat?" ¹²The man said, "The woman You put at my side—she gave me of the tree, and I ate." ¹³And the Lord God said to the woman, "What is this you have done!" The woman replied, "The serpent duped me, and I ate." ¹⁴Then the Lord God said to the serpent,

> "Because you did this,
> More cursed shall you be
> Than all cattle
> And all the wild beasts:

On your belly shall you crawl
And dirt shall you eat
All the days of your life.
15I will put enmity
Between you and the woman,
And between your offspring and hers;
They shall strike at your head,
And you shall strike at their heel."

16And to the woman He said,
"I will make most severe
Your pangs in childbearing;
In pain shall you bear children.
Yet your urge shall be for your husband,
And he shall rule over you."

17To Adam He said, "Because you did as your wife said and ate of the tree about which I commanded you, 'You shall not eat of it,'

Cursed be the ground because of you;
By toil shall you eat of it
All the days of your life:
18Thorns and thistles shall it sprout for you.
But your food shall be the grasses of the field;
19By the sweat of your brow
Shall you get bread to eat,
Until you return to the ground—
For from it you were taken.
For dust you are,
And to dust you shall return."

20The man named his wife Eve, because she was the mother of all the living. 21And the Lord God made garments of skins for Adam and his wife, and clothed them.

22And the Lord God said, "Now that the man has become like one of us, knowing good and bad, what if he should stretch out his hand and take also from the tree of life and eat, and live forever!" 23So the Lord God banished him from the garden of Eden, to till the soil from which he was taken. 24He drove the man out, and stationed east of the garden of Eden the cherubim and the fiery ever-turning sword, to guard the way to the tree of life.

8 15God spoke to Noah, saying, 16 "Come out of the ark, together with your wife, your sons, and your sons' wives. 17Bring out with you every living thing of all flesh that is with

you: birds, animals, and everything that creeps on earth; and let them swarm on the earth and be fertile and increase on earth." ¹⁸So Noah came out, together with his sons, his wife, and his sons' wives. ¹⁹Every animal, every creeping thing, and every bird, everything that stirs on earth came out of the ark by families.

²⁰Then Noah built an altar to the LORD and, taking of every clean animal and of every clean bird, he offered burnt offerings on the altar. ²¹The LORD smelled the pleasing odor, and the LORD said to Himself: "Never again will I doom the earth because of man, since the devisings of man's mind are evil from his youth; nor will I ever again destroy every living being, as I have done.

²²So long as the earth endures,
Seedtime and harvest,
Cold and heat,
Summer and winter,
Day and night,
Shall not cease."

9 ¹God blessed Noah and his sons, and said to them, "Be fertile and increase, and fill the earth. ²The fear and the dread of you shall be upon all the beasts of the earth and upon all the birds of the sky—everything with which the earth is astir—and upon all the fish of the sea; they are given into your hand. ³Every creature that lives shall be yours to eat; as with the green grasses, I give you all these. ⁴You must not, however, eat flesh with its life-blood in it. ⁵But for your own life-blood I will require a reckoning: I will require it of every beast; of man, too, will I require a reckoning for human life, of every man for that of his fellow man!

⁶Whoever sheds the blood of man,
By man shall his blood be shed;
For in His image
Did God make man.

⁷Be fertile, then, and increase; abound on the earth and increase on it."

⁸And God said to Noah and to his sons with him, ⁹"I now establish My covenant with you and your offspring to come, ¹⁰and with every living thing that is with you—birds, cattle, and every wild beast as well—all that have come out of the ark, every living thing on earth. ¹¹I will maintain My covenant with you: never again shall all flesh be cut off by the waters of a flood, and never again shall there be a flood to destroy the earth."

¹²God further said, "This is the sign that I set for the covenant between Me and you, and every living creature with you, for all ages to come. ¹³I have set My bow in the clouds, and it shall serve as a sign of the covenant between Me and the earth. ¹⁴When I bring clouds over the earth, and the bow appears in the clouds, ¹⁵I will remember My covenant

between Me and you and every living creature among all flesh, so that the waters shall never again become a flood to destroy all flesh. [16]When the bow is in the clouds, I will see it and remember the everlasting covenant between God and all living creatures, all flesh that is on earth. [17]That," God said to Noah, "shall be the sign of the covenant that I have established between Me and all flesh that is on earth."

EXODUS

23 [5]When you see the ass of your enemy lying under its burden and would refrain from raising[b] it, you must nevertheless raise it with him.

[10]Six years you shall sow your land and gather in its yield; [11]but in the seventh you shall let it rest and lie fallow. Let the needy among your people eat of it, and what they leave let the wild beasts eat. You shall do the same with your vineyards and your olive groves.

[12]Six days you shall do your work, but on the seventh day you shall cease from labor, in order that your ox and your ass may rest, and that your bondman and the stranger may be refreshed.

LEVITICUS

19 [9]When you reap the harvest of your land, you shall not reap all the way to the edges of your field, or gather the gleanings of your harvest. [10]You shall not pick your vineyard bare, or gather the fallen fruit of your vineyard; you shall leave them for the poor and the stranger: I the LORD am your God.

22 [26]The LORD spoke to Moses, saying: [27]When an ox or a sheep or a goat is born, it shall stay seven days with its mother, and from the eighth day on it shall be acceptable as an offering by fire to the LORD. [28]However, no animal from the herd or from the flock shall be slaughtered on the same day with its young.

25 The LORD spoke to Moses on Mount Sinai: [2]Speak to the Israelite people and say to them:

When you enter the land that I assign to you, the land shall observe a sabbath of the LORD. [3]Six years you may sow your field and six years you may prune your vineyard and gather in the yield. [4]But in the seventh year the land shall have a sabbath of complete rest, a sabbath of the LORD: you shall not sow your field or prune your vineyard. [5]You shall not reap the aftergrowth of your harvest or gather the grapes of your untrimmed vines; it shall be a year of complete rest for the land. [6]But you may eat whatever the land during its sabbath will produce—you, your male and female slaves, the hired and bound laborers who live with you, [7]and your cattle and the beasts in your land may eat all its yield.

26 [3]If you follow My laws and faithfully observe My commandments, [4]I will grant your rains in their season, so that the earth shall yield its produce and the trees of the field their

fruit. [5]Your threshing shall overtake the vintage, and your vintage shall overtake the sowing; you shall eat your fill of bread and dwell securely in your land.

DEUTERONOMY

20 [19]When in your war against a city you have to besiege it a long time in order to capture it, you must not destroy its trees, wielding the ax against them. You may eat of them, but you must not cut them down. Are trees of the field human to withdraw before you into the besieged city? [20]Only trees that you know do not yield food may be destroyed; you may cut them down for constructing siegeworks against the city that is waging war on you, until it has been reduced.

22 [6]If, along the road, you chance upon a bird's nest, in any tree or on the ground, with fledglings or eggs and the mother sitting over the fledglings or on the eggs, do not take the mother together with her young. [7]Let the mother go, and take only the young, in order that you may fare well and have a long life.

25 [4]You shall not muzzle an ox while it is threshing.

ISAIAH

24 [4]The earth is withered, sear;
The world languishes, it is sear;
The most exalted people of the earth languish.
[5]For the earth was defiled
Under its inhabitants;
Because they transgressed teachings,
Violated laws,
Broke the ancient covenant.

PSALMS

65 [10]You take care of the earth and irrigate it;
You enrich it greatly,
with the channel of God full of water;
You provide grain for men;
for so do You prepare it.
[11]Saturating its furrows,
leveling its ridges,
You soften it with showers,
You bless its growth.
[12]You crown the year with Your bounty;

fatness is distilled in Your paths;
    ¹³the pasturelands distill it;
    the hills are girded with joy.
¹⁴The meadows are clothed with flocks,
    the valleys mantled with grain;
    they raise a shout, they break into song.
    slow to anger, abounding in steadfast love.

104 Bless the LORD, O my soul;
    O LORD, my God, You are very great;
    You are clothed in glory and majesty,
    ²wrapped in a robe of light;
    You spread the heavens like a tent cloth.
³He sets the rafters of His lofts in the waters,
    makes the clouds His chariot,
    moves on the wings of the wind.
⁴He makes the winds His messengers,
    fiery flames His servants.
⁵He established the earth on its foundations,
    so that it shall never totter.
⁶You made the deep cover it as a garment;
    the waters stood above the mountains.
⁷They fled at Your blast,
    rushed away at the sound of Your thunder,
    ⁸—mountains rising, valleys sinking—
    to the place You established for them.
⁹You set bounds they must not pass
    so that they never again cover the earth.
¹⁰You make springs gush forth in torrents;
    they make their way between the hills,
    ¹¹giving drink to all the wild beasts;
    the wild asses slake their thirst.
¹²The birds of the sky dwell beside them
    and sing among the foliage.
¹³You water the mountains from Your[a] lofts;
    the earth is sated from the fruit of Your work.
¹⁴You make the grass grow for the cattle,
    and herbage for man's labor
    that he may get food out of the earth—
    ¹⁵wine that cheers the hearts of men
    oil that makes the face shine,
    and bread that sustains man's life.

¹⁶The trees of the L<small>ORD</small> drink their fill,
    the cedars of Lebanon, His own planting,
¹⁷where birds make their nests;
    the stork has her home in the junipers.
¹⁸The high mountains are for wild goats;
    the crags are a refuge for rock-badgers.
¹⁹ He made the moon to mark the seasons;
    the sun knows when to set.
²⁰You bring on darkness and it is night,
    when all the beasts of the forests stir.
²¹The lions roar for prey,
    seeking their food from God.
²²When the sun rises, they come home
    and couch in their dens.
²³Man then goes out to his work,
    to his labor until the evening.
²⁴How many are the things You have made, O L<small>ORD</small>;
    You have made them all with wisdom;
    the earth is full of Your creations.
²⁵There is the sea, vast and wide,
    with its creatures beyond number,
    living things, small and great.
²⁶There go the ships,
    and Leviathan that You formed to sport with.
²⁷All of them look to You
    to give them their food when it is due.
²⁸Give it to them, they gather it up;
    open Your hand, they are well satisfied;
    ²⁹hide Your face, they are terrified;
    take away their breath, they perish
    and turn again into dust;
    ³⁰send back Your breath, they are created,
    and You renew the face of the earth.
³¹May the glory of the L<small>ORD</small> endure forever;
    may the L<small>ORD</small> rejoice in His works!
³²He looks at the earth and it trembles;
    He touches the mountains and they smoke.
³³I will sing to the L<small>ORD</small> as long as I live;
    all my life I will chant hymns to my God.
³⁴May my prayer be pleasing to Him;
    I will rejoice in the L<small>ORD</small>.

³⁵May sinners disappear from the earth,
  and the wicked be no more.
Bless the LORD, O my soul.
  Hallelujah.

JOB

12 ⁷But ask the beasts, and they will teach you;
The birds of the sky, they will tell you,
⁸Or speak to the earth, it will teach you;
The fish of the sea, they will inform you.
⁹Who among all these does not know
That the hand of the LORD has done this?
¹⁰In His hand is every living soul
And the breath of all mankind.
¹⁷He makes counselors go about naked[b]
And causes judges to go mad.
¹⁸He undoes the belts of kings,
And fastens loincloths on them.
¹⁹He makes priests go about naked,
And leads temple-servants astray.
38 Then the LORD replied to Job out of the tempest and said:
²Who is this who darkens counsel,
Speaking without knowledge?
³Gird your loins like a man;
I will ask and you will inform Me.
⁴Where were you when I laid the earth's foundations?
Speak if you have understanding.
⁵Do you know who fixed its dimensions
Or who measured it with a line?
⁶Onto what were its bases sunk?
Who set its cornerstone
⁷When the morning stars sang together
And all the divine beings shouted for joy?
⁸Who closed the sea behind doors
When it gushed forth out of the womb,
⁹When I clothed it in clouds,
Swaddled it in dense clouds,
¹⁰When I made breakers My limit for it,
And set up its bar and doors,

[11]And said, "You may come so far and no farther;
Here your surging waves will stop"?
[12]Have you ever commanded the day to break,
Assigned the dawn its place,
[13]So that it seizes the corners of the earth
And shakes the wicked out of it?
[14]It changes like clay under the seal
Till [its hues] are fixed like those of a garment.
[15]Their light is withheld from the wicked,
And the upraised arm is broken.
[16]Have you penetrated to the sources of the sea,
Or walked in the recesses of the deep?
[17]Have the gates of death been disclosed to you?
Have you seen the gates of deep darkness?
[18]Have you surveyed the expanses or the earth?
If you know of these—tell Me.
[19]Which path leads to where light dwells,
And where is the place of darkness,
[20]That you may take it to its domain
And know the way to its home?
[21]Surely you know, for you were born then,
And the number of your years is many!
[22]Have you penetrated the vaults of snow,
Seen the vaults of hail,
[23]Which I have put aside for a time of adversity,
For a day of war and battle?
[24]By what path is the west wind dispersed,
The east wind scattered over the earth?
[25]Who cut a channel for the torrents
And a path for the thunderstorms,
[26]To rain down on uninhabited land,
On the wilderness where no man is,
[27]To saturate the desolate wasteland,
And make the crop of grass sprout forth?
[28]Does the rain have a father?
Who begot the dewdrops?
[29]From whose belly came forth the ice?
Who gave birth to the frost of heaven?
[30]Water congeals like stone,
And the surface of the deep compacts.
[31]Can you tie cords to Pleiades

Or undo the reins of Orion?

[32]Can you lead out Mazzaroth in its season,

Conduct the Bear with her sons?

[33]Do you know the laws of heaven

Or impose its authority on earth?

[34]Can you send up an order to the clouds

For an abundance of water to cover you?

[35]Can you dispatch the lightning on a mission

And have it answer you, "I am ready"?

[36]Who put wisdom in the hidden parts?

Who gave understanding to the mind?

[37]Who is wise enough to give an account of the heavens?

Who can tilt the bottles of the sky,

[38]Whereupon the earth melts into a mass,

And its clods stick together.

[39]Can you hunt prey for the lion,

And satisfy the appetite of the king of beasts?

Go follow the tracks of the sheep,

And graze your kids[f]

By the tents of the shepherds.

SONG OF SONGS

2 I am a rose of Sharon,

A lily of the valleys.

[2]Like a lily among thorns,

So is my darling among the maidens.

[3]Like an apple tree among trees of the forest,

So is my beloved among the youths.

I delight to sit in his shade,

And his fruit is sweet to my mouth.

[4]He brought me to the banquet room

And his banner of love was over me.

[5]"Sustain me with raisin cakes,

Refresh me with apples,

For I am faint with love."

[6]His left hand was under my head,

His right arm embraced me.

[7]I adjure you, O maidens of Jerusalem,

By gazelles or by hinds of the field:

Do not wake or rouse

Love until it please!
⁸Hark! My beloved!
There he comes,
Leaping over mountains,
Bounding over hills.
⁹My beloved is like a gazelle
Or like a young stag.
There he stands behind our wall,
Gazing through the window,
Peering through the lattice.
¹⁰My beloved spoke thus to me,
"Arise, my darling;
My fair one, come away!"

From THE QUR'AN

And the Earth have We spread forth, and thrown thereon the mountains, and caused everything to spring forth in it in balanced measure: And We have provided therein sustenance for you, and for the creature which not ye sustain: And no one thing is there, but with Us are its storehouses; and We send it not down but in settled measure; And we send for the fertilizing winds, and cause the rain to come down from the heaven, and give you to drink of it; and it is not ye who are its storers. (15: 19–22)

In the creation of the heavens and the earth, and the difference of night and day, and the ships which run upon the sea with that which is of use to people, and the water which Allah sends down from the sky, thereby reviving the earth after its death, and dispersing all kinds of beasts therein, and the ordinance of the winds, are signs for people who have sense (2: 164).

Have you not seen that unto Allah pays adoration whosoever is in the heavens and whosoever is in the earth, and the sun, and the moon, and the stars, and the hills, and the trees, and the beasts, and many of mankind . . . (22:18).

The seven heavens and the earth and all therein praise him and there is not a thing but hymns his praise. Lo! He is ever Clement, Forgiving. (17:44).

Have they not seen the earth, how we have planted therein of every fruitful pair (26:7).

And all things we have created by pairs (51:49).

Glory be to Him who created all sexual pairs, of that which the earth grows, and of themselves, and of that which they know not. (36:36).

There is not an animal in the earth, nor a flying creature flying on two wings, but they are nations like you. We have neglected nothing in the book. Then unto their Lord they will be gathered. (6:38).

Allah has created every animal of water. Of them is that which moves upon its belly and that which walks on two legs and that which walks upon four. Allah creates what He will. Lo! Allah is able to do all things. (24:45).

Have they not seen the birds obedient in mid air? None holds them save Allah. Lo! herein, verily, are signs for a people who believe. (16:79).

Have you observed the water which you drink? Is it you who shed it from the raincloud or are we the shedder? (56:68, 69).

Have you seen that which you cultivate? Is it you who foster it, or are we the fosterer? (56:63, 64).

Translated by Keyar Trad.

Let man consider his food: How we pour water in showers Then split the earth in clefts And cause the grain to grow therein And grapes and green fodder And olive trees and palm trees And garden closes of thick foliage And fruits and grasses: Provision for you and your cattle. (80: 24–32).

He it is who sends down water from the sky, and therewith we bring forth buds of every kind; we bring forth the green blade from which we bring forth the thick-clustered grain; and from the date-palm, from the pollen thereof, spring pendant bunches; and gardens of grapes, and the olive and the pomegranate, alike and unlike. Look upon the fruit thereof, when they bear fruit, and upon its ripening. Lo! herein verily are signs for a people who believe. (6:99).

"JEWS, JEWISH TEXTS, AND NATURE: A BRIEF HISTORY"

Daniel Swartz

Once upon a time—but this is neither a fairy tale nor a bedtime story—we knew less about the natural world than we do today. Much less. But we understood that world better, much better, for we lived ever so much closer to its rhythms.

Most of us have wandered far from our earlier understanding, from our long-ago intimacy. We take for granted what our ancestors could not, dared not, take for granted; we have set ourselves apart from the world of the seasons, the world of floods and rainbows and new moons. Nor, acknowledging our loss, can we simply reverse course, pretend to innocence in order to rediscover intimacy. Too much has intervened.

But we can explore the ways we once were, the times when we lived off the land, when we lived in the Land.

Our purpose in so doing is not to shake our heads in disbelief, whether at the naivete of old or the alienation of our own time. We do it in order to assess the ingredients of our loss, as also of our gain, to inquire whether here and there, perhaps even more than merely here and there, our modern sophistication can be married to the ancient intimacy, whether we can move from our discord with nature to an informed harmony with this, God's universe.

Accordingly, this is not about the good old days. It is about us, and about how we came to where we are. It is about our people and its relationship to the natural world.

Not all of us, throughout all our history, lived intimately with nature, but some of us did most of the time and most of us did some of the time.

Which of us? When? What is, in fact, the story of our shifting relationship with the natural environment? And where does that story, along with our own, point us now?

THE BIBLICAL PERIOD

Among its many facets, the Bible is the story of people who cared about and knew intimately the land around them. That knowledge is richly, even lavishly, reflected in the lan-

This essay appeared in *To Till and To Tend: A Guide to Jewish Environmental Study and Action*, published by The Coalition on the Environment and Jewish Life.

guage of the prophets and psalmists, in the poetry of the Song of Songs and Job. Indeed, the extravagant use of natural metaphor suggests that a vocabulary drawn from the world of nature was accessible to all.

Today, when we encounter God as a *nesher*, a griffin vulture (as we do in Deuteronomy 32:11), we must pause to examine just what is intended by the term. But we may surmise that then, when people first encountered that way of depicting God, they knew that the reference was to God as a fiercely protective parent, one who carries its young on its back to help them learn how to fly. Similarly, when Isaiah compares Israel to a terebinth oak in the fall (6:11–13), his listeners could appreciate immediately the two-edged nature of his metaphor. The terebinth is most glorious just before all its leaves drop—but it is also among the hardiest of trees, even sprouting again from a cut-off stump.

No modern audience can appreciate as intuitively as the listeners of old the Song of Song's lyrical description of spring flowers reappearing on the Earth or of a lily among the thorns. So, too, the psalmists' hymns to all of creation, joining with the song of heaven's birds and young lions at their hunt (see, e.g., Psalms 104 and 148). And consider the difference between a modern dweller in cities and the ancients in comprehending the sheer power of God's promise to Abraham that he would have descendants like the stars in the sky: in the one case, the stars are perceived only through a haze of light and soot; in the other, the night sky dense with brilliant stars was part of the common experience.

The language of nature came to the people naturally, as it were, for their lives were bound up with the richness of the land, with the pastoral and agricultural economy of the time. That is why they tended the land so lovingly, that is why the cycles of their celebrations followed the seasons of the land (see, e.g., Leviticus 23). And though their efforts to tame the land, to make it more productive and more dependable, were often marvels of ingenuity, they understood, as well, the limits to their mastery—for they knew God as Sovereign of the Land, and, through such institutions as the Sabbatical year and the Jubilee (Leviticus 25), they acknowledged God's ownership.

It followed that they had to treat the land well—not only to give it rest, but to respect and plant trees, keep water sources clean, create parks near urban areas, regulate sewage disposal, avoid causing pain to animals. And they understood intuitively as well the connection between their responsibility to care for the environment and justice: Since the land was God's, not only should it be protected, but its rich produce should be shared with the poorest of God's children (Leviticus 19).

In a world where warfare typically included efforts by the victor to degrade drastically the environment of the vanquished—cutting down trees, fouling waters, and salting the Earth—our forebears behaved exceptionally, in all senses of the word. They developed the principle of *bal tash-chit*, do not destroy (Deuteronomy 20:19). Do not cut down trees even to prevent ambush or to build siege engines; do not foul waters or burn crops even to cause an enemy's submission. And if, even in extremis, one is to avoid causing needless harm to the environment, *al akhat kama v'khama*—how much the more so—during the ordinary course of life.

We speak, then, of a time when people were possessed of an ideal vision of harmony, of *shlemut*, wholeness and peace. No, it was not an idyllic time, for they could not fully translate their vision into reality. No Eden, not any longer: the promised abundance had to be teased and more often wrested from the Earth by the sweat of the brow, and the seasons had a way of being fickle, not bestowing their appointed blessings. Hence work, hence prayer, hence, too, Shabbat, a time to rest from work, a time to remind themselves of God's endless beneficence, a time to dream of a time yet to come, when the world will be entirely Shabbat. And in that final and endless time, the wolf will lie down with the lamb, and humankind will be at peace with all of nature (See, e.g., Isaiah 65:21–25; Joel 2:21–24.).

In short, our ancient ancestors knew the wonderful reciprocity of Creation: Creation's sheer magnificence turns the heart towards its Creator (see, e.g., Isaiah 40), and the heart that has turned to God opens, inevitably, towards Creation, towards the awesome integrity of the natural universe that is God's gift.

ADDITIONAL QUOTES

When you reap the harvest of your land, you shall not reap all the way to the edges of your field, or gather the gleanings of your harvest . . . but you shall leave them for the poor and the stranger: I the Eternal am your God (Leviticus 19:9–20).

A time is coming . . . when the mountains shall drip with wine and all the hills shall wave with grain. I will restore My people Israel, I will plant them upon their soil (Amos 9:13–15).

Let the heavens rejoice and the earth exult! Let the sea and all within it thunder, the fields and everything in them exult! Then shall all the forest trees shout for joy, at the presence of the Eternal One, who is coming to rule the Earth; God will rule the world justly and its people in faithfulness (Psalm 96:11–13).

But ask the beasts, and they will teach you; the birds of the sky, and they will tell you; or speak to the earth and it will teach you; the fish of the sea, they will inform you. Who among all these does not know that the hand of the Eternal has done this? (Job 12:7–9)

For now the winter is past, the rains are over and gone. The blossoms have appeared in the land. The time of the song-bird has come; the song of the turtledove is heard in our land. The green figs form on the fig tree, the blossoming vines give off fragrance (Song of Songs 2:11–13).

Daniel Swartz

THE ERA OF THE MISHNAH AND THE TALMUD

During the period when the Mishnah and Talmud were developed, although many of us became dwellers in cities, our urbanization was far from complete. Farming, perhaps because a large percentage of Mishnaic sages were farmers, was considered the normative way of life. We read, for example, in *Avot d'Rabbi Nathan* (30:6) that "one who purchases grain in the market is like an infant whose mother is dry [and so needs to be taken to a wet nurse], while one who eats from what one has grown is like an infant raised at its mother's breast."

The mystics of this period wrote *bekhalot* hymns, which visionary poets recited during their attempts to ascend through the "heavenly palaces." These hymns evoked the majesty of God by reference to the wonders of the Earth, as did the prayers of the early *paytanim* (such as Yose ben Yose). Even into the late Talmudic era of the fifth and sixth centuries, our sages remained knowledgeable about the natural environment, and they wrote with great concern about it.

One testament to their concern is the panoply of blessings they developed. Through these, the experience of the natural world, as well as interactions between people and nature, became sanctified. Not only the tasting of foods, but the fragrance of blossoms, the sight of mountains, the sound of thunder were to be blessed. Talmudic sages added such rituals of blessing as the *Kiddush Levanah*, a blessing for the renewal of the moon (which was later revived by medieval mystics and still later adopted by the Hasidim of the 18th century). Such blessings showed that God was author of the wonders of nature. And as to the work of human hands, such as the baking of bread, the rabbis understood that even such work was bound up in a sacred partnership of God and humanity, as given form in the bowels of nature.

Most of all, the myriad blessings reflected and reminded those who recited them of the foundational belief: God owns everything in the world; we are but tenants in the garden, meant to till and to tend, to serve and to guard.

The premise that "you and what you possess are God's" (*Avot* 3:7) underlies most of Talmudic thinking, both about the environment and about the nature of *mitzvot* in general. The doing of *mitzvot* acknowledges that we live in a God-centered and not a human-centered universe, that because of God's ownership, we have a variety of obligations to the Divine will. The rabbis further believed that many *mitzvot*, such as the Sabbatical year, had as their *central* purpose the reaffirmation of God's ownership of the land (*Sanhedrin* 39a). Philo, writing at the same time as the Mishnaic sages, devoted a whole treatise, *De Cherubim*, to the notion that humans cannot truly own anything, for all is God's. As was true with their biblical ancestors, this understanding of ownership strengthened for them the link between treating the environment justly and justly sharing with all of God's children the products of creation.

The particular and compelling gift of these sages is that they made their concerns concrete, translated ethical principles into codes of action. While *Genesis Rabbah* and *Leviticus Rabbah*, written at roughly the same time, express general concerns about the preservation of species and the sacredness of planting trees, the Mishnah and Gemarra set definite limits on the use of any one species and regulate in detail the planting of trees in urban areas. The Talmudic sages translated the general principle of *Bal Tashchit* into a series of specific prohibitions against wasteful actions. Similarly, they developed extensive regulations on the disposal of hazardous waste, and they curtailed industries that might cause air pollution (See, e.g. *Bava Batra* 25a.). Nor did they consider these matters to be secondary or delegate these concerns to others; the heads of the *Bet Din* themselves were to inspect wells (*Tosefta Shekalim* 1:2). Only through concrete acts such as these could the vision of the age of redemption become a reality.

ADDITIONAL QUOTES

Rabbi Shimon Bar Yochai said, three things are of equal importance, earth, humans, and rain. Rabbi Levi ben Hiyyata said: . . . to teach that without earth, there is no rain, and without rain, the earth cannot endure, and without either, humans cannot exist (*Genesis Rabbah*, 13:3).

Rabbi Yohanan ben Zakkai . . . used to say: if you have a sapling in your hand, and someone should say to you that the Messiah has come, stay and complete the planting, and then go to greet the Messiah (*Avot de Rabbi Nathan*, 31b).

How can a person of flesh and blood follow God? . . . God, from the very beginning of creation, was occupied before all else with planting, as it is written, "And first of all [*mikedem*, usually translated as "in the East"], the Eternal God planted a Garden in Eden [Genesis 2:8] Therefore . . . occupy yourselves first and foremost with planting (*Leviticus Rabbah* 25:3).

MEDIEVAL AND RENAISSANCE TIMES

The urbanization of Jews continued throughout the Middle Ages. In some cases, our land was seized, or we were forbidden to own land, or we were in other ways forced off the land; in others, economic pressures, ranging from prohibitive taxes to business restrictions, as well as shifting economic opportunities, led us toward the cities.

But not all Jews became urban. In Europe, through the 1400s, many Jews cultivated vineyards. In the Islamic world, Jews played a vital role in agricultural life, first throughout the region, then, as we were displaced from the land, along its periphery.

From the beginning of this period, a number of important Jewish texts with environmental sensitivities, such as the late collections of *midrash*, Ecclesiastes *Rabbah*, *Midrash*

Daniel Swartz

Tankhuma, and *Midrash Tehillim*, were composed. Joseph Kimkhi, in his commentary on Genesis, wrote that the "us" in God's "Let *us* make humans" refers to God working together with nature and the Earth. And the expansion of Jewish mysticism and poetry also created an abundance of works concerned with the environment.

This concern was both practical and theological. Maimonides as a physician saw the ill effects environmental degradation could have on the health, and he proposed regulations to counter them (See, e.g. his *Treatise on Asthma*). Joseph Caro wrote about the responsibility of communities to plant trees (*Tur, Hoshen Mishpat* #175), while various responsa of Rabbi Yitzhak ben Sheshet (Ribash), of the early 14th century, deal with urban pollution issues, including noise pollution, and their effects on urban dwellers (See, e.g. *Responsa* 196).

But many of the sages of this period also viewed the beauty of the created world in a broader sense, as a path towards the love and contemplation of God. Both Maimonides and his son, Abraham, wrote that one could come to love God by contemplating God's great works in nature, and that such contemplation was in fact essential to spiritual development (*Sefer HaMada*, 2.2; *Ha-Mispil La-Avodat Ha-Shem*). The Jewish philosopher, Bakhya ibn Pekuda, wrote that Jews should engage in "meditation upon creation" in order to sense God's majesty (*Duties of the Heart*, 137). *Sefer Ha-Hinukh*, a compilation by medieval pietists, claimed that those who truly love God cannot bear to waste even a grain of mustard (#529).

The vast number of Kabbalistic works developed during this time took contemplation of nature a step further, for, according to the *Zohar*, nature itself is a garment of the *Shekhina*. "*Perek Shira*," a mystical poem from circa 900, has verses from all types of creatures singing God's praise. Abraham Abulafia began a tradition of Jewish mysticism that included outdoor meditation. And the mystics of Safed developed intricate *Tu B'shvat* Seders, to celebrate the presence of God in nature.

But mystics though they were, they did not restrict their relationship with nature to contemplation. Rather, they treated nature with great respect in deed as well as thought. As Moses Cordovero, author of one of these *Tu B'shvat Haggadot*, wrote in a tract about the sorts of ethical behavior in which mystics should engage, that "the principle of wisdom is to extend acts of love toward everything, including plants and animals" (*Tomer Devorah*, #3).

The particularly intense concern for and involvement with nature we find among the mystics might suggest that nature was somehow outside "mainstream" concerns. That was not the case. On the contrary, we find an abiding involvement with and appreciation of nature among some of the most "mainstream" rabbis and poets. Some of the greatest Sephardic sages, for example, were also talented nature poets. So, Moses ibn Ezra, in his poem "The Rose," wrote: "The garden put on a coat of many colors, and its grass garments were like the robes of a brocade . . . at their head advanced the rose; he came out from among the guard of leaves and cast aside his prison-clothes."

Daniel Swartz

Judah Ha-Levi, perhaps the greatest poet of his age, in "A Letter to his Friend Isaac," wrote:

> And now the Spring is here with yearning eyes; midst shimmering golden flowerbeds, on meadows carpeted with varied hues, in richest raiment clad she treads. She weaves a tapestry of blooms over all.

Nahum, a 13th-century Sephardic *paytan*, wrote:

> Winter is gone, gone is my sorrow. The fruit tree is in flower, and my heart flowers with joy. O hunted gazelle, [a reference to the *Shekhina*] who escaped far from my hut, come back. Trees of delight sway among the shadows.

And Abraham ibn Ezra, one of the great Torah commentators, wrote in his poem, "God Everywhere":

> Wherever I turn my eyes, around on Earth or to the heavens
> I see you in the field of stars
> I see You in the yield of the land
> in every breath and sound, a blade of grass, a simple flower, an echo of Your holy Name.

All these poets saw nature as beautiful and worthy in and of itself—and also as a path toward the most beautiful and worthy of all, God.

Another lasting contribution to an environmental ethic by these medieval sages is in the elaboration of the Mishnaic principle of "moderation." They elucidated a principle of moderation opposed to both a hedonism that requires ever-increasing consumption in futile attempts to satisfy ever-expanding appetites, and to an asceticism that devalues the natural world, for, as Judah Ha-Levi wrote, "the holy law imposes no asceticism, but demands rather that we grant each physical faculty . . . its due" (*Kuzari*, 2:5). Of all the medieval sages, Maimonides was the foremost exponent of moderation, writing that "good deeds are ones that are equibalanced between too much and too little" (*Eight Chapters*, 54), and that "the right way is the mean in each group of dispositions common to humanity. One should only desire that which the body needs and cannot do without. One should eat only when hungry and not gorge oneself, but leave the table before the appetite is fully satisfied. . . . This is the way of the wise" (*Hilchot Deot*, 1). Nor was Maimonides the only sage promoting the "golden mean." Ibn Gabirol wrote, "abandon both extremes and set about the right mean" (*Ethics*, 145).

ADDITIONAL QUOTES

Rabbi Shimon said, "the shade spread over us by these trees is so pleasant! We must crown this place with words of Torah" (*Zohar*, 2:127a).

When Noah came out of the ark, he opened his eyes and saw the whole world completely destroyed. He began crying for the world and said, God, how could you have done this? . . . God replied, Oh Noah, how different you are from the way Abraham . . . will be. He will argue with me on behalf of Sodom and Gomorrah when I tell him that I plan their destruction. . . . But you, Noah, when I told you I would destroy the entire world, I lingered and delayed, so that you would speak on behalf of the world. But when you knew you would be safe in the ark, the evil of the world did not touch you. You thought of no one but your family. And now you complain? Then Noah knew that he had sinned (*Midrash Tankhuma, Parashat Noach*).

It should not be believed that all the beings exist for the sake of the existence of humanity. On the contrary, all the other beings too have been intended for their own sakes, and not for the sake of something else (Maimonides, *Guide for the Perplexed*, 456).

FROM THE RISE OF MODERNITY TO TODAY

On the eve of the modern period came the rise of Hasidism. In villages throughout Eastern Europe, beginning in the 18th century and continuing through the 19th, the rebbes of this movement spoke, often ecstatically, about the importance of a close relationship with the natural environment. The Baal Shem Tov, the founder of Hasidism, said that a man should consider himself as a worm, and all other small animals as his companions in the world, for all of them are created (*Tzava'at ha-Rivash*). Rabbi Schneur Zalman, the founder of the Chabad branch of Hasidism, taught that God is in all nature, a view he based on the fact that, in *gematria*, the name of God—*Elokim*—is equivalent to *ha-teva*, nature. Rabbi Zev Wolf taught that the wonders of the soil and of growing are to be contemplated before blessing food; the Medibozer Rebbe said that "God placed sparks of holiness within everything in nature" (*Butzina DeNehorah*, 22); Rabbi Nachman of Bratzlav, the great-grandson of the Baal Shem Tov and the Hasidic rebbe most closely attuned to nature, wrote that if we quest for God, we can find God revealed in all of creation (*Likkute Mohoran*, II, #12). Nachman prescribed to his followers daily prayer in fields, teaching that their prayers would be strengthened by those of every blade of grass (*Sichot Ha-Ran*, 227).

Even the erstwhile opponents of the Hasidim, such as some of the rabbis who started the *Musar* movement, joined with them in appreciation of nature. Rabbi Joseph Leib Bloch wrote that a good Jew "will be filled with wonder and excitement at the sight of the glories of nature . . . and will know how to use these feelings for the sublime purpose of recognizing the Creator" (*Sha'arey Da'at*, I, 194).

With the dawn of the 19th century, a radical transformation of the Jewish circumstances commenced. It is doubtful whether, short of wartime, so much change in social circumstance was ever compressed in so short a period as the change we experienced in the 19th century. At the dawn of the century, Europe was home to 1.5 million of the world's then 2.5 million Jews. In the course of that century, Europe was utterly transformed, and we along with it. Old social, political, and economic structures crumbled; new possibilities emerged, enticed. Educational and economic opportunities, new places and new ideologies beckoned. And people moved: In 1813, there were some 8,000 Jews in Warsaw; by 1900, there were 219,128. In 1789, there were 114 Jews in Budapest; by 1900, there were 166,198; in 1816, there were 3,373 Jews in Berlin; by 1900, there were 92,206.

But even during this explosive time, significant rural populations remained. Thus, at the beginning of the 20th century, over 14 percent of Galician Jews were still engaged in agriculture. Many Jews emigrating to both North and South America (including, for example, the family of Rabbi Alexander Schindler) farmed during their first generation in the New World. And, perhaps more significantly, this period saw the rise of the first movements within Judaism advocating a return to the land, a reconnection with nature.

In Europe, the *Haskalah*, the "enlightenment," encouraged the establishment of thousands of farms during the 19th century in central and southern Russia. The *Haskalah* sought to reinvigorate the Jewish spirit—and many of its writers believed that there was no better way to do so than through renewed contact with nature. A number of Chaim nachman Bialik's poems reflect this contact, such as his "At Twilight": "They [our fantasies] will soar to the heights rustling like doves, and sail along into the distance and vanish. There, upon the purple mountain ridges, the roseate islands of splendor, they will silently flutter to rest."

But the *Haskalah* poet most committed to a return to nature was Saul Tchernikovsky:

And if you ask me of God, my God
'Where is God that in joy we may worship?'
Here on Earth too God lives, not in heaven alone
A striking fir, a rich furrow, in them you will find God's likeness. Divine image incarnate in
every high mountain. Wherever the breath of life flows, you will find God embodied.
And God's household? All being: the gazelle, the turtle, the shrub, the cloud pregnant with
thunder
. . . God-in-Creation is God's eternal name.

Numerous Yiddish poets, both in Europe and America, wrote nature poems, some of which were influenced by Walt Whitman, such as "A Song," by Yehoash:

A song of grass, a song of Earth, a song of gold ore in the womb of rock, a song of tin-white
brook that bathes the body of the moon, a song of famished wolves that howl upon their
snow-capped steppes.

Malka Heifetz Tussman's poems show a particular sensitivity to, perhaps even identification with, nature, as in her poem "Songs of the Priestess":

> Gather me up like wheat. Cut quickly
> and bind me
> before autumn's whirlwind sweeps me away.
> Hurry
> I am fully ripe.

Numerous Yiddish prose authors, such as Mendele Mokher Seforim in his *Of Bygone Days* and Joseph Opatoshu in his *Romance of a Horsethief*, show a great affinity for the beauties of the natural world.

But it was in the Zionist movement, particularly in elements of the *kibbutz* movement, that the return to nature found its strongest supporters. A.D. Gordon, the best-known of such advocates, wrote "And when you, O human, will return to Nature, that day your eyes will open, you will stare straight into the eyes of Nature and in its mirror you will see your image. You will know . . . that when you hid from Nature, you hid from yourself. . . . We who have been turned away from Nature—if we desire life, we must establish a new relationship with Nature" (*Mivhar Ketavim*, 57–58).

For his part, Rabbi Abraham Isaac Kook saw the return to nature as part of the sacred task of the Jew in Israel, necessary to create "strong and holy flesh" (*Orot*, 171). Some of the Zionist poets directly tied their love of nature to the return to the Land; here, religion per se was abandoned, but the secularized product was infused with spirituality. So Rachel (Rachel Blustein) wrote, in one of her most famous poems:

> Land of mine, I have never sung to you nor glorified your name with heroic deeds
> or the spoils of battle
> all I have done is plant a tree
> on the silent shores of the Jordan.

Others, such as Leah Goldberg, in her "Songs of the River," wrote of the beauty of nature in and of itself, apart from any Zionist aspirations:

> My brother the river, eternally wandering
> Renewed day by day, and changing, and one
> My brother the flow, between your banks
> Which flows like myself between spring and fall.

There was an ideological point to such expression, for the early Zionist pioneers were taken (not to say obsessed) with the idea that the health of the Jewish people depended on its reconnection with nature, from which it had been so radically cut off in Europe. From A.D. Gordon's "Religion of Labor," his desire to "strike our roots deep into its [the land's] life-giving substance, and stretch out our branches into sustaining and creating air and sunlight," up until the extraordinary passion of contemporary Israelis to know the contours of their land, endlessly hiking through it and learning its ways, we may discern the echoes of an ancient tradition.

ADDITIONAL QUOTES

Nature is of the very essence of Deity (Israel Baal Shem Tov, *Shivkhe Ha-Besht*, 329).

Master of the Universe, grant me the ability to be alone; may it be my custom to go outdoors each day among the trees and grass and all growing things, and there may I be alone, and enter into prayer (Nachman of Bratzlav, *Maggid Sichot*, 48).

On Tu B'shvat/when spring comes/An angel descends/ledger in hand/and enters each bud, each twig, each tree, and all our garden flowers./From town to town, from village to village/the angel makes a winged way/searching the valleys, inspecting the hills/flying over the desert/and returns to heaven./And when the ledger will be full/of trees and blossoms and shrubs/when the desert is turned into a meadow/and all our land a watered garden/the Messiah will appear (Shin Shalom, modern Israeli poet).

I can contemplate a tree. I can accept it as a picture. . . . I can feel it as a movement. . . . I can assign it to a species and observe it as an instance. . . . I can overcome its uniqueness and form so rigorously that I can recognize it only as an expression of law. . . . I can dissolve it into a number, into a pure relation between numbers, and externalize it. Throughout all of this the tree, the tree remains my object and has its time span, its kind and condition. But it can also happen, if will and grace are joined, that as I contemplate the tree I am drawn into a relation, and the tree ceases to be an It (Martin Buber, *I and Thou*, 57–58).

GUIDING PRINCIPLES
FOR THE PRESENT AND FUTURE

Comes the question: What relevance has that tradition today? Or, more broadly: As important as is our past relationship with the environment, as a source of both counsel and inspiration, how are we today to develop guiding principles for our present relationship to the environment?

The effort to develop such principles, tied whenever possible to our tradition—tradition here understood as an amalgam of our texts and our experiences—is open-ended. Here, we offer seven principles, asking that they be understood as we understand the Four Questions of the Passover *Haggadah*, not as an authoritative or exhaustive list but as an effort to move us forward on our journey.

One of the most basic of Jewish principles is that we are required to find ways to translate our ideals into a concrete course of action. Judaism has never been satisfied with rhetorical commitments; the *halacha* comes to give concrete shape to our most valued principles. Such concretization is not without its difficulties and controversies. We may, for example, become so overwhelmed at the complexity of the analysis and the actions it calls forth that we do nothing. How can one person help solve a global crisis?

But, as Rabbi Tarfon reminds us (*Prike Avot*, 2:21), "We are not obligated to complete the task; neither are we free to abstain from it."

And then there is the problem of translation itself. Take even the most consensual ideal, one from which virtually no one would think to dissent, translate it into an action program, and suddenly there is debate, bickering, sometimes crippling dissensus. That is the real world.

Still, it is in the work of translation that we transform ourselves from *luftmentshen* to *mentshen*. And as difficult as the process is, it also reminds us of one of the central freedoms our faith proclaims: freedom from fate. Through our actions, we can choose life and blessing. It is up to us, even if it is not always or entirely clear which paths lead where. To succumb to inaction because the problems we face are complex, because our ideals are challenging, because there is pain along the way, is to abrogate our partnership with God in creating a better world, to abandon our stewardship along with our ideals, along, finally, with our humanity.

Knowing how arduous the process, how do we muster the courage and energy to begin the translation process? One helpful metaphor might be the image Maimonides discusses in *Hilchot Teshuvah*, in the context of a discussion of preparation for the High Holidays. As one approaches the Days of Awe, he writes, one should consider the entire world as if it were exactly balanced between acts of righteousness and of evil. The very next action you take, therefore, can save or condemn the world.

Imagine, then, if we were to set aside one day a year, perhaps *Tu B'shvat* or a new Jewish holiday created around Earth Day, as an environmental holiday of reflection. In preparation for that day, we would undertake a *heshbon*, a searching account, of the environmental consequences of our actions—as individuals, as a community, as a nation. We would imagine the world's ecosystem balanced on a scale, would think of our next action in terms of how it might save or condemn. After this time of reflection, we could return, reinvigorated and renewed, to the task of the reformation of behavior—and we could plan the changes in our educational efforts, in our life-styles, and in our advocacy work that such reformation requires of us. No more than a beginning, but at least a beginning, renewed each year just as we renew ourselves, our relationships, our devotion, each year. Nor need we wait for unanimity in the Jewish community before we take action—one city's Jewish population, or one synagogue, or even one family could begin the task.

GOD'S OWNERSHIP AND THE TERMS OF OUR LEASE

How do we root our action plan in our Judaic tradition? First of all, by implementing our belief that this is God's world, not ours. To take seriously the notion that we are but leasing the planet from God is to provide ourselves with specific behavioral guidelines. One who leases is called, in general, a *shomer*, usually translated as a guardian. The specific type of lease we have on the Earth is that of a *sho'el*, a borrower. Borrowers may use any part of what they borrow—but they must ensure that, at the end of the term of the lease, and at any given moment during the lease, the property is at least as valuable as it was at the beginning of the lease (See, e.g. *Shulkhan Arukh, Hoshen Mishpat* 291, 292). This is similar to the principle of *tzon barzel*, an arrangement whereby a husband may use some of his wife's property—but only on the condition that it is never lowered in value.

Harvest a tree? Not without planting another. Farm the land? Not without allowing it periodic rest and rejuvenation. See to it that any degradation of the environment is accompanied by an equivalent restoration. Evaluate land use on the basis of how it improves or degrades the environment, so that, for example, agricultural practices that prevent soil erosion, crops that are easier on the land, requiring less irrigation and pesticides, and harvesting methods that preserve the integrity of the ecosystem are given strong preference. Attempt in each of our own lives to strike such a balance, conserving energy, supporting environmental causes, planting trees, as a path toward restoration of what we have used or abused.

While such efforts at balance are not required by present *halacha*, we should remember that the *Shulkhan Arukh* acknowledges this standard in regulating leases. (See, e.g. *Hoshen Mishpat* 308, 324).

THE UNITY OF CREATION—INESCAPABLE CONSEQUENCES AND FUTURE GENERATIONS

Through our acceptance of the one Creator, we come to realize the unity of all creation. But if we truly believe in the unity and integrity of the universe, especially of the part of creation we know as the Earth, we must begin carefully to consider the consequences of our actions on that world. We need to realize that just as there is no action that is not recorded by *Shomer Yisrael*, the Guardian of Israel, so too is there no action without consequence to God's creation, the biosphere, no "elsewhere" to dump our garbage that will not, eventually, come floating back to haunt us.

Environmental costs were once labelled "externalities" by economists, for a laissez-faire doctrine does not weigh them in its working. But we have come to realize that these costs are not "external" at all, that they affect all of us. Since all aspects of our biosphere are woven together, any tearing of the fabric of life, the *Zohar's* "garment of the *Shekhina*," is likely eventually to begin unravelling humanity's own threads.

In essence, we need to start conducting "environmental impact statements" on our daily lives. What happens when we waste water or energy? How does that affect the biosphere as a whole? Our local ecosystem? Our own health and well-being?

But what if we cannot be certain of those consequences? Is the fact that our behavior *may* be hazardous to the planet's health sufficient to make change in that behavior a moral imperative?

Rabbi Jacob Ettinger (*Responsa Binyan Zion*, 137) proposes that in such circumstances, we ask three questions: First, how "unreasonable" is the hazard, with "unreasonableness" defined in this context as a hazard that any "well-informed individual would willingly spend money to eliminate." Second, how reversible are the damages if they do occur? And last, how likely is it, in the view of the best experts, that this potential hazard will come to pass?

The question that Rabbi Ettinger does *not* include in this calculus may be even more telling than the three questions he does. He does not propose that we ask anything about the timetable of hazard, about *when* the feared consequence may unfold. That omission is conscious and fully in keeping with our tradition. Our sages, when regulating potential dangers in the public domain, or even in areas that might in the future become part of the public domain, always viewed the fate of future generations with utmost concern, always sought to avoid endangering future generations with the same zeal with which they sought to protect their own. For our covenant is not just "with those standing here with us this day," but also "with those who are not here with us this day" (Deuteronomy 29:13–14), that is, with *all* the future generations.

Tzedek, Tzedek Tirdof—The Pursuit of Seamless Justice

Our actions should also be guided by a desire for seamless justice. The rabbis interpreted the repetition of the word *tzedek*, justice, in Deuteronomy's command "justice, justice shall you pursue" (16:20), as indicating that we must seek justice in both our means and our ends, both when it is to our advantage and when it is not (See, e.g., the commentary of Bakhya Ben Asher on this verse). Ends: No individual, group, or nation, should suffer disproportionately from environmental health hazards or ecosystem degradation. Means: As we work toward repairing ecosystems, solving environment problems, we need to ensure an equitable distribution of the costs of these solutions.

But does not a heightened concern for the health of the environment impose undue burdens on the poorer nations? In conscience, how can we, whose stunning economic development took place during a time of indifference to its environmental consequences, now turn to the poorer nations, seeking so desperately to escape their grinding poverty, and insist that they incorporate into their development plans a sensitivity to the environmental impact of those plans? Can we address the human needs of poorer countries even as we work toward the solution of global environmental problems?

First, we need to realize that long-term solutions to the latter problem often help solve the former. When the environment in third world countries is degraded, no one suffers more immediately or more severely than the poor. Conversely, when the environment is protected in a thoughtful manner, it often provides health and economic benefits to these same poor communities.

Furthermore, one can infer from Jewish sources that wealthier countries should subsidize environmental protection in poorer ones. The *Shulkhan Arukh* discusses the collections of taxes from a town in order to build a wall that benefits everyone in the town. If economic factors are equal, those close to the wall, who derive more protection from it, pay more—but if economic factors are not equal, those who can afford to pay more do so, for the whole town benefits (*Hoshen Mishpat*, 163:3). By analogy, this entire globe is our "town"; the whole global community benefits when any country protects its environment—and some countries are much more able to afford such protection than others. The same concern for seamless justice should guide our environmental work in the United States as well. We should pay particular attention to communities that have been disproportionately burdened by environmental health hazards and make sure that they have the necessary resources to turn their environment from a hazard to a source of health and joy.

STEWARDSHIP—A COVENANTAL TRUST

Lately, certain followers of "deep ecology" have subjected the notion of stewardship to harsh criticism. They ask, isn't it inherently and arrogantly hierarchical, placing humanity at the center of the universe? Doesn't it assume that the world cannot function without us, when evidence suggests, in fact, that ecosystems frequently work better without human interference? In the end, doesn't stewardship serve as a justification for domination and exploitation?

Understood in context, however, the Jewish notion of stewardship is a moral category, one that speaks of responsibility rather than of unlimited privilege, of a theocentric rather than anthropocentric universe. In Genesis 2:15, the first humans are commanded "to till and to tend" the Earth. This formulation hints at a kinship with the rest of creation that becomes even clearer when we look at the Hebrew more closely. *Avad* means not only to till, or even to work in a more general sense; it means also, and more powerfully, to serve or to participate in worship of the Divine. Thus, our "tilling" is more properly understood as service to God's Earth, a service that is not only a profound responsibility but a direct and critical part of our connection with and worship of God as well. And *shamar*, or "tend," means not only to tend, but more commonly, to guard or to watch over. What these meanings have in common is that the *shomrim* guard property that does not *belong* to them, but that is *entrusted* to them.

Good *shomrim* fulfill that trust, tending to the needs of that which they steward before tending to their own (see *Berakhot* 40a for examples). And all humans can indeed live in such a harmony with that which we serve and tend. But we also have the capacity—some might say the tendency—to destroy, merely by stepping outside the ordained relationship that assigns us a covenantal trusteeship rather than raw domination.

The urge to such domination, however, not only violates the insights and commands of our tradition, a tradition that goes so far as to interpret the very words "rule" and "subdue," in Genesis 1:26 and 1:28, as signifying limited stewardship (see, e.g., *Yevamot* 65b, Genesis *Rabbah* 8:12 and the commentaries of Rashi and Sforno on these verses). It is also, in a word, stupid. For it is that urge, unencumbered by religious sensibility, unencumbered by responsibility for future generations, unencumbered by concern for our neighbors, that hastens the destruction of the very world we seek to master.

COMMUNAL RESPONSIBILITIES VS. INDIVIDUAL RIGHTS

The Jewish tradition has a strong communal orientation, one that has limited individual rights by placing them within the context of and subordinating them to communal responsibilities. For the good of the community, even "private property" could be taken, under the principle of *hefker bet din hefker*, literally, "what the court declares ownerless is ownerless," the Mishnaic version of "eminent domain." More generally, a community could both coerce its residents to take positive actions for the good of the community and prohibit them from actions held to be deleterious to the community. This prohibition went so far, for example, as to enable residents of a courtyard or sealed alley generally to prohibit any profession (excluding the teaching of Torah) from being performed in that area if it threatened, because of noise or noxious odors, to reduce the quality of life for the residents (See *Shulkhan Arukh*, Hoshen Mishpat 231:20, 161, 162, and 156 for a series of such regulations).

Such restrictions were even more stringent if a health hazard was suspected. In such cases, even if it could be demonstrated that a person's very livelihood might be lost, that bankruptcy might ensue, the practice of the endangering profession could nonetheless be prohibited. The general rule, set down by the Ribash, is that "a person is not permitted to save himself from injury by causing injury to his neighbor" (*Responsa*: 196).

What moral lessons can be inferred from these situations and applied to our contemporary global crisis? If we view the whole globe as a large community, whose citizens are as bound together through the connections of the biosphere as are residents of a courtyard, and if we factor in the undeniable health hazards of pollution, it can be argued that the community has the right, perhaps even the duty, to prohibit actions that degrade the environment—even when such prohibition imposes significant costs on the actors.

What, then, are our communal responsibilities to the environment? In general, even when human activity requires some use of, and consequent damage to, natural resources, decisions should be made in favor of the least destructive method feasible (See, e.g., *Bava Kamma* 91b). A minority opinion in *Shabbat* 140b goes even further. According to this minority view, when an individual chooses one type of food over another merely because of preference and not out of need, and when the "preferred" food is more costly to the environment, that individual is "wasting," and thus violating *bal tashchit* (the prohibition against waste), a violation that the community is entitled to prohibit. Perhaps it has come time to follow this minority opinion, to prohibit, for example, environmentally costly packaging that serves no purpose other than "convenience," or to limit consumption deemed extravagant by the community.

Many recent writers have begun to elaborate this into a principle they call "eco-kashrut," a set of guidelines for personal consumption. These guidelines ask questions such as: are fur coats "kosher?" What about styrofoam, or gas-guzzling autos?

Societal Goals—Sabbath Peace

Our final guiding principle speaks in the broadest terms, as a reminder that all the while we are engaged in detailed policy debates and behavioral adjustments, we ought not, dare not, lose sight of our ultimate goal. How may that goal be defined? At the risk of intimidating the reader, is it really not time for us to speak candidly of the tension between our lives as consumers and our lives as fully human beings—a little lower than the angels, if you will? And is it not time for us to seek, perhaps through our concern for the environment, a redirection of our own purposes and perceptions? Yes, the environment is at stake; so, also, are we.

One may prefer this economic theory or that, one may take what view one wishes of the question of "small is good" vs. "bigger is better." On virtually any reading, we in the industrialized world have allowed our appetites to outrun both our resources and our humanity (see *Pirke Avot* 2:7, 4:1, 4:21 and Maimonides' frequent teachings on the "golden mean," especially his *Eight Chapters*, for some of the many examples of calls for moderation in our tradition.). The acquisition of things becomes the measure of all value, and we are thereby diminished. More: In worshiping the idol of consumption, we do damage to the environment. More still: We do damage to our souls, to a society that might know *shalom*, might know contentment. And we have been given the first step to that *shalom* through Shabbat itself. With the pause of Shabbat, we become, as we read in Exodus (31:17), "re-ensouled" (*va-yinafash*). For the institution of Shabbat, of sacred self-imposed limits, of not working to create but of enjoying creation just as it is, helps bring us closer to peace and contentment.

Say "contentment," and some will think the very word subversive, for it suggests an end to acquisition. But this is neither an argument for asceticism nor even a deprecation of material goods. Our sages did not condemn materialism. Indeed, they wrote that without bread, there can be no Torah (*Pirke Avot* 3:21). But they were acutely aware, at the same time, of the need for balance, a balance we scarcely any longer recognize. Humankind does not, after all, live by bread alone.

ADDITIONAL RESOURCES

Cohen, Jeremy. "*Be Fertile and Increase—Fill the Earth and Master It*": The Ancient and Midrashic Career of a Biblical Text (Ithaca: Cornell University Press, 1989). An in-depth examination of the controversial Genesis 1:28 passage.

Farb, Peter, and Harry McNaught. *The Land, Wildlife, and People of the Bible.* (New York: Harper and Row, 1967). A natural history of the land of Israel, with an examination of ecological conditions in the Middle East over the past 3,000 years.

Hareuveni, Nogah. *Ecology in the Bible.* (Kiryat Ono, Israel: Neot Kedumim, 1974); *Nature in Our Biblical Heritage* (1980); *Trees and Shrubs in Our Biblical Heritage* (1984). This trio of books examines how an understanding of biblical and early rabbinic attitudes toward nature can illuminate both environmental issues and the Jewish tradition.

Rabinowitz, Louis I. *Torah and Flora.* (Sanhedrin Press, 1979). A guide, arranged by Torah portion, to the significance and symbolism of plants in the Torah.

Shochet, Elijah J. *Animal Life in Jewish Tradition: Attitudes and Relationships* (New York: KTAV, 1984). Provides history, from biblical times to modernity, of Jewish attitudes toward legal traditions about the animal kingdom.

Stein, David E., ed. *A Garden of Choice Fruits.* (Philadelphia: Shomrei Adamah, 1991). A collection (without commentary) of some 200 short quotes from Jewish texts about environmental attitudes and issues.

from *LEGENDS OF THE BIBLE*

Louis Ginzberg

ALL THINGS PRAISE THE LORD

"Whatever God created has value." Even the animals and the insects that seem useless and noxious at first sight have a vocation to fulfill. The snail trailing a moist streak after it as it crawls, and so using up its vitality, serves as a remedy for boils. The sting of a hornet is healed by the house-fly crushed and applied to the wound. The gnat, feeble creature, taking in food but never secreting it, is a specific against the poison of a viper, and this venomous reptile itself cures eruptions, while the lizard is the antidote to the scorpion.

Not only do all creatures serve man, and contribute to his comfort, but also God "teacheth us through the beasts of the earth, and maketh us wise through the fowls of heaven." He endowed many animals with admirable moral qualities as a pattern for man. If the Torah had not been revealed to us, we might have learnt regard for the decencies of life from the cat, who covers her excrement with earth; regard for the property of others from the ants, who never encroach upon one another's stores; and regard for decorous conduct from the cock, who, when he desires to unite with the hen, promises to buy her a cloak long enough to reach to the ground, and when the hen reminds him of his promise, he shakes his comb and says, "May I be deprived of my comb, if I do not buy it when I have the means." The grasshopper also has a lesson to teach a man. All the summer through it sings, until its belly burst, and death claims it. Though it knows the fate that awaits it, yet it sings on. So man should do his duty toward God, no matter what the consequences. The stork should be taken as a model in two respects. He guards the purity of his family life zealously, and toward his fellows he is compassionate and merciful. Even the frog can be the teacher of man. By the side of the water there lives a species of animals which subsist off aquatic creatures alone. When the frog notices that one of them is hungry, he goes to it of his own accord, and offers himself as food, thus fulfilling the injunction, "If thine enemy be hungry, give him bread to eat; and if he be thirsty, give him water to drink."

The whole of creation was called into existence by God unto His glory, and each creature has its own hymn of praise wherewith to extol the Creator. Heaven and earth, Paradise and hell, desert and field, rivers and seas—all have their own way of paying homage to God. The hymn of the earth is, "From the uttermost part of the earth have we heard

Louis Ginzberg, *Legends of the Bible*, 1956. Reprinted with permission of the Jewish Publication Society.

songs, glory to the Righteous." The sea exclaims, "Above the voices of many waters, the mighty breakers of the sea, the Lord on high is mighty."

Also the celestial bodies and the elements proclaim the praise of their Creator—the sun, moon, and stars, the cloud and the winds, lightning and dew. The sun says, "The sun and moon stood still in their habitation, at the light of Thine arrows as they went, at the shining of Thy glittering spear"; and the stars sing, "Thou art the Lord, even Thou alone; Thou hast made heaven, the heaven of heavens, with all their host, the earth and all things that are thereon, the seas and all that is in them, and Thou preservest them all; and the host of heaven worshippeth Thee."

Every plant, furthermore, has a song of praise. The fruitful tree sings, "Then shall all the trees of the wood sing for joy, before the Lord, for He cometh; for He cometh to judge the earth"; and the ears of grain on the field sing, "The pastures are covered with flocks; the valleys also are covered over with corn; they shout for joy, they also sing."

Great among singers of praise are the birds, and greatest among them is the cock. When God at midnight goes to the pious in Paradise, all the trees therein break out into adoration, and their songs awaken the cock, who begins in turn to praise God. Seven times he crows, each time reciting a verse. The first verse is: "Lift up your heads, O ye gates; and be ye lift up, ye everlasting doors, and the King of glory shall come in. Who is the King of glory? The Lord strong and mighty, the Lord mighty in battle." The second verse: "Lift up your heads, O ye gates; yea, lift them up, ye everlasting doors and the King of glory shall come in. Who is this King of glory? The Lord of hosts, He is the King of glory." The third: "Arise, ye righteous, and occupy yourselves with the Torah, that your reward may be abundant in the world hereafter." The fourth: "I have waited for Thy salvation, O Lord!" The fifth: "How long wilt thou sleep, O sluggard? When wilt thou arise out of thy sleep?" The sixth: "Love not sleep, lest thou come to poverty; open thine eyes, and thou shalt be satisfied with bread." And the seventh verse sung by the cock runs: "It is time to work for the Lord, for they have made void Thy law."

The song of the vulture is: "I will hiss for them, and gather them; for I have redeemed them, and they shall increase as they have increased"—the same verse with which the bird will in time to come announce the advent of the Messiah, the only difference being, that when he heralds the Messiah he will sit upon the ground and sing his verse, while at all other times he is seated elsewhere when he sings it.

Nor do the other animals praise God less than the birds. Even the beasts of prey give forth adoration. The lion says: "The Lord shall go forth as a mighty man; He shall stir up jealousy like a man of war; He shall cry, yea, He shall shout aloud; He shall do mightily against his enemies." And the fox exhorts unto justice with the words: "Woe unto him that buildeth his house by unrighteousness, and his chambers by injustice; that useth his neighbor's service without wages, and giveth him not his hire."

Yea, the dumb fishes know how to proclaim the praise of their Lord. "The voice of the Lord is upon the waters," they say, "the God of glory thundereth, even the Lord upon many waters"; while the frog exclaims, "Blessed be the name of the glory of His kingdom forever and ever!"

Contemptible though they are, even the reptiles give praise unto their Creator. The mouse extols God with the words: "Howbeit Thou art just in all that is come upon me; for Thou hast dealt truly, but I have done wickedly." And the cat sings: "Let everything that hath breath praise the Lord. Praise ye the Lord."

from "IN AND OF THE WORLD: CHRISTIAN THEOLOGICAL ANTHROPOLOGY AND ENVIRONMENTAL ETHICS"

Anna Peterson

Over thirty years ago, the historian Lynn White Jr. wrote, "Especially in its Western form, Christianity is the most anthropocentric religion the world has seen" (White, 1967: 1206). Since White's influential essay was published, a number of Christian theologians and ethicists, as well as many non-Christians, have debated his claims. Some have supported and even extended his critique. Others have argued that White's claims were too sweeping and that Christianity has, or at least can have, an ecologically positive message. A number have pointed to an ambivalence within the tradition itself, which White himself suggested with his tribute to St Francis as the "patron saint of ecology" (1967: 1207). Others have sought to defend Christianity not as a mixed bag but as powerfully, perhaps uniquely, able to generate a compelling environmental ethic in the modern West.

In this essay, I seek, first, to assess some of the reasons why White and other critics have objected to Christianity. Here I am interested in what David Laitin, following Max Weber, has termed "practical religion": "The interaction between the original doctrine and the social, political, and economic conditions of the time." As Laitin noted, practical religion "can have an independent effect on political life, often quite different from the political or economic intentions of the original propagating group" (Laitin, 1978: 571). It is, in fact, misleading to refer to "practical religion" in the singular, since it takes many forms according to different historical and geographic locations. In this essay, I am interested in a particular aspect of Christianity's "original doctrine"—its teachings on humanity's character and place in the world, i.e., its theological anthropology. It is an important theological task to reflect on what Jesus, Paul, or Augustine might have meant or intended, but it is not my task here. In other words, I am concerned with the ways these doctrines have been inter-

---

Anna Peterson, "In and of the World," *Journal of Agricultural and Environmental Ethics*, 12/3, (2000), pp. 237–261. Reprinted with permission of Kluwer Academic Publishers. This is a selection from the original essay.

preted in and through their interactions with social conditions. More specifically, I examine the ways Christian doctrines about humanness have shaped—or been perceived to shape, by critics and apologists alike—attitudes and behavior towards nature.

In the second and third sections of this article, I look at the ways some contemporary thinkers re-present and/or redefine Christian understandings of humanity's place in nature. Many of these theologians claim that Christianity's charismatic founders—Jesus, Paul, Augustine, Aquinas, among others—did not intend to instrumentalize or exploit nature, and that readings of their ideas in ecologically damaging terms are in fact misreadings. My interest, again, lies not in the historical accuracy or sacred truth of any reading—past or present, "green" or not. Rather, I hope to shed light on some of the reasons that so many traditional readings (or misreadings) of Christianity have helped legitimize environmental harm and on the issues that are most important for current efforts to redirect the practical consequences of Christian thought. I argue that among these issues, one of the most crucial is theological anthropology. In other words, any attempt at a Christian environmental ethic must come to grips with the ways that claims about God shape claims about humans, and the ways that claims about humans in turn shape understandings of nature.

Before I proceed, several further caveats are in order. First, this is not a comprehensive evaluation of the Christian tradition regarding the natural environment, a task better covered by a range of recent books (see Northcott, 1996; Santmire, 1985; Hessel, 1992, among others). In addition, when I speak of a "mainstream" Christian tradition, I am not suggesting that the tradition as a whole is either unanimous or static. Such a view, in fact, is explicitly rejected by the understanding of practical religion that I adopt. What counts as "mainstream" has changed substantially over the past two millennia. For example, in Christianity's formative period (roughly, the three centuries prior to the conversion of Constantine in 313 C.E.) and in the Middle Ages, prevailing Christian interpretations of human and non-human nature—and of many other issues—diverged widely from modern approaches. Further, throughout Christian history certain longstanding currents, notably mysticism, have challenged dominant interpretations of non-human nature. This is all to say that Christianity is a diverse, changing, and complex tradition, and I do not make any claims here to cover (or to condemn or redeem) the whole of it.

HUMAN SEPARATION FROM NATURE IN CHRISTIAN TRADITION

In one of his most important writings, Paul told the Christians of Rome: "Do not be conformed to this world" (Romans 12:2). In the almost 2000 years since, Christian theologians have continually struggled with the question of humans' place in the world. What "this world" means is ambiguous both for Paul and for later theologians. Some take it to mean only the particular social structures and institutions of their time, while others interpret it to encompass earthly life, the physical realm, and embodiment in general. A number of Christian thinkers, from Paul's time to our own, have interpreted human separation from "this world" to imply human separateness from the natural world. While this is not the only possible reading of Paul (and many theologians insist that it is not the truest or best one), the notion that humans are not ultimately at home in the natural world has undeniably shaped Christianity and, through the tradition, influenced Western culture in general.

Christian claims about human uniqueness usually rest on the assertion that humans alone possess an eternal spirit or soul, what Augustine, in *City of God*, termed the image of God and thus of the trinity within them. The soul definitively separates humans from the "non-spiritual" part of creation. It links humans in their origins, capacities, and ultimate destiny to God and, thus, forever divides them from the rest of creation. The soul is not just an added piece of equipment but a dimension that transforms the meaning of humanness. (In this sense, the soul in Christianity performs the same function that qualities such as conceptual thought and language fulfill for secular thinkers, especially those in the Cartesian lineage. In other senses, of course, the Christian notion of the soul differs significantly from these philosophical categories, especially insofar as the soul establishes humans in relationship to the sacred.)

The pre-eminent source for Christian claims about the soul, of course, is the Bible, especially creation stories. The Hebrew Bible offers two accounts of God's creation of the world and humanity. The best known and most influential, found in Genesis 1:26–28, clearly distinguishes humans from the rest of God's creatures. Humans alone are created in God's likeness and, not incidentally, given dominion over the rest of creation. According to this version, creation proceeded thus:

> [26]And God said, "Let us make man in our image, after our likeness, and let them have dominion over the fish of the sea, and over the birds of the air, and over the cattle, and over all the earth, and over every creeping thing that creeps upon the earth."
>
> [27]So God created man in His own image, in the image of God he created him; male and female he created them.
>
> [28]And God blessed them, and God said to them, "Be fruitful, and multiply, and fill the earth and subdue it; and have dominion over the fish of the sea and over the birds of the air and over every living thing that moves upon the earth."

"Having dominion" and "subduing," some Christian and Jewish thinkers argue, need not be interpreted in this context as unqualified exploitation. Interpreted in terms of stewardship, as I discuss later, human power over nature is oriented and constrained by God's ultimate authority over humans. Dominant popular and academic readings, however, take Genesis 1 as legitimating human domination over and utilization of the natural world.

In any of these interpretations of Genesis 1, it is clear that the assertion of humanity's uniqueness—its creation in the image of God—is inextricably tied to human power over the earth and other animals.[1] The soul that all other animals lack both defines humans and gives them transcendent value. The human soul also joins creation and salvation in Christian theological anthropology. In the end, the image of God implanted in the human creature returns to God. This means, crucially, that humanity's real home does not lie among the rest of creation but rather with God in heaven. It also means that humans' most important relationship is the vertical stretch to the divine rather than—or at least before—horizontal ties to other people or creatures. Thus humanity is defined first and foremost not by relations among persons, by physical embodiedness, or by embeddedness in the natural world, but by an invisible tie to an invisible God.

AMBIVALENT EMBODIMENT

Ambivalence about or even hostility to nature has been more or less prominent in different periods and movements within Christianity. It is especially strong in those dimensions of Christian thought most influenced by Greek thought, especially the Platonic idea that the essences of things or beings are more real than physical bodies. In this tradition, as Gordon Kaufman summarizes, "both man [sic] and that which was taken to be ultimately real were understood in terms of those features of man's being which most sharply distinguish us from other creatures" (1972: 352). The Hellenistic tendency to devalue the bodily and look to the transcendent has emerged in different points throughout Christian history. Perhaps the most extreme version is Gnosticism, which thrived in the first few centuries C.E. and peaked with the Manicheans, followers of the third-century prophet Mani. Manicheans defined Jesus as pure spirit and salvation as knowledge (*gnosis*) of the divine. Like a number of other early Christian movements, they rejected the notion that Jesus was fully human and died a physical death. Their Christology reflected their anthropology: what was important about Jesus and every human being was the soul, which was trapped in earth but oriented towards its true home in heaven. In heaven resided the true God, who neither created nor governed the material world. Earth, in fact, was a segment of the Divine that fell into the created world. Humans, as carriers of this divine spark, exist, like God, in radical opposition to the created world. Gnostics awaited a savior who would descend to earth to give them knowledge that would enable individual souls to leave the physical world and the body behind and reunite with the divine substance in Heaven.

The extreme dualism of Gnosticism highlights the close ties between visions of nature and human nature in Christian theology. Gnosticism, especially its Manichean form, defined what is distinctively and positively human as what transcends the material body and earth. In this perspective, just as God is radically other to the created world, so humans—as carriers of the divine spark—are other, not just more, than their bodies. On earth, humans are lost travelers, imprisoned in nature and ruled by capricious powers that enslave them, especially through the physical body. Body and soul are not just different but actively hostile to each other. In this vision, the human condition involves, first, a fundamental alienation from all that ties us to the earth and, second, a ceaseless longing for what might enable us to transcend the material realm. Humans, or at least Christians, are "strangers and pilgrims" wandering through the world, never at home in it (Santmire, 1985: 13).

While Manicheanism represented an extreme, the dualism it reflects has resurfaced again and again in Christian history, in popular movements as well as ratified theologies. In thirteenth-century France, for example, the Cathari (or Albigenses) revived the extreme division between spirit and body. They saw the body as entirely negative and the spirit as wholly good, despite its imprisonment in physicality. Like the Manicheans, the Cathari embedded their theological vision in a narrative that began with a flawed creation and ended, at least for true believers, with a return to their true home with God in heaven. The Cathari so despised physical life that they condemned having children as a sin, since it trapped more souls. The official church condemned the Albigensians as heretical, just as Augustine had condemned Manicheanism. In both cases, the extreme positions pushed mainstream theology to a fuller endorsement of physical life, reproduction, and the created world generally, as seen in various councils and doctrinal statements of both the first few centuries C.E. and the medieval period. Throughout Christian history, however, tendencies to body-spirit dualism have struggled continually with more positive valuations of human embodiment. Official Christianity has in most cases condemned extremely dualistic positions, but ambivalence about the body and nature generally has remained a strong current in both popular and academic theologies.

THE KINGDOM OF THE WORLD

Christian uneasiness about physical bodies has been closely tied to ambivalence about the created world generally. Body and world are physical and transitory in contrast to the spiritual and eternal nature of the soul and of heaven. Christian orthodoxy, however, insists that a benevolent God created both physical bodies and the cosmos itself, which means that material creation cannot simply constitute a trap for spirit. Christian thinkers' efforts to understand the relationship between soul and body reflect the tradition's larger struggle to make sense of the relationship between the spiritual and the physical, between the things of God and the things of the world. These questions raise a number of ethical questions: What is the value of "this world"? How does God will humans to act in relation to the material creation? Underlying these questions is a central concern of theological anthropology: what is the place of humans, as both physical and spiritual creatures, in the created world?

Paul inaugurated the enduring Christian effort to resolve these tensions by positing a vision of humans, or at least Christians, as "in but not of" the world. In contrast to Gnosticism and other dualistic movements, Paul saw the material world and the physical body as creations of a benevolent God. Perhaps more important, given Paul's emphasis on salvation, the world is the locus of redemption by an embodied savior. Thus humans must be in the world, and not grudgingly—but also not fully. Although Paul did not define the world and the body in their present form as evil, neither did he declare them Christians' true or final home. His primary concern was the salvific meaning of Jesus's death and resurrection and the consequences of these events for human life and history. For Paul, human redemption through Christ creates the "new man," not through the transcendence of the material world but via its actual recreation: a new earth to go with the new vision of heaven that is made possible by the crucifixion and resurrection (see, for example, Romans 8). In this context, creation serves essentially as a background for the drama of redemption. While the old earth is not evil, neither is it of permanent importance for human salvation, which alone gives meaning to human life.

Several centuries after Paul, Augustine continued to engage the dualistic tendencies in Christianity's view of nature and human nature. Like Paul, Augustine sought a balance between the conviction that the highest good lay in heaven, on the one hand, and a positive valuation of creation, on the other. Augustine was a Manichean prior to his conversion to Christianity, and his ongoing ambivalence about the body and nature reflect his—and his religion's—struggles with the seductive appeal of dualism. Augustine explicitly rejected the Gnostic notion that the earth and the body are essentially fallen. The Manicheans are wrong to despise earthly bodies as evil, in his view. He devotes large sections of *City of God* (e.g., most of Book XIII) to arguing that not the fact of embodiment but the wrong use of the will leads to sin. The fact that the body is corruptible and (as a result of original sin) mortal, not "the body itself, is heavy to the soul" (1945a: 12). All creation, including the human body, is a revelation of God's goodness, he wrote in his *Confessions*, because God created "the earth which I walk on" as well as the human body—the "earth which I carry" (*Confessions* 12.2., cited in Santmire, 1985: 66). Thus the body cannot be the prison of the soul but rather is its partner.

Although soul and body may belong together, they are far from equal partners. Augustine views both the created world and the physical body as the good works of a benevolent God, but he insists that ultimate value lies only with spiritual things. While the body is not innately evil, it is ephemeral and therefore subordinate to the eternal soul. More generally, all earthly goods are trivial in comparison to the supreme good of eternal life with God in heaven. On earth, Augustine insists, the believer remains "a heavenly pilgrim" (1945b: 252). A pilgrim, of course, is looking for something better. The end of the journey, the true fulfillment of the divinely-ordained narrative in which human life unfolds, is for Augustine the transcendence of physical existence through eternal life. Because only the fate of the soul is of ultimate importance, the non-spiritual created world lacks deep significance, and whatever significance and value it does have comes from its relation to God and eternal life. Despite his conditional valuation of creation against Gnosticism, Augustine reinforces the idea that our relations to material creation lack ultimate meaning in comparison to our relations to God and heaven.

The Augustinian tension between the things of God and the things of the world continues to mark Christianity. This is particularly evident in the Protestant tradition, beginning with Luther's reworking of Augustine's two cities metaphor. For Luther, as for Augustine and Paul, humans must live in the "kingdom of man" and strive to improve it and obey its rules. However, they must also never forget that their true home and destiny lie in the reign of God. This dual citizenship, with its sometimes-contradictory demands, stems from a deep anthropological dualism. In Luther's words, "Man has a twofold nature, a spiritual and a bodily one" (Luther, 1961:53). The former comes from and owes its allegiance to God alone, while the latter, subordinate, nature results from the temporary human condition of embodiment in a flawed material world. Humanity's two natures, as Luther sees them, never harmonize completely, within individuals or in society more generally, and when they conflict openly, the believer's duty to God and the heavenly kingdom must always come first. For Luther and for Calvin, as Michael Northcott writes, "it is not the relations between selves, and between humans and created order, which are salvifically and morally significant but the choosing of particular individual selves by the will of God to be objects of his eternal love and goodness" (Northcott, 1996: 220). The ethical demands of living in the world ultimately neither lead to nor modify the all-important goal of personal salvation and eternal life with God in heaven. Christians' spiritual citizenship ought to make them better residents of the material world, but their earthly social lives should not affect their understandings of or path to final redemption.

The Reformation ambivalence about "the world" resurfaces in the writings of neo-Orthodox theologians in the twentieth century. Reinhold Niebuhr, for example, asserts that human existence is distinguished from animal life by humans' "qualified participation in creation. Within limits it breaks the forms of nature and creates new configurations of vitality" (Niebuhr, 1964: 26). Humans, in other words, are not entirely subject to their "creatureliness" as are other animals; we alone share something of God's creativity (1964: 55). However, Niebuhr believes that people are rarely inclined to live up to their transcendent potential, because the inclination to sin is so powerful. Thus he is far from offering an unqualified celebration of human goodness and rationality. His approach to ethics rests on a conviction that the selfishness that usually drives human behavior requires social (as well as rational and religious) constraints on this inclination (Niebuhr, 1960). Still, at their core, humans have an ethical potential, grounded in their unique participation in God's creative and transforming power, which all other creatures lack. Human nature is defined by the tension, within each person, between the divine spark and the limitations of fallible, selfish embodiment.

Niebuhr does not simply reproduce the Lutheran dualism between the world and God, nor docs he consider the material realm irrelevant to Christian theology. To the contrary, Niebuhr took life in the world very seriously and brought his theological concerns to bear on concrete social projects. Still, his ethics were shaped by a vision of human nature as divided between reason, on the one hand, and emotion and self-interest, on the other. Morality involved dominating what Niebuhr understood, literally, as the baser instincts, through the combined efforts of rationality, religion, and social control. This approach refines the ambivalence evident in Augustinian and Lutheran theology: the world cannot simply be rejected as evil but must be confronted and improved to the extent possible. Like Augustine and Luther, however, Niebuhr viewed the things of the world, including the "baser" part of human nature, as separate from and ultimately detrimental to reason, transcendence, and efforts to realize humans' intrinsic connection to God.

Niebuhr's ambivalence about the world reflects the deeply rooted Protestant assumption that human nature is divided between spirit and body. The spirit, the link to the divine, which provides both what is important and what is unique in human life, exists in constant tension with the physical existence shared with other creatures. Following Luther, Protestant thinkers including Niebuhr reject a simple identification between human sinfulness and the body or the created world, while remaining uneasy about the moral and spiritual status of physical creation. This ambivalence, which sometimes becomes open hostility, toward "the world" is evident in many, though not all, variants of Pentecostal Protestant theology. Latin American Pentecostal leaders, for example, frequently warn against the dangers of the things of the world (*las cosas del mundo*), which they see as radically opposed to the things of God.

The Roman Catholic tradition, in contrast, views the created world in much more positive terms. While Protestantism has mostly seen human life on earth as radically separated from the spiritual realm or the reign of God, Catholicism has perceived greater continuity between the human and the divine and therefore between the material and the spiritual, creature and creator. This Catholic position was systematized in Thomas Aquinas's "medieval synthesis." Thomas wrote in the context of a revived interest, in the Middle Ages, in the notion of a "Great Chain of Being," which joined all creatures in a harmonious hierarchy. The medieval appropriation of the Great Chain of Being was tied both to growing confidence in humanity's mastery over nature, on the one hand, and to a grand

Anna Peterson

vision of the hierarchy of being, on the other. Linking these two themes was the idea of the human creature as microcosm. Nature, as an ordered structure, reflected the human self and vice-versa (Santmire, 1985: 81–82).

Thomas summarized the harmonious relationship between God and creation and among different aspects—human and non-human—of that creation in his notion of natural law. "The whole community of the universe," as Thomas proclaimed in the *Summa Theologica*, "is governed by the divine reason" (1948: 616). Thus the first key aspect of Thomas's thought, in relation to understandings of nature, is his insistence that "everything that in any way is, is from God" (1948: 234), and that all aspects of creation are linked together because "all things partake in some way in the eternal law" (1948: 618). Rational creatures, meaning (male) humans and angels, partake in the eternal law through the imprint of eternal law upon them (or their participation in the eternal law), which is what Thomas terms specifically natural law (in distinction from eternal and human law). Natural law frames human nature in optimistic terms, emphasizing human rationality and humans' capacity and inclination to act in harmony with God's will.

More generally, natural law refers to the entire system that links humans to God and also to the other levels of creation. A second crucial aspect of Thomistic thought is that these linkages are not only harmonious but also hierarchical. "In natural things," Thomas explains, "species seem to be arranged in a hierarchy: as the mixed things are more perfect than the elements, and plants than minerals, and animals than plants, and men more than other animals" (1948: 263). God has not only created and distinguished the creatures but also made them unequal. Humanity's place in this hierarchy is a little below the angels but clearly above the other animals. This elevation stems from humans' possession of an eternal soul, which all other animals, as well as the inanimate features of creation, lack.

Subsequent Roman Catholic thought, about nature as about so much else, builds on Thomistic foundations. Rather than opposed kingdoms or cities, Catholicism perceives creation in terms of an unbroken ascent from lowest to highest levels. God is not opposed to any part of creation, and no part of creation can be termed evil. What is crucial is understanding the nature and proper place of every element. While God creates and rules all of creation, God is not equally near to all of creation. Lower creatures can approach divine goodness only through their relationship to higher ones, and humans, as rational creatures, are superior to other animals and to all of inanimate creation. Their greater closeness to the divine makes humans not only more perfect than but also dominant over other creatures. Thus, Thomas writes, "the subjection of other animals to man is natural" (1948: 918).

Statements like these, along with later interpretations of natural law as justifying human domination, lead many environmental ethicists to conclude that Thomism inevitably reinforces human-centered and exploitative attitudes towards nature. As I discuss in the next section, however, some contemporary Roman Catholic and Anglican thinkers have argued that natural law can provide a strong basis for a positive environmental ethic. The Thomistic tradition, like most other currents within Christianity, generates ambiguous ecological consequences. This has provided ample fruit for eco-theologians and ethicists seeking to redeem Christian attitudes towards non-human nature.

NOTES

1. The second ("Jahwist") creation account in Genesis (beginning at 2:18) does not celebrate human lordship so clearly. Callicott argues that in this account, "man is neither essentially different from other animals nor separated from them by a metaphysical gulf" (Callicott, 1994: 17). This version of creation is both less well known and less influential, at least within Christianity, than Genesis I.

2. It is worth noting that Christianity never confuses the body of a chimp or tree with a mere outside cover. It does not see non-humans as spirits trapped in physical shells but rather "reduces" them to their bodies, as it also does to women. The problem, as McFague recognizes despite her confusing parenthetical clause, lies in seeing bodiliness as a "reduction" in the first place.

3. Doceticism was an early Christian movement that played a central role in the Christological controversies of the first few centuries. Doceticism insisted that Jesus was not fully human; rather, God "adopted" a human body merely as a shell or covering. Eventually another Christological model—which saw Jesus as "fully God, fully human"—won and was enshrined by ecumenical councils and official theologies.

4. This approach has affinities with an "organic" vision of the world as active, changing, perhaps even conscious that has influenced a number of Protestant thinkers, including Sallie McFague and many process theologians. Some of these authors are also influenced by the "Gaia" hypothesis, first proposed by James Lovelock and Lynn Margulis, which views the Earth itself as a conscious organism.

5. More concisely, Jung quotes a note he has posted in his bathroom: "You are not absolutely, irrevocably, personally responsible for everything. That's my job. Love, God" (19).

REFERENCES

Augustine, *City of God, Volume I* (J. M. Dent & Sons, London, 1945a).

Augustine, *City of God, Volume II* (J. M. Dent & Sons, London, 1945b).

Berry, Thomas, *The Dream of the Earth* (Sierra Club Books, San Francisco, CA, 1990).

Callicott, J. Baird, *Earth's Insights: Multicultural Environmental Ethics from the Mediterranean Basin to the Australian Outback* (University of California Press, Berkeley, CA, 1994).

Hessel, Dieter, 1992. *Nature's Revolt: Eco-Justice and Theology* (Fortress Press, Minneapolis, MN, 1992).

Kaufman, Gordon, "The Concept of Nature: A Problem for Theology," *Harvard Theological Review* 65 (1972), 337–366.

Luther, Martin, *Martin Luther: Selections from his Writings.* Edited by John Dillenberger (Anchor Books, New York, 1961).

Niebuhr, Reinhold, *Moral Man and Immoral Society* (Charles Scribner's Sons, New York, 1960).

Niebuhr, Reinhold, *The Nature and Destiny of Man: A Christian Interpretation. Volume I: Human Nature* (Charles Scribner's Sons, New York, 1964).

Northcott, Michael, *The Environment and Christian Ethics* (Cambridge University Press, Cambridge, 1996).

Santmire, Paul, *The Travail of Nature: The Ambiguous Ecological Promise of Christian Theology* (Fortress Press, Minneapolis, MN, 1985).

Thomas Aquinas, *Introduction to St. Thomas Aquinas: The Summa Theologica, The Summa Contra Gentiles* (Edited by Anton C. Pegis) (Modern Library, New York, 1948).

White, Lynn, Jr., "The Historic Roots of Our Ecologic Crisis," *Science* 155 (10 March 1967), 1203–1207.

"TRADITIONAL NATIVE HAWAIIAN ENVIRONMENTAL PHILOSOPHY"

Michael Kioni Dudley

A FISH STORY

If one meets a Hawaiian fisherman loading his nets and gear into his truck, he never asks if the man is going fishing. He might ask if the man is going *holoholo* (out for a ride) or he might ask if he is going to the mountains. But if he asks if the man is going fishing, the man will remove his gear out of the truck, and that will be the end of fishing for the day. For the fish will "hear" and know that the fisherman is coming, and they won't be there when he gets to the sea.

One also hears that senior Hawaiians are sometimes observed talking to plants and trees before picking their flowers—asking before taking—and that they often leave offerings when they take something of significance.

Many Hawaiians also believe that they have ancestral spirits (*'aumakua*) who dwell in animal or other nature forms. Among these are the *mo'o* (lizards), various birds and fish, rainbows, various cloud forms, forests, and mountains. Perhaps the best known of the ancestral spirits is Pele, the goddess who dwells in Kilauea volcano. Pele, in her lava form, flows down among the people on occasion. Hawaiians know the nature forms to which their families are related. They think of their ancestral spirits and the nature forms they inhabit as family members. When they encounter their *'aumakua*, they recognize the occurrence as special: a greeting, or possibly a warning, or an affirmation of the correctness of some action.

Actions such as these certainly reflect a different world view. In ancient *Hawai'i*, humans, gods, and nature formed a consciously interacting and interrelating cosmic community. All the species of nature were thought to be sentient—capable of knowing, choosing, and acting. Through evolution, all were related as kin. Hawaiians lived in a community in which humans, gods, and nature cared for one another and watched over and protected one another as family. There were rules to be observed in the community with

Reprinted by permission of the author. This essay originally appeared in *Ethics, Religion, and Biodiversity*, edited by Lawrence S. Hamilton (White Horse Press, 1993).

nature—environmental ethics. Humans were expected to do their part, and the gods and nature were expected to respond. A reciprocation from any of the three required its own reciprocation in return.

The world today runs according to the Western person's perspective. That perspective treats nature as a commodity, as scientifically measurable forces, and as resources to be used, rather than as fellow beings in an interrelating world community.

What doesn't correspond with a Western person's world view is seen as of little value and as something that can and probably should be ignored. But an approach to life developed over thousands of years must contain much wisdom. During the two millennia that Hawaiian people lived in these islands, they developed a complete and unique system of thought. This explained their world and how things in it interrelated with one another, and also how people fit into the complete picture. Like the Indians, Chinese, Japanese, American Indians, and others, Hawaiians approached the world from a distinctively non-Western perspective. This Hawaiian perspective or world view formed the basis for a philosophical tradition which, although very different from the modern Western view, does explain the world just as adequately. One can function in today's world while approaching it from the traditional Hawaiian-thought framework just as well as one can by approaching it from the Western-thought framework. Certainly, for island dwellers, there must be special insights and wisdom in the Hawaiian approach.

MATTER AND SPIRIT IN EVOLUTIONARY THEORY

In Hawaiian thought, there are close parallels between humans and nature. Hawaiians traditionally have viewed the entire world as being alive in the same way that humans are alive. They have thought *all* of nature as conscious—able to know and to act—and able to interrelate with humans. The Hawaiians had a quite elaborately worked out theory of evolution: its ascent of species, as told in the famous chant *Kumulipo*, corresponds surprisingly well with Darwinian theory. The *Kumulipo* speaks of spirit as well as matter: in contrast to Judeo-Christian thought, it presents both matter and spirit as existing in the beginning, existing quite separately. In further contrast to Western thought, *both* matter and spirit are seen to be conscious, if we define "conscious" as active, knowledgeable, able to make choices, and able to reduce will to action. As evolution progressed, spirit inhabited the various material species, so that they seem to have both material consciousness and spiritual consciousness. Nature, like humans, then, had the conscious ability to know and to act, to watch over, to protect, and to interrelate with humans. Humans, who stood at the top of the evolutionary ladder, formed a continuum of consciousness with nature beneath them, in sharp contrast with Western thought where humans are the anomaly, the only beings who think.

Hawaiians also viewed the land, the sky, the sea, and all the other species of nature preceding them as family—as conscious ancestral beings who had evolved earlier on the evolutionary ladder, who cared for and protected humans, and who deserved similar treatment (*aloha ʻaina* [love for the land]) in return.

THE ROLE OF THE CHIEF

In Hawaiian evolutionary theory, humans stood at the top of evolved nature. At the pinnacle of human society, and therefore of all else, stood the *aliʻi nui* (high chief or king). The *aliʻi nui* was thought to have a special relationship with nature, a nurturing and sustaining control.

The high chiefs sometimes demonstrated their power over nature in dramatic ways, such as by halting lava flows. King Kamehameha I is said to have saved his fishponds from approaching lava by standing before the flow, making offerings, and appeasing the goddess Pele, who indwelt the flowing lava.

Newspaper accounts and letters of missionaries tell of a similar event witnessed in 1881 when Princess Ruth, who rejected the Christian religion of the *haole* (white person), demonstrated the power of both her station and of the old religion by standing before a lava flow at the outskirts of Hilo, making offerings to that presence of Pele, and stopping the flow.

The Hawaiian word *ea* means "the living breath." Even more specifically, it is the "life-force" which manifests itself as breath in people, and which also exists in everything in the cosmos. For most ancient peoples, the living breath was the sign that the life-force dwelt in a person. When one stopped breathing, the life-force had gone.

The chief's relation with the lands was so intertwined that when he died, the lands also died. The chant "Fallen is the Chief" relates this. At the death of Chief Keoua, the chant says:

Puna is dead! Puna is dead!
The breath of life (*ea*) and the breathing are gone.
The spirit has fled.

The soul of the land, and "its living breath" (*ke ea o ka ʻaina*), left it just as the chief's soul and his living breath (*ea*) left his body.

The presence of the living chief held everything together: the gods, humans, and nature. When the chief died, everything came apart: people's relationship with the lands, people's relationship with the gods, and people's relationship with others—the whole societal structure. People went about nude and engaged in sexual acts in public. They gashed themselves, knocked out their teeth, shaved their heads, and burned marks on their bodies to remember the chief. The *kapu* system (the religious laws or taboos) also fell apart, completing the disorder throughout all of nature: women entered the *heiau*, ate bananas, co-

conuts, and pork, and climbed over the sacred places. And women and men ate together—all acts punishable by death under the *kapu* system.

It then devolved upon the new *ali'i nui* to renew life to the land and to restore order to nature. After the mourning period, when the new *ali'i nui* was enthroned, the direction and structure of society were restored, reestablishing order among the people by reinstating the *kapu* system. Through presence and prayers, the chief then built a new relationship with the gods and with nature, revivifying nature and setting everything right again. The chant "Fallen is the Chief" tells of a new chief as he takes over the land.

> The island was untamed, that the chief knew well.
> On his becoming guardian it was more and more tamed.
> He fed the small fish,
>   he gathered them together like bonito.
> Streams of country people of the island follow;
> Now the tail of the land wags
> Like that of a well-fed favorite dog.

Once the new chief reestablished the *kapu* system and restored order to society, and once he calmed nature and brought it under his nurturing control, then it once more could be said *Ua mau ke ea o ka 'aina* (The living breath of the land continues on) *i ka pono* (since [the king is in his place of leadership and] everything is ordered correctly again).

This whole belief system is exemplified in a situation that arose in 1843 in which King Kamehameha III was temporarily forced to cede rule of the islands to Britain. He knew when he ceded that his action would cause a rupture in his chiefly, nurturing rapport with the lands. The lands themselves would suffer during this time of cession. But he had hopes that once the lands were returned he could again bring them under his chiefly nurturing power, and they would flourish as they had.

After 5 months of British occupation, on July 31, 1843, the lands were restored to the king by Admiral Thomas. At that time King Kamehameha III came before the people again on the steps of Kawaiaha'o Church and proclaimed, *Ua mau ke ea o ka 'aina i ka pono* (The lands breathe again, nature lives on and prospers, now that the king has been restored to his proper place and has resumed his nurturing relationship with it—now that things are properly ordered again).

THE HAWAIIAN EXPERIENCE OF REALITY

The chants of the Hawaiians told them that they had descended from the cosmos itself and from its many plant and animal species. They felt a kinship with nature not experienced by people who see a break between humankind and the species of nature which have preceded them in the evolutionary advance. In the Western world, where the cleavage is most pronounced, animals are disdained as having senses but no reason; the plant world is recognized as alive, but in no way even aware; and the elements of the cosmos are treated as inert objects that follow mechanical laws. Hawaiians, on the other hand, view all these beings as sentient ancestral forms that interrelate with them as family. Therefore, they experience reality differently because of these views.

The difference in how the Hawaiian and the Westerner experience reality can be illustrated by the reaction of a person in an unfamiliar building who, rushing to a meeting late, opens one door and finds a storeroom filled with canned items, then opens another which is the front door to a lecture in session. Entering the "empty" storeroom elicits a totally different response than entering a lecture room full of people, even though one might not know a single person in the disturbed lecture. Canned items on shelves mean nothing to a person; they lack that which gives them significance: consciousness. The storeroom is "empty." The people in the lecture give meaning to the other encounter. It is their consciousness, their seeing a person blunder which makes the difference. The surprise and embarrassment the person experiences come about because of the people's consciousness, and with it their ability to relate and to help or hurt. These are all perceived immediately and undifferentiated from the appearance of their bodies in a person's total comprehension of the scene. Recognized consciousness makes demands on the perceiver, demands for correct behavior and correct relationship. For the Hawaiians, there are no empty storerooms. Confronting the world about them, they experience conscious beings at every turn, and along with this their interpersonal demands.

Further, there is also a real difference between coming upon someone recognized as a relative and meeting someone who is not. In perceiving one who is kin, a person experiences not only an added awareness of relationship, but also an emotional feeling of belongingness.

As Hawaiians view the world, what they actually *see* is the same as what Westerners see, but what they *perceive as seen* is different. It might be noted that Hawaiians of the past and many Hawaiians today are unaware that others do—or even can—perceive things without perceiving them as conscious and related to them as kin.

It is true that most Hawaiians today do not formally learn the traditional philosophy as it is described in these pages. Yet they approach the world in a Hawaiian way that fits hand-in-glove with the philosophy. Hawaiian philosophy mirrors a centuries-old approach to life which cannot be expunged from the culture. The Hawaiians who ache for the land as they watch Westerners—and now the Asians—buy it up and pave it over may not be able to say *how* they are related to the land, but they know they are in their bones. The Hawaiians who put their lives on the line standing in front of a bulldozer may not know why they must defend the land in that way, but they cannot turn away. With or without the philosophical tradition, Hawaiians know that they form a community with nature around them. Nature constantly and consciously in good faith provides for and protects them, and they are compelled from deep within to protect nature in turn. They do this with the same courage and bravery non-Hawaiians summon to defend *their* family and community from an aggressor. [A complete discussion of this topic can be found in *A Hawaiian Nation I: Man, Gods, and Nature*, by Michael Kioni Dudley, Na Kane O Ka Malo Press, P. O. Box 970, Waipahu, Hawaii 96797.]

"EARLY BUDDHIST VIEWS ON NATURE"

Chatsumarn Kabilsingh

Buddhism views humanity as an integral part of nature, so that when nature is defiled, people ultimately suffer. Negative consequences arise when cultures alienate themselves from nature, when people feel separate from and become aggressive towards natural systems. When we abuse nature, we abuse ourselves. Buddhist ethics follow from this basic understanding. Only when we agree on this common ground can we save ourselves, let alone the world.

In order to explore the connection between Buddhism and nature, Wildlife Fund Thailand has sponsored a project called Buddhism and Nature Conservation. This project is particularly interested in finding teachings of the Buddha which relate to nature and its conservation. A team of researchers has combed the texts and discovered a surprisingly large store of beautiful and valuable teachings in Buddhism relating to nature and respect for wildlife and natural resources.

The *Jataka*, the richly narrated birth stories of Buddhism, are abundant with poetic appreciations of nature. Passage after passage celebrates forests, waters, and the Earth's wild creatures. Here we find a "Garden of Delight," where grass is ever green, all trees bear fruit good to eat, and streams are sweet and clean, "blue as beryl." Nearby is "a region over-run and beautified with all manner of trees and flowering shrubs and creepers, resounding with the cries of swans, ducks and geese. . . . " Next is reported an area "yielding from its soil all manner of herbs, overspread with many a tangle of flowers," and listing a rich variety of wild animals: antelope, elephant, buffalo, deer, yak, lion, rhinoceros, tiger, panther, bear, hyena, otter, hare, and more.[1]

All Buddhist literature states that the Buddha was born in a grove of sal, lovely straight-backed trees with large leaves. According to legend, when the Buddha was born he took seven steps, and lotus flowers sprang up as he walked. As a youth, he is said to have meditated in the shade of the jambo, one of the 650 species of myrtle.

The Buddha's further study was in the company of a banyan, and his enlightenment was under the spreading branches of a tree recognized for its special place in human faith even in its scientific name, *Ficus religiosa*. Also known as the Bo, Bodhi, or peepul, this tree is sacred in both Buddhism and Hinduism.

Reprinted from *Dharma Gaia: A Harvest of Essays in Buddhism and Ecology*, edited by Allan Hunt Badiner (1990) with permission of Parallax Press, Berkeley, CA, USA.

The early Buddhist community lived in the forest under large trees, in caves, and in mountainous areas. Directly dependent on nature, they cultivated great respect for the beauty and diversity of their natural surroundings.

In the *Sutta-Nipata*, one of the earliest texts, the Buddha says:

> Know ye the grasses and the trees . . . Then know ye the worms, and the moths, and the different sorts of ants . . . Know ye also the four-footed animals small and great, the serpents, the fish which range in the water, the birds that are borne along on wings and move through the air . . . Know ye the marks that constitute species are theirs, and their species are manifold.[2]

There is a story of a monk who cut down the main branch of a tree: The spirit who resided in that tree came forward and complained to the Buddha that a monk had cut off his child's arm. From then on, monks were forbidden to cut down trees.[3]

The Buddha encouraged acting with compassion and respect for the trees, noting that they provide natural protection for the beings who dwell in the forest. On one occasion, the Buddha admonished some travelers who, after resting under a large banyan tree, proceeded to cut it down. Much like a friend, the tree had given them shade. To harm a friend is indeed an act of ingratitude.[4]

The *Anguttara Nikaya* tells a similar story:

> Long ago, Brahmin Dhamika, Rajah Koranya, had a steadfast king banyan tree and the shade of its widespread branches was cool and lovely. Its shelter broadened to twelve leagues. None guarded its fruit, and none hurt another for its fruit.
>
> Now then came a man who ate his fill of fruit, broke a branch, and went his way. Thought the spirit dwelling in that tree: How amazing, how astonishing it is, that a man should be so evil as to break a branch off the tree after eating his fill. Suppose the tree were to bear no more fruit. And the tree bore no more fruit.[5]

What about the treatment of animals? Every healthy forest is home for wildlife, so when a monk accepts the forest as his home, he also respects the animals who live in the forest. Early Buddhists maintained this kind of friendly attitude toward their natural surroundings and opposed the destruction of forests or their wildlife.[6]

The first precept in Buddhism is "Do not kill." This precept is not merely a legalistic prohibition, but a realization of our affinity with all who share the gift of life. A compassionate heart provides a firm ground for this precept.

Those who make their living directly or indirectly from killing animals will experience the karmic consequences. The resultant pain is described in the texts as being "sharp as spears" and as terrifying as being "thrown head-down into a river of fire."[7] A person who tortures or kills animals will always harbor a deep sorrow within:

When, householder, the taker of life, by reason of his taking life, breeds dread and hatred in this world, or when he breeds dread and hatred in the next world, he experiences in the mind pain and grief; but he who abstains from taking life breeds no dread and hatred in this world and in the next world . . . Thus that dread and hatred has ceased for him, who abstained from taking life.[8]

The community of monks are forbidden by the *Vinaya*, the ancient rules of conduct, from eating ten different kinds of meat, mostly animals of the forest.[9] The Buddha taught his disciples to communicate to animals their wishes for peace and happiness. This was only possible when they did not eat the animals' flesh, and harbored no thoughts of harming them. When a monk died from a snakebite, the Buddha advised the community to generate compassion and dedicate the merit to the family of snakes.[10]

When we look at the Buddha's pronouncements on water conservation, it is astonishing to see that he actually set down rules forbidding his disciples to contaminate water resources. For example, monks were dissuaded from throwing their waste or leftover food into rivers and lakes, and they were urged to guard the lives of all living beings abiding there.[11] In the *Vinaya Pitaka* there are detailed descriptions of how to build toilets and water wells.[12] One of the eight good qualities of the ocean is "cleanliness," and another is that it "must be the abode of various kinds of fish." Those who destroy or contaminate water resources do so at great karmic peril.[13] This illustrates early awareness of the need to preserve natural resources.

The early Buddhist community lived comfortably within nature, and the Buddha included many examples and similes from nature in his teachings:

> Suppose there is a pool of water, turbid, stirred up and muddied. Just so a turbid mind. Suppose there is a pool of water, pure, tranquil and unstirred, where a man can see oysters and shells, pebbles and gravel, and schools of fish. Just so an untroubled mind.[14]

Buddhism holds a great respect for and gratitude toward nature. Nature is the mother that gives rise to all the joyful things in life. Among the beautiful expressions in Buddhist literature showing mutual relation and interdependence of humankind and wildlife, there was early on a realization that survival of certain species was in danger, and that losing such creatures diminishes the Earth: "Come back, O Tigers! to the woods again, and let it not be leveled with the plain. For without you, the axe will lay it low. You, without it, forever homeless go."[15]

Another well-known and much loved teaching which exemplifies the central core of compassion in Buddhism is the *Metta Sutta*: "Thus, as a mother with her own life guards the life of her own child, let all embracing thoughts for all that lives be thine."[16]

His Holiness the Fourteenth Dalai Lama of Tibet who stands prominently among Buddhist leaders of the world who are farsighted, has repeatedly expressed his concern for environmental protection. "Our ancestors viewed the Earth as rich, bountiful and sustainable," said His Holiness. "We know this is the case, but only if we take care of it." In one of his recent speeches on the subject of ecology, he points out that the most important thing is to have a peaceful heart. Only when we understand the true nature lying within can we live harmoniously with the rest of the natural world.

In this respect, the Buddhist practice of cultivating awareness and calmness through meditation is vital. Buddhism is very much a religion of this world, this life, and the present moment. In the past it has often been misunderstood as otherworldly or life-denying. In fact, Buddhism can be meaningful only when it is relevant to our everyday lives and to our environment. The Buddhist tradition counsels us to treasure and conserve nature, of which human beings are an active part. Each of us must choose the extent to which we will bring to life the teachings of the Buddha. If we cannot hand over a better world to future generations, it is only fair that they have at least as green a world to live in as we do.

NOTES

1. *Jataka Stories*, edited by E.B. Cowell, vols. IV–V (1957).

2. *Sutta-Nipata*, translated by V. Fausboll (Delhi, India: Motilal Banarsidass, 1968).

3. *Paccittiya, Bhutagama Vagga*, Thai Tripitaka, vol. 2, p. 347.

4. Ibid., vol. 27, p. 370.

5. *Anguttara Nikaya, Gradual Sayings*, vol. 3, p. 262.

6. *Payaka Jataka, op. cit.* vol. 27:417, p. 107.

7. Ibid., vol. 28:92, p. 35.

8. *Gradual Sayings*, vol. 4, p. 273.

9. Ibid., vol. 4, p. 60–61.

10. Ibid., vol. 7, p. 9.

11. Ibid., vol. 25:300, p. 313.

12. Ibid., vol. 7, p. 48.

13. Ibid., vol. 26:104, p. 174.

14. Ibid., vol. 1, p. 6–7.

15. *Khuddakapatha* (London: Pali Text Society, 1960).

16. Ibid.

"ILLUMINATING DARKNESS: THE MONK-CAVE-BAT-ECOSYSTEM COMPLEX IN THAILAND"

Leslie E. Sponsel and Poranee Natadecha-Sponsel

INTRODUCTION

Buddhist monks and nuns dwelled and meditated in caves in northern India some 2,500 years ago. Subsequently this practice spread with Buddhism to other parts of Asia. The sacredness of a cave usually discourages, if not completely excludes, the human use of the animal species in it, and to some degree, those around it. Bats are the most important fauna in most caves. They are also keystone (critical) species in forest and other ecosystems as pollinators, seed dispersers, and insect predators while they forage widely at night. Consequently, we hypothesize that there is an ecological connection between Buddhist practices in sacred caves on the one hand, and on the other the conservation of bats and the maintenance of the ecosystems in which they forage. Given the antiquity, multitude, and widespread distribution of such sacred caves, they are a significant force in environmental and biodiversity conservation, even if previously unrecognized as such. In this essay we explore these and other propositions and provide supportive background information.

SACRED CAVES[1]

Archaeology reveals that humans have used caves opportunistically as habitation, grave, art, and ritual sites since far back into prehistory. This may help explain the attraction, fascination, and mystery that caves hold for most people (Bonsall and Tolan-Smith, 1997; Fagan, 1998). It explains one curious fact—bats and humans have in common the same cosmopolitan species of bedbug (*Cimex lectularius*) (Hill and Smith, 1984:170).

In India, the use of caves for religious practices by individuals and groups goes back in time for millennia. The Buddha dwelled and meditated in caves, forests, and other kinds of sites, practices which became common for Buddhist monks and nuns during his life-

From David Chappell, ed., *Spiritually Engaged Spirituality: Essays in Honor of Sulak Sivaraksa* (Bangkok: Sathirakoses-Nagapradipa Foundation, 2003). Reprinted by permission of the author.

time and beyond (Munier 1998). Whenever Buddhism expanded into other parts of Asia—the South, Central, East, and Southeast regions—this use of caves spread as well (Barnes, 1995; Whitfield et al., 2000).

Paintings imply that long before Buddhism came to Thailand, caves were used for ritual purposes by shamans practicing animism, a religious belief in spirit beings in nature (Munier, 1998:181–188). One of the most famous paintings is in Spirit Cave in Mae Hong Son province in the north, dating to around 9,000 years ago (Munier, 1998:155). The earliest known use of caves by Buddhists in Thailand dates back to at least the 6th to 7th centuries C.E. with Roesi, Fa Tho, Chin, and Cham caves on Khao Ngu mountain, and Narai cave in Phra Puttha Bat district (Munier, 1998:34). According to legends, the Buddha even visited some caves in either the Lamphun or Mae Sai districts, the latter including Pum, Pla, and Pleo Plong Fa caves (Munier, 1998:36, 121, 171). In Thailand, at least 112 Buddhist sacred caves (called *tham* in Thai) have been identified, and 60 of them described in some detail (Munier, 1998:153–154, 235–236). Furthermore, it is likely that there are many more caves in Thailand—hundreds, if not thousands—given the combination of several limestone mountain ranges which run from north to the south through the western portion of the country, and the heavy tropical monsoon rainfall with some acid content that can slowly erode these soluble carbonate rocks over long periods of geological time (see Pongsabutra et al., 1991). Kanchanaburi province is especially rich in caves. The caves throughout the country are all natural, except for the two at Khao Khuha, which were carved out of the rock and were used as a Hindu temple in the 6th and 7th centuries (Munier, 1998:33, 188).[2]

Munier (1998) states that a key point of Buddhism is: "to understand our human nature we need to be immersed in Nature" (p. 164) and also, "The Buddhist taste for natural places favorable to a spiritual quest often led to the worship of natural places" (p. 42). He defines a sacred place "as a space separate from the profane, a space of mystery, divine, both intimidating and appealing" (Munier, 1998:39). Munier (1998:37–42) also identifies several functions of caves as sacred places: resonance chambers for chanting; a secluded, quiet, and peaceful receptacle of spiritual energy for cultivating inner peace through meditation; places for birth and rebirth; spaces adjacent to or in the cave for reliquaries and tombs, including those of monks, the mountain containing the cave simulating a grand stupa; and gates into the subterranean world and dwelling sites of supernatural creatures like demons, ghosts, angels, and Nagas (snakelike deities). He concludes, "Today, Buddhist caves in Thailand are still part of its active Buddhist culture and even those with an archaeological or historical value are lively sanctuaries" (Munier, 1998:36).

Caves are a place in nature especially conducive to quiet seclusion for meditation (see Tiyavanich, 1997:144–148). When a monk inhabits a cave, a yellow cloth is hung at the entrance or parts where he lives. The monk meditates and sleeps in the cave. Usually he leaves only to walk the morning alms round to obtain food from villagers who may be kilometers away. A monk can occupy a cave for only a few days, for months, or even for years. Other monks and lay people may visit, the latter sometimes for short or long retreats. When the number of monks, nuns, or both grows, then they use the cave only as a sanctuary and pursue other activities in an adjacent monastery. Thus, caves are often either a part of monasteries or located near them (Munier, 1998).

Caves typically contain rows of several sizes of seated statues of the Buddha in the meditation posture, and often a huge reclining statue as well. The arrangement of the statues depends on the natural configuration of the cave. Statues are placed where sunlight illuminates them if possible; otherwise, artificial lighting is used. Other Buddha statues may be installed in various cavities or nooks in the rock formations and walls of the cave. Statues of holy hermits or monks are usually in a side chamber. In some caves, stalactites that resemble figures associated with Buddhism are worshipped as well. Naga figures are frequently placed at the entrance and inside the cave, a symbol of protection for the Buddha and for Buddhism. Over time, the number, types, and arrangement of statues and associated religious objects changes (Munier, 1998:159–170).

As Munier (1998:195) observes:

> While living in a cave seems inconceivable at the end of the 20th century, Buddhist monks in Thailand, following a 2,500-year-old Buddhist tradition, continue to practice their religion in caves for short or longer periods. It seems there is some kind of correspondence between "inside" (the cave) and "inner" (search), and that as long as Buddhism exists, so also will caves.

Some caves are famous and visited by tourists, whereas others are kept secret. Many Thais fear caves because they believe ghosts and spirits (*phi*) inhabit them (Munier, 1998:159). Some monks have seen this as a challenge to overcome, a test of their faith in the Dharma, the teachings of the Buddha (Tiyavanich, 1997:123–126). In particular, such creatures challenge the monk to demonstrate compassion and loving kindness. It is also noteworthy that the great Buddhist caves were favorite excursion sites for the kings of Thailand during the 19th and 20th centuries (Munier 1998:231).

BATS

Bats (Order Chiroptera) are one of the largest and most widely distributed group of mammals (Class Mammalia). There are nearly 1,000 species of bats in the world, comprising about one-quarter of all mammalian species. Like other mammals, including humans, bats are warm-blooded and hairy, give birth to live young, and nurse their young with milk. Bats are found on every continent except Antarctica (Bat Conservation International

2002). In Thailand, 107 species of bats have been identified thus far, comprising 38 percent of the 280 species of mammals in the country (Stewart-Cox, 1995:36). Bats are common in most terrestrial ecosystems in the nation—not only mountains and forests, but also farmlands and even inside villages, towns, and cities (Graham and Round, 1994: 95).

Bats roost in a variety of places, depending on the species. Some roost mainly or exclusively in caves which offer constant climate with protection from the weather, thereby reducing the challenge of regulating a constant body temperature. Cave roosting also avoids most predators (Hill and Smith, 1984:82). Some bat colonies are the largest concentrations of mammalian populations on Earth (Bat Conservation International 2002). In Thailand, cave colonies of the whiskered bat (*Myotis mystacinus*) contain more than 10,000 individuals, and those of the wrinkled-lipped bat (*Tadarida plicata*) more than 200,000 (Lekagul and McNeely, 1988:194, 266).

Bats are nocturnal, some species flying out from their roosts before dusk, and others well afterward. They usually follow the same narrow aerial routes (a meter or two wide) to their feeding areas and back (Lekagul and McNeely, 1988:46). Among bat species in Thailand, 89 are insectivorous (eat insects), while 18 are frugivorous (eat fruit and nectar) (Stewart-Cox, 1995:36). At the minimum, 27 species of insectivorous bats and four species of frugivorous bats roost in caves, although not necessarily exclusively (data extracted from Lekagul and McNeely, 1988).

Despite the importance of the bat fauna of Thailand, relatively little is known about their status, distribution, behavior, and ecology. There have not even been any comprehensive surveys of the bats in national parks and wildlife sanctuaries (Graham and Round, 1994:99). However, advances in technology make nocturnal observation easier with special instruments for radio tags, night vision, and even detection of echolocation sounds; the last are otherwise beyond the normal range of human hearing. Yet detailed field studies of the behavior and ecology of any bat species are rare (e.g., Fleming, 1988).[3]

ECOLOGY

Bats are a keystone species. Keystone species play a disproportionate role in an ecosystem, and the extirpation of a population or the extinction of a whole species would precipitate far-reaching ecological changes. Frugivorous bats are especially important in pollination and seed dispersal, while insectivorous bats are significant in controlling insect populations.

Distances flown in foraging vary with the type and availability of the preferred resources, and that can vary through time (daily, seasonally, annually, and so on). In tropical forests, bats fly over long distances to locate and feed on trees with appropriate fruit, because the trees of the same species are widely dispersed, different trees of the same species fruit at different times, and even on the same tree fruit can be in markedly different stages of maturity. For example, Geoffroy's rousette bat (*Rousettus aplexicaudatus*) makes nightly round trips of 40–50 kilometers between its cave and fruit-foraging areas (Lekagul and McNeely, 1988:69). Insectivorous bats, in contrast, are able to forage much closer to their diurnal roosts (Hill and Smith, 1984:70–71).

Some species of flowers and bats co-evolved; the flowers have particular morphological adaptations to facilitate pollination by bats (Graham and Round, 1994:42). Bat-pollinated flowers or flower heads are usually large and positioned singly on long, sturdy stalks which facilitate perching by bats (Graham and Round, 1994:96). Some flowers open only at night and have strong odors which attract bats (Hill and Smith, 1984:69).

Bats are also important as pollinators of human food crops. For example, the flowers of the durian tree open only at night, when they are pollinated exclusively by the cave-dwelling, nectar-eating bat (*Eonycteris spelaea*) (Graham and Round, 1994:96). Throughout Asia, the durian fruit industry is worth $100 million a year. Among the other plants that bats pollinate exclusively are wild bananas, sataw beans, and kapok. Bats as well as other animals pollinate breadfruit, mangoes, guavas, avocados, cashews, and figs (Bat Conservation International 2002). A species of mangrove tree (*Sonneratia* sp.) is pollinated exclusively by just one species of fruit bat, *Cynopterus sphinx* (Stewart-Cox, 1995:28, 36).

In tropical regions, the seedlings of most plants will not grow and mature in the shade of the parent, and the latter may even produce toxins which prevent such growth. These species are solely dependent on animal agents to disperse their seeds. Furthermore, the seeds of some, like *Ficus* species, will not germinate until they are stimulated by the chemicals in the digestive tracts of bats or birds. Most fruit-eaters do not damage the seeds they swallow. Whole seeds are simply dropped wherever the animal defecates and thus widely scattered (Hill and Smith, 1984:67). Fruit bats, unlike other frugivores, defecate in flight; thus, they often scatter seeds over degraded forests and scrublands, which in turn promotes tree growth and forest regeneration (Stewart-Cox, 1995:36). Huge bat colonies of a million individuals can disperse many millions of seeds every night.

Fruit bats, however, do not reduce the fruit crop for farm export, since unripe fruits are shipped, and the bats eat only fruit that has ripened prematurely or after the main crop is picked. Bats thereby reduce the risk of crop pests like fruit flies and fungus (Bat Conservation International 2002).

The majority of the species of bats worldwide (70 percent) and in Thailand (83 percent) are insectivores. Bats are the only major predator limiting the populations of nocturnal insects like rice-hoppers and mosquitoes. Capturing insects in flight requires fast and highly maneuverable flight styles, and that means high energy expenditure. Thus, insectivorous bats consume large quantities of insects; estimates range from one-quarter to one-half of their body weight each night (Hill and Smith, 1984:15). One foraging bat can eat up to 600 insects per hour, or 3,000 per night (Bat Conservation International 2002). The insectivorous wrinkle-lipped bat (*Tadarida plicata*) roosts in limestone caves in huge numbers of half a million or more. At Khao Chong Phran in Ratchburi Province, it is estimated that the bat population consumes 30–40 million insects each night (Lekagul and McNeely, 1988:266). A single colony of bats can consume hundreds of tons of insects annually (Hill and Smith, 1984:63). Insectivorous bats are quite beneficial to human health and economy. Indeed, extirpation of a local population or extinction of a species of bats could release mosquitoes from predation pressure and trigger an explosion of their population and consequently of malaria.

These are just some of the ways in which bats are known to be vital for the health of most terrestrial ecosystems in Thailand. Bats rarely transmit diseases to humans and normally bite only in self-defense or when handled. Otherwise, they are shy, gentle, and intelligent mammals, and avoid human contact. Because of the multifaceted role of bats as keystone species, either reduction or extirpation of populations, or extinction of whole species, could have severe negative consequences for forest ecology, farming economy, and human health.

CONSERVATION

Bats are especially vulnerable. They are the slowest reproducing mammal in the world for their body size, females of most species produce only one young annually (Bat Conservation International, 2002). Many bat species are rare, occurring in few habitat types and with restricted geographical ranges (Stewart-Cox, 1995:36). Major factors threatening or endangering bat populations and species include habitat destruction (roosting locations and depletion of critical food resources), poisoning from chemical pesticides, and human overexploitation (for food, tourism, and other economic uses). Global warming is a new threat. Bat populations have declined worldwide in recent decades (Bat Conservation International, 2002).

Prior to World War II, more than 70 percent of Thailand was forested, whereas today, estimates are less than 20 percent (e.g., Hirsch, 1997). Massive deforestation has no doubt already severely affected bat populations and species in many parts of the country. Much of this deforestation is caused by agricultural expansion. The widespread use of toxic chemical pesticides by farmers and others is increasingly concentrated as the residue flows up the food chain (biomagnification) and thus endangers bats too (Hill and Smith, 1984:63).

Limestone or karst terrain is an inherently fragile and vulnerable landscape (Williams, 1993). It is also critical for sustaining the populations of many species of bats, which use caves and other rocky areas for roosting (Graham and Round, 1994:23). For instance, the Kitti's hog-nosed or bumblebee bat (*Craseonycteris thonglongyai*) is the smallest mammal in the world, measuring about 3 centimeters in body length and 8 centimeters in wingspan, and weighing 2 grams. It is extremely rare; its roosting sites are limited to caves in Kanchanaburi province of western Thailand. Dr. Boonsong's roundleaf bat (*Hipposideros lekaguli*) is known from only a few limestone caves in Saraburi province (Graham and Round, 1994:95–96). The disc-nosed bat (genus and species not identified) is endemic to central Thailand, where it roosts in a limited number of caves (Stewart-Cox, 1995:36). Quarrying operations to mine limestone for roads and other construction purposes threaten or displace many bat colonies. Quarrying and other activities, like deforestation, can even lead to changes in the hydrological regime (surface and underground drainage systems) and to rocky desertification (Williams, 1993).

Overexploitation of bat populations by human hunters is yet another serious problem. Usually hunters can readily catch bats in nets when they exit caves at dusk to forage. Some Thais eat bats like other wildlife—the poor as a subsistence necessity, or others who can afford to buy it at special "jungle meat" market stalls or restaurants (Sponsel and Natadecha-Sponsel, 1992). The Kitti's hog-nosed bat is hunted to sell to tourists as souvenirs (Stewart-Cox, 1995:124).

However, there are economic uses of bats that do not harm them. For example, bat droppings accumulate on the cave floor of large colonies. This guano is a high-grade fertilizer which is gathered for sale by some villagers, who are thus interested in protecting the bats. Indeed, the temple of Khao Chong Pran, in Ratchaburi, has a cave housing more than two million free-tailed bats (*Rhinopoma hardwickei*). Every two weeks, local villagers are allowed to collect the guano, and the income earned is used by the monks to support a school and various development projects (Stewart-Cox, 1995:36).

Of course, government-protected areas such as national parks and wildlife sanctuaries can promote bat conservation, but only if they are effectively administered locally rather than mere "paper parks." For instance, there are at least 60 species of bats in Thung Yai National Park in western Thailand (Stewart-Cox, 1995:134). However, there are distinctive advantages and disadvantages for nature conservation with secular and sacred places (Sponsel, et al., 1998, cf. McNeely and Somchevita, 1996).

DISCUSSION

A number of hypotheses follow from the above considerations. Sacred caves usually discourage, if not completely exclude, the molestation or exploitation of the fauna therein and nearby, thus effectively promoting the conservation of roosting bats. This is turn helps guard their role as keystone species in forests and other ecosystems which may be a long distance from the caves. In turn, sacred caves are a component of a very ancient, widespread, and diverse system of sacred places throughout Thailand which have important and far-reaching significance for environmental and biodiversity conservation (Sponsel et al., 1998).

This monk-cave-bat-ecosystem complex is a complementary coincidence of three mutually reinforcing anomalies associated with caves, monks, and bats. Caves are not merely holes in the ground, but usually cavities in mountainsides, and mountains are recognized as special locations where earth and sky meet; thus, they are considered sacred in many parts of the world (Bernbaum, 1992; Einarsen, 1995). Caves are natural but anomalous features of the landscape, the interface of the underground (subterranean) and the aboveground (surface) worlds.

Monks are also something of an anomaly. They serve as intermediaries between the social and spiritual worlds. Also, they function in an anti-structural (challenging by contrast) role in relation to society, given their commitment to monasticism, selflessness, simplicity, poverty, equality, celibacy, and nonviolence.[4]

Bats are also something of an anomaly: the only true flying mammals, and of nocturnal habit. They are often thought to be blind, but are not; in fact, many species have small eyes, and these often appear to be hidden. Fruit-eating bats in the tropics have very good eyesight and sense of smell to locate ripe fruit and do not use echolocation. Furthermore, from a Thai cultural perspective, bats (*khang khao*) do not fit readily into the cultural classification of nonhuman animals (*tua*)—village/domesticated (*sad baan*) or forest/wild (*sad paa*), or other common categories like mammals (*sad kinnom*) (Tambiah, 1969). In particular, bats are neither a rodent (*nuu*) nor a bird (*nog*); they resemble a rodent, but they are equipped with wings and fly like a bird. There is also ambiguity as to whether bats are edible or inedible.

Anthropologists, such as Mary Douglas (1970), have observed that cultures recognize anomalies by affording them special symbolic and ritual status. (This has yet to be explored in the field in the case of bats in Thailand.) We hypothesize that the interdependencies among the system components of monks, caves, bats, and ecosystems are synergetic, the components being mutually reinforcing and enhancing. Furthermore, the anomalous status of monks, caves, and bats renders the complex far more powerful. This complex can be a formidable force for biodiversity and environmental conservation.

The monk-cave-bat-ecosystem complex is a previously unrecognized relationship of considerable significance, identified here for the first time (cf. McNeely and Sochaczewski, 1995). While this is an exercise in deductive reasoning, and the argument is logical, plausible, and probable, it needs to be explored systematically with field research in the future to be affirmed, explicated, and contextualized (e.g., Kunz, 1988). Nevertheless, this essay provides another example of the relevance and importance of Buddhism in spiritual ecology, sacred places, and environmental and biodiversity conservation in Thailand (Sponsel and Natadecha-Sponsel, 2001). It also has implications beyond Thailand in any area where

Buddhists use caves for religious purposes, rendering them sacred and thus protective of the fauna therein. This probably includes much of Asia.

Even though bats compose 38 percent of the mammalian species of Thailand, they are only one component of its ecosystems. A minority of bat species roost exclusively in caves, and the number of caves is limited. In any case, the monk-cave-bat-ecosystem complex assumes further importance when viewed in the wider context of the ancient and ubiquitous larger system of sacred places in the spiritual ecology of Thailand as a whole, which includes many other components, such as sacred trees, groves, forests, and mountains (Sponsel et al., 1998). This complex is further evidence of the existence of a great ancient system of nature conservation, reflecting the sacred geography of the country, something that is little recognized, let alone adequately appreciated and promoted (cf. Gesick, 1985).

Calling attention to this and its future potential for nature conservation is not necessarily a reversion to irrational superstition. There is, indeed, an eco-logic to sacred places in nature which, whether intentional or merely inadvertent, serves multiple positive sociocultural and ecological functions. In many respects, Thailand's greatest resource is its religion, and that in turn has the potential to protect natural resources and ecosystems as well as society and culture. One reason for resource depletion and environmental degradation in Thailand, in spite of a viable spiritual ecology, is the weakening of adherence to religious and cultural ideals in actual behavior as a result of wholeheartedly embracing Westernization (Sponsel and Natadecha-Sponsel, 1993:86–90).

Buddhism, nevertheless, is in principle one of the more environmentally benign religions—a fact that could be used to great advantage for nature conservation in countries like Thailand that are predominantly Buddhist, if initiatives are better promoted (Sponsel and Natadecha-Sponsel, 2002). But the study of spiritual ecology (including Buddhist ecology and environmentalism), and of the conservation relevance of sacred places in nature, has emerged mostly in the 1990s and is only now beginning to be recognized (Sponsel, 2001, 2003).

NOTES

1. Christopher Munier (1998) researched and published the most comprehensive study by far on sacred caves in Thailand, although he does not deal with the ecological aspects discussed here. We are greatly indebted to Munier's treatise for most information in this section unless otherwise indicated.

2. The oldest evidence for cave-dwelling is Zhoukoutien near Beijing, China, where the fossil skeletal remains of an early human, *Homo erectus*, were found and dated to about half a million years ago. Upper Paleolithic art in the caves at Altamira, Spain, and Lascaux, France, and other caves in southern Europe date back to about 35,000 years ago (Bonsall and Tolan-Smith, 1997; Fagan, 1998). In Thailand, the oldest human use of a rock shelter (not cave) is Lang Rongrian in the south, which dates around 37,000 years ago (Anderson, 1987).

Leslie E. Sponsel and Poranee Natadecha-Sponsel

3. For further information on bats, see Hill and Smith (1984), Kunz (1982, 1988), and the informative website of Bat Conservation International (http://www.batcon.org).

4. See Sponsel and Natadecha-Sponsel (1997) for further explication.

REFERENCES

Anderson, Douglas D., 1987. "A Pleistocene-Early Holocene Rock Shelter in Peninsular Thailand." *National Geographic Research* 3(2):184–198.

Barnes, Gina L., ed. 1995. "Buddhist Archaeology." *World Archaeology* 27(2):165–350.

Bat Conservation International. 2002. website at http://www.batcon.org.

Bernbaum, Edwin. 1992. *Sacred Mountains of the World*. San Francisco, CA: Sierra Club Books.

Bonsall, Clive, and Christopher Tolan-Smith, eds. 1997. *The Human Use of Caves*. Oxford: Archaeopress/British Archaeological Reports International Series 667.

Douglas, Mary. 1970. *Natural Symbols*. London: Barrie and Rockcliff.

Einarsen, John, ed. 1995. *The Sacred Mountains of Asia*. Boston, MA: Shambhala.

Fagan, Brian. 1998. *From Black Land to Fifth Sun: The Science of Sacred Sites*. Reading, MA: Perseus Books.

Fleming, Theodore H. 1988. *The Short-tailed Fruit Bat: A Study in Plant-Animal Interactions*. Chicago: University of Chicago Press.

Gesick, Lorraine. 1985. "Reading the Landscape: Reflections on a Sacred Site in South Thailand." *Journal of the Siam Society* 73:157–161.

Graham, Mark, and Philip Round. 1994. *Thailand's Vanishing Flora and Fauna*. Bangkok: Finance One.

Hill, John E., and James D. Smith. 1984. *Bats: A Natural History*. Austin: University of Texas Press.

Hirsch, Philip, ed. 1997. *Seeing the Forest for Trees: Environment and Environmentalism in Thailand*. Chiang Mai, Thailand: Silkworm Books.

Kunz, Thomas H., ed. 1982. *Ecology of Bats*. New York: Plenum Press.

Kunz, Thomas H., ed. 1988. *Ecology and Behavioral Methods for the Study of Bats*. Washington, D.C.: Smithsonian Institution Press.

Leakagul, Boonsong, and Jeffrey A. McNeely. 1988. *Mammals of Thailand*. Bangkok: Association for the Conservation of Wildlife.

McNeely, Jeffrey A., and Sunthad Somchevita, eds. 1996. *Biodiversity in Asia: Challenges and Opportunities for the Scientific Community*. Bangkok: Ministry of Sciences, Technology and Environment, Office of Environmental Policy and Planning.

McNeely, Jeffrey A., and Paul Spencer Sochaczewski. 1995. *Soul of the Tiger: Searching for Nature's Answers in Exotic Southeast Asia*. Honolulu: University of Hawaii Press.

Munier, Christopher. 1998. *Sacred Rocks and Buddhist Caves in Thailand*. Bangkok: White Lotus Press.

Pongsabutra, Paitoon. 1991. *Illustrated Landforms of Thailand*. Bangkok: Darnsutha Press.

Sponsel, Leslie E. 2001. "Do Anthropologists Need Religion, and Vice Versa? Adventures and Dangers in Spiritual Ecology." In *New Directions in Anthropology and Environment: Intersections*, Carole L. Crumley, ed., pp. 177–200. Walnut Creek, CA: AltaMira Press.

Sponsel, Leslie E. In preparation. *Sanctuaries of Culture and Nature: Sacred Places and Biodiversity Conservation*.

Sponsel, Leslie E., and Poranee Natadecha-Sponsel. 1992. "A Comparison of the Cultural Ecology of Adjacent Muslim and Buddhist Villages in Southern Thailand." *Journal of the National Research Council of Thailand* 23(2):31–42.

Sponsel, Leslie E., and Poranee Natadecha-Sponsel. 1993. "The Potential Contribution of Buddhism in Developing an Environmental Ethic for the Conservation of Biodiversity." In *Ethics, Religion and Biodiversity: Relations Between Conservation and Cultural Values,* Lawrence S. Hamilton, ed., pp. 75–97. Cambridge: White Horse Press.

Sponsel, Leslie E., and Poranee Natadecha-Sponsel. 1997. "A Theoretical Analysis of the Potential Contribution of the Monastic Community in Promoting a Green Society in Thailand." In *Buddhism and Ecology: The Interconnection of Dharma and Deeds,* Mary Evelyn Tucker and Duncan Ryuken Williams, eds., pp. 45–68. Cambridge: Harvard University Press/Center for the Study of World Religions.

Sponsel, Leslie E., and Poranee Natadecha-Sponsel. 2001. "Why a Tree is More than a Tree: Reflections on the Spiritual Ecology of Sacred Trees in Thailand." In *Santi Pracha Dhamma: Essays in Honour of the Late Puey Ungphakorn,* Sulak Sivaraksa, et al., eds., pp. 364–373. Bangkok: Santi Pracha Dhamma Institute, Santirakoses-Nagapradipa Foundation, and Foundation for Children.

Sponsel, Leslie E., and Poranee Natadecha-Sponsel. 2002. "Buddhist Views of Nature and Environment." In *Nature across Cultures,* Helaine Selin, ed. Boston, MA: Kluwer Academic Press (in press).

Sponsel, Leslie E., Poranee Natadecha-Sponsel, Nukul Ruttanadakul, and Somporn Juntadach. 1998. "Sacred and/or Secular Places to Biodiversity Conservation in Thailand." *Worldviews: Environment, Culture, Religion* 2(2):155–167.

Stewart-Cox, Belinda. 1995. *Wild Thailand.* Bangkok: Asia Books.

Tambiah, Stanley. 1969. "Animals Are Good to Think And Good to Prohibit." *Ethnology* 8(4):423–459.

Tiyavanich, Kamala. 1997. *Forest Recollections: Wandering Monks in Twentieth-Century Thailand.* Honolulu: University of Hawaii Press.

Whitfield, Roderick, Susan Whitfield, and Neville Agnew. 2000. *Cave Temples of Mogao: Art and History on the Silk Road.* Los Angeles: Getty Conservation Institute.

Williams, Paul W., ed. 1993. *Karst Terrains: Environmental Changes and Human Impact.* Cremlingen-Destedt, Germany: Catena Supplement 25.

"SATYAGRAHA FOR CONSERVATION: AWAKENING THE SPIRIT OF HINDUISM"

O. P. Dwivedi

The World Commission on Environment and Development acknowledged that to reconcile human affairs with natural laws "our cultural and spiritual heritages can reinforce our economic interests and survival imperatives."[1] But until very recently, the role of our cultural and spiritual heritages in environmental protection and sustainable development was ignored by international bodies, national governments, policy planners, and even environmentalists. Many fear that bringing religion into the environmental movement will threaten objectivity, scientific investigation, professionalism, or democratic values. But none of these need be displaced in order to include the spiritual dimension in environmental protection. That dimension, if introduced in the process of environmental policy planning, administration, education, and law, could help create a self-consciously moral society which would put conservation and respect for God's creation first, and relegate individualism, materialism, and our modern desire to dominate nature in a subordinate place. Thus my plea for a definite role of religion in conservation and environmental protection.

From the perspective of many world religions, the abuse and exploitation of nature for immediate gain is unjust, immoral, and unethical. For example, in the ancient past, Hindus and Buddhists were careful to observe moral teachings regarding the treatment of nature. In their cultures, not only the common person but also rulers and kings followed those ethical guidelines and tried to create an example for others. But now in the twentieth century, the materialistic orientation of the West has equally affected the cultures of the East. India, Sri Lanka, Thailand, and Japan have witnessed wanton exploitation of the environment by their own peoples, despite the strictures and injunctions inherent in their religions and cultures. Thus, no culture has remained immune from human irreverence towards nature. How can we change the attitude of human beings towards nature? Are religions the answer?

I believe that religion can evoke a kind of awareness in persons that is different from scientific or technological reasoning. Religion helps make human beings aware that there are limits to their control over the animate and inanimate world and that their arrogance and manipulative power over nature can backfire. Religion instils the recognition that human life cannot be measured by material possessions and that the ends of life go beyond conspicuous consumption.

As a matter of fact, religion can provide at least three fundamental mainstays to help human beings cope in a technological society. First, it defends the individual's existence against the depersonalizing effects of the technoindustrial process. Second, it forces the individual to recognize human fallibility and to combine realism with idealism. Third, while technology gives the individual the physical power to create or to destroy the world, religion gives the moral strength to grow in virtue by nurturing restraint, humility, and liberation from self-centeredness.[2] Directly and indirectly, religion can be a powerful source for environmental conservation and protection. Thus, we need a strategy for conservation that does not ignore the powerful influence of religions, but instead draws from all religious foundations and cultures.

World religions, each in their own way, offer a unique set of moral values and rules to guide human beings in their relationship with the environment. Religions also provide sanctions and offer stiffer penalties, such as fear of hell, for those who do not treat God's creation with respect. Although it is true that, in the recent past, religions have not been in the fore-front of protecting the environment from human greed and exploitation, many are now willing to take up the challenge and help protect and conserve the environment. But their offer of help will remain purely rhetorical unless secular institutions, national governments, and international organizations are willing to acknowledge the role of religion in environmental study and education. And I believe that environmental education will remain incomplete until it includes cultural values and religious imperatives. For this, we require an ecumenical approach. While there are metaphysical, ethical, anthropological and social disagreements among world religions, a synthesis of the key concepts and precepts from each of them pertaining to conservation could become a foundation for a global environmental ethic. The world needs such an ethic.

THE RELIGION AND ENVIRONMENT DEBATE

In 1967, the historian Lynn White, Jr., wrote an article in *Science* on the historical roots of the ecological crisis.[3] According to White, what people do to their environment depends upon how they see themselves in relation to nature. White asserted that the exploitative view that has generated much of the environmental crisis, particularly in Europe and North America, is a result of the teachings of late medieval Latin Christianity, which conceived of humankind as superior to the rest of God's creation and everything else as created for human use and enjoyment. He suggested that the only way to address the ecological crisis was to reject the view that nature has no reason to exist except to serve humanity. White's proposition impelled scientists, theologians, and environmentalists to debate the bases of his argument that religion could be blamed for the ecological crisis.

In the course of this debate, examples from other cultures were cited to support the view that, even in countries where there is religious respect for nature, exploitation of the environment has been ruthless. Countries where Hinduism, Buddhism, Taoism and Shintoism have been practised were cited to support the criticism of Thomas Derr, among others, that "We are simply being gullible when we take at face value the advertisement for the ecological harmony of nonwestern cultures." Derr goes on to say:

> Even if Christian doctrine had produced technological culture and its environmental troubles, one would be at a loss to understand the absence of the same result in equally Christian Eastern Europe. And conversely, if ecological disaster is a particularly Christian habit, how can one explain the disasters non-Christian cultures have visited upon their environments? Primitive cultures, Oriental cultures, classical cultures—all show examples of human dominance over nature which has led to ecological catastrophe. Overgrazing, deforestation and similar errors of sufficient magnitude to destroy civilizations have been committed by Egyptians, Assyrians, Romans, North Africans, Persians, Indians, Aztecs, and even Buddhists, who are foolishly supposed by some Western admirers to be immune from this sort of thing.[4]

This chapter challenges Derr's assertion with respect to the role of the Hindu religion in the ecological crisis. We need to understand how a Hindu's attitude to nature has been shaped by his religion's view of the cosmos and creation. Such an exposition is necessary to explain the traditional values and beliefs of Hindus and hence what role Hindu religion once played with respect to human treatment of the environment. At the same time, we need to know how it is that this religion, which taught harmony with and respect for nature, and which influenced other religions such as Jainism and Buddhism, has been in recent times unable to sustain a caring attitude towards nature. What are the features of the Hindu religion which strengthen human respect for God's creation, and how were these features repressed by the modern view of the natural environment and its resources?[5]

THE SANCTITY OF LIFE IN HINDUISM

The principle of the sanctity of life is clearly ingrained in the Hindu religion. Only God has absolute sovereignty over all creatures; thus, human beings have no dominion over their own lives or non-human life. Consequently, humanity cannot act as a viceroy of God over the planet, nor assign degrees of relative worth to other species. The idea of the Divine Being as the one underlying power of unity is beautifully expressed in the *Yajurveda*:

> The loving sage beholds that Being, hidden in mystery,
> wherein the universe comes to have one home;
> Therein unites and therefrom emanates the whole;

The Omnipresent One pervades souls and matter like warp and woof in created beings. (*Yajurveda* 32.8)[6]

The sacredness of God's creation means no damage may be inflicted on other species without adequate justification. Therefore, all lives, human and nonhuman, are of equal value and all have the same right to existence. According to the *Atharvaveda*, the Earth is not for human beings alone, but for other creatures as well:

> Born of Thee, on Thee move mortal creatures;
> Thou bearest them—the biped and the quadruped;
> Thine, O Earth, are the five races of men, for whom
> Surya (Sun), as he rises spreads with his rays
> the light that is immortal. (*Atharvaveda* 12.1–15)[7]

SRISHTI: GOD'S CREATION

Hindus contemplate divinity as the one in many and the many in one. This conceptualization resembles both monotheism and polytheism. Monotheism is the belief in a single divine Person. In monotheistic creeds that Person is God. Polytheism, on the other hand, believes in the many; and the concept of God is not monarchical. The Hindu concept of God resembles monotheism in that it portrays the divinity as one, and polytheism in that it contemplates the divinity as one in many. Although there are many gods, each one is the Supreme Being. This attitude we may call non-dualistic theism.

The earliest Sanskrit texts, the Veda and Upanishads, teach the non-dualism of the supreme power that existed before the creation. God as the efficient cause, and nature, *Prakriti*, as the material cause of the universe, are unconditionally accepted, as is their harmonious relationship. However, while these texts agree on the concept of non-dualistic theism, they differ in their theories regarding the creation of the universe. Why have different theories been elaborated in the Vedas and the Upanishads? This is one of the most important and intriguing questions we can ask. A suitable reply is given in the *Rigveda*:

> He is one, but the wise call him by different names; such as Indra, Mitra, Varuna, Agni, Divya—one who pervaded all the luminous bodies, the source of light; Suparna—the protector and preserver of the universe; whose works are perfect; Matriswa—powerful like wind; Garutman—mighty by nature. (*Rigveda* 1.164.46)[8]

The Hindu concept of creation can be presented in four categories. First is the Vedic theory, which is followed by further elaboration in Vedanta and Sankhya philosophies; the second is Upanishadic theory; the third is known as Puranic theory; and the fourth is enunciated in the great Hindu epics *Ramayana* and *Mahabharata*. Although the Puranic theory differs from the other three, a single thought flows between them. This unifying theory is well stated in the *Rigveda*:

> The Vedas and the universal laws of nature which control the universe and govern the cycles of creation and dissolution were made manifest by the All-knowing One. By His great power were produced the clouds and the vapors. After the production of the vapors, there intervened a period of darkness after which the Great Lord and Controller of the universe arranged the motions which produce days, nights, and other durations of time. The Great One then produced the sun, the moon, the earth, and all other regions as He did in previous cycles of creation. (*Rigveda* 10:190.1–3)

All the Hindu scriptures attest to the belief that the creation, maintenance, and annihilation of the cosmos is completely dependent on the Supreme will. In the *Gita*, Lord Krishna says to Arjuna: "Of all that is material and all that is spiritual in this world, know for certain that I am both its origin and dissolution." (*Gita* 7.6).[9] And the Lord says: again "The whole cosmic order is under me. By my will it is manifested again and again and by my will, it is annihilated at the end" (*Gita* 9.8). Thus, for ancient Hindus, both God and *Prakriti* (nature) was to be one and the same. While the *Prajapati* (as mentioned in Regveda) is the creator of sky, the earth, oceans, and all other species, he is also their protector and eventual destroyer. He is the only Lord of creation. Human beings have no special privilege or authority over other creatures; on the other hand, they have more obligations and duties.

DUTIES TO ANIMALS AND BIRDS

The most important aspect of Hindu theology pertaining to treatment of animal life is the belief that the Supreme Being was himself incarnated in the form of various species. The Lord says: "This form is the source and indestructible seed of multifarious incarnations within the universe, and from the particle and portion of this form, different living entities, like demi-gods, animals, human beings and others, are created" (*Srimad-Bhagavata* Book I, Discourse III: 5).[10] Among the various incarnations of God (numbering from ten to twenty-four depending upon the source of the text), He first incarnated Himself in the form of a fish, then a tortoise, a boar, and a dwarf. His fifth incarnation was as a manlion. As Rama he was closely associated with monkeys, and as Krishna he was always surrounded by the cows. Thus, other species are accorded reverence.

Further, the Hindu belief in the cycle of birth and rebirth where a person may come back as an animal or a bird gives these species not only respect, but also reverence. This provides a solid foundation for the doctrine of *ahimsa*—nonviolence against animals and human beings alike. Hindus have a deep faith in the doctrine of non-violence. Almost all the Hindu scriptures place strong emphasis on the notion that God's grace can be received by not killing his creatures or harming his creation: "God, Kesava, is pleased with a person who does not harm or destroy other non-speaking creatures or animals" (*Visnupurana* 3.8.15). To not eat meat in Hinduism is considered both an appropriate conduct and a duty. Yajnavalkya Smriti warns of hell-fire (*Ghora Naraka*) to those who are the killers of domesticated and protected animals: "The wicked person who kills animals which are protected has to live in hell-fire for the days equal to the number of hairs on the body of that animal" (*Yajnavalkyasmriti, Acaradhyayah*, v. 180). By the end of the Vedic and Upanishadic period, Buddhism and Jainism came into existence, and the protection of animals, birds and vegetation was further strengthened by the various kings practicing these religions. These religions, which arose in part as a protest against the orthodoxy and rituals of Hindu religion, continued its precepts for environmental protection. The Buddhist emperor, Ashoka (273–236 BCE), promoted through public proclamations the planting and preservation of flora and fauna. Pillar Edicts, erected at various public places, expressed his concerns about the welfare of creatures, plants and trees and prescribed various punishments for the killing of animals, including ants, squirrels, and rats.

FLORA IN HINDU RELIGION

As early as in the time of *Rigveda*, tree worship was quite popular and universal. The tree symbolized the various attributes of God to the Regvedic seers. Regveda regarded plants as having divine powers, with one entire hymn devoted to their praise, chiefly with reference to their healing properties. (Regveda 10.97) During the period of the great epics and Puranas, the Hindu respect for flora expanded further. Trees were considered as being animate and feeling happiness and sorrow. It is still popularly believed that every tree has a *Vriksa-devata*, or "tree deity," who is worshipped with prayers and offerings of water, flowers, sweets, and encircled by sacred threads. Also, for Hindus, the planting of a tree is still a religious duty. Fifteen hundred years ago, the *Matsya Purana* described the proper ceremony for tree planting:

> Clean the soil first and water it. Decorate trees with garlands, burn the guggula perfume in front of them, and place one pitcher filled with water by the side of each tree. Offer prayer and oblation and then sprinkle holy water on trees. Recite hymns from the Regveda, Yajur and Sama and kindle fire. After such worship the actual plantation should be celebrated. He who plants even one tree, goes directly to Heaven and obtains Moksha. (*Matsya Purana* 59.159)

The cutting of trees and destruction of flora were considered a sinful act. *Kautilya's Arthasastra* prescribed various punishments for destroying trees and plants:

> For cutting off the tender sprouts of fruit trees or shady trees in the parks near a city, a fine of six panas shall be imposed; for cutting of the minor branches of the same trees, twelve

panas, and for cutting off the big branches, twenty-four panas shall be levied. Cutting off the trunks of the same, shall be punished with the first amercement; and feeling shall be punished with the middlemost amercement. (*Kautilya's Arthasastra* III 19:197)[11]

The Hindu worship of trees and plants has been based partly on utility, but mostly on religious duty and mythology. Hindu ancestors considered it their duty to save trees; and in order to do that they attached to every tree a religious sanctity.

PRADUSHANA: POLLUTION AND ITS PREVENTION IN HINDU SCRIPTURES

Hindu scriptures revealed a clear conception of the ecosystem. On this basis a discipline of environmental ethics developed which formulated codes of conduct (*dharma*) and defined humanity's relationship to nature. An important part of that conduct is maintaining proper sanitation. In the past, this was considered to be the duty of everyone and any default was a punishable offence. Hindu society did not even consider it proper to throw dirt on a public path. Kautilya wrote:

> The punishment of one-eighth of a pana should be awarded to those who throw dirt on the roads. For muddy water one-fourth Pana, if both are thrown the punishment should be double. If latrine is thrown or caused near a temple, well, or pond, sacred place, or government building, then the punishment should increase gradually by one pana in each case. For urine the punishment should be only half. (*Kautilya's Arthasastra* II 36: 145)[12]

Hindus considered cremation of dead bodies and maintaining the sanitation of the human habitat as essential acts. When, in about 200 BCE, Caraka wrote about *Vikrti* (pollution) and diseases, he mentioned air pollution specifically as a cause of many diseases:

> The polluted air is mixed with bad elements. The air is uncharacteristic of the season, full of moisture, stormy, hard to breathe, icy cool, hot and dry, harmful, roaring, coming at the same time from all directions, badsmelling, oily, full of dirt, sand, steam, creating diseases in the body and is considered polluted. (*Caraka Samhita, Vimanastanam* III 6:1)[13]

Similarly, about water pollution, *Caraka Samhita* says:

> Water is considered polluted when it is excessively smelly, unnatural in color, taste and touch, slimy, not frequented by aquatic birds, aquatic life is reduced, and the appearance is unpleasing (*Caraka Samhita, Vimanastanam* III 6:2).[14]

Water is considered by Hindus as a powerful media of purification and also as a source of energy. Sometimes, just by the sprinkling of pure water in religious ceremonies, it is believed purity is achieved. That is why, in Regveda, prayer is offered to the deity of water: "The waters in the sky, the waters of rivers, and water in the well whose source is the ocean, may all these sacred waters protect me" (*Rigveda* 7.49.2). The healing property and medicinal value of water has been universally accepted, provided it is pure and free from all pollution. When polluted water and pure water were the point of discussion among ancient Indian thinkers, they were aware of the reasons for the polluted water. Therefore Manu advised: "One should not cause urine, stool, cough in the water. Anything which is mixed with these unpious objects, blood and poison, should not be thrown into water" (*Manusmriti* IV: 56).[15]

Still today, many rivers are considered sacred. Among these, the river Ganges is considered by Hindus as the most sacred and respectable. Disposal of human waste or other pollutants has been prohibited since time immemorial:

> One should not perform these 14 acts near the holy waters of the river Ganga: i.e., remove excrement, brushing and gargling, removing cerumen from body, throwing hairs, dry garlands, playing in water, taking donations, performing sex, attachment with other sacred places, praising other holy places, washing clothes, throwing dirty clothes, thumping water and swimming. (*Pravascitta Tatva* 1.535)

Persons doing such unsocial activities and engaging in acts polluting the environment were cursed: "A person, who is engaged in killing creatures, polluting wells, and ponds, and tanks and destroying gardens, certainly goes to hell" (*Padmapurana, Bhoomikhanda* 96: 7–8).

EFFECTIVENESS OF HINDUISM IN CONSERVATION

The effectiveness of any religion in protecting the environment depends upon how much faith its believers have in its precepts and injunctions. It also depends upon how those precepts are transmitted and adapted in everyday social interactions. In the case of the Hindu religion, which is practised as *dharma*—way of life—many of its precepts became ingrained in the daily life and social institutions of the people. Three specific examples are given below to illustrate this point.

THE CASTE SYSTEM AND SUSTAINABLE DEVELOPMENT

The Hindu religion is known for its elaborate caste system which divides individuals among four main castes and several hundred sub-castes. Over the centuries, the system degenerated into a very rigid, hereditarily determined, hierarchical, and oppressive social structure, particularly for the untouchables and lower castes. But the amazing phenomenon is that it lasted for so many millennia even with centuries of domination by Islamic and Christian cultures.

One explanation by the ecologist, Madhav Gadgil, and the anthropologist, Kailash Malhotra, is that the caste system, as continued until the early decades of the twentieth century, was actually based on an ancient concept of sustainable development which disciplined the society by partitioning the use of natural resources according to specific occupations (or castes); and "created" the right social milieu in which sustainable patterns of resource use were encouraged to "emerge."[16] The caste system regulated the occupations that individuals could undertake. Thus, an "ecological space" was created in ancient Hindu society which helped to reduce competition among various people for limited natural resources. A system of "resource partitioning" emerged whereby the primary users of natural resources did not worry about encroachment from other castes. At the same time, these users also knew that if they depleted the natural resources in their own space, they would not survive economically or physically because no one would allow them to move on to other occupations. Religious injunctions also created the psychological environment whereby each caste or sub-caste respected the occupational boundaries of the others. In a sense, the Hindu caste system can be seen as a progenitor of the concept of sustainable development.

But the system started malfunctioning during the British Raj when demands for raw materials for their fast-growing industrial economy had to be met by commercial exploitation of India's natural resources. As traditional relationships between various castes started disappearing, competition and tension grew. The trend kept on accelerating in independent India, as each caste (or sub-caste) tried to discard its traditional role and seize eagerly any opportunity to land a job. When this happened, the ancient religious injunction for doing one's prescribed duty within a caste system could no longer be maintained; this caused the disappearance of the concept of "ecological space" among Hindus. There is no doubt that the caste system also degenerated within and became a source of oppression; nevertheless, from an ecological spacing view point, the caste system played a key role in preserving India's natural riches for centuries.

BISHNOIS: DEFENDERS OF THE ENVIRONMENT

The Bishnois are a small community in Rajasthan, India, who practise a religion of environmental conservation. They believe that cutting a tree or killing an animal or bird is blasphemy. Their religion, an offshoot of Hinduism, was founded by Guru Maharaj Jambaji, who was born in 1451 CE in the Marwar area. When he was young he witnessed how, during a severe drought, people cut down trees to feed animals but when the drought continued, nothing was left to feed the animals, so they died. Jambaji thought that if trees are protected, animal life would be sustained, and his community would survive. He gave 29 injunctions and principal among them being a ban on the cutting of any green tree and killing of any animal or bird. About 300 years later, when the king of Jodhpur wanted to build a new palace, he sent his soldiers to the Bishnois area where trees were in abundance. Villagers protested, and when soldiers would not pay any attention to the protest, the Bishnois, led by a woman, hugged the trees to protect them with their bodies. As soldiers kept on killing villagers, more and more of the Bishnois came forward to honour the religious injunction of their Guru Maharaj Jambaji. The massacre continued until 363 persons were killed defending trees. When the king heard about this human sacrifice, he stopped the operation, and gave the Bishnois state protection for their belief.[17]

Today, the Bishnois community continues to protect trees and animals with the same fervour. Their community is the best example of a true Hindu-based ritual defence of the environment in India, and their sacrifices became the inspiration for the Chipko movement of 1973.

THE CHIPKO MOVEMENT

In March 1973, in the town of Gopeshwar in Chamoli district (Uttar Pradesh, India), villagers formed a human chain and hugged the earmarked trees to keep them from being felled for a nearby factory producing sports equipment. The same situation later occurred in another village when forest contractors wanted to cut trees under licence from the Government Department of Forests. Again, in 1974, women from the village of Reni, near Joshimath in the Himalayas, confronted the loggers by hugging trees and forced contractors to leave. Since then, the *Chipko Andolan* (the movement to hug trees) has grown as a grassroots ecodevelopment movement.[18]

The genesis of the Chipko movement is not only in the ecological or economic background, but in religious belief. Villagers have noted how industrial and commercial demands have denuded their forests, how they cannot sustain their livelihood in a deforested area, and how floods continually play havoc with their small agricultural communities. The religious basis of the movement is evident in the fact that it is inspired and guided by women. Women have not only seen how their men would not mind destroying nature in order to get money while they had to walk miles in search of firewood, fodder and other grazing materials, but, being more religious, they also are more sensitive to injunctions such as *ahimsa*. In a sense, the Chipko movement is a kind of feminist movement to protect nature from the greed of men. In the Himalayan areas, the pivot of the family is the woman. It is the woman who worries most about nature and its conservation in order that its resources are available for her family's sustenance. On the other hand, men go away to distant places in search of jobs, leaving women and old people behind. These women also believe that each tree has a *Vriksadevata* (tree god) and that the deity *Van Devi* (the Goddess of forests) will protect their family welfare. They also believe that each green tree is an abode of the Almighty God *Hari*.

The Chipko movement has caught the attention of others in India. For example, in Karnataka state, the Appiko movement began in September 1983, when 163 men, women, and children hugged the trees and forced the lumberjacks to leave. That movement swiftly spread to the adjoining districts. These people are against the kind of commercial felling of trees which clears the vegetation in its entirety. They do recognize the firewood needs of urban people (mostly poor) and therefore do not want a total ban on felling. However, they are against indiscriminate clearing and would like to see a consultative process established so that local people are able to participate in timber management.

These three examples are illustrative of the practical impact of Hinduism on conservation and sustainable development. While the effectiveness of the caste system to act as a resource partitioning system is no longer viable, the examples of Bishnois and Chipko/Appiko are illustrative of the fact that when appeal to secular norms fails, one can draw on the cultural and religious sources for "forest *satyagraha*." ("Satyagraha" means "insistence or persistence in search of truth." In this context, the term "forest satyagraha" means "persistence in search of truth pertaining to the rights of trees.")

LOSS OF RESPECT FOR NATURE

If such has been the tradition, philosophy, and ideology of Hindu religion, what then are the reasons behind the present state of environmental crisis? As we have seen, our ethical beliefs and religious values influence our behavior towards others, including our relationship with all creatures and plant life. If, for some reason, these noble values become displaced by other beliefs which are either thrust upon the society or transplanted from another culture through invasion, then the faith of the masses in the earlier cultural tradition is shaken. As the foreign culture, language and system of administration slowly takes root and penetrates all levels of society, and as appropriate answers and leadership are not forthcoming from the religious leaders and Brahmans, it is only natural for the masses to become more inward-looking and self-centered. Under such circumstances, religious values which acted as sanctions against environmental destruction do not retain a high priority because people have to worry about their very survival and freedom; hence, respect for nature gets displaced by economic factors.

That, it seems, is what happened in India during the 700 years of foreign cultural domination. The ancient educational system which taught respect for nature and reasons for its preservation was no longer available. On the other hand, the imported culture was unable to replace the ancient Hindu religion; consequently, a conflict continued between the two value systems. The situation became more complex when, in addition to the Muslim culture, the British introduced Christianity and Western secular institutions and values. While it is too easy to blame these external forces for the change in attitudes of Hindus towards nature, nevertheless it is a fact that they greatly inhibited the religion from continuing to transmit ancient values which encourage respect and due regard for God's creation.

The Hindu religion teaches a renunciation of worldly goods, and preaches against materialism and consumerism. Such teachings could act as a great source of strength for

Hindu societies in their struggle to achieve sustainable development. I detect in countries like India and Nepal a revival of respect for ancient cultural values. Such a revival need not turn into fundamentalism; instead it could be based on the lessons learned from environmental destruction in the West, and on the relevant precepts enshrined in the Hindu scriptures. That should not cause any damage to the secularism now practised in India. As a matter of fact, this could develop into a movement whereby spiritual guidance is made available to the secular system of governance and socioeconomic interaction.

HOPE FOR OUR COMMON FUTURE

Mahatma Gandhi warned that "nature had enough for everybody's need but not for everybody's greed." Gandhi was a great believer in drawing upon the rich variety of spiritual and cultural heritages of India. His *satyagraha* movements were the perfect example of how one could confront an unjust and uncaring though extremely superior power. Similarly, the Bishnois, Chipko, and Appiko people are engaged in a kind of "forest *satyagraha*" today. Their movements could easily be turned into a common front—"satyagraha for the environment"—to be used against the forces of big government and big business. This could include such other movements as *Mitti Bachao Abhiyan* (save the soil movement), *Van Mahotsava* (tree planting ceremony), *Chetna March* (public awareness march), *Kalpavriksha* (voluntary organization in Delhi for environmental conservation), and many others. The Hindu people are accustomed to suffering a great level of personal and physical hardships if such suffering is directed against unjust and uncaring forces. The minds of the Hindu people are slowly being awakened through the Chipko, Appiko, Bishnois, Chetna March, and other movements. *Satyagraha* for conservation could very well be a rallying point for the awakened spirit of Hinduism.

Hindu culture, in ancient and medieval times, provided a system of moral guidelines towards environmental preservation and conservation. Environmental ethics, as propounded by ancient Hindu scriptures and seers, was practised not only by common persons, but even by rulers and kings. They observed these fundamentals sometimes as religious duties, often as rules of administration or obligation for law and order, but either way these principles were properly knitted with the Hindu way of life. In Hindu culture, a human being is authorized to use natural resources, but has no divine power of control and dominion over nature and its elements. Hence, from the perspective of Hindu culture, abuse and exploitation of nature for selfish gain is unjust and sacrilegious. Against the continuation of such exploitation, the only viable strategy appears to be *satyagraha* for conservation.

NOTES

1.   World Commission on Environment and Development, *Our Common Future* (New York: Oxford University Press, 1987), 1.

2.   O.P. Dwivedi, "Man and Nature: A Holistic Approach to a Theory of Ecology," *The Environmental Professional* 10 (1987): 8–15.

3.   Lynn White, Jr., "The Historical Roots of Our Ecologic Crisis," *Science* 155 (March 1967): 1203–7.

4.   Thomas S. Derr, "Religion's Responsibility for the Ecological Crisis: An Argument Run Amok," *World View* 18 (1975): 43.

5.   These questions have been examined in detail in O.P. Dwivedi and B.N. Tiwari, *Environmental Crisis and Hindu Religion* (New Delhi: Gitanjali Publishing, 1987).

6.   *The Yajurveda*, trans. Devi Chand, (New Delhi: Munsiram Manoharlal Publishers, 1982).

7.   *The Atharvaveda*, trans. Devi Chand, (New Delhi: Munsiram Manoharlal Publishers, 1982).

8.   *Rigveda*, comp. Mahrishi Dayanand Saraswati, (New Delhi: Sarvadeshik Arya Pratinidhi Sabha, 1974), 12 vols.

9.   *The Bhagavad Gita*, commentator Swami Chidbhavananda, (Tirruchirapalli: Sri Ramakrishna Tapovanam, 1974).

10.   *Srimad Bhagavata Mahapurana*, trans. C. L. Goswami and M. A. Sastri, (Gorakhpur: Gita Press, 1982), 2 vols.

11.   R. Shamasastry, ed., *Kautilya's Arthasastra* (Mysore: Mysore Publishers, 1967), 224.

12.   Ibid., 166.

13.   *Caraka-Samhita*, trans. Priyavrat Sharma, (Varanasi: Chaukhambha Orientalia, 1983) I, 315.

14.   Ibid.

15.   *Manusmriti (The Laws of Manu)*, trans. G. Buhler, (Delhi: Motilal Banarsidass, 1975), 137.

16.   Centre for Science and Environment, *The State of India's Environment 1984–85, the Second Citizens' Report* (New Delhi: CSE, 1985), 162.

17.   Ibid., 164.

18.   Chandi Prasad Bhatt, "The Chipko Andolan: Forest Conservation Based on People's Power" in eds. Anil Agrawal, Darryl D'Monte, and Ujwala Samarth, *The Fight for Survival*, (New Delhi: Centre for Science and Environment, 1987), 51.

"ISLAMIC ENVIRONMENTAL ETHICS, LAW, AND SOCIETY"

Mawil Y. Izzi Deen (Samarrai)

Islamic environmental ethics, like all other forms of ethics in Islam, is based on clear-cut legal foundations which Muslims hold to be formulated by God. Thus, in Islam, an acceptance of what is legal and what is ethical has not involved the same processes as in cultures which base their laws on humanistic philosophies.

Muslim scholars have found it difficult to accept the term "Islamic Law," since "law" implies a rigidity and dryness alien to Islam. They prefer the Arabic word *Sharī'ah* (Shariah) which literally means the "source of water." The Shariah is the source of life in that it contains both legal rules and ethical principles. This is indicated by the division of the Shariah relevant to human action into the categories of: obligatory actions (*wājib*)— those which a Muslim is required to perform; devotional and ethical virtues (*mandūb*)— those actions a Muslim is encouraged to perform, the non-observance of which, however, incurs no liability; permissible actions (*mubāh*)—those in which a Muslim is given complete freedom of choice; abominable actions (*makrūh*)—those which are morally but not legally wrong; and prohibited actions (*haram*)—all those practices forbidden by Islam.

A complete separation into the two elements, law and ethics, is thus unnecessary in Islam. For a Muslim is obliged to obey whatever God has ordered, his philosophical questions having been answered before he became a follower of the faith.

THE FOUNDATION OF ENVIRONMENTAL PROTECTION

In Islam, the conservation of the environment is based on the principle that all the individual components of the environment were created by God, and that all living things were created with different functions, functions carefully measured and meticulously balanced by the Almighty Creator. Although the various components of the natural environment serve humanity as one of their functions, this does not imply that human use is the sole reason for their creation. The comments of the medieval Muslim scholar, Ibn Taymīyah, on those verses of the Holy Qur'ān which state that God created the various parts of the environment to serve humanity, are relevant here:

From *Ethics of Environment and Development*, edited by J. Ronald Engel and Joan Gibb Engel. Copyright 1990. Reprinted by permission of John Wiley & Sons, Ltd.

In considering all these verses it must be remembered that Allah in His wisdom created these creatures for reasons other than serving man, for in these verses He only explains the benefits of these creatures [to man].[1]

The legal and ethical reasons for protecting the environment can be summarized as follows:[2] First, the environment is God's creation and to protect it is to preserve its values as a sign of the Creator. To assume that the environment's benefits to human beings are the sole reason for its protection may lead to environmental misuse or destruction.

Second, the component parts of nature are entities in continuous praise of their Creator. Humans may not be able to understand the form or nature of this praise, but the fact that the Qur'ān describes it is an additional reason for environmental preservation:

> The seven heavens and the earth and all that is therein praise Him, and there is not such a thing but hymneth his praise; but ye understand not their praise. Lo! He is ever Clement, Forgiving (Sūrah 17:44).[3]

Third, all the laws of nature are laws made by the Creator and based on the concept of the absolute continuity of existence. Although God may sometimes wish otherwise, what happens, happens according to the natural law of God (*sunnah*), and human beings must accept this as the will of the Creator. Attempts to break the law of God must be prevented. As the Qur'ān states:

> Hast thou not seen that unto Allah payeth adoration whosoever is in the heavens and whosoever is in the earth, and the sun, and the moon, and the stars, and the hills, and the trees, and the beasts, and many of mankind (Sūrah 22: 18).

Fourth, the Qur'ān's acknowledgment that humankind is not the only community to live in this world—"There is not an animal in the earth, nor a flying creature flying on two wings, but they are peoples like unto you" (Sūrah 6: 38)—means that while humans may currently have the upper hand over other "peoples," these other creatures are beings and, like us, are worthy of respect and protection. The Prophet Muhammad (peace be upon him) considered all living creatures worthy of protection (*hurmah*) and kind treatment. He was once asked whether there will be a reward from God for charity shown to animals. His reply was very explicit: "For [charity shown to] each creature which has a wet heart there is a reward."[4] Ibn Hajar comments further upon this tradition, explaining that wetness is an indication of life (and so charity extends to all creatures), although human beings are more worthy of the charity if a choice must be made.[5]

Fifth, Islamic environmental ethics is based on the concept that all human relationships are established on justice (*'adl*) and equity (*ihsān*): "Lo! Allah enjoineth justice and kindness" (Sūrah 16: 90). The prophetic tradition limits benefits derived at the cost of animal suffering. The Prophet Muhammad instructed: "Verily Allah has prescribed equity (*ihsān*) in all things. Thus if you kill, kill well, and if you slaughter, slaughter well. Let each of you sharpen his blade and let him spare suffering to the animal he slaughters."

Sixth, the balance of the universe created by God must also be preserved. For "Everything with Him is measured" (Sūrah 13: 8). Also, "There is not a thing but with Us are the stores thereof. And We send it not down save in appointed measure" (Sūrah 15: 21).

Seventh, the environment is not in the service of the present generation alone. Rather, it is the gift of God to all ages, past, present and future. This can be understood from the general meaning of Sūrah 2:29: "He it is Who created for you all that is in the earth." The word "you" as used here refers to all persons with no limit as to time or place.

Finally, no other creature is able to perform the task of protecting the environment. God entrusted humans with the duty of viceregency, a duty so onerous and burdensome that no other creature would accept it: "Lo! We offered the trust unto the heavens and the earth and the hills, but they shrank from bearing it and were afraid of it. And man assumed it" (Sūrah 33: 72).

THE COMPREHENSIVE NATURE OF ISLAMIC ETHICS

Islamic ethics is founded on two principles—human nature, and religious and legal grounds. The first principle, natural instinct (*fitrah*), was imprinted in the human soul by God at the time of creation (Sūrah 91: 7–8). Having natural instinct, the ordinary individual can, at least to some extent, distinguish not only between good and bad, but also between these and that which is neutral, neither good nor bad.[6] However, an ethical conscience is not a sufficient personal guide. Due to the complexities of life an ethical conscience alone cannot define the correct attitude to every problem. Moreover, a person does not live in a vacuum, but is affected by outside influences which may corrupt the ability to choose between good and evil. Outside influences include customs, personal interests, and prevailing concepts concerning one's surroundings.[7]

The religious and legal grounds upon which Islamic ethics is founded were presented by the messengers of God. These messengers were possessed of a special nature, and since they were inspired by God, they were able to avoid the outside influences which may affect other individuals.

Legal instructions in Islam are not negative in the sense of forcing the conscience to obey. On the contrary, legal instructions have been revealed in such a way that the conscience approves and acknowledges them to be correct. Thus the law itself becomes a part of human conscience, thereby guaranteeing its application and its success.

An imported, alien law cannot work because, while it may be possible to make it legally binding, it cannot be made morally binding upon Muslims. Muslims willingly pay the poor-tax (*zakāh*) because they know that if they fail to do so they will be both legally and ethically responsible. Managing to avoid the legal consequences of failure to pay what is due will not help them to avoid the ethical consequences, and they are aware of this. Although a Muslim poacher may be able to shoot elephants and avoid park game wardens, if a framework based on Islamic principles for the protection of the environment has been published, he knows that he will not be able to avoid the ever-watchful divine Warden. The Muslim knows that Islamic values are all based on what God loves and wants: "And when he turns away [from thee] his effort in the land is to make mischief therein and to destroy the crops and the cattle; and Allah loveth not mischief" (Sūrah 2: 205).

When the Prophet Solomon and his army were about to destroy a nest of ants, one ant warned the rest of the colony of the coming destruction. When Solomon heard this he begged God for the wisdom to do the good thing which God wanted him to do. Solomon was obviously facing an environmental problem and needed an ethical decision; he begged God for guidance:

> Till, when they reached the Valley of the Ants, an ant exclaimed: O, ants! Enter your dwellings lest Solomon and his armies crush you, unperceiving.
>
> And [Solomon] smiled, laughing at her speech, and said: "My Lord, arouse me to be thankful for Thy favor wherewith Thou hast favored me and my parents, and to do good that shall be pleasing unto Thee, and include me among [the number of] Thy righteous slaves" (Sūrah 27: 18–19).

Ethics in Islam is not based on a variety of separate scattered virtues, with each virtue, such as honesty or truth, standing isolated from others. Rather virtue in Islam is a part of a total, comprehensive way of life which serves to guide and control all human activity.[8] Truthfulness is an ethical value, as are protecting life, conserving the environment, and sustaining its development within the confines of what God has ordered. When ʿĀisha, the wife of the Prophet Muhammad, was asked about his ethics she replied: "His ethics are the whole Qur'ān." The Qur'ān does not contain separate scattered ethical values. Rather it contains the instructions for a complete way of life. There are political, social and economic principles side by side with instructions for the construction and preservation of the earth.

Islamic ethical values are based not on human reasoning, as Aristotle claimed values to be, nor on what society imposes on the individual, as Durkheim thought, nor on the interests of a certain class, as Marxists maintain. In each of these claims values are affected by circumstances. In Islam, ethical values are held to be based on an accurate scale which is unalterable as to time and place.[9] Islam's values are those without which neither persons nor the natural environment can be sustained.

THE HUMAN-ENVIRONMENT RELATIONSHIP

As we have seen, within the Islamic faith, an individual's relationship with the environment is governed by certain moral precepts. These originate with God's creation of humans and the role they were given upon the Earth. Our universe, with all its diverse component elements was created by God and the human being is an essential part of His Measured and Balanced Creation. The role of humans, however, is not only to enjoy, use and benefit from their surroundings. They are expected to preserve, protect and promote their fellow creatures. The Prophet Muhammad (peace be upon him) said: "All creatures are God's dependents and the best among them is the one who is most useful to God's dependents."[10] The Prophet of Islam looked upon himself as responsible for the trees and the animals and all natural elements. He also said: "The only reasons that God does not cause his punishment to pour over you are the elderly, the suckling babes, and the animals which graze upon your land."[11] Muhammad prayed for rain when he was reminded that water was short, the trees suffering from drought, and animals dying. He begged for God's mercy to fall upon his creatures.[12]

The relationship between human beings and their environment includes many features in addition to subjugation and utilization. Construction and development are primary but our relationship to nature also includes meditation, contemplation and enjoyment of its beauties. The most perfect Muslim was the Prophet Muhammad, who was reported by Ibn 'Abbās to have enjoyed gazing at greenery and running water.[13]

When reading verses about the Earth in the Holy Qur'ān, we find strong indications that the Earth was originally a place of peace and rest for humans:

> Is not He [best] Who made the earth a fixed abode, and placed rivers in the folds thereof, and placed firm hills therein, and hath set a barrier between the two seas? Is there any God beside Allah? Nay, but most of them know not! (Sūrah 27: 61)

The Earth is important to the concept of interrelation. Human beings are made from two components of the Earth—dust and water.

> And Allah hath caused you to grow as a growth from the earth, And afterward He maketh you return thereto, and He will bring you forth again, a [new] forthcoming. And Allah hath made the earth a wide expanse for you That ye may thread the valleyways thereof. (Sūrah 71: 17–20)

The word "earth" (ard) is mentioned twice in this short quotation and in the Qur'ān the word occurs a total of 485 times, a simple measure of its importance.

The Earth is described as being subservient to humans: "He it is Who hath made the earth subservient unto you, so walk in the paths thereof and eat of His providence" (Sūrah 67: 15). The Earth is also described as a receptacle: "Have we not made the earth a receptacle both for the living and the dead" (Sūrah 77: 25–26).[14] Even more importantly, the Earth is considered by Islam to be a source of purity and a place for the worship of God. The Prophet Muhammad said: "The earth is made for me [and Muslims] as a prayer place (masjid) and as a purifier." This means that the Earth is to be used to cleanse oneself before prayer if water is unobtainable.[15] Ibn 'Umar reported that the Prophet of Islam said: "God is beautiful and loved everything beautiful. He is generous and loves generosity and is clean and loves cleanliness."[16]

Mawil Y. Izzi Deen (Samarrai)

Thus it is not surprising that the Islamic position with regard to the environment is that humans must intervene in order to protect the Earth. They may not stand back while it is destroyed. "He brought you forth from the earth and hath made you husband it" (Sūrah 11: 61). For, finally, the Earth is a source of blessedness. And the Prophet Muhammad said: "Some trees are as blessed as the Muslim himself, especially palm."[17]

THE SUSTAINABLE CARE OF NATURE

Islam permits the utilization of the natural environment but this utilization should not involve unnecessary destruction. Squandering is rejected by God: "O Children of Adam! Look to your adornment at every place of worship, and eat and drink, but be not prodigal. Lo! He loveth not the prodigals" (Sūrah 7: 31). In this Qur'ānic passage, eating and drinking refer to the utilization of the sources of life. Such utilization is not without controls. The component elements of life have to be protected so that their utilization may continue in a sustainable way. Yet even this preservation must be undertaken in an altruistic fashion, and not merely for its benefit to human beings. The Prophet Muhammad said: "Act in your life as though you are living forever and act for the Hereafter as if you are dying tomorrow."[18]

These actions must not be restricted to those which will derive direct benefits. Even if doomsday were expected imminently, humans would be expected to continue their good behavior, for Muhammad said: "When doomsday comes if someone has a palm shoot in his hand he should plant it."[19] This *hadīth* encapsulates the principles of Islamic environmental ethics. Even when all hope is lost, planting should continue for planting is good in itself. The planting of the palm shoot continues the process of development and will sustain life even if one does not anticipate any benefit from it. In this, the Muslim is like the soldier who fights to the last bullet.

A theory of the sustainable utilization of the ecosystem may be deduced from Islam's assertion that life is maintained with due balance in everything: "Allah knoweth that which every female beareth and that which the wombs absorb and that which they grow. And everything with Him is measured" (Sūrah 13: 8). Also: "He unto Whom belongeth the sovereignty of the heavens and the earth, He hath chosen no son nor hath He any partner in the sovereignty. He hath created everything and hath meted out for it a measure" (Sūrah 25: 2).

Humans are not the owners, but the maintainers of the due balance and measure which God provided for them and for the animals that live with them.

> And after that He spread the earth,
> And produced therefrom water thereof and the pasture thereof,
> And He made fast the hills,
> A provision for you and for your cattle. (Sūrah 79: 30–33)

The Qur'ān goes on to say:

> But when the great disaster cometh,
> The day when man will call to mind his [whole] endeavor. (Sūrah 79: 34–35)

Humans will have a different home (*ma'wā*) or place of abode, different from the Earth and what it contains. The word *ma'wā* is the same word used in modern Arabic for "environment." One cannot help but wonder if these verses are an elaboration on the concept of sustainable development, a task that humans will undertake until their home is changed.

Sayyid Qutb, commenting on these verses, observes that the Qur'ān, in referring to the origin of ultimate truth, used many correspondences (*muwāfaqāt*)—such as building the heavens, darkening the night, bringing forth human beings, spreading the earth, producing water and plants, and making the mountains fast. All these were provided for human beings and their animals as providence, and are direct signs which constitute proof as to the reality of God's measurement and calculation. Finally, Sayyid Qutb observes that every part of God's creation was carefully made to fit into the general system, a system that testifies to the Creator's existence and the existence of a day of reward and punishment.

At this point, one must ask whether it is not a person's duty to preserve the proof of the Creator's existence while developing it. Wouldn't the wholesale destruction of the environment be the destruction of much which testifies to the greatness of God?

The concept of the sustained care of all aspects of the environment also fits into Islam's concept of charity, for charity is not only for the present generation but also for those in the future. A story is told of 'Umar ibn al-Khaṭṭāb, the famous companion of the Prophet. He once saw that an old man, Khuzaymah ibn Thābit, had neglected his land. 'Umar asked what was preventing him from cultivating it. Khuzaymah explained that he was old and could be expected to die soon. Whereupon, Umar insisted that he should plant it. Khuzaymah's son, who narrated the story, added that his father and 'Umar planted the uncultivated land together.[20]

This incident demonstrates how strongly Islam encourages the sustained cultivation of the land. Land should not be used and then abandoned just because the cultivator expects no personal benefit.

In Islam, law and ethics constitute the two interconnected elements of a unified world view. When considering the environment and its protection, this Islamic attitude may constitute a useful foundation for the formulation of a strategy throughout, at least, the Muslim world. Muslims who inhabit so much of the developing world may vary in local habits and customs but they are remarkably united in faith and in their attitude to life.

Islam is a religion of submission to God, master of all worlds. The Earth and all its inhabitants were created and are dominated by God. All Muslims begin their prayers five times a day with the same words from the Holy Qur'ān: "Praise be to Allah, Lord of the Worlds" (Sūrah 1:1). These opening words of the Qur'ān have become not only the most repeated but also the most loved and respected words for Muslims everywhere. Ibn Kathīr, like many other Qur'ānic commentators, considers that the word "worlds" ('ālamī'n) means the different kinds of creatures that inhabit the sky, the land, and the sea. Muslims submit themselves to the Creator who made them and who made all other worlds. The same author mentions that Muslims also submit themselves to the signs of the existence of the Creator and His unity. This secondary meaning exists because "worlds" comes from the same root as signs; thus the worlds are signs of the Creator.[21]

A Muslim, therefore, has a very special relationship with those worlds which in modern times have come to be known as the environment. Indeed, that these worlds exist and that they were made by the same Creator means that they are united and interdependent, each a part of the perfect system of creation. No conflict should exist between them; they should exist in harmony as different parts of the whole. Their coexistence could be likened to an architectural masterpiece in which every detail has been added to complete and complement the structure. Thus the details of creation serve to testify to the wisdom and perfection of the Creator.

THE PRACTICE OF ISLAMIC ENVIRONMENTAL ETHICS

Islam has always had a great influence on the formation of individual Muslim communities and the policy making of Muslim states. Environmental policy has been influenced by Islam and this influence has remained the same throughout the history of the Islamic faith.

The concept of *himā* (protection of certain zones) has existed since the time of the Prophet Muhammad. *Himā* involved the ruler or government's protection of specific unused areas. No one may build on them or develop them in any way. The Mālikī school of Islamic law described the requirements of *himā* to be the following.[22] First, the need of the Muslim public for the maintenance of land in an unused state. Protection is not granted to satisfy an influential individual unless there is a public need. Second, the protected area should be limited in order to avoid inconvenience to the public. Third, the protected area should not be built on or cultivated. And fourth, the aim of protection (Zuhaylī 5:574) is the welfare of the people, for example, the protected area may be used for some restricted grazing by the animals of the poor.

The concept of *himā* can still be seen in many Muslim countries, such as Saudi Arabia, where it is practised by the government to protect wildlife. In a less formal way it is still practised by some bedouin tribes as a custom or tradition inherited from their ancestors.

The *harī'm* is another ancient institution which can be traced back to the time of the Prophet Muhammad. It is an inviolable zone which may not be used or developed, save with the specific permission of the state. The *harī'm* is usually found in association with wells, natural springs, underground water channels, rivers and trees planted on barren land or *mawāt*.[23] There is careful administration of the *harī'm* zones based on the practice of the Prophet Muhammad and the precedent of his companions as recorded in the sources of Islamic law.

At present the role of Islam in environmental protection can be seen in the formation of different Islamic organizations and the emphasis given to Islam as a motive for the protection of the environment.

Saudi Arabia has keenly sought to implement a number of projects aimed at the protection of various aspects of the environment, for example, the late King Khalid's patronage of efforts to save the Arabian oryx from extinction.

The Meteorology and Environmental Protection Administration (MEPA) of Saudi Arabia actively promotes the principles of Islamic environmental protection. In 1983 MEPA and the International Union for the Conservation of Nature and Natural Resources commissioned a basic paper on the Islamic principles for the conservation of natural environment.[24]

The Islamic faith has great impact on environmental issues throughout the Arab and Muslim world. The first Arab Ministerial Conference took as its theme "The Environmental Aspects of Development" and one of the topics considered was the Islamic faith and its values.[25] The Amir of Kuwait emphasized the fundamental importance of Islam when he addressed the General Assembly of the United Nations in 1988. He explained that Islam was the basis for justice, mercy, and cooperation between all humankind; and he called for an increase in scientific and technological assistance from the North to help conserve natural and human resources, combat pollution and support sustainable development projects.

Finally, it is imperative to acknowledge that the new morality required to conserve the environment which the World Conservation Strategy (Section 13.1) emphasizes, needs to be based on a more solid foundation. It is not only necessary to involve the public in conservation policy but also to improve its morals and alter its attitudes. In Muslim countries such changes should be brought about by identifying environmental policies with Islamic teachings. To do this, the public education system will have to supplement the scientific approach to environmental education with serious attention to Islamic belief and environmental awareness.

NOTES

1. Ahmad Ibn Taymīyah, *Majamū' Fatawā* (Rabat: Saudi Educational Attaché, n.d.), 11:96–97.

2. Mawil Y. Izzi Deen (Samarrai), "Environmental Protection and Islam," *Journal of the Faculty of Arts and Humanities, King Abdulaziz University* 5 (1985).

3. All references to the Holy Qur'ān are from *The Meaning of the Glorious Koran*, trans. Mohammed M. Pickthall, (New York: Mentor, n.d.).

4. Ibn Hajar al-'Asqalānī, *Fath al-Bārī' bi-Sharh Sahīh al-Bukhāri*, edited by M. F. 'Abd al-Bāqī, M. al-Khātib, and A. B. Bāz 1959; 1970 (Beirut: Dār al-Ma'rifah, 195; 197), 5:40.

5. Ibid., 5:42.

6. Muhammad 'Abd Allah Draz, *La Morale du Koran*, trans. into Arabic by A. Shahin and S. M. Badāwī (Kuwait: Dār al-Risālah, 1973), 28.

7. Ibid.

8. Sayyid, Qutb, *Muqāwamāt al-Tasawwur al-Islāmī* (Cairo: Dār al-Shurūq, 1985), 289.

9. Ibid., 290.

10. Ismā'il Ibn Muhammad al-'Ajlūnī, *Kashf al-Khafā' wa Muzīl al-Ilbās*, edited by A. al-Qallash (Syria Damascus: Mu'assasat al-Risālah, 1983), 1:458.

11. Ibid., 1:213.

12. Ibn Hajar, *Fath al Bārī*, 2:512.

13. 'Ajlūnī, *Kashf al-Khafā'*, 1:387.

14. N.J. Dawood, trans. *The Koran* (New York: Penguin, 1974): 54.

15. Muhammad Ibn Ismā'il al-Bukhāri, *Sahīh al-Bukhāri*, (Istanbul: Dār al-Tiba'ah al-Amīrah, 1897), 1:86.

16. 'Ajlūnī, *Kashf al-Khafā'*, 1:260.

17. Bukhāri, *Sahīh al-Bukhāri*, 1:22, 6:211.

18. Ahmad Ibn al-Husayn al-Bayhāqī, *Sunan al-Bayhaqī al-Kubrā* (Hyderabad, India: n.d.), 3:19.

19. Ibid., 3:184.

20. Soūti, *al-Jāmi' al-Kabīr*, manuscript (Cairo: Egyptian General Committee for Publication, n.d.).

21. M. A. al-Sabunī, *Mukhtasar Tafsīr Ibn Kathīr* (Beirut: Dār al-Qur'ān al-Karīm, 1981), 1:21.

22. Wahbah Mustafa Zuhayli, *al-Fiqh al-Islāmī wa 'Adilatuhu* (Damascus: Mu'assasat al-Risālah, 1985).

23. Ibid., 5:574.

24. A.H. Bakader, A. T. al-Sabbagh, M.A. al-Gelinid, and M.Y. Izzi Deen (Samarrai), *Islamic Principles for the Conservation of the Natural Environment* (Gland, Switzerland: International Union for the Conservation of Nature and MEPA, 1983).

25. *Habitat and the Environment* (Tunis: Economic Affairs Department of the Directorate of the Arab League, 1986).

"CENTRAL AFRICAN VOICES ON THE HUMAN-ENVIRONMENT RELATIONSHIP"

Richard B. Peterson

From a Central African perspective, human beings and nature are related in a 'both/and' dialectical manner rather than in a manner characterized by an 'either/or dualism'. Such dialectical perspectives also characterize Central African social thought, particularly in regard to the relationship between the individual and society. (Throughout this article I use the term 'dialectical' not in its formal Hegelian sense but in a more informal sense of connoting 'both/and' rather than 'either/or' thinking. 'Both/and' thinking consists of delving into the creative tension inherent in synthesizing what are seemingly opposite characteristics, propositions or processes.) These two sets of relations are themselves inextricably linked: that is, the relationship between the individual and the community holds very real implications for the human/environment relationship, and for the environment itself. This article addresses both of these key relational dilemmas. I illustrate how Central African thought can help to correct prevalent perspectives in the West regarding the relationship between the individual and the community, and that between humans and the environment.

'BOTH/AND' RELATIONS BETWEEN THE INDIVIDUAL AND THE COMMUNITY

In his recent history of the Central African forest region, Jan Vansina (1990) reveals how the human communities that inhabited the rainforests of Equatorial Africa were geniuses at maintaining a balance between their needs for autonomy and for security. Although some groups did tend toward centralization and experienced rapid growth, many more creatively intertwined both decentralization and co-operation. Historically, myriad groups were involved in a repeated dynamic of decentralizing in order to maintain their autonomy and sense of group identity, while simultaneously working to promote good relations with outsiders in order to reap the benefits of security and co-operation in the face of large-scale threats.

From *Cultural and Spiritual Values of Biodiversity*, United Nations Environment Programme (2000). Reprinted by permission of United Nations Environment Programme.

The same balancing act played out between one community and another continues to be played out, to varying degrees, within the community between the individual and the group. Any African environmental ethic rests on the same base that supports all African traditions—that of communalism. The African community is not composed of a group of individuals 'clinging together to eke out an existence' (Omo-Fadaka 1990: 178). Nor is it, as one African writer described community in the West, ' . . . a conglomeration of individuals who are so self-centred and isolated that there is a kind of suspicion of the other, simply because there isn't enough knowledge of the other to remove that suspicion' (Malidoma Somé, quoted in van Gelder 1993: 33). Rather, in Africa the community is imbued with a certain bondedness. Bondedness entails respect, which in turn entails taking responsibility for one's fellow human being, not as an atomized individual but as a member of the common fabric of life. Since life's fabric is of one piece, connections within the fabric have to be maintained. If there is social or personal disharmony or illness, something has become disconnected and needs restoration. Therefore, for the good of the whole, the responsibility to restore this broken connection falls on everyone. In such a manner African communalism provides a strong source for individual morality (Onyewuenyi 1991).

Yet, although African communalism may have much to contribute to social ethics, its influence does not necessarily mean that the individual is smothered or ignored as some Western writers have been wont to believe. Again, as in the situation with autonomy and co-operation, individualism and communalism do not exist in a dualistic and oppositional relation but in a dialectic whereby each reinforces the other (Gyekye 1987).

Pre-Westernized systems of land tenure in Central African forest environments illustrate well certain aspects of an African both/and way of thinking with regard to individuals, communities and land. Unlike our Western emphasis on individual ownership and on seeing land as a commodity, under Central African tenure systems, the goals, aspirations and property of the individual and those of the community exist hand in hand within a total system in which the two ideals are held in some degree of balance. Land is neither private property nor is it communally owned and worked in the socialist sense. Rather, land in most cases is held in communal trust; it belongs to the group, to all members of the community, extending usually at least to the level of the clan. However, within that common property ownership, each individual at the same time has their own piece of land that truly 'belongs' to them, and for which they and they alone (including family and extended family) are responsible, and to which they and they alone have usufruct.

This dialectical manner with which Central African societies treat both communal and individual drives regarding land allows the two to play themselves out in tandem. Under such methods, the community does not forgo the benefits of individual responsibility, effort and motivation that come through individual 'ownership' (but an ownership very different from our Western sense of private property). At the same time, the community keeps individualism from getting out of hand by preserving a communal sense and communal systems whereby the land belongs to everyone. With individual usufruct comes communal responsibilities and various social levelling mechanisms that keep individuals mindful of their obligations to others.

Other examples of this dialectic can be found in Central African systems of labour. Common among many societies are various communal institutions created to allow for a group sense of co-operation, helping each other out, and making sure the whole village survives. One particularly important organization of such type is what is known in Lingala and Swahili as *likilemba*—shared communal labour groups whose labour rotates from one individual's project (in this case usually garden cutting) to another's. With most *likilemba* no payment is involved; only the obligation to feed the group of workers. It is unlikely that a *likilemba* ever includes the whole village, and in villages of mixed ethnicities and families it is common to find them remaining within the extended families or among neighbours. One finds variations of the *likilemba* in urban centres—mutual aid groups (*mutualités* in French) whose members all contribute to a common pot and then rotate the use of the pot as specific needs arise.

Similar to the case of land tenure, we see that the *likilemba* and *mutualité* are means to provide space for both the individual and the communal to exist and be lived out simultaneously. What belongs to the individual is preserved—each person has their own garden or project—but at the same time, a sense of community, mutual help and co-operation is fostered by people coming together to cut each other's gardens or contribute to a common pot.

APPLICATION OF CENTRAL AFRICAN INDIVIDUAL/COMMUNITY DIALECTICS TO ACTUAL DEVELOPMENT INITIATIVES

How might these ideas translate into the very real development dilemmas facing organizations working on environmentally-sound development in Central Africa? Perhaps rather than choosing a primarily individual-based strategy or a primarily communal strategy, organizations need to find a way to combine both in a single system, a middle way that allows the individual and the communal to co-exist.

For example, rather than trying to build communal projects that are owned by everyone yet owned by no one, it would work better to encourage and support individuals in their personal projects (fishponds, vegetable gardens, fruit tree orchards, reforestation plots, agro-forestry gardens, animal husbandry, etc.), yet also encourage a communal system of labour to build such projects. Modelled after the *likilemba*, such a system could help provide the people-power often needed to get individual projects off the ground. Under such a both/and system, each person would also have the certainty that they would benefit directly from development, thus providing the necessary motivation and responsibility to make projects successful. But, at the same time, communal or co-operative labour that rotated between individual initiatives could keep development from becoming a completely individualistic money-making enterprise and enhance the communal spirit many grassroots development organizations strive for.

Efforts to improve livelihoods are difficult if not impossible to instil from the top down through a series of different committees and animators organized hierarchically. Rather, such efforts have a greater degree of success if they begin with real live individuals who truly desire to undertake certain development initiatives. Perhaps grass-roots development projects need to start with such individuals—encourage them, teach them and learn from them, and provide the seeds for them to realize their own individual projects. But they also need to promote projects that can be achieved only through individuals coming together to help each other and work co-operatively. Out of that co-operative labour, people might then begin to learn from each other, and to meet together, doing so not because it is required by the committee or centre above them in the hierarchy, but because they really have a reason to meet, they really have a desire to share ideas generated by their individual projects.

BOTH/AND RELATIONS BETWEEN HUMANS AND THE ENVIRONMENT

The same sort of dialectical relationship between the individual and the community in Central Africa can also be observed in Central Africans' relationships to the natural world itself. Again, Central Africa has a lot to teach us in regard to our Western perceptions of humans' place in nature.

Social ecologist Murray Bookchin (1990: 1930) has remarked on the tendency of Western environmental thinking to fall prone to either of two extreme and fallacious views on the relationship between human society and nature: on the one hand the view that society and nature are totally separate realms (the hallmark within both capitalist and certain conservationist schools), and at the opposite extreme, the view that dissolves all differences between nature and society such that nature absorbs society (prevalent among sociobiologists and extreme biocentrists).

Such dualistic and reductionist views would be quite foreign to Central Africans whose understanding of the relationship between society and the natural world is more complex, holistic and dialectical. For example, a mutual and complex interaction between Central African forest-dwellers and their surroundings has allowed them to develop a rich knowledge of the environment that goes beyond the purely utilitarian (Vansina 1990: 255). Widespread knowledge provides them with the room and directions in which to innovate in the face of change. If something no longer works, if a natural disaster wipes out a certain resource, they know what else to try. If one year the forest gives only a little of the preferred *asali* honey, they know where to look for the less sweet but also good *apiso*. If hunting proves poor in one locale, switching camps to a new area is not difficult. In other words, nature and humans interrelate with some degree of flexibility and slack. Unlike Western biocentrists who tend to view humans as victims under the heavy hand of nature as taskmaster, Central Africans see nature as offering them some freedom of choice rather than forcing their fate upon them. The experience of Central Africans again provides us with a lesson. It affirms that although we cannot do with nature whatever we please, neither does nature leave us freedomless. Instead there exists the opportunity and (dare we say) the responsibility for us to play a creative role in shaping the future of the natural and social evolutionary process. We are co-creators, not simply victims of natural deterministic forces.

Malawian theologian Harvey Sindima, in describing the African concept of creation writes, 'The African understanding of the world is life-centred. For the African, life is the primary category for self-understanding and provides the basic framework for any interpretation of the world, persons, nature and divinity' (Sindima 1990: 142). Elsewhere he speaks of African cosmology as stressing the 'bondedness, the interconnectedness, of all living beings' (1990: 137). Although their denotative meanings are the same, the African idea of life-centredness contrasts and corrects the Western meaning that has been given to biocentrism. The latter has not escaped the trap of dualism such that it has often come to imply a certain misanthropic and oppositional understanding of the relationship between humans and nature, or conversely a relationship offering no distinctions between the two. Environmental ethicists such as Paul Taylor uphold a biocentrism in which the human species has no special status *vis-a-vis* other species, and *Homo sapiens*, like all other species, must be judged only on a morally individualistic basis (Taylor 1986).

Instead of focusing on the either/or debate between anthropocentrism and biocentrism, lifecentredness focuses on the bondedness of all forms of life. Rather than analysing the place and standing of different human and non-human life-forms on the basis of their comparative rights, African lifecentredness focuses on life itself, in a holistic rather than analytic fashion. It is not a matter of seeing what is most important, or of deciding if one thing is more important than another, but of believing and acting on the basis that all of life is important; even more, that all of life is sacred. Further, lifecentredness is oriented less toward individual entities (rocks vs. trees vs. animals vs. people) and more toward the relations between them. More attention is paid to processes and the flow of forces between entities than to the entities themselves. Emphasis falls on relating rather than existing since it is the nature and quality of relationship that determines whether the whole will sink or swim. The relationship between any two living entities affects all the rest of life since all of life is bonded. Therefore, deciding whether humans or life is central is, in an African understanding, a non-question.

APPLICATION OF CENTRAL AFRICAN HUMAN/ENVIRONMENT DIALECTICS TO ACTUAL CONSERVATION INITIATIVES

Central African perceptions of the human/environment dialectic (that humans are part of, rather than apart from, nature) hold certain lessons for conservationists and all of us in the West who are concerned about the disappearance of the world's biodiversity. Such perceptions affirm what some Western ecologists have also come to realize: we are misguided to manage for a 'pristine' nature because nature does not exist 'pristinely'. We only place our desire for pristineness (i.e. no human influence or presence) on it. African dialectical thought reminds us that we are nature, we cannot get ourselves out of it. Such a fact also makes us aware that neither can we view nature outside of ourselves—we will always be looking at it through some degree of subjectivity. We would do well to examine and know what our own subjectivities are and how they influence what we see. When we try to manage according to the subjectivity of 'natural pristineness', we often end up moving more against nature's grain than with it.

Thus, an 'African ecology' if you will, can contribute a corrective to our Western dualistic ecology, and help to amend our disconnection with nature by emphasizing that we must manage for a whole system, humans included. Africans certainly recognize the important differences between humans and animals (as one major non-human part of nature), but they have less of a tendency than we in the West to set the two up in dualistic opposition. The two are parts of one whole, or as one forest farmer put it to me, 'God made us and animals together. If people leave from this forest, the animals will also disappear'.

An African ecology can also do much to clarify that the real problem, the real destructive glitch, is not human beings *per se*, but distinct human-created socio-economic institutions that foster unsustainable uses of the environment. Modern capitalist markets, one example of such institutions, interacting with a complex of other forces including technology and human (African as well as Western) greed, have been a key factor in destroying the relative balance that had existed between humans and the natural forest environment that supported them. One farmer shared with me a poignant example of how these 'new ways' penetrated and changed the relatively balanced systems of land use that had existed in the time of his father.

> '*This problem of poison in the waters: it came really only with this civilization of the Europeans. They have this poison to put in the soil next to the crops in order to kill pests, but crafty people have taken it and put it in the rivers and streams to kill fish. People took it for a good thing, but it is only ruining our waters, some is even killing people. These ways, they began to change . . . well some of it is due to the whites, those who came to us; it was their knowledge that began to change our knowledge. We saw how much easier it was to get things with these bad*

ways, we see the ease and we jump into it and even though the rivers may be ruined, I get my fish and I sell it and I get wealthy.' (Elanga 1995)

In destroying traditional resource use patterns, this commercialization of nature also succeeded and continues to succeed in destroying the natural ecosystems on which all of life, human and non-human, depends. Western conservation initiatives in Central Africa have tried to solve the human/non-human needs equation not by directly restraining these market forces as much as by establishing State (and in the minds of many of the villagers I talked with, 'American') control over vast areas of forest seen by local people as God's gift to them from which they can live. Given the history and philosophy of state-administered conservation in many Central African countries, such control ends up weighing the needs of the non-human ecosystem over the needs of people, not to mention the undeniable overture for state exploitation of the local population such control has always facilitated.

In short, commercialized use more than indigenous people's use of the forest lies at the root of Central Africa's environmental problems. We would do better to try and control the market forces that lead to over-exploitation of the environment rather than unjustly restrict the subsistence practices of people who have lived in these forests much longer than ourselves.

REFERENCES

Bookchin, Murray. (1990). *Remaking Society: Pathways to a Green Future*. Boston, South End Press.

Gyekye, Kwame. 1987. *An Essay on African philosophical thought: The Akan conceptual theme*. Cambridge University Press, Cambridge.

Omo-Fadaka, Jimoh. 1990. "Communalism: The Moral factor in African Development." In *Ethics of environment and development: Global Challenges, international response*, J.R. and J.G. Engel, eds. London: Bellhaven.

Onyewuwnyi, Innoxwnr. 1991. "Is there an African Philosophy?" In *African Philosophy*, T. Serequeberhan, ed. New York: Paragon House.

Sindima, H. 1990. "Community of Life: Ecology Theology in African Perspective." In W. Eakin, C. Birch, and J. McDaniel, eds., *Liberating life: Contemporary Approaches to ecological theology*. Maryknoll, NY: Orbis Books.

Taylor, Paul. 1986. *Respect for nature*. Princeton, NJ: Princeton University Press.

Van Gelder, Sarah. 1993. "Remembering our purpose: An interview with Malidoma Some." *In Context* 34:30–34.

Vansina, J. 1990. *Paths in the rainforest: Towards a history of political tradition in Equatorial Africa*. London: James Currey.

"AN ABORIGINAL PERSPECTIVE ON THE INTEGRITY OF CREATION"

Stan McKay

Aboriginal culture is passed from one generation to the next by story telling. The philosophy of life is passed on to the young mainly by their observation of the elders. Many of the most profound teachings are passed on without words.

Our elders say that when our thoughts and dreams are put into written form they lose life. We are people of the oral tradition and it is a struggle to put our teachings into written form. Thus there is a sense of compromise in writing an article which seeks to reflect our spiritual insights on paper. But the turmoil of these days has brought us to the point that our elders advise us to share the insights and even to risk writing them. It is urgent for all people to come together for a healing vision for the earth, our mother.

Art Solomon, an Annishinabe (Ontario, Canada) spiritual elder, wrote the following prayer for a 1983 World Council of Churches meeting in Mauritius which brought together people representing various faith communities to prepare for the WCC's sixth assembly in Vancouver:

> Grandfather, look at our brokenness.
> Now we must put the sanctity of life as the most sacred principle of power, and renounce the awesome might of materialism.
> We know that in all creation, only the family of man has strayed from the sacred way.
> We know that we are the ones who are divided, and we are the ones who must come back, together to worship and walk in a sacred way, that by our affirmation we may heal the earth and heal each other.
> Now we must affirm life for all that is living or face death in a final desecration with no reprieve.
> We hear the screams of those who die for want of food, and whose humanity is aborted and prevented.
> Grandfather, the sacred one,

Reprinted from David Hallman, ed., *Ecotheology: Voices from South and North* (WCC Publications, Geneva, Switzerland, 1995), pp. 213–217.

we know that unless we love and have compassion the healing cannot come.

Grandfather, teach us how to heal our brokenness.

What Art Solomon has shared in this prayer allows the reader to ponder how simple our spiritual world view is—and how profound. The purpose of this paper is to develop some themes that support the renewed ecumenical emphasis on the creation, particularly in the World Council of Churches. Much of this does affirm a Native North American view of creation, but there are also some areas which have not been developed that I could add to the scope of the discussion. Moreover, there are subtle differences in terminology and emphasis which can be confusing and at times contradictory.

"ALL MY RELATIONS" (OR ANTS AND UNCLES)

For those who come from a Judaeo-Christian background it might be helpful to view Aboriginal peoples as an "Old Testament people." Like them, we come out of an oral tradition rooted in the creator and the creation. We, like Moses, know about the sacredness of the earth and the promise of land. Our creation stories also emphasize the power of the creator and the goodness of creation. We can relate to the vision of Abraham and the laughter of Sarah. We have dreams like Ezekiel and have known people like the Pharaoh. We call ourselves "the people" to reflect our sense of being chosen.

Indigenous spirituality around the world is centred on the notion of relationship to the whole creation. We call the earth our mother and the animals are our brothers and sisters. Those parts of creation which biologists describe as inanimate we call our relatives. This naming of creation into our family is an imagery of substance, but it is more than that, because it describes a relationship of love and faithfulness between human persons and the creation. This unity as creatures in the creation cannot be expressed exclusively, since it is related to the interdependence and connectedness of all life.

The next logical reflection is that because of our understanding of the gift of creation we are called to share in the fullness of life. It is difficult to express individual ownership within the Native spiritual understanding. If the creatures and the creation are interdependent, it follows that it is not faithful to speak of ownership. Life is understood as a gift, and it makes no sense to claim ownership of any part of the creation. Our leaders have often described how nonsensical it is to lay claim to the air, the water or the land; because these are related to all life. Chief Dan George expresses it this way in *My Heart Soars*: "Of all the teachings we receive, this one is the most important: Nothing belongs to you of what there is; what you take, you must share."

Reference to the earth in our culture is not individualistic so as to indicate ownership. Our words indicate sharing and belonging to the earth. The coming of Europeans to the land which we used in North America meant a conflict of understanding which centres on the ownership of land. The initial misunderstanding is not surprising, since the first immigrants thought of themselves as coming to take "possession" of a "vacant, pagan land." The incredible fact is that this perception continues after five centuries. Equally surprising has been the historical role of the Christian church in this process of colonization, which basically was a dividing up of the earth so it could be a possession.

The developments of our own generation may alter the pattern of non-communication with indigenous peoples about the earth and life. It may be that we have entered into a time of survival which will not allow people to pursue ownership of the earth without perceiving that this path leads to destruction of life, including their own. The most obvious example has been the nuclear threat, but more important for Native people are the depletion of resources and pollution of the environment. We understand this activity to be insane, since we live in an environment which gives life but is sensitive to abuse.

Our elders have told stories about the destruction of mother earth. In their dreams and visions they have known from time immemorial about a deep caring and reverence for life. Living in very natural environments they taught that we are to care for all life or we may die. The elders say: "If you see that the top of the tree is sick you will know that it is dying. If the trees die, we too will die." The earth is our life. It is to be shared, and we know the creator intends it for generations yet unborn.

The process in political circles and in government that has come to be known as "land claims" is devastating to our cultural values. In order for us to participate in the process, our statements become sterile and technical. Our documents must be in language suggested by lawyers and understood by judges. This legal jargon contains concepts of ownership which do not carry our spiritual sense of life. As marginalized peoples, forced to live on tiny plots of land, we encounter the worldview of the wealthy and powerful and are forced to compromise or to die.

Yet we maintain the earth is to be shared, and we continue to challenge faceless corporations to be faithful to their humanity. Even as we are being pushed into the "land claims" process, we maintain our heritage and are motivated by a love of the earth and a concern for the survival of the creation. Our earth mother is in a time of pain and she sustains many thoughtless children.

THE CIRCLE OF LIFE

My remarks thus far may not make sufficiently clear what the spiritual relationships to earth are for us. It is necessary to say that we feel a sense of "Amen" to the psalmist's words, "The earth is the Lord's and all that is in it" (Ps. 24:1). The value that informs the spirituality of my people is one of wholeness. It is related to a view of life which does not separate or compartmentalize. The relationship of health with ourselves, our community and with all creation is a spiritual relationship. The need of the universe is the individual need to be in harmony with the creator. This harmony is expressed by living in the circle of life.

There is an awareness that the Spirit moves through all of life. The Great Spirit is in fact the "cosmic order." Aboriginal North American spirituality draws this cosmic order together with human life in a very experiential way. Our view of the creation and the creator is thus an attempt to unify the worldview of human beings who are interdependent. We are a part of all life. Dogmatic statements are not relevant, since the spiritual pilgrimage is one of unity in which there are many truths from a variety of experiences.

I find the image of living on the earth in harmony with the creation and therefore the creator a helpful one. It means that "faithful" living on the earth will be moving in the rhythm of the creation. It means vibrating to the pulse of life in a natural way without having to "own" the source of the music. It is our experience that the creator reveals truth to the creation and all may share in it. We have ceremonies and symbols of what may be true for us. We have developed myths and rituals which remind us of the centrality of the earth in our experience of the truth about the creator. We seek to integrate life so that there will not be boundaries between the secular and religious. For us, the Great Spirit is in the daily earthly concerns about faithful living in a relationship with the created order.

Each day we are given is for thanksgiving for the earth. We are to enjoy it and share it in service of others. This is the way to grow in unity and harmony. Central to the movement into harmony with other communities is the idea of respect. Respect allows for diversity within the unity of the creator. Dialogue can then take place in a global community which does not develop defensive arguments to protect some truth. The situation will be one of sharing stories instead of dogmatic statements and involves listening as well as talking.

MENDING THE HOOP

Many teachings of the aboriginal North American nations use the symbol of the circle. It is the symbol of the inclusive caring community, in which individuals are respected and interdependence is recognized.

The Christian church has been unclear in its relationship to the creation. The church's earliest understanding of the second coming of Christ was that it was imminent, so that we should disconnect ourselves from the things of creation. Apocalyptic thought becomes part of a philosophy of "hatred of the world," which holds up spiritual salvation as the goal. The result has been a Christology from Europe which interprets biblical references to God's love for the world as being *only* about human salvation. The North American refinement of this incomplete Christology has been to explain that this is a teaching about *individual* human salvation. This entire message of hope is detached from the creation which in the beginning was "good" and which is a part of the world that God "so loved."

The Industrial Revolution and recent technological development have brought us into a mindset which fits our theology. Economic gain is more important than caring for the creation. The pursuit of short-term gain renders the created order disposable. Materialism and militarism are served by science and technology. There is a critical imbalance in the circle of life when our life-style does not reflect a holistic and inclusive vision of the creation.

Aboriginal teachers speak of our individual wholeness which is discovered in a balance of body, mind and spirit. The discovery of the self leads to an understanding of our interdependence with the whole creation. The integrity of creation is a faith statement about our intention to live in balance and harmony with creation. The elders say "you do what you believe." Anthropocentric philosophies and theologies cannot accommodate a holistic balanced approach. They describe the natural order as enemy and seek to destroy the mystery of hope itself.

"BIODIVERSITY AND TRADITION IN MALAYSIA"

Patrick Segundad

My name is Patrick Segundad and I am from the Kadazan community. We are the main indigenous people in the State of Sabah in Malaysia, which is located in the northern part of Borneo Island.

The term 'biodiversity' does not exist in my people's understanding or language. If I were to translate the term into our language, I would say it is everything in this world, down in the sea, and things that we can touch. At the same time, it is more than this—more than just things that can be touched or things that are alive. The air, the water, and the sun also must be included. If one being or part of biodiversity is disturbed or not kept in the perfect manner, an imbalance is created which will affect all other things.

Also, there is a spiritual aspect to what is also part of biodiversity. Although our peoples embrace Christianity, Islam, or whatever, we believe in the existence of spirit. The spirit is more like a guide, something that you must respect or be conscious of. It could be the spirit of the land, the spirit of things that live on trees or rocks, or even your ancestor spirits. In our language there is something called *adat*, an unwritten understanding of common things that everybody should know.

Adat is not only important in how we deal with our resources but also in how we live. It isn't like the concept of managing but rather that two things happen in the same time. While you might manage something, what you manage is also managing you. A person is a part of a greater single action, a larger balance or harmony.

Adat is often described as a traditional legal system but, to the indigenous peoples, it is much more, encompassing a set of beliefs and values that effect all aspects of life. Further, *adat* is a set of unwritten rules and principles that extends to everything and to relationships within both the physical world and the spiritual world.

Everything is inhabited by some kind of spirit and there is a proper way to conduct relationships with them. All things are in balance and any disturbances in the spiritual world may affect other members of the earthly family or community. Indigenous communities recognize the creator, spirits of the dead, and demons. *Adat* is closely linked to agricultural practices and management of the ecosystems.

Reprinted from *Cultural and Spiritual Values of Biodiversity*, United Nations Environment Programme, 2000. Used by permission of United Nations Environment Programme.

Normally, each indigenous community has a number of elders—men and women well versed in *adat* and its rituals—and others, who command great respect within the community. Most village leaders are members of the higher social strata, although this is not a stipulation for the position. These elders form a council which takes collective decisions on important matters and also presides over village courts in which all community disputes are settled.

The Kadazandusun village or community, which is the basic unit of the traditional society, usually has a headman named *mohoingon/molohing* (old person), who is skilled in *adat*. This position has been given official recognition under both the British administrations and local governments since the formation of Malaysia. In the past, Kadazandusun communities in each area were sometimes headed by warriors. These men of wisdom and bravery were generally known amongst the Kadazandusun as *Pangazau* (head-hunter). One outstanding man would be respected throughout several areas among the various *Pangazau*. This paramount chief, generally known as *Huguan Tosiouo/Huguan Siou* ('*Huguan*' meaning 'tough leader'; '*tosiouo*' from '*osiouo*' meaning 'brave, with supernatural prowess'), is considered a 'leader', 'supreme head' or 'the one who shows the way'. These non-hereditary leadership positions involved heavy responsibilities rather than privileged status.

The concept of *adat* is also embedded in the agricultural system. There is a wealth of ritual and ceremony involved, especially with the swidden system, which aims to redress the balance of nature that agriculture temporarily interrupts. Spirit worship is practised through these ceremonies rather than in specific places, temples or at regular intervals. The whole process of work thus brings individuals into contact with the spirit world, and if this should cause conflict between the spirits, the consequences may be felt by the whole community. This, in turn, undoubtedly encourages communal work and the sharing of responsibility for any activities that may adversely affect the spirit world.

Women form the vast majority of those who exercise the priestly functions. The status of women in Kadazandusun society was high in the distant past and has changed over time due to influences from outside. The predominance of women may be due to the psychology of females who, in matters of religious belief, take a longer time to be convinced, but once they acquire conviction become more committed and faithful in their observance. Whereas man's emotion is to meet a challenge, woman's emotion is to create an atmosphere. And because of the maternal instinct in women, her nature is to transmit not only natural life but also spiritual life. Another factor is that over the centuries women have been agriculturists and men have been hunters. Because of this tradition women tend to be more consistent than men.

The function of the Priestess is to endeavour to control or alter events that are considered to be causing problems in life. This is done by appeasing the spirits or forces responsible for the crisis. The Priestess asks the spirit (in this case the devil) upset by human action to accept the sacrifice and at the same time calls on *Kinoingan id Sawat* (God in the highest) and *Id Suang Tanah* (God below the Earth) as judgee and witnesses. The offering is not made as an act of worship or adoration of the devil but rather to pacify his anger at human negligence. The ceremonies carried out by the Priestess can usually be classified into three types: (1) those connected with agriculture; (2) communal ceremonies for the benefit of the whole village; and (3) personal ceremonies for the benefit of a single individual or household, for example to cure sickness, bad dreams, and so on.

As with other indigenous societies within the region, land is not owned. The concept of land ownership is alien to indigenous peoples where they believe that land belongs to the countless number who are dead, the few who are living, and those yet to be born. They see themselves as passing their lands on unharmed to the generations that follow, and consciously manage their resources to ensure sustained yield. Individual families have well-defined farming sites where they enjoy exclusive use and are, in effect, temporary residents with protected rights. The forest, however, is almost always communal property, although individual trees may be claimed by a single family.

Communal property is not free for all to use but rather is organized within a management system where rules are developed, group size is known and enforced, incentives exist for co-owners to follow the accepted institutional arrangements, and sanctions are enforced to ensure compliance. Most areas of forest will be claimed by a community, but boundaries—particularly for hunting grounds—are often vaguely defined.

Humans are merely a transient part of this world and land belongs to God as the Creator. Indigenous peoples have strong ties with the land. The land gives the people life, it gives life to the trees which in turn, give life to various micro-organisms and a resting place for the dead. The community's rights centre on three sources of life—the land, air and water—which refer to rivers, beaches, trees, wild plants and wildlife among other things.

When we talk about land we do not distinguish between forest and other lands. Both are the same, whether used by humans to plant or where plants grow by themselves as an act of nature. Indigenous peoples know where useful forest trees are located, where the best rattans can be found, and the whereabouts of deer and other valuable game. Hunting and gathering are important not only for economic existence but also for religious and cosmological reasons.

The indigenous peoples of Sabah utilize as least a quarter of Borneo's floral species for food while most of the world relies on only 20 major crops for staple food. Plants are used in concocting traditional herbal medicines to treat a wide range of ailments from simple coughs, diarrhoea, consumption, eye infections, skin problems, sores, cuts, wounds, and so on to physiological diseases like hypertension and even malignant cancerous tumours. The method of preparation, however, also depends on tabooe and religious beliefs.

Apart from precious stones, bones and other animal by-products such as feathers, beaks and shells, Sabah's indigenous peoples also use a variety of plants for their cultural and social needs. Different parts of plants are used to make shelters, boats, hunting equipment and handicrafts, to carry out ceremonies, and to prepare dart poisons.

Adat influences the right to collect forest products and to hunt, and is often expressed as religions restrictions on over-exploitation of trees and animals. These *adat* controls are very strict, with systems of taboos which require communities to fulfil a host of activities before, during and after collection. When the individual or community violates these taboos, the community must make amends.

Guidelines expressed though *adat* for opening land for agriculture are usually very simple and practical. Farmers clear small areas of forest and burn the debris. Most plots are secondary forest that has previously been cleared for agriculture because it takes less energy to clear than primary forest. Burning the debris releases potash and phosphates immediately into the soil, prior to planting crops which will need them. Burning is done at the end of the dry season. The normal average size of a swidden plot for a family varies from 0.5 to 2.5 hectares. Only small areas are cultivated leaving most of the land in fallow. Clearing small areas is a major factor contributing to the reduction of soil erosion. The other major factor that reduces soil erosion is the variety of crops grown on any one site. Different crops are planted throughout the year, providing the farmer with a steady supply of food. Subsistence crops such as rice and corn are grown on freshly cleared sites and cash crops are grown only after the land has been cultivated for some time.

It cannot be denied that the swidden agriculture system requires relatively large tracts of land but it is labour-intensive and requires few tools. It is more appropriate to measure the system's efficiency not by output per unit labour but by yield per unit area. It should be noted here that traditional swidden agriculture within forested areas evolved to meet the needs of the local economy, not to provide raw materials for export. To this end, the swidden agriculture system is remarkably efficient.

Indigenous farmers usually have an extraordinary wealth of scientifically sound knowledge about plant species and soil qualities. This is indicative of people who are far advanced technologically. They have such a highly defined and reliable knowledge about their environment because their very survival is dependent upon the validity of their information. Their traditional practices are well adapted to local environmental conditions because these practices are the product of an intensive process of natural selection over many generations. Unlike scientific researchers in government-funded laboratories and experimental stations, farmers do not receive a monthly pay check regardless of the success or failure of their 'experiments'. Failure means hardship, even death. Consequently, selection strongly favours accurate and reliable knowledge.

Modern political, economic and cultural forces have changed indigenous peoples. Introduced religions, such as Christianity and Islam, have often failed to incorporate old beliefs which were important to the sustained use of lands and forests. Traditional agriculture is a manifestation of the indigenous peoples' concepts of a world of balance and renewal, which is rapidly eroding under modern conditions and circumstances.

In the end, traditional values are about balance and renewal and have little to do with what is called supply and demand. Biodiversity is a part of life and related to land. Without biodiversity, life would be meaningless. Without something like *adat*, it is difficult to have balance and renewal. It is similar to having a pen but no paper, or paper but no pen. Both things must be in place before we can write—just as *adat* must be in place before we can control over-use and have balance. For example, in my community we are only allowed to fish in the river for certain periods of time. So, if somebody goes and tries to catch fish before the agreed time, and is discovered, he will be asked to compensate or *sogit* which could burden him afterwards. This must be done to please and compensate both the spiritual world and the community. Because of this person's behaviour, the whole community is affected by the actions of the spiritual world.

This type of environmental control has been in operation for hundreds of years. When *adat* is not respected, you can see and feel the consequences. Today, many people don't respect *adat*. You can see this lack of respect in our forests and villages. Ten to fifty years ago when people still believed in and respected *adat*, there were forests and people who lived in the forest who appreciated and respected their surroundings. They saw no reason to change their way of life. But now they are within the influence of the modern world and there are things in the outside world that they want. Those things can be purchased with money, and the question becomes how does one get money? The majority of the younger generation are frequently influenced by money and are the ones who go and cut and over-use the forests. Because these younger people do not respect *adat*, the forests are diminished. When *adat* is in control, e.g. 'You can't cut this tree', 'You're not allowed to take more than this', 'When you cut one rattan, you plant two', 'That is for you and for your son or daughter in the future', then the forests will be preserved. By following the guidelines decided by *adat*, they are helping the forest to exist in the future for future generations.

It is like the durian tree. When you plant the tree, you're thinking about 20–30 years from now when it will bear fruit. Some people would say, 'What's the point of planting this tree? Probably your son will be old by the time of first harvest and have his own son and perhaps a grandson'. But as we eat durian today, we will remember that these are the fruits given to us by past generations. They had their own visions and their own thoughts. While they didn't go to school, they were educated in other ways. They followed what their forefathers did because they understood that this knowledge came through the actions of their forefathers. Without this knowledge they would not have enjoyed what they enjoyed in their time. It is interesting that this cultural information is like genetic information, and the evolving social and cultural forms have their analogies in biological evolution. Our ideas have evolved and served us well.

Patrick Segundad

It is bothersome that in some of the writings about indigenous peoples' knowledge, it is either presented as unchanging or as having undergone changes that leave it in a new and disorganized state. As for all peoples, change for us is all the time too. To meet new conditions as the world changes around us, *adat* must be compensated. *Adat* is permanent and ongoing, and imbalances have been created. There is no compromise with *adat:* it is not the law set up by humans but is rather something that has been negotiated between humans who are still living and the spirits.

Some people might be confused and think that *adat* is like the Ten Commandments. But the Ten Commandments are different: they are written and, when things are written, people can interpret them in different ways. But *adat* was never written. It cannot change so there is no interpretation as it is remembered with spiritual values.

Adat has been here for hundreds of years so it's already agreed that this is a 'must do' for you so that your grandchildren or the people who are going to live in the future are given the same mandate. *Adat* is always, it's a fixed one, you cannot change this thing. *Adat* is the constant that guides the way you live, the way you are going to take care of your surroundings, the animals, the air, the water, the spirits . . . everything, and you see the spiritual, your family, your community, and other things like that.

"LEARNING TO CONNECT SPIRIT, MIND, BODY, AND HEART TO THE ENVIRONMENT: A HEALER'S PERSPECTIVE"

Lea Bill-Rippling Water Woman

This contribution attempts to present the depth of relationship involved with the environment when traditional learning is applied to healing and becoming a traditional healer. I base this perspective on my own experience. My first lesson involved communication with the spirit of the self and the essence of all creation. Self understanding was acquired through experiences in visioning, fasting and utilization of all creation. The more centred with spirit I became, the more my ability to understand and apply the information received from the natural world flowed with ease. Understanding myself as a spirit essence and connecting at this level with the natural systems opened a world of understanding and knowledge that cannot be received through books or lectures. I have gained an understanding that the relationship a healer has with the environment is a reflection of the depth of understanding achieved of the personal relationship with all creation.

Communication with the environment requires a willingness to be open to the subtleties of natural communication. Prayer and the use of prayer chants were part of the initial learning about communication with the spirit. The intonations of the voice are a language in their own right, although the intellect may not register recognition of the meaning of the language. One of the greatest challenges of this process is to overcome the imprinting received through childhood learning. I was a very shy child who had experienced ridicule and discrimination both in school and in out-of-school situations. I acquired basic spiritual and healing knowledge through my grandparents, who were both traditional healers. I had to learn how to overcome fear and being self-conscious, along with the imprinting of 'you're not of any worth'. I learned to ask for guidance and help through prayer. Prayer became a way of listening to my voice and how it affected the environment. The most profound experiences have been in the mountains where I became more connected to the

Reprinted from *Cultural and Spiritual Values of Biodiversity*, United Nations Environment Programme, 2000. Used by permission of United Nations Environment Programme.

environment which continues to be a gentle and non-discriminatory supporter of my learning. There were times when the world would become silent to listen to my songs, to my prayers and to my weeping as I became connected to my spirit. I listened to the land and its patron, and I observed the movement and presence of all elements, water, wind, sky, plants and animals. These were my messengers, who brought affirmation to my prayers and applauded my songs and comforted my being as it underwent its healing. I have included here a prayer from my first language, Cree. I have translated the words of the Cree language using the most appropriate words to capture the essence of the prayer. All prayers will vary from one medicine person to another and will be particular to the ceremony and/or healing that is being conducted. This prayer is a teaching prayer. It is a prayer that reflects and sets the intent of my journey as a healer.

> Sacred Father of all Creation, thank you for the Beauty and Wonder of life. Thank you for the Beauty and Wonder of this day. I sit before you as your humble servant. Guide me in all I proceed with. Open my heart, open my mind, and clear all negative imprinting held in my body in order that my spirit may be a conduit for divine knowledge, truth and purpose.

> Sacred Mother of all Creation, with utmost love and respect, I express gratitude for the gifts you provide to humanity. Thank you for the nourishment that comes from your being. Thank you for the medicines that enhance my capacity. Thank you for the unyielding strength you reflect for me to learn perseverance. Thank you for the Beauty of your being, the synchronicity of all action, creation, cycles and evolution. Sacred Mother of all Creation, continue to be my teacher and guide as I walk upon your being. Open my heart to the beauty of your spirit. Open my mind to the abundant wisdom dwelling in all Creation. Guide my body with the principles of Love and Order. Guide my spirit in divine truth and purpose.

The second principle I learned in healing is that all living matter has spirit, and therefore must be approached as a living spirit entity. The natural world has a supreme ability to contain its spirit essence according to natural law and thereby holds the key to spirit reclamation. Humanity seeks his/her spirit in natural surroundings as they reflect the nature of his/her spirit in a physical manner through landscape, interactions of and with wildlife, and in sudden shifts of environmental elements. Vision-seeking in the natural environment is a means of reuniting with the spirit essence of life. The natural world reflects the individual aspects of spirit that become overwhelmed by day-to-day confusions and life processes. An example of the power of natural spirit is water, which is my namesake. Humanity may attempt to procure the power of water, but its spirit essence remains undaunted by manipulation or abuse. Quietly, it continues to influence life with its interactions. When its physical essence is overburdened, the spirit flows forth with unwavering and mighty strength, clearing all that is before its path, resurrecting elements that have long been submerged by the hand of man. Principles such as this one, reflected by nature, become my teaching and healing tools. It is from this perspective that I, as a traditional healer, view the world and the elements that enhance the gift of healing. During healing my assistants are the natural elements around me because I have developed a strong relationship with this world. I never cease to be filled with wonder when I have taken a client to the mountains or by a stream for healing and all becomes quiet with expectation. As I prepare and set the intent by outlining the needs of my client through prayer, all that is around me adjusts to begin with the healing. A healing ceremony has several stages.

The first phase of healing involves a prayer ceremony that encompasses all the elements for healing. The second phase involves the use of songs and rattles. This phase focuses on healing the physical body with vibration and by releasing negative imprinting and accumulated stress in the body. When the healing is performed in a natural setting there will often be complete calm: the birds will stop singing, and the winds will become gentle. There are times when the winds will pick up and swirl around my client or a bird will sing a loud or a gentle song, aiding in the healing. Once this phase is complete, a post conference is held with the client to teach and provide guidance. Teaching and counselling can sometimes take several hours and several sessions following the process outlined above.

I acknowledge and understand that there are parallels in the systems between humanity and the natural world. The systems within the world of plants, animals, trees, rocks and the atmosphere all contribute to the overall understanding of life process and the principle of cause and effect. The imbalance in one system ultimately affects the other. The natural world celebrates our healing as it means greater opportunity for increased balance and bio-diversity. Both systems strive for balance in their own manner, whether it is of mind, body, spirit or emotion. Humanity and the environment are stewards of each other.

Part III

ECOTHEOLOGY IN AN AGE OF ENVIRONMENTAL CRISIS

Transforming Tradition

The clear messages we see around us—the increased temperatures, the sickening die-off of species that may be as high as ten a day (ten chains of being stretching back to creation), the eroding ozone—these messages all tell us that we are badly out of balance. That we, the products of creation's later days, are destroying our elders. That having been given, in the words of Deuteronomy, a land of flowing streams, with springs and underground waters welling up in valleys and hills, a land of wheat and barley, of vines and fig trees and pomegranates . . . that having been given this land we are failing.

—Bill McKibben

In spite of all the worldwide concern with our deteriorating environment, very few people have yet got to grips with the deeper problems it raises. The implications are too revolutionary. They run counter to the ingrained ways of thought which have dominated the western world for the past two centuries.

The truth is that the goal of unlimited physical growth is no longer tenable. The only way out of the human predicament of our time lies in a complete and radical change, not of *methods*, but of *goals*. . . . There is only one way to avert the disaster which threatens to overwhelm mankind. *Material goals must be replaced by spiritual goals.*

—Aryeh Carmel

We told the native peoples of North America that their relationships with the land were worthless, primitive. Now we are a culture that spends millions trying to find this knowledge, trying to reestablish a sense of well-being with the earth.

—Barry Lopez

The High,
the low
all of creation,
God gives to humankind to use. If this privilege is misused,
God's Justice permits creation to punish humanity.

—Hildegard of Bingen

Lynn White's essay, which begins this part, helped initiate a fierce and searching discussion of the relation between Western religions and the environmental crisis. White's thesis—that Jewish and Christian "desacralization" of the Earth paved the way for the modern domination of nature—has been hotly debated and is referred to by many other authors in this book, some of whom find in the Bible a model of stewardship for the land rather than domination over it.

Whatever the ultimate resolution of the debate, it is clear that a host of theologians are seriously wrestling with the need to reform their traditions to face the transition from nature to environment; that is, the fact that humanity has deeply altered and continues to threaten our natural surroundings.

In this part, statements from Catholic, Lutheran, Baptist, Orthodox and Evangelical leaders indicate a "greening of the church" and a heightened awareness of issues that were rarely discussed even two decades ago. Essays by scholars and theologians Sallie McFague, John F. Haught, Arthur Waskow, John B. Cobb, Stephanie Kaza, Nawal Ammar, Christopher Chapple and Tu Weiming reveal new religious sensibilities based in Christianity, Judaism, contemporary Buddhism, Islam, Hinduism, and Confucianism. Old concepts are reinterpreted (as in the thought of an environmentally oriented "ecokosher") or challenging metaphors created (when Sallie McFague offers us the earth as the "body of God"). New forms of meditation and social practice become part of Buddhist dharma and ancient Confucian models of balance and integration between the world and the self are called upon to aid our search for a saner form of life. John F. Haught proposes a moderate reconceptualization of Christianity, which clings to basic tenets but opens to the severity of our environmental situation; and Theodore Walker looks to spiritual and ethical resources from the African-American experience to help forge a more liberating theology. Gary Kowalski and Andrew Linzey argue that animals deserve serious moral consideration—that they are "somebody, not something." Finally, my own contribution investigates the demands the environmental crisis places on people who might well consider themselves "spiritual but not religious."

To all the varieties of contemporary ecotheology—as well as to ourselves—we may ask: Will this body of thought remain merely an intellectual construct? Or will it, as in the case of the Civil Rights Movement, bring a religiously inspired vision into critical social struggles?

"THE HISTORICAL ROOTS OF OUR ECOLOGICAL CRISIS"

Lynn White

A conversation with Aldous Huxley not infrequently put one at the receiving end of an unforgettable monologue. About a year before his lamented death he was discoursing on a favorite topic: Man's unnatural treatment of nature and its sad results. To illustrate his point he told how, during the previous summer, he had returned to a little valley in England where he had spent many happy months as a child. Once it had been composed of delightful grassy glades; now it was becoming overgrown with unsightly brush because the rabbits that formerly kept such growth under control had largely succumbed to a disease, myxomatosis, that was deliberately introduced by the local farmers to reduce the rabbits' destruction of crops. Being something of a Philistine, I could be silent no longer, even in the interests of great rhetoric. I interrupted to point out that the rabbit itself had been brought as a domestic animal to England in 1176, presumably to improve the protein diet of the peasantry.

All forms of life modify their contexts. The most spectacular and benign instance is doubtless the coral polyp. By serving its own ends, it has created a vast undersea world favorable to thousands of other kinds of animals and plants. Ever since man became a numerous species he has affected his environment notably. The hypothesis that his fire-drive method of hunting created the world's great grasslands and helped to exterminate the monster mammals of the Pleistocene from much of the globe is plausible, if not proved. For six millennia at least, the banks of the lower Nile have been a human artifact rather than the swampy African jungle which nature, apart from man, would have made it. The Aswan Dam, flooding 5,000 square miles, is only the latest stage in a long process. In many regions terracing or irrigation, overgrazing, the cutting of forests by Romans to build ships to fight Carthaginians or by Crusaders to solve the logistics problems of their expeditions, have profoundly changed some ecologies. Observation that the French landscape falls into two basic types, the open fields of the north and the *bocage* of the south and west, inspired Marc Bloch to undertake his classic study of medieval agricultural methods. Quite unintentionally, changes in human ways often affect nonhuman nature. It has been noted, for example, that the advent of the automobile eliminated huge flocks of sparrows that once fed on the horse manure littering every street.

Reprinted with permission from *Science*, vol. 155, #3767, 10 March 1967, pp. 1203–1207. Copyright 1967 American Association for the Advancement of Science.

The history of ecologic change is still so rudimentary that we know little about what really happened, or what the results were. The extinction of the European aurochs as late as 1627 would seem to have been a simple case of overenthusiastic hunting. On more intricate matters it often is impossible to find solid information. For a thousand years or more the Frisians and Hollanders have been pushing back the North Sea, and the process is culminating in our own time in the reclamation of the Zuider Zee. What, if any, species of animals, birds, fish, shore life, or plants have died out in the process? In their epic combat with Neptune, have the Netherlanders overlooked ecological values in such a way that the quality of human life in the Netherlands has suffered? I cannot discover that the questions have ever been asked, much less answered.

People, then, have often been a dynamic element in their own environment, but in the present state of historical scholarship we usually do not know exactly when, where, or with what effects man-induced changes came. As we enter the last third of the 20th century, however, concern for the problem of ecologic backlash is mounting feverishly. Natural science, conceived as the effort to understand the nature of things, had flourished in several eras and among several peoples. Similarly there had been an age-old accumulation of technological skills, sometimes growing rapidly, sometimes slowly. But it was not until about four generations ago that Western Europe and North America arranged a marriage between science and technology, a union of the theoretical and the empirical approaches to our natural environment. The emergence in widespread practice of the Baconian creed that scientific knowledge means technological power over nature can scarcely be dated before about 1850, save in the chemical industries, where it is anticipated in the 18th century. Its acceptance as a normal pattern of action may mark the greatest event in human history since the invention of agriculture, and perhaps in nonhuman terrestrial history as well.

Almost at once the new situation forced the crystallization of the novel concept of ecology; indeed, the word *ecology* first appeared in the English language in 1873. Today, less than a century later, the impact of our race upon the environment has so increased in force that it has changed in essence. When the first cannons were fired, in the early 14th century, they affected ecology by sending workers scrambling to the forests and mountains for more potash, sulfur, iron ore, and charcoal, with some resulting erosion and deforestation. Hydrogen bombs are of a different order: a war fought with them might alter the genetics of all life on this planet. By 1285 London had a smog problem arising from the burning of soft coal, but our present combustion of fossil fuels threatens to change the chemistry of the globe's atmosphere as a whole, with consequences which we are only beginning to guess. With the population explosion, the carcinoma of planless urbanism, the now geological deposits of sewage and garbage, surely no creature other than man has ever managed to foul its nest in such short order.

There are many calls to action, but specific proposals, however worthy as individual items, seem too partial, palliative, negative: ban the bomb, tear down the billboards, give the Hindus contraceptives and tell them to eat their sacred cows. The simplest solution to any suspect change is, of course, to stop it, or, better yet, to revert to a romanticized past: make those ugly gasoline stations look like Anne Hathaway's cottage or (in the Far West) like ghost-town saloons. The "wilderness area" mentality invariably advocates deep-freezing an ecology, whether San Gimignano or the High Sierra, as it was before the first Kleenex was dropped. But neither atavism nor prettification will cope with the ecologic crisis of our time.

What shall we do? No one yet knows. Unless we think about fundamentals, our specific measures may produce new backlashes more serious than those they are designed to remedy.

As a beginning we should try to clarify our thinking by looking, in some historical depth, at the presuppositions that underlie modern technology and science. Science was traditionally aristocratic, speculative, intellectual in intent; technology was lower-class, empirical, action-oriented. The quite sudden fusion of these two, towards the middle of the 19th century, is surely related to the slightly prior and contemporary democratic revolutions which, by reducing social barriers, tended to assert a functional unity of brain and hand. Our ecologic crisis is the product of an emerging, entirely novel, democratic culture. The issue is whether a democratized world can survive its own implications. Presumably we cannot, unless we rethink our axioms.

THE WESTERN TRADITIONS OF TECHNOLOGY AND SCIENCE

One thing is so certain that it seems stupid to verbalize it: both modern technology and modern science are distinctively *Occidental*. Our technology has absorbed elements from all over the world, notably from China; yet everywhere today, whether in Japan or in Nigeria, successful technology is Western. Our science is the heir to all the sciences of the past, especially perhaps to the work of the great Islamic scientists of the Middle Ages, who so often outdid the ancient Greeks in skill and perspicacity: al-Râzî in medicine, for example; or ibn-al-Haytham in optics; or Omar Khayyám in mathematics. Indeed, not a few works of such geniuses seem to have vanished in the original Arabic and to survive only in medieval Latin translations that helped to lay the foundations for later Western developments. Today, around the globe, all significant science is Western in style and method, whatever the pigmentation or language of the scientists.

A second pair of facts is less well recognized because they result from quite recent historical scholarship. The leadership of the West, both in technology and in science, is far older than the so-called Scientific Revolution of the 17th century or the so-called Industrial Revolution of the 18th century. These terms are in fact outmoded and obscure the true nature of what they try to describe—significant stages in two long and separate developments. By A.D. 1000 at the latest—and perhaps, feebly, as much as 200 years earlier—the

Lynn White

West began to apply water power to industrial processes other than milling grain. This was followed in the late 12th century by the harnessing of wind power. From simple beginnings, but with remarkable consistency of style, the West rapidly expanded its skills in the development of power machinery, labor-saving devices, and automation. Those who doubt should contemplate that most monumental achievement in the history of automation: the weight-driven mechanical clock, which appeared in two forms in the early 14th century. Not in craftsmanship but in basic technological capacity, the Latin West of the later Middle Ages far outstripped its elaborate, sophisticated, and esthetically magnificent sister cultures, Byzantium and Islam. In 1444 a great Greek ecclesiastic, Bessarion, who had gone to Italy, wrote a letter to a prince in Greece. He is amazed by the superiority of Western ships, arms, textiles, glass. But above all he is astonished by the spectacle of waterwheels sawing timbers and pumping the bellows to blast furnaces. Clearly, he had seen nothing of the sort in the Near East.

By the end of the 15th century the technological superiority of Europe was such that its small, mutually hostile nations could spill out over all the rest of the world, conquering, looting, and colonizing. The symbol of this technological superiority is the fact that Portugal, one of the weakest states of the Occident, was able to become, and to remain for a century, mistress of the East Indies. And we must remember that the technology of Vasco da Gama and Albuquerque was built by pure empiricism, drawing remarkably little support or inspiration from science.

In the present-day vernacular of understanding, modern science is supposed to have begun in 1543, when both Copernicus and Vesalius published their great works. It is no derogation of their accomplishments, however, to point out that such structures as the *Fabrica* and the *De revolutionibus* do not appear overnight. The distinctive Western tradition of science, in fact, began in the late 11th century with a massive movement of translation of Arabic and Greek scientific works into Latin. A few notable books—Theophrastus, for example—escaped the West's avid new appetite for science, but within less than 200 years, effectively the entire corpus of Greek and Muslim science was available in Latin, and was being eagerly read and criticized in the new European universities. Out of criticism arose new observation, speculation, and increasing distrust of ancient authorities. By the late 13th century Europe had seized global scientific leadership from the faltering hands of Islam. It would be as absurd to deny the profound originality of Newton, Galileo, or Copernicus as to deny that of the 14th century scholastic scientists like Buridan or Oresme on whose work they built. Before the 11th century, science scarcely existed in the Latin West, even in Roman times. From the 11th century onward, the scientific sector of Occidental culture has increased in a steady crescendo.

Since both our technological and our scientific movements got their start, acquired their character, and achieved world dominance in the Middle Ages, it would seem that we cannot understand their nature or their present impact upon ecology without examining fundamental medieval assumptions and developments.

MEDIEVAL VIEW OF MAN AND NATURE

Until recently, agriculture has been the chief occupation even in "advanced" societies; hence, any change in methods of tillage has much importance. Early plows, drawn by two oxen, did not normally turn the sod but merely scratched it. Thus, cross-plowing was needed and fields tended to be squarish. In the fairly light soils and semi-arid climates of the Near East and Mediterranean, this worked well. But such a plow was inappropriate to the wet climate and often sticky soils of northern Europe. By the latter part of the 7th century after Christ, however, following obscure beginnings, certain northern peasants were using an entirely new kind of plow, equipped with a vertical knife to cut the line of the furrow, a horizontal share to slice under the sod, and a moldboard to turn it over. The friction of this plow with the soil was so great that it normally required not two but eight oxen. It attacked the land with such violence that cross-plowing was not needed, and fields tended to be shaped in long strips.

In the days of the scratch-plow, fields were distributed generally in units capable of supporting a single family. Subsistence farming was the presupposition. But no peasant owned eight oxen: to use the new and more efficient plow, peasants pooled their oxen to form large plow-teams, originally receiving (it would appear) plowed strips in proportion to their contribution. Thus, distribution of land was based no longer on the needs of a family but, rather, on the capacity of a power machine to till the earth. Man's relation to the soil was profoundly changed. Formerly man had been part of nature; now he was the exploiter of nature. Nowhere else in the world did farmers develop any analogous agricultural implement. Is it coincidence that modern technology, with its ruthlessness toward nature, has so largely been produced by descendants of these peasants of northern Europe?

This same exploitive attitude appears slightly before A.D. 830 in Western illustrated calendars. In older calendars the months were shown as passive personifications. The new Frankish calendars, which set the style for the Middle Ages, are very different: they show men coercing the world around them—plowing, harvesting, chopping trees, butchering pigs. Man and nature are two things, and man is master.

These novelties seem to be in harmony with larger intellectual patterns. What people do about their ecology depends on what they think about themselves in relation to things around them. Human ecology is deeply conditioned by beliefs about our nature and destiny—that is, by religion. To Western eyes this is very evident in, say, India or Ceylon. It is equally true of ourselves and of our medieval ancestors.

The victory of Christianity over paganism was the greatest psychic revolution in the history of our culture. It has become fashionable today to say that, for better or worse, we live in "the post-Christian age." Certainly the forms of our thinking and language have largely ceased to be Christian, but to my eye the substance often remains amazingly akin to that of the past. Our daily habits of action, for example, are dominated by an implicit faith in perpetual progress which was unknown either to Greco-Roman antiquity or to the Orient. It is rooted in, and is indefensible apart from, Judeo-Christian teleology. The fact that Communists share it merely helps to show what can be demonstrated on many other grounds: that Marxism, like Islam, is a Judeo-Christian heresy. We continue today to live, as we have lived for about 1700 years, very largely in a context of Christian axioms.

What did Christianity tell people about their relations with the environment?

While many of the world's mythologies provide stories of creation, Greco-Roman mythology was singularly incoherent in this respect. Like Aristotle, the intellectuals of the ancient West denied that the visible world had had a beginning. Indeed, the idea of a beginning was impossible in the framework of their cyclical notion of time. In sharp contrast, Christianity inherited from Judaism not only a concept of time as nonrepetitive and linear but also a striking story of creation. By gradual stages a loving and all-powerful God had created light and darkness, the heavenly bodies, and earth and all its plants, animals, birds, and fishes. Finally, God had created Adam and, as an afterthought, Eve to keep man from being lonely. Man named all the animals, thus establishing his dominance over them. God planned all of this explicitly for man's benefit and rule: no item in the physical creation had any purpose save to serve man's purposes. And, although man's body is made of clay, he is not simply part of nature: he is made in God's image.

Especially in its Western form, Christianity is the most anthropocentric religion the world has seen. As early as the 2nd century both Tertullian and St. Irenaeus of Lyons were insisting that when God shaped Adam he was foreshadowing the image of the incarnate Christ, the Second Adam. Man shares, in great measure, God's transcendence of nature. Christianity, in absolute contrast to ancient paganism and Asia's religions (except, perhaps, Zoroastrianism), not only established a dualism of man and nature but also insisted that it is God's will that man exploit nature for his proper ends.

At the level of the common people this worked out in an interesting way. In Antiquity every tree, every spring, every stream, every hill had its own *genius loci*, its guardian spirit. These spirits were accessible to men, but were very unlike men; centaurs, fauns, and mermaids show their ambivalence. Before one cut a tree, mined a mountain, or dammed a brook, it was important to placate the spirit in charge of that particular situation, and to keep it placated. By destroying pagan animism, Christianity made it possible to exploit nature in a mood of indifference to the feelings of natural objects.

It is often said that for animism the Church substituted the cult of saints. True; but the cult of saints is functionally quite different from animism. The saint is not *in* natural objects; he may have special shrines, but his citizenship is in heaven. Moreover, a saint is entirely a man; he can be approached in human terms. In addition to saints, Christianity of course also had angels and demons inherited from Judaism and perhaps, at one remove, from Zoroastrianism. But these were all as mobile as the saints themselves. The spirits *in* natural objects, which formerly had protected nature from man, evaporated. Man's effective monopoly on spirit in this world was confirmed, and the old inhibitions to the exploitation of nature crumbled.

When one speaks in such sweeping terms, a note of caution is in order. Christianity is a complex faith, and its consequences differ in differing contexts. What I have said may well apply to the medieval West, where in fact technology made spectacular advances. But the Greek East, a highly civilized realm of equal Christian devotion, seems to have produced no marked technological innovation after the late 7th century, when Greek fire was invented. The key to the contrast may perhaps be found in a difference in the tonality of piety and thought which students of comparative theology find between the Greek and the Latin Churches. The Greeks believed that sin was intellectual blindness, and that salvation was found in illumination, orthodoxy—that is, clear thinking. The Latins, on the other hand, felt that sin was moral evil, and that salvation was to be found in right conduct. Eastern theology has been intellectualist. Western theology has been voluntarist. The Greek saint contemplates; the Western saint acts. The implications of Christianity for the conquest of nature would emerge more easily in the Western atmosphere.

The Christian dogma of creation, which is found in the first clause of all the Creeds, has another meaning for our comprehension of today's ecologic crisis. By revelation, God had given man the Bible, the Book of Scripture. But since God had made nature, nature also must reveal the divine mentality. The religious study of nature for the better understanding of God was known as natural theology. In the early Church, and always in the Greek East, nature was conceived primarily as a symbolic system through which God speaks to men: the ant is a sermon to sluggards; rising flames are the symbol of the soul's aspiration. This view of nature was essentially artistic rather than scientific. While Byzantium preserved and copied great numbers of ancient Greek scientific texts, science as we conceive it could scarcely flourish in such an ambience.

However, in the Latin West by the early 13th century natural theology was following a very different bent. It was ceasing to be the decoding of the physical symbols of God's communication with man and was becoming the effort to understand God's mind by discovering how his creation operates. The rainbow was no longer simply a symbol of hope first sent to Noah after the Deluge: Robert Grosseteste, Friar Roger Bacon, and Theodoric of Freiberg produced startlingly sophisticated work on the optics of the rainbow, but they did it as a venture in religious understanding. From the 13th century onward, up to and including Leibnitz and Newton, every major scientist, in effect, explained his motivations in religious terms. Indeed, if Galileo had not been so expert an amateur theologian he would have got into far less trouble: the professionals resented his intrusion. And Newton seems to have regarded himself more as a theologian than as a scientist. It was not until the late 18th century that the hypothesis of God became unnecessary to many scientists.

It is often hard for the historian to judge, when men explain why they are doing what they want to do, whether they are offering real reasons or merely culturally acceptable reasons. The consistency with which scientists during the long formative centuries of Western science said that the task and the reward of the scientist was "to think God's thoughts after him" leads one to believe that this was their real motivation. If so, then modern Western science was cast in a matrix of Christian theology. The dynamism of religious devotion, shaped by the Judeo-Christian dogma of creation, gave it impetus.

AN ALTERNATIVE CHRISTIAN VIEW

We would seem to be headed toward conclusions unpalatable to many Christians. Since both *science* and *technology* are blessed words in our contemporary vocabulary, some may be happy at the notions, first, that, viewed historically, modern science is an extrapolation of natural theology and, second, that modern technology is at least partly to be explained as an Occidental, voluntarist realization of the Christian dogma of man's transendence of, and rightful mastery over, nature. But, as we now recognize, somewhat over a century ago science and technology—hitherto quite separate activities—joined to give mankind powers which, to judge by many of the ecologic effects, are out of control. If so, Christianity bears a huge burden of guilt.

I personally doubt that disastrous ecologic backlash can be avoided simply by applying to our problems more science and more technology. Our science and technology have grown out of Christian attitudes toward man's relation to nature which are almost universally held not only by Christians and neo-Christians but also by those who fondly regard themselves as post-Christians. Despite Copernicus, all the cosmos rotates around our little globe. Despite Darwin, we are *not*, in our hearts, part of the natural process. We are superior to nature, contemptuous of it, willing to use it for our slightest whim. The newly elected Governor of California, like myself a churchman but less troubled than I, spoke for the Christian tradition when he said (as is alleged), "when you've seen one redwood tree, you've seen them all." To a Christian a tree can be no more than a physical fact. The whole concept of the sacred grove is alien to Christianity and to the ethos of the West. For nearly two millennia Christian missionaries have been chopping down sacred groves, which are idolatrous because they assume spirit in nature.

What we do about ecology depends on our ideas of the man-nature relationship. More science and more technology are not going to get us out of the present ecologic crisis until we find a new religion, or rethink our old one. The beatniks, who are the basic revolutionaries of our time, show a sound instinct in their affinity for Zen Buddhism, which conceives of the man-nature relationship as very nearly the mirror image of the Christian view. Zen, however, is as deeply conditioned by Asian history as Christianity is by the experience of the West, and I am dubious of its viability among us.

Possibly we should ponder the greatest radical in Christian history since Christ: St. Francis of Assisi. The prime miracle of St. Francis is the fact that he did not end at the stake, as many of his left-wing followers did. He was so clearly heretical that a General of the Franciscan Order, St. Bonaventura, a great and perceptive Christian, tried to suppress the early accounts of Franciscanism. The key to an understanding of Francis is his belief in the virtue of humility—not merely for the individual but for man as a species. Francis tried to depose man from his monarchy over creation and set up a democracy of all God's creatures. With him the ant is no longer simply a homily for the lazy, flames a sign of the thrust of the soul toward union with God; now they are Brother Ant and Sister Fire, praising the Creator in their own ways as Brother Man does in his.

Later commentators have said that Francis preached to the birds as a rebuke to men who would not listen. The records do not read so: he urged the little birds to praise God, and in spiritual ecstasy they flapped their wings and chirped rejoicing. Legends of saints, especially the Irish saints, had long told of their dealings with animals but always, I believe, to show their human dominance over creatures. With Francis it is different. The land around Gubbio in the Apennines was being ravaged by a fierce wolf. St. Francis, says the legend, talked to the wolf and persuaded him of the error of his ways. The wolf repented, died in the odor of sanctity, and was buried in consecrated ground.

What Sir Steven Runciman calls "the Franciscan doctrine of the animal soul" was quickly stamped out. Quite possibly it was in part inspired, consciously or unconsciously, by the belief in reincarnation held by the Cathar heretics who at that time teemed in Italy and southern France, and who presumably had got it originally from India. It is significant that at just the same moment, about 1200, traces of metempsychosis are found also in western Judaism, in the Provençal *Cabbala*. But Francis held neither to transmigration of souls nor to pantheism. His view of nature and of man rested on a unique sort of pan-psychism of all things animate and inanimate, designed for the glorification of their transcendent Creator, who, in the ultimate gesture of cosmic humility, assumed flesh, lay helpless in a manger, and hung dying on a scaffold.

I am not suggesting that many contemporary Americans who are concerned about our ecologic crisis will be either able or willing to counsel with wolves or exhort birds. However, the present increasing disruption of the global environment is the product of a dynamic technology and science which were originating in the Western medieval world against which St. Francis was rebelling in so original a way. Their growth cannot be understood historically apart from distinctive attitudes toward nature which are deeply grounded in Christian dogma. The fact that most people do not think of these attitudes as Christian is irrelevant. No new set of basic values has been accepted in our society to displace those of Christianity. Hence we shall continue to have a worsening ecologic crisis until we reject the Christian axiom that nature has no reason for existence save to serve man.

The greatest spiritual revolutionary in Western history, St. Francis, proposed what he thought was an alternative Christian view of nature and man's relation to it: he tried to substitute the idea of the equality of all creatures, including man, for the idea of man's limitless rule of creation. He failed. Both our present science and our present technology are so tinctured with orthodox Christian arrogance toward nature that no solution for our ecologic crisis can be expected from them alone. Since the roots of our trouble are so largely religious, the remedy must also be essentially religious, whether we call it that or not. We must rethink and refeel our nature and destiny. The profoundly religious, but heretical, sense of the primitive Franciscans for the spiritual autonomy of all parts of nature may point a direction. I propose Francis as a patron saint for ecologists.

"THE ECOLOGICAL CRISIS: A COMMON RESPONSIBILITY"

Pope John Paul II

Message of His Holiness Pope John Paul II
For the Celebration of the World Day of Peace
1 January 1990
Vatican City
Peace with God the Creator, Peace with All of Creation

INTRODUCTION

1. In our day, there is a growing awareness that world peace is threatened not only by the arms race, regional conflicts and continued injustices among peoples and nations, but also by a lack of *due respect for nature*, by the plundering of natural resources and by a progressive decline in the quality of life. The sense of precariousness and insecurity that such a situation engenders is a seedbed for collective selfishness, disregard for others and dishonesty.

Faced with the widespread destruction of the environment, people everywhere are coming to understand that we cannot continue to use the goods of the earth as we have in the past. The public in general as well as political leaders are concerned about this problem, and experts from a wide range of disciplines are studying its causes. Moreover, a new *ecological awareness* is beginning to emerge which, rather than being downplayed, ought to be encouraged to develop into concrete programmes and initiatives.

2. Many ethical values, fundamental to the development of a *peaceful society*, are particularly relevant to the ecological question. The fact that many challenges facing the world today are interdependent confirms the need for carefully coordinated solutions based on a morally coherent world view.

For Christians, such a world view is grounded in religious convictions drawn from Revelation. That is why I should like to begin this Message with a reflection on the biblical account of creation. I would hope that even those who do not share these same beliefs will find in these pages a common ground for reflection and action.

Reprinted with permission of the Apostolic Nunciature, Washington, D.C.

I. "AND GOD SAW THAT IT WAS GOOD"

3. In the Book of Genesis, where we find God's first self-revelation to humanity (*Gen* 1–3), there is a recurring refrain: "*And God saw that it was good.*" After creating the heavens, the sea, the earth and all it contains, God created man and woman. At this point the refrain changes markedly: "And God saw everything that he had made, and behold, *it was very good*" (*Gen* 1:31). God entrusted the whole of creation to the man and woman, and only then—as we read—could he rest "from all his work" (*Gen* 2:3).

Adam and Eve's call to share in the unfolding of God's plan of creation brought into play those abilities and gifts which distinguish the human being from all other creatures. At the same time, their call established a fixed relationship between mankind and the rest of creation. Made in the image and likeness of God, Adam and Eve were to have exercised their dominion over the earth (*Gen* 1:28) with wisdom and love. Instead, they destroyed the existing harmony *by deliberately going against the Creator's plan*, that is, by choosing to sin. This resulted not only in man's alienation from himself, in death and fratricide, but also in the earth's "rebellion" against him (cf. *Gen* 3:17–19; 4:12). All of creation became subject to futility, waiting in a mysterious way to be set free and to obtain a glorious liberty together with all the children of God (cf. *Rom* 8:20–21).

4. Christians believe that the Death and Resurrection of Christ accomplished the work of reconciling humanity to the Father, who "was pleased . . . through (Christ) to reconcile to himself *all things,* whether on earth or in heaven, making peace by the blood of his cross" (*Col* 1:19–20). Creation was thus made new (cf. *Rev* 21:5). Once subjected to the bondage of sin and decay (cf. *Rom* 8:21), it has now received new life while "we wait for new heavens and a new earth in which righteousness dwells" (*2 Pt* 3:13). Thus, the Father "has made known to us in all wisdom and insight the mystery . . . which he set forth in Christ as a plan for the fulness of time, to unite *all things* in him, all things in heaven and things on earth" (*Eph* 1:9–10).

5. These biblical considerations help us to understand better *the relationship between human activity and the whole of creation.* When man turns his back on the Creator's plan, he provokes a disorder which has inevitable repercussions on the rest of the created order. If man is not at peace with God, then earth itself cannot be at peace: "Therefore the land mourns and all who dwell in it languish, and also the beasts of the field and the birds of the air and even the fish of the sea are taken away" (*Hos* 4:3).

The profound sense that the earth is "suffering" is also shared by those who do not profess our faith in God. Indeed, the increasing devastation of the world of nature is apparent to all. It results from the behavior of people who show a callous disregard for the hidden, yet perceivable requirements of the order and harmony which govern nature itself.

People are asking anxiously if it is still possible to remedy the damage which has been done. Clearly, an adequate solution cannot be found merely in a better management or a more rational use of the earth's resources, as important as these may be. Rather, we must go to the source of the problem and face in its entirety that profound moral crisis *of which the destruction of the environment is only one troubling aspect.*

II. THE ECOLOGICAL CRISIS: A MORAL PROBLEM

6. Certain elements of today's ecological crisis reveal its moral character. First among these is the *indiscriminate application* of advances in science and technology. Many recent discoveries have brought undeniable benefits to humanity. Indeed, they demonstrate the nobility of the human vocation to participate *responsibly* in God's creative action in the world. Unfortunately, it is now clear that the application of these discoveries in the fields of industry and agriculture have produced harmful long-term effects. This has led to the painful realization that *we cannot interfere in one area of the ecosystem without paying due attention both to the consequences of such interference in other areas and to the well-being of future generations.*

The gradual depletion of the ozone layer and the related "greenhouse effect" has now reached crisis proportions as a consequence of industrial growth, massive urban concentrations and vastly increased energy needs. Industrial waste, the burning of fossil fuels, unrestricted deforestation, the use of certain types of herbicides, coolants and propellants: all of these are known to harm the atmosphere and environment. The resulting meteorological and atmospheric changes range from damage to health to the possible future submersion of low-lying lands.

While in some cases the damage already done may well be irreversible, in many other cases it can still be halted. It is necessary, however, that the entire human community—individuals, States and international bodies—take seriously the responsibility that is theirs.

7. The most profound and serious indication of the moral implications underlying the ecological problem is the lack of *respect for life* evident in many of the patterns of environmental pollution. Often, the interests of production prevail over concern for the dignity of workers, while economic interests take priority over the good of individuals and even entire peoples. In these cases, pollution or environmental destruction is the result of an unnatural and reductionist vision which at times leads to a genuine contempt for man.

On another level, delicate ecological balances are upset by the uncontrolled destruction of animal and plant life or by a reckless exploitation of natural resources. It should be pointed out that all of this, even if carried out in the name of progress and well-being, is ultimately to mankind's disadvantage.

Finally, we can only look with deep concern at the enormous possibilities of biological research. We are not yet in a position to assess the biological disturbance that could result from indiscriminate genetic manipulation and from the unscrupulous development of new forms of plant and animal life, to say nothing of unacceptable experimentation regarding the origins of human life itself. It is evident to all that in any area as delicate as this, indifference to fundamental ethical norms, or their rejection, would lead mankind to the very threshold of self-destruction.

Respect for life, and above all for the dignity of the human person, is the ultimate guiding norm for any sound economic, industrial or scientific progress.

The complexity of the ecological question is evident to all. There are, however, certain underlying principles, which, while respecting the legitimate autonomy and the specific competence of those involved, can direct research towards adequate and lasting solutions. These principles are essential to the building of a peaceful society; *no peaceful society can afford to neglect either respect for life or the fact that there is an integrity to creation.*

III. IN SEARCH OF A SOLUTION

8. Theology, philosophy and science all speak of a harmonious universe, of a "cosmos" endowed with its own integrity, its own internal, dynamic balance. *This order must be respected.* The human race is called to explore this order, to examine it with due care and to make use of it while safeguarding its integrity.

On the other hand, the earth is ultimately *a common heritage, the fruits of which are for the benefit of all.* In the words of the Second Vatican Council, "God destined the earth and all it contains for the use of every individual and all peoples" (*Gaudium et Spes,* 69). This has direct consequences for the problem at hand. It is manifestly unjust that a privileged few should continue to accumulate excess goods, squandering available resources, while masses of people are living in conditions of misery at the very lowest level of subsistence. Today, the dramatic threat of ecological breakdown is teaching us the extent to which greed and selfishness—both individual and collective—are contrary to the order of creation, an order which is characterized by mutual interdependence.

9. The concepts of an ordered universe and a common heritage both point to the necessity of a *more internationally coordinated approach to the management of the earth's goods.* In many cases the effects of ecological problems transcend the borders of individual States; hence their solution cannot be found solely on the national level. Recently there have been some promising steps towards such international action, yet the existing mechanisms and bodies are clearly not adequate for the development of a comprehensive plan of action. Political obstacles, forms of exaggerated nationalism and economic interests—to mention only a few factors—impede international cooperation and long-term effective action.

The need for joint action on the international level *does not lessen the responsibility of each individual State.* Not only should each State join with others in implementing internationally accepted standards, but it should also make or facilitate necessary socio-economic adjustments within its own borders, giving special attention to the most vulnerable sectors of society. The State should also actively endeavor within its own territory to prevent destruction of the atmosphere and biosphere, by carefully monitoring, among other things, the impact of new technological or scientific advances. The State also has the responsibility of ensuring that its citizens are not exposed to dangerous pollutants or toxic wastes. *The right to a safe environment* is ever more insistently presented today as a right that must be included in an updated Charter of Human Rights.

IV. THE URGENT NEED FOR A NEW SOLIDARITY

10. The ecological crisis reveals the *urgent moral need for a new solidarity*, especially in relations between the developing nations and those that are highly industrialized. States must increasingly share responsibility, in complementary ways, for the promotion of a natural and social environment that is both peaceful and healthy. The newly industrialized States cannot, for example, be asked to apply restrictive environmental standards to their emerging industries unless the industrialized States first apply them within their own boundaries. At the same time, countries in the process of industrialization are not morally free to repeat the errors made in the past by others, and recklessly continue to damage the environment through industrial pollutants, radical deforestation or unlimited exploitation of non-renewable resources. In this context, there is urgent need to find a solution to the treatment and disposal of toxic wastes.

No plan or organization, however, will be able to effect the necessary changes unless world leaders are truly convinced of the absolute need for this new solidarity, which is demanded of them by the ecological crisis and which is essential for peace. *This need presents new opportunities for strengthening cooperative and peaceful relations among States.*

11. It must also be said that the proper ecological balance will not be found without *directly addressing the structural forms of poverty* that exist throughout the world. Rural poverty and unjust land distribution in many countries, for example, have led to subsistence farming and to the exhaustion of the soil. Once their land yields no more, many farmers move on to clear new land, thus accelerating uncontrolled deforestation, or they settle in urban centers which lack the infrastructure to receive them. Likewise, some heavily indebted countries are destroying their natural heritage, at the price of irreparable ecological imbalances, in order to develop new products for export. In the face of such situations it would be wrong to assign responsibility to the poor alone for the negative environmental consequences of their actions. Rather, the poor, to whom the earth is entrusted no less than to others, must be enabled to find a way out of their poverty. This will require a courageous reform of structures, as well as new ways of relating among peoples and States.

12. But there is another dangerous menace which threatens us, namely *war*. Unfortunately, modern science already has the capacity to change the environment for hostile purposes. Alterations of this kind over the long term could have unforeseeable and still more serious consequences. Despite the international agreements which prohibit chemical, bacteriological and biological warfare, the fact is that laboratory research continues to develop new offensive weapons capable of altering the balance of nature.

Today, any form of war on a global scale would lead to incalculable ecological damage. But even local or regional wars, however limited, not only destroy human life and social structures, but also damage the land, ruining crops and vegetation as well as poisoning the soil and water. The survivors of war are forced to begin a new life in very difficult environmental conditions, which in turn create situations of extreme social unrest, with further negative consequences for the environment.

13. Modern society will find no solution to the ecological problem unless it *takes a serious look at its life style*. In many parts of the world society is given to instant gratification and consumerism while remaining indifferent to the damage which these cause. As I have already stated, the seriousness of the ecological issue lays bare the depth of man's moral crisis. If an appreciation of the value of the human person and of human life is lacking, we will also lose interest in others and in the earth itself. Simplicity, moderation and discipline, as well as a spirit of sacrifice, must become a part of everyday life, lest all suffer the negative consequences of the careless habits of a few.

An education in ecological responsibility is urgent: responsibility for oneself, for others, and for the earth. This education cannot be rooted in mere sentiment or empty wishes. Its purpose cannot be ideological or political. It must not be based on a rejection of the modern world or a vague desire to return to some "paradise lost." Instead, a true education in responsibility entails a genuine conversion in ways of thought and behaviour. Churches and religious bodies, non-governmental and governmental organizations, indeed all members of society, have a precise role to play in such education. The first educator, however, is the family, where the child learns to respect his neighbor and to love nature.

14. *Finally, the aesthetic value of creation cannot be overlooked.* Our very contact with nature has a deep restorative power; contemplation of its magnificence imparts peace and serenity. The Bible speaks again and again of the goodness and beauty of creation, which is called to glorify God (cf. *Gen* 1:4ff; *Ps* 8:2; 104:1ff; *Wis* 13:3–5; *Sir* 39:16, 33; 43:1, 9). More difficult, perhaps, but no less profound, is the contemplation of the works of human ingenuity. Even cities can have a beauty all their own, one that ought to motivate people to care for their surroundings. Good urban planning is an important part of environmental protection, and respect for the natural contours of the land is an indispensable prerequisite for ecologically sound development. The relationship between a good aesthetic education and the maintenance of a healthy environment cannot be overlooked.

V. THE ECOLOGICAL CRISIS: A COMMON RESPONSIBILITY

15. Today, the ecological crisis has assumed such proportions as to be *the responsibility of everyone*. As I have pointed out, its various aspects demonstrate the need for concerted efforts aimed at establishing the duties and obligations that belong to individuals, peoples, States and the international community. This not only goes hand in hand with efforts to build true peace, but also confirms and reinforces those efforts in a concrete way. When the ecological crisis is set within the broader context of *the search for peace* within society, we can understand better the importance of giving attention to what the earth and its atmosphere are telling us: namely, that there is an order in the universe which must be respected, and that the human person, endowed with the capability of choosing freely, has a grave responsibility to preserve this order for the well-being of future generations. I wish to repeat that *the ecological crisis is a moral issue*.

Even men and women without any particular religious conviction, but with an acute sense of their responsibilities for the common good, recognize their obligation to contribute to the restoration of a healthy environment. All the more should men and women who believe in God the Creator, and who are thus convinced that there is a well-defined unity and order in the world, feel called to address the problem. Christians, in particular, realize that their responsibility within creation and their duty towards nature and the Creator are an essential part of their faith. As a result, they are conscious of a vast field of ecumenical and interreligious cooperation opening up before them.

16. At the conclusion of this Message, I should like to address directly my brothers and sisters in the Catholic Church, in order to remind them of their serious obligation to care for all of creation. The commitment of believers to a healthy environment for everyone stems directly from their belief in God the Creator, from their recognition of the effects of original and personal sin, and from the certainty of having been redeemed by Christ. Respect for life and for the dignity of the human person extends also to the rest of creation, which is called to join man in praising God (cf. *Ps* 148:96).

In 1979, I proclaimed Saint Francis of Assisi as the heavenly Patron of those who promote ecology (cf. Apostolic Letter *Inter Sanctos*: AS 71 [1979], 1509f.). He offers Christians an example of genuine and deep respect for the integrity of creation. As a friend of the poor who was loved by God's creatures, Saint Francis invited all of creation—animals, plants, natural forces, even Brother Sun and Sister Moon—to give honor and praise to the Lord. The poor man of Assisi gives us striking witness that when we are at peace with God we are better able to devote ourselves to building up that peace with all creation which is inseparable from peace among all peoples.

It is my hope that the inspiration of Saint Francis will help us to keep ever alive a sense of "fraternity" with all those good and beautiful things which Almighty God has created. And may he remind us of our serious obligation to respect and watch over them with care, in light of that greater and higher fraternity that exists within the human family.

From the Vatican, 8 December 1989.
Joannes Paulus II

"CREATION AND THE COVENANT OF CARING"

American Baptist Churches USA

Christians believe that the whole creation is God's handiwork and belongs to God (Psalm 24:1). The creation has value in itself because God created and values it (Proverbs 8:29–31). God delights in the creation and desires its wholeness and well-being.

God created the earth, affirmed that it was good, and established an everlasting covenant with humanity to take responsibility for the whole of creation. God declares all of creation good. Our proper perspective on all activity on the earth flows directly from our affirmation of God as Creator.

The earth belongs to God, as affirmed in Psalm 24:1. We are caretakers or stewards. Thus we are each related to God as one appointed to take care of someone else's possessions entrusted to us—our life, our home, the earth. The vast resources of the earth can provide for all its inhabitants, or they can be greedily swallowed up or poisoned by a few without regard for the impact of their actions.

The best understanding of the Biblical attitude of humanity's relationship with the Creation can be gained by a study of the Greek words which are the foundation of the New Testament. The word "stewardship" comes from the Greek words for house and management. The Greek word which is commonly translated "stewardship" is the root word for economics and ecology. The literal translation of steward is manager of the household. As such, we are all called to be managers of God's household, the earth and all that is in it.

Our responsibility as stewards is one of the most basic relationships we have with God. It implies a great degree of caring for God's creation and all God's creatures. The right relationship is embodied in the everlasting covenant to which Isaiah refers. There can be no justice without right relationships of creatures with one another and with all of creation. Eco-justice is the vision of the garden in Genesis—the realm and the reality of right relationship.

God has given humans tremendously creative capacities. The development of science has enabled us to understand the inherent capabilities of the resources God gave. Modern scientific technology has provided thousands of ways of applying scientific knowledge to improve our lives. It is a powerful tool, and one of the gifts God has given us.

Reprinted with permission of National Ministries, American Baptist Churches USA, from *Our Only Home: Planet Earth,* 1991, Owen D. Owens, ed., pp. 34–39.

Technology holds the possibility of both good and evil, life and death. We are given the responsibility to choose: "I set before you life or death, blessing or curse. Choose life, then so that you and your descendants may live . . . " (Deuteronomy 30:19). It is our responsibility as stewards to require that technology be used for the good and that the harmful effects of its use (or misuse) be mitigated or prevented.

RESPONSIBILITY—INDIVIDUAL AND CORPORATE

The image of God within us makes it possible for people to be aware and responsive to God's self-revelation in the creation. We have the gift of God which enables us to perceive and reflect upon the life within us and around us. The distinctive human vocation is to bring creation's beauty and order to consciousness and to express God's image within us by caring for the creation.

In the ability God has given us to make choices also lies inherent danger. We can choose to disobey, to be irresponsible, to disrupt and disturb the peaceable relationship of creature and creation. We can choose to use nature's resources only for what we perceive is our own immediate interest. Such action is sin. It is a violation of the basic covenant wherein we are called to stewardship. It is an unfaithful refusal of the responsibility entrusted to us. Often we tend to think of sin in terms of individual actions. Yet decisions and actions which we make as groups, communities and societies constitute corporate sin. These corporate decisions and actions reflect values and interests which conflict with the vision of shalom and eco-justice consistent with created order. Our task is to discern the conflict and to choose ways of living which build an eco-just community and world.

JESUS—A MODEL FOR TAKING SIDES

Jesus' ministry provides a model for choosing sides. He is clear about where his loyalty lies. In his earliest reported reading of scripture in public, he chooses, Luke tells us, to read from the prophet Isaiah. He proclaims that his mission is to serve the poor, the captives, and the downtrodden—the victims of social injury. He further states that he will "proclaim the acceptable year of the Lord." This is the Jubilee Year of Leviticus 25, a year of land reform. It is a recognition that all land basically and ultimately belongs to God, and that no person or group has the right to destroy it or to use it unendingly for unjust personal or institutional gain.

AMERICAN BAPTIST POLICY STATEMENT ON ECOLOGY

The study of ecology has become a religious, social and political concern because every area of life is affected by careless use of our environment. The creation is in crisis. We believe that ecology and justice, stewardship of creation and redemption are interdependent.

Our task is to proclaim the Good News of Jesus Christ until the coming of the Kingdom on Earth. All God's people must be guided by the balance of reverence, the acknowledgement of our interdependence, the integrity of divine wholeness and the need for empowerment by the Holy Spirit to image God by our dominion over creation (Mark 10:43–45). If we image God we will reflect in our dominion the love and the care that God has for the whole creation, "for God so loved the world . . . " (John 3:16, Romans 8:21–22, Matthew 5:43–48). Jesus told us to let your light so shine that others may see the good things you do and praise God (Matthew 5:16).

The Bible affirms, "The earth is the Lord's and the fullness thereof, the world and they that dwell therein" (Psalms 24:1). As Christians we believe that the whole universe reveals God's manifold works. God continues to create as well as to redeem. God asks us not only to call persons to redemption but also to teach them to be wise stewards, tenderly caring for God's creation.

Today the human race faces an unprecedented challenge to rediscover the role of steward in a time of extraordinary peril and promise. The explosive growth of population, the depletion of nonrenewable resources, tropical deforestation, the pollution of air, land, and water, waste of precious materials and the general assault on God's creation, springing from greed, arrogance and ignorance present the possibility of irreversible damage to the intricate, natural systems upon which life depends. At the same time nuclear weapons threaten the planet. They have the capability not only of destroying human life on a massive scale but also of poisoning and altering the environment in ways that would render much of the planet incapable of sustaining life. The danger is real and great. Churches and individual Christians must take responsibility to God and neighbor seriously and respond (Eph. 2:10).

Ironically, science and technology have multiplied many times the ecological threat. The very instruments that brought great blessing—and still hold much promise—now threaten to bring disaster unless they are used in concert rather than in conflict with the created order.

God made a world that is good in reality and potential, but our enslavement to modern industrial images of civilization hinders our ability to envision God's created order. According to our Native-American Christian sisters and brothers, we are causing the earth to self-destruct, and then we are dying of loneliness for our ruined lands. This loneliness is best understood as an alienation from Creator and creation (Job 41:1–11, 42:5–6). We are dealing with the classic theological issues of a good Creator and creation, human sin and the fall into evil which requires radical repentance in response to the saving Gospel of Jesus Christ. Salvation cannot come to creation unless we repent and turn away from former lifestyles (Romans 8:12–14, 18–23).

The Creator-Redeemer seeks the renewal of the creation and calls the people of God to participate in saving acts of renewal. We are called to cooperate with God in the transformation of a fallen world that has not fulfilled its divinely given potential for beauty, peace, health, harmony, justice and joy (Isa. 11:6–9, Micah 4:3–4, Eph. 2:10, Rev. 21:1–5). Our task is nothing less than to join God in preserving, renewing and fulfilling the creation. It is to relate to nature in ways that sustain life on the planet, provide for the essential material and physical needs of all humankind, and increase justice and well-being for all life in a peaceful world.

A wise and responsible people will recognize the increasing interdependence of all humankind in an emerging planetary society. In our time we must provide opportunities for all to grow and thrive. The fortunate who tolerate misery, strife and terrorism elsewhere, can stay safe themselves no longer. In a quest for survival, justice, and peace, we are "members one of another" (Rom. 12:5). The neighbor whom we are commanded to love is everyone (Luke 10:27), including those yet to be born who depend on us to leave them a habitable earth. Because God is our deliverer, we must recognize sin and refuse to participate in it.

Ecology and justice are inseparable. The threat to the global environment presents American Baptists with a call for prompt and vigorous response. As Christians and faithful stewards, we bear the responsibility to affirm and support programs, legislation, research and organizations that protect and restore the vulnerable and the oppressed, the earth as well as the poor. This responsibility for a habitable environment is not just for human life, but for all life. A stewardship that will fulfill this responsibility will be guided by the norms of solidarity, as we stand with the vulnerable creation and work with its defenders; sustainability, as we devise social systems that maintain the balance of nature, and sufficiency, as we give priority to basic sustenance for all life.

Therefore, we call on all of the members of the American Baptist Churches of the USA to:

1. Affirm the goodness and beauty of God's creation.

2. Acknowledge our responsibility for stewardship of the Creator's good earth.

3. Learn of the environmental dangers facing the planet.

4. Recognize that our practices and styles of life have had an effect on the environment.

5. Pursue a lifestyle that is wise and responsible in light of our understanding of the problems.

6. Exert our influence in shaping public policy and insisting that industries, businesses, farmers and consumers relate to the environment in ways that are sensible, healthy and protective of its integrity.

7. Demonstrate concern with "the hope that is within us," as despair and apathy surround us in the world (Rom. 12:21).

8. Become involved in organizations and actions to protect and restore the environment and the people in our communities.

We call upon the National Boards, Regions and institutions of our denomination to:

9. Promote an attitude affirming that all nature has intrinsic value and that all life is to be honored and reverenced.

10. Seek ways and means to alert the churches to present and impending environment threats.

Adopted by the General Board of the American Baptist Churches—June 1989, 157 For, 0 Against, 0 Abstentions (General Board Reference #7040:12/88).

"BASIS FOR OUR CARING"

Evangelical Lutheran Church in America

The world beset by environmental problems is the world created, redeemed and sustained by God. The earth system that knows many-sided crises is the earth system we are called to serve.

In the words of our responsive prayer, we know that "awesome things will you show us in your righteousness, O God of our Salvation, O hope of all the ends of the earth and of the seas that are far away" (*Lutheran Book of Worship* [*LBW*], p. 162). Since God is Lord of heaven and earth, our longing is "eager longing for the revealing of the children of God" (Rom 8:19).

GOD, EARTH AND ALL CREATURES

GOD THE CREATOR

Scripture witnesses to God as maker of the earth and all that dwells therein (Ps 24:1). The witness begins in Genesis, continues in the psalms and prophets, and stands behind the claim that Jesus Christ died and was raised for the salvation of the world.

The God revealed to us as LORD (Yahweh), the God who brought Israel out of Egypt, the God who sent Israel into exile and brought her out again, the God who spoke of old by the prophets but who has now spoken to us by a Son (Heb 1:1–2)—this is the Creator. The God who is faithful, righteous, just and loving (Ps 33:4–5; 89:8–14) attends to creation faithfully, righteously, justly and lovingly.

The creeds, which guide our reading of Scripture, proclaim God the Father of Jesus Christ to be maker of heaven and earth. Jesus Christ is also the one "through whom all things were made" (Nicene Creed; cf. Jn 1:3; 1 Cor 8:6; Col 1:16; Heb 1:2–3). And the Holy Spirit is "the Lord, the giver of life" (Nicene Creed; cf. Gen 1:2; Ps 104:30). It is the one and triune God who creates the cosmos.

VALUE OF THE WORLD

God blesses the world and calls it good. The parts of creation are "good" (Gen 1:4, 10, 12, 18, 21, 25), and the whole of creation is "very good" (Gen 1:31) solely because of the grace of its good Creator. Creation is given its own integrity. It is intact and healthy, and its parts work in harmony.

God calls aspects of creation "good" before humanity comes on the scene. *All creation, not just human beings, is declared good from a divine perspective.* And God continues to care not just for people but also for animals (Gen 6–9), plants (Ps 147:8), and even deserts and wastelands (Job 38–41, esp. 38:25–27). The New Testament, too, tells of God's faithful care for all creation (Mt 5:45; 6:26–30; Lk 12:6–7; Acts 14:17). God is at work, sustaining the world (Jn 5:17).

God is linked to all creation through covenant: to all living creatures (Gen 8–9); to beasts of the field, birds of the air, and creeping things of the ground (Hos 2:18); and to night and day (Jer 33:20). To say that God is linked to creation through covenant is also to say that God is linked to creation through promise. God's very word guarantees creation. We and all creation live by that promise.

Good, But Not God

The world is good, but it is not God. Creation is good, but is nevertheless distinct from the Creator. Even though creation has honor as the work of God, those who worship it exchange truth for a lie (Rom 1:25; cf. Job 31:26–28). Creation worships the Creator (Ps 19; 96; 148).

God is "wholly other," the final reality beyond creaturely realities, the awesome and terrible mystery. Wholly other, God stands over and against creation as judge. Wholly other, God stands *for* creation as giver of free, sustaining and saving grace.

God's creation—very good but not divine—has the limitations observed in the current environmental crisis. A creation that is good but not God is finite, and lends itself to appropriate scientific analysis.

The Presence of God in Creation

The God who is wholly other is very near. God is deeply and compassionately involved in what happens to the planet. God does not choose to dominate creation with tyrannical power, however, and works in and through natural forces (as in Ps 104) and history (as in 2 Chr 36:22–23) to lead it to fulfillment.

God is intimately and irreversibly connected to all creation through the Incarnation, where infinite grace is carried by finite creation. In Christ, God takes on the earthly material of human life. Through Christ, God is reconciled to "all things, whether on earth or in heaven" (Col 1:20). The Incarnation has saving significance for a creation that longs for fulfillment (Rom 8:18–25), seen elsewhere in the Bible as heaven coming down to earth (Rev 21).

Evangelical Lutheran Church in America

The eternal Word of God became flesh and dwelled among us, teaching us how to live and move and have our being in creation. Unlike the foxes and birds, Jesus had nowhere to lay his head (Mt 8:20). Many of his parables, however, show he understood the land (Mt 13:32; Mk 4:26–29).

Jesus presents the world as a theatre of God's grace and glory, where lilies mirror God's glory (Mt 6:28–29) and birds display God's care (Mt 6:26). And Jesus acts in accordance with God's covenant to bring peace to creation, for example, by stilling the waters (Mk 4:35–41).

The eternal Word of God became human, lived as part of earthly creation, and comes to us in, with and under the elements of bread and wine. The sacraments underscore the intimate relationship between God and a nature that is neither unclean nor unspiritual. In a variety of ways, nature imparts God's faithfulness and loving kindness.

A FAMILY PORTRAIT

The Bible tells of the goodness of creation. The first photographs of the earth relayed from space a quarter of a century ago gave us a portrait of a good planet. On a seemingly endless and void background, the earth appeared as a shimmering planet glowing in the light of the sun.

An earth-bound audience now had a portrait of the planet God made: the blue oceans, the green and brown continents, the white clouds and ice caps. We now had a portrait of the family—diverse, often divided, bound together in one earth system where every part connects with every other part.

Our planet has been through a lot in its five billion years: continental drift, ice ages, volcanic eruptions. Changes in soil, air and water have meant the appearance or disappearance of various forms of life. Predators have lived at the expense of other creatures. They, too, have received their food from God (Ps 104:21).

The earth is very good. Neither demonic nor divine, neither meaningless nor sufficient unto itself, it receives its meaning and value from God. It is filled with God's glory and permeated by God's grace (Isa 6:3).

OUR VOCATION

HUMANITY AS PART OF NATURE

Humanity (in Hebrew, 'adam) is formed from dust of the ground (in Hebrew, 'adamah) (Gen 2:7). Out of the same ground the Creator causes trees to grow and makes beasts and birds. In *creation*, humans are connected to the earth and other living things.

In Isaiah's vision of redeemed creation, animals of all kinds—wolves and lambs, lions and calves, bears and cows—live peaceably together with the child and the serpent in a world united and filled with knowledge of the LORD (Isa 11:6–9). While Isaiah's vision need not be understood literally as a prediction of the future, it does show that in *redemption*, too, the bonds between humanity and other creatures remain intact.

The great creation Psalm 104 finds people joining wild goats, lions and birds in looking to God for sustenance. The Psalmist is joined by modern scientists in a vision of human beings, in their *day to day life*, as part of the earth system.

Throughout Scripture, heaven and earth and all living creatures witness to God's lordship and power. They bless God and sing praises to their Creator (Ps 148). In our hymn of praise we "join in the hymn of all creation" (*LBW*, p. 61; cf. Easter preface).

Humans and the rest of creation are bound together in creation, redemption, sustenance, praise and thanksgiving. It is right, therefore, to include nature in our understanding of humanity's relationship to God.

We stand as God's creatures within an orderly creation, our lives woven from threads of dependence and interdependence. We depend upon God, who gives us existence through interdependence with other human beings and with the rest of creation. We cannot be persons without other persons; we cannot be humans apart from other creatures.

WHAT GOD EXPECTS OF US

Humans are a part of nature, but with a special role on behalf of the whole. We receive dignity and responsibility that distinguishes us from the rest of creation. Our status (Gen 1; 2; Deut 4:32; Ps 8; 115:16; Lk 12:6–7) is affirmed when God becomes human.

Humans relate to God in distinctive ways: we are spiritually aware and morally accountable. This includes awareness of the significance of all creation, and accountability for the earth on which we depend.

Called to Be Neighbors to Other Creatures

When we say God is Creator, we acknowledge ourselves to be part of creation. The command to love the LORD and the neighbor (Deut 6:5; Lev 19:18; Mt 22:37–40) implies love for neighbors who are the whole of creation.

Throughout Scripture we find an interplay between concern for human benefit, and concern for the land and other living things. Strongly connected to love of self and human neighbor is love of the rest of creation. Linked to social justice is care for the environment.

Leviticus 25 brings together regard for social justice and regard for the earth. Along with the admonition "you shall not wrong one another" comes a provision for the land's jubilee or sabbath rest (Lev 25:4). The Creator blesses creation through rest from work (Gen 2:2); we have a sabbath (Gen 2:3; Ex 20:8–10); the land also has sabbath rest. Additionally, jubilee and sabbath regulations seem to view the welfare of both wild and domestic animals (esp. Lev 25:6–7; cf. Ex 23:10–11).

Human beings are given some responsibility for other creatures (Gen 1:26–30; 2:19). Humans are to respect trees (Deut 20:19–20) and animals (Ex 23:12; Deut 22:6–7; 25:4). God's promise is for all of creation (Gen 9); God's compassion is for all living things (cf. the deutero-canonical Sir 18:13). This implies humane treatment of living things in activities such as laboratory experimentation, meat production and hunting.

While trees may be harvested, and animals used for work and slaughtered for food (after the entrance of sin into the world), we are to care for them. Rules on slaughter of animals, especially in post-biblical Jewish tradition, may ensure humane treatment, as well as ritual correctness.

The Bible also acknowledges that God deals with creation in some ways unknown to, and independent of us (Job 39–41). Our wonder of God, whose purposes we cannot fathom, is thereby deepened. Our esteem for other creatures, who have a value apart from what we give them, is heightened.

Called to Live According to the Wisdom of God's Creation

Scripture invites us, in fact urges us as a matter of life and death, to live according to the wisdom of God—learning prudence, paying attention, ordering our lives and our society according to the wisdom present at creation (Prov 8). The New Testament amplifies this by identifying Christ as the true Wisdom and Word of God (1 Cor 1:24; Eph 1:9; Col 2:3).

As God has called humanity to care for the earth, so God has given us the faculty for investigating the underlying wisdom and patterns of creation. In that sense, science is a modern counterpart to the wisdom of ancient Israel.

Dependent and interdependent creatures, we act correctly when we respect the wisdom and integrity of an earth system where human and other sorts of life flourish. In wisdom we know the limits of the earth system. These limits determine what we can do, and necessitate wise political, social and economic courses of action.

Although the face of the earth has changed over the centuries, often through degradation by humans, the same scientific laws are in operation. Political, social and economic conditions to which we order our lives change radically over the centuries, but they, too, have a continuity. We are no less interdependent with creation than the people of ancient Israel, no less bound by God's demand for justice.

Called to Serve and Keep the Earth

Part of humanity's job description is given in Genesis 2. There, the newly created human is placed by God in the fruitful garden and instructed to serve (in Hebrew, '*abad*) and keep (in Hebrew, *shamar*) the garden (Gen 2:15). These very verbs, often translated as "to till and to keep," are also used for serving and guarding God's temple and the tent of meeting in the wilderness (Num 3:7, 8; 4:47; 16:9).

As with the Garden of Eden, God entrusts the earth to us to serve and to protect. Serving and protecting are sacred tasks: we care for the earth as God's temple, in gratitude for God's care for us (Ps 121). Stewardship, in this environmental context, means serving life-giving cycles and rhythms of creation through restrained and creative intervention.

Called to Be God's Representatives

The cultures that surrounded ancient Israel saw only their kings—sons of the god—as an image of the divine. For Israel, all humanity was created in the image of God, after God's likeness (Gen 1:26). The myths of neighboring cultures presented humans as slaves of the gods. For Israel to say that human beings have dominion over the earth (Gen 1:28; Ps 8) was to affirm the dignity of all human beings, not to debase the rest of creation.

Made in the image of God and designated royal children of God, humans have the task of caring for the earth as representatives of God. Their dominion is to be in the image of God's dominion. "Dominion," however, is frequently removed from its proper setting and used to justify uncaring attitudes and destructive behavior toward the earth and its people.

There are other facts about dominion, a biblical yet easily misused term. *First*, having dominion does not mean that humans cease to be part of creation. We may differ qualitatively from other creatures in our ability to understand and influence the world. But we are still interdependent with the rest of creation; our power is *with* creation.

Second, the language of dominion sounded different to ancient Israelites, as compared to people with modern science and high technology. The people of biblical times were far more vulnerable to the power *of* nature. We, on the other hand, unleash considerable power *upon* nature. They could not cause global environmental disaster; we can.

Third, as God's representatives we must follow God's way of being sovereign—serving justly, loyally, compassionately (2 Sam 23; Ps 89; Isa 42:1–2; 49:1–6; 50:4–11; 52:13–53:12). As we sing at vespers: "You [God] are merciful, and you love your whole creation" (*LBW*,

p. 144). God's way of being sovereign is clearly shown on the cross; it is self-giving (Jn 3:16; Phil 2:5–11).

SIN

FALLEN HUMANITY

Humanity has been driven from the garden (Gen 3:24). We have placed our highest loyalty and trust in something other than God. We have looked to ourselves or to things of our own making for ultimate security, meaning and purpose. Sometimes we have presumed ourselves to be masters of the universe. Sometimes we have made a god of nature itself—viewing it as ultimate, and considering its welfare apart from human needs.

We have sinned. In our desire to be like God (Gen 3:5–6), we have rejected the fact that we are creatures. We have lost sight of our place in creation, and have not done what God has called us to do on behalf of creation.

Sinners all, we threaten the creation. We oppress human and other neighbors in the name of nation, race, gender or ideology. We wreak social injustice and environmental degradation upon the earth. Sloth or cowardice then prevent us from rising to defend a creation that includes ourselves from the prospect of destruction.

Some environmental destruction is the accidental consequence of well-intentioned, well-designed ideas. Even our best efforts can fail. But when ignorance becomes invincible through denial, when misinterpretation results from self-serving bias, when comfort and convenience take priority over care-giving, when demands arise from infinite greed rather than finite need—sin is at work.

Churches have often mistaken domination for dominion, and acquiesced to life-styles and structures of exploitation. By leaving unchallenged such distorted ideas of God's will for creation, or by actively promoting them, they have contributed to a sinful state of affairs.

DISRUPTION OF CREATION

Scripture sees human sin as disrupting the rest of creation. Nature witnesses to God's covenant with Israel; nature reacts to Israel's unfaithfulness (Deut 11:13–17). When Israel obeys God's commands and acts in justice, the earth is blessed. But when Israel forgets her part of the covenant and ignores God's command to do justice, all nature cries out. Curses replace blessing.

Perhaps the most dramatic reaction to human injustice is recorded in Jeremiah's haunting vision of a creation reversed so that the earth finally appears before him as wasted and void. There are no mountains or hills, no humans or birds, no fruitful land or cities, no light in the heavens. There is only desolation (Jer 4:23–28).

Today we know well the danger of desolation caused by human sin. Patterns of social injustice have led to chaos in the environment. And the converse is also true: environmental degradation has intensified social injustice.

HOPE

FORGIVENESS

Massive degradation, suffering by humanity and the rest of creation—such are the signs of our failure to follow God's call. Hope for creation is possible, nevertheless, because of God's promise. Working graciously within both natural forces and history, God overcomes our failure and brings the universe to its intended destiny.

Against the threat of desolation, God comes as Savior of the world. God loves the world, to the point of experiencing the evil and death brought about by sin. *Through the death and resurrection of Christ, God does not save us FROM the world, but saves us AND the world.*

Beginning at the cross of Christ, we give up our pursuit of security and our arrogance toward the rest of creation. God's forgiveness enables us to see what we have done to one another and to the earth. Freed by forgiveness from the paralysis of guilt, regret and remorse, we serve and protect the victims of environmental degradation.

Life in Christ gives us the vision and confidence to follow our vocation on behalf of all creation. As we live in hope, and care for creation, we know the Holy Spirit is at work within nature and history. "The Lord and giver of life" restores the broken bonds of community among people, and between human beings and the rest of creation.

FULFILLMENT

God does not just *heal* a creation wounded by human sin; God *perfects* that creation. Although nature itself has not sinned or "fallen," it looks forward to a final fulfillment. Once again: creation hopes for liberation (Rom 8:18–25); "all things" are reconciled to God through the cross (Col 1:15–20).

To say that Christ died for forests and fish as well as for human beings is admittedly rather surprising. The idea does not startle us so much when we remember our dependent and interdependent relationships. We are fully human only with our environment. Since we are saved, there must be a sense in which the environment is saved as well.

Christian hope is not for human destiny only. The Creator of all things is also the Redeemer of all things.

"EVANGELICAL DECLARATION ON THE ENVIRONMENT"

Created by the Evangelical Environmental Network and signed by hundreds of Evangelical Christian ministers, organizational leaders, theologians and lay members

ON THE CARE OF CREATION

The Earth is the Lord's, and the fulness thereof. Psalm 24:1

As followers of Jesus Christ, committed to the full authority of the *Scriptures*, and aware of the ways we have degraded creation, we believe that biblical faith is essential to the solution of our ecological problems.

Because we worship and honor the Creator, we seek to cherish and care for the creation.

Because we have sinned, we have failed in our stewardship of creation. Therefore we repent of the way we have polluted, distorted, or destroyed so much of the Creator's work.

Because in Christ God has healed our alienation from God and extended to us the first fruits of the reconciliation of all things, we commit ourselves to working in the power of the Holy Spirit to share the Good News of Christ in word and deed, to work for the reconciliation of all people in Christ, and to extend Christ's healing to suffering creation.

Because we await the time when even the groaning creation will be restored to wholeness, we commit ourselves to work vigorously to protect and heal that creation for the honor and glory of the Creator—whom we know dimly through creation, but meet fully through Scripture and in Christ. We and our children face a growing crisis in the health of the creation in which we are embedded, and through which, by God's grace, we are sustained. Yet we continue to degrade that creation.

These degradations of creation can be summed up as 1) land degradation; 2) deforestation; 3) species extinction; 4) water degradation; 5) global toxification; 6) the alteration of atmosphere; 7) human and cultural degradation.

The history of this declaration is described in *The Care of Creation: Focusing Concern and Action*, R. J. Berry, ed. (Leicester: IVP). See chapter 3 by Loren Wilkinson.

Many of these degradations are signs that we are pressing against the finite limits God has set for creation. With continued population growth, these degradations will become more severe. Our responsibility is not only to bear and nurture children, but to nurture their home on earth. We respect the institution of marriage as the way God has given to insure thoughtful procreation of children and their nurture to the glory of God.

We recognize that human poverty is both a cause and a consequence of environmental degradation.

Many concerned people, convinced that environmental problems are more spiritual than technological, are exploring the world's ideologies and religions in search of non-Christian spiritual resources for the healing of the earth. As followers of Jesus Christ, we believe that the Bible calls us to respond in four ways:

First, God calls us to confess and repent of attitudes which devalue creation, and which twist or ignore biblical revelation to support our misuse of it. Forgetting that "the earth is the Lord's," we have often simply used creation and forgotten our responsibility to care for it.

Second, our actions and attitudes toward the earth need to proceed from the center of our faith, and be rooted in the fullness of God's revelation in Christ and the Scriptures. We resist both ideologies which would presume the Gospel has nothing to do with the care of non-human creation and also ideologies which would reduce the Gospel to nothing more than the care of that creation.

Third, we seek carefully to learn all that the Bible tells us about the Creator, creation, and the human task. In our life and words we declare that full good news for all creation which is still waiting "with eager longing for the revealing of the children of God" (Rom. 8:19).

Fourth, we seek to understand what creation reveals about God's divinity, sustaining presence, and everlasting power, and what creation teaches us of its God-given order and the principles by which it works.

Thus we call on all those who are committed to the truth of the Gospel of Jesus Christ to affirm the following principles of biblical faith, and to seek ways of living out these principles in our personal lives, our churches, and society.

The cosmos, in all its beauty, wildness, and life-giving bounty, is the work of our personal and loving Creator.

Our creating God is prior to and other than creation, yet intimately involved with it, upholding each thing in its freedom, and all things in relationships of intricate complexity. God is transcendent, while lovingly sustaining each creature; and immanent, while wholly other than creation and not to be confused with it.

God the Creator is relational in very nature, revealed as three persons in One. Likewise, the creation which God intended is a symphony of individual creatures in harmonious relationship.

The Creator's concern is for all creatures. God declares all creation "good" (Gen. 1:31); promises care in a covenant with all creatures (Gen. 9:9–17); delights in creatures which have no human apparent usefulness (Job 39–41); and wills, in Christ, "to reconcile all things to himself" (Col. 1:20).

Men, women, and children have a unique responsibility to the Creator; at the same time we are creatures, shaped by the same processes and embedded in the same systems of physical, chemical, and biological interconnections which sustain other creatures.

Men, women, and children created in God's image, also have a unique responsibility for creation. Our actions should both sustain creation's fruitfulness and preserve creation's powerful testimony to its Creator.

Our God-given, stewardly talents have often been warped from their intended purpose: that we know, name, keep and delight in God's creatures; that we nourish civilization in love, creativity and obedience to God; and that we offer creation and civilization back in praise to the Creator. We have ignored our creaturely limits and have used the earth with greed, rather than care.

The earthly result of human sin has been a perverted stewardship, a patchwork of garden and wasteland in which the waste is increasing. "There is no faithfulness, no love, no acknowledgment of God in the land . . . Because of this the land mourns, and all who live in it waste away" (Hosea 4:1,3). Thus, one consequence of our misuse of the earth is an unjust denial of God's created bounty to other human beings, both now and in the future.

God's purpose in Christ is to heal and bring to wholeness not only persons but the entire created order. "For God was pleased to have all his fullness dwell in him, and through him to reconcile to himself all things, whether things on earth or things in heaven, by making peace through his blood shed on the cross" (Col. 1:19–20).

In Jesus Christ, believers are forgiven, transformed and brought into God's kingdom. "If anyone is in Christ, there is a new creation" (II Cor. 5:17). The presence of the kingdom of God is marked not only by renewed fellowship with God, but also by renewed harmony and justice between people, and by renewed harmony and justice between people and the rest of the created world. "You will go out in joy and be led forth in peace; the mountains and the hills will burst into song before you, and all the trees of the field will clap their hands" (Isa. 55:12).

We believe that in Christ there is hope, not only for men, women and children, but also for the rest of creation which is suffering from the consequences of human sin.

Therefore we call upon all Christians to reaffirm that all creation is God's; that God created it good, and that God is renewing it in Christ.

We encourage deeper reflection on the substantial biblical and theological teaching which speaks of God's work of redemption in terms of the renewal and completion of God's purpose in creation.

We seek a deeper reflection on the wonders of God's creation and the principles by which creation works. We also urge a careful consideration of how our corporate and individual actions respect and comply with God's ordinances for creation.

We encourage Christians to incorporate the extravagant creativity of God into their lives by increasing the nurturing role of beauty and the arts in their personal, ecclesiastical, and social patterns.

We urge individual Christians and churches to be centers of creation's care and renewal, both delighting in creation as God's gift, and enjoying it as God's provision, in ways which sustain and heal the damaged fabric of the creation which God has entrusted to us.

We recall Jesus's words that our lives do not consist in the abundance of our possessions, and therefore we urge followers of Jesus to resist the allure of wastefulness and overconsumption by making personal lifestyle choices that express humility, forbearance, self restraint and frugality.

We call on all Christians to work for godly, just, and sustainable economies which reflect God's sovereign economy and enable men, women and children to flourish along with all the diversity of creation. We recognize that poverty forces people to degrade creation in order to survive; therefore we support the development of just, free economies which empower the poor and create abundance without diminishing creation's bounty.

We commit ourselves to work for responsible public policies which embody the principles of biblical stewardship of creation.

We invite Christians—individuals, congregations and organizations—to join with us in this evangelical declaration on the environment, becoming a covenant people in an ever-widening circle of biblical care for creation.

We call upon Christians to listen to and work with all those who are concerned about the healing of creation, with an eagerness both to learn from them and also to share with them our conviction that the God whom all people sense in creation (Acts 17:27) is known fully only in the Word made flesh in Christ the living God who made and sustains all things.

We make this declaration knowing that until Christ returns to reconcile all things, we are called to be faithful stewards of God's good garden, our earthly home.

"ADDRESS OF HIS ALL HOLINESS ECUMENICAL PATRIARCH BARTHOLOMEW"

Our Beloved Brother in Christ, Archbishop Spyridon of America,

Our Beloved Brother in Christ, Bishop Anthony of San Francisco,

The Honorable Secretary of the Interior, Mr. Bruce Babbitt,

Distinguished Scholars, Learned Guests,

Beloved Friends and Children in the Lord,

It is with deep joy that we greet all of you, the honorable delegates and attendees of this blessed Symposium on the Sacredness of the Environment. Here in this historical city of Santa Barbara, we see before us a brilliant example of the wonder of God's creation. Recently, that God-given beauty was threatened by an oil spill. We are proud that the effort to restore the damaged beauty of Santa Barbara's seas, was led by Orthodox Christians, Dan and Candy Randopoulos.

The Ecumenical Throne of Orthodoxy, as a preserver and herald of the ancient Patristic tradition and of the rich liturgical experience of the Orthodox Church, today renews its long standing commitment to healing the environment. We have followed with great interest and sincere concern, the efforts to curb the destructive effects that human beings have wrought upon the natural world. We view with alarm the dangerous consequences of humanity's disregard for the survival of God's creation.

It is for this reason that our predecessor, the late Patriarch Dimitrios, of blessed memory, invited the whole world to offer, together with the Great Church of Christ, prayers of thanksgiving and supplications for the protection of the gift of creation. Since 1989, every September 1st, the beginning of the ecclesiastical calendar has been designated as a day of prayer for the protection of the environment, throughout the Orthodox world.

Since that time, the Ecumenical Throne has organized an Inter-Orthodox Conference in Crete in 1991, and convened annual Ecological Seminars at the historic Monastery of the Holy Trinity on Halki, as a way of discerning the spiritual roots and principles of the

Address of His All Holiness Ecumenical Patriarch Bartholomew at the Environmental Symposium at the Santa Barbara Greek Orthodox Church, Santa Barbara, California, 8 November 1997. Used by permission of His All Holiness Ecumenical Patriarch Bartholomew.

ecological crisis. In 1995, we sponsored a symposium, sailing the Aegean to the island of Patmos. The symposium on Revelation and the Environment, AD 95 to 1995, commemorated the 1900th anniversary of the recording of the Apocalypse. We have recently convened a trans-national conference on the Black Sea ecological crisis, that included participation of all the nations that border the sea.

In these and other programs, we have sought to discover the measures that may be implemented by Orthodox Christians worldwide, as leaders desiring to contribute to the solution of this global problem. We believe that through our particular and unique liturgical and ascetic ethos, Orthodox Spirituality may provide significant moral and ethical direction toward a new generation of awareness about the planet.

We believe that Orthodox liturgy and life hold tangible answers to the ultimate questions concerning salvation from corruptibility and death. The Eucharist is at the very center of our worship. And our sin toward the world, or the spiritual root of all our pollution, lies in our refusal to view life and the world as a sacrament of thanksgiving, and as a gift of constant communion with God on a global scale.

We envision a new awareness that is not mere philosophical posturing, but a tangible experience of a mystical nature. We believe that our first task is to raise the consciousness of adults who most use the resources and gifts of the planet. Ultimately, it is for our children that we must perceive our every action in the world as having a direct effect upon the future of the environment. At the heart of the relationship between man and environment is the relationship between human beings. As individuals, we live not only in vertical relationships to God, and horizontal relationships to one another, but also in a complex web of relationships that extend throughout our lives, our cultures and the material world. Human beings and the environment form a seamless garment of existence; a complex fabric that we believe is fashioned by God.

People of all faith traditions praise the Divine, for they seek to understand their relationship to the cosmos. The entire universe participates in a celebration of life, which St. Maximos the Confessor described as a "cosmic liturgy." We see this cosmic liturgy in the symbiosis of life's rich biological complexities. These complex relationships draw attention to themselves in humanity's self-conscious awareness of the cosmos. As human beings, created "in the image and likeness of God" (Gen. 1:26), we are called to recognize this interdependence between our environment and ourselves. In the bread and the wine of the Eucharist, as priests standing before the altar of the world, we offer the creation back to the creator in relationship to Him and to each other. Indeed, in our liturgical life, we realize by anticipation, the final state of the cosmos in the Kingdom of Heaven. We celebrate the beauty of creation, and consecrate the life of the world, returning it to God with thanks. We share the world in joy as a living mystical communion with the Divine. Thus it is that we offer the fullness of creation at the Eucharist, and receive it back as a blessing, as the living presence of God.

Ecumenical Patriarch Bartholomew

Moreover, there is also an ascetic element in our responsibility toward God's creation. This asceticism requires from us a voluntary restraint, in order for us to live in harmony with our environment. Asceticism offers practical examples of conservation.

By reducing our consumption, in Orthodox theology "encratia" or self-control, we come to ensure that resources are also left for others in the world. As we shift our will we demonstrate a concern for the third world and developing nations. Our abundance of resources will be extended to include an abundance of equitable concern for others.

We must challenge ourselves to see our personal, spiritual attitudes in continuity with public policy. Encratia frees us of our self-centered neediness, that we may do good works for others. We do this out of a personal love for the natural world around us. We are called to work in humble harmony with creation and not in arrogant supremacy against it. Asceticism provides an example whereby we may live simply.

Asceticism is not a flight from society and the world, but a communal attitude of mind and way of life that leads to the respectful use, and not the abuse of material goods. Excessive consumption may be understood to issue from a world-view of estrangement from self, from land, from life, and from God. Consuming the fruits of the earth unrestrained, we become consumed ourselves, by avarice and greed. Excessive consumption leaves us emptied, out-of-touch with our deepest self. Asceticism is a corrective practice, a vision of repentance. Such a vision will lead us from repentance to return, the return to a world in which we give, as well as take from creation.

We invite Orthodox Christians to engage in genuine repentance for the way in which we have behaved toward God, each other, and the world. We gently remind Orthodox Christians that the judgement of the world is in the hands of God. We are called to be stewards, and reflections of God's love by example. Therefore, we proclaim the sanctity of all life, the entire creation being God's and reflecting His continuing will that life abound. We must love life so that others may see and know that it belongs to God. We must leave the judgement of our success to our Creator.

We lovingly suggest to all the people of the earth, that they seek to help one another to understand the myriad ways in which we are related to the earth, and to one another. In this way, we may begin to repair the dislocation many people experience in relation to creation.

We are of the deeply held belief, that many human beings have come to behave as materialistic tyrants. Those that tyrannize the earth are themselves, sadly, tyrannized. We have been called by God, to "be fruitful, increase and have dominion in the earth" (Gen 1:28). Dominion is a type of the Kingdom of Heaven. Thus it is that St. Basil describes the creation of man in paradise on the 6th day, as being the arrival of a king in his palace. Dominion is not domination, it is an eschatological sign of the perfect Kingdom of God, where corruption and death are no more.

If human beings treated one another's personal property the way they treat their environment, we would view that behavior as anti-social. We would impose the judicial measures necessary to restore wrongly appropriated personal possessions. It is therefore appropriate, for us to seek ethical, legal recourse where possible, in matters of ecological crimes.

It follows that, to commit a crime against the natural world, is a sin. For humans to cause species to become extinct and to destroy the biological diversity of God's creation . . . for humans to degrade the integrity of Earth by causing changes in its climate, by stripping the Earth of its natural forests, or destroying its wetlands . . . for humans to injure other humans with disease . . . for humans to contaminate the Earth's waters, its land, its air, and its life, with poisonous substances . . . these are sins.

In prayer, we ask for the forgiveness of sins committed both willingly and unwillingly. And it is certainly God's forgiveness, which we must ask, for causing harm to His Own Creation.

Thus we begin the process of healing our worldly environment which was blessed with Beauty and created by God. Then we may also begin to participate responsibly, as persons making informed choices in both the integrated whole of creation, and within our own souls.

In just a few weeks the world's leaders will gather in Kyoto, Japan, to determine what, if anything, the nations of the world will commit to do, to halt climate change. There has been much debate back and forth about who should, and should not have to change the way they use the resources of the earth. Many nations are reluctant to act unilaterally. This self-centered behavior is a symptom of our alienation from one another, and from the context of our common existence.

We are urging a different and, we believe, a more satisfactory ecological ethic. This ethic is shared with many of the religious traditions represented here. All of us hold the earth to be the creation of God, where He placed the newly created human "in the Garden of Eden to cultivate it and to guard it" (Genesis 2:15). He imposed on humanity a stewardship role in relationship to the earth. How we treat the earth and all of creation defines the relationship that each of us has with God. It is also a barometer of how we view one another. For if we truly value a person, we are careful as to our behavior toward that person. The dominion that God has given humankind over the Earth does not extend to human relationships. As the Lord said, "You know that the rulers of the Nations lord it over them, and their great ones are tyrants over them. It will not be so among you; but whoever wishes to be great among you must be your servant, and whoever wishes to be first among you must be your slave; just as the Son of Man came not to be served but to serve, and to give his life as a ransom for many" (Mat. 20:25–28).

It is with that understanding that we call on the world's leaders to take action to halt the destructive changes to the global climate that are being caused by human activity. And we call on all of you here today, to join us in this cause. This can be our important contribution to the great debate about climate change. We must be spokespeople for an ecological ethic that reminds the world that it is not ours to use for our own convenience. It is God's gift of love to us and we must return his love by protecting it and all that is in it . . .

The Lord suffuses all of creation with His Divine presence in one continuous legato from the substance of atoms to the Mind of God. Let us renew the harmony between heaven and earth, and transfigure every detail, every particle of life. Let us love one another, and lovingly learn from one another, for the edification of God's people, for the sanctification of God's creation, and for the glorification of God's most holy Name. Amen.

"CHRISTIANITY AND ECOLOGY"

John F. Haught

Precisely why should we care about the nonhuman natural world? Most of us probably believe that it is a good thing to do, and we can even give some very convincing pragmatic answers to the question. But theology is concerned with the religious justification of any ecological concern we might have. It is the task of environmental theology to spell out, from within the context of a particular religious tradition, the *ultimate* reasons why we should care about the cosmos. In my case, the tradition is Christian, and so in this and the following chapter I would like to draw out what I think are some distinctive contributions of Christian faith to the ecological movement.

I have already suggested that the threat of global ecological collapse need not lead us to abandon our religious traditions, but that it could be a major historical stimulus to their revitalization. Yet in the case of Christianity such a suggestion may seem too optimistic. Critics of this tradition, as well as some Christian authors themselves, have complained about Christianity's complicity in the western war against nature. Hasn't Christianity been too anthropocentric, too androcentric, too otherworldly and too cavalier about the intrinsic value of nature? Hasn't its theology so overemphasized the need to repair the "fall" of humanity that it has almost completely ignored the original goodness of creation? Hasn't it heard the words of Genesis about human "dominion" over the earth as an imperative to exploit and deface it?

Whether these accusations are justified or not, it is at least certain that many Christians, perhaps even the majority of them, continue to interpret the physical universe as though it were little more than a "soul school" wherein we are challenged to develop our moral character but which itself has little intrinsic significance and no share in human destiny. In this interpretation nonhuman nature is merely a set of props for the drama of human salvation or a way-station for the human religious journey.

Because of its traditionally longing so much for another world, British philosopher John Passmore doubts that Christian theology can ever reshape itself in an ecologically helpful way without ceasing thereby to be Christian. Since Christianity actually sanctions our hostility toward nature, he argues, the only healthy alternative is a radical secularism:

Only if men see themselves . . . for what they are, quite alone, with no one to help them except their fellowmen, products of natural processes which are wholly indifferent to their survival, will they face their ecological problems in their full implications. Not by the extension, but by the total rejection, of the concept of the sacred will they move toward that sombre realization.[1]

While Passmore's indictment of Christianity may be harsh, I think we have to admit that environmentally speaking this tradition, like many others, has been at best ambiguous.[2] While the doctrines of creation and incarnation clearly affirm the value of the cosmos, most Christian spiritualities, saints and scholars have been relatively indifferent to nature. The welfare of the natural world has seldom, if ever, been a dominant concern. We can boast of St. Francis of Assisi, or of Ignatius Loyola, who urged us to see God in all things (and that would have to include nature as well). But we cannot forget other saints like Martin and John of Ephesus, each at opposite ends of the Mediterranean during the rise of Christianity, both of whom are famous for their prowess in the art of deforestation.[3] And if expressions of a deep love of nature appear in some Christian hymnody and hagiography, there are just as many indications of a desire to escape from nature in other facets of the tradition.[4]

Concern for either local or global environmental welfare is not a very explicit part of the Christian tradition. Nevertheless, I agree with Paul Santmire that there is great promise for theological renewal in the ecologically ambiguous Christian tradition.[5] In fact a rethinking of Christianity in terms of the environmental crisis is already under way, and it is the cause for some optimism that this tradition may potentially be enlivened by an ecological transformation. The new theological reflection comes in several different strains, of which I shall discuss three. I will call these respectively the *apologetic*, the *sacramental* and the *eschatological* attempts to formulate an environmental theology. None of these can be found in a perfectly pure form, and aspects of all three may be found in the work of any single author. Nevertheless, they vary considerably in theological method, and so I hope it will prove illuminating to treat them here as distinct types.

THE APOLOGETIC APPROACH

The first, and the least revisionist of the three, is the more or less apologetic enterprise of trying to show that there is already a sufficient basis in scripture and tradition for an adequately Christian response to the environmental crisis. It is exemplified by recent statements of the pope and the American Catholic bishops,[6] as well as a number of theological articles and books published in the past decade or so.[7] According to this approach, which runs the range from biblical literalism to very sophisticated theological scholarship, we have simply ignored the wealth of ecologically relevant material in the tradition. Therefore, what we need to do now in order to have an adequate environmental theology is simply dig up the appropriate texts and allow them to illuminate the present crisis. Sometimes this apologetic method merely scours the scriptures for nuggets of naturalism in order to show that the Bible cares about the cosmos after all. At its most simplistic extreme it does little more than recite the psalms and other biblical passages that proclaim creation as God's handiwork. But at a more erudite level of interpretation it excavates the themes of incarnation and creation as theological warrants for an ecological theology. In addition it digs out environmentally sensitive, and previously overlooked passages in the early Christian and other theological writings.[8] More than anything else, though, the apologetic approach emphasizes the biblical notion that God has given humanity "dominion" and "stewardship" over creation, and that this is reason enough for us to take care of our natural environment.

This first type of ecological theology also argues that if only we practiced the timeless religious virtues we could alleviate the crisis. Since one of the main sources of our predicament is simple human greed, the solution lies in a renewed commitment to humility, to the virtue of detachment, and to the central religious posture of gratitude by which we accept the natural world as God's gift and treat it accordingly. If we allowed our lives to be shaped by genuinely Christian virtues, our relation to nature would have the appropriate balance, and we could avert the disaster that looms before us.

I call this approach apologetic because it defends the integrity of biblical religion and traditional theology without requiring their transformation. It holds, at least implicitly, that Christianity is essentially okay as it is, that environmental abuse stems only from perversions of pure faith and not from anything intrinsic to it, and therefore that Christianity does not need to undergo much of a change in the face of the present emergency. Rather, we need only to bring our environmental policies into conformity with revelation and time-tested doctrine. With respect to the present state of our environment, the fault is not with Christianity but with our failure to accept its message.

How are we to evaluate this apologetic approach (which is probably the one most Christians, and I suspect most Christian theologians, take today)? On the positive side, I would say that it does develop an indispensable component of an ecological theology: it turns our attention to significant resources in the Christian classics that have not been sufficiently emphasized. Its highlighting the environmental relevance of traditional teachings, forgotten texts and religious virtues is very helpful. We need this retrieval as we begin the work of shaping a theology appropriate to the contemporary crisis.

Moreover, a good dose of apologetics is certainly called for today in the face of many incredibly simplistic complaints by some historians that Christianity is the sole or major cause of the environmental crisis. A sober analysis of the historical roots of the crisis will show that some of the antinature attitudes associated with Christianity comprise only one aspect of a very complex set of ingredients leading to the present destruction of the ecosphere. An unbiased historical analysis can also demonstrate that major aspects of Christianity have firmly resisted the dominating practices that led us to the present situation. Thus, some defending of Christianity seems entirely appropriate.

However, I do not think that this apologetic type goes far enough in opening Christian faith to the radical renewal the ecological crisis seems to demand. I seriously doubt that we can adequately confront the problems facing our natural environment, theologically speaking, simply by being more emphatic about familiar moral exhortations or by endlessly exegeting scriptural passages about the goodness of nature or the importance of stewardship. Such efforts are not insignificant; indeed they are essential. But I wonder if they are fundamental enough. In the face of the chastisement Christianity has received from secular environmentalists, the apologetic quest for relevant texts, teachings and virtues does not go far enough. I doubt that even the most impressive display of biblical or patristic passages about God and nature will allay this criticism or, for that matter, turn many Christians into serious environmentalists. In order to have an adequate environmental theology Christianity, I think, will need to undergo a more radical internal change.

THE SACRAMENTAL APPROACH

The beginnings of such a change are now taking place in what I shall call the sacramental approach to Christian ecological theology. This second type focuses less on normative religious texts or historical revelation than does the apologetic approach, and more on the allegedly sacral quality of the cosmos itself. It is more willing to acknowledge the revelatory character of nature. It comes in a variety of theological forms ranging from what has been called "natural theology," which focuses on the apparent evidence for God's existence in nature, to the cosmic spirituality of Thomas Berry[9] and Matthew Fox and their followers.[10] It is also found, in different ways and degrees, in non-Christian religions, as well as in the spirituality of eco-feminists and some so-called "deep ecologists."[11]

In its typical form this sacramental approach interprets the natural world as the primary symbolic disclosure of God. Religious texts and traditions are still important, but the cosmos itself is the primary medium through which we come to know the sacred. Today the sacramental approach usually accommodates evolutionary theory and aspects of contemporary physics. It embraces a holistic view of the earth as an organism comprised of a delicately balanced web of interdependent relationships. Rejecting mechanism, it regards the entire universe organismically, that is, as an intricate network of dynamic interconnections in which all aspects are internal to each other. Hence, it also places particular emphasis on the continuity of humans with the rest of the natural world.

Accordingly, it views our spiritual traditions not as activities that we humans "construct" on the face of the earth, but as functions that the cosmos performs through us. According to Thomas Berry, for example, the universe is the primary subject, and humanity is one of many significant developments of the universe. Cultures and religions are simply natural extensions of the cosmic process rather than unnatural creations of lonely human exiles on earth.

In the Christian context today I think this revisionist approach finds its most compelling expression in what has been called "creation-centered" theology. As the prime example of our second type it goes beyond the apologetic variety of environmental theology by arguing that our present circumstances require a whole new interpretation of what it means to be Christian. In the face of the environmental crisis it will not do simply to take more seriously our inherited texts and teachings. These are still important, but they must be carefully sifted and reinterpreted in terms of a cosmological, relational, nonhierarchical, nonpatriarchal, nondualistic and more organismic understanding of the universe. We must pay more attention to the sacral quality of the universe and not place such a heavy burden on premodern religious texts to give us the foundations of our environmental ethic.

In Christian circles this creation-centered outlook accepts the doctrines of the creed but gives them a cosmological interpretation. It may be helpful to look briefly at several of the results of its recosmologizing of traditional Christian teachings.

1.   As the label suggests, this new theological emphasis brings the biblical theme of *creation* to the center of theology instead of subordinating it, as it has been in the past, to the theme of redemption. Theology's focusing primarily on the redemption of a "fallen" world has distracted us from an adequate reverencing of the intrinsic goodness of nature. Moreover, our understanding of redemption has been too anthropocentric. We have been so obsessed with overcoming our human sinfulness and suffering, that we have forgotten about the travail of nature as a whole.

2.   Creation-centered theology also argues that we need a correspondingly broader understanding of that from which we are said to be redeemed, namely, *sin*. It insists that sin means not just our estrangement from God or from each other, but also the present condition of severe alienation of the cosmos from ourselves. Reconciliation then implies not only the restoration of human communion but, just as fundamentally, our reintegration with the earth-community and the whole of the universe. In order to experience this reconciliation we must abandon all forms of religious dualism which have sanctioned our self-distancing from nature.

3.   Creation-centered theology insists also that we need to rethink what we mean by *revelation*. Revelation is not just God's self-manifestation in history, let alone the communication of divine information in propositional form. We need to think of revelation in more cosmic terms. The universe itself is the primary revelation. In its 15 billion-year evolution the cosmos is the most fundamental mode of the unfolding of divine mystery. The mys-

tery of God is revealed gradually in the evolution of matter, life, human culture and the religions of the world (and not just in biblical religion either). Viewed in terms of cosmic evolution our religions can no longer be explained or explained away as simple heartwarming gestures that estranged humans engage in on an alien terrain as we look toward some distant far-off eternity. Rather, religions are something that the universe does through us as it seeks to disclose its mysterious depths. The fact of there being a plurality of religions is in perfect keeping with evolution's extravagant creation of variety and difference. Hence, an ecological spirituality should be no less committed to preserving the plurality of religions in the world than it is to the salvaging of biodiversity. We should lament the loss of religious diversity since religions are also products of cosmic evolution and just as deserving of conservation as the multiple species of plants and animals.

4.   Viewing things in this cosmological way, creation-centered theology appreciates both ancient and modern efforts to understand the *Christ* also as a cosmic reality, and not simply as a personal historical savior. Cosmic Christology, already present in ancient Christian theology, needs to be recovered today in terms of an evolutionary and ecological worldview. The entire cosmos (and not just human society) is the body of Christ. A cosmic Christology then provides the deepest foundations of a distinctively Christian environmental spirituality. And in keeping with this cosmic Christology the eucharistic celebration ideally represents the healing not only of severed human relationships, but also of the entire universe.

5.   The theological experiment of creation-centered theology culminates in an ecological understanding of *God*. Here the trinitarian God is the supreme exemplification of ecology, a term which refers to the study of relationships. Creation in the image of God then means that the world itself has being only to the extent that, like God, it exists in relationship. An ecological theology is congruent both with contemporary science and the classic doctrine of the Trinity, a doctrine which renounces the idea that God exists only in isolated aseity.

6.   This ecological contextualization of Christian teaching leads us in the direction of a whole new *spirituality*. Creation-centered theology encourages an enjoyment of the natural world as our true home. Traditional spiritualities, often characterized by a discomfort with bodily existence, received parallel expression simultaneously in the sense of humanity's fundamental homelessness in nature. The classic texts of Christianity have unfortunately been tainted by a dualistic bias that has sanctioned our hostility toward nature and the body. For this reason a purely apologetic type of environmental theology is inadequate, for it is not sufficiently alert to such ideological flaws in the classic sources.

7.   Moreover, an ecological spirituality requires its own kind of *asceticism*. This asceticism prescribes a renunciation not of the natural world but of the Enlightenment ideal of autonomous, isolated selfhood. It subjects us to the arduous discipline of taking into full account the fact of our being inextricably tied into a wider earth-community. A full life, one in which we acknowledge our complex relation to the universe, widens our sense of re-

sponsibility toward ourselves and others. Above anything else, this means adopting a continually expanding posture of inclusiveness toward all otherness that we encounter, including the wildness of the natural world.

8.   Creation-centered spirituality in turn inspires a restructuring of Christian *ethics* in terms of an environmental focus. Ethics cannot be grounded only in the classic moral traditions which usually left the welfare of the cosmos out of the field of concern. An environmental awareness gives a new slant to social ethics and life ethics. In place of (or alongside of) social justice, it advocates a more inclusive "eco-justice" according to which we cannot repair human inequities without simultaneously attending to the prospering of the larger earth-community. And being "pro-life" means going beyond the focus simply on the ethics of human reproduction. An environmentally chastened life ethic questions aspects of current moral teachings that tolerate policies which, while protective of human fertility, ignore the complex life-systems in which human fertility dwells.[12]

9.   Finally, creation-centered theology advocates the reshaping of *education* from the earliest years so that it pays closer attention to the natural world. At the level of secondary and college education, including the core curriculum, this would mean making environmental education central and not just an afterthought. Our students should be required to look carefully at what both science and religion have to say about the universe, and yet remain critical of scientism and materialism, both of which are no less ecologically disastrous ideologies than are dualistic and patriarchal forms of religion.

The most characteristic feature of this contemporary revision of theology is its focus on the sacramentality of nature. (By "sacrament," let us recall, we mean any aspect of the world through which a divine mystery becomes present to religious awareness.) Ever since the Old Stone Age aspects of nature such as clean water, fresh air, fertile soil, clear skies, bright light, thunder and rain, living trees, plants and animals, human fertility, etc., have symbolically mediated to religious people at least something of the reality of the sacred. As we saw in the previous chapter, sacramentalism recognizes the transparency of nature to the divine, and it therefore gives to the natural world a status that should evoke our reverence and protectiveness. The sacramental perspective reads in nature an importance or inherent value that a purely utilitarian or naturalist point of view cannot discern. Nature, then, is not primarily something to be used for human purposes or for technical projects. It is essentially the showing forth of an ultimate goodness and generosity.

In principle the sacramental features of Christianity (and of other religions) protect the integrity of the natural world. According to our second type of environmental theology, therefore, the nurturing of a sacramental vision is one of the most important contributions Christianity and other religions can make to the preservation of the natural world. If biodiversity eventually decays into a homogeneity similar, say, to the lunar landscape (and this is the direction in which things are now moving) we will lose the richness

John F. Haught

of our sacramental reference to God. And if we lose the environment, Thomas Berry is fond of saying, we will lose our sense of God as well.

By way of evaluation, I would say that this second type of environmental theology is another important step toward an acceptable Christian environmental theology. It goes beyond the more superficial efforts of our first type which consist primarily of an apologetic search for texts that allegedly contain a ready-made environmental theology adequate to our contemporary circumstances. Our second type seeks a radical transformation of all religious traditions, including Christianity, in the face of the present crisis. The creation-centered approach is aware that religious texts, like any other classics, can sometimes sanction policies which are socially unjust and ecologically problematic. So it allows into its interpretation of the classic sources of Christian faith a great deal of suspicion about some of the same motifs that our first approach holds to be normative.

To give one example, the ideal of human dominion or stewardship over creation, which is fundamental in our first type of environmental theology, turns out to be quite inadequate in the second. Stewardship, even when it is exegetically purged of the distortions to which the notion has been subjected, is still too managerial a concept to support the kind of ecological ethic we need today. Most ecologists would argue that the earth's life-systems were a lot better off before we humans came along to manage them. In fact, it is almost an axiom of ecology that these systems would not be in such jeopardy if the human species had never appeared in evolution at all. So, even if we nuance the notions of stewardship and dominion in the light of recent scholarship, the biblical tradition is still too anthropocentric. And since anthropocentrism is commonly acknowledged to be one of the chief causes of our environmental neglect, creation-centered theology seeks to play down those theological themes that make us too central in the scheme of things. In the shadow of the environmental crisis it seeks a more cosmic understanding of Christianity.

At the same time, this approach acknowledges that we humans still play a very important role in the total cosmic picture. Our presence enriches and adds considerable value to life on earth. However, the concept of dominion or stewardship, important as it is, fails to accentuate that we belong to the earth much more than it belongs to us, that we are more dependent on it than it is on us. If in some sense we "transcend" the universe by virtue of our freedom and consciousness, in another sense this same universe is taken up as our constant companion in our own transcendence of it. Christian theology now needs to emphasize more than ever before the inseparable and (as we shall develop in the next chapter) the everlasting connection between ourselves and the cosmos.[13]

THE ESCHATOLOGICAL APPROACH

As I have already hinted, I have much stronger sympathies with the second approach than with the first (although the exegetical work that accompanies the first is also quite fruitful). Any attempt to construct a Christian environmental theology today must build on the sacramental interpretation of nature. Today Christianity desperately needs to bring the cosmos back into the center of its theology, and creation-centered theology is an important contribution to this process.

However, if we are looking for Christianity's possible significance in the global project of bringing an end to the crisis that threatens all of humanity as well as life on earth, I think in all honesty we have to ask whether the Bible's most fundamental theme, that of a divine promise for future fulfillment, is of any relevance here. In other words, we need to ask whether the *eschatological* dimension of Christianity, its characteristic hope for future perfection founded on the ancient Hebrew experience of God's promise and fidelity, can become the backbone of an environmentally sensitive religious vision. If a return to cosmology is theologically essential today, then from the point of view of Christian faith, we need assurance that this cosmology remains adequately framed by eschatology.

During the present century, we have rediscovered the central place of eschatology in Christian faith. Hope in God's promise upon which Israel's faith was built is now also seen to be the central theme in Christian faith as well, a fact that bonds Christianity very closely to its religious parent. The faith of Jesus and his followers was steeped in expectation of the coming of the reign of God. Reality is saturated with promise, and the authentic life of faith is one of looking to the fulfillment of God's promise, based on a complete trust that God is a promise keeper. True faith scans the horizon for signs of promise's fulfillment. For this faith present reality, including the world of nature in all of its ambiguity, is pregnant with hints of future fulfillment.

Until recently this way of looking at the cosmos, namely, as the embodiment of promise, had almost completely dropped out of Christian understanding. It had been replaced by a dualism that looked vertically above to a completely different world as the place of fulfillment. The cosmos itself had no future. Only the immortal human soul could look forward to salvation, and this in some completely different domain where all connection with nature and bodiliness would be dissolved. That such an interpretation of human destiny could arise in a community of faith which from the beginning professed belief in the resurrection of the body is indeed ironic. But more than that, it is tragic. For by suppressing awareness of the bodiliness of human nature dualism was inclined also to disregard the larger matrix of our bodiliness, the entire physical universe which is inseparable from our being. By excepting nature and its future from the ambit of human hope Christianity left the cosmos suspended in a state of hopelessness. It had forgotten St. Paul's intuition that the entire universe yearns for redemption. Fortunately theology has begun to retrieve this inspired idea. Now any ecological theology worked out in a Christian context must make this motif of nature's promise the very center of its vision.

It is easy enough to argue that Christianity's sacramental quality, which it shares with many other religions, affirms the value of nature. But the Bible, because of the multiplicity of traditions it embodies, has an eschatologically nuanced view of sacramentality. It is aware, for example, that something is terribly wrong with the present world and that any sacraments based on the present state of nature inevitably participate in this imperfection. Pure sacramentalism, therefore, is not enough. Biblical faith looks less toward a God transparently revealed in present natural harmony than toward a future coming of God in the eschatological perfection of creation. It is especially this hopeful tone, and not just its sacramentalism, that can ground an ecological spirituality. As we seek a Christian theology of the environment, therefore, we need to ask how the future-oriented, promissory aspect of this tradition connects with contemporary ecological concern. Most recent attempts by Christians to build an environmental theology have made only passing reference to the eschatological vision of nature as promise.[14]

Hence, as an alternative to the apologetic and the sacramental types, I am proposing a more inclusive eschatological cosmology as the foundation of a Christian environmental theology. Here the cosmos is neither a soul-school for human existence nor a straightforward epiphany of God's presence. Rather, it is in its deepest essence a promise of future fulfillment. Nature is promise. If we are sincere in proposing a theology of the environment that still has connections with biblical religion, we need to make the topic of promise central, and not subordinate, in our reflections. In order to do this in an ecologically profitable way we must acknowledge that the cosmos itself is an installment of the future, and for that reason deserves neither neglect nor worship, but simply the kind of care proportionate to the treasuring of a promise.

A Christian environmental theology, I am maintaining, is ideally based on the promissory character of nature. But some religious thinkers will complain that the biblical theme of promise is not very helpful in theological efforts to ground ecological ethics. Following Arnold Toynbee, Thomas Berry, for example, argues that it is precisely the biblical emphasis on the future that has wreaked ecological havoc. For Berry the future orientation of the Bible has bequeathed to us the dream of progress, and it is the latter that has caused us to bleed off the earth's resources while we have uncritically pursued an elusive future state of perfection. Berry holds that biblical eschatology, with its unleashing of a dream of future perfection, is inimical to environmental concern. According to this leading creation-centered geologian, hoping in a future promise can lead us to sacrifice the present world for the sake of some far-off future fulfillment. Although he is a Catholic priest himself, Berry considerably distances himself from the prophetic tradition that many of us still consider to be the central core of biblical faith and the bedrock of Christian ethics.[15]

But would our environmental theology be consonant with biblical tradition if we left out the prophetic theme of future promise? The sacramental accent taken by Berry and many other religiously minded ecologists has the advantage of bringing the cosmos back into our theology, and this is essential today. But Berry seems to be embarrassed by eschatology. Hence, in spite of his many valuable contributions to environmental thinking, I would have to question whether his and some other versions of creation-centered theology have adequately tapped the ecological resources of biblical eschatology.

In the preceding chapter's general depiction of religion I argued that the sacramental component present in Christianity and other religions is ecologically significant. Preserving religion's sacramentality contributes to the wholeness of both nature and religion. But we cannot forget that in the Bible sacramentality is taken up into eschatology. Biblical hope diverts our religious attention away from exclusive enrapturement with any present world-harmony and from nature's alleged capacity to mediate an epiphany of the sacred through its present forms of beauty. Instead, the Bible's eschatology encourages us to look toward the future coming of God. In terms of this particular religious accent any reversion to pure sacramentalism is suspect. It has, in fact, been condemned outright by prophets and reformers as faithless idolatry.

Christianity, aided by its roots in biblical monotheism, and owing to its unique emphasis on the promise of history, may itself be partly responsible for the demotion of the sacramental attitude which some religious ecologists now wish to make paramount. By understanding the promising God of history to be alone holy, Judaism and Christianity (as well as Islam) seem to have divested any present state of nature of its supposedly sacral character. Belief in God's radical transcendence of nature, and the location of absolute reality in the realm of the historical or eschatological future—these seem to have relativized present cosmic realities, at times to the point of insignificance. The biblical desacralization of nature may even have helped open up the natural world to human domination and exploitation. Biblical religion expels the gods from the forests and streams once and for all, and because of its "disenchantment" of nature, along with its focus on the historical future, it is problematic to some religious ecologists of a more sacramental or cosmological persuasion.

Adding to this environmentally controversial character of biblical religion is the fact that, in terms of the fourfold typology of religion presented in the previous chapter, prophetic faith falls predominantly in the active or transformative type. The Bible not only gives thanks for present creation, but it also seeks to change it. It celebrates the Sabbath on one day, but it permits work on the other six. Because it is based fundamentally on the sense of promise it can never remain totally satisfied with present reality, including any present harmoniously balanced state of nature. This is because it looks toward the future perfection of creation. That is, it moves beyond any merely vertical sacramentalism that seeks to make the divine fully transparent in presently available nature. It acknowledges the imperfection of the present state of creation and seeks to reshape the world, including the natural world, so that it will come into conformity with what it takes to be God's vision of the future. Some writers have sensed herein an ecologically dangerous feature of Christianity. The Bible's prophetic tradition is then itself blamed for unleashing the dream of a transforming "progress" that has ended up wrecking the earth rather than perfecting it.

This is a serious charge, and I simply cannot respond to it adequately here. I might just point out that apologists of our first type rightly indicate that though the biblical texts emphasize God's transcendence of nature they do not sanction the kind of exploitation of nature that some historians have traced to this doctrine. Even so, it seems appropriate for us to ask whether a pure sacramentalism would itself guarantee that we will save the environment. And, on the other hand, is it self-evident that actively transforming nature will lead inevitably to its degradation? John Passmore, whom I quoted earlier, says that

> . . . the West needs more fully to . . . "glorify" nature. But it cannot now turn back [to a sacralization of nature] . . . ; only by transforming nature can it continue to survive. There is no good ground, either, for objecting to transformation as such; it can make the world more fruitful, more diversified, and more beautiful.[16]

At the same time, he goes on to say that

> . . . societies for whom nature is sacred have nonetheless destroyed their natural habitation. Man does not necessarily preserve . . . the stream he has dedicated to a god; simple ignorance . . . can be as damaging as technical know-how.[17]

Thus an immoderate sacramentalism may be not only religiously but also environmentally irresponsible. If carried to an extreme, Passmore insists, the sacramental view can even precipitate environmental neglect. It may do so by causing us naively to trust that nature can always take care of itself. And he argues that one of the main causes of ecological destruction is the human ignorance which only a heavy dose of scientific learning can help to dispel.[18]

While many ecologists will certainly take issue with Passmore on this matter, he helpfully forces us to ask whether we need to think of nature itself as sacred, as many religious environmentalists are now suggesting, in order to ground its intrinsic value. Can the sacramental vision proposed by Berry and creation-centered theology all by itself motivate us religiously to take care of our planet?

My own suggestion is that, without denying the ecological importance of the sacramental approach, we may follow the Bible's lead by holding close to the theme of promise. For to suppress the theme of hope and promise whenever we do any kind of theologizing from a Christian point of view, no matter what the occasion or the issue, is to fail to engage the heart and soul of this tradition. I am more sympathetic, therefore, with the theological program of Jürgen Moltmann who for almost three decades now has consistently argued that all Christian theology must be eschatology.[19] Theology must be saturated with hope for the future. And what this means for our purposes here is that environmental theology must also be future oriented, no matter how tendentious this may initially appear from the point of view of a pure sacramentalism.

I am afraid that the creation-centered approach, valuable as it is in retrieving the cosmos that has been tragically lost to our theology, has not paid sufficient attention to the radically eschatological, promise-laden, character of Christian faith. It has helpfully promulgated what has been called a "lateral transcendence," that is, a reaching out beyond the narrow boundaries of our isolated selfhood in order to acknowledge the ever-expanding field of present relationships that comprise the wider universe.[20] But this horizontal transcendence must be complemented by a looking-forward-beyond-the-present. Transcendence, understood biblically, means not only a movement beyond narrowness toward a wider inclusiveness, but also a reaching toward the region of what Ernst Bloch calls "not-yet-being," toward the novelty and surprise of an uncontrollable future.[21]

Consequently, I would like to persist in my suggestion that the distinctive contribution Christian theology has to offer to ecology (since many of its sacramental aspects are present in other traditions) is a vision of nature as promise. A biblical perspective invites us to root ecology in eschatology. It reads in cosmic and sacramental reality an intense straining toward the future. It obliges us to keep the cosmos in the foreground of our theology without removing the restlessness forced on the present by a sense of the yet-to-come.

The Bible, in fact, includes not only human history but also the entire cosmos in its vision of promise. The universe, as St. Paul insinuates, is not a mere point of departure, a *terminus a quo*, which we leave behind once we embark on the journey of hope. Modern science has also demonstrated that our roots still extend deep down into the earth and fifteen billion years back in time to the big bang. Hence, our own hoping carries with it the whole universe's yearning for its future.

The natural world is much more than a launching pad that the human spirit abandons as it soars off toward some incorporeal absolute. Through the sacramental emphasis of creation-centered spirituality (as well as the powerful voices of deep ecology, ecofeminism and the many varieties of contemporary naturalism) the cosmos now claims once again that it, too, shares in our hope. Billions of years before our own appearance in evolution it was already seeded with promise. Our own religious longing for future fulfillment, therefore, is not a violation but a blossoming of this promise.

Human hoping is not simply our own constructs of imaginary ideals projected onto an indifferent universe, as much modern and postmodern thought maintains. Rather, it is the faithful carrying on of the universe's perennial orientation toward an unknown future. By looking hopefully toward this future we are not being unfaithful to the cosmos, but instead we are allowing ourselves to be carried along by impulses that have always energized it. If we truly want to recosmologize Christianity then we do well also to "eschatologize" our cosmology. Eschatology invites us to make more explicit nature's own refusal to acquiesce in trivial forms of harmony. It persuades us to understand the universe as an adventurous journey toward the complexity and beauty of a future perfection.

IMPLICATIONS FOR ENVIRONMENTAL ETHICS

In the light of an eschatological cosmology let us then ask once again: why should we be concerned about our natural environment? Not only because it is sacramentally transparent to the sacred, but even more fundamentally because it is the incarnation of a promise yet to be fulfilled. It is because nature is not only sacrament but also promise that we are obliged to revere it. In the sacramental view we condemn environmental abuse because it is a sacrilege. But in the eschatological perspective the sin of environmental abuse is one of despair. To destroy nature is to turn away from a promise. What makes nature deserve our care is not that it is divine but that it is pregnant with a mysterious future. When looked at eschatologically its value consists not so much of its sacramentally mediating a divine "presence," as of its nurturing a promise of future perfection.

Nature is not yet complete, nor yet fully revelatory of God. Like any promise it lacks the perfection of fulfillment. To demand that it provide fulfillment now is a mark of an impatience hostile to hope. Nature is wonderful, but it is also incomplete. We know from experience that it can also be indifferent and ugly at times. A purely sacramental or creation-centered theology of nature cannot easily accommodate the shadow side of nature. By focusing on ecological harmony it expects us to see every present state of nature as an epiphany of God. This is a projection which neither our religion nor the natural world can bear.

An eschatological view of nature, on the other hand, allows ambiguity in as a partner to promise. Nature's harshness, which so offends both religious romantics and cosmic pessimists, is entirely in keeping with its being the embodiment of promise. The perspective of hope allows us to be realistic about what nature is. We do not have to cover up its cruelty. We can accept the fact that the cosmos is not a paradise but only the promise thereof.

The world, including that of nonhuman nature, has not yet arrived at the final peace of God's kingdom, and so it does not merit our worship. It does deserve our valuation, but not our prostration. If we adopt too naive a notion of nature's significance we will inevitably end up being disappointed by it. If we invest in it an undue devotion we will eventually turn against it, as against all idols, for disappointing us—as it inevitably will. For that reason an exclusively sacramental interpretation of nature is theologically inadequate, and it can even prepare the way for our violating the earth. I think that a biblical vision invites us to temper our devotion with a patient acceptance of nature's unfinished status. Understanding the cosmos as a promise invites us to cherish it without denying its ambiguity.

SUMMARY AND CONCLUSION

The Christian story of hope embraces the entirety of cosmic occurrence as part of its promise. Looking toward the future in hope requires that we preserve nature for the promise it carries. A religion of hope allows us to accept nature as imperfect precisely because it is promise. A sacramental theology is all by itself unable to accommodate the fact of nature's fragility. To accept nature's intrinsic value we can learn from primal sacramental traditions much that we had forgotten. But in order to accommodate both its ambiguity and its promise we are usefully instructed not only by the spirituality of primal traditions, but also by the story of Abraham.

NOTES

1. John Passmore, *Man's Responsibility for Nature* (New York: Scribner, 1974), p. 184.

2. See Paul Santmire, *The Travail of Nature* (Philadelphia, Fortress Press, 1985).

3. Robin Lane Fox, *Pagan and Christian* (San Francisco: Harper & Row, 1988), p. 44.

4. Very early in the history of Christianity there appeared the "heresies" of docetism and monophysitism, which denied the incarnation of God in Christ, and gnosticism, which advocated escape from the allegedly evil material world. In spite of their being officially condemned by the Christian church, however, docetism and monophysitism still hover over our Christology, and gnosticism continues to infect Christian spirituality. The previous failure of Christianity effectively to confront the ecological crisis is in part the result of its continuing flirtation with these excessively spiritualist perspectives, both of which are embarrassed at our historicity, our "naturality" and our embodied existence.

5. Paul Santmire, *The Travail of Nature* (Philadelphia: Fortress Press, 1985).

6. See the World Day of Peace Message by Pope John Paul II entitled *The Ecological Crisis: A Common Responsibility* (1990), and the American Catholic bishops' recent statement, *Renewing the Earth* (1992).

7. One of the best examples of the apologetic type, from a quite conservative Catholic standpoint, is Charles M. Murphy's *At Home on Earth* (New York: Crossroad, 1989). From a more "liberal" Catholic perspective, but still within the framework of what I am calling the apologetic kind of environmental theology, is John Carmody's provocative *Religion and Ecology* (New York: Paulist Press, 1983). Most current Christian theology of the environment is apologetic in nature.

8. See, for example, Bernard J. Przewozny, "Elements of a Catholic Doctrine of Humankind's Relation to the Environment," in B. J. Przewozny, C. Savini and O. Todisco, *Ecology Francescana* (Rome: Edizioni Micellanea Francescana, 1987), pp. 223–255.

9. Thomas Berry, *The Dream of the Earth.*

10. Matthew Fox, *Original Blessing* (Santa Fe: Bear & Co., 1983); and Brian Swimme, *The Universe Is a Green Dragon* (Santa Fe: Bear & Co., 1984).

11. For a compendium of such viewpoints see Charlene Spretnak, *States of Grace* (San Francisco: Harper & Row, 1991).

12. Whenever it ignores the fact that overpopulation adds enormously to every kind of ecological degradation, Christian moral teaching ironically contributes to what the Irish missionary to the Philippines, Sean McDonagh, has called the "death of birth," and therefore does not deserve to be called "pro-life" in the deepest sense of the term. See his *The Greening of the Church* (Maryknoll: Orbis Books, 1990), pp. 38–73.

13. See Fritjof Capra and David Steindl-Rast, *Belonging to the Universe* (San Francisco: HarperCollins).

14. A major exception is Jürgen Moltmann, *God in Creation*, trans. Margaret Kohl (San Francisco: Harper & Row, 1985).

15. Berry, p. 204.

16. Passmore, p. 179.

17. Ibid., pp. 175–76.

18. Ibid.

19. Jürgen Moltmann, *Theology of Hope*, trans. James W. Leitch (New York: Harper & Row, 1967).

20. The concept of lateral transcendence is that of Linda Holler, cited by Spretnak, p. 155.

21. See Ernst Bloch, *The Principle of Hope*, Vol. I, trans. Neville Plaice, Stephen Plaice and Paul Knight (Oxford: Basil Blackwell, 1986).

"PROTESTANT THEOLOGY AND DEEP ECOLOGY"

John B. Cobb, Jr.

THE FAILURE OF ANTHROPOCENTRISM

All of the "higher religions," when viewed against the background of the primal religions, are anthropocentric and even individualistic. They are religions of human salvation, and they have focused on the salvation of individuals. This salvation has been disconnected from physical well-being and thus from changes in the physical world.

These great traditions all strike other notes as well. In this book, we are emphasizing these other notes. As we have become aware of our historic failures in relation to ecological matters, we have rightly recovered these other elements and sought to give them a central role. These efforts have important contributions to make, but it is best to begin with the acknowledgment that a truly ecological consciousness was far more clearly and effectively present in hunting and gathering societies than in our traditions. When we look for religious versions of deep ecology, it is to them that we should turn.

Although this weakness characterizes all the great world religions, as a Protestant Christian I am impelled to move quickly to the acknowledgment that Protestant theology has been an extreme case. Christianity as a whole has emphasized the interior relation of the individual to God, but the Eastern Church down to the present has kept in view the larger setting of God's relation to the whole of creation. Even in the Western church, in the Patristic and Medieval periods the church's teaching incorporated the whole of society and of the natural world. The Eastern and Roman Catholic traditions have resources today for responding to our new awareness of the ecological crisis that require separate treatment. As a Protestant I will limit myself, as the title of this essay indicates, to the situation of ecumenical Protestantism.

The feature of traditional teaching that disturbed the Reformers and led to their break with Rome had to do quite narrowly with the roles of God, the church, and persons in the salvation of individuals. As a result the writings of the Reformers focused overwhelmingly on these topics. Furthermore, they believed that what they regarded as distortions on these topics came in large part from the broader philosophical traditions incorporated into Christian teaching. Rejecting these led to still further concentration on issues of personal redemption. Calvin built his theology around God and the human soul. The broader creation provided only background and context.

The situation became worse in the nineteenth century. Following Kant, Protestant theologians abandoned the world of nature to the sciences and took history as their only domain, usually emphasizing the moral and spiritual spheres and focusing attention on the individual person. The doctrine of creation that had previously connected Christian thought to the whole of nature was reinterpreted to express the individual's radical dependence on God.

Of course, Protestantism is not a monolithic movement, and many Protestants in the nineteenth and twentieth centuries continued to find God in and through nature. To many of them, creation continued to mean the whole of nature, and the wonder of this nature often grounded their faith in its Creator. Indeed, this appreciation of nature has been more characteristic of popular Protestant piety than was the Kantianism of the theologians. But because it did not receive theoretical expression, its influence on church leadership was negligible. Thus, the Kantian move in theology had enormous effects. What would-be ministers learned in the course of their studies was that attention to nature was sentimental and irrelevant. Their energies should be directed to dealing with the human condition. The options among which they were to choose were alternative ways of understanding human salvation: sociohistorical or otherworldly, psychological or existential, moral or mystical.

My own theological teachers were not Kantian. At the University of Chicago Divinity School we learned that theology should not be separated from the study of the natural world. We learned that there are continuities between natural and historical processes as well as differences. Some of the professors called themselves neonaturalists in order to emphasize this opposition to Kantian theology. Some of them called for deep changes in the Western sensibility.

Nevertheless, we had to learn to operate in the wider theological scene and to express our distinctive views in that context. In that wider scene the spectrum of possibilities was largely defined by Karl Barth's neo-Calvinist theology and Rudolf Bultmann's Christian existentialism. For us it was far easier to relate to Bultmann. In Bultmann's existentialist theology, the focus was on personal decision, and individualistic anthropocentrism reached a pinnacle. Although we sometimes engaged in argument with Bultmann and his followers, his framing of the issues, and the broader neo-Orthodox context tended to shape our agenda and the topics of our reflection. What was happening to the biosphere did not even appear on our radar screen.

At least, this is how it worked out in my case. In the mid-sixties I wrote a book called *A Christian Natural Theology* to express the non-Kantian philosophical theology I had internalized, especially under the influence of the writings of Alfred North Whitehead. But "natural theology" has not been defined in Christian history as reflection about the natural world, although it often included that. It has meant theology within the bounds of reason, that is, independent of appeal to supernatural revelation. The topics I treated were those that were standard in Protestant theology: "man" and God.

I write this to indicate how deeply I was socialized into anthropocentrism by the dominant character of Protestant theology even when the philosophical and theological sources on which I drew offered a very different option. It was not until the end of the sixties, when my eyes were opened to the seriousness of the environmental crisis, that I became aware of this paradox. At that point I realized that my teachers had not been as blind as I. But this openness to the natural world on their part had not affected me, and I think it safe to say that I was not unusual among their students.

When I read Lynn White's famous essay, "The Historical Roots of Our Ecologic Crisis," I saw at once that he was correct, at least as far as the Christian traditions that had informed my thinking were concerned. He extended his charge to the mainstream of the whole of Western Christianity, and despite the fact that pre-Kantian theology was not as extreme in its anthropocentrism as post-Kantian theology, and that Patristic and Medieval Roman Catholic theologies were more inclusive of nature than were the Reformers, I judged then, and I judge now, that he was correct.

White himself pointed out that the tradition included other voices. In particular he pointed to St. Francis as offering another vision, far more suited to our current needs. He wrote as a Protestant layman, calling for reform and suggesting how that could come about.

Western Christianity has always been anthropocentric, and over the centuries it became increasingly so. This is especially true of Protestantism. It was this Protestantism that provided the most important context for the rise of anthropocentric and individualistic philosophy, ethics, economics, and political thought. Together with these, it has supported practices that were consistent with this individualistic anthropocentrism. These practices have changed the face of the Earth. Whatever the failures of the other great religious traditions in these respects, it is our failure that bears the chief responsibility for the degradation of the planet.

THE WAY OF PROCESS THEOLOGY

Fortunately, Christianity is not a static phenomenon. For me its greatest strength is its ability to repent. We Protestants have had much of which to repent, not only in relation to the natural world. Repentance does not mean primarily remorse, although some remorse is no doubt appropriate. It means changing direction. It consists, therefore, of rethinking our theology.

John B. Cobb, Jr.

The easiest form of repentance for Protestants is the recovery of neglected biblical themes. The most apparent biblical theme, obviously relevant to our current concern, that has been seriously neglected in mainstream Protestant theology is that of creation. The Bible begins with the account of how God made the heavens and the earth. In the nineteenth century, Protestant theologians dismissed this story to the periphery in order to accent the covenant relation of God with Israel and also to avoid debates with biologists about evolution.

Now the story has been recovered, not for scientific information, but for its clear affirmation of the whole of nature as important to God and as good in God's eyes. What God appreciates, we should appreciate also. Instead of seeing nature as simply a stage on which the human drama is played out, Protestants have been recovering the more biblical vision that the whole of human history takes place in the context of nature and in continuity with nature. What happens in the natural world is of intrinsic importance as well as having vast instrumental importance for human beings.

These teachings are reinforced by the story of the flood. In particular the story of Noah and his ark had been marginalized as a nice story for children. But today we appreciate how it emphasized that human history is interconnected with and dependent upon the conditions of nature. In particular it shows God's concern for the preservation of species, or, in contemporary parlance, for biodiversity.

Once the Kantian spectacles are removed, it is clear that within the Bible the concern for the whole of nature and its interaction with human beings is persistent. Even the eschatological vision, that is, the hope for final salvation, includes the natural world. The salvation that is celebrated is not so much of individual souls from the world as of the world itself, including, of course human beings. Protestant Biblical scholars have reread and reinterpreted extensively.

I speak as a particular type of Protestant theologian, a "process" one. The University of Chicago Divinity School was for many years the chief place where this more naturalistic form of theology was taught. Process theologians have given some leadership in the recovery of creation thinking. In the World Council of Churches, Charles Birch, a biologist as well as a process theologian, provided important leadership in the official affirmation of environmental "sustainability" as a central concern in 1975 at Nairobi. Official acknowledgment of the theological importance of the natural world in Protestant circles dates only from then.

The World Council held a meeting at the Massachusetts Institute of Technology in 1979, on "Faith, Science and the Future." Birch played another role there still more significant for clarifying the distinctiveness of process theology in the Protestant context. The participants were to be divided into groups to discuss diverse issues, such as atomic energy, education, transfer of technology, and economics. Planners recognized that there should also be one group dealing with the underlying theological questions. This they entitled "Faith and Science." Birch proposed an additional group dealing with "nature, humanity, and God." Because of the support of an Eastern Orthodox bishop, this proposal was accepted. I ended up chairing that group.

The difference between the two topics indicates that between Kantian and non-Kantian theology. Under the influence of Kant, most professional Protestant theology had fallen into the modern philosophical bias of defining issues epistemologically. Faith and science are two ways of knowing. The question is, then, how they are related.

Process theology, on the other hand, argues that even epistemology has ontological assumptions; it does not provide a neutral, foundational point of departure. It is just as important to articulate what we believe about the real world as to focus on how we know what we know. Neither approach transcends our always partial perspectives, and, indeed, no such transcendence is possible. This means that process theologians develop our theories about nature and about God as having their reality independently of how they are known by human beings. It also means that we recognized the speculative or hypothetical character of all our affirmations.

The mainstream of Western thought, including the mainstream of Protestant theology, is more comfortable to remain epistemological in focus. Since the epistemological focus is inherently anthropocentric, the mainstream has not adequately overcome anthropocentrism even when it reconnects faith with science. From the perspective of process theologians, the rediscovery of biblical ways of thinking helps to overcome this anthropocentrism of the mainstream, but until the problem with the epistemological starting point is directly faced, the improvement will not have full effect.

These comments indicate that Protestant theology is changing. Process theologians hope that it will change much more. Any sociohistorical movement changes slowly, and those that deal with matters of ultimate concern may be peculiarly slow. There is the danger that the sense of ultimacy be attached to existing beliefs and practices rather than to the object of ultimate devotion.

Nevertheless, change does occur. Protestantism began as change in Christian teaching based on recursion to biblical authority against the way doctrine and practice had developed in fifteen hundred years of tradition. Protestants emphasized the fallibility of human interpretation of God's revelation. Calvinists, especially, insisted that reformation could not be once-for-all; it must be a continuing process. Because the authority of the Bible exceeds for Protestants the authority of any interpretation of the Bible or particular philosophical commitment, changes in biblical interpretation call for changes in doctrine and practice. To whatever extent a concern for creation as a whole is found in the Bible, in principle Protestants must repent of their neglect of this concern. That repentance is far advanced.

From the perspective of process theology, change needs to be embraced on other grounds as well. The Bible itself points us forward to new truth. When Christians encounter wisdom in any source, we should be open to learning. This means that we should assimilate what the natural sciences have to teach us, modifying our teaching accordingly. On the whole, we have done this. It means that we should be open to new understanding coming from the psychological and sociological fields, and changes have occurred in these areas as well. Recently we have been deeply challenged by recognizing that our inherited perspective, including most of that in the Bible, is masculine, and we have been seeking to open ourselves to the different sensibility and insight of women. This has proved more controversial, but much has happened nevertheless. We are now also challenged to learn from other religious traditions as well, including the primal ones.

Much of the change we need in relation to the understanding of the natural world is called for by the Biblical texts themselves. But indirectly the Bible calls us to learn about this from the natural sciences, sociology and psychology, feminists, and other religious traditions as well. To limit ourselves to the biblical texts and what tradition has drawn from them is not truly faithful to the Bible.

PROCESS THEOLOGY AND DEEP ECOLOGY

Theological environmentalism cannot be placed simply under the heading of "shallow ecology." That is usually understood as dealing with particular practical ecological problems in terms of inherited anthropocentric categories. The recognition of the importance of rethinking our intellectual, cultural, and religious heritage is central to current Protestant thought about creation. In this sense it is a form of "deep ecology," and this is especially true of process ecological theology.

Nevertheless, there are tendencies among those who identify themselves as "deep ecologists" that separate Protestant theology, including Protestant process theology, from them. I will identify five such tendencies and indicate why and how Protestant ecological theology, and especially its process form, moves in a different direction. Whether this theology is not "deep ecology" at all, or is a different form of "deep ecology," is a terminological question. But for simplicity's sake, I will use the term "deep ecology" to mean what those who founded this tradition have meant by it.

Writing as a Protestant theologian, I will not only describe the Protestant view but make a case for it. That does not mean that on all points of difference I believe Protestants to be right and deep ecologists wrong. Instead, I believe that there is a place for both approaches and hope for mutual respect.

First, those who have led in defining "deep ecology" often direct attention away from issues of justice and liberation in human relations. Protestant Christians, immersed in the Bible, cannot accept this. Especially from the perspective of process theologians, our concerns can and should extend far beyond the human species to the well-being of God's creation as a whole. But process theologians agree with other Protestants that this must not be allowed to reduce concern for human beings individually and collectively. And concerns for human beings focus on those people who are least able to meet their own needs.

My intention here is not to accuse all deep ecologists of indifference to human suffering and oppression. It is only to say that what is called "deep ecology" usually begins with the condition of the earth and moves from that to the well-being of the human species and its members. This is a rational approach to be fully respected. But it is not the Christian one.

Christians typically begin with the "neighbor" who is in need. A great deal of Christian love is expressed in a very individualistic way. But many Christians have recognized that the condition of the neighbor is bound up with wider systems—political, social, and economic. Accordingly, a great deal of attention is paid also to these systems.

All of this remained, until quite recently as we have seen, limited to the human scene. Prior to the repentance described above, Christian habits, and especially Protestant habits, and still more emphatically those habits informed by Kantian philosophy, paid very little attention to the wider ecological system in which the neighbor lives. For Protestants in general, and process theologians in particular, the shift to include this system as well takes place as an extension of neighbor love.

When this occurs, two positions are possible. Christians may recognize the importance of the ecological system because of human dependence on it. This was all that was necessarily implied when the World Council of Churches affirmed that Christians should be just as concerned that human societies be sustainable as that they be participatory and just. This is the dominant position among those for whom the influence of Kant, consciously or unconsciously, remains strong.

But Christians may recognize that the other creatures that make up the ecosystem are also valuable in themselves and to God, and this is especially emphasized by process theologians. The importance of the well-being of nonhuman creatures is, then, not simply because of their contribution to human beings. This is implied by the shift in World Council rhetoric from the sustainability of human societies to the integrity of creation. For example, the extinction of species is now opposed not only because something of value to human beings may be lost but also because each species is of value to its own members, and each species is of value to God. This leads in the direction of deep ecology.

Nevertheless, the heavy emphasis on humanity remains. The full slogan of the World Council since 1982 has been "peace, justice, and the integrity of creation." The Council knows that sometimes there are tensions among these goals. Efforts to attain justice often disrupt peace, when "peace" means the absence of violent conflict. Virtually all Christians affirm that every effort should be made to attain justice through peaceful means, but most Christians recognize that there are times when violence in the cause of justice is preferable to real alternatives.

More directly relevant to this essay is the fact that there can be tensions between the quest for justice for human beings and the quest to provide for other creatures. For example, to maintain habitat for African animals, poor human beings are sometimes denied the use of lands they need. There are also conflicts between those animal rights organizations that oppose experimentation on animals and supporters of medical research seeking a cure for AIDS by means of such research.

The natural response among Christians is to seek some way of meeting both sets of needs rather than choosing between them. But if a choice must be made, one will expect most Protestants to come down quite consistently for the poor and for sick human beings. Commitment to the human neighbor who is in need has not been significantly compromised by commitment to the integrity of creation.

There are, thus, times when there are tensions between the short-term good of human beings and the health of the natural environment. Tradeoffs are inevitable and, at least for now, most Christians remain sufficiently anthropocentric that they will tend to support meeting the immediate human need. From the perspective of process theology, the dominant Protestant community needs to move farther and become more explicit that human beings should be prepared to make sacrifices for the sake of other animals, but we agree that we should take care that these sacrifices not be imposed on those human beings who are already poor and powerless.

On the other hand, it is a serious mistake to set up the well-being of humanity and that of other creatures dualistically. Far more often, what damages one damages the other, and what helps one helps the other. If we are concerned with the future of the natural world, we must be concerned with peace as well as with justice and participation in human affairs, and if we are concerned with peace as well as justice and participation in human affairs, we must be concerned with the health of the natural world.

For process theologians even that terminology separates humanity too far from nature. It reflects the influence of Kantian dualism rather than deeper Christian traditions. The biblical language of creation unites the human and the natural, and it is with the whole of creation, with its integrity, that we are now to concern ourselves.

Second, whereas Christians see humanity as part of creation, we still see human beings as playing a distinctive role within that creation. The distinction between human beings and the remainder of creation—for convenience I will call it "nature" despite the misleading impression that human beings are not part of nature—continues to be important not only because of our special concern for justice and liberation but also because of our need to reflect about our distinctive role. Deep ecology seems to view the human species as simply one among others in a way that minimizes consideration of its special responsibility for the whole.

Of course, the human species is, for Protestant theology as well, one among others. But for those shaped by the Bible, it is that species that plays the dominant role in the whole and which, therefore, has responsibility for the well-being of the whole. The reality of dominance seems to us confirmed by the actual situation. Indeed, the totality of our dominion over most other species has been realized in truly disturbing ways. Habitable wilderness exists today only where human beings determine that some fragments should survive. The very fact that we have exercised our dominion so disastrously calls us now to exercise it responsibly—not to suppose that we do not have dominion.

Deep ecologists rightly point out that talk of dominion has been part and parcel of an attitude and sensibility that has done enormous harm. They seek a different spirituality, one in which ideas of management and control would be replaced by the sense of connectedness, kinship, and reverence for otherness. They prize letting things be rather than changing them into what suits us. From the point of view of process theologians, they are correct in all this.

But Christians cannot accept the conclusions that deep ecologists sometimes draw from this. The fate of the earth in fact lies in human hands. It is certainly true that unless there are basic changes in the way human beings behave, we are destined for a terrible end. It is also true that this change can only occur if deep-seated attitudes, or our basic spirituality, change. But the change should not be away from responsibility for what happens.

One important way of exercising dominion is to withdraw from controlling presence where that is possible—to leave wilderness alone. But that is an exercise of human responsibility, not the abandonment of the dominant role for which deep ecologists sometimes seem to call. To us it seems that we can counter the still dominant exploitative mentality, if at all, only with a mentality of responsible concern.

Third, deep ecology often speaks of nature or the earth as sacred. Process theologians affirm that against the treatment of other creatures as simply means to human ends this is a valuable reaction. We believe also that for those Protestants who, under the influence of Enlightenment humanism, have become accustomed to speaking of human personality as sacred, this extension of sacredness to all creation is salutary. It is wrong to draw a line between the human and the natural that is supposed also to separate the sacred and the profane. If we connect the sacred with intrinsic value and the profane with instrumental value, we can recognize in this distinction the anthropocentrism that has had such devastating effects. Hence, process theologians can celebrate the growing sense of the sacredness of all creatures.

Nevertheless, that language is, from a historic Protestant perspective, dangerously misleading. Speaking rigorously, the line between the sacred and the profane is better drawn between God and creatures. To place any creatures on the sacred side of the line is to be in danger of idolatry. For many Protestants, including process theologians, the right way to speak is incarnational, immanental, or sacramental. God is present in the world—in every creature. But no creature is divine. Every creature has intrinsic value, but to call it sacred is in danger of attributing to it absolute value. That is wrong.

Deep ecologists in general are not theists. Indeed, with much justification, they see most forms of theism as having directed attention away from the natural world and fo-

John B. Cobb, Jr.

cused it on the relation of the individual believer to a transcendent Other. The concentration of the sacred in this Other is a major cause of the disenchantment of nature and hence of its ruthless exploitation. The denial of this transcendent God opens the way to the renewed sacralization of nature which inhibits human arrogance in relation to it.

Here, too, the position of deep ecologists is deserving of full respect. Their picture of what has happened and what can happen is correct. But the move they make is one that Protestants, including those in the process traditions, cannot follow. And from the Protestant perspective, it is a dangerous one.

Once something is viewed as sacred, judgments of relative value or importance cease to function. Within Protestantism, we have seen something like this in the thought of Albert Schweitzer. His doctrine of reverence for life precluded any judgments with respect to the relative value of one form of life and another. On the other hand, in practice he made such judgments all the time. He killed bacteria for the sake of the health of his human patients. To nurse a bird back to health, he fed it fish. In these acts he expressed normal Protestant values.

But for most Protestants, and certainly for process theologians, there is an advantage in articulating the principles by which one acts so that they can be criticized and discussed. One problem with having declared human life to be sacred is that it has made very difficult the many decisions that have to be made in the area now known as bioethics. If all human life is sacred, how can we articulate the basis on which we make decisions about which life to save when we must choose?

It seems better to many Protestants, and certainly to process theologians, to affirm that only God is sacred but that God's Spirit is present in every creature. All creatures have intrinsic value. In addition, they have value for God and for other creatures. Recognizing this has the effect of checking our casual exploitation of others for narrowly selfish purposes. But it also allows us to think about the intrinsic value of different creatures, their contributions to the divine life, and their importance in the biosystem as a whole. On the basis of such reflection, we can decide which of the many needs we confront are of greatest urgency.

Fourth, in reaction to anthropocentrism, deep ecology typically opposes all judgments about gradations of value. These gradations are often defined in terms of a hierarchy of value. Hierarchy is associated with power or authority as well as with gradation; so the use of that language has further intensified the opposition of deep ecologists. As one who has sometimes spoken of a hierarchy of value, I acknowledge the appropriateness of the deep ecology critique.

It would be too much to say that Protestants as a whole or through their institutional expressions have dealt clearly with this question. My comments here, more than elsewhere in this essay, project the implication of positions taken rather than explicit affirmations. Furthermore, they do so from the perspective of a process theologian.

Process theologians cannot give up the affirmation of gradations of value. All creatures have intrinsic value, but some have greater intrinsic value than others. That is to say, the inner life of some creatures is more complex, deeper, and richer than that of others. More positive value is lost and more suffering is inflicted in killing a whale than in destroying some plankton. Of course, this is a human judgment, but that does not make it anthropocentric in the way we should avoid. We are called to exercise our best judgment about the consequences of our actions in relation to other creatures.

The charge of anthropocentrism here is often supported by pointing out that we typically judge that creatures more like ourselves have greater value than those that differ greatly from us. There is truth in this account of how judgments work out, but similarity is not as such the basis of judgment. We do know that human beings are capable of remarkable scope and depth of experience, and that, accordingly, human experience often has great intrinsic value. Other creatures that are like us in relevant respects, we judge, also have rich experience and thus great intrinsic value.

But our judgment is about the probable richness of experience of other animals, not about the similarity of their experience to our own. Because of our limited imagination, this judgment may be distorted by similarities. We may underestimate the richness of a dolphin's experience and overestimate that of a monkey because the latter is more like us. But this would be an error in judgment; it is not built into the basis for judgment.

Furthermore, we judge God's experience to be incomparably richer than our own. If judgments of the intrinsic value of the experience of other animals is to be made on resemblance, it is resemblance to God's perfect inclusion of all that is and creative integration of this into a new whole. An experience that includes more of the world is of greater value than one that includes less. One that integrates this complexity into an effective unity is better than one that is left in discord.

I have chosen the example of whales and plankton so as to bring out a second important point. Intrinsic value is quite different from value for others or for the whole. If whales become extinct, life in the ocean will continue. They play a role in the ecology of the seas, but it is not an essential role. If plankton disappear, the whole system will collapse.

In addition to this practical interdependence, in which some creatures and species are more important than others for the well-being of the whole, there is an ontological interdependence. Each of us is constituted by relationships to all others. Even when we know nothing about the others, what happens to them affects us in some way, however slight. We are, in Paul's language, members one of another.

There are other value considerations as well. For process theologians diversity is valuable in itself. Thus, the loss of a species is important beyond the loss of individual members or the damage to the ecosystem. This is true because the diversity of creatures contributes to some extent to the richness of the experience of all, but decisively and universally to the all-inclusive divine experience.

John B. Cobb, Jr.

My point is that responsible action for the sake of the creation must be based on complex judgments of value. These are inhibited by the refusal to acknowledge gradations of value. Since as Protestants we are committed to accepting responsibility for what happens—this is sometimes called stewardship—we also need to reflect on the bases on which we make judgments.

Fifth, as a process theologian I find it necessary to address a question on which thus far very few Protestant institutions have spoken clearly. It is the concern for individual animals, especially for those judged to have significant subjective experience.

The World Council language about the integrity of creation translates into recognition that our concern for the well-being of creation should not be simply anthropocentric and that other species are of importance to God. Thus far, however, the Council has not spelled out the implications for concern about the suffering of individual nonhuman animals.

Deep ecologists, also, for the most part do not attend to the question of individual animal suffering. Their concern for the health of the biosystem leads them to accept animal suffering as the natural course of things. That humans share in inflicting suffering on other animals is not of special importance. Interest in "humane" treatment of domesticated animals seems to many deep ecologists to be sentimental. Their concern is directed chiefly to the wild and to how human beings rightly fit into the order of the wild.

As a Protestant process theologian I am critical of both my fellow Protestants and deep ecologists on this score. I share their concern for the system as a whole and the species that make it up. But that is no reason to be indifferent to the vast amount of unnecessary suffering inflicted by human beings on helpless fellow creatures.

If we had to choose between preserving a viable biosphere and reducing the suffering of domesticated animals, I would accept the priority of the former without question. But neglecting an issue because it is not the *most* important one is a serious mistake. From the point of view of a process theologian, the suffering of our fellow creatures, whether human or not, causes suffering to God. This view has good Biblical warrant. To cause unnecessary pain to others, whether they are human or not, is to inflict pain, unnecessarily, both on them and on God. There is nothing sentimental about the commitment to reduce such pain and suffering.

Since the recent move beyond anthropocentrism in Protestant leadership has not yet expressed itself explicitly in concern for the suffering of individual animals, I have not posed this as a conflict between Protestant theology and deep ecology. Nevertheless, there is a difference that is brought out more clearly in the process form of Protestant theology than elsewhere but is implicit in Protestant thought generally.

Protestants emphasize the subjectivity of the other. When one person relates to another, the other is understood not primarily as what appears in one's sense experience of the other but as a partly independent subject of experience—as a thou. How the thou feels is important. Hence, inflicting unnecessary pain and suffering on another individual human being is self-evidently wrong. Even though there are theoretical issues stemming from traditional doctrines of divine impassability, most Protestants understand from the Bible that God cares about this pain and suffering.

When Protestants affirm, with the Bible, that God's care is not for human beings alone, there is a very natural extension of the concern about individual human suffering to those other creatures about whom God cares. Indeed, until this extension is made explicit, one will have to suspect that the grip of anthropocentric thinking has not been fully broken. Furthermore, millions of Protestants have long since made this move and provide much of the support and even leadership of organizations committed to the betterment of the condition of domesticated animals.

Finally, it is noteworthy that an organization such as the Humane Society of the United States, headed by a former Protestant minister, has expanded its concerns and commitments far beyond the humane treatment of domesticated animals. It now places that concern in a wider context. Just as concern for the individual neighbor has led Protestants to systemic analysis; so concern for individual nonhuman animals is leading to such systemic analysis. Thus far I have not seen a similar move from the side of deep ecology to sympathetic interest in animal suffering.

We find it dangerous, also, to react so strongly against anthropocentrism as to minimize the distinctive value of individual human beings. For those informed by the Bible, individual persons have a special preciousness for God and should be held in that way by other human beings. Repentance for destructive anthropocentrism should not be allowed to reduce our sensitive concern for the human neighbor who is in need.

CONCLUSION

All of these qualifications of the basic agreements with deep ecology often lead deep ecologists to reject our position and to hold that it continues to be anthropocentric. This, too, is a matter of definition. As a Protestant process theologian, I reject anthropocentrism in the following ways.

1. God cares for all creatures, not just for human beings, and human beings should follow in that universal care.
2. The value of other creatures is not limited to their value for us. Their value for God, for one another, and for themselves is also important. Human values should sometimes be sacrificed for the sake of others.
3. Reality is what it is in itself and not restricted to how it is experienced by human beings.
4. Individual human beings and even humanity as a whole are not self-contained. We are physically and psychically embedded in a matrix that includes the other crea-

tures. Our relations to them are internal to our being. Destruction and loss anywhere diminishes me.

As a process Protestant theologian, I retain what deep ecologists call anthropocentrism in the following respects.

1. In all probability individual human beings are the greatest embodiments of intrinsic value on the Earth.
2. Human beings have a responsibility for other creatures in a way that is shared by no other species. A great deal depends on how we exercise that responsibility, and that means that we should acknowledge and affirm it as well as repent of the way we have exercised dominion in the past.
3. In order to exercise our responsibility well, we must make judgments of relative value about other creatures. We know these are human judgments, and this knowledge should lead us to be particularly careful not to make the judgments anthropocentrically. At the same time, there is no basis for making these or any other judgments that does not depend on distinctively human experience.

The accent in this essay has been on places at which Protestant theologians, including Protestant process theologians, disagree with what is usually called deep ecology. But from the point of view of those Protestants who are trying to move Protestant practice to catch up with the best Protestant thinking, the work of deep ecologists is to be celebrated and they are to be thanked for their leadership. We Protestants must do our own thinking out of our own heritage. But in doing that we are indebted to the stimulus of those who stand outside our community, who point out our faults, and who provide alternatives that at least on some issues are far ahead of us.

It is important also to recognize that in the broader scene the differences between us are minor in comparison with the agreements. We cannot merge forces; the differences are too great for that. But on most of the issues that face humankind so urgently today, we *can* and should learn to appreciate one another's contributions.

On many fronts, furthermore, we can work together. No one group of those concerned for the fate of the earth has the power to save it. It is far from clear that even if we work together wherever our agreements allow, pooling our resources to accomplish what most needs to be done, we can succeed. But it is very clear that if we fall into academic habits of endless debate, instead of appreciating one another in our differences and supporting one another's efforts when that is possible, the united forces of exploitation will continue to rape the earth.

"THE SCOPE OF THE BODY: THE COSMIC CHRIST"

Sallie McFague

The suffering of creation—undoubtedly the greater reality for most creatures, human as well as nonhuman—is addressed by the scope of the body or the cosmic Christ. *Whatever happens*, says our model, happens to God also and not just to us.[1] The body of God, shaped by the Christic paradigm, is also the cosmic Christ—the loving, compassionate God on the side of those who suffer, especially the vulnerable and excluded. All are included, not only in their liberation and healing, but also in their defeat and despair. Even as the life-giving breath extends to all bodies in the universe, so also does the liberating, healing, *and* suffering love of God. The resurrected Christ is the cosmic Christ, the Christ freed from the body of Jesus of Nazareth, to be present in and to all bodies.[2] The New Testament appearance stories attest to the continuing empowerment of the Christic paradigm in the world: the liberating, inclusive love of God for all is alive in and through the entire cosmos. We are not alone as we attempt to practice the ministry of inclusion, for the power of God is incarnate throughout the world, erupting now and then where the vulnerable are liberated and healed, as well as where they are not. The quiescent effect on human effort of the motif of sacrificial suffering in the central atonement theory of Christianity has made some repudiate any notion of divine suffering, focusing entirely on the active, liberating phase of God's relation to the world.[3] But there is a great difference between a sacrificial substitutionary atonement in which the Son suffers for the sins of the world and the model of the God as the body within which our bodies live and who suffers with us, feeling our pain and despair. When we have, as disciples of Jesus' paradigmatic ministry, actively fought for the inclusion of excluded bodies, but nonetheless are defeated, we are not alone, even here. And the excluded and the outcast bodies for which we fought belong in and are comforted by the cosmic Christ, the body of God in the Christic paradigm.

THE DIRECTION OF CREATION
AND THE PLACE OF SALVATION

The immediate and concrete sense of the cosmic Christ—God with us in liberation and in defeat—is the first level of the scope or range of God's body. But there are two additional dimensions implied in the metaphor that need focused and detailed attention. One is the relationship between creation and salvation in which salvation is the *direction* of creation and creation is the *place* of salvation. The metaphor of the cosmic Christ suggests that the cosmos is moving *toward* salvation and that this salvation is taking place *in* creation. The other dimension is that God's presence in the form or shape of Jesus' paradigmatic ministry is available not just in the years 1–30 C.E. and not just in the church as his mystical body, but everywhere, in the cosmic body of the Christ. Both of these dimensions of the metaphor of the cosmic Christ are concerned with *place* and *space*, with where God's body is present in its Christic shape.[4] Christian theology has not traditionally been concerned with or interested in spatial matters, as we have already noted, priding itself on being a historical religion, often deriding such traditions as Goddess, Native, and "primitive" for focusing on place, on sacred spaces, on the natural world. But it is precisely place and space, as the common creation story reminds us, that must now enter our consciousness. An ecological sensibility demands that we broaden the circle of salvation to include the natural world, and the practical issues that face us will, increasingly, be ones of space, not time. On a finite, limited planet, arable land with water will become not only the symbol of privilege but, increasingly, the basis of survival. Geography, not history, is the ecological issue. Those in the Christian tradition who have become accustomed to thinking of reality in a temporal model—the beginning in creation; the middle in the incarnation, ministry, and death of Jesus Christ; and the end at the eschaton when God shall bring about the fulfillment of all things—need to modify their thinking in a spatial direction. We need to ask where is this salvation occurring here and now, and what is the scope of this salvation?

In regard to the first dimension of the cosmic Christ, what does it mean to say that salvation is the *direction* of creation and creation is the *place* of salvation? To say that salvation is the direction of creation is a deceptively simple statement on a complex, weighty matter. It is a statement of faith in the face of massive evidence to the contrary, evidence that we have suggested when we spoke of the absurdity of such a claim in light of both conventional standards and natural selection. Some natural theologies, theologies that begin with creation, try to make the claim that evolutionary history contains a teleological direction, an optimistic arrow, but our claim is quite different. It is a retrospective, not a prospective claim; it begins with salvation, with experiences of liberation and healing that one wagers are from God, and reads back into creation the hope that the whole creation is included within the divine liberating, healing powers. It is a statement of faith, not of fact;

it takes as its standpoint a concrete place where salvation has been experienced—in the case of Christians, the paradigmatic ministry of Jesus and similar ministries of his disciples in different, particular places—and projects the shape of these ministries onto the whole. What is critical, then, in this point of view about the common creation story is not that this story tells us anything about God or salvation but, rather, that it gives us a new, contemporary picture with which to remythologize Christian faith. The entire fifteen-billion-year history of the universe and the billions of galaxies are, from a Christian perspective, from this concrete, partial, particular setting, seen to be the cosmic Christ, the body of God in the Christic paradigm. Thus, the direction or hope of creation, all of it, is nothing less than what I understand that paradigm to be for myself and for other human beings: the liberating, healing, inclusive love of God.

To say that creation is the place of salvation puts the emphasis on the here-and-now aspect of spatiality. While the direction motif takes the long view, speaking of the difficult issue of an evolutionary history that appears to have no purpose, the place motif underscores the concrete, nitty-gritty, daily, here-and-now aspect of salvation. In contrast to all theologies that claim or even imply that salvation is an otherworldly affair, the place motif insists that salvation occurs *in* creation, in the body of God. The cosmic Christ is the physical, available, and needy outcast in creation, in the space where we live. In Christian thought creation is often seen as merely the backdrop of salvation, of lesser importance than redemption, the latter being God's main activity. We see this perspective in such comments as "creation is the prologue to history" or "creation provides the background and setting for the vocation of God's people,"[5] and in Calvin's claim that nature is the stage for salvation history. In this way of viewing the relation between creation and redemption, creation plays no critical role: it is only the stage on which the action takes place, the background for the real action. But in our model of the body of God as shaped by the Christic paradigm, creation is of central importance, for creation—meaning our everyday world of people and cities, farms and mountains, birds and oceans, sun and sky—is the place where it all happens and to whom it happens. Creation as the place of salvation means that the health and well-being of all creatures and parts of creation is what salvation is all about—it is God's place and our place, the one and only place. Creation is not one thing and salvation something else; rather, they are related as scope and shape, as space and form, as place and pattern. Salvation is for all of creation. The liberating, healing, inclusive ministry of Christ takes place *in* and *for* creation.

These two related motifs of the direction of creation and the place of salvation both underscore expanding God's liberating, healing, inclusive love to all of the natural world. This expansion does not eclipse the importance of needy, vulnerable human beings, but it suggests that the cosmic Christ, the body of Christ, is not limited to the church or even to human beings but, as coextensive with God's body, is *also* the direction of the natural world and the place where salvation occurs.

NATURE AND THE COSMIC CHRIST

These comments lead us into the second dimension of the metaphor of the cosmic Christ, which also concerns spatiality. The world in our model is the sacrament of God, the visible, physical, bodily presence of God. The cosmic Christ metaphor suggests that Jesus' paradigmatic ministry is not limited to the years 1–30 C.E. nor to the church, as in the model of the church as the mystical body of Christ, but is available to us throughout nature. It is available everywhere, it is unlimited—with one qualification: it is mediated *through bodies*. Our model is unlimited at one end and restrictive at the other: the entire cosmos is the habitat of God, but we know this only through the mediation of the physical world. The world as sacrament is an old and deep one in the Christian tradition, both Eastern and Western. The sacramental tradition assumes that God is present not only in the hearing of the Word, in the preaching and reading of Scripture, and not only in the two (or seven) sacraments of the church, but also in each and every being in creation. While Christian sacramentalism derives from the incarnation ("the Word became flesh"), the sense of the extraordinary character of the ordinary or the sacredness of the mundane is scarcely a Christian insight. In fact, it is more prevalent and perhaps more deeply felt and preserved in some other religious traditions, including, for instance, Goddess, Native, and Buddhist ones.[6] Moreover, Christian sacramentalism has usually been utilitarian in intent, that is, using the things of the world as symbols of religious states. They are often not appreciated in their own integrity as having intrinsic value but rather as stepping stones on one's pilgrimage to God. This perspective is evident in a famous passage from Augustine's *Confessions*, in which all the delights of the senses are transmuted into symbols of divine ecstasy: "But what is it I love when I love You? Not the beauty of any bodily thing . . . Yet in a sense I do love light and melody and fragrance and food and embrace when I love my God—the light and the voice and the fragrance and the food and embrace in the soul. . . ."[7] This tradition is rich and powerful, epitomized in a sensibility that sees God in everything and everything full of the glory of God: the things of this earth are valuable principally as vehicles for communication with the divine. A different sensibility is evident in this Navajo chant:

> May it be delightful my house;
> From my head may it be delightful;
> To my feet may it be delightful;
> Where I lie may it be delightful;
> All above me may it be delightful;
> All around me may it be delightful.[8]

The delight here is in and not through the ordinary; the ordinary is not chiefly a symbol of the divine delight. The difference between these sensibilities is epitomized in two lines, one from Hildegard of Bingen, a medieval German mystic ("Holy persons draw to themselves all that is earthly") and one from Abraham Heschel, a contemporary Jewish theologian ("Just to be is a blessing, Just to live is holy").[9] The first perspective transmutes all things earthly into their holy potential, while the second finds ordinary existence itself to be holy.

Nevertheless, in spite of its limitations, traditional sacramentalism is an important perspective, for it is the major way Christianity has preserved and developed an appreciation for nature. It has encouraged Christians to look upon the world as valuable—indeed, as holy—and has served as a counterforce to two other perspectives on nature within Christian history, one that divorces it totally from God through secularizing it and one that dominates and exploits it. Traditional sacramentalism has, in its own way, supported the principal thesis of this essay: the model of the world (universe) as God's body means that the presence of God is not limited to particular times or places but is coextensive with reality, with all that is. It has been one of the few traditions within Christianity that has encouraged both a spatial and a historical perspective; that is, Christian sacramentalism has included nature as a concern of God and a way to God rather than limiting divine activity to human history. For these and other reasons Christian sacramentalism should be encouraged. It is a distinctive contribution of Christianity. From its incarnational base, it claims that in analogy with the body of Jesus the Christ all bodies can serve as ways to God, all can be open to and give news of the divine presence. But it does not claim, at least primarily, that bodies have intrinsic value. The great theologians and poets of the Christian sacramental tradition, including Paul, John, Irenaeus, Augustine, the medieval mystics (such as Julian of Norwich, Meister Eckhart, Hildegard of Bingen), Gerard Manley Hopkins, and Pierre Teilhard de Chardin, love the things of this world principally *as expressions of* divine beauty, sustenance, truth, and glory.[10] It is not a sensibility that in a homey phrase wants "to hold on hard to the huckleberries."[11] The value of huckleberries as huckleberries is not a major concern of Christian sacramentalism.

Again, we need to remind ourselves that for the purposes of the planetary agenda, no one tradition needs to claim universality or the whole truth. What is more helpful is to specify the *kind* of insights that are distinctive of different traditions. The Christian tradition does not underscore the intrinsic value of all things earthly but does express richly and deeply the symbolic importance of each and every body on the earth: each in its own way expresses divine reality and is valuable for this reason. Unfortunately, traditional sacramentalism is not a central concern for many Christians; in fact, some Protestant churches scarcely attend to it. Yet it can be a way that Christians, at least, might begin to change their exploitative, utilitarian attitudes toward nature—as well as toward other humans whose bodies are also expressions of God. As Hopkins puts it, "Christ plays in ten thousand places, lovely in limbs, lovely in eyes not his."[12] If use is to be made of our earth

Sallie McFague

and its people and other creatures, it can only be a use, says Christian sacramentalism, for God's glory, not for our profit.

Nevertheless, we suggest two qualifications of traditional sacramentalism. The first is implicit in the direction of this entire essay: the need to replace the utilitarian attitude toward other beings that accompanies anthropocentrism with a perspective that values them intrinsically. If we are not the center of things, then other beings do not exist for our benefit—even for our spiritual growth as ways to God. They exist within the vast, intricate web of life in the cosmos, of which they and we are all interdependent parts, and each and every part has both utilitarian and intrinsic value. Within our model of the world as God's body, all of us, human beings included, exist as parts of the whole. Some parts are not merely means for the purposes of other parts, for all parts are valued by God and hence should be valued by us. We do have a distinctive role in this body, but it is not as the ones who use the rest as a ladder to God; rather, it is as the ones who have emerged as the caretakers of the rest.

The second qualification of traditional sacramentalism picks up on this note of care and might be called "negative sacramentalism." It focuses on bodies not as expressions of divinity, but as signs of human sin and destruction. It is a perspective on the earth and its many bodies that sees them not as telling of the glories of God but of human destruction. The bodies of the earth, human and nonhuman, that are vulnerable and needy cry out for compassion and care. These bodies appear to us, in the closing years of the twentieth century, not primarily as expressions of divine loveliness, but as evidence of human neglect and oppression. The focus is not on their use to help us in our religious pilgrimage but on our misuse of them, our refusal to acknowledge these bodies as valuable in and for themselves and to God. One of the motifs of our analysis of the model of the world as God's body from the perspective of the common creation story is that all bodies are united in webs of interrelatedness and interconnectedness. This motif has been radicalized by the Christic paradigm that reaches out to include especially the vulnerable, outcast, needy bodies. Hence, I would suggest that a form of Christian sacramentalism for an ecological era should focus not on the use of all earthly bodies but on our care of them, in the ways that the Christic paradigm suggests. We are suggesting that the Christic shape to God's body be applied to the full scope of that body, especially to the new poor, the natural world. Nature, its flora and fauna, therefore would not simply be addenda to human salvation, avenues providing deeper communion between God and human beings; rather, the Christic salvific paradigm would also be applied to the earth and its many creatures. This is what a cosmological or ecological context for theological reflection demands: the whole cosmos is God's concern, not just its human inhabitants and not merely as our habitat.

In what ways, then, should the Christic paradigm be applied to the natural world? In the same ways as applied to other outcasts: the deconstructive phase (liberation from oppressive hierarchies as seen in the parables), the reconstructive (physical sustainability as suggested by the healing stories), and the prospective (inclusion of all as manifest in the eating practices). These primary, active dimensions of the Christic paradigm—the shape of the cosmic Christ given to God's body—are balanced by a secondary, passive phase, the suffering of God with the despairing and defeated. What does each of these themes suggest to us as we reflect on the deteriorating, needy body of our planet earth?

Just as, in the overturning of oppressive, dualistic hierarchies, poor people are liberated from their enslavement by the rich, people of color are liberated from discrimination by whites, so also the earth and its many nonhuman creatures are liberated from oppression and destruction by human beings. The dualistic hierarchy of people over nature is an old and profound one, certainly as ancient as the patriarchal era that stretches back some five thousand years.[13] Until the sixteenth-century scientific revolution, however, and the subsequent marriage of science with technology, human beings were not sufficiently powerful to wreak massive destruction on nature. But we now are. The first phase, then, of extending the Christic paradigm beyond human beings is the recognition, which involves a confession of sin, of our oppressive misuse of the major part of God's creation in regard to our planet, that is, everything and every creature that is *not* human. The destructive phase is a breaking down of our "natural" biases against nature; our prejudices that it is, at best, only useful for our needs; our rationalizations in regard to activities that profit us but destroy it. The hierarchy of humans over nature has been, at least in the West, so total and so destructive for the last several hundred years that many people would deny that nature merits a status similar to other oppressed "minorities." Nature is, of course, the *majority* in terms of both numbers and importance (it can do very well without us, but not vice versa). Bracketing that issue for the moment, however, many would still claim that it does not, like poor or oppressed people, deserve attention as intrinsically valuable. Nature is valuable insofar as and only insofar as it serves human purposes. Thus, in a telling phrase, many speak of wilderness as "undeveloped" land, that is, of course, undeveloped for human profit, though it is excellently developed for the animals, trees, and plants that presently inhabit it.

The liberation of nature from our oppressive practices, the recognition that the land and its creatures have rights and are intrinsically valuable, is by no means easy to practice, since immediately and inevitably, especially on a finite planet with limited resources and increasing numbers of needy human beings, conflicts of interest will occur. These conflicts are real, painful, and important, but the point that our model underscores is that the resolution of them from a Christian perspective cannot ignore the value and rights of 99 percent of creation on our planet. The model of the world as God's body denies this attitude, and the model of the cosmic Christ intensifies that denial. Whether we like it or not, these models say that all parts of the planet are parts of God's body and are included in the

Christic liberation from dualistic hierarchies. It is for us to figure out what this must, can, mean in particular situations where conflicts arise. The preferential option for the poor is uncomfortable wherever it is applied; it will be no less so when applied to the new poor, nature.

The second phase of the Christic paradigm, the healing phase, is especially appropriate to the nonhuman dimensions of creation. It is increasingly evident that the metaphors of sickness, degeneration, and dysfunction are significant when discussing the state of our planet. The pollution of air and water, the greenhouse effect, the depletion of the ozone layer, the desertification of arable land, the destruction of rainforests are all signs of the poor health of the earth. One of the great values of the organic model is that it not only focuses on bodies and includes the natural world (unlike many models in the Christian tradition), but it also implies that salvation includes, as the bottom line, the health of bodies. While the model helps us to focus on basic justice issues for human beings—the need for food, clean air and water, adequate housing, education and medical benefits—it also insists that we focus on the basics for other creatures and dimensions of our planet. The organic model focuses on the basics of existence: the healthy functioning of all inhabitants and systems of the planet. Jesus' healing stories are extremely valuable in a time of ecological deterioration and destruction such as we are experiencing. They refuse any early and easy spiritualizing of salvation; they force us, as Christians, to face the deep sickness of the many bodies that make up the body of God. These embarrassing stories are part of the mud of our tradition, the blood-and-guts part of the gospel that insists that whatever more or else Christian faith might be and mean, it includes as a primary focus physical well-being. And nature, in our time, is woefully ill.

Most of us, most of the time, refuse to acknowledge the degree of that sickness. It is inconvenient to do so, since curing the planet's illnesses will force human inhabitants to make sacrifices. Hence, denial sets in, a denial not unlike the denial many people practice in relation to serious, perhaps terminal, illness when it strikes their own bodies. But denial of the planet's profoundly deteriorating condition is neither wise nor Christian: it is not wise because, as we increasingly know, we cannot survive on a sick planet, and it is not Christian because, if we extend the Christic healing ministry to all of creation, then we must work for the health of its many creatures and the planet itself.

This brings us to the third and final phase of the Christic paradigm as extended to the whole body of God: the inclusive fulfillment epitomized in Jesus' eating practices. As with the healing stories, the stories of Jesus feeding the multitudes and inviting the excluded to his table are embarrassments, perhaps scandals, in their mundanity and inclusivity. Neither conventional standards nor natural selection operates on the themes of sharing and inclusion; these stories are countercultural and counterbiological, but they are hints and clues of a new stage of evolution, the stage of our solidarity with other life-forms, especially with the needy and outcast forms. The time has come, it appears, when our competition with various other species for survival will not result in a richer, more complex and diverse community of life-forms. The human population is already so dominant that it is likely to wipe out many other forms and probably seriously harm its own, if predictions of our exponential growth prove true and the profligate life-style of many of us continues. The good life rests in part, then, on human decisions concerning sharing and inclusion, with food as an appropriate and powerful symbol of both bare existence as well as the abundant life. In the Christian tradition food has always served these dual functions, though the emphasis has often been on the latter meaning, especially in the eucharist as a foretaste of the eschatalogical banquet. But in our time, the value of food is precisely its literal meaning: sustainability for bodies, especially the many bodies on our planet that Christians as well as others in our society think of as superfluous. In a telling reversal of the need of all bodies for food, many people assume that other creatures not only do not *deserve* food but are themselves *only* food—food for us.[14]

The paradigmatic Christic shape of the body of the world, then, suggests some hints and clues for Christians as we, in an ecological age, extend that shape to be coextensive with the world, superimposing, as it were, the cosmic Christ on the body of God. We look at the world, our planet and all its creatures, through the shape of Christ. As we do so, we acknowledge the distinctive features of that form, especially liberation from our destructive oppression, the healing of its deteriorating bodies, and the sharing of basic needs with all the planet's inhabitants, that the Christian tradition can contribute to the planetary agenda.

But we are not left alone to face this momentous, indeed, horrendous, task. Ecological despair would quickly overwhelm us if we believed that to be the case. The cosmic Christ as the shape of God's body also tells us that God suffers with us in our suffering, that divine love is not only with us in our active work against the destruction of our planet but also in our passive suffering when we and the health of our planet are defeated. An attitude of sober realism, in view of the massiveness of ecological and human oppression that faces us in our time, is the appropriate—perhaps the only possible—attitude. We and our planet may, in fact, be defeated, or, at least life in community, life worth living, may no longer be possible. The situation we face is similar in many respects to that portrayed in Albert Camus's powerful allegorical novel, *The Plague*, in which a mysterious and devastating plague overwhelmed and destroyed most of the inhabitants of a contemporary Algerian town. It was a symbol of the modern malaise, but for our purposes "the plague" can serve as a literal description of deepening planetary sickness. The response of one of the book's chief activists fighting the plague is a soberly realistic one: "All I maintain is that on this earth there are pestilences and there are victims, and it's up to us, so far as possible, not to join forces with the pestilences."[15] When the work of healing fails in spite of all efforts to make it work, one must, Christians must, not "join forces with the pestilences." The cross in the Christic paradigm does not, in our model, promise victory over the pestilences, but it does assure us that God is with the victims in their suffering. That is the last word, however, not the first.

Actually, the cross is not the last word. The enigmatic appearance stories of the risen Christ, the Christ who appeared in bodily form to his disciples, is the witness to an ancient, indelible strain within the Christian community. It is the belief and the hope that diminishment and death are not the last word, but in some inexplicable manner, the way to new life that, moreover, is physical. This is an important point for an embodiment theology. The death and resurrection of Jesus Christ are paradigmatic of a mode of change and growth that only occurs on the other side of the narrow door of the tomb. Often that pattern has been absolutized as occurring completely and only in Jesus of Nazareth: his death and resurrection are the answer to all the world's woes. In his death all creation dies; in his resurrection all arise to new life. The absolutism, optimism, and universalism of this way of interpreting the ancient and recurring relationship between death and new life—a relationship honored in most religious traditions as well as in evolutionary biology—are problematic in a postmodern, ecological, and highly diverse cultural and religious era. What is possible and appropriate, however, is to embrace these strains in Christian thought as a deep pattern within existence to which we cling and in which we hope—often as the hope against hope. We must believe in the basic trustworthiness at the heart of existence; that life, not death, is the last word; that against all evidence to the contrary (and most evidence is to the contrary), all our efforts on behalf of the well-being of our planet and especially of its most vulnerable creatures, including human ones, will not be defeated. It is the belief that the source and power of the universe is on the side of life and its fulfillment. The "risen Christ" is the Christian way of speaking of this faith and hope: Christ is the firstborn of the new creation, to be followed by all the rest of creation, including the last and the least.

NOTES

1. See John Hick's analysis of major theodicies; he supports the contemporary one in which God suffers with those who suffer (*Evil and the God of Love* [New York: Macmillan, 1966]).

2. For a brief but excellent treatment of the cosmic Christ in the tradition, see Rosemary Radford Ruether, *Gaia and God: An Ecofeminist Theology of Earth Healing* (San Francisco: HarperCollins, 1992), 321ff. For two very different twentieth-century reconstructions of the cosmic Christ, see various works by Pierre Teilhard de Chardin, and Matthew Fox, *The Coming of the Cosmic Christ* (San Francisco: Harper and Row, 1988).

3. This tendency is evident in some forms of liberation theology, especially reform feminism, which is understandably cautious about embracing motifs of divine sacrifice and suffering that might encourage similar passive behavior among the oppressed.

4. One of the few instances of serious attention to the notion of space by a Christian theologian is interesting treatment by Jürgen Moltmann in *God in Creation: A New Theology of Creation and the Spirit of God* (San Francisco: Harper and Row, 1985), chap. 6.

5. Bernhard W. Anderson, "Creation in the Bible," in *Cry of the Environment: Rebuilding the Christian Creation Story*, ed. Philip N. Joranson and Ken Butigan (Santa Fe, N. M.: Bear and Co., 1984), 25.

6. Two collections of poems and prayers illustrate this point: Marilyn Sewell, ed., *Cries of the Spirit: A Celebration of Women's Spirituality* (Boston: Beacon Press, 1991); Elizabeth Roberts and Elias Amidon, eds., *Earth Prayers from Around the World* (San Francisco: Harpers, 1991).

7. *The Confessions of St. Augustine*, Bks. I–X, trans. F. J. Sheed (New York: Sheed and Ward, 1942), 10.6.

8. *Earth Prayers*, 366.

9. *Earth Prayers*, 360, 365.

10. This is a complex issue to which we cannot here do justice. There are at least two directions within this tradition, one from Augustine's Neoplatonism, which tends to absorb the things of the world into God, and the other from Thomas's Aristotelianism, which supports greater substance for empirical reality. One sees the former epitomized in the extreme realism of the doctrine of transubstantiation in which the eucharistic elements are wholly converted into the body and blood of Christ, and the latter in a poet such as Gerard Manley Hopkins with his notion of "inscape," the particular, irreducible, concrete individuality of each and every aspect of creation that is preserved and heightened in its sacramental role as a sign of God's glory. But between these poles are many other positions, with the unifying factor being that in some way or other the things of this world are valuable because of their connection to God.

11. The phrase is from an essay by the literary critic, R. W. B. Lewis, and refers to the "suchness" and "thereness" of ordinary things in the world that stand against all attempts to translate them into or use them for spiritual purposes.

12. Gerard Manley Hopkins, *Poems and Prose*, introd. by W. H. Gardner (London: Penguin Books, 1953), 51.

13. See an analysis by Gerda Lerner, *The Creation of Patriarchy* (New York: Oxford University Press, 1986).

14. On animal rights and vegetarianism, see the following: Carol J. Adams, *The Sexual Politics of Meat: A Feminist-Vegetarian Critical Theory* (New York: Continuum, 1991); Tom Regan, *The Case for Animal Rights* (Berkeley, Calif.: University of California Press, 1983).

15. Albert Camus, *The Plague*, trans. Stuart Gilbert (New York: Alfred A. Knopf, 1954), 229.

"WHAT IS ECO-KOSHER?"

Arthur Waskow

Over thousands of years, Judaism has evolved a series of precepts intended to govern the Jewish community and to keep it in internal harmony and in harmony with other peoples and the Earth. Twice in Jewish history, profound changes in society have required changes in the content of these precepts in order to achieve a new harmony in the new situation. One of those times was 2,000 years ago, when Hellenism swept across the Mediterranean basin, greatly increasing the ability of human beings to control their own history and the forces of nature, and dispersed the Jewish people into many lands.

The second time is now. Modernity has shattered the Jewish life that had become traditional, has liberated and empowered women, has transformed the very chemistry and biology of the Earth, and threatens to bring about a mass death of many species. Under these conditions, we must reexamine the content of the precepts that sought for harmony under old conditions, while drawing on the wisdom of the entire Jewish past in order to shape the new content.

Part of that wisdom was the code of eating kosher food in which only the meat of non-predatory animals and birds was kosher to eat; the food of mammalian life (milk) and mammalian death (meat) could not be eaten together; even this restricted kind of meat could only be eaten if the animal had been slaughtered in a painless way with prayerful consciousness and ritual; and vegetarianism was viewed as the higher, but not compulsory, path.

Today we must ask ourselves a broader question: Is it food alone that is subject to the precepts of a kosher life-path? If we wish to protect the Earth, then today we must explore a broader set of questions about what might be considered an "eco-kosher" life.

Are tomatoes that have been grown by drenching the earth in pesticides "eco-kosher" to eat at a wedding reception?

Is newsprint that has been made by chopping down an ancient and irreplaceable forest "eco-kosher" to use for a newspaper?

Are windows and doors so carelessly built that the warm air flows out through them and the furnace keeps burning all night "eco-kosher" for a home or a public building?

Is a bank that invests the depositors' money in an oil company that befouls the ocean an "eco-kosher" place to deposit money?

If by "kosher" we mean a broader sense of "good practice" that draws on the deep well-springs of Jewish wisdom and tradition about protecting the Earth, then none of these ways of behaving is eco-kosher.

"Eco-kosher" might as an approach speak to two kinds of Jews—both those who now live by the traditional code of kosher food and those who have decided the traditional code is no longer important to them. It might speak to other communities as well.

Why does "eco-kosher" transcend these differences? Because the Earth and the human race are in serious danger. Not economic progress but the *way* we have pursued economic progress has brought this danger. For the sake of our children and our children's children, it is crucial to address the issues. And the Jewish people has its own wisdom on these matters, rooted in our own ancient tradition of ourselves as a pastoral and agricultural people that nourished the Earth, as well as in our modern efforts to nurture the Land of Israel. So it may be of value to the human race to examine and draw on this sense of sacred practically.

Shabbat—the Sabbath—is the great challenge of the Jewish people to technology run amok. It asserts that although work can be good, it becomes good only when crowned by rest, reflection, re-creation, and renewal. The Sabbaths of the seventh day, the seventh month, the seventh year, and in principle the seventh cycle (the Jubilee at the fiftieth year) give not only human beings but animals and even plants and minerals, the entire Earth, the right to rest.

The modern age has been the greatest triumph of work, technology, in all of human history. This triumph deserves celebration. But instead of pausing to celebrate and reevaluate, we have become addicted to the work itself. For five hundred years, the human race has not made Shabbat, has not paused to reflect and reconsider, to take down this great painting from its easel and catch our breaths before putting up a new canvas to begin a new project.

Torah teaches that if we deny the Earth its Shabbats, the Earth will make Shabbat anyway—through desolation. The Earth *does* get to rest. Our only choice is whether the rest occurs with joy or disaster.

The Earth and the human race are now faced with such a moment of Shabbat denied. Triumphant human technology, run amok without Shabbat, brings the danger of impending desolation. We can quickly identify several specific areas in which these dangers are already clear:

The multiplication of thousands of nuclear-weapons warheads that, if exploded in a short period, could devastate the planet; the creation from nuclear energy plants of radioactive wastes that will need to be contained and controlled for thousands of years; the galloping destruction of the ozone layer; the overproduction of carbon dioxide from massive deforestations and the extensive burning of fossil fuels, in such a way as to make much more likely a major rise in world temperatures; the destruction of many species through destruction of their habitats.

Torah teaches not that we abandon technology but that we constrain it with Shabbat and all the implications of Shabbat. Instead, we have used technological progress to poison the earth and air and water, so that they poison us with cancer at the very moment when we take in their nourishment.

What we sow is what we reap.

If what we sow is poison, what we reap is also poison.

The planetary biosphere cannot long endure the treatment we are now giving it. Nor can the human race.

Our technology has also transformed the medium of the relationship between Earth and human earthling. Originally, food was the great connection. But that is no longer so. The human race has created an economy in which *energy*, *minerals*, and *money* take on many of the roles that land and food originally had.

That is why an eco-kosher approach to life requires us to look beyond food to such other consumable items as wood, oil, and aluminum, and to where and how we save and invest our money.

And the new conditions of the planet may also point toward changes in the content of precepts outside the arena of kosher or eco-kosher consuming of goods from the Earth.

The most important of these is the area of population and the sexual ethics that bear on population. Traditionally, Jewish sexual ethics operated under the rubric of "Be fruitful and multiply, and fill up the Earth." It strongly encouraged sexuality that was likely to procreate and rear more children, and frowned both on celibacy and on all sexuality outside a heterosexual marriage, and even then on sexual relations outside the two most fertile weeks of the woman's ovulation cycle. So traditional Jewish sexual precepts opposed gay or lesbian sexuality, masturbation, most forms of birth control, and sexual relations for the sake of loving pleasure between two adult, unmarried people.

But once the Earth is already "filled up" with human beings, where shall we look for a sexual ethic to balance one that is focused on bearing and nurturing children?

In the books of Jewish wisdom, one that looks to such a time is the *Song of Songs*. It celebrates a Garden of Eden that is no longer peopled by a childish human race that is just entering rebellious adolescence, but by adults.

Its sexual ethic is one of loving pleasure and flowing relationship between human beings and each other, and human beings and the Earth. Instead of opposing sexual expression except when it is focused on the bearing or rearing of children, the *Song of Songs* celebrates sexual expression except when it is coerced or demeaning.

In the new era of the Earth, the human race needs to balance a sexual ethic focused on children and the family with one focused on love and joy. The new "eco-kosher" sexual ethic might affirm sexual relationships between adults of any sexual orientation where there is honesty, caring, no coercion or other misuse of an imbalance in power between the parties, and no deceit of others or an attack on other relationships. And it might affirm

as well the special relationship of two people who have decided to make a more permanent commitment, including one to have and rear children, so long as they have made a
careful judgment in the light of the Earth's needs about how many children will suffice.

Why should the Jewish people and religious community bother to do all this, and why
should other communities encourage the Jews to do it? Why is this a Jewish issue and why
is it a Jewish-renewal issue? For two reasons:

We must draw on the wisdom, energy, and commitment of all peoples, each of them in
the specificity and uniqueness of its own world view, if we are to heal the Earth, nurture all
living beings, and protect our children from environmentally caused cancer, famine, and
other disasters.

Just as every unique species of plant and animal brings a sacred strand into the sacred
web of life, so does the unique wisdom of each human culture. Just as modernity threatens
to narrow and crush the diversity of species, so it threatens to narrow and crush the diversity of cultures. Both Jews and others are helping to heal that web of life if they give new
heart and new life to endangered cultures as well as endangered species. The Jewish people
is one such endangered culture.

The shift from Biblical to Rabbinic Judaism is one of the most useful histories of how a
culture can renew and transform itself without losing its own identity. Now when the
world is being profoundly transformed, every religious tradition needs to examine how
best to renew and transform itself, neither abandoning its own deepest wisdom nor getting stuck in the transient versions of itself that worked in a departed past. [For further information on "eco-kosher," write the author at ALEPH: Alliance for Jewish Renewal, 7318
Germantown Ave., Philadelphia, PA 19119, and see his book *Down-to-Earth Judaism*
(Morrow, 1995).]

"AFRICAN-AMERICAN RESOURCES FOR A MORE INCLUSIVE LIBERATION THEOLOGY"

Theodore Walker, Jr.

Black theology is a form of liberation theology which holds that we are morally obliged to contribute to the well-being of all, and most especially to the well-being of the poor and oppressed. Black theology, on account of its appropriation of the philosophy of black power, sometimes describes contribution to the well-being of others in terms of empowerment. And most often, black theology's main social ethical concern is with the well-being and empowerment of people, i.e., "power to the people." This essay emphasizes what is occasionally but not frequently emphasized by black and other liberation theologians, that our moral obligation to contribute to the well-being and empowerment of others includes obligation to plants and animals.

In the foreword to Jay B. McDaniel's *Of God and Pelicans: A Theology of Reverence for Life*, John B. Cobb, Jr., notes that until recently the church was largely silent in regard to environmental issues. Cobb accounts for this "deafening silence" in terms of churchly fear that "attention to ecological issues would distract from that given to justice" (p. 11). But, as Cobb notes, "this has changed" because the church is coming to see that both justice and ecological sustainability "are essential and that in fact neither is possible without the other" (p. 11).

Like other churches and theologies, black churches and black theologians have been less than consistently outspoken about support for ecological and animal rights issues. Again, it would be correct to account for this relative silence by reference to the need for increased attention to human rights issues, and while it is true that John Cobb, Jay McDaniel, Sallie McFague, Thomas Berry, Tom Regan and others have done much to increase the conceptual and moral ground for unity between concern with justice and concern with the environment, there are some causes of black churchly and theological reluctance to adopt ecological and animal rights agenda which have yet to be overcome. From the perspective of many black and colored peoples, there are racial and racist aspects of modern white eco-

Reprinted from *Good News for Animals?: Christian Approaches to Animal Well-Being*, edited by Charles Pinches and Jay B. McDaniel, © 1993, by permission of the author and Orbis Books.

logical/animal rights thinking which make it somewhat more difficult for us to adopt their ecological/animal rights agenda as our own. One recent example from the literature of environmental and animal rights/protection will serve to illustrate our difficulty.

Douglas H. Chadwick's "Elephants—Out of Time, Out of Space," in *National Geographic* (vol. 179, no. 5, May 1991) includes a photograph of two white persons shooting a family of elephants in Zimbabwe (pp. 44–45). In the text we are told that the riflemen are members of a "culling team," and: "Culling, unlike poaching and trophy hunting, attempts to maintain the herd's natural age and gender balance. Still, critics emphasize the inevitable loss of genetic diversity and the horror of slaughtering great and intelligent beings" (p. 45).

Here it is reported that regard for the well-being of elephants and a sense of horror over their slaughter, produces criticism of shooting elephants, even when killing individual elephants is thought to benefit elephant life in general. In this very same article, there is a photograph of black men shooting black men. The text tells us this is Richard Leakey's "anti-poaching unit in Kenya," and that they are armed with automatic rifles, helicopter gunships, and "shoot-to-kill orders" (pp. 30–31). And we are told that as a result of Leakey's command, "more than a hundred poachers have been killed, giving Kenya's elephants a fighting chance" (p. 31). *National Geographic* reports nothing horrible, regrettable, or even critical of killing more than a hundred humans.

Obviously, this example of animal protection policy is morally problematic. Moreover, the fact that Mr. Leakey's anti-poaching unit has shoot-to-kill orders that pertain to predominantly if not exclusively black poachers in Africa, but no such homicidal power over the predominantly nonblack buyers and distributors of ivory, indicates that this valuing of elephant life over human life is helped by the fact that the humans being shot are black. This uncritical valuing of elephant life over black human life is helped by the fact that the modern West is victim of a racist heritage that regards black and colored humans as less than fully human. For instance, at one point in United States legal history, a black man was counted as "three-fifths of a man." This racist heritage no doubt helps to enable white environmentalists and animal rights advocates to experience no horror when Mr. Leakey's unit shoots to kill black humans for the sake of elephants, and when in fact they do experience horror when elephants are shot for the sake of elephants, and when in fact they would be much horrified if Mr. Leakey's antipoaching unit were to start shooting to kill the white consumers, investors, and distributors who profit from this and other destruction of wildlife.

From our perspective, many calls by white persons for an extension of the range of moral concern so as to include regard for the well-being of plants and animals are morally suspect on account of failure to include adequate regard for the well-being of black and colored humans—such as, for example, the more than one hundred persons killed by Mr. Leakey's antipoaching unit. When those who value the lives of black humans less than they value the lives of elephants, and less than they value the lives of white humans, ask us to join them in expressing their newfound concern for the well-being and rights of animals, we are not overly eager to join them. When we see environmentalists and animal rights proponents expressing criticism and concern with the well-being of elephants and other life while at the same time being utterly unconcerned about human life, just as when we see "right-to-life" activists showing much concern for the well-being of the unborn and no concern for the already born, we find it difficult, even impossible at times, to adopt their social ethical agenda as our own. Too often what passes for a wider concern inclusive of the environment is in fact a white racially gerrymandered concern which reaches out to include plants and animals while continuing to exclude black and colored peoples. These difficulties have yet to be overcome, and they must be overcome if white environmentalists and animal rights activists expect to receive the support of black and colored peoples.[1]

In the meantime, it is important for black theologians to consult nonracist traditions and resources in order to develop our own independent black churchly environmental agenda. Moreover, we must work to help our white sisters and brothers in the various environmental and ecological movements overcome the racial exclusions that continually retard the development of more inclusive efforts to contribute to ecological sustainability and liberation of other life.

Katie Geneva Cannon has an essay in a book titled *Inheriting Our Mothers' Gardens*, the language of mothers' gardens being an inheritance from Alice Walker's black womanist *In Search of Our Mothers' Gardens*. In her essay, Katie Cannon speaks about "surviving the blight" of hard times and oppression by attending to the inheritance from our mothers' gardens.[2] When black theologians attend to the inheritance from the gardens of Mother Africa, we learn that righteous social ethical reflection must take due account of the cross-generational character of human existence.

According to traditional African thought, we are morally obliged to remember and venerate the contributions of previous generations, most notably the ancestors; we are morally obliged to contribute to the well-being of our neighbors in this generation, and our neighborhood includes other life, human and nonhuman; and we have a moral responsibility to contribute to the well-being of future life (including our own future lives) and future generations. Traditional African social ethical reflection is characterized by a strong emphasis upon the need to contribute to the well-being of future life, including especially the well-being of those who are called "the beautiful ones" by Ayi Kwei Armah in his classic novel *The Beautyful Ones Are Not Yet Born*.[3] We have a moral responsibility to contribute to the well-being and empowerment of the beautiful ones who are not yet born.

This cross-generational vision of social ethical obligation is an important resource for black theological social ethical reflection. It is also a very much needed resource for modern western ethical thought. For it is clear that much of modern western ecological irresponsibility is a function of the failure to consider the well-being of future life and future generations. The well-being of other life and of future generations is regularly sacrificed for the sake of immediate monetary gain. Modern western ethical calculus seldom reaches beyond consequences which obtain for the present generation. Let us, then, cultivate among ourselves and others the habit of being explicitly attentive to the cross-generational aspects of human existence and social ethical responsibility. This is essential to the development of more ecologically responsible social ethical reflection and behavior.

Another insight essential to more ecologically responsible social ethical reflection and behavior which we can glean from traditional African sources is a more holistic vision of life and of our place within the web of life. Harvey Sindima's essay "Community of Life: Ecological Theology in African Perspective" teaches us that traditional African thought offers an alternative to the traditional western "mechanistic perspective that views all things as lifeless commodities to be understood scientifically and to be used for human ends."[4] Sindima describes the African alternative to this western-mechanistic-commodity-oriented way of seeing the world as "a life-centered way" which "stresses the bondedness, the interconnectedness, of all living beings" (p. 137). According to this African alternative, the nonhuman world of nature is not merely a collection of exploitable lifeless commodities; instead, the whole world (including nonhuman animals, plants, the earth, and its ecosystem) is seen as a living and sacred part of one divine life. Specifically, Sindima says that for Malawians, "nature and persons are one, woven by creation into one texture or fabric of life, a fabric or web characterized by an interdependence between all creatures. This living fabric of nature—including people and other creatures—is sacred" (p. 143).

For Sindima, this traditional African perspective upon the community of life calls for a more inclusive understanding of justice. Sindima defines justice in terms of "how we live in the web of life in reciprocity with people, other creatures, and the earth, recognizing that they are part of us and we are part of them" (p. 146).

Also among the important resources inherited from the gardens of Mother Africa are the ancient and antiquitous religions on North Africa, greater North Africa, and the Afro-Mediterranean world, including ancient Egyptian, Hebrew, Christian, and Moslem religions. Scripture scholars and historians of religion are already teaching us that according to these sources, the modern western habit of excluding and failing to reverence other life, including nonhuman and future life, is contrary to right relationship to God. According to early religious insights that grew out of Afro-Mediterranean soil and water, right relation to God entails right relation to creation. We must contribute to the well-being of those who are and will be loved by God, and God's love includes all creation. No creature, species, race, or gender is excluded.

The philosophy of black power is another important resource for black theological social ethical reflection. The philosophy of black power is defined by an attempt to answer the question, What must we black folk do with the resources that we control in order to contribute to the well-being and empowerment of all the people? The most recent scholarly reflection upon this question includes an attempt to correct what Harold Cruse identifies as the failed tradition of "noneconomic liberalism."[5] Noneconomic liberalism is a social strategy which focuses upon political empowerment without adequate attention to economic empowerment. During the 1980s, Cruse and other black social analysts became increasingly critical of failure to give adequate attention to economic empowerment. We should remain mindful of this criticism when thinking about environmental issues and animal rights.

Social ethical reflection upon contribution to ecological sustainability and animal protection must take account of the fact that pollution and environmental exploitation and oppression of animals and other life are financially profitable. Noneconomic or financially unprofitable environmental animal-protection policies are likely to be no more successful than noneconomic liberalism has been for African-Americans. Given the relentless pursuit of short-term financial profit, significant improvement cannot be achieved until it becomes financially profitable to be ecologically responsible. Like with struggles for human liberation, the quest for liberation of other life requires serious attention to economic matters.

Another resource related to the philosophy of black power is the inclusive conception of freedom symbolized by our liberation colors—red, black, green, and gold. Our red-black-green liberation flag was first popularized in the United States by Marcus Garvey (1887–1940) and the Universal Negro Improvement Association.[6] The color red is a symbol for blood, especially blood sacrificed in the struggle for liberty. Black symbolizes people. Green symbolizes land, particularly the motherland of Africa, and, more broadly, the whole earth. During the 1980s, African-Americans in the United States and other black people became increasingly inclined to add a fourth liberation color—gold. Gold is for the wealth and resources stolen from Mother Africa and from the earth as a whole. These colors—red, black, green, gold—symbolize a conception of freedom and a black liberation agenda which includes concern for the well-being of Mother Earth and all her creatures. Other life and life-forms—including our own future lives, the lives of the beautiful ones not yet born, the earthly ecosystem, and nonhuman lives or creatures inclusive of plants and animals—are important parts of the liberation agenda called for by our black liberation flag and colors.

Our black liberation flag and colors are conceptual resources also in that by inviting our attention to the land and its wealth, they remind us to be attentive to the plight of our farmers. Green is for the land. Gold is for the wealth and resources stolen from the land, most especially from the land of Africa. We Africans in the Americas are part of that stolen wealth. We were stolen from the land of Africa so that we could be forced to work the land that was stolen from red people in the Americas. When we were emancipated from slavery, we were driven from the rural land we had worked and farmed for others, and into the cities. Some few of us were able to stay on the land as landowners and farmers, but, in recent years, the forces of racial oppression and exploitation have joined with the forces of agribusiness and factory farming to drive us from farmland and from farming altogether. In 1910 there were approximately one million minority farmers in the United States. By 1978, there were only 57,000 black farmers in the United States. Between 1910 and 1978, African-American farmers suffered the loss of over nine million acres of land. Given the continuation of these trends, it is estimated that there will be virtually no black farmowners in the United States by the year 2000.[7]

Of course, one of the most basic resources available to us is data from the black experience of suffering and oppression. The witness of our people is that the experience of suffering is such as to entail desire to be liberated from suffering. Insofar as animals suffer, there is no doubt that they experience desire to be free of suffering. There is, then, no good reason for failure to take account of this experience in our social ethical reflection and behavior. Howard Thurman made the point about animals experiencing desire to be free of suffering and oppression by narrating an experience from his youth in Daytona Beach, Florida. Thurman recalled that on one occasion during his childhood, he happened upon a tiny green snake crawling along a dirt path. In the mischievous way that is typical of a boy child, he pressed his bare foot on top of the little snake. Immediately, the little snake began to struggle against this oppression. Young Thurman felt the tremor of the snake's struggle as it vibrated up his leg and through his body. Thurman reasoned that struggle against suffering and oppression is divinely given to the nature of all living creatures, including even little green snakes.[8]

Attention to the cross-generational character of existence and moral obligation; a more holistic vision of life, and a more inclusive understanding of justice; the ancient and antiquitous religions of North Africa, greater North Africa, and the Afro-Mediterranean world; the philosophy of black power, including attention to economic empowerment; the conception of freedom and the inclusive liberation agenda called for by our liberation colors, including attention to the land, especially farmland; and the witness of the black experience of suffering and of other experiences of suffering are all important resources for developing a liberation agenda that includes concern for the well-being of other and future life. The religious and moral reflection of Native American peoples, Korean Minjung theologies, Buddhism, process/neoclassical philosophies, and many other helpful resources are also available. The harvest is plentiful, and there is great need for our labor in these fields and gardens. It is important that black churches and black theology contribute to the growth of more ecologically responsible reflection and behavior. We African-Americans in the United States are not without a measure of responsibility for the global ecological crisis. While it is historically true that through recent generations we have been and continue to be victim of the same Euro-American oppression that has victimized the global environment, nonetheless, it is also true that at this time and in this generation and for our social location in the Euro-American world, many of us are beneficiaries of environmental exploitation. Our piano keys also contain ivory. We also drive cars, eat butchered animal flesh, use animal-tested cosmetics, and otherwise benefit from the misuse and abuse of other and future life.

Moreover, the well-being of earthly creatures and the life-sustaining capacity of the ecosystem are much too important for us to leave entirely to the resources of white people. Given the unfortunate heritage of much Western thought, they are not likely to do well without help. Environmental and animal-protection efforts are very much in need of contributions from Native Americans, Latin American campesinos, traditional Africans, and other colored and black peoples. I believe, for example, the Environmental Protection Agency would be a more diligent protector of the environment if it were heavily peopled with Native Americans. Given sufficient economic resources, native South Americans could protect the Amazon rain forests from the destruction that is presently financed by North Atlantic interests. And I am certain that African elephants would be better served if Africans were paid more to protect elephants than they are paid for ivory. For the sake of other life, including elephants, pelicans, buffalo, and humans—black and white and colored, born and yet to be born—and for the sake of right relation to God, all of us are called to help in this important work.

NOTES

1. Cain Hope Felder provides another example of ecological concern failing to include the well-being of black and colored humans in an unpublished paper—"Technology, Ecology, and the Eclipse of the Biblical Vision: Theological Reflections on the State of the Environment"—presented at the Fourth Annual Theodore Roosevelt Environment and Conservation Symposium, October 23, 1989. Felder says "It is proper to highlight President Theodore Roosevelt's concern about aspects of the natural environment. . . . Yet, we cannot forget his safaris nor those thousands of Blacks imported to Panama as cheap labor to build the Panama Canal. Anonymous hundreds of them were killed in the blasting areas, their bodies in pieces buried under the soil, unmarked; while others were crushed under boulders or became victims of malaria. Rarely does anyone dare to mention the lack of human ecology for/of African Americans during his presidency. In the area of moral human ecology, the Roosevelt legacy itself is quite mixed" (pp. 3,4).

2. See Katie Geneva Cannon, "Surviving the Blight," *Inheriting Our Mothers' Gardens: Feminist Theology in Third World Perspective*, Letty M. Russell, Kwok Puilan, Ada Maria Isasi-Diaz, Katie Geneva Cannon, eds. (Philadelphia: Westminster Press, 1988). And see Alice Walker, "In Search of Our Mothers' Gardens," in *Black Theology: A Documentary History, 1966–1979*, Gayraud S. Wilmore and James H. Cone, eds. (Maryknoll, N.Y.: Orbis Books, 1984) (originally published in *MS.*, vol. 2, no. 11, May 1974), and Alice Walker, *In Search of Our Mothers' Gardens: Womanist Prose* (San Diego: Harcourt Brace Jovanovich, 1983).

3. See Ayi Kwei Armah, *The Beautyful Ones Are Not Yet Born* (New York: Collier Books, 1969).

4. Harvey Sindima's "Community of Life: Ecological Theology in African Perspective" appears in *Liberating Life: Contemporary Approaches to Ecological Theology*, edited by Charles Birch, William Eakin, and Jay B. McDaniel (Maryknoll, N.Y.: Orbis Books, 1990), p. 137.

5. See Harold Cruse, *Plural But Equal: Blacks and Minorities in America's Plural Society* (New York: William Morrow, 1987).

6. In March 1921, the Universal Negro Improvement Association (UNIA) issued a "Universal Negro Catechism" prepared by the Reverend George Alexander McGuire (founder of the African Orthodox Church). According to this catechism, red, black, and green were established as the "National Colors of the Negro Race" at the UNIA's First International Negro Convention in New York in August 1920. See Robert Hill, ed., *Marcus Garvey Universal Negro Improvement Association Papers*, vol. 3. (Los Angeles: University of California Press, 1984), p. 319.

7. These statistics come from David M. Graybeal's 1986 film, "From This Valley: On Defending the Family Farm" (Jo Bales Gallagher, executive producer). Drawing upon data from the March 1986 report to Congress by the Office of Technology Assessment, Graybeal reports a national trend toward the increase of large corporate farms and toward decreasing numbers of medium and small family farms. In the U.S. generally, there were 7 million family farms in 1930. By 1986 that had become 2.2 million. The Office of Technology Assessment expects that very large farms will get larger, with only 50,000 of them producing three-fourths of all U.S. agricultural output, while on the other hand, moderate size and smaller farms will decline in number, market share, and net income. The plight of black and minority farmers is a very much more severe instance of this general trend. Graybeal reports that churches are coming to recognize that defense of family farming, including defense of black and minority farming, is an important item on the churchly liberation agenda. Here we are told that: "The churches are concerned by the centralization of corporate control over the national supplies of food and fiber, and by the transformation of agriculture into agribusiness. They are concerned by the pushing of dispossessed farmers into an economy that already has much unemployment. This is especially painful for black and other minority farm families and workers. The churches are concerned about a democracy in which nearly all the land is owned by the white race. They are concerned by tax policies that reward speculation in farm land by investors interested only in quick gains . . . In short, the churches are concerned about future generations and the sustainability of a food production system when land, water, and other natural resources are threatened. . . . The churches intend to resist the growth of a new feudalism."

8. Howard Thurman narrated this story on the occasion of his visit to Livingstone College in Salisbury, North Carolina, during the spring of 1978.

"AN ISLAMIC RESPONSE TO THE MANIFEST ECOLOGICAL CRISIS: ISSUES OF JUSTICE"

Nawal H. Ammar

INTRODUCTION

The crisis of an earth bleeding and burning to accommodate a fivefold economic expansion in just the last forty years is, by definition, global, and not specific to Muslims per se. Nonetheless, the manifestations of the crisis in Muslim communities and countries are as alarming as anywhere else in the world and illustrate some of the problems that afflict other religions. Some argue that the ecological crisis is the divine will of God as revealed by the Qur'an denoting the nearing of the end of life on earth. As such all this discussion about avoiding an ecological crisis is futile since it is predestined. The collective human disapproval of the crisis is of no consequence and it is actually discredited as a standard of value by some in Islam.[1] This view of predestination in Islam is not, however, maintained by all believers, although it dominates today. Islam also includes a progressive view wherein humans impact and change the world in ways that are not predestined. This debate between predestination and human free will in Islam is known as the *naql* (knowledge transmitted from revelation and tradition) versus *aqal* (knowledge transmitted from independent reason) debate. The proponents of *naql* see morality and values as not subject to human free will because only God can know what is good and what is bad.[2] The *aqal* view proponents, on the other hand, maintain that reason, guided by revelation, can provide the basis for a progressive Islamic vision of human action. Evidence supporting this progressive view can be found as early as the seventh century. The party of Unity and Justice, or the *Mu'tazilites*, insisted that God gave humans intellect to "choose conduct to decide and even to create their own acts free from predestination."[3] Reason guides in accordance with general principles and revelation gives particular parables of such principles.[4] The Qur'an emphasizes rationalism for example "Say (unto them Muhammad): Are those who know equal to those who know not? It is those who are endued with understanding that receive admonition."[5] Hence, humans, according to this school, when punished in the hereafter will be punished for sins they could have avoided. This chapter will be framed by arguments proposed by *ahl al-aqal* (the rationalists) with revelation guiding the general principles of reason.

A MUSLIM RESPONSE TO THE ECOLOGICAL CRISIS: FRAMING THE ISSUES

It is not difficult to understand the ecological crisis in its apparent manifestations as polluted air, radiation, contamination of water, and the eradication of entire species of animals and plants. It is, however, more difficult to ascertain that the processes that lead to environmental depletion and thus an ecological crisis of the magnitude we are experiencing on our earth today are the result of human injustices and greed. This type of correlation between behavior and the resulting ecological crisis is particularly difficult for a group of people, such as the Muslims in the world, who view themselves as victims of postcolonialism, racism, poverty, enslavement, and an unfair demonization. In this chapter, I am proposing, based on a rational basis, a retrieval of an Islamic response to the ecological crisis that has been long forgotten. This response assumes a confident and responsible world community of Muslims that sees itself engaged in the problems on this earth as active contributors to a global solution. This response views the reasons underlying human crisis (including the ecological one) to be behaviors of greed, lack of moderation, inequity, and disrespect (or, as Loy says in his chapter, believing in the religion of the market). Islamic history is full of examples of how such behavior has lead to losing battles against the pagans, making bad judgements, and losing the Islamic empire and hence, the Islamic identity altogether in the nineteenth century. Contemporary behavior of Muslims is also full of examples of greed, lack of moderation, and hence nonreverence to God's creation. In recent years Muslims have extracted eightfold their level of consumption of oil for export to the United States, Western Europe, and Japan.[6] The extraction of oil and its byproducts is undertaken with minimal controls on toxic emissions and hazards. The Muslim world owns 800 billion barrels of oil in future reserves.[7] To keep the price of oil at a competitive level for global consumption, stringent pollution controls are not likely to be introduced. Muslims must join other world religions in recovering the sense of the sacred, which, as Daniel Maguire says, is at the heart of all religion. The false sacreds of the market religion are invading and pervading all cultures and are the modern idols challenging all world religions today.

The polluting effect of oil reaches far beyond its production. We were all reminded of this in 1990 by the "Desert Shield/Desert Storm" war. The Iraqi invasion of Kuwait meant a loss of 25 percent of world oil reserves and a future threat to 54 percent of the world's oil reserves held by Saudi Arabia and the Emirates (Tanzer 1991, 271–72). In a war that the British press dubbed "the real estate war," 93 percent of the "precision" bombs dropped were misguided and 75 percent missed their target. At least two hundred thousand people were killed and injured. More than ten thousand Kurds were displaced. Today, a large number of U.S. Desert Storm veterans suffer from what is feared to be the consequences of a germ warfare.[8]

The setting ablaze of over six hundred oil wells on 22 February 1991 exemplifies the environmental impact of war. Toukani and Barnaby, two British scientists, summarized the global environmental effects by stating "Close to Kuwait, the plume could cause a considerable reduction in daylight; the obstruction of sunlight might significantly reduce the surface temperature locally. This in turn could reduce the rainfall over parts of South East Asia during the period of summer monsoon. If the smoke reaches the ozone layer, the smoke could lead to small reductions in ozone concentrations within the northern hemisphere."[9] Once again, the maldistribution of resources and the desire to maintain or extend access to them is directly implicated in this "real estate" war.

More than thirty Muslim nations were directly involved in this war that environmentalists are calling the "Nuclear Winter," because the effects of the oil burning has reduced sunlight and temperatures throughout the region. The future does not look any brighter for Muslims. In the last world Arms Proliferation Treaty (1995), two among the countries that refused to sign the treaty were Muslim, Pakistan and Turkey.

War, however, is not the only polluting factor in Muslim countries and communities. Water is also polluted in Muslim countries. Waste dumping into rivers, seas, or nearest streams is common and the state apparatus cannot control it. Explosives are also used to fish, thus eradicating the symbiotic environment in the habitat. Air pollution results from unregulated industrial waste disposal, the use of leaded gasoline, and the overcrowding in cities. A recent study conducted by the U.S. Agency of International Development (AID) in Egypt shows that air in Cairo is ten times more polluted than a city equal to its size in the United States. Industries discharge 1,350 tons of lead yearly into the air in Egypt. Drinking water has at its lowest estimate 9.3 milligrams more lead than the average acceptable rate globally.[10]

The behaviors illustrated above that lead to human crisis can be understood through the Arabic word *hay'a*. The word is virtually untranslatable to English. It actually denotes behaviors that reflect shyness out of respect and reverence rather than out of fear. It is behavior that reflects balance, honorable manners, and protection of God's glory including his creatures and other creation. For the purpose of this chapter I will translate the word as "dignified reserve." I am proposing that we revive this conceptual framework of *hay'a* as a guiding theological principle that could avert an ecological crisis. I suggest that the absence of *hay'a* has contributed to a livelihood among Muslims that is causing the ecological crisis. This is reflected in the disparity between the poor and the rich, a production system that is entirely dependent on the monopolies and big corporations, which in turn leads to maldistribution of resources and overconsumption, authoritarian leadership, wars, disrespect of human diversity, and finally a way of life that depletes natural and human resources. In this livelihood that lacks dignified reserve Muslims have also dehumanized women, which in turn has contributed to reducing their status to reproductive apparatuses only, hence causing the overpopulation that Muslim communities experience today. This overpopulation in turn has led to the manifest results of environmental depletion in the forms of pollution, disease, infant mortality, and crime.

In the balance of this chapter I will look at how the behaviors that lack *hay'a* in production and consumption, and toward women have contributed to the manifestations of ecological depletion. I will suggest throughout some ethical responses that are Islamic in principle and hope that their retrieval provides a solid response to averting the doomsday approach that some Muslims believe is beyond human free will and reason.

THE ISSUES IN DETAIL: MUSLIMS' ECONOMIC AND POLITICAL LIVELIHOOD AND THE ECOLOGICAL CRISIS

Islamic teachings from the Qur'an, Hadith, Sunna, and history all emphasize the need for moderation and modesty in a Muslim's life. The integration of Muslim countries and communities into the larger market economy as a consequence of national modernization, development, and desegregation have left them with maldeveloped patterns of production and consumption that do not function by moderation principles. Although Muslim countries and communities are considered as peripheral in terms of their production capacity—that is, they are marginal contributors to manufacturing markets—the way Muslim countries produce and consume creates glaring disparities between the poor and the rich, makes them dependent on monopolies, leads to authoritarian leadership, and creates an elite class that overconsumes and overproduces and, hence, contributes to depleting the environment. By and large the forty-six Muslim countries mainly extract raw materials, oil being the most important (56 percent of the world's oil export). Although Muslim countries have some manufacturing industries such as cement, textile, and light armaments, it is not at a level to move them into a competitive advantage within the global market.[11] Hence, most of the trade (95 percent) that occurs is with non-Muslim countries. The oil industry, although nationalized, is heavily dependent on foreign technology, expertise, and security (as the Gulf War lately showed), and the maintenance of an elite group with which foreign heads of state can interact.

Robert Reich notes this structure of elites benefitting from the global economies wherever they are by stating, "the economic globalization . . . has served to delink the interests of the wealthy classes from a sense of national interest and thereby from a sense of concern for an obligation to their less fortunate neighbors . . . It is no longer meaningful to speak about this delinking in terms of a North-South divide. . . . It is class."[12]

For Muslim countries, the problem involves the uneven development in the global capitalist system that has led to extreme disparities between the elites and nonelites both among and within nations. Understood in terms of disparity between the poor and the rich, Islam has a very clear response to how Muslims should produce and consume. Hourani, a famous scholar of Islam writes "Islam could also be a basis of economic life . . . and if accepted that will ensure social justice and liberate humans from servitude."[13] The Islamic economic system has been set forth as a "third way" that differs from both "laissez-faire capitalism and Marxist socialism."[14] The basis of the system is set out in general terms in the Qur'an, but the details have been worked out by legal scholars. The system, ideally, creates a society of private ownership and enterprise without the vast accumulation and concentration of wealth. Two principles summarize the Islamic economic system. The first sees that income, exchange, and trade should be based on just transaction and not claims on natural or market resources. The second is similar to the ideas presented in Coward's chapter in this volume, and sees that the community has an overriding priority over individuals. Adherence to these principles would serve to constrain the unequal distribution of resources and, hence, the overconsumption and overproduction of resources among the few. The following outlines these principles.

PRINCIPLE ONE: INCOME, EXCHANGE, AND TRADE SHOULD BE BASED ON JUST TRANSACTION AND NOT CLAIMS ON NATURAL OR MARKET RESOURCES

Just interaction in the Islamic perspective should not be confused with the Buddhist concept of eliminating desire as mentioned in Gross's chapter. Actually Islam sees desire as a source of happiness, but what is problematic with desire is its attainment. In Islam individual desires should be attained in ways that permit everyone in the community to fulfill his/her individual desires and individual desires take a lower priority over community desires. Hence, there are conditions that regulate individual and communal fulfillment of desire.

Work is one of the conditions of just interaction. The Qur'an is very clear about issues of reward and revenues. For example it states "Humans shall have nothing but what they strive for."[15] People who work are not equal to those who do not in Islam.[16] Work in the Islamic tradition includes more than a "job," and the word would translate as "labor."

Equal, exact, and honest exchange is another condition of the just transaction in Islam. The Qur'an emphasizes "O my people give full measure and full weight with equity, and wrong not people in respect of their things, and act not corruptly in the land making mischief."[17] This concept becomes clearer to many of us living in the West when we consider the madness of Christmastime and the desire to buy toys for children during this time. In 1996 in the United States, a toy called 'Tickle Me Elmo' from the *Sesame Street* children's show that sells normally for $26 became so rare in the market that some people were auctioning it for over $1,500. This kind of exchange that is based on creating an artificial need and crazed desire is not permitted in the Islamic system. All exchange in the Islamic system ought to be of *use value*—that is, a good, or service for another equivalent in value. Exchange should never be of *surplus value*—i.e., a commodity with a value altered for some humanly imposed reason. Surplus-value exchanges (i.e., values determined not by the real use value of the good or service, but by the value imposed by supply/demand forces of the market) are considered usury.

Usury, *riba*, is forbidden in Islam. The rule governing *riba* in Islam states that any profit or interest accrued without working for it, or without being a full partner in the risks of gain and loss makes the transaction unjust. *Riba*, thus, is defined as "asking something for nothing in an interaction . . . it is not equal for equal."[18] As such the Qur'an warns "that they used usury though it was forbidden and that they usurped human wealth with falsehood."[19]

Interest accrued from Western-style banking is considered *riba*. The client in Western-style banking, according to Islamic interpretation, is at a disadvantage. As a depositor his/her money is used to create more money under false guarantees of delivery. As a borrower, she/he pays interest on imaginary assets that the banks do not have. The imaginary money that banks have creates artificial wealth by exploiting the hardworking depositor and the needy borrower. In addition this artificial wealth is not redistributed equitably, but remains concentrated in the hands of a small minority of financiers. The Qur'an refers to such practices by saying "That which you lay out for increase through the property of [other] people, will have no increase with God: but that which you lay out for charity seeking the countenance of God, [will increase], it is these who will get a recompense multiplied."[20]

Cummings, Askari, and Mustafa note that the Islamic banking system operates on the principle of equity ownership not interest.[21] Money invested in a bank as though it were a business venture without guarantees of profit or loss would be Islamic. Hence, the investor gains interest only if the business produces profit. This kind of investment guarantees more conservative risk-taking ventures and thereby reduces creation of vast sums of artificial wealth and its concentration in few hands.

Nawal H. Ammar

PRINCIPLE TWO: THE RIGHT OF
THE COMMUNITY OVER INDIVIDUALS

Islam emphasizes the concept of communal good and duties to the community in a way that is similar to Coward's suggestion in his chapter on the we-self. This community of believers has a collective ethos of goodness: "let there arise out of you a band of people inviting to all that is good, enjoining what is right and forbidding what is wrong."[22] It is a community where Muslims protect each other, hold together tightly, and cooperate on generosity and righteousness.[23] Islam's emphasis on the right of the community over the individual is demonstrated through its position on issues of distributive justice in general. The particularities of this position can be best illustrated in Islam's treatment of the three issues of: (*a*) taxation, (*b*) community leadership, and (*c*) its vision of the "other" in the community.

a. Taxation. Islam outlines three tax structures: one for Muslims, one for non-Muslims, and one that is universal and applies to all regardless of religion. All taxes aim to redistribute the wealth and power of the rich to the poor. *Zakat* is a tax that all Muslims should pay. It is a tax that has become a religious obligation and it is particularly intended for the rich to fulfill the needs of the poor in the community. This fulfillment is not charity in the Western sense but a community obligation. The state, *dar al-Islam*, oversees the collection of *zakat*. The exact levy of the *zakat* varies in accordance with different legal schools of thought. Generally, a 2.5 percent tax on one's wealth is applied. Some Islamic jurists include taxation on mines as part of the *zakat*, others assess it as a separate tax. Regardless all Muslims must pay a tax for extracting the land's wealth. Some jurists also argue that if *zakat* is inadequate to meet the demands of the needy, then the state can impose additional taxes.

Muslims also pay taxes on agricultural land, *ushur*. The levy on land is applied to the gross production before deduction of production costs.[24] The Qur'anic injunction recommending this tax states: "O you who have attained to faith spend on theirs out of the good things which you may have acquired and out of that which we bring forth for you from the earth."[25] Non-Muslims living in an Islamic state pay a poll tax (*jiziyah*). This tax is paid as compensation for being defended by and included in the state. The tax rate is based on a community consensus (*ijma'*) and should be assessed on the ability to pay.[26] Finally, all citizens of the Islamic state must pay a land tax (*kharaj*). The tax is levied on two bases. The first is assessed on a fixed rate regardless of the output, and the second is paid only if there is output from the land.

Islam's prescriptions on taxation offer an economic mechanism for limiting the disparities in access to resources the economic system otherwise generates. Nonetheless, two noneconomic prescriptions concerning community leadership and respect for human diversity are also critically important for an Islamic economic system and further serve to diminish inequities in the Islamic community.

b. Distributive justice beyond utilitarian economies: Leadership qualities. The Imam, Caliph, or Sultan is the person who leads the Islamic community and who would be responsible to facilitate and promote distribution within it. The quality of the leader is a very important element in securing a just community. Mernissi writes: "It is difficult to imagine a weaker political leader than a Muslim one. The ideal leader is modest, trembling with fear before his God and terrified before those he/she governs for making an unjust decision will lead him directly to hell."[27] The legitimacy of the Muslim leader is based on the will of the community (*ummah*) according to Islamic jurisprudence.[28] In Islam the leader has no divine powers.[29] The leader of the Islamic state ought to guarantee freedom for the subjects.[30] The leader ought to treat subjects equitably, and consult the community on the affairs of the state. The Qur'an states clearly the issue of justice as the working ideology of the leader in many verses.[31] Ibn Taymiya, a famous Muslim thinker who based his interpretations on reason, stated that "people have never disagreed on the negative consequences of injustice and the positive impact of justice. As such God will render a just nation victorious even if its citizens were non-believers, while the unjust state will be defeated even if its citizens were believers."[32]

The above-mentioned characteristics of the Islamic leader have disappeared in our modern day. Most leaders today in the Islamic world exercise some kind of authoritarianism. According to Mernissi: "The vulnerability has disappeared from the scene through the combined effect of the separation of Muslim memory from the rationalist tradition and the modern media that have created an unchallenged leader."[33] As such the issue of disparity between the poor and the rich in Islamic countries that are the result of maldevelopment requires the restoration of a just leader who is accountable to the community he/she rules. Once the leaders are ruling under Islamic precepts—justice, equality, and humility—rather than manipulating them, economic policies aimed at distributive justice could work and the ecological crisis resulting from the lack of distributive justice could be checked.

The above response, however, partially disregards the fact that Muslims do not live alone in this world. The relationship between Muslims and non-Muslims is very important to ensure equitable distribution of resources. Since I am writing an Islamic response I will focus on Islam's position toward non-Muslims. (Others in this volume have considered the other side of this relationship, see especially Keller and Múnera.)

c. Distributive justice beyond utilitarian economies: The vision of the "other" in Islam. In addition to the need of having a just leader, Islam enjoins Muslims to treat others peacefully and kindly if distributive justice is to be a characteristic of their community. There is some confusion about what Islam says concerning the relationship of Muslims to non-Muslims. Visions of the "other" are often tainted by three verses of Surah 9, Al Tawbah in the Qur'an.[34] The three verses enjoin Muslims to fight those who do not believe in Allah. Chapter 9 of the Qur'an is among the last that was revealed to the Prophet Muhammad.

Nawal H. Ammar

Sayed Qutb, a well-known Egyptian Islamist and a prominent thinker among the Muslim Brotherhood, argues that this chapter provides a final and absolute injunction. He argues that all other verses enjoining mercy, justice, tolerance toward non-Muslims were voided by this revelation.[35] This interpretation leads a number of Muslims to believe that Islam is the religion of the sword in its relationship to the non-Muslims. Numerous Muslim scholars (Abdu, Rida, Shaltout), however, disagree strongly with Qutb's interpretation. They argue that this chapter was revealed to address one specific historic instance. Al-Ghazzali notes that the Qur'an contains 120 verses related to respecting the non-Muslims including pagans, and that three verses cannot void so many injunctions.[36]

Difference and diversity in Islam must be understood as God's will.[37] This will of God for diversity among humans has to be respected: "We have indeed created humans in the best mold."

The Prophet's tradition and Islamic history are also full of stories about respect for non-Muslims. "Upon the passing of a funeral procession near where the Prophet gathered with some of his friends, he stood up in respect and so did the rest of the gathered. After the procession passed, one person in the crowd said: O Messenger of God did you know that this was the funeral of a Jew? The Prophet replied: Wasn't he human and had a human soul? Was he not a human created and made by God? Wasn't he a being with dignity?"[38] Another well-known story in Islamic history about the fourth Orthodox Caliph Ali is indicative of respect of the "other." Ali told the ruler he sent to Egypt, Malik al-Ashtar: "fill your heart with mercy and love to your subjects since they are two kinds: A sibling in belief or a human created by God the same way you were."

Islam not only prescribes respect of the "other," but urges cooperation with all peoples and nations.[39] Muslims are very clearly ordered to befriend the "other." The Qur'an states: "If one amongst the pagans sought asylum or refuge grant it to him."[40]

To summarize, the maldevelopment in the economic systems of Muslim communities that led to maldistribution of resources, overconsumption, disparity between the rich and the poor, dependency, authoritarianism among leaders, and disrespect of human diversity are at the basis of the ecological crisis. Islam prescribes an economic system that constrains the extent of the maldistribution of resources through its principles of taxation and distributive justice. Once Muslims practice these principles of equity in distribution of resources and treatment of others, which are at the heart of Islamic teachings, we will be moving one more step toward averting the ecological crisis.

The economic and political principle of *hay'a* (dignified reserve) has implications for other social and cultural relationships that pertain to the ecological crisis, namely the relationship between men and women. It is to this that I now turn.

ABSENCE OF *HAY'A* TOWARD WOMEN
AND THE ECOLOGICAL CRISIS

Scientists have ascertained that overpopulation is a major contributing factor in the ecological crisis. The population growth rate in Muslim countries is among the highest in the world. The crude birth rate of the forty-six Muslim countries is 1 percent higher than that of the developing world as a whole.[41] In the mid-1980s even countries that adopted family planning programs (with the exception of Indonesia) in the early 1960s had very high natural increase rates of the population. For example, Pakistan's rate of increase was 2.8 percent, Egypt's rate was 2.6 percent, while the rate of increase in non-Muslim countries such as India and Colombia was 2.3 and 2.1 percent.[42]

Islam is indisputably a pronatal religion.[43] Nonetheless, family planning programs have also used Islamic teachings to convince people to use contraception. Various verses from the Qur'an that favor family planning outcomes were stressed. These included injunctions concerned with leaving heirs in good conditions, educating children to be useful, the quality and not the quantity of children, and how children are an enormous responsibility for parents.[44] Other interpretations based on reason were reiterated. For instance, in the Arab Muslim world distinctions between lifetime family planning (*Tahdid al-nasl*) versus family planning as the spacing of children (*Tanzim al-nasl*) were made to sanction the use of contraception.

Although Islam sanctions the use of various methods of family planning and many Muslim countries and communities have adopted family planning as a state policy, only one country, Indonesia, has succeeded in curtailing its population increase significantly. What accounts for the limited success of these attempts to reduce population growth through the adoption of family planning programs and hence reduce the pressure on environmental resources?

The root of the reproductive problems for most Muslim women lies in the fact that they live either in the less developed world or the less affluent parts of the developed world. As such their social and material conditions inhibit following family planning programs successfully. While women are the target of most family planning programs, seldom do they participate directly in their design and implementation (i.e., they remain "invisible"). The human context of women in the programs ought to be emphasized and brought to the forefront. Data has shown that the empowerment of women through higher education, active involvement in the labor force, legislative policies, and increased access to health services often serve to delay marriage, reduce the number of offspring, and diminish the incidence of polygamy.[45] In Egypt, for example, 60 percent of women who cannot read and write had at least one co-wife, while the incidence of polygamy was reduced to 0.01 percent among women who had university degrees.[46] In most Muslim countries the patriarchal, misogynist local cultures favor interpretations of the Qur'an that debase women. Islam, however, sees women as equal to men and deserving of the same treatment; and both men and women will be judged on equal grounds before God.[47]

The equity that Islam grants women is not reflected in popular culture, economic opportunities, or formal substantive law. For instance, popular culture, as reflected in some Arabic proverbs, encourages violence against women ("if you break a girl's rib, twenty-four other ribs will grow"), glorifies male offspring ("those who bear boys never die"), and encourages women's dependence on men ("a straw husband is better than none").

Women's participation in the paid labor force still remains marginal in most Muslim countries and the jobs they do take typically offer little power, prestige, or income. According to statistics from the 1990 UN report on the Situation of Women, women constituted only 6 percent of the labor force in the United Arab Emirates (one of the wealthiest Muslim countries) and 62 percent of women above the age of fifteen were illiterate. Similarly, women made up only 10 percent of the labor force in Egypt (one of the poorest Muslim countries), and of these 20 percent worked in agriculture (a low-paying job) and 41 percent were self-employed (a less secure job).

Legal codes in Muslim countries, whether totally dependent on divine law (Shari'a) or partially dependent at the level of personal status codes, very clearly debase women. In all these countries, codes are legislated to favor men over women even if the punishment was un-Islamic. For example, in fornication cases, women are punished more severely than men, a practice that goes against the letter of the Qur'an. In cases where the texts are silent, the codes derived from the spirit of the text also favor men. Hence, a Muslim woman from an Islamic country cannot give her citizenship to her children if she is married to a foreign man. A man from a Muslim country, however, can give his children his citizenship even if his wife is foreign and he does not live in his native country. Women cannot divorce their husbands except in court, while men can declare a wife divorced by verbally uttering the words "I divorce you" three times. In many Muslim countries a Muslim man can divorce his wife or take a co-wife without any legal requirements to inform the concerned wife.

The empowerment of Muslim women as humans is central to the discussion about population increase and its impact on the ecology. Unless we improve the conditions of Muslim women according to Islamic teachings, the discussion of family planning would be as relevant as talking to an incubator. This means including women as active participants in family, economic, and political decision making. This can only be made possible by improving the conditions under which they live and bringing equity and dignity to women.

The improvement of Muslim women's status applies to both the rich and the poor. Islam has its own share of powerful women both in its history and in the contemporary world. Consequently, a return to Islamic teachings about women is essential to make family planning successful. Muslims, hence, need to remember how the Qur'an emphasizes the dignity of women by stating "Never will I suffer to be lost the work of any of you be he male or female ye are members of one of another" and behave with hay'a toward them.[48]

In sum, Islam offers much in response to the manifest ecological crisis of population growth. This response, however, focuses on a behavior toward women as humans rather than simply permitting a technological fix such as family planning. While Islam leaves open several avenues for family planning, traditional approaches using education about contraception have achieved limited success in most Muslim countries. This suggests that the population problem runs deeper than merely extending the knowledge about and availability of contraceptive devices. Rather, the empowerment of women (or lack thereof) lies at the core of the population problem, and hence, the ecological crisis. Islam views women and men as equal participants in the Muslim community, even if, in most Muslim (and, I might add, non-Muslim) countries this equity has not been realized. The population problem, then, appears to stem from un-Islamic behaviors and attitudes that lead to inequity between men and women. I am thus suggesting a revival of the Islamic behaviors of dignified respect toward women as mentioned in the Qur'an and Hadith.

CONCLUSION

Progressive Islam has several effective responses toward the ecological crisis. These responses have action-oriented components toward averting evil and promoting the good. Hence, the Qur'an emphasizes: "Verily never will Allah change the condition of a people until they change themselves."[49] The orientation of action in progressive Islam toward averting the ecological doom is one of dignified reserve: *hay'a*.

In relation to distributive justice between the poor and the rich that creates an elite that overconsumes and overproduces, and hence contributes to the ecological crisis by depleting the environment, *hay'a* is reflected in the ethic of hard work. *Hay'a* is also reflected in the economic system of exchange that is based solely on use value versus surplus value of a good. Such an exchange value would bring equity among community members, reduce concentration of wealth and diminish the maldistribution of resources. The leader's humility and consultative duties with the community also bring forth the issue of respect of the leader to his/her subjects, which would eventually promote distributive justice. Further Islam advises the respect for human diversity, something that is necessary for averting wars and for ensuring distributive justice within and outside the community.

In relation to population increase that also puts pressure on the ecology, *hay'a* requires action toward empowering women to have family planning programs, which would contribute to a reduction in natural growth rates in population.

Islam has a very clear and unequivocal response to the depletion and destruction of the environment and nature. Nature was created by God in an orderly fashion.[50] This nature is given to humans as a trust (*ammanah*). Thus, the Qur'anic injunction says "I am setting on earth a vice-regent."[51]

This vice-regent is a manager of the trust and not an owner. Depending on how humans manage this trust, they will be judged in the hereafter. Hence, there is a direct relationship between the utilization of nature and rewards on the day of judgment. The relationship not only emphasizes a "no-harm" principle to nature, but insists on the doing of good. The Prophet, for example, said: "anyone who witnesses evil should remonstrate upon it by hand, mouth or heart, the last is the weakest of faith."

Islam counsels Muslims to use of environmental resources in accordance with five rules:[52]

1. The use of nature and its resources in a balanced, not excessive manner;
2. Treat nature and its resources with kindness;
3. Do not damage, abuse or distort nature in any way;
4. Share natural resources with others living in the habitat; and
5. Conserve.

These rules are set forth by jurors to ensure that nature and its resources are managed well by humans who are the executors of God's trust. Balance, admonitions against excess, justice, and the sharing of resources are, once more, found at the core of the Islamic attitude toward the environment. *Hay'a* of God's creation requires that Muslims use earth's resources in moderation and conserve it.

The dignified reserve prescribed by Islam toward life on earth is not only the responsibility of some people, but it is every Muslim's duty. Muslim jurists have set forth a rule stating that "the executor is a guarantor even if the act is not deliberate or intentional." On account of this rule, every Muslim and every community claiming the faith ought to listen. Regardless of one's ethical preference to human free will or predestination, given the state of the earth's warming climate, increasing pollution, rates of deforestation, state of war, and disease due to the ecological imbalance, Muslims will be and are responsible on the day of judgment for this crisis.

NOTES

1. The following format will be utilized to denote reference to Qur'anic chapters and verses: Fatir: 8.

2. Al Ra'd: 17.

3. G. F. Hourani, 1985, *Reason and Tradition in Islamic Ethics* (Cambridge: Cambridge University Press), p. 7.

4. M. Khadduri, 1984, *The Islamic Conception of Peace* (Baltimore, MD: Johns Hopkins University Press), pp. 41–48.

5. Al Zumar: 9.

6. *BP Statistical Review of World Energy*, 1990, (London: British Petroleum Educational Service).

7. *BP Statistical Review of World Energy*, 1990.

8. The *Presidential Gulf War Illnesses Commission Report* has shown that a large number of U.S. Desert Storm veterans have been exposed to germ warfare during combat.

9. Penny Kemp, 1991, "For Generations to Come: The Environmental Catastrophe," in *Beyond the Storm: A Gulf Crisis Reader*, ed. P. Bennis and M. Moushabeck (New York: Olive Branch Press), p. 331.

10. "Al-Qahira Akhthar Mudin al'Alam Talwitha" (Cairo is the most polluted city in the world), *Al-Akhbar Daily News*, 6 June 1995, p. 8.

11. Quoted in Pervez Houdbhoy, 1991, *Islam and Science* (London: Zed Books), p. 30.

12. Quoted in David Korten, 1994, "Sustainability and the Global Economy: Beyond Bretton Woods" (Opening Plenary Presentation to Fall Retreat, 13–15 October 1994, the Environmental Grantmakers Association, Mount Washington Hotel & Resort, Bretton Woods, New Hampshire), p. 7.

13. Hourani, *Reason and Tradition in Islamic Ethics*, p. 372.

14. J. T. Cummings, H. Askari, and A. Mustafa, 1980, "Islam and Modern Economic Change," in *Islam and Development: Religion and Sociopolitical Change*, ed. John Esposito (Syracuse, NY: Syracuse University Press, pp. 25–48), p. 44.

15. Al Najm: 39.

16. Al Nisa': 95.

17. Hud: 85.

18. Umar Vadillo and Fazlun Khalid, 1992, "Trade and Commerce in Islam," in *Islam and Ecology*, eds. Fazlun Khalid and Joanne O'Brien (New York, NY: Cassell), p. 73.

19. Al Baqarah: 161.

20. Al Rum: 39.

21. Cummings, Askari, and Mustafa, "Islam and Modern Economic Change."

22. Ali Imaran: 104.

23. Tawbah: 71; Ali Imran: 103; Al Mai'dah: 2.

24. Cummings, Askar, and Mustafa, "Islam and Modern Economic Change," p. 27–29.

25. Al Baqarah: 267.

26. Cummings, Askar, and Mustafa, "Islam and Modern Economic Change," p. 30.

27. Fatima Mernissi, 1992, *Islam and Democracy: Fear of the Modern World* (translated by Mary Jo Lakeland, New York: Addison-Wesley), p. 27.

28. Fahmi Houidi, *Al-Islam wa al-Democratiah* (Islam and Democracy; Cairo: Markaz al-Ahram Llitargamah wa al-Nashr), p. 124.

29. Al Ghashiyah: 21–22.

30. Al Kahf: 29.

31. Al Nisa: 58; Al Mai'dah: 8; Al Nahl: 90; Al Shura: 15, 38; Al Hujurat: 9, 13.

32. Houidi, *Al-Islam wa al-Democratiah*, p. 122.

33. Mernissi, *Islam and Democracy*, p. 22–23.

34. Verses 5, 29, 36.

35. Houidi, *Al-Islam wa al-Democratiah*, p. 33–35.

36. Houidi, p. 24.

37. Yunus: 99; Hud: 18.

38. Houidi, p. 27.

39. Al Nahl: 92; Al Qasas: 18, 38.

40. Al Tawbah: 6.

41. I use the word *countries* because I can obtain statistics only from such geopolitical designations. It is essential to remember that Islam sees its adherents and those who live with them as a community (*ummah*).

42. Indonesia has had the most successful family planning programs in the developing world. See Hayim Adid, 1987, "Islamic Leaders' Attitudes Towards Family Planning in Indonesia 1950s–1980s," a master's thesis, Australian National University, Canberra.

43. Al Nahl: 72; Al Kahf: 46.

44. Al Nisa: 9; Al Tur: 21; Al Anfal: 28.

45. Hamed Abu Gamrah, 1980, "Fertility and Childhood Mortality by Mother's and Father's Education in Cairo," in *Population Bulletin of the Economic Commission of Western Asia* (Beirut, Lebanon), p. 81.

46. "Aqed al-Jawaz al-Jadid" (The new marriage contract), in *Nisf al-Dunia* (a weekly magazine), 15 June 1995, pp. 21–26.

47. Al Nisa: 1, 32.

48. Ali Imran: 195.

49. Al Ra'd: 11.

50. Al Ra'd: 8; Al Sajdah: 4; Al Mulk: 3, 4.

51. Al Baqarah: 30.

"HINDUISM AND DEEP ECOLOGY"

Christopher Key Chapple

The grammar not only of language, but of culture and civilization itself, is of the same order as this mossy little forest creek, this desert cobble.

— Gary Snyder, *The Practice of the Wild*

Deep ecology speaks of an intimacy with place, a sense of being in the world with immediacy, care, and frugality. Gary Snyder, drawing from an American tradition that stretches back to Thoreau, writes of how the wild enriches the human spirit and sacralizes the process of survival. Establishing oneself within in a sense of place gives meaning to one's existence; for a deep ecologist, this becomes a way of life, encompassing "an attempt to uncover the most profound level of human-nature relationships, stressing the need for personal realization as accomplished by integrating the self with nature."[1] Deep ecology also urges the examination of the underlying political and economic structures that work against intimacy with nature and thwart the development of a sustainable society.

Ecological thinkers in India proclaim the need for social change that includes the sustenance and uplift of the masses as integral to the process of environmental healing. They have been somewhat reluctant to embrace the concept of deep ecology as expressed through American authors, largely due to the particular situation of India's overwhelming population and suspicions that the deep ecology rhetoric smacks of neocolonialism, romanticism, and religion. The environmental movement on the part of India's intellectuals has been largely a secular movement; deep ecology moves into the realm of affectivity and a ritualization of life. Its near-religiosity would render deep ecology suspect for many contemporary Indian thinkers, for whom religion connotes fundamentalism, nationalism, and a return to a caste-bound past.[2]

In recent years, some scholars and activists within the Hindu tradition, inspired by industrial tragedies such as the Bhopal explosion, the depletion of forests, and the fouling of India's air and water, have started to reconsider traditional Hindu lifeways in terms of ecological values. In earlier writings, I have explored various modalities of environmental ac-

Reprinted by permission from *Deep Ecology and World Religions: New Essays on Sacred Ground*, edited by David Landis Barnhill and Roger S. Gottlieb, State University of New York Press. © 2001, State University of New York. All rights reserved.

tivism in India, including educational programs, the emphasis on social ecology by the post-Gandhians, and Brahminical and renouncer models for the development of an indigenous Indian environmentalism.[3] In this essay I will more fully explore how the Hindu tradition, broadly interpreted, might further its contribution to both a localized and a globalized sense of deep ecology.

DEFINING HINDU RELIGION

To look at deep ecology in light of Hindu religion, we must probe the term *Hinduism*. First of all, the term *Hindu* is inherently a non-Indian construct, first coined by Persians to describe those persons living on the other side of the Indus River. Another definition of Hinduism links the term to a cluster of religious faiths and theological schools that ascribe truth to the earliest of India's sacred texts, the Vedas, and the various texts and traditions stemming therefrom. Such persons might call themselves followers of Viu (*Vaiṣqvas*), Śiva (*Śaivas*), or the Devī or Goddess (*Úakti*) or some other deity or of no deity in particular. This definition would include several million persons living outside India in such places as Sri Lanka, Singapore, Britain, and the United States. It would, in a sense, also include many persons of non-Indian descent who ascribe to the monistic Vedanta philosophy and to the many practitioners of Indian physical and spiritual disciplines such as Yoga.[4] The term Hindu could also refer in a general way to the people who live in the subcontinental region. This would include Jains, Buddhists, and Sikhs, as well as Indian Christians and Muslims, all of whom exhibit at least some common cultural traits associated with "Hindustan."

Hinduism does not operate in the manner of many traditional religions. It includes multiple doctrines, multiple deities, and many different types of people from various levels of society. Hence, rather than attempting to present a monolithic view of Hinduism and deep ecology, I prefer to suggest some ways in which I have discovered that Hinduism, broadly defined, espouses a philosophy akin to the core sensibilities of deep ecology. Specifically, the following essay will begin with a discussion of the importance of the five elements in the Hindu world view and the relationship between meditative practices and the natural world. Ritual worship will be explored as providing a context for understanding the function of "embedded ecology" in Hindu life, with special reference to the Mannarassala Temple in Kerala. I will then turn to a discussion of sacred groves in India, with mention of some of the successes and difficulties encountered by those involved with tree planting in India. The essay will close with reflections on the challenge posed by contemporary consumer pressures in India and the suggestion that the meditative and ritual deep structures of India life and culture can help support an indigenous form of Hindu deep ecology.

THE FIVE ELEMENTS (PAÑCA-BHŪTA)

Hindu religious literature, from the Vedas to contemporary theorists, takes up a discussion of the natural world through a systematic approach to the five elements. This tradition provides an analysis of material reality in terms of its manifestation through earth (*pṛthivī*), water (*āp*), fire (*agni*), air (*vāyu*), and space (*ākāśā*). These elements find mention not only in the earliest of India's oral texts, the *Ṛg Veda*, but also play a prominent role in the later philosophical systems of Sāmkhya, Vedānta, as well as the non-Hindu systems of Jainism and Buddhism. For instance, the *Vāna Purāṇa* (12.26) states:

> Let all the great elements bless the dawning day:
> Earth with its smell, water with its taste,
> fire with its radiance, air with its touch,
> and sky with its sound.

These elements are not seen as abstractions or metaphors but literally compose the reality of the world and of one's own body. The *Mokṣadharmaparvan*, one of the books of the *Mahābhārata* epic, summarizes the relationship between body and cosmos first articulated in the *Ṛg Veda* and the *Bṛhadāraṇyaka Upaniṣad*:

> The Lord, the sustainer all beings, revealed the sky.
> From space came water and, from water, fire and the winds.
> From the mixture of the essence of fire and wind arose the earth.
> Mountains are his bones, earth his flesh, the ocean his blood.
> The sky is his abdomen, air his breath, fire his heat, rivers his nerves.
> The sun and moon, which are called Agni and Soma, are the eyes of Brahman.
> The upper part of the sky is his head. The earth is his feet and the directions are his hands.[5]

This vision of the relationship between the body, divinity, and the order of the things becomes both descriptive and prescriptive in terms of the human relationship with nature in India. The world cannot be separated from the human body nor can the human body be separated from the world.

In the traditional Hindu view, the world exists as an extension of the body and mind; the body and mind reflect and contain the world. In describing the women of the Garwhal region of the Himalayas, Carol Lee Flinders notes that they "enjoy a connection with trees, rivers, mountains, livestock, and plants that is simultaneously their connection with divinity, and that connection is seen as absolutely reciprocal."[6] From the texts above, we can understand this continuity as an expression of what Vandana Shiva calls "embedded in nature" and Vijaya Nagarajan refers to as "embedded ecology." This notion of intimacy with the natural world, culturally supported by a anthropocosmic vision of the earth, instantiates a person in immediate and intimate contact with one's surroundings. Just as the

Christopher Key Chapple

Hymn of the Person in the *Ṛg Veda* identifies human physiology with the cosmos, correlating the feet with the earth and the head with the sky, so also a vision of deep ecology in the context of Hindu faith will seek to integrate and include its understanding of the human as inseparable from and reflective of nature.

MEDITATIVE MASTERY

Hinduism, while revering the five elements and venerating many gods and goddesses, places ultimate importance on the attainment of spiritual liberation *(mokṣa)*. The path toward liberation requires a skillful reciprocity between spirit and materiality. Yogic practice *(sādhana)* cultivates an awareness of and intimacy with the realm of manifestation and materiality *(prakṛti)*. Just as the *Bṛhadāraṇyaka Upaniṣad* proclaims a relationship between the body and the universe, so also the Yoga system urges one to gain mastery over how the body stands in relationship to the cosmos. The Yoga Sūtras of Patanjali state, "From concentration on significance and connection of the subtle [body] and the essence of gross manifestation, there is mastery over the elements."[7] This statement acknowledges a linkage between the realm of bodily sensation and the experience of the physical world. By concentrating on this relationship, one gains an intimacy with the elements that results in an understanding of one's embeddedness with one's environment.

The yogic accomplishment of mastery over the elements *(bhūtajaya)* entails a detailed training that focuses on the elements over a period of several months. In this regimen, one begins with concentration on the earth, moving toward an appreciation of the special relationship between the sense of smell residing in the subtle body *(sūkṣma śarīra)* and the earth *(pṛthivī)*. Moving up in subtlety, the practitioner then concentrates on the link between subtle taste *(rasa)* and water *(āp)*; between visible form *(rūpa)* and light and heat *(tejas)*; between touch *(sparśa)* and the wind *(vāyu)*; and between sound *(śabda)* and space *(ākāśa)*. Beginning with earth, the most gross aspect of manifestation, one progresses to the lightest. This insight into the relationship between the senses and the elements leads to an ability to acknowledge and withhold the outflow of the senses *(prapñca)*. Through this mastery, one gains freedom from compulsive attachment; this lightness *(sattva)* ultimately leads to liberation *(mokṣa)*.

On the one hand, it might be argued that this process leads one away from intimacy to an introspective distancing from nature. On the other hand, it could also be stated that this meditative practice entails a greater rapport with nature, an entry into a purified, immediate state of perception freed from residues of past attachment. In the words of David Abram, "The recuperation of the incarnate, sensorial dimension of experience brings with it a recuperation of the living landscape in which we are corporeally embedded. As we return to our senses, we gradually discover our sensory perceptions to be simply our part of a vast, interpenetrating webwork. . . . "[8] By entering fully into a reflection on the workings of the senses through the practices of yogic meditation, one gains an intimacy with the foundational constructs of objects that transcends their specificity, leading one to a state of unity with the natural world.

RITUAL WORSHIP (PŪJĀ) AND ECOLOGY

Ritual worship performed by meditators and temple priests includes a veneration and internalization of the elements, a sanctification of the body that leads to identity with divine power. Anthropologist James Preston describes the experience of one temple priest at the Chandi Temple in Cuttack, Orissa:

> One of the first steps in the *puja* is for the priest to transform his body into a microcosm of the universe. This is accomplished by combining the five elements represented within it. Kumar Panda explained the correspondences between nature and the human body; *earth* is equated with that part of the human body below the waist; *water* is symbolized by the stomach region; *fire* is represented by the heart; *wind* is equivalent to the throat, nose, and lungs; *sky* corresponds to the brain. As these elements are mixed together in symbolic rites, the priest is filled with divine power or *shakti*, which is the goddess herself. . . . Kumar Panda describes his inner vision during meditation: "After performing meditation and the ritual for two or three hours, lightning flashes before my eyes . . . I become the goddess. She who is *Ma* (Mother) is me . . . Water and the coldness of water, fire and the burning capacity of fire, the sun and the rays of the sun; there is no difference between all these things, just as there is no difference between myself and the goddess."[9]

This journey through the relationship between the body and the elements to the point of unity with the goddess brings the meditator to a point of visionary immersion, a form of profound and deep ecological awareness.

Within the context of celebrating the special relationship between the human person and nature, each region of India has developed an extensive ritual cycle. These festivals often coincide with times of harvest or renewal. For instance, the Pongal festival in South India takes place each January to acknowledge the rice harvest. Many Hindu rituals include reverence for sacred traditional plants such as the Tulsi tree; many explicitly invoke the elements as mentioned above and many celebrate the earth goddess or Bhū Devi. Vijaya Nagarajan has extensively described how the practice of the Kolam morning ritual establishes in Tamil women a sense of connectedness with their environment.[10] Madhu Khanna writes about how rituals practiced in the urban context maintain significant agricultural and hence ecological meanings. Ritual acknowledges and invokes one's position in the order of things and connects the worshipper directly with fecundity cycles.[11]

I would like to describe a fertility ritual in South India that provides a living example of embedded ecology in the state of Kerala. In 1997, I visited the Mannarassala Temple, between the cities of Cochin and Trivandrum. We spent many hours in the cool shade of this sylvan retreat and learned, through observation and friendly informants, of the mythic history and ritual cycles associated with this temple. My companion, Professor Surinder Datta, a retired biologist from the University of Wisconsin, Parkside, sought out this particular site because of its renowned sacred grove. Adjacent to its buildings, behind a walled enclosure, the temple maintains a fourteen acre preserve of forest. No one is allowed to enter this towering woods except a small group of Brahman priests who enter once each year to gather medicinal herbs, to be used in Ayurvedic treatments. The forest stretches as high as the eye can see, a remarkable remnant of the tropical forests that once covered the entire state of Kerala. Though not far from the main road, this compound stands in stark contrast to the densely populated and cultivated surrounding landscape, which, though green and lush with rice paddies and coconut groves, has been thoroughly domesticated by the many people that live in Kerala. Similarly, even in the mountains, what at first glance appears to be wild forest at a closer examination turns out to be terraces of spice and coffee trees, creeping vines of black pepper, and bushes of cardamom, all under cultivation.

According to the local tale, this particular temple arose on the spot where Parasurama, an incarnation of Vishnu, met with the snake god Nagaraja to obtain blessings to ensure the fertility of Kerala's soil. Years prior, the mountains of Kerala were formed when Parasurama had thrown his ax *(paraśu)* into the ocean. The plain below the mountains, though seemingly rich, was too salty to support life. Parasurama pleaded with the snake king to purify the land. Now, in return, offerings are made to the snake king to thank him for granting Parasurama's request and snakes, particularly in the wild areas, are protected. This story divinizes the land of Kerala and offers a local rationale for preserving both forest and wildlife in honor and respect for a viable ecosystem.

The Mannarassala Temple serves as a sacred place for human reproduction. Our visit to Mannarassalla Temple coincided with a fertility thanksgiving in the form of a first name and first solid food ceremony to bless several babies. For several decades, one woman, Valia Amma, served as priestess of the temple. She was born in 1903 and, according to our informants, she married a temple priest when she was thirteen or fourteen years old. At the age of fifteen, in 1918, she renounced the carnal aspects of her marriage and dedicated her life to serving the temple. She instituted *pūjā* or worship ceremonies at the temple that continue to the present day, including weddings and the Kalasam tantric rite.[12]

During our visit, we witnessed a portion of the special rituals known as the Choronu ceremony associated with the successful birth and nurturance of babies. Young couples come to the temple priestess for fertility blessings when they decide it is time to bear children. After the birth of a child, the family returns when the baby reaches six months, for the naming and first solid food ceremonies. The parents first place the baby in a basket attached to a scale and fill the opposite basket with grain. When the scale balances, the proper payment is accepted by the temple staff. Midst the smoke and light of the oil lamps and the blaring trumpets of a circumambulating band of musicians, we saw several children receive the name acknowledging their survival through the first six months of life. We also witnessed these babies being fed their first meal of cooked rice. A woman temple musician playing a one-stringed instrument held with her toe then sings a song in honor of the baby and then the family proceeds to receive *darshan* or blessing from the temple priestess, who greets people from the family quarter within the temple compound. Valia Amma died in 1993; we received blessings from her husband's brother's wife, who assumed the priestess duties upon her passing.

The ritual life of this temple complex exhibits the qualities of embedded ecology in its story of cosmic origins, its grounding in nature, and its function as promoting the good health and well-being of future generations.

SACRED GROVES

In her work on sacred groves, Frederique Apffel-Marglin describes such ritual centers as source of rejuvenation. She writes that "the network of sacred groves in such countries as India has since time immemorial been the locus and symbol of a way of life in which humans are embedded in nature. . . . It stands for the integration of the human community in nature. . . . The sacred grove, with its shrine to the local embodiment of the Great Goddess, is the permanent material sign of these periodic processes of regeneration."[13] Though Apffel-Marglin writes of her experiences in a sacred grove in northeast coastal Orissa, the grove parallels and mirrors that of Kerala, more than a thousand miles to the southwest. Both affirm the process of fertility. Both celebrate feminine powers of reproduction. Both serve as symbols of community and continuity, a place where, in Apffel-Marglin's words, "culture and society are embedded in nature, and the spiritual is embedded in the material."[14]

Ramachandra Guha notes that "sacred groves and sacred ponds . . . protection of keystone species . . . and the moderation of harvests from village wood-lots have persisted in Indian society over the historical period, sometimes to the present day."[15] He tells the story of the Bishnois sect, a group in the Rajasthan desert for whom the Khejadari tree became sacred. This tree, described as a "multi-purpose leguminous tree of great utility to the villagers" was never to be uprooted or killed.[16] In the 1650s a prince of Jodhpur attempted to cut a grove of Khejadari trees to fire a kiln to manufacture bricks for a new palace. The Bishnois revolted, laying down their lives to protect the sacred tree. Even today, the Khejadari serves as the backbone for desert subsistence; I have seen women in Rajasthan lopping its limbs to provide food for their goats; they also harvest its leaves and pods. Unlike the Joshua tree of the western United States which has lost its utility since the decimation of indigenous populations, the Khejadari reciprocally supports the people who sustain it through their protective customs.

WATER HARVESTING

Anil Agarwal and Sunita Narain have written of water catchment systems employed throughout India that have allowed human life to flourish in what otherwise would be arid wastelands. This system, like the prudent pruning of the Khejadari tree by desert women, works with the immediate available resources on a small scale. They note that "[a]ncient texts, inscriptions, local traditions and archaeological remains refer to a wide range of techniques—canals, huge tanks, embankments, wells and reservoirs—to harvest every possible form of water: rainwater, ground-water, stream water, river water and flood water."[17]

One of the tragic consequences of the British colonial period was a dismantling of many traditional water catchment systems. Before the British period, each village supported the workers who maintained the irrigation systems. The British, in an attempt to increase revenues, deemed these to be merely "religious and charitable allowances" and discontinued allocation for these functions. In time, the systems fell into disrepair, leading to "the disintegration of village society, its economy and its polity."[18]

Following independence from Britain, India initiated huge irrigation projects inspired by the example of the Soviet Union. Massive water projects have been and continue to be destructive to traditional life in India, disrupting indigenous ways of desert survival, as in the case of the Narmada Dam project in western India.[19] As the dry lands of Gujarat open to wetter styles of cultivation through the various planned irrigation channels, and as more desert dwellers and displaced tribals from the flooded valleys flock to the cities in search of employment in a cash-based economy, the age-old deep ecology based on a traditional economy of living within available means will disappear. Some have argued that progress is inevitable, that the benefits of wealth and increased nutrition outweigh clinging to an outdated lifestyle. However, from a religious point of view and from the perspectives of deep ecology, a sense of connectedness with the land becomes lost when large-scale development prevails. The World Bank has grappled with this issue and has put their funding of the Narmada Dam projects on hold.

NATURE AS ROMANCE?

Guha has argued against the romanticization of Western-style deep ecology, claiming that it merely extends the imperialism of a culture of abundance that can afford to set aside vast tracts of land in convenient preserves. Guha's position, unfortunately and probably unintentionally, can play into the hands of modern developers who would argue for "Wise Use," taking the position that progress is desirable and inevitable. However, for traditional India, Wise Use would entail protecting the sacred grove. For Nehruvian, progress-oriented contemporary India, Wise Use has led to the uprooting of people from their habitats, increased urbanization, and, ultimately, increased pollution.

In a probing analysis and critique of colonialism, Guha notes that British land use policies marginalized and impoverished the hunter-gatherers of India. The British usurped many common lands and required they be converted to food production and the production of cash crops for export such as indigo. Guha explains that the literate castes of India were able to move into clerical jobs and to operate as trading partners, but that "the others—hunter-gatherers, peasants, artisans, and pastoral and non-pastoral nomads— had all to squeeze into the already diminishing niche space for food production. And they, we have seen, suffered great impoverishment."[20] The emotional and material toll on great masses of the Indian population has been devastating. He writes:

> The consequence has been a scramble for resources and intense conflict, in the countryside and in the cities where people who have been driven out from elsewhere are flocking. . . . Endogamous caste groups remain cultural entities [in the cities], but have no common belief system to hold them together. No longer functional entities in the present scenario of shrinking niche space, castes and communities are set up against each other, with frighteningly high levels of communal and caste violence being the result.[21]

The cities of India teem with millions of street dwellers displaced from rural life who, having flocked to the cities without the benefit of education, perform menial tasks to eke out a survival living.

ESTABLISHING A NEW GROVE

Australian environmental activist John Seed paints a somewhat sobering picture of on-the-ground conservation in the Indian context. In 1987, Seed received a plea from Apeetha Aruna Giri, an Australian nun living near Arunachala mountain in Tiruvanamalai, Madras. She lived at Sri Ramana Ashram, a spiritual hermitage named after the famed Indian sage Ramana Maharshi, whose life energized spirituality in India during the first part of the twentieth century. She noticed that the surrounding areas had become stripped clean of vegetation due to local scavenging for firewood and fodder to feed the goats. Seed raised money for the development of a new NGO established by Apeetha: the Annamalai Reforestation Society. Through the efforts of this organization,

The space between the inner and outer walls of the vast 23-acre temple complex has been transformed from a wasteland into the largest tree nursery in the south of India. Hundreds of people have received environmental education, and a 12-acre patch of semidesert was donated to the project and transformed into a lush demonstration of permaculture and the miraculous recuperative powers of the earth. Hundreds of Tamil people have been trained in reforestation skills—tree identification, seed collection, nursery techniques, watershed management, erosion control, sustainable energy systems. Shiva's robes are slowly being rewoven.[22]

However, despite Seed's enthusiasm, this project has not been universally well received. Guards must be maintained to prevent local people from scavenging for fuel and fodder in the preserve, a practice that is enforced in various of India's national preserves and at other temple sites. Pilgrims to the sacred mountain complain that the trees block their view of the sunset. Clearly, the affection for trees in the Anglo-Australian love for nature movement does not necessarily work in the Indian context, where trees are seen as an economic resource necessary for human survival.

Seed himself speaks and writes of his own affirmation of the importance of this preservation work through a special quiet moment he experienced in the Arunachala forest with a troop of scores of monkeys:

They groomed each other, they made love, mothers breast-fed their babies, children played and cavorted, utter unself-consciously living their everyday lives in my astonished and grateful presence. . . . I had never felt more accepted by the nonhuman world. I knew that Shiva had answered my prayer, had acknowledged my efforts, and was giving me his sign of approval.[23]

For Seed, this shamanic moment established a link between his work and the life of the mountain. For others, this fencing of the forest might be seen as an extension of colonialist attitudes that seek to ban Adivasi or aboriginal peoples from their source of livelihood, an example of "the colonials having saved the forests of South Asian from certain destruction by indigenous forest users."[24]

Recognizing the encroachment of desert lands in areas that were once forested and then under cultivation, the Indian government and several NGOs have promoted tree planting. Balbir Mathur, founder of Trees for Life, has planted thousands of trees in India.[25] Visheswar Saklani, recipient of the Vrikshamitra or Friend of Trees award bestowed by Indira Gandhi in 1987, has planted more than 200,000 trees.[26] Banwari, a contemporary environmentalist writer in India, attributes India's abundance and traditional economic strength to its magical forests, its sacred groves, and its medicinal trees. He writes of the care for forests and trees in India's ancient cities and towns and celebrates the forests that once stood in India as "the land of no war."[27] The tree and the grove provide a foundation through which some ideas akin to deep ecology might be appreciated or understood in the Indian context.

In my own travels to India over the past several years, I have been alarmed by the increase in air pollution, saddened by the lack of resolve to effectively clean India's rivers, and heartened by the extensive planting of trees on the northern plains. In 1980, one could gaze over lentil and vegetable fields for what seemed like miles, with no hedgerow, only a raised furrow to separate one field from another. Twenty years later, the same landscape vista now offers tall Asokha and Champa trees along the roadsides and throughout the fields. These new trees are not sheltered within sacred groves nor does one see them adorned or revered. Their quiet and pervasive presence nonetheless bears witness to a regreening of the landscape.

THE CONTEMPORARY CHALLENGE

In this chapter, we have surveyed meditative and ritual practices, and the ancient tradition of preserving sacred groves, as possible models for deep ecology within Hinduism. However, just as we mentioned at the beginning of this essay that deep ecology might be a hard sell for secular intellectuals in India, so also it might be difficult to champion the old ways in light of the advent of modern consumerism. The automobile has arrived in full force in India. There has been a threefold increase in automobiles in the past ten years. Vehicles contribute more than 70 percent of India's urban air pollution. According to the Tata Institute, "air pollution in India caused an estimated 2.5 million premature deaths in 1997—equivalent to wiping out the entire population of Jamaica or Singapore."[28] Consumerism can be seen in all its splendor and allure. And with consumerism come the accompanying difficulties of waste disposal, air pollution, and water pollution. Can a deep ecological sensibility inspired by the Hindu tradition help counter these recent harmful developments? Most likely it will not for the urban peoples who have little touch with traditional ways and little interest in the meditative model presented by the wandering *sadhu* or renouncer.

The rising prevalence of urban life (and the imitation of urban life in rural areas) threatens to undermine the very embeddedness that has so characterized the underlying Hindu ecological sensibility. Vasudha Narayan laments that "a burgeoning middle class in India is now hungry for the consumer bon-bons of comfortable and luxurious living . . . The rich in India can easily surpass the middle class and the rich of the industrialized nations in their opulent life-styles . . . unbridled greed reigns."[29] While visiting alumni and their families in India, I have noted that the number of electronic gadgets such as VCR players, TVs, and CD players in the average upper-middle-class Indian home far exceed the modest accumulations in my own small American home.

Informants have told Vijaya Nagarajan that since inorganic substances (plastic, stone) are used in the Kolam (household threshold artistry) in place of rice plaster,

Christopher Key Chapple

We do not know why we do the Kolam anymore. We have forgotten. If we had not, we would not make the Kolam out of plastic or white stone powder. Now everything is modern, modern, modern. Before we would make it with rice . . . to feed a thousand souls . . . ants, birds, small worms, insects, maggots. . . . How ungenerous we are becoming![30]

Just as modernity moved the American masses from the countryside to the cities and suburbs, robbing its populace of operative barnyard metaphors and knowledge of basic pastoralism, the Indian urbanized population potentially will lose touch with some of its embedded relationship with nature. A woman from India, observing a fully lit football field at night, once commented that such uses of electricity "rob the sun of its power," a poignant statement laden with multiple meanings.

On a more optimistic note, environmental writer Bill McKibben has suggested the world consider the state of Kerala as a model for sustainable development. We have already discussed one ritual aspect of life in Kerala that seems to indicate a living example of embedded ecology. Melinda Moore has written about how even the architectural design of a house in Kerala takes into account one's place in the cosmic scheme.[31] Along with maintaining ancient rituals, sacred places, and an integrated sense of the human's niche in nature, Kerala has developed a society that in quality of life equals that of most First World countries, but with a Third World economy. Specifically, of the twenty-nine million living in the state of Kerala, nearly 100 percent are literate, though the per capita income in Kerala ranges from $298 to $350 per year. The seventy-year life expectancy of the Keralese male nearly equals that of a North American male (seventy-two years), and during a recent visit one Kerala promoter boasted that home ownership in Kerala stands at over 90 percent. Essayist Bill McKibben, who has spent time in Kerala, writes:

> Kerala demonstrates that a low-level economy can create a decent life, abundant in things—health, education, community—that are most necessary for us all. . . . One recent calculation showed that for every American dollar spent or its equivalent spent anywhere on earth, half a liter of oil was consumed in producing, packaging, and shipping the goods. One-seventieth the income means one-seventieth the damage to the planet. So, on balance, if Kerala and the United States manage to achieve the same physical quality of life, Kerala is the vastly more successful society.[32]

Unlike most of the subcontinent, two monsoons visit Kerala each year, which allows for denser foliage than most of India. Consequently, women spend less time collecting fodder and firewood, allowing time for educational pursuits, a hallmark of Kerala's success. And its abundant spices have provided ready cash in the world economy for nearly three millennia. Nonetheless, the region's ability to maintain harmony with the land despite great population density, and to balance three powerful religions (Hinduism, Islam, and Christianity) stands as a beacon of hope for an operative, simple, deep ecology.

In India, the issues of social context, historical realities, and survival in a country with huge population pressures demand a different definition of deep ecology. Hundreds of millions of people in India live by subsistence, without certain access to clean water or adequate food. In some ways, this population lives according to the precepts of deep ecology. These people do not consume petroleum; their diet is largely grain and vegetable based; they own next to no consumer products or luxuries. India's middle class (of several hundred million), on the other hand, has developed an elaborate urban lifestyle replete with packaged foods, private scooters and automobiles, and numerous consumer luxuries. India's poor live in a deep ecology mandated by circumstance not design. The middle class has embraced all that America can offer; in the words of one Indian intellectual, "We want what we see on Star (satellite) TV"; many Indians have joined wholeheartedly the American consumerist model.

Between these two extremes of utter material poverty and material excess lies the possibility of a deep ecology that improves health, nutrition, and education for the poor and offers thoughtways, perhaps along the Gandhian model, to inspire restraint from overconsumption. Deep ecology in India must be linked to sustainable development with a focus on universal education (as in Kerala), adequate food supplies, and the development of appropriate technology and transportation systems.

People overpower the landscape, the place of India. Even in remote rural areas, stay still for a minute or two and a person will appear, off on a distant hill or in a hedgerow nearby. Ecologist Patricia C. Wright has commented that China and India have not willfully stumbled into pollution and overpopulation; they simply have been settled and civilized far longer than Europe or the Americas, which has led to a greater density of people. Consequently, any "nature policy" or sensitivity to the core values of deep ecology as outlined in this book must by necessity be instrumental. The human person will not disappear from the subcontinent, nor can one effectively escape from people into a pristine forest; even the sacred grove exists in reciprocity with human use. Gary Snyder has suggested that "[s]ome of us would hope to resume, reevaluate, re-create, and bring into line with complex science that old view that holds the whole phenomenal world to be our own being: multicentered, 'alive' in its own manner, and effortlessly self-organizing in its own chaotic way."[33] In a sense, India and the Hindu approach to environmental issues operates in a careening, inventive fashion, drawing from the tradition, yet recognizing the complexity of distinguishing between human need and human greed.

CONCLUSION

Deep ecology in the American context requires personal struggle to resist the temptations of overconsumption. For a middle-class American, a move toward an ecological lifestyle might include riding a bicycle to work and adopting a vegetarian diet. Such changes reduce harmful emissions into the air, improve one's health, and allow one to consume fewer natural resources by eating low on the food chain. One might also find inspiration in beautiful landscapes and in reading literature from the burgeoning field of nature writing.

In a Hindu context, deep ecology can be affirmed through reflection on traditional texts that proclaim a continuity between the human order and nature, through ritual activities, and through applying meditative techniques that foster a felt experience of one's relationship with the elements. Long ago, India developed yogic techniques for self-awareness, self-control, and the cultivation of inner peace. These techniques have been practiced by Hindus, Buddhists, Jainas, Sikhs, and Sufis throughout the world, and, as mentioned at the beginning of this chapter, have been embraced by many individuals in the Americas and Europe. The principles of abstemiousness and harmlessness associated with these meditative practices can help cultivate an awareness of one's place in the ecosystem and inspire one to live within the confines of a wholesome ritual simplicity.

These features of Indian thought can also inspire an environmental approach that acknowledges the significant needs of a large and growing population. Deep ecology in a Hindu context must take into account the harmful effects of urbanization due to pollution and use its insights to encourage earth-friendly attitudes in the villages and the cities.

NOTES

1. Mitchell Thomashow, *Ecological Identity: Becoming a Reflective Environmentalist* (Cambridge, MA: MIT Press, 1995), 58.

2. One reason for the underdevelopment of deep ecology in India lies in the absence of both religious and environmental studies as academic disciplines in the universities of South Asia. Religious instruction takes place in the observance of home rituals, story telling, and media presentations such as the literatalist television versions of the Ramayana, Mahabharata, and other religious tales. The rote and somewhat static nature of the conveyance of religion in South Asia has resulted in its rejection by many of the educated elite, who prefer to embrace secularism as their primary world view.

3. See Christopher Key Chapple, *Nonviolence to Animals, Earth, and Self in Asian Traditions* (Albany: State University of New York Press, 1993); "India's Earth Consciousness," in *The Soul of Nature: Visions of a Living Earth*, ed. Michael Tobias and Georgianne Cowan (New York: Continuum, 1994), 145–151; and "Toward an Indigenous Indian Environmentalism," in *Purifying the Earthly Body of God: Religion and Ecology in Hindu India*, ed. Lance E. Nelson (Albany: State University of New York Press, 1998), 13–38.

4. A. R. Victor Raj, *The Hindu Connection: Roots of the New Age* (Saint Louis: Concordia Publishing House, 1995), 62–119.

5. 182: 14–19, adapted from O. P. Dwivedi and B. N. Tiwari, *Environmental Crisis and Hindu Religion* (New Delhi: Gitanjali Publishing House, 1987), 126.

6. Carol Lee Flinders, *At the Root of This Longing: Reconciling a Spiritual Hunger and a Feminist Thirst* (San Francisco: Harper SanFrancisco, 1998), 260.

7. Christopher Key Chapple and Yogi Anand Viraj (Eugene P. Kelly Jr.), *The Yoga Sȳtras of Patanjali: An Analysis of the Sanskrit with English Translation* (Delhi: Satguru Publications, 1990), 99.

8. David Abram, *The Spell of the Sensuous: Perception and Language in a More-Than-Human World* (New York: Pantheon Books, 1996), 65.

9. James J. Preston, *Cult of the Goddess: Social and Religious Change in a Hindu Temple* (Prospect Heights, IL: Waveland Press, 1985), 52, 53.

10. Vijaya Rettakudi Nagarajan, "The Earth as Goddess Bhu Devi: Toward a Theory of 'Embedded Ecologies' in Folk Hinduism," in *Purifying the Earthly Body of God: Religion and Ecology in Hindu India*, ed. Lance Nelson (Albany: State University of New York Press, 1998), 269–296.

11. Madhu Khanna, "The Ritual Capsule of Purgā Pūjā: An Ecological Perspective," in *Hinduism and Ecology: The Intersection of Earth, Sky, and Water*, ed. Christopher Key Chapple (Cambridge: Harvard University Center for the Study of World Religions, 2000).

12. Moozhikkulam Chandrasekharam Pillai, *Mannarassala: The Serpent Temple*, trans. Ayyappa Panikker (Harippad: Manasa Publication, 1991), 33.

13. Frederique Apffel-Marglin, "Sacred Groves: Regenerating the Body, the Land, the Community," in *Global Ecology: A New Arena of Political Conflict*, ed. Wolfgang Sachs (London: Zed Books, 1993), 198.

14. Ibid., 206.

15. Madhav Gadgil and Ramachandra Guha, *This Fissured Land: An Ecological History of India* (Delhi: Oxford University Press, 1992), 106.

16. Ibid., 108.

17. Anil Agawal and Sunita Narain, "Dying Wisdom: The Decline and Revival of Traditional Water Harvesting Systems in India," *Ecologist 27*, no. 3 (1997): 112.

18. Ibid., 115.

19. William F. Fisher, *Toward Sustainable Development: Struggling Over India's Narmada River* (Armonk, NY: M. E. Sharpe, 1995).

20. Gadgil and Guha, *This Fissured Land*, 243.

21. Ibid., 244.

22. John Seed, "Spirit of the Earth: A Battle-Weary Rainforest Activist Journeys to India to Renew His Soul," *Yoga Journal*, no. 138 (January/February 1998): 135.

23. Ibid., 136.

24. Mahesh Rangarajan, *Fencing the Forest: Conservation and Ecological Change in India's Central Provinces 1860–1914* (Delhi: Oxford University Press, 1961), 5.

25. Ranchor Prime, *Hinduism and Ecology: Seeds of Truth* (London: Cassell, 1992), 90.

26. Carolyn Emett, "The Tree Man," *Resurgence: An International Forum for Ecological and Spiritual Thinking*, no. 183 (July/August 1997): 42.

27. Banwari, *Pancavati: Indian Approach to Environment*, trans. Asha Vora (Delhi: Shri Vinayaka Publications, 1992).

28. Payal Sampat, "What Does India Want?" *World Watch* 11 (July/August 1998): 36.

29. Vasudha Narayanan, "One Tree Is Equal to Ten Sons: Hindu Responses to the Problems of Ecology, Population, and Consumption," *Journal of the American Academy of Religion* 65, no. 2 (January 1997): 321.

30. Narayan, "One Tree Is Equal to Ten Sons," 275.

31. Melinda A. Moore, "The Kerala House as a Hindu Cosmos," *India through Hindu Categories*, ed. McKim Marriott (New Delhi: Sage Publications, 1990), 169–202.

32. Bill McKibben, *Hope, Human and Wild: True Stories of Living Lightly on the Earth* (Saint Paul: Hungry Mind Press, 1995), 121, 163.

33. Gary Snyder, *A Place in Space: Ethics, Aesthetics, and Watersheds* (Washington, DC: Counterpoint, 1996), 241.

"BEYOND THE ENLIGHTENMENT MENTALITY"

Tu Weiming

The Enlightenment mentality underlies the rise of the modern West as the most dynamic and transformative ideology in human history.[1] Virtually all major spheres of interest characteristic of the modern age are indebted to or intertwined with this mentality: science and technology, industrial capitalism, market economy, democratic polity, mass communication, research universities, civil and military bureaucracies, and professional organizations. Furthermore, the values we cherish as definitions of modern consciousness—including liberty, equality, human rights, the dignity of the individual, respect for privacy, government for, by, and of the people, and due process of law—are genetically, if not structurally, inseparable from the Enlightenment mentality. We have flourished in the spheres of interest and their attendant values occasioned by the advent of the modern West since the eighteenth century. They have made our life-world operative and meaningful. We take it for granted that, through instrumental rationality, we can solve the world's major problems and that progress, primarily in economic terms, is desirable and necessary for the human community as a whole.

We are so seasoned in the Enlightenment mentality that we assume the reasonableness of its general ideological thrust. It seems self-evident that both capitalism and socialism subscribe to the aggressive anthropocentrism underlying the modern mind-set: man is not only the measure of all things but also the only source of power for economic well-being, political stability, and social development. The Enlightenment faith in progress, reason, and individualism may have been challenged by some of the most brilliant minds in the modern Western academy, but it remains a standard of inspiration for intellectual and spiritual leaders throughout the world. It is inconceivable that any international project, including those in ecological sciences, not subscribe to the theses that the human condition is improvable, that it is desirable to find rational means to solve the world's problems, and that the dignity of the person as an individual ought to be respected. Enlightenment as human awakening, as the discovery of the human potential for global transformation, and as the

Reprinted from *Worldviews and Ecology*, Mary Evelyn Tucker and John A. Grim, eds. Copyright © 1994, Associated University Presses, Inc.

realization of the human desire to become the measure and master of all things is still the most influential moral discourse in the political culture of the modern age; for decades it has been the unquestioned assumption of the ruling minorities and cultural elites of developing countries, as well as highly industrialized nations.

A fair understanding of the Enlightenment mentality requires a frank discussion of the dark side of the modern West as well. The "unbound Prometheus," symbolizing the runaway technology of development, may have been a spectacular achievement of human ingenuity in the early phases of the industrial revolution. Despite impassioned reactions from the romantic movement and insightful criticisms of the forebears of the "human sciences," the Enlightenment mentality, fueled by the Faustian drive to explore, to know, to conquer, and to subdue, persisted as the reigning ideology of the modern West. It is now fully embraced as the unquestioned rationale for development in East Asia.

However, a realistic appraisal of the Enlightenment mentality reveals many faces of the modern West incongruous with the image of "the Age of Reason." In the context of modern Western hegemonic discourse, progress may entail inequality, reason, self-interest, and individual greed. The American dream of owning a car and a house, earning a fair wage, and enjoying freedom of privacy, expression, religion, and travel, while reasonable to our (American) sense of what ordinary life demands, is lamentably unexportable as a modern necessity from a global perspective. Indeed, it has now been widely acknowledged as no more than a dream for a significant segment of the American population as well.

An urgent task for the community of like-minded persons deeply concerned about ecological issues and the disintegration of communities at all levels is to insure that both the ruling minorities and cultural elites in the modern West actively participate in a spiritual joint venture to rethink the Enlightenment heritage. The paradox is that we cannot afford to accept uncritically its inner logic in light of the unintended negative consequences it has engendered on the life-support systems; nor can we reject its relevance, with all of the fruitful ambiguities this entails, to our intellectual self-definition, present and future. There is no easy way out. We do not have an "either-or" choice. The possibility of a radically different ethic or a new value system separate from and independent of the Enlightenment mentality is neither realistic nor authentic. It may even appear to be either cynical or hypercritical. We need to explore the spiritual resources that may help us to broaden the scope of the Enlightenment project, deepen its moral sensitivity, and, if necessary, transform creatively its genetic constraints in order to realize fully its potential as a worldview for the human condition as a whole.

A key to the success of this spiritual joint venture is to recognize the conspicuous absence of the idea of community, let alone the global community, in the Enlightenment project. Fraternity, a functional equivalent of community in the three cardinal virtues of the French Revolution, has received scant attention in modern Western economic, political, and social thought. The willingness to tolerate inequality, the faith in the salvific power of self-interest, and the unbridled affirmation of aggressive egoism have greatly poisoned the good well of progress, reason, and individualism. The need to express a universal intent for the formation of a "global village" and to articulate a possible link between the fragmented world we experience in our ordinary daily existence and the imagined community for the human species as a whole is deeply felt by an increasing number of concerned intellectuals. This requires, at a minimum, the replacement of the principle of self-interest, no matter how broadly defined, with a new Golden Rule: "Do not do unto others what you would not want others to do unto you."[2] Since the new Golden Rule is stated in the negative, it will have to be augmented by a positive principle: "in order to establish myself, I have to help others to enlarge themselves."[3] An inclusive sense of community, based on the communal critical self-consciousness of reflective minds, is an ethico-religious goal as well as a philosophical ideal.

The mobilization of at least three kinds of spiritual resources is necessary to ensure that this simple vision is grounded in the historicity of the cultural complexes informing our ways of life today. The first kind involves the ethico-religious traditions of the modern West, notably Greek philosophy, Judaism, and Christianity. The very fact that they have been instrumental in giving birth to the Enlightenment mentality makes a compelling case for them to reexamine their relationships to the rise of the modern West in order to create a new public sphere for the transvaluation of typical Western values. The exclusive dichotomy of matter/spirit, body/mind, sacred/profane, human/nature, or creator/creature must be transcended to allow supreme values, such as the sanctity of the earth, the continuity of being, the beneficiary interaction between the human community and nature, and the mutuality between humankind and Heaven, to receive the saliency they deserve in philosophy, religion, and theology.

The Greek philosophical emphasis on rationality, the biblical image of man having "dominion" over the earth, and the Protestant work ethic provided necessary, if not sufficient, sources for the Enlightenment mentality. However, the unintended negative consequences of the rise of the modern West have so undermined the sense of community implicit in the Hellenistic idea of the citizen, the Judaic idea of the covenant, and the Christian idea of fellowship that it is morally imperative for these great traditions, which have maintained highly complex and tension-ridden relationships with the Enlightenment mentality, to formulate their critique of the blatant anthropocentrism inherent in the Enlightenment project. The emergence of a communitarian ethic as a critique of the idea of the person as a rights-bearing, interest-motivated, rational economic animal clearly indicates the relevance of an Aristotelian, Pauline, Abrahamic, or Republican ethic to current moral self-reflexivity in North America. Jürgen Habermas's attempt to broaden the scope of rational discourse by emphasizing the importance of "communicative rationality" in social intercourse represents a major intellectual effort to develop new conceptual apparatuses to enrich the Enlightenment tradition.[4]

The second kind of spiritual resource is derived from non-Western, axial-age civilizations, which include Hinduism, Jainism, and Buddhism in South and Southeast Asia, Confucianism and Taoism in East Asia, and Islam. Historically, Islam should be considered an essential intellectual heritage of the modern West because of its contribution to the Renaissance. The current practice, especially by the mass media of North America and Western Europe, of consigning Islam to radical otherness is historically unsound and culturally insensitive. It has, in fact, seriously undermined the modern West's own self-interest as well as its own self-understanding. Islam and these non-Western ethico-religious traditions provide sophisticated and practicable resources in worldviews, rituals, institutions, styles of education, and patterns of human-relatedness. They can help to develop ways of life, both as continuation of and alternative to the Western European and North American exemplification of the Enlightenment mentality. Industrial East Asia, under the influence of Confucian culture, has already developed a less adversarial, less individualistic, and less self-interested modern civilization. The coexistence of market economy with government leadership, democratic polity with meritocracy, and individual initiatives with group orientation has, since the Second World War, made this region economically and politically the most dynamic area of the world. The significance of the contribution of Confucian ethics to the rise of industrial East Asia offers profound possibilities for the possible emergence of Hindu, Jain, Buddhist, and Islamic forms of modernity.

The Westernization of Confucian Asia (including Japan, the two Koreas, mainland China, Hong Kong, Taiwan, Singapore, and Vietnam) may have forever altered its spiritual landscape, but its indigenous resources (including Mahāyāna Buddhism, Taoism, Shinto-ism, shamanism, and other folk religions) have the resiliency to resurface and make their presence known in a new synthesis. The caveat, of course, is that, having been humiliated and frustrated by the imperialist and colonial domination of the modern West for more than a century, the rise of industrial East Asia symbolizes the instrumental rationality of the Enlightenment heritage with a vengeance. Indeed, the mentality of Japan and the Four Mini-Dragons (South Korea, Taiwan, Hong Kong, Singapore) is characterized by mercantilism, commercialism, and international competitiveness. The People's Republic of China (the motherland of the Sinic world) has blatantly opted for the same strategy of development and has thus exhibited the same mentality since the reform was set in motion in 1979. Surely the possibility for these nations to develop more humane and sustainable communities should not be exaggerated; nor should it be undermined.

The third kind of spiritual resource involves the primal traditions: Native American, Hawaiian, Maori, and numerous tribal indigenous religious traditions. They have demonstrated, with physical strength and aesthetic elegance, that human life has been sustainable since Neolithic times. The implications for practical living are far-reaching. Their style of human flourishing is not a figment of the mind but an experienced reality in our modern age.

A distinctive feature of primal traditions is a deep experience of rootedness. Each indigenous religious tradition is embedded in a concrete place symbolizing a way of perceiving, a mode of thinking, a form of living, an attitude, and a worldview. Given the unintended disastrous consequences of the Enlightenment mentality, there are obvious lessons that the modern mind-set can learn from indigenous religious traditions. A natural outcome of indigenous peoples' embeddedness in concrete locality is their intimate and detailed knowledge of their environment; indeed, the demarcations between their human habitat and nature are muted. Implicit in this model of existence is the realization that mutuality and reciprocity between the anthropological world and the cosmos at large is both necessary and desirable. What we can learn from them, then, is a new way of perceiving, a new mode of thinking, a new form of living, a new attitude, and a new worldview. A critique of the Enlightenment mentality and its derivative modern mind-set from the perspective of indigenous peoples could be thought-provoking.

An equally significant aspect of indigenous lifeways is the ritual of bonding in ordinary daily human interaction. The density of kinship relations, the rich texture of interpersonal communication, the detailed and nuanced appreciation of the surrounding natural and cultural world, and the experienced connectedness with ancestors point to communities grounded in ethnicity, gender, language, land, and faith. The primordial ties are constitutive parts of their being and activity. In Huston Smith's characterization, what they exemplify is participation rather than control in motivation, empathic understanding rather than empiricist apprehension in epistemology, respect for the transcendent rather than domination over nature in worldview, and fulfillment rather than alienation in human experience. As we begin to question the soundness or even sanity of some of our most cherished ways of thinking—such as regarding knowledge as power rather than wisdom, asserting the desirability of material progress despite its corrosive influence on the soul, and justifying the anthropocentric manipulation of nature even at the cost of destroying the life-support system—indigenous perspectives emerge as a source of inspiration.

Of course, I am not proposing any romantic attachment to or nostalgic sentiments for "primal consciousness," and I am critically aware that claims of primordiality are often modernist cultural constructions dictated by the politics of recognition. Rather, I suggest that, as both beneficiaries and victims of the Enlightenment mentality, we show our fidelity to our common heritage by enriching it, transforming it, and restructuring it with all three kinds of spiritual resources still available to us for the sake of developing a truly ecumenical sense of global community. Indeed, of the three great Enlightenment values embodied in the French Revolution, fraternity seems to have attracted the least attention in the subsequent two centuries. The re-presentation of the *Problematik* of community in recent years is symptomatic of the confluence of two apparently contradictory forces in the late twentieth century: the global village as both a virtual reality and an imagined community in our information age and the disintegration and restructuring of human togetherness at all levels, from family to nation.

It may not be immodest to say that we are beginning to develop a fourth kind of spiritual resource from the core of the Enlightenment project itself. Our disciplined reflection, a communal act rather than an isolated struggle, is a first step toward the "creative zone" envisioned by religious leaders and teachers of ethics. The feminist critique of tradition, the concern for the environment, and the persuasion of religious pluralism are obvious examples of this new corporate critical self-awareness. The need to go beyond the Enlightenment mentality, without either deconstructing or abandoning its commitment to rationality, liberty, equality, human rights, and distributive justice, requires a thorough reexamination of modernity as a signifier and modernization as a process.

Underlying this reexamination is the intriguing issue of traditions in modernity. The dichotomous thinking of tradition and modernity as two incompatible forms of life will have to be replaced by a much more nuanced investigation of the continuous interaction between modernity as the perceived outcome of "rationalization" defined in Weberian terms and traditions as "habits of the heart" (to borrow an expression from Alexis de Tocqueville), enduring modes of thinking, or salient features of cultural self-understanding. The traditions in modernity are not merely historical sedimentation passively deposited in modern consciousness. Nor are they, in functional terms, simply inhibiting factors to be undermined by the unilinear trajectory of development. On the contrary, they are both constraining and enabling forces capable of shaping the particular contour of modernity in any given society. It is, therefore, conceptually naïve and methodologically fallacious to relegate traditions to the residual category in our discussion of the modernizing process. Indeed, an investigation of traditions in modernity is essential for our appreciation of modernization as a highly differentiated cultural phenomenon rather than as a homogeneous integral process of Westernization.

Talcott Parsons may have been right in assuming that market economy, democratic polity, and individualism are three inseparable dimensions of modernity.[5] The post–Cold War era seems to have inaugurated a new world order in which marketization, democratization, and individualism are salient features of a new global village. The collapse of socialism gives the impression that market rather than planned economy, democratic rather than authoritarian polity, and individualist rather than collectivist style of life symbolize the wave of the future. Whether or not we believe in the "end of history," a stage of human development in which only advanced capitalism—characterized by multinational corporations, information superhighways, technology-driven sciences, mass communication, and conspicuous consumption—dominates, we must be critically aware of the globalizing forces which, through a variety of networks, literally transform the earth into a wired discourse community. As a result, distance, no matter how great, does not at all inhibit electronic communication and, ironically, territorial proximity does not necessarily guarantee actual contact. We can be frequent conversation partners with associates thousands of miles apart, yet we are often strangers to our neighbors, colleagues, and relatives.

The advent of the global village as virtual reality rather than authentic home is by no means congenial to human flourishing. Contrary to the classical Confucian ideal of the "great harmony" (*ta-t'ung*), what the global village exhibits is sharp difference, severe differentiation, drastic demarcation, thunderous dissonance, and outright discrimination. The world, compressed into an interconnected ecological, financial, commercial, trading, and electronic system, has never been so divided in wealth, influence, and power. The advent of the imagined, and even anticipated, global village is far from a cause for celebration.

Never in world history has the contrast between the rich and the poor, the dominant and the marginalized, the articulate and the silenced, the included and the excluded, the informed and the uninformed, and the connected and the isolated been so markedly drawn. The rich, dominant, articulate, included, informed, and connected beneficiaries of the system form numerous transnational networks making distance and, indeed, ethnic boundary, cultural diversity, religious exclusivism, or national sovereignty inconsequential in their march toward domination. On the other hand, residents of the same neighborhood may have radically different access to information, ideas, tangible resources (such as money), and immaterial goods (such as prestige). People of the same electoral district may subscribe to sharply conflicting political ideologies, social mores, and worldviews. They may also experience basic categories of human existence (such as time and space) in incommensurable ways. The severity of the contrast between the haves and the have-nots at all levels of the human experience—individual, family, society, and nation—can easily be demonstrated by hard empirical data. The sense of relative deprivation is greatly intensified by the glorification of conspicuous consumption by the mass media. Even in the most economically advanced nations, notably North America, the Scandinavian countries and other nations of Western Europe, and Japan and the Mini-Dragons, the pervasive mood is one of discontent, anxiety, and frustration.

If we focus our attention exclusively on the powerful megatrends that have exerted shaping influences on the global community since the end of the Second World War—science, technology, communication, trade, finance, entertainment, travel, tourism, migration, and disease—we may easily be misled into believing that the world has changed so much that the human condition is being structured by newly emerging global forces without any reference to our inherited historical and cultural praxis. One of the most significant *fin-de-siècle* reflections of the twentieth century is the acknowledgment that globalization does not mean homogenization and that modernization intensifies as well as lessens economic, political, social, cultural, and religious conflict in both inter- and intra-national contexts. The emergence of primordial ties (ethnicity, language, gender, land, class, and faith) as powerful forces in constructing internally defensive cultural identities and externally aggressive religious exclusivities compels practical-minded global thinkers to develop new conceptual resources to understand the spirit of our time. The common practice of internationalists, including some of the most sophisticated analyzers of the world scene, of condemning the enduring strength of primordial ties as a parochial reaction to the inevitable process of globalization is simple-minded and ill-advised. What we witness in Bosnia, Africa, Sri Lanka, and India is not simply "fragmentization" as opposed to global integration. Since we are acutely aware of the explosive potential of ethnicity in the United States, language in Canada, and religious fundamentalism in all three major monotheistic religions, we must learn to appreciate that the quest for roots is a worldwide phenomenon.

Nowadays we are confronted with two conflicting and even contradictory forces in the global community: internationalization (globalization) and localization (communization). The United Nations, which came into being because of the spirit of internationalization, must now deal with issues of rootedness (all those specified above as primordial ties). While globalization in science, technology, mass communication, trade, tourism, finance, migration, and disease is progressing at an unprecedented rate and to an unprecedented degree, the pervasiveness and depth of communal (or tribal) feelings, both hidden and aroused, cannot be easily transformed by the Enlightenment values of instrumental rationality, individual liberty, calculated self-interest, material progress, and rights consciousness. The resiliency and explosive power of human-relatedness can be better appreciated by an ethic mindful of the need for reasonableness in any form of negotiation, distributive justice, sympathy, civility, duty-consciousness, dignity of person, sense of intrinsic worth, and self-cultivation.

In the Confucian perspective, human beings are not merely rational beings, political animals, tool-users, or language-manipulators. Confucians seem to have deliberately rejected simplistic reductionist models. They define human beings in terms of five integrated visions:

1. Human beings are sentient beings, capable of internal resonance not only between and among themselves but also with other animals, plants, trees, mountains, and rivers, indeed nature as a whole.
2. Human beings are social beings. As isolated individuals, human beings are weak by comparison with other members of the animal kingdom, but if they are organized to form a society, they have inner strength not only for survival but also for flourishing. Human-relatedness as exemplified in a variety of networks of interaction is necessary for human survival and human flourishing. Our sociality defines who we are.

3. Human beings are political beings in the sense that human-relatedness is, by biological nature and social necessity, differentiated in terms of hierarchy, status, and authority. While Confucians insist upon the fluidity of these artificially constructed boundaries, they recognize the significance of "difference" in an "organic" as opposed to "mechanic" solidarity—thus the centrality of the principle of fairness and the primacy of the practice of distributive justice in a humane society.

4. Human beings are also historical beings sharing collective memories, cultural memories, cultural traditions, ritual praxis, and "habits of the heart."

5. Human beings are metaphysical beings with the highest aspirations not simply defined in terms of anthropocentric ideas but characterized by the ultimate concern to be constantly inspired by and continuously responsive to the Mandate of Heaven.

The Confucian way is a way of learning, learning to be human. Learning to be human in the Confucian spirit is to engage oneself in a ceaseless, unending process of creative self-transformation, both as a communal act and as a dialogical response to Heaven. This involves four inseparable dimensions—self, community, nature, and the transcendent. The purpose of learning is always understood as being for the sake of the self, but the self is never an isolated individual (an island); rather, it is a center of relationships (a flowing stream). The self as a center of relationships is a dynamic open system rather than a closed static structure. Therefore, mutuality between self and community, harmony between human species and nature, and continuous communication with Heaven are defining characteristics and supreme values in the human project.[6]

Since Confucians take the concrete living human being here and now as their point of departure in the development of their philosophical anthropology, they recognize the embeddedness and rootedness of the human condition. Therefore, the profound significance of what we call primordial ties—ethnicity, gender, language, land, class, and basic spiritual orientation—which are intrinsic in the Confucian project, is a celebration of cultural diversity (this is not to be confused with any form of pernicious relativism). Often, Confucians understand their own path as learning of the body and mind (*shen-hsin-chih-hsüeh*) or learning of nature and destiny (*hsing-ming-chih-hsüeh*). There is a recognition that each one of us is fated to be a unique person embedded in a particular condition. By definition, we are unique particular human beings, but at the same time each and every one of us has the intrinsic possibility for self-cultivation, self-development, and self-realization. Despite fatedness and embeddedness as necessary structural limitations in our conditionality, we are endowed with infinite possibilities for self-transformation in our process of learning to be human. We are, therefore, intrinsically free. Our freedom, embodied in our responsibility for ourselves as the center of relationships, creates our worth. That alone deserves and demands respect.

In discussing the "spirit" of the Five Classics in the concluding section of *The World of Thought in Ancient China*, Benjamin Schwartz, referring to the central issue of the Neo-Confucian project, observes:

> In the end the root problem was to be sought where Confucius and Mencius had sought them—in the human heart/mind. It is only the human heart/mind . . . which possesses the capacity to "make itself sincere" and having made itself sincere to extend this transcendent capacity to realize the *tao* within the structures of human society. When viewed from this perspective, this is the essential gospel of the Four Books. At a deeper level, the Four Books also point to an ontological ground for the belief in this transcendental ethical capacity of the individual in the face of the ongoing challenge of a metaethical Taoist and Buddhist mysticism.[7]

The ontological grounding of the Neo-Confucian project on the learning of the heart-and-mind enabled Confucian intellectuals in late imperial China, premodern Vietnam, Chosŏn Korea, and Tokugawa Japan to create a cultural space above the family and below the state. This is why, though they never left home, actively participated in community affairs, or deeply engaged themselves in local, regional, or "national" politics, they did not merely adjust themselves to the world. Max Weber's overall assessment of the Confucian life-orientation misses the point. The spiritual resources that sustained their social activism came from minding their own business and included cultivating themselves, teaching others to be good, "looking for friends in history," emulating the sages, setting up cultural norms, interpreting the Mandate of Heaven, transmitting the Way, and transforming the world as a moral community.

As we are confronted with the issue of a new world order in lieu of the exclusive dichotomy (capitalism and socialism) imposed by the super powers, we are easily tempted to come up with facile generalizations: "the end of history,"[8] "the clash of civilizations,"[9] or "the Pacific century." The much more difficult and, hopefully, in the long haul, much more significant line of inquiry is to address truly fundamental issues of learning to be human: Are we isolated individuals, or do we each live as a center of relationships? Is moral self-knowledge necessary for personal growth? Can any society prosper or endure without developing a basic sense of duty and responsibility among its members? Should our pluralistic society deliberately cultivate shared values and a common ground for human understanding? As we become acutely aware of our earth's vulnerability and increasingly wary of our own fate as an "endangered species," what are the critical spiritual questions to ask?[10]

Since the Opium War (1840–1842), China has endured many holocausts. Prior to 1949, imperialism was the main culprit, but since the founding of the People's Republic of China, erratic leadership and faulty policies must also share the blame. Although millions of Chinese died, the neighboring countries were not seriously affected and the outside world was, by and large, oblivious to what actually happened. Since 1979, China has been rapidly becoming an integral part of the global economic system. More than 30 percent of the Chinese economy is tied to international trade. Natural economic territories have emerged between Hong Kong and Chuan Chou, Fujian and Taiwan, Shantung and South Korea. Japanese, European, and American, as well as Hong Kong and Taiwanese, investments are present in virtually all Chinese provinces. The return of Hong Kong to the PRC, the conflict across the Taiwan Straits, the economic and cultural interchange among overseas Chinese communities and between them and the motherland, the intraregional communication in East Asia, the political and economic integration of the Association for Southeast Asian Nations, and the rise of the Asia-Pacific region will all have substantial impact on our shrinking global community.

The revitalization of the Confucian discourse may contribute to the formation of a much needed communal critical self-consciousness among East Asian intellectuals. We may very well be in the very beginning of global history rather than witnessing the end of history. And, from a comparative cultural perspective, this new beginning must take as its point of departure dialogue rather than clash of civilizations. Our awareness of the danger of civilizational conflicts, rooted in ethnicity, language, land, and religion, makes the necessity of dialogue particularly compelling. An alternative model of sustainable development, with an emphasis on the ethical and spiritual dimensions of human flourishing, must be sought.

The time is long overdue to move beyond a mind-set shaped by instrumental rationality and private interests. As the politics of domination fades, we witness the dawning of an age of communication, networking, negotiation, interaction, interfacing, and collaboration. Whether or not East Asian intellectuals, inspired by the Confucian spirit of self-cultivation, family cohesiveness, social solidarity, benevolent governance, and universal peace, will articulate an ethic of responsibility as Chinese, Japanese, Koreans, and Vietnamese emigrate to other parts of the world is profoundly meaningful for global stewardship.

We can actually envision the Confucian perception of human flourishing, based upon the dignity of the person, in terms of a series of concentric circles: self, family, community, society, nation, world, and cosmos. We begin with a quest for true personal identity, an open and creatively transforming selfhood which, paradoxically, must be predicated on our ability to overcome selfishness and egoism. We cherish family cohesiveness. In order to do that, we have to go beyond nepotism. We embrace communal solidarity, but we have to transcend parochialism to realize its true value. We can be enriched by social integration, provided that we overcome ethnocentrism and chauvinistic culturalism. We are committed to national unity, but we ought to rise above aggressive nationalism so that we can be genuinely patriotic. We are inspired by human flourishing, but we must endeavor not to be confined by anthropocentrism, for the full meaning of humanity is anthropocosmic rather than anthropocentric. On the occasion of the international symposium on Islamic-Confucian dialogue organized by the University of Malaya (March 1995), the Deputy Prime Minister of Malaysia, Anwar Ibrahim, quoted a statement from Huston Smith's *The World's Religions*. It very much captures the Confucian spirit of self-transcendence:

> In shifting the center of one's empathic concern from oneself to one's family one transcends selfishness. The move from family to community transcends nepotism. The move from community to nation transcends parochialism and the move to all humanity counters chauvinistic nationalism.[11]

We can even add: the move towards the unity of Heaven and humanity (*t'ien-jen-ho-i*) transcends secular humanism, a blatant form of anthropocentrism characteristic of the Enlightenment mentality. Indeed, it is in the anthropocosmic spirit that we find communication between self and community, harmony between human species and nature, and mutuality between humanity and Heaven. This integrated comprehensive vision of learning to be human serves well as a point of departure for a new discourse on the global ethic.

The case against anthropocentrism through the formulation of an anthropocosmic vision embodied in the Neo-Confucian learning of the heart-and-mind is succinctly presented by Wang Yang-ming. Let me conclude with the opening statement in his *Inquiry on the Great Learning*:

> The great man regards Heaven and Earth and the myriad things as one body. He regards the world as one family and the country as one person. . . . That the great man can regard Heaven, Earth, and the myriad things as one body is not because he deliberately wants to do so, but because it is natural to the humane nature of his mind that he do so. Forming one body with Heaven, Earth, and the myriad things is not only true of the great man. Even the mind of the small man is no different. Only he himself makes it small. Therefore when he sees a child about to fall into a well, he cannot help a feeling of alarm and commiseration. This shows that his humanity (*jen*) forms one body with the child. It may be objected that the child belongs to the same species. Again, when he observes the pitiful cries and frightened appearance of birds and animals about to be slaughtered, he cannot help feeling an "inability to bear" their suffering. This shows that his humanity forms one body with birds and animals. It may be objected that birds and animals are sentient beings as he is. But when he sees plants broken and destroyed, he cannot help . . . feeling . . . pity. This shows that his humanity forms one body with plants. It may be said that plants are living things as he is. Yet even when he sees tiles and stones shattered and crushed, he cannot help . . . feeling . . . regret. This shows that his humanity forms one body with tiles and stones. This means that even the mind of the small man necessarily has the humanity that forms one body with all. Such a mind is rooted in his Heaven-endowed nature, and is naturally intelligent, clear and not beclouded. For this reason it is called "clear character."[12]

For Confucians to fully realize themselves, it is not enough to become a responsible householder, effective social worker, or conscientious political servant. No matter how successful one is in the sociopolitical arena, the full measure of one's humanity cannot be accommodated without a reference to Heaven. The highest Confucian ideal is the "unity of man and Heaven," which defines humanity not only in anthropological terms but also in cosmological terms. In the *Doctrine of the Mean* (*Chung yung*), the most authentic manifestation of humanity is characterized as "forming a trinity with Heaven and Earth."[13]

Yet, since Heaven does not speak and the Way in itself cannot make human beings great—which suggests that although Heaven is omnipresent and may be omniscient, it is certainly not omnipotent—our understanding of the Mandate of Heaven requires that we fully appreciate the rightness and principle inherent in our heart-minds. Our ability to transcend egoism, nepotism, parochialism, ethnocentrism, and chauvinistic nationalism must be extended to anthropocentrism as well. To make ourselves deserving partners of Heaven, we must be constantly in touch with that silent illumination that makes the rightness and principle in our heart-minds shine forth brilliantly. If we cannot go beyond the constraints of our own species, the most we can hope for is an exclusive, secular humanism advocating man as the measure of all things. By contrast, Confucian humanism is inclusive; it is predicated on an "anthropocosmic" vision. Humanity in its all-embracing fullness "forms one body with Heaven, Earth, and the myriad things." Self-realization, in the last analysis, is ultimate transformation, that process which enables us to embody the family, community, nation, world, and cosmos in our sensitivity.

The ecological implications of the Confucian anthropocosmic worldview are implicit, yet need to be more carefully articulated. On the one hand, there are rich philosophical resources in the Confucian triad of Heaven, Earth, and human. On the other hand, there are numerous moral resources for developing more comprehensive environmental ethics. These include textual references, ritual practices, social norms, and political policies. From classical times Confucians were concerned with harmonizing with nature and accepting the appropriate limits and boundaries of nature. This concern manifested itself in a variety of forms cultivating virtues that were considered to be both personal and cosmic. It also included biological imagery used for describing the process of self-cultivation. To realize the profound and varied correspondences of the person with the cosmos is a primary goal of Confucianism: it is a vision with vital spiritual import and, at the same time, it has practical significance for facing the current ecological crisis. This volume itself begins to chart a course for realizing the rich resources of the Confucian tradition in resituating humans within the rhythms and limits of the natural world.

NOTES

1. I wish to acknowledge, with gratitude, that Mary Evelyn Tucker and John Berthrong were instrumental in transforming my oral presentation into a written text. I would also like to note that materials from three published articles of mine have been used in this paper: "Beyond the Enlightenment Mentality," in *Worldviews and Ecology: Religion, Philosophy, and the Environment*, ed. Mary Evelyn Tucker and John A. Grim (Maryknoll, N.Y.: Orbis Books, 1994), 19–28; "Global Community as Lived Reality: Exploring Spiritual Resources for Social Development," *Social Policy and Social Progress: A Review Published by the United Nations, Special Issue on the Social Summit, Copenhagen, 6–12 March 1995* (New York: United Nations Publications, 1996), 39–51; and "Beyond the Enlightenment Mentality: A Confucian Perspective on Ethics, Migration, and Global Stewardship," *International Migration Review* 30 (spring 1996):58–75.

2. *Analects*, 12:2.

3. *Analects*, 6:28.

4. Jürgen Habermas, "What Is Universal Pragmatics?" in his *Communication and the Evolution of Society*, trans. Thomas McCarthy (Boston: Beacon Press, 1979), 1–68.

5. Talcott Parsons, "Evolutionary Universals in Sociology," in his *Sociological Theory and Modern Society* (New York: The Free Press, 1967), 490–520.

6. See Thomé H. Fang, "The Spirit of Life," in his *The Chinese View of Life: The Philosophy of Comprehensive Harmony* (Taipei: Linking Publishing, 1980), 71–93.

7. Benjamin I. Schwartz, *The World of Thought in Ancient China* (Cambridge, Mass.: Belknap Press of Harvard University Press, 1985), 406.

8. Francis Fukuyama's use of this Helena expression may have given the misleading impression that, with the end of the Cold War, the triumph of capitalism necessarily led to the homogenization of global thinking. Dr. Fukuyama's recent emphasis on the idea of "trust" by drawing intellectual resources from East Asia clearly indicates that, so far as shareable values are concerned, the West can hardly monopolize the discourse.

9. Samuel P. Huntington, "The Clash of Civilizations?" *Foreign Affairs* 72, no. 3 (summer 1993):22–49.

10. These questions are critical issues for my course, "Confucian Humanism: Self-Cultivation and the Moral Community," offered in the "moral reasoning" section of the core curriculum program at Harvard University.

11. Quoted by Anwar Ibrahim in his address at the opening of the international seminar entitled "Islam and Confucianism: A Civilizational Dialogue," sponsored by the University of Malaya, 13 March 1995. It should be noted that Huston Smith's remarks, in this particular reference to the Confucian project, are based on my discussion of the meaning of self-transcendence in Confucian humanism. If we follow my "anthropocosmic" argument through, we need to transcend "anthropocentrism" as well. See Huston Smith, *The World's Religions* (San Francisco: Harper San Francisco, 1991), 182, 193, and 195 (notes 28 and 29).

12. *A Source Book in Chinese Philosophy*, trans. Wing-tsit Chan (Princeton: Princeton University Press, 1963), 659–60.

13. *Chung yung* (Doctrine of the Mean), chap. 22. For a discussion of this idea in the perspective of Confucian "moral metaphysics," see Tu Wei-ming, *Centrality and Commonality: An Essay on Chung-yung* (Honolulu: The University Press of Hawaii, 1976), 100–141.

"TO SAVE ALL BEINGS: BUDDHIST ENVIRONMENTAL ACTIVISM"

Stephanie Kaza

Meditators form a circle at the base camp of the Headwaters Forest. All are invited to join the Buddhists sitting still in the flurry of activity. While others drum, talk, dance, and discuss strategy, the small group of ecosattvas—Buddhist environmental activists—focus on their breathing and intention amidst the towering trees. They chant the *Metta Sutta* to generate a field of loving-kindness. Here in volatile timber country they renew their pledges to the most challenging task of Buddhist practice—to save all beings.

In this action, old-growth redwoods are the beings at risk, slated for harvest on the Maxxam company property in northern California. Until recently the sixty-thousand-acre ecosystem was logged slowly and sustainably by a small family company. Then in 1985 logging accelerated dramatically following a hostile corporate buyout. Alarmed by the loss of irreplaceable giants, forest defenders have fought tirelessly to halt clear-cutting and preserve these ancient stands of redwoods. They have been joined by Hollywood stars, rock singers, and Jewish rabbis, many willing to practice civil disobedience in protest. How is it that Buddhists have become involved with this effort?

Motivated by ecological concerns, the ecosattvas formed as an affinity group at Green Gulch Zen Center in Marin County, California. As part of their practice they began exploring the relationship between Zen training and environmental activism. They wanted to know: What does it mean to take the bodhisattva vow as a call to save endangered species, decimated forests, and polluted rivers? What does it mean to engage in environmental activism from a Buddhist perspective?[1] The ecosattvas are part of an emerging movement of ecospiritual activism, backed by a parallel academic development which has become the field of Religion and Ecology.[2] Christian scholars, Jewish social justice groups, Hindu tree-planting projects, and Islamic resistance to usurious capitalism are all part of this movement. Buddhist efforts in the United States like those of the ecosattvas are matched by monks in Thailand protesting the oil pipeline from Burma and Tibetans teaching environmental education in Dharamsala.[3]

Activist scholar Joanna Macy suggests these actions are all part of the "third turning of the wheel [of Dharma]," her sense that Buddhism is undergoing a major evolutionary shift at the turn of the millennium.[4] In today's context, one of the oldest teachings of the Buddha—*paticca samuppada* or dependent co-arising—is finding new form in the ecology movement. If ecosystem relationships are the manifestation of interdependence, then protecting ecosystems is a way to protect the Dharma: "with the Third Turning of the Wheel, we see that everything we do impinges on all beings."[5] Acting with compassion in response to the rapidly accelerating environmental crisis can be seen as a natural fruit of Buddhist practice.

Is there a Buddhist ecospiritual movement in North America? Not in any obvious sense, at least not yet. No organizations have been formed to promote Buddhist environmentalism; no clearly defined environmental agenda has been agreed upon by a group of self-identified American Buddhists. However, teachers are emerging, and Buddhist students of all ages are drawn to their writings and ideas. Writers Joanna Macy and Gary Snyder have made ecological concerns the center of their Buddhist practice. Teachers Thich Nhat Hanh and His Holiness the Dalai Lama have frequently urged mindful action on behalf of the environment. Activists John Seed, Nanao Sakaki, and others are beginning to define a Buddhist approach to environmental activism. There is a strong conversation developing among Western and Eastern Buddhists, asking both practical and philosophical questions from this emerging perspective. With environmental issues a mounting global concern, Buddhists of many traditions are creatively adapting their religious heritage to confront these difficult issues.

In this chapter I begin the preliminary work of documenting the scope of Buddhist environmentalism in the late 1990s, gathering together the historical and philosophical dimensions of what has been called "green Buddhism." This study will be necessarily limited to Western Buddhism, in keeping with the focus of this volume. However, it is important to note the strong relationship with other global initiatives. Buddhist tree-ordaining in Thailand, for example, has inspired similar ceremonies in California.[6] Environmental destruction by logging and uranium mining in Tibet has prompted the formation of the U.S.-based Eco-Tibet group.[7] Environmental issues in Buddhist countries have been a natural magnet for Buddhist activists in the West. But Western Buddhists have taken other initiatives locally, bringing their Buddhist and environmental sensibilities to bear on nuclear waste, consumerism, animal rights, and forest defense.[8] Out of these impulses Buddhist environmental activism is taking shape, based on distinct principles and practices.

One of the most challenging aspects of documenting these developments is finding the hidden stories. In the United States today, environmentalism has grown so strong as a political and cultural force that it is suffering the impact of "brownlash," as biologists Paul and Anne Ehrlich call it. Christian fundamentalism is often allied with the wing of the conservative right that promulgates anti-environmental views. Taking a strong environmental position as a self-proclaimed Buddhist can be doubly threatening. My personal experience is that the environmental arena is a place to act as a small "b" Buddhist. This means concentrating on the message of the Buddha by cultivating awareness, tolerance, and understanding, and acting from a loving presence. "In Buddhism, we say that the presence of one mindful person can have great influence on society and is thus very important."[9] Mindful Buddhist practitioners engaging difficult environmental issues may not proclaim their Buddhism to help solve the problem at hand. Yet they can bring inner strength and moral courage to the task at hand, drawing on the teachings of the Buddha as a basic framework for effective action.

LOOKING BACK

When Buddhism arrived in the West in the mid-1800s, there was little that could be called an environmental movement. Although Henry David Thoreau had written *Walden* in 1854, it was not until the end of the century that a serious land conservation movement coalesced. Advocates recognizing the unique heritage of such landforms as Yellowstone, Yosemite, and the Grand Canyon pressed for the establishment of the National Park system. Conservationists alert to the ravaging of eastern forests and the rush to cut the West spurred the formation of the National Forest Service. But serious concern about overpopulation, air and water pollution, and endangered species did not ignite until the 1960s. Since then the list of dangerous threats has only increased—toxic wastes, ozone depletion, global climate change, genetic engineering, endocrine disrupters—fires are burning on all fronts.

The most recent Western wave of interest in Buddhism coincides almost exactly with the expansion of the environmental movement.[10] Young people breaking out of the constrictions of the 1950s took their curiosity and spiritual seeking to India, Southeast Asia, and Japan; some discovered Buddhist meditation and brought it back to the United States.[11] During this period, Gary Snyder was probably the most vocal in spelling out the links between Buddhist practice and ecological activism. His books of poetry, *Turtle Island* (1974) and *Axe Handles* (1983), expressed a strong feeling for the land, influenced by his seven years of Zen training in Japan. His 1974 essay "Four Changes" laid out the current conditions of the world in terms of population, pollution, consumption, and the need for social transformation. Core to his analysis was the Buddhist perspective "that we are interdependent energy fields of great potential wisdom and compassion."[12] Snyder's ideas were adopted by the counterculture through his affiliation with beat writers Jack Kerouac and

Allen Ginsberg and then further refined in his landmark collection of essays, *The Practice of the Wild*.[13]

Interest in Buddhism increased steadily through the 1970s along with the swelling environmental, civil rights, and women's movements. While Congress passed such landmark environmental laws as the Marine Mammal Protection Act, the Endangered Species Act, and the National Environmental Protection Act, Buddhist centers and teachers were becoming established on both coasts. San Francisco Zen Center, for example, expanded to two additional sites—a wilderness monastery at Tassajara, Big Sur, and a rural farm and garden temple in Marin County. By the 1980s the Buddhist Peace Fellowship was well along in its activist agenda and a number of Buddhist teachers were beginning to address the environmental crisis in their talks. In his 1989 Nobel Peace Prize acceptance speech His Holiness the Dalai Lama proposed making Tibet an international ecological reserve.[14] Thich Nhat Hanh, the influential Buddhist peace activist and Vietnamese Zen monk, referred often to ecological principles in his writings and talks on "interbeing," the Buddhist teaching of interdependence.[15]

The theme was picked up by Buddhist publications, conferences, and retreat centers. Buddhist Peace Fellowship featured the environment in *Turning Wheel* and produced a substantial packet and poster for Earth Day 1990.[16] The first popular anthology of Buddhism and ecology writings, *Dharma Gaia*, was published by Parallax Press that same year, following the more scholarly collection, *Nature in Asian Traditions of Thought*.[17] World Wide Fund for Nature brought out a series of books on five world religions, including *Buddhism and Ecology*.[18] *Tricycle* magazine examined green Buddhism and vegetarianism in 1994;[19] *Shambhala Sun* interviewed Gary Snyder and Japanese anti-nuclear poet-activist Nanao Sakaki.[20] The Vipassana newsletter *Inquiring Mind* produced an issue on "coming home"; *Ten Directions* of Zen Center Los Angeles, *Mountain Record* of Zen Mountain Monastery, and *Blind Donkey* of Honolulu Diamond Sangha also took up the question of environmental practice.

Some retreat centers confronted ecological issues head on. Green Gulch Zen Center in northern California had to work out water use agreements with its farming neighbors and the Golden Gate National Recreation Area. Zen Mountain Monastery in New York faced off with the Department of Environmental Conservation over a beaver dam and forestry issues. In earlier days when vegetarianism was not such a popular and commercially viable choice, most Buddhist centers went against the social grain by refraining from meat-eating, often with an awareness of the associated environmental problems. Several Buddhist centers made some effort to grow their own organic food.[21] Outdoor walking meditation gained new stature through backpacking and canoeing retreats on both coasts.

By the 1990s, spirituality and the environment had become a hot topic. The first "Earth and Spirit" Conference was held in Seattle in 1990, and Buddhist workshops were part of the program. Middlebury College in Vermont hosted a "Spirit and Nature" conference that same year with the Dalai Lama as keynote speaker, sharing his Buddhist message for protection of the environment.[22] More interfaith conferences followed and Buddhism was always represented at the table. By 1993, human rights, social justice, and the environment were top agenda items at the Parliament of the World's Religions in Chicago. Buddhists from all over the world gathered with Christians, Hindus, pagans, Jews, Jains, and Muslims to consider the role of religion in responding to the environmental crisis.

Parallel sparks of interest were ignited in the academic community. Though both environmental studies and religious studies programs were well established in the academy, very few addressed the overlap between the two fields. In 1992 religion and ecology scholars formed a new group in the American Academy of Religion and began soliciting papers on environmental philosophy, animal rights, Gaian cosmology, and other environmental topics. Out of this initiative, colleagues generated campus interreligious dialogues and new religion and ecology courses. In the spring of 1997, Mary Evelyn Tucker and John Grim of Bucknell University convened the first of a series of academic conferences with the aim of defining the field of religion and ecology.[23] The first of these addressed Buddhism and Ecology; the volume of collected papers was the first publication in the series.[24] The spring 1998 meeting of the International Buddhist-Christian Theological Encounter also focused on the environment, looking deeply at the impacts of consumerism.[25]

For the most part, the academic community did not address the *practice* of Buddhist environmentalism. This was explored more by socially engaged Buddhist teachers such as Thich Nhat Hanh, Bernie Glassman, the Dalai Lama, Sulak Sivaraksa, Christopher Titmuss, John Daido Loori, and Philip Kapleau.[26] One leader in developing a Buddhist ecological perspective for activists was Joanna Macy. Her doctoral research explored the significant parallels and distinctions between Western general systems theory and Buddhist philosophy.[27] In her sought-after classes and workshops, Macy developed a transformative model of experiential teaching designed to cultivate motivation, presence, and authenticity.[28] Her methods were strongly based in Buddhist meditation techniques and the Buddhist law of dependent co-arising. She called this "deep ecology work," challenging participants to take their insights into direct action. Working with John Seed, a Buddhist Australian rainforest activist, she developed a ritual "Council of All Beings" and other guided meditations to engage the attention and imagination on behalf of all beings.[29] Thousands of councils have now taken place in Australia, New Zealand, the United States, Germany, Russia, and other parts of the Western world.

Following in the footsteps of these visionary thinkers, a number of Buddhist activists organized groups to address specific issues—nuclear guardianship, factory farming, and forest protection. Each initiative has had its own history of start-up, strategizing, attracting interest, and, in some cases, fading enthusiasm. When these groups work with well-

Stephanie Kaza

established environmental groups, they seem to be more successful in accomplishing their goals. Some Buddhist environmental activists have been effective in helping shape the orientation of an existing environmental group. The Institute for Deep Ecology, for example, which offers summer training for activists, has had many Buddhists among its faculty, especially on the West Coast.

Though the history of Buddhist environmentalism is short, it has substance: bright minds suggesting new ways to look at things, teachers and writers inspiring others to address the challenges, and fledgling attempts to practice ecospiritual activism based in Buddhist principles. As Western interest in Buddhism grows, it affects wider social and political circles. As other Buddhist activists take up the task of defining the principles and practices of socially engaged Buddhism, environmental Buddhism can play a vital role. As Buddhist teachers come to see the "ecosattva" possibilities in the bodhisattva vows, they can encourage such practice-based engagement. The seeds for all this are well planted; the next ten years of environmental disasters and activist responses will indicate whether Buddhist environmental activism will take its place among other parallel initiatives.

PHILOSOPHICAL GROUND

During its two-thousand-year-old history, Buddhism has evolved across a wide range of physical and cultural geographies. From the Theravada traditions in tropical South and Southeast Asia, to the Mahayana Schools in temperate and climatically diverse China and Japan, to the Vajrayana lineages in mountainous Tibet—Buddhist teachings have been received, modified, and elaborated in many ecological contexts. Across this history the range of Buddhist understandings about nature and human-nature relations has been based on different teachings, texts, and cultural views. These have not been consistent by any means; in fact, some views directly contradict each other.

Malcolm David Eckel, for example, contrasts the Indian view with the Japanese view of nature.[30] Indian Buddhist literature shows relatively little respect for wild nature, preferring tamed nature instead; Japanese Buddhism reveres the wild but engages it symbolically through highly developed art forms. Tellenbach and Kimura take this up in their investigation of the Japanese concept of nature, "what-is-so-of-itself"; Ian Harris discusses the difficulties in comparing the meaning of the word "nature" in different Asian languages.[31] When Harris reviews traditional Buddhist texts, he does not find any consistent philosophical orientation toward environmental ethics. He also challenges claims that Buddhist philosophies of nature led to any recognizable ecological awareness among early Buddhist societies, citing some evidence to the contrary. Lambert Schmithausen points out that according to early Buddhist sources, most members of Buddhist societies, including many monks, preferred the comforts of village life over the threats of the wild.[32] Images of

Buddhist paradises are generally quite tame, not at all untrammeled wilderness. Only forest ascetics chose the hermitage path with its immersion in wild nature.

Even with these distinctions, Buddhist texts do contain many references to the natural world, both as inspiration for teachings and as source for ethical behavior. For Westerners tasting the Dharma in the context of the environmental crisis, all the Buddhist traditions are potential sources for philosophical and behavioral guidelines toward nature. The newest cultural form of Buddhism in the West will be different from what evolved in India, Thailand, China, and Japan. In seeking wisdom to address the world as it is now, Westerners are eagerly, if sometimes clumsily, looking for whatever may be helpful. From the earliest guidelines for forest monks to the hermitage songs of Milarepa, from the Jataka tales of compassion to Zen teachings on mountains and rivers, the inheritance is rich and diverse.[33] In this section, I lay out the principal teachings identified by leading Buddhist environmental thinkers in the late twentieth century as most relevant to addressing the current environmental situation.

INTERDEPENDENCE

In the canonical story of the Buddha's enlightenment, the culminating insight comes in the last hours of his long night of deep meditation. According to the story, he first perceived his previous lives in a continuous cycle of birth and death, then saw the vast universe of birth and death for all beings, gaining understanding of the workings of karma. Finally he realized the driving force behind birth and death, and the path to release from it. Each piece of the Buddha's experience added to a progressive unfolding of a single truth about existence—the law of mutual causality or dependent origination (in Sanskrit *pratityasamutpada*, in Pali *paticca samuppada*). According to this law, all phenomena, that is, all of nature, arise from complex sets of causes and conditions, each set unique to the specific situations. Thus, the simple but penetrating Pali verse:

> This being, that becomes;
> from the arising of this, that arises;
> this not being, that becomes not;
> from the ceasing of this, that ceases.[34]

Ecological understanding of natural systems fits very well within the Buddhist description of interdependence. This law has been the subject of much attention in the Buddhism and Ecology literature because of its overlapping with ecological principles.[35] Throughout all cultural forms of Buddhism, nature is perceived as relational, each phenomenon dependent on a multitude of causes and conditions. From a Buddhist perspec-

Stephanie Kaza

tive these causes include not only physical and biological factors but also historical and cultural factors, that is, human thought forms and values.

The Hua-Yen School of Buddhism, developed in seventh-century China, placed particular emphasis on this principle, using the jewel net of Indra as a teaching metaphor. This cosmic net contains a multifaceted jewel at each of its nodes. "Because the jewels are clear, they reflect each other's images, appearing in each other's reflections upon reflections, ad infinitum, all appearing at once in one jewel."[36] To extend the metaphor, if you tug on any one of the lines of the net—for example, through loss of species or habitat—it affects all the other lines. Or, if any of the jewels become cloudy (toxic or polluted), they reflect the others less clearly. Likewise, if clouded jewels are cleared up (rivers cleaned, wetlands restored), life across the web is enhanced. Because the web of interdependence includes not only the actions of all beings but also their thoughts, the intention of the actor becomes a critical factor in determining what happens. This, then, provides a principle of both explanation for the way things are, and a path for positive action.

Modern eco-Buddhists working with this principle have taken various paths. Using the term "interbeing," Thich Nhat Hanh emphasizes nonduality of view, encouraging students to "look at reality as a whole rather than to cut it into separate entities."[37] Gary Snyder takes up the interdependence of eater and eaten, acknowledging the "simultaneous path of pain and beauty of this complexly interrelated world."[38] Feminist theologian Rita Gross looks at the darker implications of cause and effect in the growing human population crisis.[39] Activist Joanna Macy leads people through their environmental despair by steadily reinforcing ways to work together and build more functional and healing relationships with the natural world.[40]

The law of interdependence suggests a powerful corollary, sometimes noted as "emptiness of separate self." If all phenomena are dependent on interacting causes and conditions, nothing exists by itself, autonomous and self-supporting. This Buddhist understanding (and experience) of self directly contradicts the traditional Western sense of self as a discrete individual. Alan Watts called this assumption of separateness the "skin-encapsulated ego"—the very delusion that Buddhist practices seek to cut through. Based on the work of Gregory Bateson and other systems theorists, Macy describes a more ecological view of the self as part of a larger flow-through.[41] She ties this to Arne Naess's deep ecology philosophy, derived from a felt shift of identification to a wider, more inclusive view of self. Buddhist rainforest activist John Seed described his experience of no-self in an interview with *Inquiring Mind*: "All of a sudden, the forest was inside me and was calling to me, and it was the most powerful thing I have ever felt."[42] Gary Snyder suggests this emptiness of self provides a link to "wild mind," or access to the energetic forces that determine wilderness. These forces act outside of human influence, setting the historical, ecological, and even cosmological context for all life. Thus "emptiness" is dynamic, shape-shifting, energy in motion—"wild" and beyond human imagination.[43]

THE PATH OF LIBERATION

The Buddhist image of the Wheel of Life contains various realms of beings; at the center are three figures representing greed, hate, and delusion. They chase each other around, generating endless suffering, perpetrating a false sense of self or ego. Liberation from attachment to this false self is the central goal in Buddhist practice. The first and second of the four noble truths describe the very nature of existence as suffering, due to our instincts to protect our own individual lives and views. The third and fourth noble truths lay out a path to liberation from this suffering of self-attachment, the eight-fold path of morality, awareness, and wisdom.

Buddhist scholar Alan Sponberg argues that green Buddhism has overemphasized interdependence or the relational dimension almost to the exclusion of the developmental aspect of practice.[44] By working to overcome ego-based attachments and socially conditioned desires, students cultivate the capacity for insight and compassion. This effort, he says, is crucial to displacing the hierarchy of oppression that undermines the vision of an ecologically healthy world. Sponberg suggests that a Buddhist environmental ethic is a virtue ethic, based fundamentally on development of consciousness and a sense of responsibility to act compassionately for the benefit of all forms of life. This is the basis for the Mahayana archetype of the bodhisattva, committed to serving others until suffering is extinguished. Macy argues that this responsibility need not be some morally imposed self-righteous action (often characteristic of environmentalists) but rather an action that "springs naturally from the ground of being."[45]

The path of liberation includes the practice of physical, emotional, and mental awareness. Such practice can increase one's appreciation for the natural world; it can also reveal hidden cultural assumptions about privilege, comfort, consumption, and the abuse of nature. When one sees one's self as part of a mutually causal web, it becomes obvious that there is no such thing as an action without effect. Through the practice of green virtue ethics, students are encouraged to be accountable for all of their actions, from eating food to using a car to buying new clothes. Likewise, they can investigate the reigning economic paradigm and see how deeply it determines their choices. Through following the fundamental precepts, environmentally oriented Buddhists can practice moderation and restraint, simplifying needs and desires to reduce suffering for others. For Westerners this

Stephanie Kaza

may mean withdrawal from consumer addictions to products with large ecological impacts, such as coffee, cotton, computers, and cars.

PRACTICE IN ACTION

Buddhist environmental teachers and writers point to three primary arenas of practice that can serve the environment: compassion, mindfulness, and nonharming. In the Theravada tradition, one practices loving-kindness, wishing that all beings be free from harm and blessed by physical and mental well-being. In the Mahayana tradition one takes up the bodhisattva path, vowing to return again and again to relieve the suffering of all sentient beings—the life work of an environmentalist! Both practices are impossible challenges if interpreted literally; the environmental implications of these prayers or vows can be overwhelming. Yet the strength of intention offers a substantial foundation for Buddhist environmental activism. Budding eco-Buddhists struggle with the application of these spirituall vows in the very real contexts of factory farms, pesticide abuse, genetic engineering, and loss of endangered species habitat.

Mindfulness practice, a natural support to Buddhist environmentalism, can take a range of forms. Thich Nhat Hanh teaches the basic principles of the *Satipatthana Sutta* or the mindfulness text, practicing awareness of breath, body, feelings, and mind. Walking and sitting meditation generate a sense of grounded presence and alertness to where one actually is. Environmental educators stress mindfulness through nature appreciation exercises and rules of respect toward the natural world. Environmental strategists use promotional campaigns to generate awareness of threatened species and places. These efforts take mindfulness practice off the cushion and out into the world where alarming situations of great suffering require strong attention.

The practice of *ahimsa* or non-harming derives naturally from a true experience of compassion. All the Buddhist precepts are based fundamentally on non-harming or reducing the suffering of others. Practicing the first precept, not killing, raises ethical dilemmas around food, land use, pesticides, pollution, and cultural economic invasion. The second precept, not stealing, suggests considering the implications of global trade and corporate exploitation of resources. Not lying brings up issues in advertising and consumerism. Not engaging in abusive relations covers a broad realm of cruelty and disrespect for nonhuman others. As Gary Snyder says, "The whole planet groans under the massive disregard of ahimsa by the highly organized societies and corporate economies of the world."[46] Thich Nhat Hanh interprets the precept prohibiting drugs and alcohol to include the toxic addictions of television, video games, and junk magazines.[47] Practicing restraint and non-harming is a way to make Buddhist philosophy manifest in the context of rapidly deteriorating global ecosystems. Zen teacher Robert Aitken offers this vow:

> With resources scarcer and scarcer, I vow with all beings—
> To reduce my gear in proportion even to candles and carts.[48]

BUDDHIST ENVIRONMENTAL ACTIVISM

How is green Buddhism being practiced? What is the evidence of green Buddhism on the front lines? Macy suggests three types of activism that characterize environmentalism today: 1) holding-actions of resistance, 2) analysis of social structures and creation of new alternatives, and 3) cultural transformation.[49] Some of the best examples of Buddhist environmentalism come from outside the West, but here I report only on local efforts in North America.

Holding-actions aim primarily to stop or reduce destructive activity, buying time for more effective long-term strategies. The small group of ecosattvas protesting the logging of old growth redwood groves is part of the holding-actions in northern California. They draw on local support from Buddhist deep ecologist Bill Devall and his eco-sangha in Humboldt County as well as support from the Green Gulch Zen community and the Buddhist Peace Fellowship. For the big 1997 demonstration, the ecosattvas invited others to join them in creating a large prayer flag covered with human handprints of mud. This then served as visual testimony of solidarity for all those participating in Headwaters actions. Six months after the protest, several ecosattvas made a special pilgrimage deep into the heart of the Headwaters, carrying a Tibetan treasure vase. Activists used the vase to bring attention to the threatened trees at various Bay Area sangha meetings. People were invited to offer their gifts and prayers on behalf of the redwoods. On a rainy winter's day, the vase was ceremonially buried beneath one of the giants to strengthen spiritual protection for the trees.[50]

Resistance actions by Buddhists Concerned for Animals were initiated by Brad Miller and Vanya Palmers, two Zen students in the San Francisco area. Moved by the suffering of animals in cages, on factory farms, and in export houses, they joined the animal rights movement, educating other Buddhists about the plight of monkeys, beef cattle, and endangered parrots. Vanya has continued this work in Europe, where he now lives, focusing on the cruelty in large-scale hog farming.[51]

When the federal government proposed burial of nuclear waste deep under Yucca Mountain, a group of Buddhists and others gathered together under Joanna Macy's leadership and met as a study group for several years. They took the position that nuclear waste was safer above ground where it could be monitored, and they developed an alternate vision of nuclear guardianship based in Buddhist spiritual practices.[52] At about the same time, Japan arranged for several shipments of plutonium to be reprocessed in France and then shipped back to Japan. Zen student and artist Mayumi Oda helped to organize Pluto-nium-Free Future and the Rainbow Serpents to stop these shipments of deadly nuclear material. One ship was temporarily stopped, and although shipments resumed, the actions raised awareness in Japan and the United States, affecting Japanese government policies.[53]

The second type of activism, undertaking structural analysis and creating alternative green visions, has also engaged twentieth-century Buddhists. Small "b" Buddhist Rick Klugston directs the Washington, D.C.-based Center for Respect of Life and the Environment, an affiliate of the Humane Society of the United States. He and his staff work on sustainability criteria for humane farming, basing their work in religious principles of nonharming. In 1997 the Soka Gakkai-affiliated group, Boston Research Center for the 21st Century, held a series of workshops addressing the people's earth charter, an internationally negotiated list of ethical guidelines for human-earth relations. The center published a booklet of Buddhist views on the charter's principles for use in discussions leading up to United Nations adoption.[54] A subgroup of the International Network of Engaged Buddhists and the Buddhist Peace Fellowship, called the "Think Sangha," is engaged in structural analysis of global consumerism. Collaborating between the United States and Southeast Asia, they have held conferences in Thailand on alternatives to consumerism, pressing for moderation and lifestyle simplification.[55] One of the boldest visions is the Dalai Lama's proposal that the entire province of Tibet be declared an ecological reserve. Sadly, this vision, put forth in his Nobel Peace Prize acceptance speech, is nowhere close to actualization.[56]

Scholars have offered structural analyses using Buddhist principles to shed light on environmental problems. Rita Gross, Buddhist feminist scholar, has laid out a Buddhist framework for considering global population issues.[57] I have compared eco-feminist principles of activism with Buddhist philosophy, showing a strong compatibility between the two.[58] Through Buddhist-Christian dialogue, process theologian and meditator Jay McDaniel has developed spiritual arguments for compassionate treatment of animals as a serious human responsibility.[59] Sociologist Bill Devall integrated Buddhist principles into his elaboration of Arne Naess's Deep Ecology philosophy urging simplification of needs and wants.[60] Joanna Macy likewise draws on Buddhist philosophy and practices to analyze the paralyzing states of grief, despair, and fear that prevent people from acting on behalf of the environment.

As for the third type of activism, transforming culture, these projects are very much in progress and sometimes met with resistance. Two Buddhist centers in rural northern California, Green Gulch Zen Center and Spirit Rock, already demonstrate a serious commitment to the environment through vegetarian dining, land and water stewardship efforts, an organic farm and garden at Green Gulch, and ceremonies that include the natural world.[61] On Earth Day 1990, the abbot led a tree-ordaining precepts ceremony and an animal memorial service. Other environmental rituals include special dedications at the solstices and equinoxes, a Buddha's birthday celebration of local wildflowers, Thanksgiving altars from the farm harvest, and participation in the United Nations Environmental Sabbath in June. The ecosattvas meet regularly to plan restoration projects that are now part of daily work practice. When people visit Green Gulch, they can see ecological action as part of a Buddhist way of life. Similar initiatives have been undertaken at Spirit Rock Meditation Center, also in the San Francisco Bay area.

In the Sierra foothills, Gary Snyder has been a leader in establishing the Yuba River Institute, a bioregional watershed organization working in cooperation with the Bureau of Land Management. They have done ground survey work, controlled burns, and creek restoration projects, engaging the local community in the process. "To restore the land one must live and work in a place. To work in a place is to work with others. People who work together in a place become a community, and a community, in time, grows a culture."[62] Snyder models the level of commitment necessary to reinhabit a place and build community that might eventually span generations. Zen Mountain Center in Southern California is beginning similar work, carrying out resource management practices such as thinning for fire breaks, restoring degraded forest, and limiting human access to some preserve areas.[63] Applying Buddhist principles in an urban setting, Zen teacher Bernard Glassman has developed environmentally oriented small businesses that employ local street people, sending products to socially responsible companies such as Ben and Jerry's.[64]

As the educational element of cultural transformation, several Buddhist centers have developed lecture series, classes, and retreats based on environmental themes. Zen Mountain Monastery in the Catskills of New York offers "Mountains and Rivers" retreats based on the center's commitment to environmental conservation. These feature backpacking, canoeing, nature photography, and haiku as gateways to Buddhist insight. Ring of Bone Zendo at Kitkitdizze, Gary Snyder's community, has offered back-packing *sesshins* in the Sierra Mountains since its inception. Green Gulch Zen Center co-hosts a "Voice of the Watershed" series each year with Muir Woods National Monument, including talks and walks across the landscape of the two valleys. At Manzanita Village in southern California, Caitriona Reed and Michele Benzamin-Masuda include deep ecology practices, gardening, and nature observation as part of their Thich Nhat Hanh-style mindfulness retreats.

Most of these examples represent social change agents working within Buddhist or non-Buddhist institutions to promote environmental interests. But what about isolated practitioners, struggling to consider the implications of their lifestyles in consumer America and other parts of the West? Independent of established groups, a number of Buddhists are taking small steps of activism as they try to align their actions with their Buddhist practice. One growing area of interest is ethical choices in food consumption, prompted both by health and environmental concerns. Many people, Buddhists included, are turning to vegetarianism and veganism as more compassionate choices for animals and ecosystems. Others are committing to eat only organically grown food, in order to support pesticide-free soil and healthy farming. Thich Nhat Hanh has strongly encouraged his students to examine their consumption habits, not only around food and alcohol, but also television, music, books, and magazines. His radical stance is echoed by Sulak Sivaraksa in Thailand, who insists the Western standard of consumption is untenable if extended throughout the world. Some Buddhists have participated in "International Buy Nothing" Day, targeted for the busiest shopping day right after Thanksgiving. Others have joined support groups for reducing credit card debt, giving up car dependence, and creating work cooperatives. Because Buddhism is still so new in the Western world, the extent of Buddhist lifestyle activism is very hard to gauge. But for many students, environmental awareness and personal change flow naturally from a Buddhist practice commitment.

ELEMENTS OF GREEN BUDDHIST ACTIVISM

What makes Buddhist environmentalism different from other environmental activism or from other eco-religious activism? The answer in both cases lies in the distinctive orientation of Buddhist philosophy and practice. Buddhist environmentalists turn to principles of nonharming, compassion, and interdependence as core ethics in choosing activism strategies. They aim to serve all beings through equanimity and loving-kindness. Though activists may not fulfill the highest ideals of their Buddhist training, they at least struggle to place their actions in a spiritual context. This reflects an underlying premise that good environmental work should also be good spiritual work, restoring both place and person to wholeness.

To be sure, there are significant challenges. Engaged Buddhist scholar Kenneth Kraft outlines four dilemmas a generic American Buddhist environmentalist ("Gabe") might encounter.[65] First, he or she would likely encounter some gaps between the traditional teachings and current political realities. Most of the Buddha's advice to students deals with individual morality and action; but today's environmental problems require *collective* action and a conscious sense of group responsibility. It is not so easy to find guidelines for global structural change within these ancient teachings. Second, Gabe must make some tough decisions about how to use his or her time. Meditate or organize a protest? When political decisions are moving at a rapid rate, activists must respond very quickly for effective holding action. Yet cultivating equanimity, patience, and loving-kindness requires regular hours of practice on the cushion. The yearning for time dedicated to Buddhist retreats can compete with time needed for soul-renewing wilderness. Third, Gabe may question the effectiveness of identifying his or her efforts as specifically Buddhist. It may be easier just to "blend in" with others working on the same issue. Fourth, Gabe may also begin to wonder about the effectiveness of some forms of practice forms in combatting environmental destruction. How can meditation or ceremony stop clear-cut logging? Can spiritually oriented activists make a difference in the high pressure political world? Given these and other challenges, green Buddhists nonetheless try to carry out their work in a manner consistent with Buddhist practice and philosophy.

Characteristic ideals for green Buddhism can be described in terms of the Three Jewels: the Buddha, Dharma, and Sangha. The Buddha exemplified a way of life based on spiritual practice, including meditation, study, questioning and debate, ceremony and ritual. Each Buddhist lineage has its own highly evolved traditional practice forms that encourage the student to "act like Buddha." At the heart of the Buddha's path is reflective inquiry into the nature of reality. Applying this practice in today's environmental context, eco-activists undertake rigorous examination of conditioned beliefs and thought patterns regarding the natural world. This may include deconstructing the objectification of plants and animals, the stereotyping of environmentalists, dualistic thinking of enemy-ism, the impacts of materialism, and environmental racism.

In addition, the green Buddhist would keep his or her activist work grounded in regular engagement with practice forms—for example, saying the precepts with other activists, as Thich Nhat Hanh has encouraged, or reciting sutras that inspire courage and loving-kindness (that is, the *Metta Sutta* for example, or the Zen chant to Kanzeon). Ring of Bone Zen students chant Dogen's "Mountains and Rivers" treatise on their backpacking retreats. Mindfulness practice with the breath can help sustain an activist under pressure, during direct political action or in the workplace. Green Buddhist ceremonies are evolving, often as variations on standard rituals—for example, the Earth Day precepts at Green Gulch, and the earth relief ceremony at Rochester Zen Center.[66] If the Buddha's path is foundational to Buddhist environmental activism, it means each engaged person undertakes some form of spiritual journey toward insight and awakening. Activism is the context in which this happens, but the Buddha's way serves as the model.

Of the Buddha's teachings, or Dharma, several core principles contribute to a green Buddhist approach. First, it is based on a relational understanding of interdependence and no-self. This may mean, for example, assessing the relationships of the players in an environmental conflict from a context of historical and geographical causes and conditions. It may also mean acknowledging the distribution of power across the human political relationships, as well as learning about the ecological relationships that are under siege. Second, green Buddhist activism could reflect the teachings of ahimsa, nonharming, with compassion for the suffering of others. For the Buddhist environmentalist this may extend to oppression based on race, class, or gender discrimination as well as to environmental oppression of plants, animals, rivers, rocks, and mountains. This recognition of suffering in the non-human world is rarely acknowledged by the capitalist economy. Voicing it as a religious point of view may open some doors to more humane policies. This green Buddhist teaching is congruent with many schools of ecophilosophy that respect the intrinsic value and capacity for experience of each being.

A third Buddhist teaching applicable to activism is the *nondualistic* view of reality. Most political battles play out as confrontations between sworn enemies: loggers vs. spotted owl defenders, housewives vs. toxic polluters, birdlovers vs. pesticide producers. From a Buddhist perspective, this kind of hatred destroys spiritual equanimity; thus, it is much better to work from an inclusive perspective, offering kindness to all parties involved, even while setting firm moral boundaries against harmful actions. This approach is quite rare among struggling, discouraged, battle-weary environmentalists who, in fact, are being attacked by government officials, sheriffs, or the media. A Buddhist commitment to nondualism can help to stabilize a volatile situation and establish new grounds for negotiation.

A fourth Buddhist teaching reinforces the role of *intention*. Buddhist texts emphasize a strong relationship between intention, action, and karmic effects of an action. If a campaign is undertaken out of spite, revenge, or rage, that emotional tone will carry forth into all the ripening of the fruits of that action (and likely cause a similar reaction in response). However, if an action is grounded in understanding that the other party is also part of Indra's jewel net, then things unfold with a little less shoving and pushing.

Perhaps the most significant teaching of the Dharma relevant to Buddhist activism is the practice of detachment from the ego-generating self. Thus, a green Buddhist approach is not motivated primarily by the need for ego identity or satisfaction. Strong intention with less orientation to the self relieves the activist from focusing so strongly on results.[67] One does what is necessary in the situation, not bound by the need for it to reinforce one's ideas or to turn out a certain way. By leaning into the creative energies moving through the wider web but holding to a strong intention, surprising collaborative actions take place. Small 'b' Buddhists have been able to act as bridge-builders in hostile or reactive situations by toning down the need for personal recognition.

Sangha, the third of the Three Jewels, is often the least recognized or appreciated by American Buddhists. As newcomers to the practice in a speedy, product-driven society, most students are drawn to the calming effects of meditation practice and the personal depth of student-teacher relationships. Practicing with community can be difficult for students living away from Buddhist centers. Building community among environmental Buddhists is even harder, since they are even more isolated geographically from each other and sometimes marginalized even by their own peers in Buddhist centers. From a green Buddhist perspective, sangha work presents not only the challenges of personal and institutional relations, but also ecological relations. Some of the leading green Buddhist thinkers have suggested ways to move toward this work in an integrated way.

Gary Snyder brings his sangha work home through the framework of bioregional thinking and organizing. His foundation for this is more than ecological; it is aesthetic, economic, and practice-based. He suggests that "by being in place, we get the largest sense of community." The bioregional community "does not end at the human boundaries; we are in a community with certain trees, plants, birds, animals. The conversation is with the whole thing."[68] He models and encourages others to take up the practice of *rein-habitation*, learning to live on the land with the same respect and understanding as the original indigenous people. He expects this will take a number of generations, so the wisdom gathered now must be passed along to the young ones. Spiritual community on the land offers one place to do this.

Others can participate in eco-sangha through supporting and lobbying for ecological practices at their local Buddhist centers. The hundreds of people who come to Green Gulch Zen Center or Spirit Rock Meditation Center, for example, follow the centers' customs regarding water conservation, recycling, vegetarianism, and land protection. With each step toward greater ecological sustainability, local community culture takes on a greener cast. These actions need not be only a painful commitment to restraint, rather they can become a celebration of environmental awareness. Printed materials such as the booklet on environmental practices at Green Gulch can help to educate visitors about institutional commitments.

Joanna Macy recommends sangha-building as central to deep ecology work. Through trust-building exercises, brainstorming, and contract-making, Macy helps people find ways to support each other in their activist efforts. Learning networks of Buddhists and non-Buddhists often stay together after her workshops for mutual support and prevention of activist burnout. Macy helps people taste the power of *kalyana mitta*, or spiritual friendship—acting together in the web to help others practice the Dharma and take care of this world.

CONCLUSION

How might Buddhist environmentalism affect the larger environmental movement and how might it influence Western Buddhism in general? Will Buddhist environmentalism turn out to be more environmental than Buddhist?[69] The answers to these questions must be largely speculative at this time, since green Buddhism is just finding its voice. It is possible that this fledgling voice will be drowned in the brownlash against environmentalists, or in the Western resistance to engaged Buddhism. Environmental disasters of survival proportions may overwhelm anyone's capacity to act effectively. The synergistic combination of millennialism and economic collapse may flatten green Buddhism as well as many other constructive social forces.

But if one takes a more hopeful view, it seems possible to imagine that green Buddhism will grow and take hold in the minds and hearts of young people who are creating the future. Perhaps some day there will be ecosattva chapters across the world affiliated with various practice centers. Perhaps Buddhist eco-activists will be sought out for their spiritual stability and compassion in the face of extremely destructive forces. Buddhist centers might become models of ecological sustainability, showing other religious institutions ways to encourage ecological culture. More Buddhist teachers may become informed about environmental issues and raise these concerns in their teachings, calling for moderation and restraint. Perhaps the next century will see Buddhist practice centers forming around specific ecological commitments.

Making an educated guess from the perspective of the late 1990s, I predict that the influence of green Buddhism may be small in numbers, but great in impact. Gary Snyder, for example, is now widely read by college students in both literature and environmental studies classes. Joanna Macy has led workshops for staff at the White House and the Hanford nuclear reactor in Washington State. Thich Nhat Hanh has shared his commentaries on the interbeing of paper, clouds, trees, and farmers with thousands of listeners on lecture tours throughout the West. Some practicing Buddhists already hold influential positions in major environmental groups such as the Natural Resources Defense Council, Rainforest Action Network, and Greenpeace. Perhaps in the near future they will also hold cabinet positions or Congressional committee chairs or serve as staff for environmental think tanks.

Buddhist centers and thinkers will not drive the religious conversation in the West for quite some time, if ever. The Judeo-Christian heritage of the West is still a prominent force in Western thinking, laws, and religious customs. However, Buddhists are already significant participants in interfaith dialogue regarding the environment. This could have an increasing impact on public conversations by raising ethical questions in a serious way. Right now, decisions that affect the health and well-being of the environment are often made behind closed doors. To challenge these in a public way from a religious perspective could shed some much needed light on ecologically unethical ways of doing business.

What happens next lies in the hands of those who are nurturing this wave of enthusiasm for green Buddhism and those who will follow. It may be religious leaders, writers, teachers, or elders; it may be the younger generations, full of energy and passion for protecting the home they love. Because the rate of destruction is so great now, with major life systems threatened, any and all green activism is sorely needed. Buddhists have much to offer the assaulted world. It is my hope that many more step forward boldly into the melee of environmental conflict. Side by side with other bodhisattvas, may they join the global effort to stop the cruelty and help create a more respectful and compassionate future for all beings.

NOTES

1. For information on ecosattva activity, see "Universal Chainsaw, Universal Forest," *Turning Wheel* (winter 1998): 31–33.

2. See, for example, such recent volumes as Steven C. Rockefeller and John C. Elder, *Spirit and Nature: Why the Environment Is a Religious Issue* (Boston: Beacon Press, 1992); Mary Evelyn Tucker and John A. Grim, eds., *Worldviews and Ecology* (Lewisburg, PA: Bucknell University Press, 1993); Fritz Hull, ed., *Earth and Spirit: The Spiritual Dimensions of the Environmental Crisis* (New York: Continuum, 1993); David Kinsley, *Ecology and Religion: Ecological Spirituality in Cross-Cultural Perspective* (Englewood Cliffs, NJ: Prentice Hall, 1995); Dieter T.

Hessel, ed., *Theology for Earth Community: A Field Guide* (Maryknoll, NY: Orbis Books, 1996); Roger Gottlieb, ed., *This Sacred Earth: Religion, Nature, and Environment* (New York: Routledge, 1996).

3.   Parvel Gmuzdek, "Kalayanamitra's Action on the Yadana Pipeline," *Seeds of Peace* 13.3 (September–December 1997): 23–26.

4.   Joanna Macy, "The Third Turning of the Wheel," *Inquiring Mind* 5.2 (winter 1989): 10–12.

5.   Ibid., p. 11.

6.   Wendy Johnson and Stephanie Kaza, "Earth Day at Green Gulch," *Journal of the Buddhist Peace Fellowship* (summer 1990): 30–33.

7.   See reports on their activities in Bay Area Friends of Tibet newsletters.

8.   Stephanie Kaza and Kenneth Kraft, eds., *Dharma Rain: Sources of Buddhist Environmentalism* (Boston: Shambhala Publications, 1999).

9.   Sulak Sivaraksa, "Buddhism with a Small 'b,'" *Seeds of Peace* (Berkeley, CA: Parallax Press, 1992), p. 69.

10.   Peter Timmerman, "It Is Dark Outside: Western Buddhism from the Enlightenment to the Global Crisis," in Martine Batchelor and Kerry Brown, eds., *Buddhism and Ecology* (London: Cassell, 1992), pp. 65–76.

11.   See Rick Fields, *How the Swans Came to the Lake: A Narrative History of Buddhism in America* (Boston: Shambhala Publications, 1986), for a thorough history of these and earlier forays to the East by Westerners.

12.   Gary Snyder, *A Place in Space* (Washington, D.C.: Counterpoint Press, 1995), p. 41.

13.   Gary Snyder, *The Practice of the Wild* (San Francisco: North Point Press, 1990).

14.   "The Nobel Peace Prize Lecture," in Sidney Piburn, ed., *The Dalai Lama: A Policy of Kindness* (Ithaca, New York: Snow Lion Publications, 1990), pp. 15–27.   ·

15.   Thich Nhat Hanh, *Love in Action* (Berkeley, CA: Parallax Press, 1993).

16.   Issues on the theme of environmental activism were published in spring 1990, spring 1994, and spring 1997.

17.   Alan Hunt-Badiner, ed., *Dharma Gaia* (Berkeley, CA: Parallax Press, 1990); J. Baird Callicott and Roger T. Ames, eds., *Nature in Asian Traditions of Thought* (Albany: State University of New York Press, 1989).

18.   The other four books in the series address Christianity, Hinduism, Islam, Judaism, and Ecology.

19.   See *Tricycle* 4.2 (winter 1994): 2, 49–63.

20.   For Gary Snyder interviews, see "Not Here Yet" 2.4 (March 1994): 19–25; "The Mind of Gary Snyder" 4.5 (May 1996): 19–26; for Nanao Sakaki, see "Somewhere on the Water Planet" 4.2 (November 1995): 45–47.

21.   For a detailed study of two Buddhist centers see Stephanie Kaza, "American Buddhist Response to the Land: Ecological Practice at Two West Coast Retreat Centers," in Mary Evelyn Tucker and Duncan Ryuken Williams, eds., *Buddhism and Ecology: The Interconnectedness of Dharma and Deeds* (Cambridge: Harvard University Press, 1997), pp. 219–48.

22.   See conference talks in Rockefeller and Elder, eds., *Spirit and Nature*.

23.   Mary Evelyn Tucker, "The Emerging Alliance of Ecology and Religion," *Worldviews: Environment, Culture, and Religion* 1.1 (1997): 3–24.

24.   Tucker and Williams, eds., *Buddhism and Ecology*.

25.   See one of the lead papers from the meeting: Stephanie Kaza, "Overcoming the Grip of Consumerism," forthcoming in *Journal of Buddhist-Christian Studies*.

26.   See, for example, such works as Thich Nhat Hanh, "The Individual, Society, and Nature," in Fred Eppsteiner, ed., *The Path of Compassion* (Berkeley, CA: Parallax Press, 1988), pp. 40–46; Dalai Lama, "The Ethical Approach to Environmental Protection," in Piburn, ed., *The Dalai Lama: A Policy of Kindness* (Ithaca, NY: Snow Lion Publications, 1990), pp. 118–28; Sulak Sivaraksa, *Seeds of Peace* (Berkeley, CA: Parallax Press, 1992);

Christopher Titmuss, "A Passion for the Dharma," *Turning Wheel* (fall 1991): 19–20; John Daido Loori, "River Seeing River," in *Mountain Record* 14.3 (spring 1996): 2–10; and Philip Kapleau, *To Cherish All Life: A Buddhist Case for Becoming Vegetarian* (San Francisco: Harper and Row, 1982).

27. Joanna Macy, *Mutual Causality in Buddhism and General Systems Theory: The Dharma of Natural Systems* (Albany: State University of New York Press, 1991).

28. Joanna Macy, *Despair and Personal Power in the Nuclear Age* (Philadelphia: New Society Publishers, 1983).

29. John Seed, Joanna Macy, Pat Fleming, and Arne Naess, *Thinking Like a Mountain: Towards a Council of All Beings* (Philadelphia: New Society Publishers, 1988).

30. Malcolm David Eckel, "Is There a Buddhist Philosophy of Nature?" in Tucker and Williams, eds., *Buddhism and Ecology*, pp. 327–50.

31. Ian Harris, "Buddhism and the Discourse of Environmental Concern: Some Methodological Problems Considered," in Tucker and Williams, eds., *Buddhism and Ecology*, pp. 377–402; and Hubertus Tellenbach and Bin Kimura, "The Japanese Concept of 'Nature,'" in *Nature in Asian Traditions of Thought*, ed. J. Baird Callicott and Roger T. Ames (Albany: State University of New York Press, 1989).

32. Lambert Schmithausen, "The Early Buddhist Tradition and Ecological Ethics," *Journal of Buddhist Ethics* 4 (1997): 1–42.

33. Represented in Stephanie Kaza and Kenneth Kraft, eds., *Dharma Rain*.

34. *Samyutta Nikaya* II.28,65; *Majjhima Nikaya* II.32.

35. See, for example, Francis H. Cook, "The Jewel Net of Indra," in Callicott and Ames, eds., *Nature in Asian Traditions of Thought*, pp. 213–30; Bill Devall, "Ecocentric Sangha," in Hunt-Badiner, ed., *Dharma Gaia*, pp. 155–64; Paul O. Ingram, "Nature's Jeweled Net: Kukai's Ecological Buddhism," *The Pacific World* 6 (1990): 50–64; Joanna Macy, *Mutual Causality in Buddhism*; and Gary Snyder, *A Place in Space*.

36. Tu Shun, in Thomas Cleary, *Entry into the Inconceivable: An Introduction to Hua-Yen Buddhism* (Honolulu: University of Hawaii Press, 1983) p. 66.

37. Thich Nhat Hanh, "The Individual, Society, and Nature," in Eppsteiner, ed., *The Path of Compassion*, p. 40.

38. Snyder, *A Place in Space*, p. 70.

39. Rita Gross, "Buddhist Resources for Issues of Population, Consumption, and the Environment," in Tucker and Williams, eds., *Buddhism and Ecology*, pp. 291–312.

40. Joanna Macy and Molly Young Brown, *Coming Back to Life: Practices to Reconnect Our Lives, Our World* (Gabriola Island, British Columbia: New Society Publishers, 1998).

41. Macy, *Mutual Causality in Buddhism*.

42. Interview with John Seed, "The Rain Forest as Teacher," *Inquiring Mind* 8.2 (spring 1992): 1.

43. Gary Snyder, "The Etiquette of Freedom," in *The Practice of the Wild*, p. 10.

44. Alan Sponberg, "Green Buddhism and the Hierarchy of Compassion," in Tucker and Williams, eds., *Buddhism and Ecology*, pp. 351–76.

45. Joanna Macy, "Third Turning of the Wheel," *Inquiring Mind* 5.2 (winter 1989): 10–12.

46. Snyder, *A Place in Space*, p. 73.

47. See his discussion of the fifth precept in Thich Nhat Hanh, *For a Future to Be Possible* (Berkeley, CA: Parallax Press, 1993).

48. Robert Aitken, *The Dragon Who Never Sleeps* (Berkeley, CA: Parallax Press, 1992), p. 62.

49. Macy and Brown, *Coming Back to Life*.

50. Wendy Johnson, "A Prayer for the Forest," *Tricycle* 8.1 (fall 1998): 84–85.

51. Vanya Palmers, "What Can I Do," *Turning Wheel* (winter 1993): 15–17.

52. Joanna Macy, "Guarding the Earth," *Inquiring Mind* 7.2 (spring 1991): 1, 4–5, 12.

53. Kenneth Kraft, "Nuclear Ecology and Engaged Buddhism," in Tucker and Williams, eds., *Buddhism and Ecology*, pp. 269–90.

54. Amy Morgante, ed., *Buddhist Perspectives on the Earth Charter* (Cambridge, MA: Buddhist Research Center for the 21st Century, November 1997).

55. See 1998–1999 issues of *Seeds of Peace* for reports and announcements of these events.

56. Tenzin Gyatso, "The Nobel Peace Prize Lecture," in Piburn, ed., *The Dalai Lama: A Policy of Kindness*, pp. 15–27.

57. Gross, "Buddhist Resources for Issues of Population, Consumption, and the Environment," in Tucker and Williams, eds., *Buddhism and Ecology*, pp. 291–312.

58. Stephanie Kaza, "Acting with Compassion: Buddhism, Feminism, and the Environmental Crisis," in Carol Adams, eds., *Ecofeminism and the Sacred* (New York: Continuum, 1993).

59. Jay B. McDaniel, *Earth, Sky, Gods, and Mortals: Developing an Ecological Spirituality* (Mystic, CT: Twenty-Third Publications, 1990).

60. Bill Devall, *Simple in Means, Rich in Ends: Practicing Deep Ecology* (Salt Lake City: Peregrine Smith Books, 1988).

61. Stephanie Kaza, "American Buddhist Response to the Land: Ecological Practice at Two West Coast Retreat Centers," in Tucker and Williams, eds., *Buddhism and Ecology*, pp. 219–48.

62. Snyder, *A Place in Space*, p. 250. See also David Barnhill, "Great Earth Sangha: Gary Snyder's View of Nature as Community," in Tucker and Williams, *Buddhism and Ecology*, pp. 187–217.

63. Jeff Yamauchi, "The Greening of Zen Mountain Center: A Case Study," in Tucker and Williams, eds., *Buddhism and Ecology*, pp. 249–65.

64. Interviewed by Alan Senauke and Sue Moon, "Monastery in the Streets: A Talk with Tetsugen Glassman," *Turning Wheel* (fall 1996): 22–25.

65. Kenneth Kraft, "Nuclear Ecology and Engaged Buddhism," in Tucker and Williams, eds., *Buddhism and Ecology*, pp. 280–83.

66. A selection of such evolving practice forms are presented in the forthcoming anthology by Kaza and Kraft, *Dharma Rain*.

67. See Christopher Titmuss, "A Passion for the Dharma," *Turning Wheel* (fall 1991): 19–20; also Chogyam Trungpa, *Shambhala: The Sacred Path of the Warrior* (Boston: Shambhala Publications, 1988).

68. David Barnhill, "Great Earth Sangha: Gary Snyder's View of Nature as Community," in Tucker and Williams, *Buddhism and Ecology*, p. 192.

69. As Ian Harris suggests in "Buddhism and the Discourse of Environmental Concern: Some Methodological Problems Considered," in Tucker and Williams, eds., *Buddhism and Ecology*, pp. 377–402.

"SOMEBODY, NOT SOMETHING: DO ANIMALS HAVE SOULS?"

Gary A. Kowalski

The word "animal" comes from a Latin root that means "soul." To ancient thinkers, soul was the mysterious force that gave life and breath to the myriad of the earth's creatures. Some even spoke of a "world soul" or anima mundi *that enlivened the whole of nature. Later, theologians restricted the possession of a soul to human beings. But what is soul or spirit? Spirit is the channel through which we become conscious of the essence—the inward beauty—that dwells within another living being.*

Above the first edition of his book *Daniel*, Martin Buber inscribed the words of the medieval theologian Scotus Erigena: "In a wonderful and inexpressible way God is created in his creatures."

Animals were sacred to Buber. It was through his rapport with a horse he befriended on a visit to his grandfather's country estate when he was eleven years old that the Jewish thinker first awakened to "the immense otherness of the Other."

The barn, filled with the warmth and closeness of other living beings, became a temple for the young boy, where he sensed the presence of the ineffable. When he stroked the horse's "mighty mane" and felt the life beneath his hand "it was as though the element of vitality itself" bordered on his skin. There was a bond of understanding between him and the mare, as if they both, without saying, knew that the other had glimpsed the same wonderful secret, or heard the same murmuring currents of being. The horse very gently raised his massive head in greeting to the child, ears flicking, then snorted quietly, "as a conspirator gives a signal meant to be recognizable only by his fellow conspirators: and I was approved."[1]

Such experiences are not uncommon. For many children, even today, it is an animal that first introduces them to the sanctities of birth and death and invites them to ponder what it means to be alive. Buber was unusual, perhaps, in never allowing the years to dim that youthful awareness of the *mysterium* that resides in other living beings. For him a

---

From *The Souls of Animals* (Walpole, NH: Stillpoint, 1991). Reprinted with permission of Stillpoint Publishing.

creature as domestic and seemingly mundane as a housecat remained a wild and unfathomed cosmos.

"The eyes of an animal have the capacity of a great language," Buber testified, and the cat's glance bore for him a question: "Can it be that you mean me? Do you actually want that I should not merely do tricks for you? Do I concern you? Am I there for you?"[2] This instant of communication with another species, though fleeting, left a powerful impression. Such one-on-one encounters with animals were for him epiphanies: revelations into the very essence of reality.

The living world is responsive and charged with feeling, which flows like a sympathetic current between all sentient beings. Other creatures, as we have seen, can be astonishingly complex and subtle. Their emotional lives are nuanced with moods that range from grief and sadness to gaiety and glee. Their family structures and relationships can be as intricate and their bonds with one another as strong and tender as our own.

Cats and horses, as Buber realized, are creatures like ourselves, and the same is true of other animals. They are not an entirely different order of creation, but like us they have rich and spacious interiors. They contain inner landscapes: desert places and lonely canyons, cliffs of madness and rivers of serene awareness that merge in tranquil seas. They share with us a heart and mind and soul.

Animals are not our property or chattel, therefore, but our peers and fellow travelers. Like us, they have their own likes and dislikes, fears and fixations. They have plans and purposes as important to them as our plans are to us. Animals not only have biologies; they also have biographies.[3] We can appreciate the lives of animals, but not appropriate them, for they have their own lives to lead.

We have been long accustomed to regard animals as things: as objects, tools, commodities, or resources. Thus we raise and slaughter them for food; we use their furs and hides for clothing and decoration; we dissect their bodies for research; we study their anatomy with detached interest. We regard other creatures as means to our own fulfillment, not as ends in themselves. One might say that we "de-humanize" animals, but this would not be accurate, since animals are not human. Rather, we "de-sacralize" animals—rob them of their holy qualities—and in the process de-humanize ourselves. For animals cannot be relegated to the status of objects. When we treat them as if they were mere biological machines—collections of conditioned reflexes—we injure both their nature and our own.

Animals are our spiritual colleagues and emotional companions. We know this to be true less through debate than through direct experience. Whatever we may say about it, people have truly mutual relationships with animals and do encounter the sacred in non-human form. As a child, for instance, Martin Buber often visited the stall of the dapple-grey mare that he found so stirring. He and the beast had a special affinity for each other. One day, as he stroked its side, he thought what fun he was having and became aware of his own hand. Then, with a start, he realized that the spell of camaraderie was broken. His attention had wandered from the horse itself to his own thoughts about the horse. And in that instant, he had ceased to relate to the mare as a friend and instead turned the animal into a thing: an object of gratification rather than a partner in pleasure. The horse also sensed the change. The next day when Martin returned to the stall at feeding time the horse no longer raised its head in greeting. Martin continued to pet the mare, but the relationship had changed.[4]

When we relate to another as a thing our experience is flat and lacking in depth. We never really share ourselves; we touch on surfaces alone. When we relate to others as spiritual beings, our experience opens into a "vertical dimension" that stretches toward infinity. Our world becomes softer and more intimate. We become confidantes—literally, those who come together with faith. And it is through faith—not the faith of creeds or dogmas, but the simple "animal faith" of resting in communion with each other and with the natural world of soil and sunlight—that we touch the divine.

There is an inwardness in other living beings that awakens what is innermost in ourselves. I have often marveled, for instance, watching a flock of shore birds. On an invisible cue, they simultaneously rise off the beach and into the air, then turn and bank seawards in tight formation. They are so finely coordinated and attuned in their aeronautics it is as though they share a common thought, or even a group mind, guiding their ascent. At such moments, I feel there are depths of "inner space" in nature that can never be sounded. And it is out of those same depths, in me, that awe arises as I contemplate the synchronicity of their flight.

To contain such depths is to participate in the realm of spirit. To be "made of the image of God" is to be *somebody* rather than *something*. A thing is merely the sum of its parts. Bricks and buildings are good examples of things. They can be reduced to molecules and atoms without losing much in the analysis. A *somebody*, on the other hand, is greater than the sum of its part—people, deer, bears, and horses are examples here—and when we try to dissect or reduce them to their underlying components, we miss their very essence. Just as a symphony is more than the individual notes that compose it, a *somebody* is more than a set of behaviors or biochemical reactions.

It is impossible to define precisely what gives a great piece of music its beauty and power; when we try to define it, the magic is gone. Nor can we precisely define the soul, yet if we open our hearts we can respond to its allure. Soul is the magic of life. Soul is what gives life its sublimity and grandeur.

There is a glimmering of eternity about our lives. In the vastness of time and space, our lives are indeed small and ephemeral, yet not utterly insignificant. Our lives do matter. Because we care for one another and have feelings, because we can dream and imagine, because we are the kinds of creatures who make music and create art, we are not merely disconnected fragments of the universe but at some level reflect the beauty and splendor of the whole. And because all life shares in One Spirit, we can recognize this indwelling beauty in other creatures. Animals, like us, are microcosms. They too care and have feelings; they too dream and create; they too are adventuresome and curious about their world. They too reflect the glory of the whole.

Can we open our hearts to the animals? Can we greet them as our soul mates, beings like ourselves who possess dignity and depth? To do so, we must learn to revere and respect the creatures who, like us, are a part of God's beloved creation, and to cherish the amazing planet that sustains our mutual existence. We must join in a biospirituality that will acknowledge and celebrate the sacred in all life.

No longer can we discount the lives of sensitive and intelligent creatures merely because they assume nonhuman form. The things that make life most precious and blessed—courage and daring, conscience and compassion, imagination and originality, fantasy and play—do not belong to our kind alone.

Animals, like us, are living souls. They are not things. They are not objects. Neither are they human. Yet they mourn. They love. They dance. They suffer. They know the peaks and chasms of being.

Animals are expressions of the Mind-at-Large that suffuses our universe. With us, they share in the gifts of consciousness and life. In a wonderful and inexpressible way, therefore, God is present in all creatures.

NOTES

1. Maurice Friedman, *Martin Buber's Life and Work: Volume I, The Early Years, 1878–1923* (Detroit, MI: Wayne State University Press, 1981), p. 14.

2. Martin Buber, *I and Thou* (New York: Scribner, 1970), p. 145.

3. For this contrast of "biology" versus "biography," I am indebted to Tom Regan, Professor of Religion and Philosophy at North Carolina State University.

4. Friedman, *op. cit.*, p. 15.

"THE THEOLOGICAL BASIS OF ANIMAL RIGHTS"

Andrew Linzey

Secretary of Health and Human Services Louis Sullivan recently told a Vatican conference that animal rights "extremists" threaten the future of health research and that churches "cannot remain on the periphery in this struggle. . . . Any assertion of moral equivalence between humans and animals is an issue that organized religion must refute vigorously and unambiguously." Sullivan went on to say that world religious leaders possess the authority to "affirm the necessity of appropriate and humane uses of animals in biomedical research."

At first sight, Sullivan has backed a winner. What better than conservative theology and who better than conservative churches to respond to the rallying call for human superiority over animals—even and especially if this "superiority" involves inflicting pain and suffering? Christian theology has, it must be admitted, served long and well the oppressors of slaves, women and animals. Only 131 years ago, William Henry Holcombe wrote confidently of slavery as the "Christianization of the dark races." It took 1900 years for theologians to question seriously the morality of slavery, and even longer the oppression of women. Keith Thomas reminds us that over the centuries theologians debated "half frivolously, half seriously, whether or not the female sex had souls, a discussion which closely paralleled the debate about animals." Apparently the Quaker George Fox encountered some who thought women had "no souls, no more than a goose."

Who better to look to then but the Roman Catholic Church, which in its approved *Dictionary of Moral Theology* of 1962 confidently proclaims that "Zoophilists often lose sight of the end for which animals, irrational creatures, were created by God, viz., the service and use of man. . . . In fact, Catholic moral doctrine teaches that animals have no rights on the part of man"? In practice, Catholic countries are among the worst in the world as far as animals are concerned. Bullfighting and the Spanish fiestas in which animals are gratuitously mutilated (with the compliance of priests and nuns) are examples of how historical theology lives on. Surely Sullivan could not have chosen a more agreeable ally in his fight against "extremists" who believe that animals have rights.

And yet, there are signs that Christian theology and Christian churches cannot be so easily counted upon to support the standard line that humans are morally free to do as they like with animals. Anglican Archbishop Donald Coggan in 1977 stated the unthinkable: "Animals, as part of God's creation, have rights which must be respected. It behooves us always to be sensitive to their needs and to the reality of their pain." Archbishop Robert Runcie went further in 1988 and specifically contradicted historical anthropocentrism. His words deserve to be savored:

> The temptation is that we will usurp God's place as Creator and exercise a *tyrannical* dominion over creation. . . . At the present time, when we are beginning to appreciate the wholeness and interrelatedness of all that is in the cosmos, preoccupation with humanity will seem distinctly parochial. . . . Too often our theology of creation, especially, here in the so-called "developed" world, has been distorted by being too man-centered. We need to maintain the value, the preciousness of the human by affirming the preciousness of the nonhuman also—of all that is. For our concept of God forbids the idea of a *cheap creation*, of a throwaway universe in which everything is expendable save human existence. . . . The value, the worth of natural things is not found in Man's view of himself but in the goodness of God who made all things good and precious in his sight. . . . As Barbara Ward used to say, "We have only one earth." Is it not worth our love? ["Address to the Global Forum of Spiritual and Parliamentary Leaders on Human Survival" (his emphases).]

Even at the very center of conservative theology there are indications of movement. The pope's 1984 encyclical *Solicitudo Rei Socialis* speaks of the need to respect "the nature of each being" within creation. It underlines the modern view that the "dominion granted to man . . . is not an absolute power, nor can one speak of a freedom to use and misuse or to dispose of things as one pleases."

It would be silly to pretend that Pope John Paul II and Archbishops Coggan and Runcie are card-carrying members of the animal rights movement (there are no membership cards in any case). Yet for Sullivan, desperately hoping for moral assurance in the face of animal rights "extremists," these cannot be encouraging signs. Is the ecclesiastical bastion of human moral exclusivity really going to tumble? Might there be, in 50 or 100 years, a Roman encyclical defending the worth, dignity and rights of the nonhuman world? The *National Catholic Reporter* noted that Pope John Paul II had only "cautiously" defended animal experimentation. In 1982, the paper recalled, the pope argued that "the diminution of experimentation on animals, which has progressively been made ever less necessary, corresponds to the plan and well-being of all creation." The true reading of Sullivan's overture might be not confidence but desperation. Perhaps the most worrying thing for Sullivan is that the churches *won't* remain on the periphery in this struggle.

Sullivan has a counterpart in the United Kingdom: agriculture minister and fellow Anglican John Selwyn Gummer, who tried to bolster the meat trade by asserting that vegetarianism is a "wholly unnatural" practice. Like Sullivan he thought Christian theology would be of some help—in his case, against 5 million British vegetarians. "I consider meat to be an essential part of the diet," argued Gummer. "The Bible tells us that we are masters of the fowls of the air, and the beasts of the field and we very properly eat them."

Alas, biblical theology cannot be so easily wheeled in to rescue the minister of agriculture. The creation saga in Genesis I does indeed give humans dominion over animals (v. 28) but just one verse later commands vegetarianism (vv. 29–31). As Karl Barth observed: "Whether or not we find it practicable and desirable, the diet assigned to men and beasts by God the Creator is vegetarian" (*Church Dogmatics*, III/1, p. 208). Bystanders may marvel at how Gummer could in all innocence hurl himself not at the weakest but the strongest part of his enemy's armor.

Sullivan and Gummer seem united in the view that if theology is to speak on animal rights, it will speak not on the side of the oppressed but on behalf of the oppressor. Indeed, the view somehow seems to have got about that there can be no mainstream theological basis for animal rights. As well as accusing the movement of being "philosophically flawed and obscurantistic—based on ignorance and emotion, not reason and knowledge—and antihuman and even antianimal," the magazine *Eternity* produced by Evangelical Ministries Inc., claimed in 1985 that "the true religious underpinning of animal-rights consists in a kind of vague neopantheism" (Lloyd Billingsley, "Save the Beasts, Not the Children? The Dangerous Premises of the Animal-Rights Crusade," February 1985).

To begin to construct an adequate theological understanding of animals, we should recall Runcie's statement about the "value, the preciousness of the nonhuman." Secular thinkers are free to be agnostic about the value of the nonhuman creation. They could argue, for example, that creation has value only insofar as humankind is benefited or insofar as other creatures can be classed as utilities. Not so, however, for Christians. If, as Runcie observes, "our concept of God forbids the idea of a cheap creation" because "the whole universe is a work of love" and "nothing which is made in love is cheap," Christians are precluded from a purely humanistic, utilitarian view of animals. This point will sound elementary, but its implications are profound.

At its most basic it means that animals must not be viewed simply as commodities, resources, tools, utilities for human use. If we are to grapple with real theology, we must abandon purely humanocentric perspectives on animals. What may be the use of animals to us is a totally separate question from what their value is to almighty God. To argue that the value and significance of animals in the world can be circumscribed by their value and significance to human beings is simply untheological. I make the point strongly because there seems to be the misconception—even and especially prevalent among the doctrinal advocates of Christian faith—that theological ethics can be best expressed by a well-meaning, ethically enlightened humanism. Not so. To attempt a theological understanding must involve a fundamental break with humanism, secular and religious. God alone is the source of the value of all living beings.

This argument is usually countered in one of two ways. The first is to say that if this is so, it should follow that all creation has value, so we cannot rate animals of greater value than rocks or vegetables, let alone insects or viruses. Increasingly this argument seems to be made by "conservationists" and "green thinkers" who want to exclude animals from special moral consideration. They argue that the value of animals, and therefore what we owe them, is really on a par with the value of natural objects such as trees or rivers. One can immediately see how this view falls in neatly with the emerging green view of "holistic interdependence" and holistic appeals to respect "earth as a whole." God loves the whole creation holistically, so it is claimed.

But is it true that God loves everything equally? Not so, I think. Christian tradition clearly makes a distinction between humans and animals, and also between animals and vegetables. Scholars eager to establish the preeminence of humans in Scripture have simply overlooked ways in which animals exist alongside humans within the covenant relationship. The Spirit is itself the "breath of life" (Gen. 1:30) of both humans and animals. The Torah delineates animals within its notion of moral community. After having surveyed the ways in which animals are specifically associated, if not identified, with humans themselves, Barth concludes: " 'O Lord, thou preservest man and beast' (Ps. 36:6) is a thread running through the whole of the Bible; and it first emerges in a way which is unmistakable when the creation of man is classified in Gen. 1:24f with that of the land animals" (*Church Dogmatics*, III/1, p. 181n).

The second way in which my argument may be countered is by proposing that while animals have some value, it is incontestably less than the special value of humans. But this objection only adds fuel to my thesis. I, for one, do not want to deny that humans are unique, superior, even, in a sense, of "special value" in creation. Some secular animal rightists, it is true, have argued in ways that appear to eclipse the uniqueness of humanity. But Christian animal rights advocates are not interested in dethroning humanity. On the contrary, the animal rights thesis requires the re-enthroning of humanity.

The key question is, What kind of king is to be reenthroned? Gummer's utterances show only too well how "dominion" has come to mean little more than despotism. But the kingly rule of which we are, according to Genesis, the vice-regents or representatives is not the brutalizing regime of a tyrant. Rather, God elects humanity to represent and actualize the loving divine will for all creatures. Humanity is the one species chosen to look after the cosmic garden (Gen. 2:15). This involves having power over animals. But the issue is not whether we have power over animals but how we are to use it.

It is here that we reach the christological parting of the ways. Secularists may claim that power is itself the sufficient justification for our use of it. But Christians are not so

Andrew Linzey

free. No appeal to the power of God can be sufficient without reference to the revelation of that power exemplified in Jesus Christ. Much of what Jesus said or did about slaves, women or animals remains historically opaque. But we know the contours even if many of the details are missing. The power of God in Jesus is expressed in *katabasis*, humility, self-sacrifice, powerlessness. The power of God is redefined in Jesus as practical costly service extending to those who are beyond the normal boundaries of human concern: the diseased, the poor, the oppressed, the outcast. If humans claim a lordship over creation, then it can only be a lordship of service. There can be no lordship without service.

According to the theological doctrine of animal rights, then, humans are to be the servant species: the species given power, opportunity and privilege to give themselves, nay sacrifice themselves, for the weaker, suffering creatures. According to Sullivan, the churches must refute "any assertion of moral equivalence between humans and animals." But I, for one, have never claimed any strict moral equality between humans and animals. I have always been a bit worried by Peter Singer's view that animal liberation consists in accepting "equal consideration of interests" between humans and animals. In my view, what we owe animals is more than equal consideration, equal treatment or equal concern. The weak, the powerless, the disadvantaged, the oppressed should not have equal moral priority but greater moral priority. When we minister to the least of all we minister to Christ himself. To follow Jesus is to accept axiomatically that the weak have moral priority. Our special value as a species consists in being of special value for others.

No one has enumerated this doctrine better than that 19th-century pioneer of social reform for both humans and animals, the seventh Earl of Shaftesbury:

> I was convinced that God had called me to devote whatever advantages He might have bestowed upon me to the cause of the weak, the helpless, both man and beast, and those who had none to help them. . . . What I have done has been given to me; what I have done I was enabled to do; and all happy results (if any there be) must be credited, not to the servant, but to the great Master, who led and sustained him.

The relevance of such theology to animal rights should be clear. Readers will have noticed I have assiduously used the term "animal rights" rather than "animal welfare" or "animal protection." Some Christians are still apt to regard "rights" terminology as a secular import into moral theology. They are mistaken. The notion of rights was first used in explicitly theological contexts. Moreover, animal rights is explicitly a problem of Christian moral theology for this reason: Catholic scholasticism has specifically and repeatedly repudiated animal rights. It is the tradition, not its so-called modern detractors, that insists on the relevance of the concept of rights. The problem is only now compounded because, unaware of history, Christians want to talk boldly of human rights yet quibble about the language when it comes to animals. For me the theological basis of rights is compelling.

God is the source of rights, and indeed the whole debate about animals is precisely about the rights of the Creator. For this reason in *Christianity and the Rights of Animals* (New York: Crossroad, 1987) I used the ugly but effective term "theos-rights." Animal rights language conceptualizes what is objectively owed the Creator of animals. From a theological perspective, rights are not something awarded, granted, won or lost but something recognized. To recognize animal rights is to recognize the intrinsic value of God-given life.

I do not deny that the rights view involves a fundamental reorientation. This is one of its merits. The value of living beings is not something to be determined by human beings alone. Part of the reason rights language is so controversial is that people sense from the very outset that recognizing animal rights must involve personal and social change. Whatever else animal rights means it cannot mean that we can go on consuming their flesh, destroying their habitats, wearing their dead skins and inflicting suffering. Quite disingenuously some church people say that they do not "know" what "animal rights" are. Meanwhile, by steadfastly refusing to change their lifestyles, they show a precise understanding of what animal rights are.

Earlier I compared the oppression of slaves and women to that of animals. Some may regard that comparison as exaggerated, even offensive. But at the heart of each movement of reform has been a simple yet fundamental change of perception. Slaves should not be thought of as property but as human beings with dignity and rights. Women should not be regarded as second-class humans but as humans with dignity and rights. At the heart of the animal rights movement is a change of moral perception, simple, yet profound: animals are not our property or utilities but living beings with dignity and rights.

To recognize animal rights is a spiritual experience and a spiritual struggle. One homely example may suffice. The university where I work is situated amid acres of 18th-century parkland. Wildlife abounds. From my study window I observe families of wild rabbits. Looking up from my word processor from time to time, I gaze in wonder, awe and astonishment at these beautiful creatures. I sometimes say half-jokingly, "It is worth coming to the university for the rabbits." Occasionally I invite visitors to observe them. Some pause in conversation and say something like, "Oh yes," as though I had pointed out the dust on my bookshelves or the color of my carpet. What they see is not rabbits. Perhaps they see machines on four legs, "pests" that should be controlled, perhaps just other "things." It is difficult to believe that such spiritual blindness and impoverishment is the best that the superior species can manage.

Sullivan makes free with calling animal rightists "extremists." The reality is, however, that moral theology would hardly advance at all without visionaries and extremists, people who see things differently from others and plead God's cause even in matters that others judge insignificant. I don't think there are many moderates in heaven.

Andrew Linzey

"NO PLACE TO HIDE: SPIRITUALITY, AVOIDANCE, AND DENIAL"

Roger S. Gottlieb

Spiritual teachings offer us peace in place of pain. Or at least they offer us a way to accept the inevitable distress that comes from being alive. Yet if we choose to follow those teachings, we face a dilemma. On the one hand, awareness of the generalized suffering which afflicts people in the world—and of environmental or political threats to my own life—makes me feel decidedly *unpeaceful*. I'd rather not be aware of them. Various forms of escape are so attractive, and seem so natural, in a world like ours. On the other hand, spiritual growth cannot be accomplished while I'm screening out the pains and dangers around me. This response will thwart my spiritual aspirations and leave me no better off than when I began.

What am I to do?

People respond to this dilemma in different ways. I will focus here on avoidance and denial. These forms of escape are important because they permeate not only our personal lives but society as a whole. Sadly (but not surprisingly) it is not just our individual minds that want to look the other way. Many of our most prestigious and influential institutions are built on doing just that. The spiritual task that faces us as individuals is therefore made especially difficult by the fact that it would be so easy simply to conform to the escapist style of our surroundings.

Any painful or threatening reality—from unnecessary poverty to the abuse of women, from AIDS to breast cancer—may give rise to the desire to escape. However, this desire is especially likely to surface in response to the environmental crisis. This is so because the scope of the environmental crisis dwarfs other social problems, no matter how important they may be.* What is at stake is of such immense value that the prospect of its ruin is very hard to take in. Even in our technologically overburdened times, we have a special relation to the "more-than-human."[1] The complex and often disappointing world of human relationships is for many of us offset by the simple delight and comfort that we get from ocean or forest, birdsong or sunset. When we think of species made extinct, or particular places altered (for the worse!) forever, we find ourselves overcome by feelings of helplessness and

---

Reprinted from *A Spirituality of Resistance* (New York: The Crossroad Publishing Company, 1999).

*With the possible exception of war—which in our time includes a strong element of environmental destruction.

hopelessness. The prospect that nature's powers to heal and comfort might be eroded or eliminated is just too painful to bear.

Also, our own well-being is so tied up with the environment that its deterioration threatens us directly. It is not easy to really acknowledge all the dangers lurking in the food, the water, and the air. Unlike wars or poverty, environmental threats can be silent and hidden. Often created by technical powers of which the average person has little understanding, they are pervasive and long-lasting. We often don't know how and why they begin, or—from the lead in our backyard gardens to the pesticides leeching into our drinking water—if they are still around us.

Perhaps most frustratingly, there commonly seems to be so little we can do about these far-reaching problems. Unless by profession we are environmental lawyers or Sierra Club staffers, it appears virtually impossible to make a real difference in what is going on. We can recycle, drive less, and eat organic foods. But while these responses are good, they have limited effects on the major sources of environmental destruction. So it may be hard to accept that our individual actions are so inadequate to the real scope of the problem. Alternatively, it might appear that the only way to do anything is to overturn society, renounce everything we have, and sever all ties. When we fail to take such steps, our own sense of inadequacy and guilt grows. We realize that we are behaving just like everyone else, and that there is nothing to be done. If this is indeed true, we may again move toward various forms of escape. After all, why should we pay attention if we can't change anything?

Usually, such motivations to escape thinking and feeling about the environmental crisis exist well below the level of conscious awareness. To acknowledge that these feelings exist would in fact be to begin the process of overcoming our tendency to run away. It is our unconscious drive not to know or feel the truth that prompts us to try to escape in the first place!

Yet no matter what short-term composure we gain from our flight, we lose much more. Psychic and institutional retreats cast a shadow over any attempt to really be happy with one's own life. We cannot feel at home on this earth if we are not ready to take in what it is. In the end, we will be stifled both morally and spiritually.

Many years ago, I was part of a small group that researched, wrote, and produced a theatrical presentation on Jewish resistance during the Holocaust. In the early months of working together we shared the results of our initial inquiries. Each of us volunteered to study a different area, for example, causes of the Holocaust, resistance in the ghettos, life and death in the concentration camps. At each meeting we were to report to the group on what we'd found, as part of a preliminary process toward writing a script for the final presentation.

Several times people who had committed themselves to doing a particular piece of research would show up empty-handed, having failed even to do the reading. Later my wife, who was also part of the group, heard me fume: "I just don't understand. How can they promise to do the reading and then not do it?" "What do you expect," she would reply, "Reading about the Holocaust raises all kinds of painful feelings. These are so hard to deal with that it's easy to forget or avoid the whole thing."

At that time I really couldn't understand. After all, I never missed an assignment, never failed to study one site of mass death or another; and I had little patience for the people who couldn't handle the material. They didn't do what they said they would. I did. They were avoiding. I wasn't.

It was only years later, as I began to concentrate on humanity's relation to nature, that I became aware that in regard to environmental issues I had done exactly the same thing for years.

It was a simple process, really. In an almost physical way, I would simply move over or around what I didn't want to know. For instance, I would be reading the newspaper, going through stories on congressional activity, Middle East violence, welfare mothers, drug policy. Then a small story would catch my eye: "Rash of Wild Frogs Born with Abnormalities, Environmental Causes Suspected," or "Long Island Beaches Closed for Seventh Day, Runoff from Area Sewage Plants Blamed." Now the trick is that in the very moment of seeing the headline, I would turn away. My seeing was a kind of purposeful, yet barely conscious, not seeing. There would be a scarcely perceptible tightening of my face, a surreptitious pulling back in my chest, a split-second unconscious decision that this was not what I wanted to read about. My avoidance was a jerky psychic movement, the mental equivalent of a small animal who finds himself on a hot surface: a series of jumps and sideways shuffles until it escapes the threat.

During those years I was a graduate student or college teacher: a scholar, a professional intellectual. I wrote on the history of the Middle East conflict, compared different theories of the transition from feudalism to capitalism, and plowed through text and commentary of dense works by Marx and Hegel. I was at home with vast library resources, professional journals, obscure and detailed accounts of all sorts of things. I was, in short, no stranger to doing research and informing myself about how things stood.

Yet for those years of my adult intellectual life, from my late twenties through my early forties, I had read only one short book on environmental issues: and I had never consulted a single specialty magazine or journal—not even the glossy ones aimed at general readers. What I knew came from odd bits of information overheard on radio news, from casual glances at the headlines, and from the material that events like Earth Day pumped into the general culture. Of course, as a card-carrying member of the sixties generation, I had no trouble believing that large corporations and militaristic governments could trash the environment to further their short-term ends. I could easily imagine that things were bad—and I didn't want to know any of the details.

If I had been asked, "Why don't you find out what is going on?" I might have answered, "Well, it's not really my area" or "I don't have time" or "Later." But no one did ask. If I'd actually had to offer such answers, I now realize, I might have sensed how ridiculous they were. In just this way, my own avoidance was buttressed by that of just about everyone I knew. (And we were all politically correct types who constantly discussed sexism, corporate abuse, and racism.) We all managed not to ask each other: "Why aren't you finding out?" In retrospect, I can see that I—we—were simply avoiding. On a rational level, of course, this made no sense. After all, if air and water and toxic poisoning are not everyone's concern, part of every group's "special interests," part of every academic's "field," what is? (Years later, when I appealed directly to some colleagues to include environmental issues in their courses, courses into which the material would have fit easily, I got precisely that response. "It's great that you are doing this, Roger, but it's not my field.")

The simple fact of the matter was that I was afraid to find out more than the bare minimum. I didn't want to have anything like an adequate awareness of what was really going on. Because I was scared to know more, I managed to be content with the little I knew.

There were many reasons for my fear. From a young age I had been in love with the natural world and the threat to it frightened me deeply. The house in which I grew up had a large backyard, with many trees and a muddy little brook. Beyond our wire mesh fence there were—before being developed into another suburban enclave—a few acres of woods. And at the foot of my dead-end street there was a whole little forest, with rock outcroppings to climb over and little hollows in which I would make small fires on cold November afternoons. These were the places I went when my childhood loneliness grew especially painful. The trees, muddy brooks, and rich breezes of late autumn or early spring made me feel I had a place where I belonged. They soothed me, in a way no person I knew would. The pseudo-wildness of my suburban youth—and as an adult the really wild settings of Wyoming national forests or the Himalayas—gave me an emotional support I couldn't get anywhere else. At the times when I felt most at one with everything that breathed or grew or shone in the sunlight, the natural world seemed like part of my true family, as connected to me and the people I loved as any favorite aunt or good-humored cousin. So for years the thought that this family was being poisoned was more than I had the courage to endure.

What does this story of my own personal avoidance, which I believe might be representative of many people's experience, have to do with spiritual life?

To begin with, consider that it is impossible to avoid something without, in some sense or other, knowing what it is you are avoiding. If I hadn't "known" or "sensed" or "believed" that the environment was in bad shape, I wouldn't have had to exert that spontaneous little movement to avoid the threatening news stories.[2] With the same peculiar combination of stoicism and eagerness with which I studied sexism and the Holocaust, I would have examined what pesticides were doing to migrant workers or what clear-cuts were doing to forest ecosystems. I didn't pursue the matter in all its gory details because I was scared: of the truth, and of how the truth would make me feel. But to the extent that I had to know—to sense, to intuit—the truth in order to avoid it, I was having the emotional response already. Buried in the back of my mind, under the floorboards of a consciousness ever so occupied with other things, was a barely discernible anguish over what was going on. The emotions were there; I just wasn't willing to face them. I was closed to a part of my own reality as well as to a part of the world. There was what I somewhere "knew" and didn't acknowledge; and there was the limited reality that I tried to pass off as all I needed to think and talk about. Psychologically and spiritually, I was split.

Such a split mind is a profound barrier to spiritual development. Emotions hidden are not really gone. Whether or not we realize it they have pernicious effects on our lives. Unacknowledged anger becomes hostility directed inward or outward. A grief suppressed becomes a quiet depression, numbness of spirit. It can lead to what Kierkegaard called "a disorder of feelings, the disorder consisting in not having any."[3] If spiritual life means a quiet enjoyment of what we have, a spontaneous gratitude for what God has given us, an open-hearted empathy for both the joy and the suffering that exists around us, then spirituality will be diminished if I give my energy over to avoiding the world and choking off my reactions to it.

Are our prayers of spiritual appreciation to read something like: "Thank you God, for the beauties of my life (and please let me not think about the high cancer rate in the next town, or what might happen to me if I don't use a #45 sun block)"? Am I to "do unto my neighbor as I would have him do unto me" without thinking about what I am actually doing? (For instance, that the smoke from my factory is killing his forests?) Can I manifest authentic gratitude for what I have if I'm also spending a lot of energy avoiding looking at what other people (or species) are going through? The comparable point can be made, without too much trouble, for other spiritual virtues. Compassion, humility, integrity, equanimity, and all the rest require as a bare beginning that we be able to confront the truth.

In avoidance we approach and, quickly, run away. We avert our eyes, as we sometimes do when we glimpse someone with a crippling disease or a facial deformity. And the hidden message to ourselves in all this is that we are too frail to live with the facts. By avoiding we are acting as if we must absolutely have something that doesn't exist: in this case, a world without an environmental crisis. We thus commit ourselves to being the kind of person who is incapable of taking in what is going on. Like the family member from whom some horrible secret must be hidden ("Don't tell dad, you know he just couldn't handle it"), we require protection. Our consciousness becomes a defensive window and we experience the world as through a glass darkly.

Such a stance diminishes our capacity for either spontaneous joy or confidence that we really can be at home in this world. Ultimately, it is an aesthetic message. It suggests that we must have a restricted realm of experiences in order to live well. And if the world doesn't have the properly limited range, we'll limit it ourselves by avoiding what threatens our precarious grip on happiness and well-being.

The first day of my environmental philosophy course I tell students of my own fear, grief, and rage about the ecological crisis. I admit to years of avoiding information about just how bad things are, share my helpless anger over the threats to my daughter's health, acknowledge a temptation to despair for the wilderness forever lost.

I then ask them to speak in turn about what they feel. They respond slowly and hesitantly, emboldened by my example but still somewhat unsure that a university classroom is the proper place for emotions. As the hour progresses, however, their statements become increasingly more revealing.

"I'm pissed off," one will say, "because the field where I used to hunt for grasshoppers was turned into a parking lot for a mall, and they hardly even use it. What a waste."

"I'm scared," a young woman admits. "Every time I go out in the sun in the summer I think about skin cancer. My aunt died from it."

Several young men tell me they don't see much use in thinking about all these problems. I ask one: "What would happen if you did think about it?"

"I don't know," he replies. "I'm not sure I could go on with what I'm supposed to do in this life. If I started to cry, I might never stop."

People's spiritual lives do not unfold in a vacuum. The surrounding culture shapes our tastes in music, food, and clothes, our beliefs about history and the physical world, our expectations concerning romantic love or friendship. In exactly the same way, we are spiritually affected by the way the major institutions of our time confront—or avoid—the most serious and threatening aspects of the environmental crisis. To a significant extent these institutions offer models for how to deal with what is going on in the world.

Government, media, and schools do not really talk about environmental issues very much; and when they are talked about, the conversation is often superficial. This chapter is not the place to try to prove this assertion—which might strike the reader as yet another overblown claim by another hysterical tree hugger! To test it, however, you might try the following simple experiment. Put this book down, go to any bookstore or library, and get a copy of any one of several solid, but hardly technical or arcane, environmental magazines: *E Magazine, Sierra Club, Audubon, WorldWatch, The Ecologist, Garbage*, and *Buzzworm* are all good. Read the magazine from cover to cover: every story, news byte, ad, and letter to the editor. Then ask yourself: "Did I know about much of this? Did I have any idea how serious it was in the [pick one or more] forests, third world coastlines, fishing industry, use of chemicals in agriculture, environmental effects of militarism, other?" And, presuming that you are a reasonably educated, reasonably aware person, you might ask yourself: "I listen to public radio, I watch the news, I read a newspaper, I subscribe to [pick all that apply] *Time, Newsweek, Ms., The Nation, The New Republic, New Age Journal, Yoga Journal, Sports Illustrated, Mother Jones, Cosmopolitan*, other, . . . yet how little I knew about all this. Why is that?"

This exercise is the first reading I have students perform in my environmental philosophy class. Having made it into one of the top engineering colleges in the U.S., these students are scientifically and technically gifted. They typically score above 650 on their Math SATs, they are not afraid of science, and they have all been educated decades after the first Earth Day—decades into a period in which public schools are (supposedly) including environmental issues as part of the curriculum. After doing the reading, many of them end up in a state of semi-shock.

For a number of reasons, environmental issues do not get the attention they deserve. For one thing, some of the richest, most powerful institutions in the world both cause a lot of the damage and also own a good deal of the media. Yet there is also the fact that particular reporters and editors are, like the rest of us, scared. For too many of us, too often, the facts are emotionally overwhelming, and responding to them would require basic changes in how all of us live. And so avoidance wins the day.

The second dimension of institutional denial is in some ways even more pernicious. It occurs at those times when the environment becomes yet another part of the ever-changing spectacle of our media-saturated times. We have the "year of the environment," pop stars for the rainforest, TV specials for clean air, Disney movies highlighted by songs which reject putting a price tag on nature, and pious declamations from politicians, corporations, and anyone else who has access to advertising, a microphone, or a web site. Our own personal concerns are reflected back to us through media images of public concern. These images seem to promise action to redress wrongs, solve problems, and restore public safety. Experts galore provide analysis and devise programs. We start to believe that the authorities are willing and able to handle the problem.

Often, however, no really significant action is taken. To begin with, much of corporate action in these areas takes the form of "green-washing." Corporations mount large-scale public relations campaigns to obscure what they've actually done or take credit for improvements mandated by laws against which they themselves vigorously lobbied! Perception of change, not change itself, is often what they are after most. Further, by the time the commissions of inquiry and studies of the problem are concluded, our attention is focused somewhere else. The environment will have had its fifteen minutes of fame, until of course we get another really, really hot summer, or the beaches are once again littered with dirty syringes. The rainforest in Brazil had, I just read, two of its most destructive years in 1995–97[4]—and this after how many conferences, stories, rainforest benefit CDs, and boxes of rainforest crunch sold at health food stores? We thought something would change, yet an entire country (world?) afflicted with Attention Deficit Disorder is just not capable of focusing long and hard enough to keep one problem before our eyes. We look, we look hard, one might even say with a touch of hysteria—and then we look away again.

Some years ago, my avoidance of environmental issues began to break down. There were a number of reasons, including a little more emotional maturity on my part and the examples of people like Joanna Macy, Miriam Greenspan, and Bill McKibben, who were willing to face the facts and the emotions that went along with them. In person or through their writing they asked me: "Well, why *don't* you think about it?"

I immersed myself in all the material I had avoided: studies of toxic waste dumps causing raised leukemia rates, descriptions of the burning, chemical-filled rivers of Poland, and long dispassionate lists of lost species. I wept bitterly as the facts were paraded before my eyes, and started carrying around both a deep anger at those in power and a nagging guilt over my own years of complicity, complacency, and ignorance.

But there was something else: something powerful, liberating, and astonishingly joyful. The energy I had poured into avoidance was freeing up. I could cover my desk with books like *Toxic Nation* and *Who'll Save the Forests?* and know that I'd read them soon. I was no longer (subconsciously) telling myself: "Watch out, here comes something you can't handle." I was no longer acting as if what was happening was so bad that I couldn't even think about it! I was no longer crippled by fear. Like Rachel Carson, my joy in the natural world was renewed just because I was no longer hiding from what was happening to it. Instead, I felt determined to find out and respond. While I had always believed that spiritual development required some engagement with the world, I finally developed the courage to apply this insight to environmental issues.

Perhaps most important, happiness in my own (actually very limited) ability to do something about these problems was fueled by admiration for those strong souls who were fighting back against the devastation. As in the case of my earlier study of the Holocaust, the bravery of resisters altered the spiritual meaning of the situation. My sense of horror remained, but that sense was now accompanied by a kind of wonder at what people could face and do under the most difficult of circumstances. As the Holocaust was not

Roger S. Gottlieb

only a time when people were murdered, but also a time when they resisted, so the environmental crisis comprised not only the destruction of the earth but also its protection.

The change I underwent when I put my avoidance away was, and can only be described as, a kind of spiritual awakening. There was a lightness in my step and a new twinkle in my eye. The world, with all its pains and problems, seemed fresh and vibrant. I was "reborn" as someone who no longer had to live in fear of finding out what the truth was, as downright scary as that truth might be. I felt, in a way I hadn't in years, truly at home.

When reality threatens us directly, when the little movements of avoidance don't suffice, we may turn to denial. The difference between avoidance and denial is the difference between passivity and activity, or between the tacit and the overt. While avoidance takes those little hops and jumps away from what frightens us, in denial we look it right in the face and say it isn't there. And then that thought guides how we live.

At bottom, the many forms of denial have a simple message in common: "It's not that bad." "It's not that bad" can mean, for instance, that there is a place to go where we can get away. It's too bad about the cities, we might think, but there is always the country. Or: it's too bad about the U.S., but there is the rainforest (the mountains of Canada, at least the Arctic?). Or: it's too bad about what's happening somewhere else, but here (in this suburb with green lawns and big trees, or nature reserve, or national forest) we are safe.

In reality, of course, there is no safe place and no place left unchanged. In the most general terms, as Bill McKibben devastatingly argued in *The End of Nature*, now that we've altered the climate and thinned the ozone layer, all of the earth has been affected by human actions. If we think of "nature" as something which functions without our intervention, we must acknowledge that nature is lost forever.

Less abstractly, there is also the painful truth that pollution is everywhere. Arctic seals have PCBs in their fat cells, Antarctic air carries toxins, litter can be found at the bottom of the ocean and on the tops of mountains. (And if it's a *famous* mountain, there are liable to be huge mounds of trash left from the glossy, high-tech expeditions that come to climb them, right alongside the ever-increasing telecommunications towers that make the cell phones work.)

Consider my friend Jack, who moved from metropolitan Boston to a peninsula on the coast of Maine. He and his wife let their income drop by 50 percent in order to live a more rural life and to establish a small spiritual community with some friends. The tiny town they settled in had a population of five hundred; the nearest "city," with a population of twelve hundred, was fourteen miles away. The only local industry was small-boat fishing, seafood processing, and a summer ferry to a small offshore island. Jack was two hundred miles from Boston, a hundred from Portland.

Yet there is a strange confluence of winds in Tenants Harbor, Maine, an unpredictable pattern that can cause different kinds of air pollution to collect along the coast. This barren, rocky, and beautifully evocative place, graced by seabirds and lobster beds, can have bouts of terrible air quality. When Jack went jogging, pains in his chest made him wonder if he was developing heart problems or lung disease. "No," said his doctor, "your heart and lungs are fine." While reading a story in the local paper about other people experiencing trouble breathing, especially while exercising, he discovered that it was something else. As the local air quality monitoring station revealed, his tiny village often had more ground level ozone than Boston. Ground level ozone is a prime component of classic smog. And here it was, miles from nowhere.

This story is less about Jack than it is about all of us. Green with envy, I and his other friends saw him as someone who had left pollution behind. While each of us had our own reasons to stay tied to the city or the suburban sprawl, he (we thought) had gotten out. And if he had gotten out, then it was at least possible that we could too. Yet the sad truth, the one we were all denying, is that there is no more "out."

Another form of denial rests on the idea that scientific and technical wizardry will take care of these problems. Sadly, however, we can no more place uncritical trust in scientists and engineers than we can expect to find a totally pristine seacoast. Just like the rest of us, those with highly specialized knowledge can get caught up in an institutional temptation to put what is ugly or threatening out of the way.

As an example, consider the history of CFCs (chlorofluorocarbons). Most of us have learned that these chemicals, so useful to modern refrigeration and auto air conditioning, do something destructive to the atmosphere. As they escape in the process of production or in worn-out units, they release chlorine molecules that make their way inexorably up to the ozone layer, a band of special oxygen molecules at eighty thousand feet above the earth's surface. Once they reach the ozone, the chlorine molecules begin to break it down, with each chlorine molecule able to destroy tens of thousands of ozone molecules. The result is less protection from the sun's ultraviolet radiation. The consequence of decreased protection is, at least, higher incidence of skin cancer and cataracts. This we are sure of. Less certain, but perhaps even more frightening, is the possibility that increased UV radiation will weaken the phytoplankton, the basis of the ocean's food chain, or that it might have unforeseen effects on animal (and, therefore, human) reproduction. There is some suspicion that a worldwide decrease in various species of frogs, especially ones whose eggs sit in sunlight, is a result of increases in UV radiation.

My focus here is not principally on the factual details of such environmental disasters, but on their spiritual meaning—and especially on how we deny them. What is striking about the disaster of CFC production—a production that continues as of this moment, aimed at distribution in the third world rather than in Europe and the U.S.—are two remarkable examples of denial that mark its history.[5]

The first example comes from the times when the potentially damaging effects of CFCs were first under serious study. Two chemists, whose work was shadowed by fears of the professional ostracism that often attends scientists who challenge large corporations on matters of public safety, began to be convinced that CFCs would impair the ozone layer. They offered an elegant theoretical model of how this could be occurring. The ozone producers replied that these claims were simply speculative science that could not be taken seriously without some confirmation in the real world. Years passed, during which the lead scientist of the pair, Sherry Rowland, found his career under a cloud for having gone public in a "policy" matter instead of staying in the realm of "pure science." Despite his status as a nationally recognized senior chemist, invitations to present his research to business and academia dwindled to the vanishing point. (Ironically, twenty years after he asked the simple question of what happens when CFCs get released at ground level, Rowland got a Nobel Prize for this work; by then, however, the damage to our world had been done.)

In fact, however, the confirmation the chemical companies said they were waiting for was already in existence. For some years data from British Antarctic Survey instruments had been registering a thinning of the ozone layer. But this information had been so shocking that it had been disbelieved, written off as a failure of the satellite's instruments rather than as an indication that the ozone was really being depleted. The evidence directly in front of the researchers' eyes was denied. They thought: this just can't be happening. Yet it was.

In this particular instance the chemist Rowland was the professional victim of a generalized form of institutional denial: the notion that science is (or should be) detached from the rest of society, that it is a perfectly neutral source of knowledge and technical expertise. Unlike politics, commerce, or personal interests, we are sometimes told, science will give us the direct, unvarnished truth. This idea ignores how the vast majority of contemporary scientific research is funded by corporations or the government. It is therefore governmental or corporate interests that determine the direction and content of research. The truths that are known are those that are sought after by researchers who must conceive of problems in the way that is congenial to those paying the bills. Of course many times this works to everyone's advantage. The knowledge that is gained is equally relevant and valuable for us all. In other cases, however, the results are partial, biased, or damaging. Research on energy is conducted on sources of power that can be centrally owned by large utilities; health research focuses on finding expensive drugs rather than on low-cost prevention. In such cases (and many more could be described), it is not that the scientific or technical claims are necessarily false. It is that someone had to choose what would be investigated—which questions would be raised and answered. In other words, all science has to fit into somebody's image of what is important or good, for it is always somebody other than the scientist who is paying for it. Any suggestion that scientists should leave policy issues alone presupposes that other policy makers are not already influencing it. Unfortunately, this is not the case.

The second example of denial in the history of CFCs goes back to its origins. The Dupont chemists who developed the stuff had tried to be reasonably cautious. In theoretical models and lab tests they sought to find out what would happen when CFCs entered the atmosphere. There is only one problem with their studies: they stopped at a level of forty thousand feet. The ozone layer, however, is at eighty thousand feet. What did they think would happen after the stuff hit forty thousand? How could they have ignored what would happen next?

We live in a civilization permeated by this kind of denial—of our vulnerability, of the limited scope of our knowledge, of how badly things can turn out. The fruits of such denial can be found in many other cases: the "miracle" pesticides which ten years later are made illegal, the anti-miscarriage drugs which cause birth defects, the economic development that poisons those whose lives it is supposed to enrich.

This kind of denial continues in the illusion that we can have anything money can buy. What CFCs are about, after all, is refrigerated foods and cars that are cool in 95-degree weather. To have used the chemicals as we did requires that we believe that these things can be had without some corresponding loss. In this and comparable cases, substances are developed, produced, and distributed while their potential real cost has been denied. For example, the vast majority of man-made chemicals which we inject into our surroundings have never been tested for their carcinogenic effects. They are innocent until proven guilty, that is, until it can be proven that they are harming people. And almost none of these chemicals are examined for what they will do to us in combination—which is, after all, how they are experienced by our bodies. When they are regulated, the corporations who make them exercise frightening control over how the regulations are observed (or eluded). They authorize biased research, bribe regulators, pay off legislators, or end up getting asked to write the regulations themselves.[6] Is it any wonder that despite the great orchestrated public denial embodied in trumpeted claims about the powers of medical research and high-tech treatment, in many if not most areas we are losing the "war on cancer"? Is it any wonder that in the 1990s the rates of breast, colorectal, brain, testicle, and kidney cancer continued to rise?[7] Or that we can now expect that between one-third and two-fifths of us will get cancer in our lifetimes? What the frequent public campaigns of medical self-congratulations offer is the denial of our frailty, our vulnerability, our imperfection. They deny the simple truth that we will not win the war on cancer unless we change the way we live.

Roger S. Gottlieb

As I write this chapter, the movie *Titanic* is enjoying great success. The film tells the story of the ship that was supposed to be invulnerable, which had no use for lifeboats—and which sank on its maiden voyage. As I watched the film I sensed that the whole tale is a disquieting metaphor for much of our own time. In the self-confident folly that said the sea had been mastered, a folly so clearly based in a denial of who we really are, was inscribed the deaths of fifteen hundred people. Our shortcomings of knowledge, competence, and foresight—and of the actual complexity of the world—were denied. Does this remind us of anything that has happened and continues to happen in the realm of the environment?

In fact, countless other examples can be found of a mistaken, irrational confidence that our actions won't have negative effects. What occurs, time after time, is a kind of willful refusal to see what we are doing. Not so much an avoidance—which, as I understand it, is a movement away from, a skipping over, a leaving out—as an active act of exclusion. To deny is simultaneously to confront, to reject, and to obscure. To deny is to look the truth in the face and say: "this isn't so." And then, if we can, to hide that truth out of sight. World Bank "development" projects which devastated the rainforest and poisoned the natives would sometimes plant a line of trees around the local helicopter landing spot, so visiting dignitaries would not witness the ruin that had taken place.[8] The favored response to oil spills is often to apply a chemical that simply makes the oil sink out of sight. The damaging effects of the oil continue, but on the bottom of the sea, where they can't be easily seen.[9] Environmental offensives against native peoples typically take place away from TV cameras or adequate news coverage.[10] Consequently, some of the most terrible assaults never get reported. This invisibility of the environmental victims, especially if they are not white, is itself taken for granted by some of the major players. When Exxon sought to locate a new mine in Indian territory in Minnesota, for instance, it had to prepare an environmental impact statement. It did so, but managed to omit any mention of possible effects on Indians living immediately downstream from where the mine would be located.[11]

Under the regime of denial, when the truth does surface, people attempt to hide it. Thus we have countless examples of companies or the government authorizing studies of products or procedures, and then asking (or telling) the authors to rewrite their documents. For instance, a mining company hired a scientist to evaluate workers' complaints that widespread ulcers were related to handling radium. After the research confirmed the workers' claims, the company barred the researcher from publishing his results and lied to the government about the findings.[12] Pesticide manufacturers, who also threatened to sue her publisher, called Rachel Carson, now hailed as the saint of modern environmentalism, a communist. While Carson's attackers proved too weak to accomplish much, thirteen states now have laws holding people liable for damages if they make (vaguely defined) "false" statements about agricultural products. The goal of these "food disparagement laws" is to create a psychic climate of fear and a public atmosphere of blanket denial over the dangers of and lack of reassuring research about hi-tech food processes like irradiation and genetic engineering.[13] These laws may in fact be unconstitutional, but they nevertheless have made people wary of facing major corporate food producers in a lawsuit. (Oprah won her case against the beef industry, but how many of us have her clout?) In another situation, a time- and money-consuming freedom of information lawsuit by a pesticide manufacturer has harassed a leading researcher studying the presence and effects of the pesticide toxaphene in the Great Lakes. The goal is to warn her and other researchers that if they speak too directly about the effects of chemicals in the environment, every scrap of paper they ever used in their work can be subpoenaed.[14]

Of course, it is not hard to see why people might want to protect their jobs, their corporations, their income—and lie to do so. What is critical here from the spiritual point of view is that at this time in history all of us are implicated in denial. When avoidance fails, we all, at one time or another, use denial in its stead. The corporate defenders of CFCs were in denial about their—and their children's—vulnerability to UV rays; as if people of wealth don't live in the sun's neighborhood. The defenders of questionable food processing forget that they too eat, and that if exposing meat to radioactive waste isn't the safest of all ways to sterilize food, they too will suffer as a result. When those of us who are not corporate spokesmen or well-defended bureaucrats simply continue with business as usual, we too are part of our culture's denial. At times even the most environmentally conscious, bogged down in the demands of daily life, turn away from what is right in front of their faces. I remember making light of an asbestos-wrapped pipe in my house, refusing for a while to acknowledge how much the dust it was shedding could be harming my family. "Don't worry about it so much," I told my wife. "Half the houses in our town have pipes wrapped like that." "So," she asked, "why should that reassure me?"

And of course there was no reason for her to be reassured. I was just whistling in the wind, hiding my real fear under a false confidence.

What is the spiritual problem with denial? It is, I think, the pain, confusion, and sense of unreality that arises when we both know the truth and refuse to acknowledge it. It is another kind of "double consciousness," one which takes an enormous amount of effort to live in. Our minds have to grapple with a reality split between what actually exists and what we would like to exist. We cannot fully engage with what is, because we are constantly picking and choosing between the parts of reality we will accept and those we will deny. Spiritual development, however, requires that we engage with reality. And that we be able to see it for what it is. As avoidance leads to the repression of energy, denial cuts us off

Roger S. Gottlieb

from the truth, makes us doubt our own sense of how things are, keeps us from listening to others or the world and from changing the way things are.

After the Holocaust, a Polish worker who kept track of the number of people entering Treblinka concentration camp said: "Of course, one had no conception of what 'extermination camp' really meant. I mean, it was beyond—not just experience, but imagination, wasn't it?"[15] This man saw, and kept a record of what he saw. He allowed himself to be changed, to develop a new "imagination." In denial, by contrast, we reject what we are seeing and refuse to extend ourselves.

Or, in our effort to hide away that which is true, we simply foist it off on others. So the toxic incinerators are concentrated in poor and black communities; the uranium mines are on Native American property. As a result the cancer rates in both communities far exceed the national average. Or, in a different setting, we find that many inner-city kids in Los Angeles have stunted lung growth due to air pollution. These Others carry the stuff that those of us who are richer and luckier don't want to see or breathe, that which we deny in our minds and our social policies. The truth of our society's collective denial is written in their bodies.

If avoidance leads to a kind of sickness of the self, a diminished sense of who we are, denial corrodes our ability to stand for something. It sucks the integrity right out of us. We say things that somewhere in our minds we suspect are untrue. Harboring a lurking fear that what has been repressed will return to haunt us, we try to banish the offending realities. The sad truth is that to the extent that we live in denial our lives are a little empty, just because (as with avoidance) somewhere we sense what we are doing. And thus we sense that at any time something can come along and bust right through the denial that has been (we think) sustaining us. We are haunted by suppressed anxiety and dishonesty, and our ability to live in spiritual truth is diminished.

Alternatively, denial represents a kind of frantic childish fantasy of omnipotence. "I will close my eyes," we seem to be saying, "and it will disappear." If we just continue on as if the wolf is not at the door, if we don't pay too much attention to the millions of pounds of toxins in the air and water, if we put the destructive effects of chemical agriculture out of our minds, if we continue to say "this can't be changed, don't be an alarmist, let's be practical"—if all these things are done, then, in fact, there is no crisis.

Finally, if all else fails, we can pass the whole thing off as a problem faced by separate individuals. "Isn't it too bad," we say, "that his wife died of breast cancer. So young, so vibrant, so special. What bad luck (karma, fate, God's will . . .)." And then we don't have to think about all those chemicals stressing the DNA in our own breast cells, or those of our mothers or wives or daughters. We don't have to think about how breast cancer is a collective problem, not some huge collection of individual hard luck stories. That, in fact, we've brought a lot of it on ourselves.

In a culture shaped by denial and avoidance, spiritual truth will often arise from strange sources: dreams, madmen, shrill political groups making all sorts of proclamations about the end of the world. The more our dominant institutions avoid and deny, and so many of us manifest the same response in our personal lives, the more a real awareness of the truth will necessarily often exist only on the margin. Part of the spiritual task of facing the truth about the world in which we live, part of living on *this* earth (and not one sanitized by the attempt to escape from the pain) is to begin to be aware of these sources of the truth— both within ourselves and from others.

Consider Elie Wiesel's classic memoir *Night*, in which he tells of Moche, the janitor from his little town's synagogue. While Wiesel and his neighbors remained in the town, Moche had been expelled back to Poland and had miraculously escaped when the Nazis had murdered his companions. He returned and tried to tell the townspeople what he had seen. The janitor had always been a strange man, poor and unassuming. Now, in the confusion and despair of wartime, people in the town wrote off his strange and frightening story. "What an imagination he has," people said. Or: "Poor fellow, he's gone mad." Perhaps what he had seen had driven him a little out of his mind. Nevertheless, he alone knew the truth.[16]

Or consider the story told by Terry Tempest Williams, in her haunting essay "The Clan of One-Breasted Women"—so named because of the epidemic of breast cancer that runs through her extended family. For years she had a strange, frequently recurring dream. She is in the Utah desert not far from her childhood home. Each time she is there she witnesses a strange flash of light against the night sky. After years of having this dream seared into her consciousness she mentioned it to her father. His answer shocked her:

> "You did see it. . . . The bomb. The cloud. We were driving home. . . . It was an hour or so before dawn, when this explosion went off. We not only heard it, but felt it. . . . We pulled over and suddenly, rising from the desert floor, we saw it, clearly, this golden-stemmed cloud, the mushroom. The sky seemed to vibrate with an eerie pink glow. Within a few minutes, a light ash was raining on the car. . . . I thought you knew that . . . it was a common occurrence in the fifties."
>
> It was at this moment that I realized the deceit I had been living under. Children growing up in the American Southwest, drinking contaminated milk from contaminated cows, even from the contaminated breasts of their mothers—members, years later, of the Clan of One-Breasted Women.[17]

Of course it is not as if there aren't a lot of respected and respectable voices, from the Audubon Society to Al Gore, who claim to speak to the environmental crisis. Too often these voices are drowned out by the collective forces of avoidance and denial, but they do exist.

Perhaps more dangerously, at times the dominant powers in our society create the illusion that they are heeding the call of environmental sanity. Attention is being paid, we think, and it seems that those of us who do not control the economy or the courts or the EPA can leave it to others. "After all," we might be saying to ourselves, "wasn't there just a huge international conference in Kyoto about global warming? Surely, they'll take care of the problem. And didn't a bunch of countries meet years ago in Montreal to take care of the threat to the ozone layer? They had foreign ministers and top scientists and all the rest. Surely they'll know what to do, now that they are thinking about it!"

Sadly, this too can be a kind of denial. For as much as we would like to believe that all the headlines and TV stories and loud speeches mean that things have been taken care of, if we look very carefully we will see that this is often not the case. Indeed, the Kyoto agreement was a step forward. Yet even if abided by, it would only roll back the emissions of greenhouse gases to what they were in the mid-1980s. But those levels were already sufficiently high to warm the earth. What was needed at Kyoto, most responsible observers said, was a fundamental commitment to decrease dependence on fossil fuels, the only step that might really reduce the warming trend. Such a step would require a full public acknowledgement of just how significant the threat is. In fact, we would have to admit that it is so significant that in transportation, energy production, agriculture, and housing (to name a few) we cannot go on with business as usual. To avoid this conclusion is to perpetuate the denial, if even in a slightly reduced form. Even worse, I discover as I finish this chapter that many members of Congress are so opposed to reducing our greenhouse gases that they are trying to eliminate funding for even the discussion of climate change, education about global warming, or preparation for the passage of the Kyoto treaty. If successful, denial-as-enforced-silence would be imposed on the administration, on the EPA, and on other government agencies.[18]

Further, to find an account of Kyoto that reveals these truths, we have to look beyond the most accessible sources of information and dig deeper: to the environmental journals and news services and on-line information sources.[19] Just as Wiesel's town should have listened to its mad janitor, and Williams needed to find the truth in her dreams, so spiritual seekers who want to overcome denial in an age of ecocide need to pursue information and analysis that is not quite so readily accessible as the TV news or the local newspaper. But this search, I am suggesting, is as much a part of our spiritual journey as the more traditional examination of our personal moral failings. Without it, we will never really be part of the world in which we live.

At the same time, we need to listen to our own doubts and fears, our own intuitions and common sense. Even without graduate degrees in environmental science or an exhaustive knowledge of global warming, we may well have access to some of the critical truths we need to know.

The notion of an inner truth is basic to spiritual traditions. It is frequently suggested that we can find the most important of truths within ourselves, if only we devote sufficient devotion to prayer, meditation, and honest introspection. Consider, for example, the "Arhat," the sage of Theravada Buddhism. In his religious practices the Arhat seeks an end to the confinement imposed by an identification with a self bound to desires that inevitably cause suffering. The question that arises for such a person is, of course, whether it is possible to be alive as a human being and not identify with such a self. Spiritual wisdom arises when the student directly experiences a state of mind in which identification with self dissipates. As one early practitioner is reputed to have said, when questioned by a fellow seeker: "During my meditation I reached a point where I had no thought that 'I am this; this is mine; this is my self.'"[20]

Or consider the prophet Elijah. Fleeing for his life from Jezebel's wrath after he put to death the prophets of Baal, he encounters God not in a mighty wind, an earthquake, or a fire, but in a "still, small voice."

Consider how the poet William Blake saw Christ suspended in air, dancing outside his window. Or the states of ecstatic no-self produced by Sufi dancing or tribal chanting; or the transformations of consciousness which come on a Native American Vision Quest, prepared for by days of fasting and isolation.

In all these, examples, and in the many more which could be discussed, spiritual teachings tell us that wisdom can be found within ourselves, if only we open ourselves to it. This wisdom provides an alternative to the ego's twisted identification with permanent dissatisfaction, greed, or violence. In it, we find truths that are usually inaccessible to a mind bound by the conventional social order.

And it is just this wisdom which can be sought, and followed, in regard to what is around us as well as what is within us, in regard to social conditions as well as to our own personal spiritual condition. Our senses, our intelligence, and our emotional wisdom can instruct us about the wider relationships in which we live. The truth of these intuitions is not guaranteed (any more than they are certain to be true when they concern our inner life.) But like Williams's dream or the stories of Moche the beadle, they deserve our attention.[21]

When the urban summer air is called "unhealthy" for the seventh straight day, and once again nothing is being done to reduce car traffic in favor of public transportation or bikes, doesn't some part of ourselves sense that our political and industrial leaders are making a huge mistake? When we find researchers making the exact same plea—first in 1955 and then, after forty years of near silence, in 1995—for an investigation into the relation between cancer and chemicals in the environment, isn't there some part of us that knows that our scientists, for all their brilliance, are simply not doing what so terribly

Roger S. Gottlieb

needs to be done?[22] In instances such as these we sense that things aren't right. Our inner voices prompt us to awareness. And it is part of our spiritual discipline to pay attention to these feelings, to use them as we might use the information from an environmental magazine or the revelation that our drinking water is not as safe as we thought.

For spiritual development to take place, we cannot ignore our own inner knowledge. When we sense that something is wrong—in ourselves, in the world—we must respond. If we do not, then the prayer and meditation, the listening to the voice of God and exploring our own hearts, will count for little. The point of those practices is to find, and heed, the most basic truths. If we are going to listen and search, we had better take seriously what turns up, no matter how scary it is. We need to attend to the truths known by others, no matter how shrill and marginalized they may be, and to the truth as we know it ourselves, even when it is fragmented, confused, and unfinished.

How are we to live with the truth? When we do move beyond avoidance and denial, how are we to retain any sense of joy in life? How can we keep from succumbing to dread or despair?

In essence, I believe that only if we become increasingly aware of the resistance of others and resist ourselves can we regain the sense of peace that necessarily leaves us when we end our own flight from reality. While a more developed answer to this question will be offered later, a few thoughts are relevant here.

First of all, from the point of view of a spirituality of resistance, it is necessary that we not be afraid of the depths of our feelings about the environmental crisis. While these feelings are painful, they also reveal the depth of our connections to the rest of the world. As sources of precious information and measures of our love, they deserve to be honored. They teach us that despite everything we can still care for the world and mourn the many deaths around us. In directly experiencing our feelings about these matters, our souls may recover some strength and vitality: qualities that are very much essential to any real spiritual growth and that have been eroded by avoidance and denial.

To realize these qualities anew we may need to go through a period, which in fact may recur, of focusing on the desperate, terrifying truth.

I remember, for instance, what happened to me when I was doing the detailed research for the Holocaust presentation I mentioned earlier. Immersed in historical material about deportations and mass killings, I began to see boxcars carrying Jews when I took the subway, and to think of SS vans when I heard sirens in the night. I had entered another world. Similarly, when years later I focused my attention on the environmental crisis, I would bore people at parties and give my wife nightmares, compulsively sharing the latest ecological horror story just before bedtime. Walking among beautiful birch trees, I thought of what the ravages of acid rain were doing to the forests of New England. A trip to the beach reminded me of the tumor-afflicted whales in the Bay of Newfoundland. I was shot through with grief and anger.

At this point I, and perhaps anyone else who goes through this process, faced, paradoxically, two more temptations to slip into denial.

The first temptation is that of despair. So much has been lost forever: so many people and animals poisoned, so many beautiful places turned barren. Once the denial and avoidance recede, a tide of hopeless gloom naturally starts to inch forward. While a temptation to conscious despair is inevitable at this point, it can be resisted. For what despair obscures is that the matter at hand is not closed, not finished. It is, in fact, still in doubt. The attraction of despair is that we no longer have to make the effort of hope, an effort which could give rise to further pain and disappointment. In despair, after all, we need care no longer because everything has been settled. As deeply as such despair might be felt, it too is a kind of denial. For while the environment has suffered greatly, there is still much to treasure and protect. Grief can legitimately become despair only when there is no hope left: nothing, that is, which is still worth saving.

A spirituality of resistance can build here on the countless spiritual teachings from a variety of traditions which have told us quite simply: there is no grief which cannot be endured, no loss that need become the sole meaning of our lives, no emotional pain that will not heal if it is entered into fully. We can feel the fear and grief and still do what needs to be done. Despite our losses, we can still resist—if, that is, we do not succumb to the rejection of hope which is the hidden message of despair.

From a spiritual point of view the steadfastness of hope is essential, just because it expresses our capacity to think beyond the pain we ourselves are experiencing in any particular moment and to delight in the prospect that someone, somewhere, can still find some happiness. The Italian Marxist Antonio Gramsci coined the telling phrase "pessimism of the intellect, optimism of the will." He meant by it that we must seek to know the bitterest of truths but can embody in our actions our continuing commitment to create new, and different realities. If we can still mourn, then we can still act. And while there is the capacity for action, there is the possibility that what we do will bring some happiness to some of our fellow beings. The persistence of this thought is the essence of hope, even in the darkest of times. We do not have to believe in some power greater than ourselves that is overseeing what is going on. To have hope we need not have faith. All we need is to admit that despite all the pains of the present, the future is still in doubt. That ignorance may be our greatest source of hope.

The second temptation is a kind of suppression of the self. We adopt a purely factual, business-like, pseudo-rational approach to the crisis. We accept the facts but start to deny the emotional pain by pouring everything we have into information, information, information and action, action, action. We focus on facts and figures, policies and procedures.

Roger S. Gottlieb

We make a lot happen and fight the good fight. For a while this type of denial is quite useful. It helps us Get a Lot Done, wins us a lot of (well-deserved) admiration, and seems to keep the demons at bay.

But how long will it be until we become shrill and a little crazy, burn out, or lose any sense of joy? How long can we ignore the feelings that got us here in the first place? The simple truth of the matter is that we are human, and human beings have feelings about their lives: about their families and friends and about the world in which they live. We cannot separate the facts of the matter from what we feel about them. Quite simply, the feelings we have are part of the facts: that we feel this much grief and fear about what is happening is something which needs to be attended to, just as much as the DDT level in the Arctic snow or the decline in water quality. We need to share our sadness and rage, to get some solace so that what we know doesn't eat away at our souls. Once we face the truth of what humanity has done to the world, we carry a permanent grief. This grief will not cripple us if we honor it, but it will poison our hearts if we pretend it is not there.

My times of being overwhelmed by the environmental crisis passed. I survived, none the worse for wear and in fact basically happier, more alive, and more in touch with the world and my feelings about it. If we open up a dam of feelings, is it surprising that a great rush comes forth? Rather than avoid this rush and keep the best parts of ourselves suppressed, we can ride it—knowing that a much healthier balance will surely follow. In this balance we will not forget about what acid rain is doing to forests, but will find a newly fresh joy in the trees around us. We will savor the birds before our eyes, even as we grieve for the ones dying because their meadows have been turned into parking lots. We will feel, and this may be the greatest blessing, a new and profound connection to nonhuman nature in all its brilliant diversity, and to our comrades and partners in the struggle to turn things around. Putting aside our own denial and avoidance, we can sense much more clearly the greatness of those who—from the Brazilian rainforest to the Afro-American factory towns to the California redwoods—have fought back to protect themselves and this earth on which we all must live.

NOTES

1. This wonderful phrase comes from David Abram's *The Spell of the Sensuous* (New York: Pantheon, 1995).

2. This line of reasoning is indebted to Jean-Paul Sartre's critique of Freud's theory of the unconscious, in *Being and Nothingness* (New York: Pocket Books, 1966).

3. Søren Kierkegaard, *Concluding Unscientific Postscript* (Princeton, N.J.: Princeton University Press, 1966).

4. World Resources Institute, *World Resources 1998–99* (New York: Oxford University Press, 1998), 186.

5. John Nance, *What Goes Up: The Global Assault on our Atmosphere* (New York: Morrow, 1991).

6. Dan Fagin, Marianne Lavell, and the Center for Public Integrity, *Toxic Deception: How the Chemical Industry Manipulates Science, Bends the Law and Endangers Your Health* (Secaucus, N.J.: Birch Lane Press, 1996).

7. Robert Proctor, *Cancer Wars* (New York: Basic Books, 1995), 73.

8. Bruce Rich, *Mortgaging the Earth: The World Bank, Environmental Impoverishment, and the Crisis of Development* (Boston: Beacon Press, 1994), 120.

9. Dashka Slater, "Dress Rehearsal for Disaster," *Sierra* (May–June 1994).

10. Al Gedicks, *The New Resource Wars: Native and Environmental Struggles against Multinational Corporations* (Boston: South End Press, 1993).

11. Gedicks, *The New Resource Wars*, 43, 62.

12. Proctor, *Cancer Wars*, 80, 179.

13. See "Food Slander Laws in the U.S.: The Criminalization of Dissent," *The Ecologist* 27, no. 6 (December 1997).

14. "Researcher Investigating Toxin Becomes Subject of Investigation," *Minneapolis Star Tribune*, May 17, 1998.

15. Gita Sereny, *Into That Darkness: From Mercy Killing to Mass Murder* (New York: McGraw Hill, 1974), 151.

16. Elie Wiesel, *Night* (New York: Avon Books, 1958), 16–18.

17. Terry Tempest Williams, *Refuge* (New York: Vintage, 1991), 283.

18. "Lawmakers want to bar talk about global warming," *Boston Globe*, July 7, 1998.

19. See the journals mentioned earlier in this chapter, as well as the wonderful on-line newsletter *Rachel's Environment and Health Weekly* (erf@rachel.org).

20. See, for example, Edward Conze, *Buddhism: Its Essence and Development* (New York: Harper, 1951), and Lucien Stryk, ed., *World of the Buddha* (New York: Anchor, 1969).

21. The next paragraphs are indebted to Miriam Greenspan's work, especially her forthcoming *Healing through the Dark Emotions.*

22. Sandra Steingraber, *Living Downstream: An Ecologist Looks at Cancer and the Environment* (Reading, Mass.: Addison-Wesley, 1997), 232.

PART IV

ECOTHEOLOGY IN AN AGE OF ENVIRONMENTAL CRISIS

Ecofeminist Spirituality

The Goddess in all her manifestations was a symbol of the unity of all life in Nature. Her power was in water and stone, in tomb and cave, in animals and birds, snakes and fish, hills, trees, and flowers. Hence the holistic and mythopoetic perception of the sacredness and mystery of all there is on Earth.

. . . The Goddess gradually retreated into the depths of forests or onto mountaintops, where she remains to this day in beliefs and fairy stories. Human alienation from the vital roots of earthly life ensued, the results of which are clear in our contemporary society. But the cycles never stop turning, and now we find the Goddess reemerging from the forests and mountains, bringing us hope for the future, returning us to our most ancient human roots.

—Marija Gimbutas

People often ask me if I *believe* in the Goddess. I reply, "Do you believe in rocks?" . . . In the Craft, we do not *believe* in the Goddess—we connect with Her; through the moon, the stars, the ocean, the earth, through trees, animals, through other human beings, through ourselves. She is here. She is within us all.

—Starhawk

. . . for more than twenty thousand years, a Great Goddess existed in our mythic and religious imagination, art, rituals, and lives. What these images tell us is that in earliest periods of human consciousness, the creative impulse was imagined as female. . . . In clay, bone, and stone, her body is sculpted with great egg shapes—breast, belly, and buttocks—images of fullness and potential becoming.

—Patricia Reis

The mother of us all,
the oldest of all,
hard,
        splendid as rock
Whatever there is that is of the land
                  it is she
                    who nourishes it,
      It is the Earth
      that I sing.
          —Homer

In the beginning, people prayed to the Creatress of Life, the Mistress of Heaven. At the very dawn of religion, God was woman. Do you remember?

          —Merlin Stone

Since the 1960s a worldwide feminist movement has called into question virtually every cherished institution and belief system of patriarchal culture. In 1974, French feminist Françoise d'Eaubonne coined the term "ecofeminism" to express a theoretical perspective that sees critical links between the domination of nature and the exploitation of women. Early texts by Carolyn Merchant *(The Death of Nature)* and Susan Griffin *(Women and Nature)* documented how modern Western culture associated women and nature, contrasting both to the self-proclaimed rationality, moral superiority, and scientific prowess of "man."

Simultaneously, thinkers such as Mary Daly, Rosemary Radford Ruether, Carol Christ, and Judith Plaskow—as well as countless grassroots activists—brought feminist claims into the realm of established religions. They questioned male power in religious institutions, sexist teachings about gender relationships, and exclusively male images of divinity.

These two tendencies are connected in spiritual ecofeminism, which builds on the premise that patriarchal society dominates women and nature with parallel ideologies and practices. Further, ecofeminism self-consciously values those aspects of women's social and natural experience which allow them to sense and value their connections to the non-human world. Ecofeminist spirituality tends to celebrate the body and the earth. It is highly critical of the familiar hierarchies of Western metaphysics, which privilege the eternal, the immaterial and the (supposedly) rational over the changing, the physical body and the realm of emotional response and empathic connection.

Part IV begins with Rosemary Radford Ruether's overview of the subject, as she traces the lineage of patriarchy in the history of Western religion. Ivone Gebara reinterprets the Trinity from an ecofeminist perspective rooted in Latin America. Shamara Shantu Riley and Karen Baker-Fletcher, in very different ways, relate ecofeminism to the social situation of African-Americans, reminding us that while all people share environmental concerns, the experience of racism, no less than sexism, is often instrumental in determining how and to what degree those concerns are manifest. Irene Diamond and David Seidenberg challenge the conventional wisdom that there is no basis of ecological and feminist wisdom in Judaism. Riane Eisler highlights the feminist attempt to recover in the worship of the goddess a religious form that treasures both women and the earth, and Brooke Medicine Eagle describes her own spiritual initiation. Vandana Shiva describes how women in northern India have defended the forest which is essential to both their physical and cultural existence.

A comparatively recent perspective, spiritual ecofeminism (like all bold new philosophies) faces serious questions. For instance, is the turn to Goddess worship really a rediscovery of the past or simply an invention of the present? Is the association of women with nature likely to support rather than weaken patriarchy's devaluation of women's capacity for instrumental reason and public power? How much of traditional religious life can be transformed by feminism, and how much is beyond redemption?

"ECOFEMINISM: SYMBOLIC AND SOCIAL CONNECTIONS OF THE OPPRESSION OF WOMEN AND THE DOMINATION OF NATURE"

Rosemary Radford Ruether

What is ecofeminism? Ecofeminism represents the union of the radical ecology movement, or what has been called "deep ecology," and feminism. The word "ecology" emerges from the biological science of natural environmental systems. It examines how these natural communities function to sustain a healthy web of life and how they become disrupted, causing death to the plant and animal life. Human intervention is obviously one of the main causes of such disruption. Thus ecology emerged as a combined socioeconomic and biological study in the late sixties to examine how human use of nature is causing pollution of soil, air, and water, and destruction of the natural systems of plants and animals, threatening the base of life on which the human community itself depends (Ehrlich et al. 1973).

Deep ecology takes this study of social ecology another step. It examines the symbolic, psychological, and ethical patterns of destructive relations of humans with nature and how to replace this with a life-affirming culture (Devall and Sessions 1985).

Feminism also is a complex movement with many layers. It can be defined as only a movement within the liberal democratic societies for the full inclusion of women in political rights and economic access to employment. It can be defined more radically in a socialist and liberation tradition as a transformation of the patriarchal socioeconomic system, in which male domination of women is the foundation of all socioeconomic hierarchies (Eisenstein 1979). Feminism can be also studied in terms of culture and consciousness, charting the symbolic, psychological, and ethical connections of domination of women and male monopolization of resources and controlling power. This third level of feminist analysis connects closely with deep ecology. Some would say that feminism is the primary expression of deep ecology (see Doubiago 1989, 40–44).

Yet, although many feminists may make a verbal connection between domination of women and domination of nature, the development of this connection in a broad historical, social, economic, and cultural analysis is only just beginning. Most studies of ecofeminism, such as the essays in *Healing the Wounds: The Promise of Ecofeminism*, are brief and evocative, rather than comprehensive (Plant 1989).

Fuller exploration of ecofeminism probably goes beyond the expertise of one person. It needs a cooperation of a team that brings together historians of culture, natural scientists, and social economists who would all share a concern for the interconnection of domination of women and exploitation of nature. It needs visionaries to imagine how to construct a new socioeconomic system and a new cultural consciousness that would support relations of mutuality, rather than competitive power. For this, one needs poets, artists, and liturgists, as well as revolutionary organizers, to incarnate more life-giving relationships in our cultural consciousness and social system.

Such a range of expertise certainly goes beyond my own competence. Although I am interested in continuing to gain working acquaintance with the natural and social sciences, my primary work lies in the area of history of culture. What I plan to do in this essay is to trace some symbolic connections of domination of women and domination of nature in Mediterranean and Western European culture. I will then explore briefly the alternative ethic and culture that might be envisioned, if we are to overcome these patterns of domination and destructive violence to women and to the natural world.

PRE-HEBRAIC ROOTS

Anthropological studies have suggested that the identification of women with nature and males with culture is both ancient and widespread (Ortner 1974, 67–88). This cultural pattern itself expresses a monopolizing of the definition of culture by males. The very word "nature" in this formula is part of the problem, because it defines nature as a reality below and separated from "man," rather than one nexus in which humanity itself is inseparably embedded. It is, in fact, human beings who cannot live apart from the rest of nature as our life-sustaining context, while the community of plants and animals both can and, for billions of years, did exist without humans. The concept of humans outside of nature is a cultural reversal of natural reality.

How did this reversal take place in our cultural consciousness? One key element of this identification of women with nonhuman nature lies in the early human social patterns in which women's reproductive role as childbearer was tied to making women the primary productive and maintenance workers. Women did most of the work associated with child care, food production and preparation, production of clothing, baskets, and other artifacts of daily life, cleanup, and waste-disposal (French 1985, 25–64).

Although there is considerable variation of these patterns cross-culturally, generally males situated themselves in work that was both more prestigious and more occasional, demanding bursts of energy, such as hunting larger animals, war, and clearing fields, but allowing them more space for leisure. This is the primary social base for the male monopolization of culture, by which men reinforced their privileges of leisure, the superior prestige of their activities, and the inferiority of the activities associated with women.

Perhaps for much of human history, women ignored or discounted these male claims to superiority, being entirely too busy with the tasks of daily life and expressing among themselves their assumptions about the obvious importance of their own work as the primary producers and reproducers (Murphy and Murphy 1974, 111–41). But, by stages, this female consciousness and culture was sunk underneath the growing male power to define the culture for the whole society, socializing both males and females into this male-defined point of view.

It is from the perspective of this male monopoly of culture that the work of women in maintaining the material basis of daily life is defined as an inferior realm. The material world itself is then seen as something separated from males and symbolically linked with women. The earth, as the place from which plant and animal life arises, became linked with the bodies of women, from which babies emerge.

The development of plow agriculture and human slavery very likely took this connection of woman and nature another step. Both are seen as a realm, not on which men depend, but which men dominate and rule over with coercive power. Wild animals which are hunted retain their autonomy and freedom. Domesticated animals become an extension of the human family. But animals yoked and put to the plow, driven under the whip, are now in the new relation to humans. They are enslaved and coerced for their labor.

Plow agriculture generally involves a gender shift in agricultural production. While women monopolized food gathering and gardening, men monopolize food production done with plow animals. With this shift to men as agriculturalists comes a new sense of land as owned by the male family head, passed down through a male line of descent, rather than communal landholding and matrilineal descent that is often found in hunting-gathering and gardening societies (Martin and Voorhies 1975, 276–332).

The conquest and enslavement of other tribal groups created another category of humans, beneath the familiar community, owned by it, whose labor is coerced. Enslavement of other people through military conquest typically took the form of killing the men and enslaving the women and their children for labor and sexual service. Women's work becomes identified with slave work (Lerner 1986, ch. 4). The women of the family are defined as a higher type of slave over a lower category of slaves drawn from conquered people. In patriarchal law, possession of women, slaves, animals, and land all are symbolically and socially linked together. All are species of property and instruments of labor, owned and controlled by male heads of family as a ruling class (see Herlihy 1988, 1–28).

Rosemary Radford Ruether

As we look at the mythologies of the Ancient Near Eastern, Hebrew, Greek, and early Christian cultures, one can see a shifting symbolization of women and nature as spheres to be conquered, ruled over, and finally, repudiated altogether.

In the Babylonian Creation story, which goes back to the third millennium B.C.E., Marduk, the warrior champion of the gods of the city states, is seen as creating the cosmos by conquering the Mother Goddess Tiamat, pictured as a monstrous female animal. Marduk kills her, treads her body underfoot, and then splits it in half, using one half to fashion the starry firmament of the skies, and the other half the earth below (Mendelsohn 1955, 17–46). The elemental mother is literally turned into the matter out of which the cosmos is fashioned (not accidentally, the words *mother* and *matter* have the same etymological root). She can be used as matter only by being killed; that is, by destroying her as "wild," autonomous life, making her life-giving body into "stuff" possessed and controlled by the architect of a male-defined cosmos.

THE HEBRAIC WORLD

The view of nature found in Hebrew Scripture has several cultural layers. But the overall tendency is to see the natural world, together with human society, as something created, shaped, and controlled by God, a God imaged after the patriarchal ruling class. The patriarchal male is entrusted with being the steward and caretaker of nature, but under God, who remains its ultimate creator and Lord. This also means that nature remains partly an uncontrollable realm that can confront human society in destructive droughts and storms. These experiences of nature that transcend human control, bringing destruction to human work, are seen as divine judgment against human sin and unfaithfulness to God (see Isaiah 24).

God acts in the droughts and the storms to bring human work to naught, to punish humans for sin, but also to call humans (that is, Israel) back to faithfulness to God. When Israel learns obedience to God, nature in turn will become benign and fruitful, a source of reliable blessings, rather than unreliable destruction. Nature remains ultimately in God's hands, and only secondarily, and through becoming servants of God, in male hands. yet the symbolization of God as a patriarchal male and Israel as wife, son, and servant of God, creates a basic analogy of woman and nature. God is the ultimate patriarchal Lord, under whom the human patriarchal lord rules over women, children, slaves, and land.

The image of God as single, male, and transcendent, prior to nature, also shifts the symbolic relation of male consciousness to material life. Marduk was a young male god who was produced out of a process of theogony and cosmogony. He conquers and shapes the cosmos out of the body of an older Goddess that existed prior to himself, within which he himself stands. The Hebrew God exists above and prior to the cosmos, shaping it out of a chaos that is under his control. Genesis 2 gives us a parallel view of the male, not as the child of woman, but as the source of woman. She arises out of him, with the help of the male God, and is handed over to him as her Master.[1]

THE GREEK WORLD

When we turn to Greek philosophical myth, the link between mother and matter is made explicit. Plato, in his creation myth, the *Timaeus*, speaks of primal, unformed matter as the receptacle and "nurse" (Plato, 29). He imagines a disembodied male mind as divine architect, or Demiurgos, shaping this matter into the cosmos by fashioning it after the intellectual blueprint of the Eternal Ideas. These Eternal Ideas exist in an immaterial, transcendent world of Mind, separate from and above the material stuff that he is fashioning into the visible cosmos.

The World Soul is also created by the Demiurgos, by mixing together dynamics of antithetical relations (the Same and the Other). This world soul is infused into the body of the cosmos in order to make it move in harmonic motion. The remnants of this world soul are divided into bits, to create the souls of humans. These souls are first placed in the stars, so that human souls will gain knowledge of the Eternal Ideas. Then the souls are sown in the bodies of humans on earth. The task of the soul is to govern the unruly passions that arise from the body.

If the soul succeeds in this task, it will return at death to its native star and there live a life of leisured contemplation. If not, the soul will be reincarnated into the body of a woman or an animal. It will then have to work its way back into the form of an (elite) male and finally escape from bodily reincarnation altogether, to return to its original disincarnate form in the starry realm above (Plato, 23). Plato takes for granted an ontological hierarchy of being, the immaterial intellectual world over material cosmos, and, within this ontological hierarchy, the descending hierarchy of male, female, and animal.

In the Greco-Roman era, a sense of pessimism about the possibility of blessing and well-being within the bodily, historical world deepened in Eastern Mediterranean culture, expressing itself in apocalypticism and gnosticism. In apocalypticism, God is seen as intervening in history to destroy the present sinful and finite world of human society and nature and to create a new heaven and earth freed from both sin and death.[2] In gnosticism, mystical philosophies chart the path to salvation by way of withdrawal of the soul from the body and its passions and its return to an immaterial realm outside of and above the visible cosmos.[3]

CHRISTIANITY

Early Christianity was shaped by both the Hebraic and Greek traditions, including their alienated forms in apocalypticism and gnosticism. Second-century Christianity struggled

Rosemary Radford Ruether

against gnosticism, reaffirming the Hebraic view of nature and body as God's good creation. The second-century Christian theologian Irenaeus sought to combat gnostic anticosmism and to synthesize apocalypticism and Hebraic creationalism. He imaged the whole cosmos as a bodying forth of the Word and Spirit of God, as the sacramental embodiment of the invisible God.

Sin arises through a human denial of this relation to God. But salvific grace, dispensed progressively through the Hebrew and Christian revelations, allows humanity to heal its relation to God. The cosmos, in turn, grows into being a blessed and immortalized manifestation of the divine Word and Spirit, which is its ground of being (Richardson 1953, 1:387–98).

However, Greek and Latin Christianity, increasingly influenced by Neoplatonism, found this materialism distasteful. They deeply imbibed the platonic eschatology of the escape of the soul from the body and its return to a transcendent world outside the earth. The earth and the body must be left behind in order to ascend to another, heavenly world of disembodied life. Even though the Hebrew idea of resurrection of the body was retained, increasingly this notion was envisioned as a vehicle of immortal light for the soul, not the material body, in all its distasteful physical processes, which they saw as the very essence of sin as mortal corruptibility.[4]

The view of women in this ascetic Christian system was profoundly ambivalent. A part of ascetic Christianity imagined women becoming freed from subordination, freed both for equality in salvation and to act as agents of Christian preaching and teaching. But this freedom was based on woman rejecting her sexuality and reproductive role and becoming symbolically male. The classic Christian "good news" to woman as equal to man in Christ was rooted in a misogynist view of female sexuality and reproduction as the essence of the sinful, mortal, corruptible life (see Vogt, 1990).

For most male ascetic Christians, even ascetic woman, who had rejected her sexuality and reproductive role, was too dangerously sexual. Ascetic women were increasingly deprived of their minor roles in public ministry, such as deaconess, and locked away in convents, where obedience to God was to be expressed in total obedience to male ecclesiastical authority. Sexual woman, drawing male seminal power into herself, her womb swelling with new life, became the very essence of sin, corruptibility, and death, from which the male ascetic fled. Eternal life was disembodied male soul, freed from all material underpinnings in the mortal bodily life, represented by woman and nature.

Medieval Latin Christianity was also deeply ambivalent about its view of nature. One side of medieval thought retained something of Irenaeus's sacramental cosmos, which becomes the icon of God through feeding on the redemptive power of Christ in the sacraments of bread and wine. The redeemed cosmos as resurrected body, united with God, is possible only by freeing the body of its sexuality and mortality. Mary, the virgin Mother of Christ, assumed into heaven to reign by the side of her son, was the representative of this redeemed body of the cosmos, the resurrected body of the Church (Semmelroth 1963, 166–68).

But the dark side of Medieval thought saw nature as possessed by demonic powers that draw us down to sin and death through sexual temptation. Women, particularly old crones with sagging breasts and bellies, still perversely retaining their sexual appetites, are the vehicles of the demonic power of nature. They are the witches who sell their souls to the Devil in a satanic parody of the Christian sacraments (Summers 1928).

THE REFORMATION AND THE SCIENTIFIC REVOLUTION

The Calvinist Reformation and the Scientific Revolution in England in the late sixteenth and seventeenth centuries represent key turning points in the Western concept of nature. In these two movements, the Medieval struggle between the sacramental and the demonic views of nature was recast. Calvinism dismembered the Medieval sacramental sense of nature. For Calvinism, nature was totally depraved. There was no residue of divine presence in it that could sustain a natural knowledge or relation to God. Saving knowledge of God descends from on high, beyond nature, in the revealed World available only in Scripture, as preached by the Reformers.

The Calvinist reformers were notable in their iconoclastic hostility toward visual art. Stained glass, statues, and carvings were smashed, and the churches stripped of all visible imagery. Only the disembodied Word, descending from the preacher to the ear of the listener, together with music, could be bearers of divine presence. Nothing one could see, touch, taste, or smell was trustworthy as bearer of the divine. Even the bread and wine were no longer the physical embodiment of Christ, but intellectual reminders of the message about Christ's salvific act enacted in the past.

Calvinism dismantled the sacramental world of Medieval Christianity, but it maintained and reinforced its demonic universe. The fallen world, especially physical nature and other human groups outside of the control of the Calvinist church, lay in the grip of the Devil. All who were labeled pagan, whether Catholics or Indians and Africans, were the playground of demonic powers. But, even within the Calvinist church, women were the gateway of the Devil. If women were completely obedient to their fathers, husbands, ministers, and magistrates, they might be redeemed as goodwives. But in any independence of women lurked heresy and witchcraft. Among Protestants, Calvinists were the primary witch-hunters (Perkins 1590, 1596; see also Carlsen 1980).

The Scientific Revolution at first moved in a different direction, exorcizing the demonic powers from nature in order to reclaim it as an icon of divine reason manifest in natural law (Easlea 1980). But, in the seventeenth and eighteenth centuries, the more animist natural science, which unified material and spiritual, lost out to a strict dualism of transcendent intellect and dead matter. Nature was secularized. It was no longer the scene of a struggle between Christ and the Devil. Both divine and demonic spirits were driven out of it. In Cartesian dualism and Newtonian physics, it becomes matter in motion, dead stuff moving obediently, according to mathematical laws knowable to a new male elite of scientists. With no life or soul of its own, nature could be safely expropriated by this male elite and infinitely reconstructed to augment its wealth and power.

In Western society, the application of science to technological control over nature marched side by side with colonialism. From the sixteenth to the twentieth centuries, Western Europeans would appropriate the lands of the Americas, Asia, and Africa, and reduce their human populations to servitude. The wealth accrued by this vast expropriation of land and labor would fuel new levels of technological revolution, transforming material resources into new forms of energy and mechanical work, control of disease, increasing speed of communication and travel. Western elites grew increasingly optimistic, imagining that this technological way of life would gradually conquer all problems of material scarcity and even push back the limits of human mortality. The Christian dream of immortal blessedness, freed from finite limits, was translated into scientific technological terms (Condorcet 1794).

ECOLOGICAL CRISIS

In a short three-quarters of a century, this dream of infinite progress has been turned into a nightmare. The medical conquest of disease, lessening infant mortality and doubling the life span of the affluent, insufficiently matched by birth limitation, especially among the poor, has created a population explosion that is rapidly outrunning the food supply. Every year 10 million children die of malnutrition.[5] The gap between rich and poor, between the wealthy elites of the industrialized sector and the impoverished masses, especially in the colonized continents of Latin America, Asia, and Africa, grows ever wider (Wilson and Ramphele 1989).

This Western scientific Industrial Revolution has been built on injustice. It has been based on the takeover of the land, its agricultural, metallic, and mineral wealth appropriated through the exploitation of the labor of the indigenous people. This wealth has flowed back to enrich the West, with some for local elites, while the laboring people of these lands grew poorer. This system of global affluence, based on exploitation of the land and labor of the many for the benefit of the few, with its high consumption of energy and waste, cannot be expanded to include the poor without destroying the basis of life of the planet itself. We are literally destroying the air, water, and soil upon which human and planetary life depend.

Rosemary Radford Ruether   395

In order to preserve the unjust monopoly on material resources from the growing protests of the poor, the world became more and more militarized. Most nations have been using the lion's share of their state budgets for weapons, both to guard against one another and to control their own poor. Weapons also become one of the major exports of wealthy nations to poor nations. Poor nations grow increasingly indebted to wealthy nations while buying weapons to repress their own impoverished masses. Population explosion, exhaustion of natural resources, pollution, and state violence are the four horsemen of the new global apocalypse.

The critical question of both justice and survival is how to pull back from this disastrous course and remake our relations with one another and with the earth.

TOWARD AN ECOFEMINIST ETHIC AND CULTURE

There are many elements that need to go into an ecofeminist ethic and culture for a just and sustainable planet. One element is to reshape our dualistic concept of reality as split between soulless matter and transcendent male consciousness. We need to discover our actual reality as latecomers to the planet. The world of nature, plants, and animals existed billions of years before we came on the scene. Nature does not need us to rule over it, but runs itself very well, even better, without humans. We are the parasites on the food chain of life, consuming more and more, and putting too little back to restore and maintain the life system that supports us.

We need to recognize our utter dependence on the great life-producing matrix of the planet in order to learn to reintegrate our human systems of production, consumption, and waste into the ecological patterns by which nature sustains life. This might begin by revisualizing the relation of mind, or human intelligence, to nature. Mind or consciousness is not something that originates in some transcendent world outside of nature, but is the place where nature itself becomes conscious. We need to think of human consciousness not as separating us as a higher species from the rest of nature, but rather as a gift to enable us to learn how to harmonize our needs with the natural system around us, of which we are a dependent part.

Such a reintegration of human consciousness and nature must reshape the concept of God, instead of modeling God after alienated male consciousness, outside of and ruling over nature. God, in ecofeminist spirituality, is the immanent source of life that sustains the whole planetary community. God is neither male nor anthropomorphic. God is the font from which the variety of plants and animals well up in each new generation, the matrix that sustains their life-giving interdependency with one another (McFague 1987, 69–77).

In ecofeminist culture and ethic, mutual interdependency replaces the hierarchies of domination as the model of relationship between men and women, between human groups, and between humans and other beings. All racist, sexist, classist, cultural, and anthropocentric assumptions of the superiority of whites over blacks, males over females, managers over workers, humans over animals and plants, must be discarded. In a real sense, the so-called superior pole in each relation is actually the more dependent side of the relationship.

But it is not enough simply to humbly acknowledge dependency. The pattern of male-female, racial, and class interdependency itself has to be reconstructed socially, creating more equitable sharing in the work and the fruits of work, rather than making one side of the relation the subjugated and impoverished base for the power and wealth of the other.

In terms of male-female relations, this means not simply allowing women more access to public culture, but converting males to an equal share in the tasks of child nurture and household maintenance. A revolution in female roles into the male work world, without a corresponding revolution in male roles, leaves the basic pattern of patriarchal exploitation of women untouched. Women are simply overworked in a new way, expected to do both a male workday, at low pay, and also the unpaid work of women that sustains family life.

There must be a conversion of men to the work of women, along with the conversion of male consciousness to the earth. Such conversions will reshape the symbolic vision of salvation. Instead of salvation sought either in the disembodied soul or the immortalized body, in a flight to heaven or to the end of history, salvation should be seen as continual conversion to the center, to the concrete basis by which we sustain our relation to nature and to one another. In every day and every new generation, we need to remake our relation with one another, finding anew the true nexus of relationality that sustains, rather than exploits and destroys, life (Ruether 1984, 325–35).

Finally, ecofeminist culture must reshape our basic sense of self in relation to the life cycle. The sustaining of an organic community of plant and animal life is a continual cycle of growth and disintegration. The western flight from mortality is a flight from the disintegration side of the life cycle, from accepting ourselves as part of that process. By pretending that we can immortalize ourselves, souls and bodies, we are immortalizing our garbage and polluting the earth. In order to learn to recycle our garbage as fertilizer for new life, as matter for new artifacts, we need to accept our selfhood as participating in the same process. Humans also are finite organisms, centers of experience in a life cycle that must disintegrate back into the nexus of life and arise again in new forms.

These conversions, from alienated, hierarchical dualism to life-sustaining mutuality, will radically change the patterns of patriarchal culture. Basic concepts, such as God, soul-body, and salvation will be reconceived in ways that may bring us much closer to the ethical values of love, justice, and care for the earth. These values have been proclaimed by patriarchal religion, yet contradicted by patriarchal symbolic and social patterns of relationship.

These tentative explorations of symbolic changes must be matched by a new social practice that can incarnate these conversions in new social and technological ways of organizing human life in relation to one another and to nature. This will require a new sense of urgency about the untenability of present patterns of life and compassionate solidarity with those who are its victims.

NOTES

1. Phyllis Trible (1973) views the story of Eve's creation from Adam as essentially egalitarian. For an alternative view from the Jewish tradition, see Reik 1960.

2. For the major writings of inter-testamental apocalyptic, see Charles 1913.

3. For the major gnostic literature, see Robinson 1977.

4. Origen (1966, Bk. 2, ch. 3, 83–94). Also Nyssa, 464–65.

5. Cited in a talk in London, May 29, 1989, by Dr. Nafis Sadik, head of the United Nations Fund for Population Activities. See Broder, 1989.

BIBLIOGRAPHY

Broder, David, 1989. *Chicago Tribune* (May 31), sec. 1, 17.

Carlsen, Carol F. 1980. *The Devil in the Shape of a Woman: The Witch in 17th-Century New England.* Ph.D. Diss. New Haven, Conn.: Yale University.

Charles, R. H. 1913. *The Pseudepigrapha of the Old Testament.* Oxford: Clarendon Press.

Condorcet, Antoine-Nicholas de. 1794. *Sketch for a Historical Picture of the Progress of the Human Mind.*

Devali, Bill, and George Sessions. 1985. *Deep Ecology: Living as if Nature Mattered.* Salt Lake City: Peregrine Smith Books.

Doubiago, Sharon. 1989. "Mama Coyote Talks to the Boys." In Judith Plant, ed. *Healing the Wounds: The Promise of Ecofeminism.* Philadelphia, Pa.: New Society Publishers.

Easlea, Brian. 1980. *Witchhunting, Magic and the New Philosophy.* Highlands, N.J.: Humanities Press.

Ehrlich, Paul R., et al. 1973. *Human Ecology: Problems and Solutions.* San Francisco: W. H. Freeman Co.

Eisenstein, Zillah, ed. 1979. *Capitalist Patriarchy and the Case for Socialist Feminism.* New York: Monthly Review Press.

French, Marilyn. 1985. *Beyond Power: On Women, Men and Morals.* New York: Summit Books.

Gregory of Nyssa. 1893. *On the Soul and the Resurrection.* In *Nicene and Post-Nicene Fathers,* 2nd series, vol 5. New York: Parker.

Herlihy, David. 1988. *Medieval Households.* Cambridge, Mass.: Harvard University Press.

Lerner, Gerda, ed. 1986. *The Creation of Patriarchy.* New York: Oxford University Press.

McFague, Sallie, 1987. *Models of God: Theology for an Ecological, Nuclear Age.* Philadelphia: Fortress Press.

Martin, M. Kay, and Barbara Voorhies. 1975. *Female of the Species.* New York: Columbia University Press.

Mendelsohn, Isaac, ed. 1955. *Religion in the Ancient Near East.* New York: Liberal Arts Press.

Murphy, Yolanda, and Robert Murphy. 1974. *Women of the Forest.* New York: Columbia University Press.

Origen. G. W. Butterworth, ed. 1966. *On First Principles.* New York: Harper and Row.

Rosemary Radford Ruether

Ortner, Sherry. 1974. "Is Female to Male as Nature Is to Culture?" In Michelle Zimbalist Rosaldo and Louise Lamphere, eds. *Woman, Culture and Society*. Stanford, Calif.: Stanford University Press.

Perkins, William. 1590. *Christian Oeconomie*. London.

Plant, Judith, ed. 1989. *Healing the Wounds: The Promise of Ecofeminism*. Philadelphia: New Society Publishers; Toronto: Between the Lines.

Plato. 1937. Timaeus. In B. Jowett, ed. *The Dialogues of Plato*. vol. 2. New York: Random House.

Reik, Theodor. 1960. *The Creation of Woman*. New York: McGraw-Hill.

Richardson, Cyril, ed. 1953. *Early Christian Fathers* 1. Philadelphia: Westminster Press.

Robinson, James M., ed. 1977. *The Nag Hammadi Library*. San Francisco: Harper and Row.

Ruether. 1984. "Envisioning Our Hope: Some Models for the Future." In Janet Kalven and Mary Buckley, eds. *Women's Spirit Bonding*. New York: Pilgrim Press.

Semmelroth, Otto. 1963. *Mary: Archetype of the Church*. New York: Sheed and Ward.

Summers, Montague, ed. 1928. *Malleus Maleficarum*. London: J. Rodker.

Trible, Phyllis. 1973. "Depatriarchalizing in Biblical Interpretation." *Journal of the American Academy of Religion* 41(1) (March).

Vogt, Kari, 1990. "Becoming Male: A Gnostic and Early Christian Metaphor." In Kari Borresen, ed. *Image of God and Gender Models in Judaeo-Christian Tradition*. Oslo: Solum Forlag.

Wilson, Francis, and Mamphela Ramphele, 1989. *Uprooting Poverty: The South African Challenge*. Capetown: David Philip.

"THE TRINITY AND HUMAN EXPERIENCE: AN ECOFEMINIST APPROACH"

Ivone Gebara[1]

> Human beings are a part of the whole we call the Universe, a small region in time and space. They regard themselves, their ideas and their feelings as separate and apart from all the rest. It is something like an optical illusion in their consciousness. This illusion is a sort of prison; it restricts us to our personal aspirations and limits our affective life to a few people very close to us. Our task should be to free ourselves from this prison, opening up our circle of compassion in order to embrace all living creatures and all of nature in its beauty.
>
> —Albert Einstein[2]

When we hear the word Trinity, we immediately associate it with unfathomable mystery. It is part of our faith, but we have trouble relating to it. We've been told that our God is a Trinity who has overcome all loneliness and isolation. We've heard that it is the communion among Father, Son, and Holy Spirit, a beautiful and perfect sharing that we should imitate in our own relationships. Today, this "imitation" seems more and more difficult to understand. It seems to take place so far from ourselves: from our own flesh, our concerns, our limitations. In the final analysis it is a sharing among "persons" who are totally spiritual and perfect. It is, after all, a divine communion.

There is a real fear in all of us of daring to doubt certain ideas, of raising questions about things we were taught that have been set forth as truths we have to accept. Religious institutions often create this fear in us, fettering our ability to think critically about faith issues. The Trinity, and the words Father, Son, and Holy Spirit are like a code that needs to be broken and translated anew. They are symbols that refer to life experiences but their symbolism has grown hazy and has been absolutized within a closed, eminently masculine and arcane theoretical system. I invite you to *dare to think*, above all because this is a deci-

---

Reprinted by permission from *Women Healing the Earth: Third World Women on Ecology* (Maryknoll: Orbis Books, 1996).

sive moment in our history, a moment full of difficult questions and institutional crises, a moment in which the very survival of life is at stake.

For all these reasons, the perspective I adopt in this reflection is *ecofeminism*. In simple and practical terms, I'd like to show that there is a need to rediscover and reflect on the truly universal aspects of life, on dimensions that reflect what the earth and the cosmos are telling us about themselves, and the things women are vehemently affirming with regard to their own dignity and that of all humanity.

Before I speak of the Trinity I'd like to say a few words about the wonder of being human. I want to remind you that human beings are a fruit of a long process, the evolution of life itself. Life evolved for thousands and thousands of years before the creation of the species to which we belong and which we call human. Within us, life continues to be created: it develops, folds back, and reveals itself in differing cultures and economic, political, social, and cultural organizations. Life itself led humanity to arise from within the whole creative evolutionary process, which is both earthly and cosmic.

The human race carries on this creative expression of life both in itself and in its works. Participating in the creative evolution of life, we re-create ourselves. This is manifest in our ability to reflect and love, in our ethical behavior, and in all the other capabilities that make us what we are.

Living within the context of nature as a whole, we have gradually accumulated significant learnings. We have responded, for example, to the challenge of rivers that stretched before us, separating one place from another: we learned to build bridges. To move on water we built boats, then ships. To cross great distances we built airplanes, and so on. We learned to closely examine our human experience, as well as the lives of insects, animals, and plants; and thus we found ways of living and developing our creativity as we responded to the challenges posed by each situation.

Our learning led us to discover the social causes of poverty, and then to formulate hypotheses aimed at explaining and interpreting history and responding with concrete actions. Our learning also led us to cultivate a sense of wonder and perplexity in the face of the astounding order that marks all of reality.

We ourselves continually re-create the life that is in us. Human culture, in its multiple artistic and literary expressions, bears witness to our admirable creativity. This creativity also exists, albeit in a different form, in the vegetable and animal worlds. We have often been taught, however, that these "other worlds" have little creativity. The real reason for this attitude is that we always think of creativity in human terms and judge everything else on that basis. It would be good, however, if human beings would stop once in a while and reflect on the creativity that is manifest in an orange seed: the memory present in this small, vital center; its ability to develop when conditions are favorable; its ability to adapt to different soils and situations; to become a tree; to produce flowers and fruit, and then once again seeds. The seed's creativity is surely not the same as human creativity, but it clearly participates in the ongoing and awesome creativity of the universe.

The seed planted in the depths of the earth goes through a complex process of transformation, of changes in life and in death, before it breaks through the soil's surface. And when we discover that the seed has become a small plant, we do not remember the entire, arduous process it went through in the bowels of the earth and in its own innermost recesses; neither do we remember its multiple interactions with all the forces of nature.

The same is true of human beings. The things we produce, even the most precious among them, sublime creations such as our religious beliefs, emanate from a long maturation process in which our concern for our immediate needs has always been present. Our extraordinary creativity acquired the ability to produce meanings capable of helping us live out this or that situation. But these meanings are not static realities; they are part of the dynamism of life, and thus they change as well. Of necessity, they undergo transformations in order to respond to life's demands and adapt to new situations as they arise.

The important thing, if we are going to be able to take the next step in our reflection, is to get a clear sense that the *human* meanings of things come from ourselves, as does the human meaning of the entire universe. It is we ourselves who construct our interpretations, our science, our wisdom, our knowledge. It is we ourselves who today affirm one thing and tomorrow correct what we have said. It is we who affirm the image of God as warrior-avenger or as tender and compassionate. It is we, in our ancestors and traditions, who have construed the Trinity as three distinct persons in one God; so too, we can change our way of portraying it as we develop new perceptions.

The Trinity is an expression of our history, of human history, which is both tragic and challenging; but it is a unified Trinity, as if in that unity we were expressing our own desire for harmony and communion with all that exists. It is a communion to which we aspire in the midst of tears, of the experience of pain and suffering, as if that Holy Trinity of which we speak was the expression of a world that is both plural and transformed, harmonized, in which all suffering and pain are overcome, separation and division overcome, every tear wiped away; and in the end God, that is, the One, Love, is all in all.

The Trinity brings multiplicity and the desire for unity into one single and unique movement, as if they were moments within the same breath. Trinity is a name we give to ourselves, a name that is the synthesis of our perception of our own existence. Trinity is a language we build in an attempt to express our awareness of being a multitude and at the same time a unity. Trinity is a word that points to our common origin, our shared substance, our universal breathing within the immense diversity that surrounds each and every one of us, each a unique and original creation, a path along the great road of life.

Trinity is also a word about ourselves, about what we know and live out in our own flesh-and life-stories.

A baptism of fire is one we go through as a result of our inner faithfulness to ourselves. It is a reality that envelops us by virtue of our rediscovery of our deepest self. Within that rediscovery we are reborn in God; we are reborn to the earth, to the cosmos, to history, and to service in the construction of human relationships grounded in justice and mutual respect.

Today, if we are to recover the dynamism of the Trinity, we need to recover the dynamism of our own existence—even at the risk of not managing to formulate our ideas in clear and precise terms. Our great challenge is to accept the insecurity involved in discussing what is real and to seek only the security that comes from dealing with the here and now, with daily life, with our own experiences and with our questions, heeding that wise phrase from the Hebrew world, "sufficient to the day is its own task."

The Trinity, then, is not three separate persons living in a heaven we cannot locate. It is not three persons different from one another the way we differ as persons. The Father, Son, and Holy Spirit are not of divine stuff as opposed to our human stuff; rather, they are *relationships*, that is, relationships we human beings experience. These relationships are expressed in anthropomorphic style; but the expression is metaphorical and not primarily metaphysical. Within Christian experience, Father, Son, and Holy Spirit are symbolic expressions we use to speak of the profound intuition that all of us share, along with everything that exists, in the same divine breath of life.

RECONSTRUCTING THE MEANING OF THE TRINITY

We speak of "reconstruction" when a human relationship, a piece of land, a city, or even a society needs to remake itself, re-create itself, renew its relational life. Something has happened that has weakened an edifice, a relationship, a bond of friendship. In this sense I'd like to offer a somewhat tentative effort at rebuilding Trinitarian meanings—a reconstruction demanded by the present historical situation. I'd like to propose five reflections on this reconstruction: the Trinity in the cosmos; the Trinity on earth; the Trinity in relationships among peoples and cultures; the Trinity in human relationships; and the Trinity in every person.

The Trinity in the Cosmos

"This universe is a single multiform energetic unfolding of matter, mind, intelligence and life."[3] So says Brian Swimme, a North American astrophysicist who has worked hard to tell the story of the universe in empirical language. He tries to show that as we approach the end of this century, humanity has acquired the ability to tell the story of the universe itself. This is a fundamental step in coming to understand our shared history and in the effort to create a new relationship with the earth, the cosmos, and with all peoples.

At this point I merely want to draw your attention to the unique and multiform structure of the universe that in symbolic and metaphorical terms we could call a "Trinitarian" structure. By Trinitarian structure I mean the reality that constitutes the entire cosmos and all life forms, a reality marked at the same time by multiplicity and by unity, by the differences among all things and their interdependence.

Stars, galaxies, heavenly bodies, planets, satellites, the atmosphere, the seas, rivers, winds, rain, snow, mountains, volcanos—all are expressions of the multiple creativity of the universe; they are profoundly interdependent and interrelated. They are diversity and unity, existing and interrelating in a unique and single movement of continual creativity.

THE TRINITY ON EARTH

Plants, animals, forests, mountains, rivers, and seas form the most diverse combinations in the most remote and varied places. They attract one another, couple with one another, blend with one another, destroy one another, and recreate themselves in species of pale or exuberant colors. They grow and feed on one another's lives, transforming and adapting to one another, dying and rising in many ways within the complex life process to which we all belong. In its stunning mutations, the earth sometimes threatens us and sometimes awes us, sometimes makes us shiver and at other times inspires cries of joy. Spinning around the sun and on its own axis, the earth creates days and seasons and brings forth the most varied forms of life.

The Earth as Trinity: The Trinitarian earth is a movement of continuous creativity, unfolding processes of creation and destruction that are expressions of a single vital process. To grasp the immense creative force in which we are immersed and of which we are an integral part, we need only think of the succession of geological eras, the birth of the continents, the transformation of seas into deserts, the flowering of forests, and the emergence of manifold expressions of vegetable and animal life.

THE TRINITY IN RELATIONSHIPS AMONG PEOPLES AND CULTURES

Whites, blacks, indigenous peoples, Asiatics and *mestizos*, all with different languages, customs, statures and sexes, make up the awesome and diverse human symphony in which, once again, multiplicity and unity are constitutive expressions of the single vital process that sustains us all. Life, in its complex process of evolution, brings about the variety of human groups and invites us to contemplate the luxuriance of our diversity.

If we accept this diversity as part of the Trinitarian structure itself and take it seriously as the basic make-up of all beings, there is no way to justify the idea of any being's superiority or inferiority. What we have now is cosmic citizenship. We are merely "cosmics," terrestrials, members of the cosmos and of the earth; we need one another, and can exist only on the basis of a community of being, of interdependence among our differences.

I am convinced that if we were to try to develop this idea of cosmic citizenship, we could more easily overcome the different strains of racism, anti-racisim, xenophobia, exclusion, violence, and sexism that are rife in our culture. A new sense of citizenship needs to be born and grow in us, without denying the national affiliations that are still part of our history.

The pluralism that makes us a human species is Trinity: it is the symbolic expression of a single and multiple reality that is an essential component of our living tissue. This plurality is essential if human life itself is to continue on, if the different races and cultures are to develop, support one another and enter into communion.

THE TRINITY IN HUMAN RELATIONSHIPS

The Trinitarian mystery is also found in intimate I-thou relationships. We are I-thou and mystery—the mystery of our presence to the world, to the universe, to ourselves. We are the mystery of our stories, our traditions, our questions. We are I, thou, and mystery, and therefore Trinity, in the closeness and allure of a profound relationship that leads us to a deeper level of intimacy, of desire to know one another, of tender sharing. For this reason, knowing one another requires not only time, patience and dialogue but a constant and challenging investment of ourselves. We are challenged to enter into a process of shared self-revelation, of unmasking ourselves, of manifesting an ever greater part of ourselves. We will find that what we reveal is drawn from those things that are known and unknown to ourselves, and therefore to others.

THE TRINITY IN EVERY PERSON

Our own personal being is Trinitarian: it is mysteriously multiple at the same time that it is one. And most important, this extraordinary reality can be seen in the lives of all peoples; it is present in all biological functions, in all cultural and religious processes. This vision gives us a new worldview and a different anthropology, on the basis of which we see ourselves as persons who are *of* the earth and *of* the cosmos, participants in the extraordinary process of life's evolution. "The new heavens and the new earth" are always on the way: they were coming to be yesterday, they are coming to be today, and they will be on the way tomorrow. Heaven is not opposed to earth; it does not present itself as something superior or as the final aim of our efforts, the place where we will at last enter into a state of divine peace and harmony.

THE CELEBRATION OF LIFE

By trying to understand the Trinity as a human experience, as an experience of the earth and of the cosmos, we are able to celebrate life in a new way. "In a new way" means we ourselves are celebrated as we celebrate life in the Trinity. It means, too, that we experience a broader oneness with the life processes that are beyond our own boundaries. We praise ourselves; we praise the earth; we praise all beings as we raise our voices in praise of the Trinity, using the symbolic language that is most dear to us. We include ourselves in the celebration. It is not just something apart from us; it starts with our own existential experience, in our communion with all forms of life and all the cosmic energies.

THE TRINITY AND THE PROBLEM OF EVIL

The ancient problem of evil is very much with us today, above all because, as I pointed out previously, we see an increase in the destruction of persons, of groups, and of the earth itself. Our society seems ever less capable of devising formulas that permit dignified human sharing and the possibility of survival on the earth. We have the impression that our present world, despite its theories, its analyses and its designs, has turned ever more often to violence and exclusion in order to solve its problems. This in turn has brought about a growing wave of destruction, greater than at any other time in history. The wretched of the earth, the hungry, the landless, the unemployed—those who thirst for justice—feel ever more acutely the silence of God even when, hoping beyond all hope, they continue to speak of God's justice.

A Trinitarian vision of the universe and of humanity does not identify evil, destruction, and suffering as realities that are outside ourselves and need to be eliminated through violence; neither does it say they should be accepted as God's will. Rather than point to "the other" as the source of evil, it recognizes that what we call evil is in ourselves; in a certain sense evil is also our body. Evil is a relationship we ourselves construct; it leads to the destruction not only of the individual but of the entire fabric of human life.

The Trinitarian view of the universe places us at the very energy source of all that exists. At the same time it makes a distinction: on the one hand is the creative-destructive process that is inherent in the evolution of life itself; on the other is moral evil, evil defined in ethical terms. The latter refers to human evil, the evil worked by ourselves: actions that, when combined with our inherent frailty, can make us murderers of life in all its multiple expressions.

When we speak of human beings, we always speak in terms of good and evil. But when we speak of the cosmos, of the universe, we need to speak of forces that are at once creative and destructive. This constitutive reality of the universe, these positive and negative poles (we use these terms with an awareness of the limitations of our language) are inseparable in all the life processes. The birth of our solar system required the destruction of others. The appearance of a desert region may mean the death of a river. The use of fish as food may require the destruction of many of them, and so on.

The fact that we are the "consciousness" or the thinking process of the universe leads us to label things good or evil according to the way they affect us. Today we need to have another look at these reflections in the light of our contemporary historical situation and our more global and articulated sense of the life processes.

Ethical evil is evil wrought by human beings. On the one hand, it arises from the dynamics of life itself and from our human condition of frailty, dependence, and interdependence. On the other, the Christian tradition has always taught that evil actions arise out of our selfishness and the excesses of our passions.

But ethical evil is also a result of our very limited understanding of ourselves and our relationship with all other beings. We have acquired a highly developed sense of our individuality, of our superiority or inferiority, but have relatively little sense of our collective nature, of the way in which our communion with everything else assures our survival and shared happiness.

Because of our narrow affirmation of our personal, racial, religious, and even class identity, we have created systems to protect ourselves from one another—the systems based on greed or on the perceived superiority of those who regard themselves as "the strongest" or "the finest." These systems do not allow us to perceive the ephemeral nature of our individual lives and projects. Instead, we exalt the individual and regard the most powerful, wealthy, or brilliant individuals as absolutes, quasi-divinities to be protected against all the ebbs and flows of history.

From this perspective we developed the idea of a God who is above and presides over history. This in turn led us to construct an image of a just divinity outside our world—a powerful deity often fashioned in the image of the powerful of this world. This God, who is also an "individual," is always just, strong and good—the very opposite of our fragility and depravity. This is the God of theodicy, a God who is very difficult to reconcile with the tragic reality of human history. It is a God whose goodness "in itself" must always be affirmed and defended, as if in defending the goodness of a supreme being we could guarantee our escape from our own tragic iniquity.

The poor continue to bend their knees before this deity, begging for mercy, clemency, and help in satisfying their most basic needs and harboring the spark of hope in their daily lives. They act toward this God much the way they act toward the powerful of this world, hoping to be treated with consideration and left with some prospect of earning their bread with dignity. The poor are slaves of many masters and, by analogy, also of a supreme master.

To leave behind this crude and highly patriarchal, hierarchical, materialistic, individualistic, dependent, and class-biased understanding of God and of the Trinity seems to me an essential step for the present and the future. Above all this is a spiritual path, a personal and collective empowerment that opens us to a wider and freer perspective. By "spiritual path" I mean a path that transforms our inner convictions, a demanding path that goes beyond adherence to a political party's program or obedience to a code of canon law. It is a spiritual path because it is the path of the Spirit, which blows freely where it will; no one can hold back its movement. It is a spiritual path because it is the path of God in each and all of us.

We are constantly being invited to return to our roots: to communion with the earth, with all peoples and with all living things; to realize that transcendence is not a reality "out there," isolated, "in itself," superior to all that exists, but a transcendence within us, among us, in the earth, in the cosmos, everywhere. That transcendence is here and now, among those who are similar to us and different from us, among plants and animals, rivers and seas. That transcendence invites us to reach beyond the limitations of our selfishness and respond to our call to a new collective ethic centered on saving all of life. That transcendence is a canticle, a symphony unceasingly played by the infinite creativity of *Life*.

What, then, is evil in this traditional yet novel perspective? Within this perspective, what we call evil is the unbalanced situation in which we find ourselves, our millennial thirst for individual power and our millennial hunger to eat more and more while preventing others from consuming their rightful share.

The basic evil propagated by our species originates in the desire to possess life and make it our own—selfishly. It is the appropriation of goods by individuals and groups— the self-appointed proprietors of the earth—of other persons and groups, whom the dominant regard as of secondary importance. Evil is the growing dysfunctionality in both personal and social life that leads me to the narcissistic cultivation of my own individuality and my ecclesiastical, political, or business interests.

Evil is the excess or abundance that is held back and hoarded, whether it be food, land, power, knowledge, or pleasure. It remains in the hands of the owners of capital: those who, with the support of their direct and indirect accomplices, present themselves as veritable gods upon the earth.

Evil is the idolatry of the individual, of the "pure" race, of the messianic people, of the empire that dominates by insinuating itself into everything, even into people's inner being, inducing them to believe in their own inferiority. Evil is the ascendancy of one sex over another, its domination over all personal, social, political, and economic realms.

Evil is the proclamation and imposition of my gods as eternal and exclusive, capable of saving all of humanity. Evil is the claim that some people know the will of God and are commissioned to teach it as irrefutable dogma, while others are obligated to humbly recognize and accept their own ignorance.

Human evil leaves us perplexed. It poses innumerable questions, many of them unanswerable. Cosmic "evil," on the other hand, is the creation-destruction process inherent in the universe, and it only frightens us when we suffer its consequences.

Cosmic evil has two faces: it is rooted in the Trinity we are and in the humanity and divinity we participate in. This evil is the negative aspect or, to use a different term, the emptiness found everywhere in the universe, on earth, and among human persons. This emptiness opens the way for opposition, conflict, tension, and destruction; but at the same time it bears extraordinary creative possibilities for the unfolding of our sensitivities and the opening of our inner being to that which is beyond ourselves.

In some way, too, things that appear negative have an energy capable of developing within us the capacity for loving others, bending to those who have fallen in the street, taking in an abandoned child, replanting a ravaged forest, cleaning up a polluted river, or feeding animals during a time of drought. Out of the garbage we accumulate, a flower can bloom; dry bones can return to life; the horror of war can become a cradle of compassion. We ourselves and the whole universe are made up of the same energy, an energy that is both positively and negatively charged. This very energy continually creates and re-creates the earth and human existence.

Human history bears witness to the fact that great gestures of mercy and tenderness are born of dramatic, life-threatening situations. When another's pain becomes unbearable, it becomes my pain and stimulates the birth of loving gestures. The Buddha, Jesus, Mohammed, the thousand Francises, Clares and Theresas, the ever-present unnamed saints turn pain into a source of compassion, mercy, and new prospects for life.

This new vision, which is present in our reflection on the Trinity, helps us leave behind the dualistic and confining anthropocentrism that has characterized our Western Christian tradition, a dualism that not only regards the dyad God and humanity as opposites but does the same to the dyads spirit and matter, man and woman, and good and evil. Throughout the course of our history, dualism has engendered a thousand and one antitheses.

The saying attributed to Jesus of Nazareth, "Love your neighbor as yourself," should be taken up by us and understood as the way back to a Trinitarian balance. If we have excessive love for ourselves, we will fall into a sort of unlimited narcissism and the virtually implacable destruction of others. We will continue to build empires: Nazism, fascism, racism, classism, *machismo*, and all kinds of excesses that end up turning back on us, and above all, on the poor. A balance between I and thou, I and we, we and they, ourselves and the earth is the way to turn around and allow the human, as well as plants and animals and all the creative energies of the earth, to flourish anew.

This new vision calls on us to see the universe as our body, the earth as our body, the variety of human groups as our body—a body that is in evolution, in creative ecstasy, in the midst of destructive and regenerative labor, of death and resurrection. Everything is our body, our Trinitarian body: it is a continual tension and communion of multiplicity and unity, all within the ecstatic and mysterious adventure of Life.

CONCLUSION

In conclusion I want to express a hope-filled certainty. At the end of this millennium we are beginning to work together, as peoples from many parts of the earth, to build a new spirituality. It looks, in fact, like a new Pentecost; but it is a slow-moving Pentecost: patient, universal, at times almost imperceptible. It is an inner and outer Pentecost that bursts open our religious boundaries. It begins not only to change our understanding of the world and of ourselves, but to modify our behavior. All this is spirituality, that is, an energy that puts order in our lives, that gives meaning, that awakens in us the desire to help others to discover the "pearl of great price" hidden in our own bodies and in earth's body. We know that when people find their personal and collective "pearl," they "sell all they have" in order to obtain it. The pearl is the symbolic expression of the new spirituality that is growing in our own bodies, nourished by our human energies, by the earth, by the cosmos—in the last analysis, by the indissoluble one and multiple Trinitarian energy that is present in all that exists.

The Trinity is our primary creative reality, a constitutive reality, a reality that permeates all we do and are. A Trinity of things old and new, of stories and tales that evolve and are organized in many creative ways. The ecofeminist perspective, which is an intimate connection between feminist thought and ecology, opens us not only to the possibility of real equality between men and women of different cultures, but to a different relationship between ourselves, the earth, and the entire cosmos. This new relationship, which is still in its embryonic stages, aims at going beyond merely speculative discussions, which do not lead to a change in relationships.

We are tired of sterile religious-scientific discourse, of its powers grounded in an All-Powerful, One and Trinitarian God, distant and apart from ourselves. We are tired, to use the words of Arnaldo Jabor, of seeing the world "divided between those who bewail hell and those who live in it."[4] This refers to the hell of our society, which kills Indians, children, and entire peoples; but which can also produce individuals who designate themselves as the "conscience" of society and as critics of its ills, and who speak in the name of God but fail to recognize either the blasphemy they commit or the complicity that flaws their beliefs.

410   *Ivone Gebara*

The important thing is to renew our lives daily, with tenderness, responsibility, keenness, and great passion, to experience daily our struggle to defend the extraordinary Life that is within us, in the unity in multiplicity of all things.

—Translated by David J. Molineaux

NOTES

1. An abridged version of a long essay originally published in Portuguese as *Trinidade, palavra sobre coisas velhas e novas: Uma perspectiva ecofeminista.* São Paulo: Paulinas, 1994.

2. Cited by Peter Russel in *Odespertar da terra: O cerebro global.* São Paulo: Ed. Cultrix, 1991.

3. Swimme, Brian, *The Universe Is a Green Dragon.* Santa Fe: Bear & Co., 1984, p. 28.

4. Jabor, Arnaldo, "*Todos temos inveja da paz dos ianomamis,*" in *Jornal do Commercio,* Recife: Aug. 25, 1993.

"ECOLOGY IS A SISTAH'S ISSUE TOO: THE POLITICS OF EMERGENT AFROCENTRIC ECOWOMANISM"

Shamara Shantu Riley

Black womanists, like everyone in general, can no longer overlook the extreme threat to life on this planet and its particular repercussions on people of African descent.[1] Because of the race for increased "development," our world continues to suffer the consequences of such environmental disasters as the Chernobyl nuclear meltdown and Brazil's dwindling forests. Twenty percent of all species are at risk of extinction by the year 2000, with the rate of plant and animal extinction likely to reach several hundred per day in the next ten to thirty years (Worldwatch 1987, 3). Manufacturing chemicals and other abuses to the environment continue to weaken the ozone layer. We must also contend with the phenomenon of climate change, with its attendant rise in sea levels and changes in food production patterns.

Along with these tragic statistics, however, are additional environmental concerns that hit far closer to home than many Black people realize. In the United States, poor people of color are disproportionately likely to be the victims of pollution, as toxic waste is being consciously directed at our communities. The nation's largest hazardous-waste dump, which has received toxic material from 45 states, is located in predominantly black Sumter County, Alabama (de la Pena and Davis 1990, 34). The mostly African-American residents in the 85-mile area between Baton Rouge and New Orleans, better known as Cancer Alley, live in a region which contains 136 chemical companies and refineries. A 1987 study conducted by the United Church of Christ's Commission for Racial Justice found that two-thirds of all Blacks and Latinos in the United States reside in areas with one or more unregulated toxic-waste sites (Riley 1991, 15). The CRJ report also cited race as the most significant variable in differentiating communities with such sites from those without them. Partly as a result of living with toxic waste in disproportionate numbers, African-Americans have higher rates of cancer, birth defects, and lead poisoning than the United States population as a whole.[2]

On the African continent, rampant deforestation and soil erosion continue to contribute to the hunger and poverty rates in many countries. The elephant population is rapidly being reduced as poachers kill them to satisfy industrialized nations' ivory trade demands (Joyce 1989, 22). Spreading to a dozen African nations, the Green Belt Movement is seeking to reverse the environmental damage created by the European settlers during colonialism, when the settlers brought nonindigenous trees on the continent. As with United States communities of color, many African nations experience "economic blackmail," which occurs when big business promises jobs and money to "impoverished areas in return for these areas' support of or acquiescence to environmentally undesirable industries" (Meyer 1992, 32).

The extinction of species on our ancestral continent, the "mortality of wealth," and hazardous-waste contamination in our backyards ought to be reasons enough for Black womanists to consider the environment as a central issue of our political agendas.[3] However, there are other reasons the environment should be central to our struggles for social justice. The global environmental crisis is related to the sociopolitical systems of fear and hatred of all that is natural, nonwhite, and female that has pervaded dominant Western thought for centuries.[4] I contend that the social constructions of race, gender, class and nonhuman nature in mainstream Western thought are interconnected by an ideology of domination. Specific instances of the emergent Afrocentric ecowomanist activism in Africa and the United States, as well as West African spiritual principles that propose a method of overcoming dualism, will be discussed in this paper.

THE PROBLEM OF NATURE FOR BLACK WOMANISM

Until recently, few Black womanists gave more than token attention to environmental issues. At least in the United States, the origins of such oversight stem from the traditional Black association of environmentalism as a "white" concern. The resistance by many United States Blacks to the environmental movement may partly originate from a hope of revenge. Because of our acute oppression(s), many Blacks may conclude that if the world comes to an end because of willful negligence, at least there is the satisfaction that one's oppressors will also die. In "Only Justice Can Stop a Curse," author Alice Walker discusses how her life experiences with the Eurocentric, masculinist ideology of domination have often caused her to be indifferent to environmental issues:

> I think . . . Let the earth marinate in poisons. Let the bombs cover the ground like rain. For nothing short of total destruction will ever teach them anything. (Walker 1983b, 341)

However, Walker later articulates that since environmental degradation doesn't make a distinction between oppressors and the oppressed, it should be very difficult for people of color to embrace the thought of extinction of all life forms simply for revenge.

In advocating a reformulation of how humans view nonhuman nature, ecofeminist theorist Ynestra King states that from the beginning, women have had to grapple with the historical projection of human concepts onto the natural, which were later used to fortify masculinist notions about females' nature (King 1989, 118). The same problem is applicable to people of color, who have also been negatively identified with the natural in white supremacist ideologies.

Black women in particular have historically been associated with animality and subsequently objectified to uphold notions of racial purity; bell hooks articulates that since the 1500s, Western societies have viewed Black women's bodies as objects to be subdued and controlled like nonhuman nature:

> From slavery to the present day, the Black female body has been seen in Western eyes as the quintessential symbol of a "natural" female presence that is organic, closer to nature, animalistic, primitive. (hooks and West 1991, 153)

Patricia Hill Collins asserts that white exploitation of Black women as breeders during the Slave Era "objectified [Black women] as less than human because only animals can be bred against their will" (Collins 1990, 167). Sarah Bartmann, an African woman also known as the Hottentot Venus, was prominently displayed at elite Parisian parties. While being reduced to her sexual parts, Bartmann's protruding buttocks were often offered as "proof" that Blacks were closer to animals than whites. After her death in 1815, Bartmann was dissected, and her genitalia and buttocks remain on display in Paris (Gilman 1985). Bartmann's situation was similar to the predicament of Black female slaves who stood on auction blocks as masters described their productive body parts as humans do cattle. The historical dissection of Black women, be it symbolic or actual, to uphold white supremacist notions is interconnected with the consistent human view of nonhuman animals as scientific material to be dissected through an ideology that asserts both groups are inferior.

Because of the historical and current treatment of Blacks in dominant Western ideology, Black womanists must confront the dilemma of whether we should strive to sever or reinforce the traditional association of Black people with nature that exists in dominant Western thought. However, what we need is not a total disassociation of people from nature, but rather a reformulation of *everyone's* relationship to nature by socially reconstructing gender, class, and ethnic roles.

Environmentalism is a women's issue because females (especially those of color) are the principal farm laborers around the world, as well as the majority of the world's major consumers of agricultural products (Bizot 1992, 36). Environmentalism is also an important issue for people of color because we disproportionately bear the brunt of environmental degradation. For most of the world's population, reclaiming the Earth is not an abstract state of affairs but rather is inextricably tied to the survival of our peoples.

Womanism and ecology have a common theoretical approach in that both see all parts of a matrix as having equal value. Ecology asserts that without each element in the ecosystem, the biosphere as a whole cannot function properly. Meanwhile, womanism asserts the equality of races, genders, and sexual preferences, among other variables. There is no use in womanists advocating liberation politics if the planet cannot support people's liberated lives, and it is equally useless to advocate saving the planet without addressing the social issues that determine the structure of human relations in the world. If the planet as a whole is to survive, we must all begin to see ourselves as interconnected with nonhuman nature and with one another.

THE POLITICS OF NATURE-CULTURE DUALISM

At the foundation of dominant Western thought exists an intense ambivalence over humankind's place in the biosphere, not only in relation to one another, but also in relation to nonhuman nature. The systematic denigration of men of color, women, and nonhuman nature is interconnected through a nature-culture dualism. This system of interconnectedness, which bell hooks labels "the politic of domination," functions along interlocking axes of race, gender, species, and class oppression. The politic of domination "refers to the ideological ground that [the axes] share, which is a belief in domination, and a belief in the notions of superior and inferior, which are components of all those systems" (hooks 1989, 175). Although groups encounter different dimensions of this matrix based on such variables as species or sexual orientation, an overarching relationship nevertheless connects all of these socially constructed variables.

In discussing the origins of Western dualism, Dona Richards articulates the influence of dominant Jewish and Christian thought on Western society's conceptions about its relationship to nonhuman nature:

> Christian thought provides a view of man, nature, and the universe which supports not only the ascendancy of science, but of the technical order, individualism and relentless progress. Emphasis within this world view is placed on humanity's dominance over *all* other beings, which become "objects" in an "objectified" universe. Humanity is separated from nature. (Richards 1980, 69)

With dualistic thinking, humans, nonhuman nature, and ideas are categorized in terms of their difference from one another. However, one part is not simply deemed different from its counterpart; it is also deemed intrinsically *opposed* to its "Other" (Collins 1990, 69). For instance, speciesists constantly point to human neocortical development and the ensuing civilization that this development constructs as proof of human superiority over nonhuman animals. Women's position as other in Western patriarchies throughout the histories of both psychological theory and Christian thought has resulted in us being viewed as defective men.

Women, the nonelite, and men of color are not only socially constructed as the "Others," but the elite, white, male-controlled global political structure also has the power—through institutions such as the international media and politics—to extensively socialize us to view ourselves as others to be dominated. By doing so, the pattern of domination and subjugation is reinforced. Objectification is also central to the process of oppositional difference for all entities cast as other. Dona Richards claims that in dominant Western thought, intense objectification is a "prerequisite for the despiritualization of the universe and through it the Western cosmos was made ready for ever increasing materialization" (Richards 1980, 72). Since one component is deemed to be the other, it is simultaneously viewed as an object to be controlled and dominated, particularly through economic means.

Because nature-culture dualism conceives of nature as an other that (male) human undertakings transcend and conquer, women, nonhuman nature, and men of color become symbolically linked in Eurocentric, masculinist ideology. In this framework, the objectification of the other also serves as an escape from the anxiety of some form of mortality. For instance, white supremacists fear that it will be the death of the white race if people of color, who comprise the majority of the world's population, successfully resist the current global relations of power. Objectifying nonhuman nature by technology is predicated on an intense fear of the body, which reminds humans of death and our connection with the rest of nature. By making products that make tasks easier, one seeks to have more opportunities to live one's life, with time and nature converted into commodities.

World history can be seen as one in which human beings inextricably bind the material domination of nonhuman nature with the economic domination of other human beings. The Eurocentric, masculinist worldview that dominates Western thought tends to only value the parts of reality that can be exploited in the interest of profit, power and control. Not only is that associated with nature deemed amenable to conquest, but it is also a conquest that requires no moral self-examination on the part of the prospective conqueror. For instance, there is very little moral examination by research laboratories that test cosmetics on animals, or by men who assault women. There was also very little moral examination on the part of slave owners on the issue of slavery or by European settlers on colonialism in "Third World" nations.

By defining people of color as more natural and animalistic, a political economy of domination has been historically reinforced. An example of this phenomenon is the founding of the United States and the nation's resultant slave trade. In order for the European colonialists to exploit the American land for their economic interests, they first needed to subjugate the Native American groups who were inhabiting the land. While this was being accomplished, the colonists dominated Blacks by utilizing Africans as slave labor (and simultaneously appropriating much of Mexico) in order to cultivate the land for profit and expand the new capitalist nation's economy. Meanwhile, the buffalo almost became extinct in the process of this nation building "from sea to shining sea."

A salient example of the interconnectedness of environmental degradation and male supremacy is the way many societies attach little value to that which can be exploited without (economic) cost. Because nonhuman nature has historically been viewed by Westerners as a free asset to be possessed, little value has been accredited to it. Work traditionally associated with women via cultural socialization has similarly often been viewed as having little to no value. For instance, in calculating the Gross Domestic Product, no monetary value is attached to women's contributions to national economies through reproduction, housework, or care of children.

THE ROLE OF THE ENVIRONMENTALISMS IN PROVIDING THE FOUNDATION FOR AN AFROCENTRIC WOMANIST AGENDA

While serving as executive director of the United Church of Christ's Commission for Racial Justice in 1987, Reverend Benjamin Chavis, Jr., coined the term *environmental racism* to explain the dynamics of socioeconomic inequities in waste-management policies. Peggy Shephard, the director of West Harlem Environmental Action, defines United States environmental racism as "the policy of siting potentially hazardous facilities in low-income and minority communities" (Day and Knight 1991, 77). However, environmental racism, which is often intertwined with classism, doesn't halt at the boundaries of poor areas of color. Blacks in Africa and the United States often have to contend with predominantly white environmental groups that ignore the connection between their own values and the struggles of people of color to preserve our future, which is a crucial connection in order to build and maintain alliances to reclaim the earth. For instance, because the Environmental Protection Agency is often seen as another institution that perceives elite white communities' complaints as more deserving of attention than poor communities of color, many United States social activists are accusing the EPA of "environmental apartheid" (Riley 1991, 15).

In "Granola Boys, Eco-Dudes, and Me," Elizabeth Larsen articulates how race, class, and gender politics are interconnected by describing the overwhelmingly white middle-class male leadership of mainstream United States environmental groups. In addition to being indifferent to the concerns of people of color and poor whites, the mainstream organizations often reinforce male supremacy by distributing organizational tasks along traditional gender roles (Larsen 1991, 96). The realization that only we can best represent our interests, an eco-identity politics, so to speak, lays the foundation for an Afrocentric ecowomanist agenda.[5] Even though many Black women have been active in the environmental movement in the past, there appears not to be much *published* analysis on their part about the role of patriarchy in environmental degradation. The chief reason for this sentiment may stem from perceiving race as the "primary" oppression. However, there is an emergent group of culturally identified Black women in Africa and the United States who are critically analyzing the social roles of white supremacy, patriarchy, and classism in environmental degradation.

EMERGENT AFROCENTRIC ECOWOMANISM: ON THE NECESSITY OF SURVIVAL

There are several differences between ecofeminism and Afrocentric ecowomanism. While Afrocentric ecowomanism also articulates the links between male supremacy and environmental degradation, it lays far more stress on other distinctive features, such as race and class, that leave an impression markedly different from many ecofeminists' theories.[6]

Many ecofeminists, when analyzing the links between human relations and ecological degradation, give primacy to gender and thus fail to thoroughly incorporate (as opposed to mere tokenism) the historical links between classism, white supremacy, and environmental degradation in their perspectives. For instance, they often don't address the fact that in nations where such variables as ethnicity and class are a central organizing principle of society, many women are not only viewed in opposition to men under dualism, but also to other women. A salient example of this blind spot is Mary Daly's *Gyn/Ecology*, where she implores women to identify with nature against men and live our lives separately from men. However, such an essentialist approach is very problematic for certain groups of women, such as the disabled and Jews, who must ally themselves with men (while simultaneously challenging them on their sexism) in order to combat the isms in their lives. As writer Audre Lorde stated, in her critique of Daly's exclusion of how Black women use Afrocentric spiritual practices as a source of power against the isms while connecting with nonhuman nature:

> to imply, however, that women suffer the same oppression simply because we are women, is
> to lose sight of the many varied tools of patriarchy. It is to ignore how these tools are used by
> women without awareness against each other. (Lorde 1983, 95)

Unlike most white women, Black women are not limited to issues defined by our femaleness but are rather often limited to questions raised about our very humanity.

Although they have somewhat different priorities because of their different environments, Afrocentric ecowomanists in the United States and Africa nevertheless have a common goal—to analyze the issues of social justice that underlie environmental conflict. Not only do Afrocentric ecowomanists seek to avoid detrimental environmental impacts, we also seek to overcome the socioeconomic inequalities that led to the injustices in the first place.

Emergent United States Afrocentric Ecowomanist Activism

Contrary to mainstream United States media claims, which imply that African-Americans are not concerned about ecology, there has been increased environmental activism within Black communities since the early 1980s. Referred to as the environmental equity movement by Robert Bullard, predominantly Black grassroots environmental organizations tend to view environmentalism as an extension of the 1960s civil rights movement. In *Yearning*, bell hooks links environmentalism with social justice while discussing Black radicals and revolutionary politics:

> We are concerned about the fate of the planet, and some of us believe that living simply is part of revolutionary political practice. We have a sense of the sacred. The ground we stand on is shifting, fragile, and unstable. (hooks 1990, 19)

On discussing how the links between environmental concerns and civil rights encouraged her involvement with environmentalism, arts writer and poet Esther Iverem states:

> Soon I began to link civil rights with environmental sanity. . . . Because in 1970 Black folks were vocally fighting for their rightful share of the pie, the logical question for me became "What kind of shape will that pie be in?" (Iverem 1991, 38)

Iverem's question has been foremost in many African-American women's minds as we continue to be instrumental in the Black communities' struggle to ensure that the shape of the social justice pie on our planet will not be increasingly carcinogenic. When her neighborhood started to become dilapidated, Hattie Carthan founded the Magnolia Tree Earth Center of Bed-Stuy in Brooklyn in 1968, to help beautify the area. She planted more than 1,500 trees before her death in 1974. In 1986, the city council of Los Angeles decided that a 13-acre incinerator, which would have burned 2,000 tons of city waste daily, was to be built in a low-income Black and Latino neighborhood in South Central Los Angeles. Upon hearing this decision, residents, mostly women, successfully organized in opposition by forming Concerned Citizens of South Central Los Angeles. While planning direct actions to protest the incinerator, the grass roots organization didn't have a formal leadership structure for close to two years. Be it a conscious or unconscious decision, Concerned Citizens accepted a relatively nonhierarchical, democratic process in their political activism by rotating the chair's position at meetings, a form of decision making characteristic of many ecofeminist groups.[7]

The Philadelphia Community Rehabilitation Corporation (PCRC), founded by Rachel E. Bagby, operates a village community to maintain a nonhierarchical relationship between human and nonhuman nature for its working-class-to-poor urban Black residents. About 5,000 reside in the community, and there is communalistic living, like that of many African villages. PCRC has a "repeopling" program that renovates and rents more than 50 previously vacant homes and also created a twelve-unit shared house. PCRC also takes vacant lots and recycles them into gardens to provide food, and oversees literacy and employment programs. Hazel and Cheryl Johnson founded People for Community Recovery (PCR), which is operated from a storefront at the Altgeld Gardens housing project, after they became aware that their community sits atop a landfill and has the greatest concentration of hazardous waste in the nation. In its fight against environmental racism, PCR has insisted that the Chicago Housing Authority remove all asbestos from the Altgeld homes and has helped lobby city government to declare a moratorium on new landfill permits. PCR also successfully prevented the establishment of another landfill in Altgeld Gardens.

One Black women's organization that addresses environmental issues is the National Black Women's Health Project. The NBWHP expresses its Afrocentric ecowomanist sentiment primarily through its SisteReach program, which seeks to connect the NBWHP with various Black women's organizations around the world. On urging African-American women to participate in the environmental movement and analyze the connections between male supremacy and environmental degradation, Dianne J. Forte, the SisteReach coordinator, makes the following statement:

> At first glance and with all the major problems demanding our energy in our community we may be tempted to say, "this is not my problem." If however, we look at the ominous connection being made between environmental degradation and population growth; if we look at the same time at trends which control women's bodies and lives and control the world's resources, we realize that the same arguments are used to justify both. (Forte 1992, 5)

For instance, women are increasingly being told that we should not have control over our own bodies, while the Earth is simultaneously deemed feminine by scientists who use sexual imagery to articulate their plans to take control over the Earth. Meanwhile, dominant groups often blame environmental degradation on overpopulation (and with their privileged status, usually point at poor women of color), when industrial capitalism and patriarchal control over women's reproduction are among the most pronounced culprits.

The most salient example of practical United States Afrocentric ecowomanism combating such claims is Luisah Teish, a voodoo priestess. In connecting social justice issues with spiritual practices rooted in the West African heritage, Teish articulates the need for everyone to actively eliminate patriarchy, white supremacy, and classism, along with the domination of nonhuman nature. Members of Teish's altar circle have planned urban gardening projects both to supply herbs for their holistic healing remedies and to assist the poor in feeding themselves. They have also engaged in grassroots organizing to stop gentrification in various communities.

EMERGENT AFROCENTRIC ECOWOMANIST ACTIVISM IN AFRICA

On the African continent, women have been at the forefront of the movement to educate people about environmental problems and how they affect their lives. As with much of the African continent, environmental problems in Kenya particularly influence rural women's lives, since they comprise 80 percent of that nation's farmers and fuel gatherers (Maathai 1991, 74). Soil erosion directly affects the women, because they depend on subsistence agriculture for their families' survival. The lack of firewood in many rural areas of Kenya because of deforestation disproportionately alters the lives of women, who must walk long distances to fetch firewood. The lack of water also makes a negative imprint on Kenyan women's lives, because they have to walk long distances to fetch the water.

However, many Kenyan women are striving to alter these current realities. The most prominent Afrocentric ecowomanist in Africa is Wangari Maathai, a Kenyan microbiologist and one of Africa's leading activists on environmental issues. Maathai is the founder and director of the Green Belt Movement (GBM), a fifteen-year-old tree-planting project designed to help poor Kenyan communities stop soil erosion, protect their water systems, and overcome the lack of firewood and building materials.

Launched under the auspices of the National Council of Women of Kenya, the majority of the Green Belt Movement's members are women. Since 1977, these women have grown 10 million trees, 80 percent of which have survived, to offset Kenya's widespread deforestation.[8] Although the Green Belt Movement's primary practical goal is to end desertification and deforestation, it is also committed to promoting public awareness of the relationship between environmental degradation and social problems that affect the Kenyan people—poverty, unemployment, and malnutrition. However, one of the most significant accomplishments of the GBM, Maathai asserts, is that its members are "now independent; had acquired knowledge, techniques; had become empowered" (Maathai 1991, 74).

Another Kenyan dedicated to environmental concerns is Wagaki Mwangi, the founder and coordinator of the International Youth Development and Environment Network. When she visited the University of Illinois at Urbana-Champaign, Mwangi discussed how Kenya suffers economic and environmental predicaments primarily because her homeland is trying to imitate Western cultures. "A culture has been superimposed on a culture," Mwangi said, but there are not enough resources for everyone to live up to the new standards of the neocolonial culture (Schallert 1992, 3). She asserted that in attempts to be more Western, "what [Kenyans] valued as our food has been devalued, and what we are valuing is what they value in the West" (Schallert 1992, 3). For instance, Kenyans used to survive by eating a variety of wild foods, but now many don't consider such foods as staples because of Western influences. In the process, many areas of Kenya are deemed to be suffering from food shortages as the economy has been transformed to consumer capitalism with its attendant mechanization of agriculture.

In Kourfa, Niger, women have been the primary force behind preventing the village from disappearing, a fate that many surrounding villages have suffered because of the Sahel region's desertification. Reduced rainfall and the drying up of watering places and vegetation, combined with violent sandstorms, have virtually deprived Kourfa of harvests for the past five years. As a result, the overwhelming majority of Kourfa's men have had to travel far away for long periods of time to find seasonal work.

With the assistance of the Association of Women of Niger and an agricultural advisor, the women have laid out a small marketgarden around the only well in Kourfa. Despite the few resources at their disposal, the Kourfa women have succeeded in supporting themselves, their children, and the village elders. In response to the survival of the village since these actions, the Kourfa women are now calling for increased action to reverse the region's environmental degradation so "the men won't go away" from the village (Ouedraogo 1992, 38).

AFROCENTRIC ECOMOTHERISTS: ECOWOMANIST POTENTIAL?

The environmental activism of some Black women brings up the question of whether community-oriented Black women who are addressing environmental issues are genuinely Afrocentric ecowomanists or possibly Afrocentric ecomotherists.[9] According to Ann Snitow, motherists are women who, for various reasons, "identify themselves not as feminists but as militant mothers, fighting together for survival" (Snitow 1989, 48). Snitow also maintains that motherism usually arises when men are absent or in times of crisis, when the private sphere role assigned to women under patriarchy makes it impossible for the collective to survive. Since they are faced with the dictates of traditional work but face a lack of resources in which to fulfill their socially prescribed role, motherists become a political force.

Since they took collective action to secure the survival of the village's children and elders only after the necessary absence of Kourfa's men, the activism of the Kourfa women may possibly be based on a motherist philosophy. One can only conjecture whether the

Kourfa women criticized the social role of motherhood in Niger as they became a political force, or if womanist consciousness emerged after their political experiences. Because of their potential to transform into ecowomanists after they enter the political realm, Afrocentic ecomotherists shouldn't be discounted in an analysis of Black women's environmental activism. For instance, Charlotte Bullock contends that she "did not come to the fight against environmental problems as an intellectual but rather as a concerned mother" (Hamilton 1990, 216). However, she and other women in Concerned Citizens of South Central Los Angeles began to notice the sexual politics that attempted to discount their political activism while they were protesting. "I noticed when we first started fighting the issue how the men would laugh at the women . . . they would say, 'Don't pay no attention to them, that's only one or two women . . . they won't make a difference.' But now since we've been fighting for about a year the smiles have gone" (Hamilton 1990, 215). Robin Cannon, another member of Concerned Citizens, asserts that social relations in her home, specifically gender roles on caretaking, were transformed after she began participating in the group's actions (Hamilton 1990, 220).

MOVING BEYOND DUALISM: AN AFROCENTRIC APPROACH

In utilizing spiritual concepts to move beyond dualism, precolonial African cultures, with their both/and perspectives, are useful forms of knowledge for Afrocentric ecowomanists to envision patterns toward interdependence of human and nonhuman nature. Traditional West African cultures, in particular, which also happen to be the ancestral roots of the overwhelming majority of African-Americans, share a belief in nature worship and view all things as being alive on varying levels of existence (Haskins 1978, 30). One example of such an approach in West African traditions is the *Nyam* concept. A root word in many West African languages, *Nyam* connotes an enduring power and energy possessed by all life (Collins 1990, 220). Thus, all forms of life are deemed to possess certain rights, which cannot be violated at will.

In *Jambalaya*, Luisah Teish writes of the *Da* concept, which originates from the Fon people of Western Africa. *Da* is "the energy that carries creation, the force field in which creation takes place" (Teish 1985, 61). In the Fon view, all things are composed of energy provided by *Da*. For example, "the human is receptive to the energy emanating from the rock and the rock is responsive to human influence" (Teish 1985, 62). Because West Africans have traditionally viewed nonhuman nature as sacred and worthy of praise through such cultural media as song and dance, there is also a belief in *Nommo. Nommo* is "the physical-spiritual life force which awakens all 'sleeping' forces and gives physical and spiritual life" (Jahn 1961, 105).

However, with respect for nonhuman nature comes a different understanding of *Ache*, the Yoruba term for human power. *Ache* doesn't connote "power over" or domination, as it often does in mainstream Western thought, but rather power *with* other forms of creation. With *Ache*, Teish states that there is "a regulated kinship among human, animal, mineral, and vegetable life" (Teish 1985, 63). Humans recognize their *Ache* to eat and farm, "but it is also recognized that they must give back that which is given to them" (Teish 1985, 63). In doing so, we respect the overall balance and interdependence of human and nonhuman nature.

These concepts can be useful for Afrocentric ecowomanists not only in educating our peoples about environmental issues, but also in reclaiming the cultural traditions of our ancestors. Rachel Bagby states the positivity of humans connecting with nonhuman nature, a view that is interwoven in her organization's work:

> If you can appreciate the Earth, you can appreciate the beauty of yourself. The same creator created both. And if I learned to take care of that I'll also take care of myself and help take care of others. (Bagby 1990, 242)

Illustrating an outlook of planetary relations that is parallel to the traditional West African worldview, Bagby simultaneously reveals the continuous link between much of the African–American religious tradition and African spirituality.

In light of the relations of power and privilege that exist in the world, the appropriation of indigenous cultures by some ecofeminists must be addressed. Many womanists, such as Andy Smith and Luisah Teish, have criticized cultural feminists for inventing earth-based feminist spiritualities that are based on the exploitation of our ancestral traditions, while we're struggling to reclaim and defend our cultures from white supremacy. In "For All Those Who Were Indian in Another Life," Smith asserts that this appropriation of non-Western spiritual traditions functions as a way for many white women to avoid taking responsibility for being simultaneously oppressive as well as oppressed (see her article, pp. 168–71). White ecofeminists can reclaim their own pre-Christian European cultures, such as the Wiccan tradition, for similar concepts of interconnectedness, community, and immanence found in West African traditions.[10]

Adopting these concepts would transform humans' relationship to nonhuman nature in a variety of ways. By seeing all components of the ecosystem affecting and being affected by one another, such a world perspective demonstrates a pattern of living in harmony with the rest of nature, instead of seeking to disconnect from it. By viewing ourselves as a part of nature, we would be able to move beyond the Western disdain for the body and therefore not ravage the Earth's body as a result of this disdain and fear. We would realize that the Earth is not merely the source of our survival, but also has intrinsic value and must be treated with respect, as it is our elder.

The notion of community would help us to appreciate the biological and cultural diversity that sustains life. Because every entity is viewed as embodying spirituality under immanence, culture wouldn't be viewed as separate from, and superior to, nature, as it is seen in mainstream Western religions. Communalism would also aid us in reformulating the social constructions of race, gender, species, class (among other variables), which keep groups separate from one another. And finally, the environmental movement in particular would view politics as rooted in community and communally take actions to reclaim the Earth and move toward a life of interdependence for generations to come.

NOTES

I would like to acknowledge the help that Carol Adams has given me with this essay. Her reading suggested valuable changes in the structure of the paper as well as clearing up minor flaws in writing. She also suggested some references that would augment my claims.

1.   Alice Walker's definition of womanist is a feminist of color who is "committed to the survival and wholeness of entire people, male *and* female" (Walker 1983a, xi–xii). University of Ibadan (Nigeria) English senior lecturer Chikwenye Okonjo Ogunyemi contends that "black womanism is a philosophy that celebrates black roots . . . It concerns itself as much with the black sexual power tussle as with the world power structure that subjugates blacks" (Ogunyemi 1985, 72). Since feminism often gives primacy to gender, and race consciousness often gives primacy to race, such limitations in terminology have caused many women of color to adopt the term *womanist*, which both Walker and Ogunyemi independently coined in the early 1980s. Although some of the women in this paper refer to themselves as feminists rather than womanists, or use both terms interchangeably, I am using the term *womanist* in an interpretative sense to signify a culturally identified woman of color who also critically analyzes the sexual politics within her respective ethnic group.

2.   For a discussion of how toxic waste has affected the environmental health of United States Black communities, see Day and Knight (1991).

3.   Robert Bullard (1990) contends that the mortality of wealth involves toxic-waste dumping to pursue profits at the expense of others, usually low-income people of color in the United States. Because this demographic group is less likely to have economic resources and political clout, it can't fight back as easily as more affluent communities that possess white skin privileges. I think this term is also applicable to the economic nature of toxic dumping in "Third World" countries, which are basically disempowered in the global political process.

4.   For an ecofeminist text that makes a similar claim, see King (1989).

5.   My definition of an Afrocentric ecowomanist is a communalistic-oriented Black woman who understands and articulates the interconnectedness of the degradation of people of color, women, and the environment. In addition to articulating this interconnectedness, an Afrocentric ecowomanist also strives to eradicate this degradation. For an extensive discussion of Afrocentrism, see Myers (1988).

6.   An example of this distinction can be seen in Davies (1988). In her article, Davies only discusses the interconnections between gender and nature and completely avoids analyzing how such variables as ethnicity and class influence the experience of gender in one's life.

7.   For several descriptions of the political decision making within feminist peace organizations, see the essays in Harris and King (1989).

8.   It is noteworthy that the seedlings come from over 1,500 tree nurseries, 99 percent of which are operated by women. In addition, the women are given a small payment for the trees that survive.

9.   In comparison to an Afrocentric ecowomanist, I define an Afrocentric ecomotherist as a communalistic-oriented Black woman who is involved in saving the environment and challenging white supremacy, but who does not challenge the fundamental dynamics of sexual politics in women's lives.

10.   For instance, Starhawk, a practitioner of the Wiccan tradition, has written about her spiritual beliefs (1990).

BIBLIOGRAPHY

Bagby, Rachel. 1990. "Daughters of Growing Things." In Irene Diamond and Gloria Feman Orenstein, eds., *Reweaving the World: The Emergence of Ecofeminism.* San Francisco: Sierra Club Books.

Bullard, Robert. 1990. *Dumping in Dixie: Race, Class and Environmental Quality.* Boulder, Colo.: Westview Press.

Collins, Patricia Hill. 1990. *Black Feminist Thought: Knowledge, Consciousness, and the Politics of Empowerment.* Boston: Unwin Hyman.

Davies, Katherine. 1988. "What Is Ecofeminism?" *Women and Environments* 10(3): 4–6.

Day, Barbara, and Kimberly Knight. 1991. "The Rain Forest in Our Back Yard." *Essence* 21 (Jan.): 75–77.

de la Pena, Nonny, and Susan Davis. 1990. "The Greens Are White: And Minorities Want In." *Newsweek* 116 (Oct. 15): 34.

Forte, Dianne J. 1992. "SisteReach . . . Because 500 Years Is Enough." *Vital Signs: News from the National Black Women's Health Project* 1 (Spring): 5.

Gilman, Sander L. 1985. "Black Bodies, White Bodies: Toward an Iconography of Female Sexuality in Late Nineteenth-Century Art, Medicine and Literature." *Critical Inquiry* 12 (Autumn): 205–43.

Hamilton, Cynthia. 1990. "Women, Home and Community: The Struggle in an Urban Environment." In Irene Diamond and Gloria Feman Orenstein, eds. *Reweaving the World: The Emergence of Ecofeminism.* San Francisco: Sierra Club Books.

Harris, Adrienne, and Ynestra King, eds., 1989. *Rocking the Ship of State: Toward a Feminist Peace Politics.* Boulder, Colo.: Westview Press.

hooks, bell. 1989. *Talking Back: Thinking Feminist, Thinking Black.* Boston: South End Press.

———. 1990. *Yearning: Race, Gender and Cultural Politics.* Boston: South End Press.

hooks, bell, and Cornell West. 1991. *Breaking Bread: Insurgent Black Intellectual Life.* Boston: South End Press.

Iverem, Esther. 1991. "By Earth Obsessed." *Essence* 22 (Sept.): 37–38.

Jahn, Janheinz. 1961. *Muntu: The New African Culture.* New York: Grove Press.

Joyce, Christopher. 1989. "Africans Call for End to the Ivory Trade." *New Scientist* 122 (June 10): 22.

King, Ynestra. 1989. "Healing the Wounds: Feminism, Ecology, and the Nature/Culture Dualism." In Alison M. Jaggar and Susan R. Bordo, eds. *Gender/Body/Knowledge: Feminist Reconstructions of Being and Knowing.* New Brunswick, N.J.: Rutgers University Press.

Larsen, Elizabeth. 1991. "Granola Boys, Eco-Dudes, and Me." *Ms.* 2 (July/Aug.), 96–97.

Lorde, Audre. 1983. "An Open Letter to Mary Daly." In Cherríe Moraga and Gloria Anzaldua, eds. *This Bridge Called My Back: Writings by Radical Women of Color.* New York: Kitchen Table Press.

Maathai, Wangari. 1991. "Foresters Without Diplomas." *Ms.* 1 (Mar./Apr.), 74–75.

Meyer, Eugene L. 1992. "Environmental Racism: Why Is It Always Dumped In Our Backyard? Minority Groups Take a Stand." *Audubon* 94 (Jan./Feb.): 30–32.

Myers, Linda James. 1988. *Understanding an Afrocentric Worldview: Introduction to an Optimal Psychology*. Dubuque, Iowa: Kendall/Hunt.

Ogunyemi, Chikwenye Okonjo. 1985. "Womanism: The Dynamics of the Contemporary Black Female Novel in English." *Signs: Journal of Women in Culture and Society* 11 (Autumn): 63–80.

Ouedraogo, Josephine. 1992. "Sahel Women Fight Desert Advance." *UNESCO Courier* 45 (March): 38.

Richards, Dona. 1980. "European Mythology: The Ideology of 'Progress.'" In Molefi Kete Asante and Abdulai Sa Vandi, eds. *Contemporary Black Thought*. Beverly Hills, Calif.: Sage.

Riley, Shay. 1991. "Eco-Racists Use Fatal Tactics." *Daily Illini* 121 (Sept. 4), 15.

Schallert, K. L. 1992. "Speaker Examines Impact of the West on Africa" (Wagaki Mwangi). *Daily Illini* 121 (April 3), 3.

Smith, Andy. 1991. "For All Those Who Were Indian in Another Life." *Ms.* (Nov./Dec.), 44–45.

Snitow, Ann. 1989. "A Gender Diary." In Adrienne Harris and Ynestra King, eds. *Rocking the Ship of State: Towards a Feminist Peace Politics*. Boulder, Colo: Westview Press.

Starhawk, 1990. "Power, Authority, and Mystery: Ecofeminism and Earth-Based Spirituality." In Irene Diamond and Gloria Feman Orenstein, eds. *Reweaving the World: The Emergence of Ecofeminism*. San Francisco: Sierra Club Books.

Teish, Luisah. 1985. *Jambalaya: The Natural Woman's Book of Personal Charms and Practical Rituals*. San Francisco: Harper & Row.

——. 1983b. "Only Justice Can Stop a Curse." In *In Search of Our Mothers' Gardens: Womanist Prose*. New York: Harcourt Brace Jovanovich.

Walker, Barbara. 1983. *The Woman's Encyclopedia of Myths and Secrets*. San Francisco: Harper & Row.

Worldwatch. 1987. "On the Brink of Extinction." Quoted in *World Development Forum* 5 (Nov.), 3.

"SOMETHING OR NOTHING: AN ECO-WOMANIST ESSAY ON GOD, CREATION, AND INDISPENSABILITY"

Karen Baker-Fletcher

Tears and
Breath
Swirl
Dust into
Oases of mud
And green
And blue
Kissing
Lips to
Truth

In the beginning God created the heaven and the earth. And the earth was without form, and void; and darkness was upon the face of the deep. And the Spirit of God moved upon the face of the waters. (Genesis 1:1–2)

So begins creation according to the Hebrew scripture which we Christians have inherited through adoption. The birth of the cosmos, nature, creatures—all that we call "the world"—begins with divine creativity interacting with a formless, empty, yet-to-be earth. All that we have come to know as our cosmos begins with the Spirit of God hovering over the dark, deep waters.[1] Genesis 1:1–2 offers an account of the cosmic and ecological nativity of the planet we rely on for sustenance.

When we lived in southern California, my family and I spent many summer days at local beaches. One of our favorite beaches was in Crystal Cove State Park, a natural, conserved setting with trails winding through native brush and wildflowers. Living in northern Texas, which has its own beauty, we often miss the seagulls, sea otters, seals, herons, and sea anemones of the California ocean. Also missed are the red-tailed hawks in the mountains.

When I wrote *Sisters of Dust, Sisters of Spirit*, all of these things were just a short drive away. Now I have Gulf waters several hours away which I have yet to explore but will eventually find and write about. In the meantime, the live oak trees planted by settlers, the expanse of blue sky, and the lakes with freshwater herons soothe my eyes in my new home.

Yet I turn to memories of the ocean to articulate my understanding of divine creativity. Passages of my book *Sisters of Dust, Sisters of Spirit* preserve rich memories and keep me grounded in my love for this planet. I recall the shades of yellow and purple that delighted my senses as I found my way to the beach at the bottom of high, grassy cliffs where "Lizards and squirrels rustle, skittering away from our intrusive steps along a trail that looks like a subtle slash through their land," and I am there again where "the previously invisible ocean appears below us, seemingly still from a distance, vast, deep, blue" and "the rush of ocean air seems like an embodiment of Spirit itself, opening our eyes to infinity . . . a broad splash of color between earth and vast canvas of sky."[2]

I continue to ask, "Where did all this come from?" Were we humans, our planet, our solar system, and our universe created out of nothing, as classical Christianity tells us? Or were we created from disorganized matter and energy that was already present? Christians often think our cosmos and this planet were created from nothing, in part because John and Paul offer that interpretation. In Genesis 1:1–2, however, the Spirit of God hovers over the waters. The earth was "without form." It was "void or empty." There were waters for the Spirit of God to hover over. It does not say "nothing." On the one hand, Christian tradition emphasizes the chaos from which our becoming was shaped; on the other, there is a claim that we were created from nothing. Chaos is traditionally understood as evil, writes Susan Niditch:

> Traditional, patriarchal Christian interpretations of Genesis 1 paint "formlessness," "emptiness," "darkness," and "the waters" as *chaos*. Chaos is seen as evil, and the Spirit of god brings order and goodness out of chaos. One can tell from such interpretations that ancient peoples were familiar with the unpredictability of oceanic waters. On the one hand such waters provide sustenance, rich with fish. On the other hand fishers have been know to perish in ocean storms. People have always appreciated and feared the deep. It is understandable that some would see the unpredictability of the ocean as chaotic and deep darkness as nothingness. The Hebrew term for "deep waters" in Genesis 1:1–2 is *tehom*, which is related to *Tiamat,* the name of the mother goddess, the salt waters of Chaos, in the Mesopotamian creation myth, the *Enuma Elish*. In the *Enuma Elish*, Tiamat is killed and split like a mussel by Marduk, who builds the world out of her dead body. The deep, yawning, salt waters of chaos, in this myth, represent the mystery and power of female deity.[3]

The void, the formlessness, and the deep of Genesis are a remnant from the *Enuma Elish*. These terms refer to the body of deity as Goddess. They are a remnant of the maternal in divine creativity. Again, quoting from *Sisters of Dust, Sisters of Spirit*: "Tiamat's destruction by a male deity represents a misogynist, destructive perspective on women's sexual and creative power."[4] While there is no explicit reference to a matriarchal goddess in the Hebrew scripture, Bible scholar Susan Niditch notes that "if the Genesis account lacks a matriarchal goddess, it also does not present the creation of the world as dependent on her death or on a primal battle."[5]

My early analysis of Genesis in *Sisters of Dust, Sisters of Spirit* has grown, but it remains grounded in an interpretation that positively values the feminine aspects of divine creativity. It is true that "a careful reading of Genesis does not associate the formlessness, emptiness, darkness, the deep, or the waters with evil."[6] We are simply informed that these things were present:

> They were present and the Spirit of God was present. From the deep, the formlessness, the darkness, the waters, and the Spirit of God emerged all of creation, and abundance of life. The creation story in Genesis is a birth story, a story about the nativity of the solar system, the earth and its creatures, including women and men. The deep, the darkness, the waters dance in co-creative activity with the Spirit of God. Out of mutual, loving creative activity, all that we call life came into being. By the creative power of spirit ecosystems emerged in which special creatures, earth creatures *(Adam)* could live. A wildness, a free natural growth, is therefore part of all that lives. Like the waters, the wind, and the groaning of the earth when it quakes, it frightens us with its fury, its ability to turn and stir into storminess and chaos. Such freedom is necessary for life. To abuse it or attempt to eradicate it results in death.[7]

Such creativity, freedom, wildness, and depth are revealed in the first verses of Genesis 1 as the Spirit of God hovers over the waters. Genesis 1 begins with remnants of feminine descriptions of the divine. Earth creatures are created in "our image," says the divine. But by the time we reach the end of Genesis 3, other writers have given different accounts in which this imagery is lost. As one reads through the first three books of Genesis, with its two creation accounts and story of distracted desire, there is more to say about the types of questions that may have been raised by the audiences for whom these books of Genesis were written. The audiences for whom the authors of Genesis wrote, like we today, wanted to know why they were there and why their lives were full of pain and suffering. Why was there good and evil? And in the battle between men and women, surely one came first, so who was it? Thus the conflict between two accounts: one with God creating Adam, earth creature, in "our image," and another with the woman being taken from Adam's rib. Thus the development of a theory to offer a response to who is to blame for evil, and questions of which gender is to blame. For better or for worse, with conflicting accounts, their questions were social-relational questions, whereas many of our questions are scientific questions. In the midst of the complications Genesis 1 and 2 have wrought in our understanding of gender relations and how we came to be, the heart of it is that neither men nor women are gods. The attempt to become like gods results in imbalance, disharmony, and suffering.

In Genesis 1, God created and it was good! Genesis 1 and 2 respond to the question of why there is pain and suffering—evil—in our cosmos. This account is concerned about the fact that we humans, created from the dust of the earth and the breath or spirit of God, are deeply connected to the rest of creation. Yet there is an evil tendency to violate the earth and one another. We are somehow different in our consciousness and relationship to God, yet we are dust. In Genesis 1:20–24, God commands the elements—the waters and earth—to bring forth every living creature of a kind to live in watery and earthy ecosystems. According to Ecclesiastes 4:19, animals and humans alike are made from the dust of the earth and will return to it. The text, attributed to Solomon, says that what befalls the beasts, befalls humankind. As one dies, so dies the other. They all have one breath, so that a human being has no preeminence above a beast, the text states. After all, the wisdom writer cautions, all is vanity. We don't like to remember Ecclesiastes. In the Jewish tradition, it is given less weight than the Torah and the books of the prophets. Christians rarely preach from it. But Ecclesiastes returns us to the truths of Genesis. God created us *last from the dust of the earth.*

My interpretation of Genesis 1, like that of other eco-theologians, suggests that God created the earth out of something. This is a neo-classical approach. Classical theologians, in contrast, employ John 1 to interpret Genesis 1 as suggesting that God created something out of nothing. This is the *creatio ex nihilo* theory. Because Genesis 1 is vague and the author is not concerned about these questions, both interpretations are in effect a kind of *midrash* (commentary) on the possibilities, informed by later philosophies and scientific knowledge.

It is the later Johannine interpretation, with its gnostic philosophical influences and Pauline hyperbole, that suggests God created out of "nothing." Early Christian writers employed such philosophical and poetic interpretation to develop the *creatio ex nihilo* theory. The author of the book of John claims that all things were made by God and that nothing was made without God. Even John 1:1–3 does not say that there was nothing before the creation of this particular cosmos; it says that without God, nothing was made. Neo-classical theologians, like Charles Hartshorne, Schubert Ogden, and the eco-feminist Rosemary Ruether, insist on a different approach. There was something there—inert matter, then hydrogen and the dust of stars, making possible the dust of earth, later nitrogen in soil, with oxygen existing only billions of years later to support algae, then more complex vegetation, then oxygen-dependent carbon-producing events.

I share with such theologians an integrative understanding of spirit and matter, influenced in part by African Bantu Muntu philosophy, which sees spirit in all that is. I am asked by neo-classicists who appreciate my work "to come out as a neo-classicist" and to propound with radical, metaphysical philosophical fervor that the *creatio ex nihilo* theory is nonsense. But I am a womanist, a Black feminist or feminist of color, who cares little for either-or thinking when interpreting texts.[8] I am also a poet who finds less nonsense in *creatio ex nihilo* doctrine than some of my neo-classical colleagues, who aptly recognize that poetry is not meant to be taken literally but in the process sometimes forget the truth in the poetry. From my African-American heritage, I have learned what it means to live with a scarcity of resources, a kind of nothingness, and make something out of it. This is part of the heritage of the descendants of slaves. This heritage leads me to maintain that there is something of value in the expression "God made something out of nothing." It is a poetic representation of truth.

Womanists write from the wisdom of African-American women whose survival has depended on a God who can make something out of nothing. The poor in this country and globally have an experiential, not simply theoretical, understanding of God in this way. When we have been raised by parents and grandparents who talked about "making something out of nothing," "making a way out of no way," and "making do with what you've got," taking the word "nothing" figuratively comes naturally. My grandmother could make something out of what looked like nothing to me and many a bystander. There was always something to eat, no matter who came over. She'd take a scrap of this and a piece of that, a little flour, the last egg or two, and neck bones or a left-over carcass to create a feast—chicken and dumplings with recooked greens from her garden that she froze last summer. She made bedspreads from old curtains purchased at a yard sale. In the early days, before my college-educated parents had much to speak of, my mother could create a wonder with rice, okra, corn meal, and navy beans. We did not know that we were eating a rather generous "third world" meal. Nor did we know that we were eating sustainably, ecologically, and from "low on the food chain." What seemed like "nothing" in the days of steak and potatoes was plenty of something and much healthier for us "back in the day." It was kinder to the planet.

Coming from such a cultural heritage, one can conclude that what looks like nothing to us is something to God. Isn't this the truth behind the story of Hagar in the desert, so often cited by Delores Williams and other womanist theologians?[9] In the biblical story, Hagar is the servant of Sarai, Abram's wife. Later God renames her Sarah, and Abram becomes Abraham.[10] Abraham is seen as blessed by God to be the father of Israel, God's chosen people, with Sarah as mother. Muslims call Abraham "Father" also, because they regard themselves as descendants of his son Ishmael. Christians claim to be descendants of Abraham and Sarah as heirs that have been "grafted on." In the story of Hagar and Sarai, however, Abraham was not able to produce a single child with Sarai after many years of marriage. God had promised Abraham, however, that his descendants would be "like the

Karen Baker-Fletcher

dust of the earth, so that if anyone could count the dust, then [his] offspring could be counted."[11] Still childless, but thinking she could intervene to fulfill this promise, Sarai asked Abraham to lie with her servant or slave,[12] Hagar, to bear a child with her. When Hagar found she was pregnant, she began to resent Sarai. Sarai mistreated her. Hagar ran into the desert. An angel of God told Hagar to return and submit to Sarai, promising Hagar many descendants. Hagar named God "El Roi," or "God of Seeing," because God had seen her. Hagar bore a son for Abraham and Sarai, calling him Ishmael. Years later, through a covenant marked by male circumcision, God renamed Abram "Abraham" to change Sarai's name to Sarah, promising that Sarah would bear him a son. Sarah and Abraham, in their old age, had a son named Isaac. There were now two sons, in a culture where inheritance goes to the oldest son. Conflict emerged between the two mothers. Sarah accused Hagar of mocking her and told Abraham to get rid of Hagar and her son. Commanded by God to do so, but probably weary of the conflict, Abraham sent Hagar and Ishmael into the wilderness with a skin of water and some food. When she ran out of water, Hagar despaired of her own life and her crying son's. She sat down to die. At that moment a messenger of God, having heard Ishmael's cry, appeared to Hagar, and God "opened her eyes." She saw a spring of water in the desert.[13] There is something where it seems nothing exists. The God of seeing has made a way out of no way. Oppressed peoples, people bereft of adequate food and water, care, and respect, know what it means to look to a God who makes something from the dust of the earth. We know our survival depends on finding sustenance even in desert places and that our bodies are as earthy as the soil from which desert springs and sparse vegetation emerge.

My love for the evangelical and liberationist heart of historically Black churches, with their emphasis on the power of a God who makes a way out of no way and something out of nothing, leads me to refuse sheer dismissal of *creatio ex nihilo*. I suspect the truth lies somewhere between the *creatio ex nihilo* and chaos accounts. One can argue that theologians on either side of these debates engage in eisegesis—the practice of reading things into the text that are not there. There is also a tendency to treat the text as if it were closed when it is open-ended. When you are the daughter of a people for whom God has made a way out of no way and something out of nothing, you cannot dismiss what you have come to know from generations of experience. The intellectual debates of my conservative, liberal, and progressive colleagues are not so easily resolved for me. Yet I am not confused. I am a womanist, a Black feminist, who is deeply committed to the spiritual wisdom of Black culture and a both/and way of thinking, particularly when it is apparent that both sides have worth, value, and truth.

The problem in the debate is that theologians from both conservative and liberal camps fail to acknowledge that we are engaged in *midrash*—creative, theoretical interpretation of possibilities as to how we came to be. One can argue that theologians on either side of these debates engage in eisegesis. Early Christian writers, the Church Fathers, and theologians committed to classical interpretations read the word "nothing" into Genesis when it is not in the text. Modern and postmodern theologians from liberal to reformist read "something" into the text. But if we focus on the first three words of Genesis, that does not seem to be the author's concern. In fact, the author appears to be concerned with neither our arguments about "nothing" nor our arguments that there was "something" prior to our existence. We treat the text as if it were closed when it is open-ended.

My love for the Jewish tradition of *midrash*, respect for multiple possibilities in what is written and unwritten in biblical accounts, affects my readings of texts. As one who appreciates neo-classical process-relational and eco-feminist persuasive arguments that in the dance of divine creative activity all existence emerges from something, I am asked to agree that this argument is the only sensible, possible, and correct one. However, my love for the evangelical heart of historically Black churches, with their emphasis on the power of a God who makes a way out of no way and something out of nothing, leads me to refuse sheer dismissal of the classical understanding. I suspect there is an element of truth in both interpretations of the text, and that there are possibilities we have not imagined. The text, after all, is vague and open-ended.

The *midrash* account that God creates something out of nothing reminds us that without the Spirit of God we are nothing, unable to breathe or love. It relativizes our sense of power. We are not equal with God in power or ability. The *midrash* account that God creates something out of chaotic, disorganized matter reminds us that God as Creative Activity Itself created something before the universe as we know it. It de-centers our sense of power. The *refusal* to consider that there was something or some event, made possible by God, prior to the creation of *our* universe affects our sense of self-importance and our ability to respond to that which is not us. When we believe we are the center of all possible universes, we think of ourselves more highly than we ought. This leads to oppression of the earth and all who are in it. Whatever dominion one might speak of is fragile and tentative, and it requires sharing power with others rather than holding power over others. Such dominion can only mean that we are called to self-control and care for the environments that sustain us. Our relationship with the earth is one of elemental interrelationship. We are dust and spirit, people of the land who belong to God.

For those who claim to be followers of Jesus, if Jesus exemplifies our full humanity in flesh and spirit, then Jesus is dust and spirit. To imitate the life of Jesus, then, requires a loving and just relationship with the earth and one another. It means that we need to remember that the very dust of the earth is an intrinsic part of God who creates something out of seeming nothingness. It means that we need to remember that "nothing" is "something" in this vast universe of ours, and that life begins with the infinitesimal. And yet all too many are bent on disregarding this truth. The will to dominate the earth and its peoples—especially the poor, people of color, and women in general—competes destructively with the call to mutual care, respect, justice, and liberation. According to Matthew 25, Jesus calls humankind to love "the least of these" and the stranger. Through the will to power, human beings proudly make excuses to continue oppressing the least. Many of us who are affected by environmental injustice have awakened to participate in grassroots movements for nontoxic environments, but many of us have also failed to wake up to the realities of how toxins affect us. Some of us would become active if we were more informed. Education in our communities is vital. Yet some of us have chosen not to listen or give conscious effort to these problems, suspecting that ecology is "the white man's issue." There are very deep historical reasons for such suspicion and mistrust; however, when we are reluctant to listen and are silent on these issues, we reinforce our own oppression. We reinforce the assumption that we are dispensable, nothing, because it appears that we do not care. When we are silent, only we know that we do care, that we are tired of losing family members to cancer. We silently care, but the dance of dispensability continues. In the meantime, the rocks cry out for us.

As a child, during humid Indian summers on days when it was too hot to play outside, I looked from the windows of my urban, middle-class childhood home onto the street. As I wrote in *Sisters of Dust, Sisters of Spirit*, "I would imagine that the heat wavering in exhaust fumes from the pavement was instead a world of blue coolness and green grass, waterfalls shimmering in the daylight. Sometimes night was magic with jewel-bedecked buildings draped like necklaces against a purple, velvet skyline. But always the roaring of the cars, the sour-smelling smoke from old exhaust pipes would wake me from my daydreams. Or the sunlight filtering into the haze from nearby factories in odorous hues of pink, yellow, and red would assault my senses and turn last night's precious jewels into the cheap, cut and broken glass of pop bottles. Over the years, cancer has taken away the lives of many loved ones who trusted the water they drank, the air they breathed, the asbestos they worked with, the pesticides they used, the food they ate."[14] Some of these loved ones came from communities that were urban, others suburban, and others rural. Some are black, some brown, some white, yellow, or mixed. Environmental abuse, racism, sexism, and classism are interlocking forms of evil and oppression. I continue to believe that "no matter where we live, the products of industry gone awry, fueled by class-biased and racialized attitudes meet us to inaugurate a cruel dance of dispensability. Air currents rush into air currents and waters into waters to soak the soil. There is no hiding place."[15]

I aver today, as I did in *Sisters of Dust, Sisters of Spirit*, that there is no such thing as dispensability in our interdependent, embodied, spiritual lives. As African-American preachers and church mothers often say, "God don't make no junk!" Everything has intrinsic worth and value. Every cell of an organism, each creature in an ecosystem, the very dust of stars and earth hold secrets of life and sustenance. But in practice, there is a tendency to deny the interdependence of life. We are each so inevitably caught up in the machines of industry, technology, and development that have become part of the postmodern world that the prospect of change seems daunting. Trapped in the bonds of broken relationship, it is all too easy to place toxins in the neighborhoods of the poor and the colored in the United States and globally, because current sociopolitical and economic systems allow it. There is no requirement that those who are not directly affected think about it.

In the United States there are numerous poor black and brown communities who are concerned about one another and their environment. They love their neighborhoods. They invest time in organizing and participating in neighborhood associations to confront industries that endanger their lives. They are concerned about smog, toxic dust in air and soil, high-voltage power lines, and maintaining their neighborhoods as places of beauty. Some of our churches are involved, providing transportation for community members to participate in civic meetings on toxic sites and to confront manufacturers. Little is heard about us in presidential and national legislative addresses, giving us the impression once again that we are dispensable. Refusing to accept our supposed dispensability, knowing that God does not make junk and we need not live in poisonous atmospheres on deadly soil, drinking lethal water, we continue to protest and change policies at the grassroots level.

War is another way in which human beings reduce the earth and its peoples to "nothingness." It is a way of denying that no matter how dispensable we may view another life, that life is something of intrinsic value of God. We close our hearts to realizing our full humanity. The fact that our earthy, elemental bodies so often meet with violent destruction is troubling. These earthy bodies and the earth itself resist the violence and the destruction. Violent acts are desecrating acts. They literally violate the sacred. Is the earth sacred? Are our bodies sacred? If God created it and it was good, then yes, all that lives is created sacred and continuously sacralized in the life-giving power of a creating God. Desecration is contemptuous of the sacred. Bodies, air, waters, and soil are dishonored, poisoned, dispensed of, blown to the winds, stuck in the rubble, vaporized.

The earth is our common ground. We are each made from the earth and depend on it. This common ground is not something we need to find. This common ground is *something*; we must learn to see we are on it and it is in us. We are it and to it we all shall return. In returning to it, our bodies do not return to "nothingness" in the literal sense of the word, but rather to the original elements that make up the natural cycle of life, death, and rebirth. How willing are we to liberate ourselves as the earth, to participate in healing renewal in the here and now? I ask *will*, because *can* always comes when we decide what we will do to participate in God's initial aim for the wellbeing of creation. To what extent are we *willing* to participate in this initial aim? If we are willing, we will each, in community, see and create what we need to do.

NOTES

1. An original version of this section on the ocean as a symbol of the formlessness from which God creates life may be found in Karen Baker-Fletcher, "Nativity and Wildness," in *Sisters of Dust, Sisters of Spirit* (Minneapolis: Fortress Press, 1998), 21–25.

2. Karen Baker-Fletcher, "Nativity and Wildness," 21.

3. Susan Niditch, "Genesis," in *The Women's Bible Commentary*, Carol A. Newsome and Sharon H. Ringe, eds. (Louisville, KY: Westminster John Knox Press, 1992), 13.

4. Karen Baker-Fletcher, *Sisters of Dust, Sisters of Spirit*, 25.

5. Ibid.

6. Ibid.

7. Karen Baker-Fletcher, "Nativity and Wildness," *Sisters of Dust, Sisters of Spirit*, 21–25.

8. Alice Walker coined the term "womanist" in 1983. Most succinctly, a womanist is a "black feminist or feminist of color." The term is derived from the Black folk expression "you acting womanish" as in "grown up," "responsible," "in charge," and not "girlish." See Alice Walker, *In Search of Our Mothers' Gardens*, (New York: Harcourt, Brace, Jovanovich, 1983), xi–xii.

9. See Delores Williams, *Sisters in the Wilderness: The Challenge of Womanist God-Talk*, (Maryknoll, New York: Orbis, 1993), 198. The experience of a God who makes a way out of no way is poignantly described in Williams's exegesis of the story of Hagar. God provides Hagar and African-American women with "*new vision* to see revival resources where [they] saw none before." Williams's account of what God does for Hagar is accurate, but her interpretation of Sarah is so deeply affected by African-American women's experience of oppression during slavery that Sarah is portrayed like a 19th-century slave mistress, which she was not. Moreover, by focusing on Hagar's Egyptian ethnicity, Williams makes Hagar sound "blacker" than Sarah. Since they were from the same region and of mixed ethnicity, they may have looked similar. Some Jewish readers have found Williams's interpretation anti-Semitic. Black women have argued that Sarah plays some role in Hagar's oppression. What is most important is Williams's emphasis on Black women's experience of God as one who provides vision for survival resources. I hope, however, that womanists and Jewish feminists will seriously consider Jewish/Womanist dialogue on the story of Hagar in order to better understand one another's traditions and reshape the ones we belong to.

10. Genesis 17:15.

11. Genesis 13:16, New International Version. Compare with Genesis 22:17: "descendants as numerous as the stars in the sky."

12. Some interpretations read "servant" and others "slave." While slavery is always problematic, the system of slavery or servanthood among the ancient Hebrew people was different from modern trans-Atlantic slavery. Slave status did not extend from the mother (or father) to the child. Servants and their children could inherit from their "masters." Hebrew slaves had more rights and freedom than modern slaves. Every fifty years was a "year of Jubilee" when slaves/servants were freed from their debts to their masters.

13. Genesis 16:1–15, 17:15 and 21:1–20.

14. Karen Baker-Fletcher, *Sisters of Dust, Sisters of Spirit*, 60.

15. Ibid.

"SENSUOUS MINDS AND THE POSSIBILITIES OF A JEWISH ECOFEMINIST PRACTICE"

Irene Diamond and David Seidenberg

> There is no defense against an open heart and a supple body in dialogue with wildness. Internal strength is an absorption of the external landscape. We are informed by beauty, raw and sensual. Through an erotics of place our sensitivity becomes our sensibility. If we ignore our connection to the land and deny our relationship to the pansexual nature of earth, we will render ourselves impotent as a species.
>
> —*An Unspoken Hunger*,
> Terry Tempest Williams

We come to the questions of ecological practice as politically committed Jews whose passions, and search for truth tell us that at this juncture, neither feminist theory nor Jewish theory can rest on an understanding of humanity, sexuality, or carnality which does not take account of the life of the planet that nourishes our spirit and flesh. Like Terry Tempest Williams, we find ourselves compelled to examine human desiring bodies within the context of the earth.

Our work together is part of a conversation in process in which we are exploring understandings of human embodiment through a specifically Jewish sensibility. We believe that such a project is important not only in terms of transforming Judaism but also in terms of the alternative models it might suggest to the disembodied approach to knowing and being that has prevailed in the West since the time of Hellenism. We will suggest that embedded within Judaism is an understanding of sensuous minds that points to a path beyond human/animal, culture/nature, mind/body dualisms. That is the promise. Each of us will trace the individual paths through which we entered these questions. At the same time we should clarify that as the dialogue has developed the boundaries between voices have blurred and the voices as presented do not necessarily represent particular authors. We have maintained the form of distinct voices both to invert the tradition of male voices speaking about female bodies and to play with the boundedness of subjectivity. This

Reprinted by permission from *Ethics and the Environment* 4:2 (Indiana University Press, 2000).

438

seems particularly important in a project devoted to understanding human embodiment and desire in relationship to the more than human world.

Irene: As a fairly typical Jewish intellectual for much of my adult life, I lived through daily practices that had nothing to do with the intricate Jewish rituals that mark virtually every aspect of bodily life. My reading and writing was focused on rethinking the feminist philosophical assumption and political strategy that freedom for women was to be achieved through gaining control over our bodies. This work was primarily informed by the ecofeminist insistence on women and men's dependence on the earth and by Michel Foucault's (1978) analysis of the operation of power/knowledge in societies governed by the human sciences. In *Fertile Ground* (Diamond 1994), I explored how the production of what I termed the sexuated body through technologies of control diminishes our access to the sensuousness of life.

To the extent that my life had anything to do with the world of ritual, it was through rituals that are a part of ecofeminist political and cultural activities. In my limited and intermittent involvement, I found these rituals interesting and meaningful primarily as opportunities for frivolity, camaraderie among humans in the here and now, and tools for creating political unity and effective political strategies. A shift occurred with the passing of my mother, when I found myself immersed in the intricacies of Jewish burial practices. Suddenly Judaism, with its emphasis on bringing the dead body in direct contact with the earth, appeared to have important ecological traces. I began to see that Judaism was a repository of ritual practices whose character starkly contrasted with those of a dominant culture bent on staving off the decay and withering integral to the cyclical nature of life on earth. This disrupted for me the indigenous/nonindigenous and monotheistic/pagan dualisms that frame much of contemporary ecofeminism.[1]

Something was amiss with the dominant ecological narrative that railed against a so-called "Judeo-Christian" ethic. Attention to the actual Hebrew of the Jewish Bible pointed to an understanding of embodiment and sentience in which body and mind are one and intimately related to and dependent on the elemental force of breath. I discovered an understanding of bodies that was far more corporeal and involved with a sensuous living earth than is commonly understood through the lens of most Hellenistic and Western Christian thought. For example, the body and mind, which are one, are called by the one word, "nefesh" in the Torah. These insights led me directly to formulating an idea of "the sensuous mind" in my latest work, a concept which I use to explore the openness of the human body as a disciplined formation of awareness. The sensuous mind is the sensuous body.

Searching for paths for my own grounding, I discovered the Jewish concept of shabbat, when we let both ourselves and the earth rest while engaging in the sensual pleasures of learning, eating, and sexual play. In the process of immersing myself in Jewish texts and practices, I began to see that feminist discourse is primarily focused on the sexed openings of the body. My immersion in Jewish rituals generated an enriched understanding of the many ways human bodies open to the world—the diverse creatures, plants, and elemental forces that nourish all flesh. I learned to pause for blessings for eating foods that came from the ground and those that came from trees, for the wonder of a rainbow, for hearing thunder, and most amazingly, even for the proper opening and closing of the holes that allow for elimination. What I had written about as the limitations of the sexuated body standardized by genital sex became grounded in a set of practices in which my body was palpably connected to the earth.

Looking back, I would now argue that Foucault's account of how sex became the truth of ourselves is inadequate because it is derived primarily from an analysis of human institutions vis-à-vis human bodies. His polemics are directed at the human sciences; he takes little note of how new models of the natural world in the physical and biological sciences had rendered the earth into an inert machine, a process the ecofeminist historian Carolyn Merchant (1980) wrote about as "the death of nature."

Foucault's analysis only pertains to shifting inscriptions on bodies understood as surfaces.[2] If, however, we understand human bodies as constituted by a multitude of openings that provide for orientation, pleasure, and communion with the life-world, then the intensified focus on the specifically sexed openings of human bodies Foucault identifies may actually have been produced by a deprivation of opening or awareness of the nonhuman natural world. Although Foucault focuses on the re-inscribing of surfaces, the most important shift may well have been the diminishment of the body's erotic depth.

The short-sightedness which Foucault displays with respect to the natural world is recapitulated in most feminist critiques of gender. Contemporary feminism has surely complicated our understanding of bodies and human desire in profound ways. However, between the prevalence on the one hand of poststructuralist theorizing that undermines any truth of the body, and on the other hand the popularity of Catherine MacKinnon's (1987) radical feminist science of domination which reifies sexual desire, the central debates of feminist theory have little to say about the vitally important relations between body and earth. For example, when Judith Butler (1990) writes that "gendering is, among other things, the differentiating relations by which speaking subjects come into being" (7), the speaking subjects to which she refers are clearly human subjects, and gender emerges strictly from a constructing of human differences.

Ecofeminist theory and practice is one of the most important places where such ideas about the body are challenged. Simply put, it is not just human relationships that enable us to become aware, speaking, consciously alive subjects, but our relationships with all beings and all dimensions of being. Feminism in general regards gender, sex, standpoint, and embodiment from within a strictly human context. Consideration of the more-than-human world points to the necessity of a broader context for both our theory and practice. Such a turn might well enable us to move beyond the essentialist and antiessentialist abstractions of the gendered body. What is needed is a framework that allows us to speak of species-being as well as the specificity of male and female bodies in their divers relationships to creation and fertility.

Carol Bigwood (1993) and David Abram (1996) both use Merleau-Ponty's phenomenology of the body in order to map out important new directions in feminism and ecology. Their work helps us to complexify our understanding of sensuous embodiment and to go beyond the idea of the body as a self-enclosing container. For Bigwood, "The phenomenological body is not fixed but continually emerges anew out of everchanging weave of relations to earth and sky, things, tasks, and other bodies. The living world . . . is not merely external to the body. The world-earth-home is the ever-present horizon latent in all our experiences" (51).

Abram (1996) expresses a similar idea when he writes:

> [T]he boundaries of the body are open and indeterminate; more like membranes than barriers, they define a surface of metamorphosis and exchange. The breathing, sensing body draws its sustenance and its very substance from the soils, plants, and elements that surround it; it continually contributes itself, in turn, to the air, to the composting earth, to the nourishment of insects and oak trees and squirrels, ceaselessly spreading out of itself as well as breathing the world into itself, so that it is very difficult to discern, at any moment precisely where this living body begins and ends. (46)

In short, the body is sensitive to its environs and is neither contained nor constituted by finite surfaces.

David: I'd like to flesh out what this means by using an example from the fall harvest festival called Sukkot. Traditionally, Jews construct a simple booth, called a sukkah, which we live in for seven days starting with the seventh full moon after Passover. The sukkah becomes a place where we eat, sometimes sleep, and even make love.

The practice of constructing a sukkah on the full moon after Yom Kippur is carefully regulated and becomes a lesson in creating a sense of place. It must have two-and-a-half or three or almost four walls (minus the door)—enough to feel enclosed. The space under the roof must be big enough to cover "a person's head and most of the body," because the sukkah is like a body. The roof itself made of leaves and branches must give more shade than light, without a gap larger than a hand's breadth, but through which one can see stars. These definitions teach us to bind the inside and the outside, the internal and the external, the physical and the spiritual, the sensible, and the sensual.

The sukkah is a precise physical form for the way we sense the world, through a latticework of sense and interpretation, through openness and limitation, through the "interweaving" of the senses. The profound depth of this ritual, like all rituals, is found in the physical experience of it, sharing meals with friends, watching the moon through the leaves, feeling both protected and open to the world. And finally, this framework of a body, like all bodies, must be temporary: at the end of the holiday we break it down, turn it back to its constituent parts.

Such a phenomenological understanding of ritual is not foreign to the rabbinic tradition. For example, the sukkah is interpreted as an embodiment of God's desire for us by Meishulam Feibush (1975), the Chassidic rebbe of Zbarazh. He writes:

> Embrace is hinted at in the sukkah: Just as a person embraces his child in love, encircling him with his arms, and sheltering him with his head, so here for the arm there are the two [walls according to] their rule/halakhah, plus a third [wall at least as wide as a] handbreadth, and the third, the handbreadth, is the hand, and all of it is a parable for the situation of being embraced . . . (36a, sec. 5)

Traditionally, the sukkah ritual is done to commemorate the Jewish people's wandering in the desert after leaving Egypt, where they were protected by the presence of God, called "Shekhinah." Theologically, the sukkah becomes an incarnating of God's presence sheltering each of us. On a shamanic level it succeeds because it manifests the phenomenology of conscious embodiment. The sukkah frames for us the moment of ingathering, of sense and meaning and smell and sight, of earth, wind, and starlight, which is the embrace between our sense of home and sense of self.

For me, dwelling in a sukkah with this openness of body and mind is an experience of profound joy. It was this kind of experience of Jewish earth-based ritual that first deeply attracted me to the Jewish path as a college student. The joy I felt enabled me to connect the two sources of my earliest experiences of wonderment: my intimacy with the animals and insects I loved to study and the holy magic of the rituals I shared with my great-grandfather and extended family. Making this connection helped me to move beyond the alienating fifties vision of American maleness which structured my nuclear family. Up until then my intellectual pursuit had been focused on junctures between science, eastern spirituality, and meditation. When I first began to practice the rituals of Judaism I found the escape from suburban culture I had searched for in Buddhism and Taoism. Like Irene, I had the opportunity and privilege to develop a perspective on Judaism far from institutionalised Jewish life. Living in rural New England, there were no obstacles to prevent my pagan persona, my sense of animism, from flowing directly into the forms of Jewish practice and the sensuality of its texts.

Irene and I are collaborating as Jews, not just as theorists. We know that there are many other paths besides Judaism which may teach the discipline of a sensuous relationship to the world. However, Judaism is privileged for us by arbitrary facts of birth, family, and culture. Furthermore, it is these very elements of identity, history, and place which constitute the ethos and Eros of being. In Judaism, from a liberal perspective or anthropological perspective, it is clear that sacredness is constructed by ritual actions which mark the sacred as different from the common. Each time we learn Torah sacredly, we reinscribe the text as sacred and at the same time create new openings in the text for sacredness. Each time we withdraw from creating on Shabbat, we create the possibility for revisioning the world on new terms, outside the law of labor and production.

This is not so different from what Judith Butler (1990) calls "performativity." She writes: "Performativity is thus not a singular 'act,' for it is always a reiteration of a norm or set of norms . . . " (12). But, where for Butler such an act is simply a repetition which deceptively conceals its conventions, within a living ritual system an act which repeats norms can also create meaning. An act of ritual can therefore become a transformative way of knowing and constituting knowledge. More than this, the nature of learning and knowing as constituted by Jewish ritual practices is one which completely circumvents the usual binary construction of rationality which is of such great concern for feminism.

The physicality of ritual provides a kind of screen or vortex through which divinity, humanity, and nature are drawn into a single embodiment. The phenomenology of ritual can help us understand something about the nature of our consciousness and self. Rituals in Judaism are firstly physical, not spiritual, embodiments of awareness rather than ideas. Ritual can teach us to open our thinking to this intertwining, to think "sensuously." If our body is destined to the world, then somehow we can understand the world through our bodies. The human body, as we have understood it, is really a form for awareness or consciousness, a form which connects rather than contains. We open out to touch other creatures, other forms, and most importantly, the earth itself.

For us in a Jewish context, ritual has been one of the primary ways we encounter the opening of the body. It is only because we are animals, "packaged" to move, as it were, that we do not normally see all our fractal branching, that our bodies appear to be smooth and rounded surfaces. Every surface of the body, despite its apparent smoothness, is also a branching out, an extension of the senses, of breath and sweat and fluid, a casting out upon the world beyond the apparent boundary it represents. It is this openness, and our ability to reflect on this openness through the gift of insight and imagination, which allows us to see the infinity which unfolds within the finite. Ritual, along with science and simple meditation, is among the many ways we begin to see and continue to see the wonder of what we call nature.

Irene: We cannot enter into this discussion without acknowledging that Judaism is a tradition whose sensuality has been arbitrarily gendered according to the needs of men. Even on the most basic level, David's body is marked as a Jewish body because it has been cut ritually as part of a covenant. But my female body is not Jewishly marked. Even though only the body of a Jewish woman traditionally has the power to pass on tribal peoplehood, the covenant itself is carried out through men acting on male bodies through the ritual obligation of circumcision. Therein lies much of the challenge for Jewish ecofeminist practice. As feminism reclaims the fullness of Jewish ritual for men and women, it awakens the possibility of a Jewish body which is equally female and male. The problem is that straightforward egalitarianism minimizes the specificities of sexedness and ignores the many ways bodies open to the world, thereby rendering the body neutered and sensually diminished. How then do we evolve a cultural practice that acknowledges and gives meaning to sexedness and specifics-being without essentializing or codifying these meanings?

As Jews confront this dilemma which we inherited from our ancestors, we are also confronted with radical accusations about Judaism which come from outside of our experience as Jews: Among both feminists and ecological thinkers, Judaism is understood to have killed the Goddess, to have created in monotheism the foundation for patriarchy's domination over both women and the land.

This line of reasoning mimics the accusations made against Jews of being "Christ-killers." It is used by some Christian feminists to pardon Christianity or Greco-Roman culture for their patriarchal imperialism. However, we know that, historically, Judaism evolved in the shadow of patriarchal polytheistic cultures. The matriarchal religions of the Near East had already died out or been subverted.[3]

Nonetheless, it is true that medieval Judaism largely rejected the biblical conception of living nature and in some ways intensified the biblical subjugation of women. Even until contemporary times, exile and persecutions have led much of Jewish culture more and more deeply into the written text and away from the sensuousness of the natural world. Concurrently, the inner dynamics of rabbinic cultures led to a state in which the "textuated body" became synonymous with the sexuated male body. Learning became an extraordinarily eroticized and sensual activity between men, equaling sexuality in both pleasure and intensity. Daniel Boyarin (1997) has written extensively about this phenomenon as a liberating feminization of masculinity in his book, *Unheroic Conduct*. Elliot Wolfson, in his many books on Kabbalah, however, sees the same phenomenon as strictly misogynist. We believe that any resolution of these conflicting perspectives depends on taking the more-than-human world into account.

David: This sensuousness of ancient Judaism, a sensuousness of minds and bodies, was saved by rabbinic culture in a coded and gendered form called Halakha, or Jewish law, or more literally the "way." In the 20th century, as learning has become opened up to women as well as men it continues to be forged and reforged as sacred and sensual. But the code itself must be radically invigorated and transformed. Jewishly informed ecofeminist insights and teachings are particularly important in this regard. One might say that the code must be decoded, unraveled, and rewoven. The ritual of mikveh provides a particularly stark example.

The rituals concerning fertility and sexuality, especially mikveh, the immersion in "living water," are among the most difficult for many Jews in the liberal movements. Yet these

Irene Diamond and David Seidenberg

rituals have the potential to bring the most powerful transformation. A mikveh is a "gathering" of "living waters," waters which flow from a spring or river or from the ocean, or which are gathered directly by rainfall. Mikveh water must always be flowing in and out, it cannot be left standing; in other words, it must be connected to the cycle which joins water to the intimate process of life, evolution, and birth. Immersion, in which every surface of the body must come in simultaneous contact with the water, returns a person to a state of bodily wholeness by connecting to the flow which began at creation. Our texts teach about an ancient ritual which was in constant use by men and women to help them cope with the disruption of the body through normal contact with life processes in the world.

Centuries of practice, however, have confined the ritual of immersion to a process for making women sexually available to their husbands after menstruation. The physical state which brings a woman to the mikveh is associated with sin and impurity by the Prophets, and by normative strands of rabbinic and medieval Jewish culture.

Irene: This gender difference in ritual practice happens to correspond with most modern models of sexuality, which portray fertility as primarily a concern of women's bodies and interiors and male ejaculation as a straightforward, machine-like process. The idea of the male body as a hydraulic machine accepts male seed as inert, lifeless, and therefore fully expendable.[4] From an ecofeminist perspective, we can easily see this as a deprivation of sensuousness and aliveness to the body. Biblical stories and rabbinic injunctions against the spilling of seed could help us to complicate the idea of male sexuality, but in cultural contexts where the fullness of human sensuality has atrophied and the sexuated body permeates consciousness, the notion of not wasting seed as one would not waste any element of life is associated with an increase in sexual fear rather than an increase in sensuality. It is important to remember here that the mikveh ritual was once applied to both men and women after contact with either semen or menses. If men were to reclaim the mikveh as a ritual for restoring their relationship to fertility, it could help Jewish culture to go beyond a drive model for male sexuality, freeing men and women to experience fertility as a divine blessing which encompasses both male and female.

We are confronted with a ritual that has great potential to teach ecological wisdom. This cannot happen as long as the mikveh ritual is carried out exclusively under the determinations of medieval Halakhah which is narrowly concerned only with the oscillation of women's bodies between the categories of permitted and forbidden. This also cannot happen within a Jewish feminism that is not deepened by ecological insight and a covenantal connection to creation. Only if the Jewish people develop the capacity to reach back to the primitive source of our obligations in the compulsion to unite our bodies with the elements of water and earth, will we be able to draw out the wisdom encoded in the mikveh ritual.

David: In the ritual of mikveh, the male and female body are renewed through contact with waters whose movement can be traced back to the first tide, the first upwelling of life in the ocean. The teaching about the body in mikveh connects the flows of the body to the emergence of creation itself. Judaism has another powerful ritual that connects the body and creation, the ritual of not-doing, the Sabbath, which we enter into when the sun sets every seventh day. On the mythical level, Judaism commands the weekly celebration of creation. It is one of the few particularistic Jewish rituals which has been adopted by numerous Christian sects, the only ritual law to take a place among the Ten Commandments, perhaps the only Jewish ritual that has universal significance.

The Sabbath, Shabbat in Hebrew, offers the simple contemplation which can come with the discipline of resting. It is this dimension of discipline which escapes so many modern Jews, who interpret rest as "relaxation," pursuing entertainment, shopping, gardening, and so forth, as distractions from everyday labors. But the discipline of rest requires more than this: it is the discipline of refraining from human manipulation, of relinquishing the powers we accumulate through culture and human endeavor, even when it does not bring pleasure. This brings us to the heart of the difference between being pleased by things, and contemplating the world which gifts them.

On Shabbat, Judaism commands that we give up the powers which make us seem so different from the other animals. This means two things: we become more like the other animals, who do not bake bread, build fire, plow fields, and so forth, but we become more like God, who rested after the first week of creation. On the mythical tribal level, we allow the hierarchies which divide the theistic world to lapse, we set a limit on expansion, acquisition, aggression, domination.

All of our rituals of ecological consciousness, not only Shabbat but even practical actions like tree planting or recycling, are probably not enough to change the way we live in the rest of our lives. Our civilization seems to be directed toward the destruction of the more-than-human world by human activity, and dedicated to the retreat of humans into an artificial lifeworld that does not acknowledge its sources in nature. But even if the Sabbath is not sufficient, the simple act of stopping is essential if we are to believe in the possibility of altering the course of human development.

According to Halakhah, what is forbidden on the Sabbath is the work necessary to build the Tent of Meeting. This Tent was a movable temple where the ancient Israelites made their sacrifices, and God's presence was manifested as they wandered through the desert. The implication of this is that all of our work during the week is related to building a sacred place. Rabbinic commentary teaches that the pattern of the Tent reproduced the structure of creation. Later mystics said that not only did the tent represent all of creation, but that when the menorah was first lit within it, the tent achieved consciousness—the consciousness of creation itself. The deep teaching of Shabbat is that all of human activity must have this same goal.

Irene: We recognize in these interpretations not just nice sermons or ancient legends, but a practical tribal wisdom about preserving the sacredness of the world amidst all the busy upheaval of human action. Even in the contemporary practice of rituals, such as mikveh, there is a deep echo and trace of wisdom about connecting to the sacred living body of the world. One might explain the power of ritual using Foucault's ideas about micro-resistance to regimes of surveillance.

Ancient ritual in particular becomes an act of resistance to the constant onslaught of technology and labor, modernity and machine. (A better model, however, might be the so-called butterfly effect of chaos theory in which small actions can effect large changes independent of hierarchical human power relations.) Many of us believe that we must turn to exactly this kind of knowledge, which is commonly termed "indigenous," in order to chart a different path for Western and human civilization.

The Jewish people stand between being indigenous and being without a home, between sharing the ancient roots of nomadic herdsman and embracing modern industrial society, between spreading universalist ideas of truth and preserving a particular tribal knowledge of the world. Perhaps now we will begin to unfold the wisdom encoded by ancient rituals and laws and to distill a language for revivifying the connectedness with each land that must have been the starting point for every culture. We believe that such a turn would entail opening up human culture through a sensuous mind that knowingly lives in the embrace of nonhuman creatures and the more-than-human world. We believe that ritual can be a teacher of this sensuousness.

The sensuous mind is none other than the sensuous body aware of what Terry Tempest Williams called "the pan-sexual nature of the world." We recognize its movement when we exert internal self-discipline in what we take from the bounty of the world and in how we express our passion towards others. We recognize its shape in our awareness of the future, in seeking to balance desires of the moment with an awareness of the needs and desires of other creatures and other times. We recognize its flow in taking pleasure in the discipline of simply being, rather than needing to transcend; in loving the humility of learning. The writer Grace Paley said, "It is essential to love the natural world before you can understand it." We submit to that discipline, rigor, joy, fertility, loss, and the willingness to experience these through the matrix of ritual and cultural inheritance are critical components of this love.

Can the restraint, withdrawal and disciplining of human needs inspired by ecological questions or inspired by ritual obligations restore what has been deprived or destroyed in a world where we share neither one cultural history nor one set of cultural practices?

NOTES

1. For some guidelines to the internal Jewish debates about these questions, see Schwartz, E. "Jewish Theology and the Environmental Crisis," *Judaism*, Fall 1995; Antonelli, J. "Beyond Nostalgia: Rethinking the Goddess Myth," *On The Issues*.

2.   Elizabeth Grosz's (1993) work attempts to reconceptualize the idea of surface. She writes, "Inscriptions mark the surface of the body, dividing it into zones of intensified or de-intensified sensations . . . .These Surface effects however are not superficial, for they generate an interior, an underlying, depth." From "Bodies and Knowledges: Feminism and the Crisis of Reason." In *Feminist Epistemologies*, edited by L. Alcoff and E. Potter, pp. 197, 198. NY: Routledge. Grosz's is one of several attempts to get beyond the idea of the body as enclosure which is nonetheless still dependent upon the idea of surface.

3.   Tikva Fymer-Kensky's (1991) *In the Wake of the Goddesses*, NY: Basic Books, is essential on this point.

4.   Donna Haraway (1990) writes, "For Western men in reproduction, setting aside the 'problem' of death, the loss of self seems so tiny, the degrees of freedom so many." From "Investment Strategies for the Evolving Portfolio of Primate Females." In *Women and the Discourse of Science*, edited by M. Jacobus, E. F. Keller, and S. Shuttleworth, p. 43, NY: Routledge. Haraway's words are an example of how feminist theory typically accepts this mechanistic understanding of male bodies even when it critiques male reproductive consciousness.

REFERENCES

Abram, D. 1996. *The Spell of the Sensuous*. New York: Random House.

Bigwood, C. 1993. *Earth Muse*. Philadelphia: Temple University Press.

Boyarin, D. 1997. *Unheroic Conduct*. Berkeley: University of Califonria.

Butler, J. 1990. *Gender Trouble*. New York: Routledge.

Diamond, I. 1994. *Fertile Ground*. Boston: Beacon Press.

Diamond, I. and G. Orenstein, eds. 1990. *Reweaving the World*. San Francisco: Sierra Club Books, foreword.

Foucault, M. 1978. *History of Sexuality, Vol. 1*. New York: Pantheon. *Power/Knowledge: Selected Interviews and Other Writings, 1972–77* ed. Colin Gordon. New York: Pantheon.

Feibush, M. Meishulam 1975. *Yosher Divray Emet*. Jerusalem, Hebrew University Press, 36a, sec. 5.

MacKinnon, C. 1987. *Feminism Unmodified*. Cambridge: Harvard University Press.

Merchant, C. 1980. *The Death of Nature*. New York: Harper and Row.

Williams, T. T. 1994. *An Unspoken Hunger*. New York: Pantheon.

Wolfson, E. 1995. *Circle in the Square*. Albany: State University of New York Press; 1994. *Through the Speculum that Shines*. Princeton: Princeton University Press.

"MESSAGES FROM THE PAST: THE WORLD OF THE GODDESS"

Riane Eisler

What kind of people were our prehistoric ancestors who worshiped the Goddess? What was life like during the millennia of our cultural evolution before recorded or written history? And what can we learn from those times that is relevant to our own?

Because they left us no written accounts, we can only infer, like Sherlock Holmes turned scientist, how the people of the Paleolithic and of the later, more advanced Neolithic, thought, felt, and behaved. But almost everything we have been taught about antiquity is based on conjecture. Even the records we have from early historic cultures, such as Sumer, Babylon, and Crete, are at best scanty and fragmentary and largely concerned with inventories of goods and other mercantile matters. And the more detailed later written accounts about both prehistory and early history from classical Greek, Roman, Hebrew, and Christian times are also mainly based on inferences—made without even the aid of modern archaeological methods.

Indeed, most of what we have learned to think of as our cultural evolution has in fact been interpretation. Moreover, as we saw in the preceding chapter, this interpretation has more often than not been the projection of the still prevailing dominator worldview. It has consisted of conclusions drawn from fragmentary data interpreted to conform to the traditional model of our cultural evolution as a linear progression from "primitive man" to so-called "civilized man," who, despite their many differences, shared a common preoccupation with conquering, killing, and dominating.

Through scientific excavations of ancient sites, archaeologists have in recent years obtained a great deal of primary information about pre-history, particularly about the Neolithic, when our ancestors first settled in communities sustained by farming and the breeding of stock. Analyzed from a fresh perspective, these excavations provide the data base for a re-evaluation, and reconstruction, of our past.

One important source of data is excavations of building and their contents—including clothing, jewelry, food, furniture, containers, tools, and other objects used in daily life. Another is the excavation of burial sites, which tell us not only about people's attitudes about death but also about their lives. And overlapping both of these data sources is our richest source of information about prehistory: art.

Even when there is a written as well as an oral literary tradition, art is a form of symbolic communication. The extensive art of the Neolithic—be it wall paintings about daily life or about important myths, statuary of religious images, friezes depicting rituals, or simply vase decorations, pictures on seals, or engravings on jewelry—tells us a great deal about how these people lived and died. It also tells us a great deal about how they thought, for in a very real sense Neolithic art is a kind of language or shorthand symbolically expressing how people in that time experienced, and in turn shaped, what we call reality.[1] And if we let this language speak for itself, without projecting on it prevailing models of reality, it tells a fascinating—and in comparison to the stereotype, a far more hopeful— story of our cultural origins.

NEOLITHIC ART

One of the most striking things about Neolithic art is what it does *not* depict. For what a people do not depict in their art can tell us as much about them as what they do.

In sharp contrast to later art, a theme notable for its absence from Neolithic art is imagery idealizing armed might, cruelty, and violence-based power. There are here no images of "noble warriors" or scenes of battles. Nor are there any signs of "heroic conquerors" dragging captives around in chains or other evidences of slavery.

Also in sharp contrast to the remains of even their earliest and most primitive male-dominant invaders, what is notable in these Neolithic Goddess-worshiping societies is the absence of lavish "chieftain" burials. And in marked contrast to later male-dominant civilizations like that of Egypt, there is here no sign of mighty rulers who take with them into the afterlife less powerful humans sacrificed at their death.

Nor do we here find, again in contrast to later dominator societies, large caches of weapons or any other sign of the intensive application of material technology and natural resources to arms. The inference that this was a much more, and indeed characteristically, peaceful era is further reinforced by another absence: military fortifications. Only gradually do these begin to appear, apparently as a response to pressures from the warlike nomadic bands coming from the fringe areas of the globe, which we will examine later.

In Neolithic art, neither the Goddess nor her son-consort carry the emblems we have learned to associate with might—spears, swords, or thunderbolts, the symbols of an earthly sovereign and/or deity who exacts obedience by killing and maiming. Even beyond this, the art of this period is strikingly devoid of the ruler-ruled, master-subject imagery so characteristic of dominator societies.

What we do find everywhere—in shrines and houses, on wall paintings, in the decorative motifs on vases, in sculptures in the round, clay figurines, and bas reliefs—is a rich

Riane Eisler

array of symbols from nature. Associated with the worship of the Goddess, these attest to awe and wonder at the beauty and mystery of life.

There are the life-sustaining elements of sun and water, for instance, the geometric patterns of wavy forms called meanders (which symbolized flowing waters) incised on an Old European altar from about 5000 B.C.E. in Hungary. There are the giant stone heads of bulls with enormous curled horns painted on the walls of Catal Huyuk shrines, terra-cotta hedgehogs from southern Romania, ritual vases in the form of does from Bulgaria, egg-shaped stone sculptures with the faces of fish, and cult vases in the form of birds.[2]

There are serpents and butterflies (symbols of metamorphosis) which are in historic times still identified with the transformative powers of the Goddess, as in the seal impression from Zakro, in eastern Crete, portraying the Goddess with the wings of an eyed butterfly. Even the later Cretan double axe, reminiscent of the hoe axes used to clear farm lands, was a stylization of the butterfly.[3] Like the serpent, which sheds its skin and is "reborn," it was part of the Goddess's epiphany, yet another symbol of her powers of regeneration.[4]

And everywhere—in murals, statues, and votive figurines—we find images of the Goddess. In the various incarnations of Maiden, Ancestress, or Creatrix, she is the Lady of the waters, the birds, and the underworld, or simply the divine Mother cradling her divine child in her arms.[5]

Some images are so realistic that they are almost lifelike, like the slithering snake on a dish found in an early fifth millennium B.C.E. cemetery in western Slovakia. Others are so stylized that they are more abstract than even our most "modern" art. Among these are the large stylized sacramental vase or chalice in the shape of an enthroned Goddess incised with ideograms from the Tisza culture of southeastern Hungary, the pillar-headed Goddess with folded arms from 5000 B.C.E. Romania, and the marble Goddess figurine from Tell Azmak, central Bulgaria, with schematized arms and an exaggerated pubic triangle, dating from 6000 B.C.E. Still other images are strangely beautiful, such as an 8000-year-old horned terra-cotta stand with female breasts, somehow reminiscent of the classical Greek statue called the Winged Victory, and the painted Cucuteni vases with their graceful shapes and rich geometric snake-spiral designs. And others, such as the crosses incised on the navel or near the breasts of the Goddess, raise interesting questions about the earlier meanings of some of our own most important symbols.[6]

There is a sense of fantasy about many of these images, a dreamlike and sometimes bizarre quality suggestive of arcane rituals and long-forgotten myths. For example, a bird-faced woman on a Vinca sculpture and a bird-faced baby she is holding would seem to be masked protagonists of ancient rites, probably enacting a mythological story about a bird Goddess and her divine child. Similarly, a terra-cotta head of a bull with human eyes from 4000 B.C.E. Macedonia suggests a masked protagonist of some other Neolithic ritual and myth. Some of these masked figures seem to represent cosmic powers, either benevolent or threatening. Others have a humorous effect, such as the masked man with padded knickers and exposed belly from fifth millennium B.C.E. Fafkos, described by Gimbutas as probably a comic actor. There are also what Gimbutas calls cosmic eggs. These too are symbols of the Goddess, whose body is the divine Chalice containing the miracle of birth and the power to transform death into life through the mysterious cyclical regeneration of nature.[7]

Indeed, this theme of the unity of all things in nature, as personified by the Goddess, seems to permeate Neolithic art. For here the supreme power governing the universe is a divine Mother who gives her people life, provides them with material and spiritual nurturance, and who even in death can be counted on to take her children back into her cosmic womb.

For instance, in the shrines of Catal Huyuk we find representations of the Goddess both pregnant and giving birth. Often she is accompanied by powerful animals such as leopards and particularly bulls.[8] As a symbol of the unity of all life in nature, in some of her representations she is herself part human and part animal.[9] Even in her darker aspects, in what scholars call the chthonic, or earthy, she is still portrayed as part of the natural order. Just as all life is born from her, it also returns to her at death to be once again reborn.

It could be said that what scholars term the chthonic aspect of the Goddess—her portrayal in surrealistic and sometimes grotesque form—represented our forebears' attempt to deal with the darker aspects of reality by giving our human fears of the shadowy unknown a name and shape. These chthonic images—masks, wall paintings, and statuettes symbolizing death in fantastic and sometimes also humorous forms—would also be designed to impart to the religious initiate a sense of mystical unity with both the dangerous as well as the benign forces governing the world.

Thus, in the same way that life was celebrated in religious imagery and ritual, the destructive processes of nature were also recognized and respected. At the same time that religious rites and ceremonies were designed to give the individual and the community a sense of participation in and control over the life-giving and preserving processes of nature, other rites and ceremonies attempted to keep the more fearful processes at bay.

But with all of this, the many images of the Goddess in her dual aspect of life and death seem to express a view of the world in which the primary purpose of art, and of life, was not to conquer, pillage, and loot but to cultivate the earth and provide the material and spiritual wherewithal for a satisfying life. And on the whole, Neolithic art, and even more so the more developed Minoan art, seems to express a view in which the primary function of the mysterious powers governing the universe is not to exact obedience, punish, and destroy but rather to give.

We know that art, particularly religious or mythical art, reflects not only peoples' attitudes but also their particular form of culture and social organization. The Goddess-centered art we have been examining, with its striking absence of images of male domination or warfare, seems to have reflected a social order in which women, first as heads of clans and priestesses and later on in other important roles, played a central part, and in which both men and women worked together in equal partnership for the common good. If there was here no glorification of wrathful male deities or rulers carrying thunderbolts or arms, or of great conquerors dragging abject slaves about in chains, it is not unreasonable to infer it was because there were no counterparts for those images in real life.[10] And if the central religious image was a woman giving birth and not, as in our time, a man dying on a cross, it would not be unreasonable to infer that life and the love of life—rather than death and the fear of death—were dominant in society as well as art.

THE WORSHIP OF THE GODDESS

One of the most interesting aspects of the prehistoric worship of the Goddess is what the mythologist and religious historian Joseph Campbell calls its "syncretism."[11] Essentially, what this means is that the worship of the Goddess was both polytheistic and monotheistic. It was polytheistic in the sense that she was worshiped under different names and in different forms. But it was also monotheistic—in the sense that we can properly speak of faith in the Goddess in the same way we speak of faith in God as a transcending entity. In other words, there are striking similarities between the symbols and images associated in various places with the worship of the Goddess in her various aspects of mother, ancestress or creatrix, and virgin or maid.

One possible explanation for this remarkable religious unity could be that the Goddess appears to have been originally worshiped in all ancient agricultural societies. We find evidence of the deification of the female—who in her biological character gives birth and nourishment just as the earth does—in the three main centers for the origins of agriculture: Asia Minor and southeastern Europe, Thailand in Southeast Asia, and later on also Middle America.[12]

In many of the earliest known creation stories from very different parts of the world, we find the Goddess-Mother as the source of all being. In the Americas, she is the Lady of the Serpent Skirt—of interest also because, as in Europe, the Middle East, and Asia, the serpent is one of her primary manifestations. In ancient Mesopotamia this same concept of the universe is found in the idea of the world mountain as the body of the Goddess-Mother of the universe, an idea that survived into historic times. And as Nammu, the Sumerian Goddess who gives birth to heaven and earth, her name is expressed in a cuneiform text of circa 2000 B.C.E. (now in the Louvre) by an ideogram signifying sea.[13]

The association of the feminine principle with the primal waters is also a ubiquitous theme. For example, in the decorated pottery of Old Europe, the symbolism of water— often in association with the primal egg—is a frequent motif. Here the Great Goddess, sometimes in the form of the bird or snake Goddess, rules over the life-giving force of water. In both Europe and Anatolia, rain-bearing and milk-giving motifs are interwoven, and ritual containers and vases are standard equipment in her shrines. Her image is also associated with water containers, which are sometimes in her anthropomorphic shape. As the Egyptian Goddess Nut, she is the flowing unity of celestial primordial waters. Later on, as the Cretan Goddess Ariadne (the Very Holy One), and the Greek Goddess Aphrodite, she rises from the sea.[14] In fact, this image was still so powerful in Christian Europe that it inspired Botticelli's famous Venus rising from the sea.

Although this too is rarely included in what we are taught about our cultural evolution, much of what evolved in the millennia of Neolithic history is still with us today. As Mellaart writes, "it formed the basis on which all later cultures and civilizations have built."[15] Or as Gimbutas put it, even after the world they represented was destroyed, the mythic images of our Goddess-worshiping Neolithic forebears "lingered in the substratum which nourished further European cultural developments," enormously enriching the European psyche.[16]

Indeed, if we look closely at the art of the Neolithic, it is truly astonishing how much of its Goddess imagery has survived—and that most standard works on the history of religion fail to bring out this fascinating fact. Just as the Neolithic pregnant Goddess was a direct descendant of the full-bellied Paleolithic "Venuses," this same image survives in the pregnant Mary of medieval Christian iconography. The Neolithic image of the young Goddess or Maiden is also still venerated in the aspect of Mary as the Holy Virgin. And of course the Neolithic figure of the Mother-Goddess holding her divine child is still everywhere dramatically in evidence as the Christian Madonna and Child.

Images traditionally associated with the Goddess, such as the bull and the bucranium, or horns of the bull, as symbols of the power of nature, also survived well into classical, and later Christian, times. The bull was appropriated as a central symbol of later "pagan" patriarchal mythology. Still later, the horned bull god was in Christian iconography converted from a symbol of male power to a symbol of Satan or evil. But in Neolithic times, the bull horns we now routinely associate with the devil had a very different meaning. Images of bull horns have been excavated in both houses and shrines at Catal Huyuk, where horns of consecration sometimes form rows or altars under representations of the Goddess.[17] And the bull itself is here also still a manifestation of the ultimate power of the Goddess. It is a symbol of the male principle, but it is one that, like all else, issues from an all-giving divine womb—as graphically depicted in a Catal Huyuk shrine where the Goddess is shown giving birth to a young bull.

Even the Neolithic imagery of the Goddess in two simultaneous forms—such as the twin Goddesses excavated in Catal Huyuk—survived into historic times, as in the classical Greek images of Demeter and Kore as the two aspects of the Goddess: Mother and Maid as symbols of the cyclical regeneration of nature.[18] Indeed, the children of the Goddess are all integrally connected with the themes of birth, death, and resurrection. Her daughter survived into classical Greek times as Persephone, or Kore. And her son-lover/husband likewise survived well into historic times under such diverse names as Adonis, Tammutz, Attis—and finally, Jesus Christ.[19]

This seemingly remarkable continuity of religious symbolism becomes more understandable if we consider that in both the Neolithic-Chalcolithic of Old Europe and the later Minoan-Mycenaean Bronze Age civilization the religion of the Great Goddess appears to have been the single most prominent and important feature of life. In the Anatolian site of Catal Huyuk the worship of the Goddess appears to permeate all aspects of life. For example, out of 139 rooms excavated between 1961 and 1963, more than 40 appear to have served as shrines.[20]

This same pattern prevails in Neolithic and Chalcolithic Europe. In addition to all the shrines dedicated to various aspects of the Goddess, the houses had sacred corners with ovens, altars (benches), and offering places. And the same holds true for the later civilization of Crete, where, as Gimbutas writes, "shrines of one kind or another are so numerous that there is reason to believe that not only every palace but every private house was put to some such use. . . . To judge by the frequency of shrines, horns of consecration, and the symbol of the double-axe, the whole palace of Knossos must have resembled a sanctuary. Wherever you turn, pillars and symbols remind one of the presence of the Great Goddess."[21]

To say the people who worshiped the Goddess were deeply religious would be to understate, and largely miss, the point. For here there was no separation between the secular and the sacred. As religious historians point out, in prehistoric and, to a large extent, well into historic times, religion was life, and life was religion.

One reason this point is obscured is that scholars have in the past routinely referred to the worship of the Goddess, not as a religion, but as a "fertility cult," and to the Goddess as an "earth mother." But though the fecundity of women and of the earth was, and still is, a requisite for species survival, this characterization is far too simplistic. It would be comparable, for example, to characterizing Christianity as just a death cult because the central image in its art is the Crucifixion.

Neolithic religion—like present-day religious and secular ideologies—expressed the worldview of its time. How different this worldview was from ours is dramatically illustrated if we contrast the Neolithic religious pantheon with the Christian one. In the Neolithic, the head of the holy family was a woman: the Great Mother, the Queen of Heaven, or the Goddess in her various aspects and forms. The male members of this pantheon—her consort, brother, and/or son—were also divine. By contrast, the head of the Christian holy family is an all-powerful Father. The second male in the pantheon—Jesus Christ—is another aspect of the godhead. But though father and son are immortal and divine, Mary, the only woman in this religious facsimile of patriarchal family organization, is merely mortal—clearly, like her earthly counterparts, of an inferior order.

Religions in which the most powerful or only deity is male tend to reflect a social order in which descent is patrilinear (traced through the father) and domicile is patrilocal (the wife goes to live with the family or clan of her husband). Conversely, religions in which the most powerful or sole deity is female tend to reflect a social order in which descent is matrilinear (traced through the mother) and domicile is likewise matrilocal (a husband goes to live with his wife's family or clan).[22] Moreover, a male-dominated and generally hierarchic social structure has historically been reflected and maintained by a male-dominated religious pantheon and by religious doctrines in which the subordination of women is said to be divinely ordained.

IF IT ISN'T PATRIARCHY IT MUST BE MATRIARCHY

Applying these principles to the mounting evidence that for millennia of human history the supreme deity had been female, a number of nineteenth- and early twentieth-century scholars came to a seemingly earthshaking conclusion. If prehistory was not patriarchal, it must have been matriarchal. In other words, if men did not dominate women, women must have dominated men.

Then, when the evidence did not seem to support this conclusion of female dominance, many scholars returned to the more conventionally accepted view. If there never was a matriarchate, they reasoned, male dominance must, after all, always have been the human norm.

The evidence, however, supports neither one of these conclusions. To begin with, the archaeological data we now have indicate that in its general structure prepatriarchal society was, by any contemporary standard, remarkably equalitarian. In the second place, although in these societies descent appears to have been traced through the mother, and women as priestesses and heads of clans seem to have played leading roles in all aspects of life, there is little indication that the position of men in this social system was in any sense comparable to the subordination and suppression of women characteristic of the male-dominant system that replaced it.

From his excavations of Catal Huyuk, where the systematic reconstruction of the life of the city's inhabitants was the primary archaeological goal, Mellaart concluded that though some social inequality is suggested by sizes of buildings, equipment, and burial gifts, this was "never a glaring one."[23] For example, there are in Catal Huyuk no major differences between houses, most of which show a standardized rectangular plan covering about twenty-five square meters of floor space. Even shrines are not structurally different from houses, nor are they necessarily larger in size. Moreover, they are intermingled with the houses in considerable numbers, once again indicating a communally based rather than a centralized, hierarchic social and religious structure.[24]

The same general picture emerges from an analysis of Catal Huyuk burial customs. Unlike the later graves of Indo-European chieftains, which clearly bespeak a pyramidal social structure ruled by a feared and fearful strongman on the top, those of Catal Huyuk indicate no glaring social inequalities.[25]

As for the relationship between men and women, it is true, as Mellaart points out, that the divine family of Catal Huyuk is represented "in order of importance as mother, daughter, son, and father,"[26] and that this probably mirrored the human families of the city's inhabitants, which were evidently matrilineal and matrilocal. It is also true that in Catal Huyuk and other Neolithic societies the anthropomorphic representations of the Goddess—the young Maid, the mature Mother, and the old Grandmother or Ancestress, all the way back to the original Creatrix—are, as the Greek philosopher Pythagoras later noted, projections of the various stages of the life of woman.[27] Also suggesting a matrilineal and matrilocal social organization is that in Catal Huyuk the sleeping platform where the woman's personal possessions and her bed or divan were located is always found in the same place, on the east side of the living quarters. That of the man shifts, and is also somewhat smaller.[28]

But despite such evidence of the preeminence of women in both religion and life, there are no indications of glaring inequality between women and men. Nor are there any signs that women subjugated or oppressed men.

In sharp contrast to the male-dominated religions of our time, in which in almost all cases until quite recently only men could become members of the religious hierarchy, there is here evidence of both priestesses and priests. For instance, Mellaart points out that although it seems likely that it was primarily priestesses who officiated at the worship of the Goddess in Catal Huyuk, there is also evidence pointing to the participation of priests. He reports that two groups of objects found only in burials in shrines were mirrors of obsidian and fine bone belt fasteners. The former were found only with the bodies of women, the latter only with men. This led Mellaart to conclude that these were "attributes of certain priestesses and priests, which would explain both their rarity and their discovery in shrines."[29]

It is also revealing that sculptures of elderly men, sometimes fashioned in a position reminiscent of Rodin's famous *The Thinker*, suggest that old men as well as old women had important and respected roles.[30] Equally revealing is that the bull and the bucranium, or horns of consecration, which have a central place in the shrines of Neolithic Anatolia, Asia Minor, and Old Europe and later in Minoan and Mycenaean imagery, are symbols of the male principle, as are the images of phalluses and boars, which make their appearance in the later Neolithic, particularly in Europe. Moreover, some of the earlier Goddess figurines are not only hybrids of human and animal features, but often also have features, such as exaggerated long necks, that can be interpreted as androgynous.[31] And of course the young god, the son-consort of the Goddess, plays a recurring part in the central miracle of pre-patriarchal religion, the mystery of regeneration and rebirth.

Clearly, then, while the feminine principle as the primary symbol of the miracle of life permeated Neolithic art and ideology, the male principle also played an important role. The fusion of these two principles through the myths and rituals of the Sacred Marriage was in fact still celebrated in the ancient world well into patriarchal times. For example, in Hittite Anatolia, the great shrine of Yazilikaya was dedicated to this purpose. And even later, in Greece and Rome, the ceremony survived as the *hieros gamos*.[32]

It is interesting in this connection that there is Neolithic imagery indicating an understanding of the joint roles of women and men in procreation. For example, a small stone plaque from Catal Huyuk shows a woman and man in a tender embrace; immediately next to them is the relief of a mother holding a child, the offspring of their union.[33]

All this imagery reflects the markedly different attitudes prevailing in the Neolithic about the relationship between women and men—attitudes in which linking rather than ranking appears to have been predominant. As Gimbutas writes, here "the world of myth was not polarized into female and male as it was among the Indo-Europeans and many other nomadic and pastoral peoples of the steppes. Both principles were manifest side by side. The male divinity in the shape of a young man or male animal appears to affirm and strengthen the forces of the creative and active female. Neither is subordinate to the other: by complementing one another, their power is doubled."[34]

Again and again we find that the debate about whether there once was or was not a matriarchate, which still periodically erupts in academic and popular works, seems to be more a function of our prevailing paradigm than of any archaeological evidence.[35] That is, in our culture built on the ideas of hierarchy and ranking and in-group versus out-group thinking, rigid differences or polarities are emphasized. Ours is characteristically the kind of if-it-isn't-this-it-has-to-be-that, dichotomized, either/or thinking that philosophers from earliest times have cautioned can lead to a simplistic misreading of reality. And, indeed, psychologists today have discovered it is the mark of a *lower* or less psychologically evolved state of cognitive and emotional development.[36]

Mellaart apparently tried to overcome this either/or, if-it-isn't-patriarchy-it-has-to-be-matriarchy tangle when he wrote the following passage. "If the Goddess presided over all the various activities of the life and death of the Neolithic population of Catal Huyuk, so in a way did her son. Even if his role is strictly subordinate to hers, the males' role in life seems to have been fully realized."[37] But in the contradiction between a "fully realized" and a "strictly subordinate" role we again find ourselves tangled up in the cultural and linguistic assumptions inherent in a dominator paradigm: that human relations must fit into some kind of superior-inferior pecking order.

However, looked at from a strictly analytical or logical viewpoint, the primacy of the Goddess—and with this the centrality of the values symbolized by the nurturing and regenerating powers incarnated in the female body—does not justify the inference that

Riane Eisler

women here dominated men. This becomes more apparent if we begin by analogizing from the one human relationship that even in male-dominant societies is not generally conceptualized in superiority-inferiority terms. This is the relationship between mother and child—and the way we perceive it may actually be a remnant of the prepatriarchal conception of the world. The larger, stronger adult mother is clearly, in hierarchic terms, superior to the smaller, weaker child. But this does not mean we normally think of the child as inferior or less valued.

Analogizing from this different conceptual framework, we can see that the fact that women played a central and vigorous role in prehistoric religion and life does not have to mean that men were perceived and treated as subservient. For here both men and women were the children of the Goddess, as they were the children of the women who headed the families and clans. And while this certainly gave women a great deal of power, analogizing from our present-day mother-child relationship, it seems to have been a power that was more equated with responsibility and love than with oppression, privilege, and fear.

In sum, in contrast to the still prevailing view of power as the power symbolized by the Blade—the power to take away or to dominate—a very different view of power seems to have been the norm in these Neolithic Goddess-worshiping societies. This view of power as the "feminine" power to nurture and give was undoubtedly not always adhered to, for these were societies of real flesh-and-blood people, not make-believe utopias. But it was still the normative ideal, the model to be emulated by both women and men.

The view of power symbolized by the Chalice—for which I propose the term *actualization power* as distinguished from *domination power*—obviously reflects a very different type of social organization from the one we are accustomed to.[38] We may conclude from the evidence of the past examined so far that it cannot be called matriarchal. As it cannot be called patriarchal either, it does not fit into the conventional dominator paradigm of social organization. However, using the perspective of Cultural Transformation theory we have been developing, it does fit the other alternative for human organization: a partnership society in which neither half of humanity is ranked over the other and diversity is not equated with inferiority or superiority.

. . . [T]hese two alternatives have profoundly affected our cultural evolution. Technological and social evolution tend to become more complex regardless of which model prevails. But the *direction* of cultural evolution—including whether a social system is warlike or peaceful—depends on whether we have a partnership or a dominator social structure.

NOTES

1. Marija Gimbutas, *Goddesses and Gods of Old Europe, 7000–3500 B.C.* (Berkeley and Los Angeles: University of California Press, 1982), 37–38.

2. See illustrations in James Mellaart, *Catal Huyuk* (New York: McGraw-Hill, 1967); Gimbutas, *Goddesses and Gods of Old Europe.*

3. *Goddesses and Gods of Old Europe,* plate 17 and text figure 148.

4. Nicolas Platon, *Crete* (Geneva: Nagel Publishers, 1966), 148.

5. For examples, see illustrations in Erich Neumann, *The Great Mother* (Princeton, NJ: Princeton University Press, 1955); Mellaart, *Catal Huyuk,* Gimbutas, *Goddesses and Gods of Old Europe.*

6. Gimbutas, *Goddesses and Gods of Old Europe,* examples (in order) from plates 58, 59, 105–7, 140, 144; plate 53, text figures 50–58 on pp. 95–103; 114, 181, 173, 108, 136.

7. Ibid., 66; plates 132, 341, 24, 25; pp. 101–7.

8. Mellaart, *Catal Huyuk,* 77–203.

9. Gimbutas, *Goddesses and Gods of Old Europe,* see, e.g., plates 179–81 for bee Goddess, plates 183–85 for Goddess with animal mask, p. 146 for Minoan snake Goddess with a bird's beak.

10. The absence of these images is also striking in the art of Minoan Crete. See, e.g., Jacquetta Hawkes, *Dawn of the Gods: Minoan and Mycenaean Origins of Greece* (New York: Random House, 1968), 75–76. The double ax of the Minoan Goddess is reminiscent of the hoe axes used to clear farmland and was, according to Gimbutas, also a symbol of the butterfly, part of the Goddess's epiphany. As Gimbutas notes, the image of the Goddess as a butterfly continued to be engraved on double axes (Gimbutas, *Goddesses and Gods of Old Europe,* 78, 186).

11. Joseph Campbell, "Classical Mysteries of the Goddess" (workshop at Esalen Institute, California, May 11–13, 1979). The cultural historian Elinor Gadon also stresses this aspect of the prehistoric worship of the Goddess but takes it one important step further. Gadon writes that the reemergence of the Goddess in our time is a key to "the radical pluralism so urgently needed to counteract the prevailing ethnocentrism and cultural imperialism" (prospectus for Elinor Gadon, *The Once and Future Goddess: A Symbol for Our Time* [San Francisco: Harper & Row, 1988]; and private communications with Gadon, 1986).

12. Ibid.

13. See, e.g., Joseph Campbell, *The Mythic Image* (Princeton, NJ: Princeton University Press, 1974), 157, 77.

14. Gimbutas, *Goddesses and Gods of Old Europe,* 112–50, 112, 145; figs. 87, 88, 105, 106, 107; p. 149.

15. Mellaart, *Neolithic of the Near East* (New York: Scribner, 1975), 279.

16. Gimbutas, *Goddesses and Gods of Old Europe,* 238.

17. Mellaart, *Catal Huyuk.* See, e.g., 108–9.

18. Ibid., 113.

19. See, e.g., Neumann, *The Great Mother.*

20. Mellaart, *Catal Huyuk,* 77.

21. Gimbutas, *Goddesses and Gods of Old Europe,* 80.

22. See, e.g., Jane Harrison, *Prolegomena to the Study of Greek Religion* (London: Merlin Press, 1903, 1962), 260–63.

23. Mellaart, *Catal Huyuk,* 225.

24. Mellaart, *Neolithic of the Near East,* 100; Mellaart, *Catal Huyuk,* chap. 6.

25. Mellaart, *Catal Huyuk,* chap. 9.

26. Ibid., 201.

27. Harrison, *Prolegomena to the Study of Greek Religion,* 262.

28. Mellaart, *Catal Huyuk,* 60.

29. Ibid., 202, 208.

30. Gimbutas, *Goddess and Gods of Old Europe*, 232, fig. 248. See also figs. 84–91 in Mellaart, *Catal Huyuk*, for examples of male figurines.

31. Gimbutas, *Goddesses and Gods of Old Europe*, 217, where Gimbutas notes that seventh and sixth millennium B.C.E. Goddess figurines often had long, cylindrical necks reminiscent of a phallus, that there were also phallic representations in the form of simple clay cylinders that sometimes had female breasts, and that the combining of female and male characteristics in one figure did not completely die out after the sixth millennium B.C.E.

32. Edwin Oliver James, *The Cult of the Mother Goddess* (London: Thames & Hudson, 1959), 87.

33. Mellaart, *Catal Huyuk*, 184.

34. Gimbutas, *Goddesses and Gods of Old Europe, 237.*

35. See, e.g., "the caveat that such a social order need not imply the domination of one sex, which the term 'matriarchy' would by its semantic analogue to patriarchy infer," in Kate Millett, *Sexual Politics* (New York: Doubleday, 1970), 28, n. 9; or Adrienne Rich's comment that "the terms 'matriarchy,' 'mother-right,' or 'gynocracy' tend to be used imprecisely, often interchangeably," in *Of Woman Born* (New York: Bantam, 1976), 42–43. Rich also notes that "Robert Briffault goes to some pains to show that matriarchy in primitive societies was not simply patriarchy with a different sex in authority" (p. 43). For a discussion of how the term *gylany* avoids this semantic confusion, see chapter 8.

36. Abraham Maslow, *Toward a Psychology of Being*, 2d ed. (New York: Van Nostrand-Reinhold, 1968).

37. Mellaart, *Catal Huyuk*, 184.

38. This distinction will be discussed at length in Riane Eisler and David Loye, *Breaking Free* (forthcoming). It is a distinction that is central to the new feminist ethic now being developed by many thinkers. See, e.g., Jean Baker Miller, *Toward a New Psychology of Women* (Boston: Beacon, 1976); Carol Gilligan, *In a Different Voice* (Cambridge: Harvard University Press, 1982); Wilma Scott Heide, *Feminism for the Health of It* (Buffalo: Margaretdaughters Press, 1985). Of particular interest in this context is Anne Barstow, "The Uses of Archaeology for Women's History: James Mellaart's Work on the Neolithic Goddess at Catal Huyuk," *Feminist Studies* 4 (October 1978): 7–18, who independently arrived at a similar conclusion about the way power was probably conceptualized in the societies that worshiped the Goddess (see p. 9).

"THE RAINBOW BRIDGE"

Brooke Medicine Eagle

> I found some dry, bleached bones today,
> and gathered them to put into a bag
> for casting to ask the future,
> when modern means have failed me.

The vision quest that I have done was with my teacher who is a Northern Cheyenne woman. She is eighty-five years old and is known as The Keeper of the Sacred Buffalo Hat. Her people call her The Woman Who Knows Everything. She and a younger medicine woman took me to a place called Bear Butte, South Dakota; it's plains country that goes up into the Black Hills. That's the traditional fasting, vision-questing place of the Sioux and Cheyenne and has been for centuries and centuries. What is usually done among the Cheyenne is that you fast and cleanse yourself bodily, emotionally, and psychically. Then you go atop a mountain for four days and nights with just a breechcloth on and a buffalo robe, and you stay there without food or water, praying for vision. This is the kind of quest that I did.

The younger medicine woman took me up the butte. She prepared and blessed a bed of sagebrush on a very rocky hill halfway up the mountain. This was to be my bed. After we smoked a pipe and offered prayers, she left me. So I spent the time there fasting and praying for vision.

It was just getting to be dark. Up on the mountain, I can look down over the country: There's a lake down below me; in the far-off distance are the Black Hills, and I can see the lights of Rapid City. I'm hoping it won't rain because I really don't want to be rained on up here. A few little clouds are flitting across the sky, but it is relatively warm, the late fall. I'm just lying here very peacefully. And beside me there comes a woman, older than me, but not really an old woman. She's dressed very simply, buckskin. And I'm surprised that she doesn't have beading on her dress. She has raven black hair in long braids. And she stands beside me and begins to talk to me. As she talks to me, her words come, but not in my ears; I don't really hear her say anything. It's as though she's feeding something in at my navel, and it comes through me, and I can interpret part of it in words but not all of it, like she's

---

Reprinted by permission of the author. This essay appeared in *Shamanic Voices: A Survey of Visionary Narratives*, edited by Joan Halifax (Dutton, 1979).

giving me something through my stomach and letting it come up. So the words that I put to it have to be my own, and I have discovered more and more of what she told me as time has gone on.

Just then the little clouds that were over the moon move off, and as they move away, the moonlight shining on her dress creates a flurry of rainbows, and I can see that her dress is beaded with crystal beads, hundreds of tiny crystal beads; the slightest movement she makes sends little flurries of soft rainbows all over. About this time, something else starts to happen. Down off the high part of the mountain, it starts to become light, and I hear soft drumbeats begin, very soft. There's a kind of dance that the women do that is very soft. And down off that mountain in a slow, soft, and gentle step come the old women, spirits of that land, that mountain, old gray-haired women, Indian women, dancing down. They either *are* light or carry light. They wind down the mountain and then circle around the hill I am on. And as they dance around in a circle, very quickly, into that circle comes another circle, this of young women, of my age and time, young women that I know, and they, too, are dancing. Those two circles are dancing and moving, and then they begin to weave in and out of each other, sway in and out of each other. And then inside of that circle comes another circle of seven old grandmothers, white-haired women, women who are significant to me, powerful old women.

In the Native American tradition, there is an amazing amount of humor. And the humor comes when all this very solemn, very slow, and very beautiful ceremony is taking place. Running off the mountain, with her hair flying, is this friend of mine. She's always late. She is a very high person, but she is very unstable. Into the circle comes Dianne, flying, with her hair streaming, late as always. And on her hand she is carrying a dove. The Rainbow Woman looks down on me and says, "Her name is Moon Dove," and she smiles. Dianne then lets the dove fly. The circles around me disappear, and I am again alone with the Rainbow Woman.

She said to me that the earth is in trouble, that the land is in trouble, and that here on this land, this Turtle Island, this North American land, what needs to happen is a balancing. She said that the thrusting, aggressive, analytic, intellectual, building, making-it-happen energy has very much overbalanced the feminine, receptive, allowing, surrendering energy. She said that what needs to happen is an uplifting and a balancing. And because we are out of balance, we need to put more emphasis on surrendering, being receptive, allowing, nurturing. She was speaking to me as a woman, and I was to carry this message to women specifically. But not only do women need to become strong in this way; we all need to do this, men and women alike.

Women are born into that kind of space. It's more natural for us to be receptive and nurturing. That's what being a woman in this body is about. But even the women in our society don't do that very well. None of us has ever been taught how to do that. We know how to *do* something; we know how to *make* something, how to *do*, how to *try*. But we need to allow, to be receptive, to surrender, to serve. These are things we don't know very well. So she told me that women especially need to find that place, to find the strength of their place, and that also the whole society, men and women, need that balance to bring ourselves into balance.

Another thing she said to me was that we on this North American continent are all children of the rainbow, all of us; we are mixed-bloods. And especially me she was speaking to, saying that she felt that I would be a carrier of the message between the two cultures, across the rainbow bridge, from the old culture to the new, from the Indian culture to the dominant culture, and back again. And in a sense, all of us in this generation can be that. We can help bridge that gap, build that bridge into the new age of balance.

Those are the kind of things that she talked about, about cleansing ourselves so that we can allow love and light and surrender to come through us. And when she finished talking, she stood quietly for a moment. Her feet stayed where they were, but she shot out across the sky in a rainbow arc that covered the heavens, her head at the top of that arc. And then the lights that formed that rainbow began to die out, almost like fireworks in the sky, died out from her feet and died out and died out. And she was gone.

When I woke up the next morning, on the other side of the sky was the completion of the rainbow that had started the night before. And for days and days after that, rainbows kept appearing in my life.

There are very few women who are on the path of the shaman, and yet, this is my way. I was raised on the Crow Reservation in Montana. My blood is Sioux and Nez Percé. The Indian tradition was very much hidden when I was growing up on the reservation. However, I am getting back, more and more, to the tribal way. This happened as I began to have visions; I was drawn back to the old ways by my visions. I did not choose it outwardly. It just came about.

One of the things that I feel about the quest for vision: The traditional Indians, when they prayed, their prayers were always "Not only for myself do I ask this, but that the people may live, the people may live." Any of us can dream, but when you seek a vision, you do this not only for yourself but that the people may live, that life might be better for all of us, not only for me but for all people.

I feel my purpose is to help in any way I can to heal the earth. I feel that we are in a time when the earth is in dire need of healing. We see it everywhere, the droughts, earthquakes, storms, pollution. Yes, the earth itself is in need of healing. And I feel that any way that I can help, that is my mission: to make it whole, to pay attention to that wholeness, not only in ourselves but also in relation to the earth.

The Indian people are the people of the heart. When the white man came to this land, what he was to bring was the intellect, that analytic, intellectual way of being. And the Indian people were to develop the heart, the feelings. And those two were to come together to build the new age, in balance, not one or the other.

It has been only a couple of hundred years now, and I think we're beginning to see the force of this land, that receptive force, come back again, and that balance is beginning to happen. And I feel that what we are is that land. We are those children Rainbow Woman talked about. We are the ones who are going to have to do it. We are that blend.

In the philosophy of the true Indian people, Indian is an attitude, a state of mind; Indian is a state of being, the place of the heart. To allow the heart to be the distributor of energy on this planet; to allow your heart, your feelings, your emotions to distribute your energy; to pull that energy from the earth, from the sky; to pull it down and distribute it from your heart, the very center of your being—that is our purpose.

Several different traditions talk about four or five different worlds and say that the Creator made all these worlds with one simple law: that we shall be in harmony and in balance with all things, including the sun. And time and again people have destroyed that harmony; we have destroyed that harmony. And we have done it again needlessly. Unless we bring about that balance again, this is our last chance.

We need to achieve a clarity and lack of resistance before we seek vision—a surrendering, a relinquishing. If you are unwilling to be in your experience now, then vision will not open for you. You need to get on that circle where there is no resistance, no up, no down, where there are no square corners to stumble on. Then, someday, you become that circle.

"THE CHIPKO WOMEN'S CONCEPT OF FREEDOM"

Vandana Shiva

On 30 November 1986, Chamundeyi, a woman of Nahi-Kala village in Doon Valley, was collecting fodder in the forest when she heard trucks climbing up the mountain toward the limestone quarry in the area. But since September 1986 there had been a Chipko camp on the road to the quarry set up by the village communities of Thano region, to stop the mining operations which have created ecological havoc in the region; the trucks should not, therefore, have been there. The quarry workers had attacked the protesters, removed them from the blockade, and driven the trucks through. Chamundeyi threw down her sickle, raced down the slope and stood in front of the climbing trucks, telling the drivers that they could go only over her dead body. After dragging her for a distance, they stopped and reversed.

In April 1987 the people of Nahi-Kala were still protesting because the government had been tardy in taking action to close the mine although the lease had expired in 1982. The mining operations were also in total violation of the 1980 Forest Conservation Act. People's direct action to stop the mining was an outcome of the government's failure to implement its own laws. The quarry contractor meantime tried to take the law into his own hands. On 20 March 1987, he brought about 200 hired thugs to the area who attacked the peaceful protesters with stones and iron rods. But the children, women and men did not withdraw from the blockade. They are their own leaders, their own decision-makers, their own source of strength.

The myth that movements are created and sustained by charismatic leaders from outside is shattered by the non-violent struggle in Nahi-Kala in which ordinary women like Itwari Devi and Chamundeyi have provided local leadership through extraordinary strength. It is the invisible strength of women like them that is the source of the staying power of Chipko—a movement whose activities in its two decades of evolution have been extended from embracing trees to embracing living mountains and living waters. Each new phase of Chipko is created by invisible women. In 1977, Bachni Devi of Advani created Chipko's ecological slogan: 'What do the forests bear? Soil, water and pure air.'

A decade later, in Doon Valley, Chamundeyi inspired the Chipko poet Ghanshyam 'Shailani' to write a new song:

Reprinted from *Ecofeminism* (Zed Books, 1993).

A fight for truth has begun
  At Sinsyaru Khala
A fight for rights has begun
  In Malkot Thano
Sister, it is a fight to protect
Our mountains and forests.
  They give us life
Embrace the life of the living trees
  And streams to your hearts
Resist the digging of mountains
Which kills our forests and streams
  A fight for life has begun at
  Sinsyaru Khala

On 29 March during a meeting of friends of Chipko, I spent a day with Chamundeyi and Itwari Devi—to learn about their hidden strengths, to learn from them about the hidden strengths of nature. Here are some extracts from our exchange of experiences:

Vandana: *What destruction has been caused by limestone mining in Nahi-Kala?*

Chamundeyi: When I came to Nahi 17 years ago, the forests were rich and dense with ringal, tun, sinsyaru, gald, chir, and banj. Gujral's mine has destroyed the ringal, the oak, the sinsyaru. Our water sources which are nourished by the forests have also dried up. Twelve springs have gone dry. Two years ago, the perennial waterfall, Mande-Ka-Chara which originates in Patali-ka-Dhar and feeds Sinsyaru Khala went dry. Mining is killing our forests and streams, our sources of life. That is why we are ready to give up our lives to save our forests and rivers.

Itwari: Sinsyaru-ka-Khala was a narrow perennial stream full of lush sinsyaru bushes. Today it is a wide barren bed of limestone boulders. With the destruction caused by mining our water, mills, forests and paddy fields have been washed away. When Gujral first came he was in rags. I remember I had come to the water mill to get flour ground. Gujral had come with a dilapidated truck, and his lunch was a dry chappati, with raw onion. Today, after having robbed our mountain for 26 years, Gujral is a rich man with 12 trucks who can hire armies of thugs to trouble and attack us, as he hired armies of labour to dig our mountain. We have been camping on the road for seven months now to stop his mine, and his efforts to hurt us and threats to kill us keep increasing.

First he started picking limestone boulders from the river bed. Then he climbed the mountain. He has done ten years of very intensive mining and turned our rich and productive mountain into a desert. The source of Sinsyaru has become a desert. We decided then that the mine must be closed if our children were to survive.

The young boys of the Yuvak Mandal who are working with our Mahila Mandal to get the mine closed, were six months or one year old when Gujral first came to our village.

They have spent a lifetime watching him treat our land and resources as his private property. The Chipko protest was precipitated when the boys went to demand royalty payment for the mining in Gram Sabha land. Gujral said to them, 'You have grown on crumbs I have thrown to you—how dare you demand royalty from me.' The boys said, 'We have grown with the nurturance of our mothers—and the mountains and forests and streams which are like our mothers—and we will no longer let you destroy our sources of sustenance. We will not let your trucks go to the mine.'

C: On 20 March we saw Gujral's truck come. They pushed out the five people who were at the Satyagraha camp—meantime the women rushed down to the camp. We held on to the trucks and said, 'Please stop, listen to us.' They had hired women from the Dehra Dun slums to assault us—they pushed us aside and went to the line. Eight thugs stayed with us and said, 'Listen, mothers and sisters, you have been sitting on a Chipko protest for six months now with the Chipko activists. What facilities have they created for you in six months?' I said, 'Listen brothers, Gujral has been digging our mountain for 26 years, what has he done for us? The Chipko people have been with us for only six months of struggle—come back in 26 years and find out what they helped us create.' Gujral's people said, 'Ask for whatever you need—we will provide it.' We replied, 'We have only one need and one demand, that the mine be closed.' They said they would stop mining and only take what has already been mined. We told them, 'No, those stones came from the mountain and we will put them back to stabilize it. We will make check-dams with them. We will protect our forests and mountain with the boulders. These boulders are the flesh of *Dharti Ma* (Mother Earth). We will return them to where they belong, and heal her wounds.' Then they said, 'For each trip we make, we will give you earnings from our truckload of limestone.' We continued to insist that we wanted the mine closed, that nothing could tempt us. They said 'We will give you a truck for transport. Bahuguna cannot give you that.' We answered 'We are our own transport, our feet are our most dependable transport. We do not need your trucks. We only want the mine closed.'

V: *This is the third time they have attacked you; what happened in the November* [1986] *incident?*

C: I had just fed my children and was going to the forest for fodder with my sons Suraj Singh and Bharat Singh. I saw a truck coming. I sent Suraj Singh to inform the Satyagrahis at the Camp, but they had already been attacked and removed from the road. I met the trucks half way up the mine and put myself in front of them and said, 'The trucks can go only over my dead body.' They finally turned back.

V: *What are the three most important things in life you want to conserve?*

C: Our freedom and forests and food. Without these, we are nothing, we are impoverished. With our own food production we are prosperous—we do not need jobs from businessmen and governments—we make our own livelihood—we even produce crops for sale like rajma and ginger; two quintals of ginger can take care of all our needs. Forests are central as sources of fertilizer and fodder. Our freedom to work in the forests and to farm is very important. Gujral's mine is destroying our work and our prosperity while they talk of mining and 'creating' work and prosperity.

V: *Do you feel tempted by his bribes?*

I: Gujral offered my son Rs. 500,000 if he would remove me from the Chipko protest. My son replied, 'Money I can get anywhere, but my mother's dignity and respect comes from the village community, and we can never sacrifice that.'

C: They went to my brother and said, 'Get your sister away.' Gujral himself came and said he would make a school and hospital for us. We asked him why it had taken him 26 years to think of all this? Now it was too late. We are determined to close his mine and protect ourselves.

V: *What is your source of strength (shakti)? What is Chipko's strength?*

I: *Shakti* comes to us from these forests and grasslands, we watch them grow, year in and year out through their internal *shakti* and we derive our strength from it. We watch our streams renew themselves and we drink their clear, sparkling water, that gives us shakti. We drink fresh milk, we eat ghee, we eat food from our own fields. All this gives us not just nourishment for the body but a moral strength, that we are our own masters, we control and produce our own wealth. That is why it is 'primitive', 'backward' women who do not buy their needs from the market but produce for themselves, who are leading Chipko. Our power is nature's power. Our power against Gujral comes from these inner sources and is strengthened by his attempts to oppress and bully us with his false power of money. We have offered ourselves, even at the cost of our lives, for a peaceful protest to close this mine, to challenge and oppose the power that Gujral represents. Each attempt to violate us has strengthened our integrity. They stoned us on 20 March when they returned from the mine. They stoned our children and hit them with iron rods, but they could not destroy our *shakti.*

Part V

ECOTHEOLOGY IN AN AGE OF ENVIRONMENTAL CRISIS

Spiritual Deep Ecology

Love animals, God has given them the rudiments of thought and joy untroubled. Do not trouble their joy, don't harass them, don't deprive them of their happiness.

—Fyodor Dostoyevsky

The deep ecology sense of self-realization goes beyond the modern Western sense of "self" as an isolated ego striving for hedonistic gratification. . . . Self, in this sense, is experienced as integrated with the whole of nature.

—Bill Devall and George Sessions

Familiarity with basic ecology will permanently change your world view. You will never again regard plants, microorganisms, and animals (including people) as isolated entities. Instead you will see them—more accurately—as parts of a vast complex of natural machinery—as, in the dictionary definition, "related elements in a system that operates in a definable manner."

—Paul Ehrlich

Being rock, being gas, being mist, being Mind,
Being the mesons travelling among the galaxies with the speed of light,
You have come here, my beloved one . . .
You have manifested yourself as trees, as grass, as butterflies, as single-celled beings, and as chrysanthemums;
but the eyes with which you looked at me this morning tell me you have never died.

—Thich Nhat Hanh

Deep ecology is both an orientation within environmental ethics and a spiritually based rethinking of human identity. The term was first used by environmental philosopher Arne Naess to signal the view that nature has value in its own right, and is not simply an instrument to meet human needs.

For deep ecology people's "selves" are not bounded solely by individuality or social group, but partly constituted by our connections to and at times identity with the natural world. In this regard, spiritual deep ecology echoes religious perspectives that ask us to "love our neighbor as ourselves," or that deny the essential reality of the isolated ego. Here, however, the expansion of identity has to do with connections to the nonhuman. As Joanna Macy writes in *World as Lover, World as Self*:

> In our infancy as a species, we felt no separation from the natural world around us. Trees, rocks, and plants surrounded us with a living presence as intimate and pulsing as our own bodies . . . Now . . . having gained distance and sophistication of perception, we can turn and recognize who we have been all along . . . we are our world knowing itself.

The selections which follow express a variety of deep ecological perspectives. Through a compelling account of personal experiences David Abram shows how a deep ecological sensibility is something we manifest as cultures and communities—or not at all. Thomas Berry, a Catholic monk cited by many as a leading teacher of deep ecology, tells a new story about humanity's place in the universe. Joanna Macy's perspective is rooted in Buddhism as well as deep ecology. Here she continues her profoundly important "despair and empowerment" work—in which she seeks to have us acknowledge both the pain and the healing power of our emotional responses to the environmental crisis. Paul Shepard, whose intellectual commitment to the human-nature bond goes back more than thirty years, argues for the centrality of animals to human cultural evolution.

The great gift of a deep ecological sensibility—whether it goes under that term or not—is to acquaint us with our most profound connections to the natural world, and to suggest a way beyond the limitations of the conventional social ego. Nevertheless, deep ecology faces some significant dilemmas. Even if we accept every deep ecological claim, we still will not know how we should interact with the natural world in any given situation. While nature may be sacred, a person must eat to live, and must necessarily displace other parts of nature in order to dwell in a house, warm his body, feed her children, and cultivate the land. To live is to use and be used. Further, is reverence for all of nature to be extended to ghetto rats and the AIDS virus? Is personal or human survival necessarily human centered rather than nature-loving?

Perhaps a deep ecological point of view can simply ask us to question carefully before we consume and displace; and to experience our utilization of nature as a sacred exchange rather than as casual consumption in a cosmic shopping mall.

"THE FAWN"

Edna St. Vincent Millay

There it was I saw what I shall never forget
And never retrieve.
Monstrous and beautiful to human eyes, hard to believe,
He lay, yet there he lay,
Asleep on the moss, his head on his polished cleft small ebony hooves,
The child of the doe, the dappled child of the deer.

Surely his mother had never said, "Lie here
Till I return," so spotty and plain to see
On the green moss lay he.
His eyes had opened; he considered me.
I would have given more than I care to say
To thrifty ears, might I have had him for my friend
One moment only of that forest day:

Might I have had the acceptance, not the love
Of those clear eyes;
Might I have been for him the bough above
Or the root beneath his forest bed,
A part of the forest, seen without surprise.

Was it alarm, or was it the wind of my fear lest he depart
That jerked him to his jointy knees,
And sent him crashing off, leaping and stumbling
On his new legs, between the stems of the white trees?

"THE ECOLOGY OF MAGIC"

David Abram

Late one evening I stepped out of my little hut in the rice paddies of eastern Bali and found myself falling through space. Overhead the black sky was rippling with stars, densely clustered in some regions, almost blocking out the darkness between them, and loosely scattered in other areas, pulsing and beckoning to each other. Behind them streamed the great river of light with its several tributaries. But the Milky Way churned beneath me as well, for my hut was set in the middle of a large patchwork of rice paddies, separated from each other by narrow two-foot-high dikes, and these paddies were all filled with water. By day, the surface of the pools reflected perfectly the blue sky, or the monsoon clouds, a reflection broken only by the thin, bright green tips of new rice. By night, the stars glimmered from the surface of the paddies, and the river of light whirled through the darkness underfoot; there seemed to be no ground in front of my feet, only the abyss of star-studded space falling away forever.

I was no longer simply beneath the night sky, but also above it—the immediate impression was of weightlessness. I might perhaps have been able to reorient myself, to regain some sense of ground and gravity, were it not for a fact that confounded my senses entirely: between the galaxies below and the constellations above drifted countless fireflies, their lights flickering like the stars, some drifting up to join the clusters of stars overhead, others, like graceful meteors, slipping down from above to join the constellations underfoot, and all these paths of light upward and downward were mirrored in the still surface of the paddies. I felt myself at times falling through space, at other moments floating and drifting. I could not dispel the profound vertigo and giddiness; the paths of the fireflies and their reflection in the water's surface held me in a sustained trance. Even after I crawled back to my hut and shut the door on this whirling world, the little room in which I lay seemed itself to be floating free of the earth.

Fireflies! It was in Indonesia that I was first introduced to the world of insects, and there that I first learned of the great influence that such diminutive entities could have upon the human senses. I had traveled to Indonesia on a research grant to study magic—more precisely, to study the relation between magic and medicine, first among the tradi-

Originally published in *Orion*, Summer 1991. Reprinted from chapter 1 in *Spell of the Sensuous: Perception and Language in a More-Than-Human World* (Pantheon, 1996; Vintage, 1997).

tional sorcerers, or *dukuns*, of the Indonesian archipelago, and later among the *dzankris*, the traditional shamans of Nepal.

The grant had one unique aspect: I was to journey into rural Asia not outwardly as an anthropologist or academic researcher, but as an itinerant magician, in hopes of gaining a more direct access to the local sorcerers. I had been a professional sleight-of-hand magician for five years back in the United States, helping put myself through college by performing in clubs and restaurants throughout New England. I had also taken a year off from my studies to travel as a street magician through Europe, and toward the end of that journey had spent some months in London, where I explored the use of sleight-of-hand magic in a therapeutic setting, as a way to open communication with distressed individuals largely unapproachable by clinical healers. As a result of this work I became interested in the relation, largely forgotten in the West, between folk medicine and magic.

It was this interest that eventually led to the grant, and to my sojourn in rural Asia. There my sleight-of-hand skills proved invaluable as a means of stirring the curiosity of the local shamans. Magicians, whether modern entertainers or indigenous, tribal sorcerers, have in common the fact that they work with the malleable texture of perception. When the local sorcerers gleaned that I had at least some rudimentary skill in altering the common field of perception, I was invited into their homes, asked to share secrets with them, and eventually encouraged—even urged—to participate in various rituals and ceremonies.

But my interest gradually shifted from a concern with the application of magical techniques in medicine and ritual curing toward a deeper pondering of the relation between traditional magic and the natural world. This broader concern seemed to hold the key to the earlier one. For *none* of the several island sorcerers that I came to know in Indonesia, nor any of the *dzankris* with whom I lived in Nepal, considered their work as ritual healers to be their major role or function within their communities. Most of them, to be sure, *were* the primary healers or "doctors" for the villages in their vicinity, and they were often spoken of as such by the inhabitants. But the villagers *also* sometimes spoke of them, in low voices and in very private conversations, as witches (or "leyaks" in Bali)—as dark magicians who at night might well be practicing their healing spells backwards, or, by turning to the left instead of to the right, might be afflicting people with the very diseases that they would later work to cure. I myself never saw any of those magicians or shamans with whom I became acquainted engage in magic for harmful purposes, nor any convincing evidence that they had ever done so. (Few of the shamans that I came to know even accepted money in return for their services, although they did accept gifts in the way of food, blankets, and the like.) Yet I was struck by the fact that none of them ever did or said anything to counter such disturbing rumors and speculations. Slowly I came to recognize that it was through the agency of such rumors, and the ambiguous fears these rumors engendered, that the sorcerers were able to maintain a basic level of privacy. By allowing the inevitable suspicions and fears to circulate unhindered in the region (and sometimes even by encouraging and contributing to such rumors), the sorcerers ensured that only those who were in real and profound need of their skills would dare approach them for help. This privacy, in turn, left the magicians free to attend to their primary craft and function.

A clue to this role may be found in the circumstance that shamans rarely live at the heart of their village; rather, their dwellings are commonly at the spatial periphery of the community or, most often, out beyond the edges of the village, amid the rice fields, or in a forest, or a wild cluster of boulders. We can easily attribute this location to the just-mentioned need for privacy, yet for the magician in a traditional culture it also serves another purpose, providing a spatial expression of his or her symbolic position with regard to the community. For the magician's intelligence is not encompassed within the society—its place is at the edge, mediating between the human community and the larger community of beings upon which the village depends for its nourishment and sustenance. This larger community includes, along with the humans, the multiple nonhuman entities that inhabit and constitute the local landscape, from the myriad plants and diverse animals—birds, mammals, fish, reptiles, insects—of the region, to the particular winds and weather patterns that inform the local geography, as well as the various land-forms—rivers, forests, mountains, caves—that lend their specific character to the surrounding earth.

The traditional shaman, as I came to discern in the course of my twelve months in Asia, is in many ways the "ecologist" of a tribal society. He or she acts as intermediary between the human community and the larger ecological field, regulating the flow of nourishment, not just from the landscape to the human inhabitants, but from the human community back to the local earth. By his or her constant rituals, trances, ecstasies, and "journeys," the shaman ensures that the relation between human society and the larger society of beings is balanced and reciprocal, and that the village never takes more from the living land than it returns—not just materially, but with prayers, propitiations, and praise. The scale of a harvest or the size of a hunt is ever negotiated between the tribal community and the natural world that it inhabits. To some extent every adult in the community is engaged in this process of listening and attuning to the other presences that surround and influence daily life. But the shaman or sorcerer is the exemplary voyager in the intermediate realm between the human and the more-than-human worlds, the primary strategist and negotiator in any dealings with the Others.

It is only as a result of his or her ongoing engagement with the animate powers that dwell beyond the human community that the traditional magician is able to alleviate many illnesses that arise *within* that community. Disease, in most such cultures, is conceptualized as a disequilibrium within the sick person, or as the intrusion of a demonic or malevolent presence into his or her body. There are, at times, destructive influences within the village or tribe that may disrupt the health and emotional well-being of susceptible individuals. Yet such influences are commonly traceable to an imbalance between the human community and the larger field of forces in which it is embedded. Any healer who is not attending to the relations between the human community and the larger field will likely dispel an illness from one person only to have it arise, perhaps in a new guise, somewhere else in the community. Hence the traditional magician or medicine-person functions primarily as an intermediary between human and nonhuman worlds, and only secondarily as a healer. Without a continually adjusted awareness of the relative balance or imbalance between the local culture and its nonhuman environs, along with the skills necessary to modulate that relation, any "healer" is worthless, indeed, not a healer at all. The medicine-person's primary allegiance, then, is not to the human community, but to the earthly web of relations in which that community is entwined, and it is from this that his or her power to alleviate human illness derives.

The primacy of the magician's relation to other species and to the earth is not always evident to Western researchers. Countless anthropologists have managed to overlook the ecological dimension of the shaman's craft, while writing at length of the shaman's rapport with "supernatural" entities. We must attribute much of this oversight to the modern assumption that nonhuman nature is largely determinate and mechanical, and that that which is regarded as mysterious, powerful, and beyond human ken must therefore be of some other, nonphysical realm outside nature—"supernatural." The oversight becomes still more comprehensible when we recognize that many of the earliest ethnologists were Christian missionaries, for the church has long assumed that only human beings have souls, and that the (other) animals, to say nothing of trees and rivers, were "created" for no other reason than to serve humankind. It is not surprising that most of these early ethnologists, steeped in the dogma of institutionalized Christianity, assumed a belief in supernatural, other-worldly powers among those tribal persons whom they observed awestruck and entranced by nonhuman (but nevertheless natural) forces. What is remarkable is the extent to which contemporary attitudes preserve their anthropocentric bias. We no longer dismiss the shaman's "spirit-helpers" as the superstitious claptrap of heathen primitives, yet we still refer to these enigmatic presences, respectfully now, as "supernaturals"—for we are unable to shed the sense, so endemic to our civilization, that nature is a rather prosaic and predictable realm, unsuited to such mysteries. Nevertheless, that which is regarded with the greatest awe and wonder by indigenous, oral cultures is, I suggest, none other than what we view as *nature* itself. The deeply mysterious powers and beings with whom the shaman enters into a rapport are ultimately the same entities—the very same plants, animals, forests, and winds—that to literate, "civilized" Europeans are just so much scenery, the pleasant backdrop to our more pressing human concerns.

To be sure, the shaman's ecological function, his or her role as intermediary between human society and the land, is not always obvious at first, even to a sensitive observer. We

see the shaman being called upon to cure an ailing tribesperson of sleeplessness, or to locate some missing goods; we witness the shaman entering into a trance and sending his or
her awareness into other dimensions in search of insight and aid. Yet we should not be so
ready to interpret these dimensions as "supernatural," nor as realms entirely "internal" to
the personal psyche of the practitioner. For it is likely that the "inner world" of our Western psychological experience, like the supernatural heaven of Christian belief, originated
in the loss of our ancestral reciprocity with the living landscape. When the animate presences with whom we have evolved over several million years are suddenly construed as
having less significance than ourselves, when the fecund earth that gave birth to us is interpreted as a soulless or determinate object devoid of sensations and feelings, then the numinous mysteries with which we have always been in touch must migrate, either into a
supersensory heaven beyond the natural world, or else into the human skull itself—the
only allowable refuge, in this world, for what is ineffable and unfathomable.

But in genuinely oral, tribal cultures, the sensuous world itself remains the dwelling
place of the gods, the mysterious powers that can either sustain or extinguish human life.
It is not by sending awareness out *beyond* the natural world that the shaman makes contact with the purveyors of life and health, nor by journeying into the personal psyche;
rather it is by propelling awareness *laterally*, outward into the depths of a landscape at
once sensuous and psychological, the living dream that we share with the soaring hawk,
the spider, and the stone silently sprouting lichens on its coarse surface.

The sorcerer's intimate relation to nonhuman nature becomes most evident when we
attend to the easily overlooked background of his or her practice, not just to the more visible tasks of curing and ritual aid to which the sorcerer is called by individual clients, or to
the larger ceremonies at which he or she presides and dances, but to the content of the
prayers made in preparation for such ceremonies and the countless ritual gestures enacted
when alone, the daily propitiations and praise that flow from the sorcerer toward the land
and its many voices.

The most sophisticated definition of "magic" that circulates today through the American
counterculture is "the ability or power to alter one's consciousness at will." No mention is
made of any reason for altering one's state of consciousness. In tribal cultures, however,
that which we call "magic" takes all of its meaning from the fact that humans in an oral
context experience their own intelligence as simply one form of awareness among many
others. The traditional magician cultivates an ability to shift out of his or her common
state of consciousness precisely in order to enter into rapport with the other organic forms
of sensitivity and awareness that animate the local landscape. Only by temporarily shedding the accepted perceptual logic of his or her culture can the sorcerer hope to enter into

relation with other species on their own terms. It is this, we might say, that defines a shaman: the ability to readily slip out of the perceptual boundaries that demarcate his or her particular culture—boundaries reinforced by social customs, taboos, and most importantly, the common speech or language—in order to make contact with and learn from the other powers in the land. The shaman's magic is precisely this heightened receptivity to the meaningful solicitations—songs, cries, gestures—of the larger, more than-human field.

Magic, then, in its perhaps more primordial sense, is the experience of living in a world made up of multiple intelligences, the institution that every natural form one perceives—from the swallows swooping overhead to the fly on a blade of grass and indeed the blade of grass itself—is an experiencing form, an entity with its own predilections and sensations, albeit sensations that are very different from our own.

The magician's relation to nonhuman nature was not at all my intended focus when I embarked on my research into the medical uses of magic in Indonesia, and it was only gradually that I became aware of this more subtle dimension of the native magician's craft. The first shift in my preconceptions came when I was staying for some days in the home of a young "balian," or magic practitioner, in the interior of Bali. I had been provided with a simple bed in a separate, one-room building in the balian's family compound (most homes in Bali are comprised of several separate small buildings set in a single enclosed plot of land). Early each morning the balian's wife came by to bring me a small plate of delicious fruit, which I ate by myself, sitting on the ground outside, leaning against my hut and watching the sun slowly climb through the rustling palm leaves.

I noticed, when she delivered the plate of fruit, that my hostess was also balancing a tray containing many little green bowls—small, boat-shaped platters, each of them woven neatly from a freshly cut section of palm frond. The platters were two or three inches long, and within each was a small mound of white rice. After handing me my breakfast, the woman and the tray disappeared from view behind the other buildings, and when she came by some minutes later to pick up my empty plate, the tray was empty as well.

On the second morning, when I saw the array of tiny rice-platters, I asked my hostess what they were for. Patiently, she explained to me that they were offerings for the household spirits. When I inquired about the Balinese term that she used for "spirit," she repeated the explanation now in Indonesian, that these were gifts for the spirits of the family compound, and I saw that I had understood her correctly. She handed me a bowl of sliced papaya and mango and slipped around the corner of the building. I pondered for a minute, then set down the bowl, stepped to the side of my hut, and peered through the trees. I caught sight of her crouched low beside the corner of one of the buildings, carefully setting what I presumed was one of the offerings on the ground. Then she stood up with the tray, walked to the other corner, and set down another offering. I returned to my bowl of fruit and finished my breakfast.

That afternoon, when the rest of the household was busy, I walked back behind the building where I had seen her put the two offerings. There were the green platters resting neatly at the two rear corners of the hut. But the little mounds of rice were gone.

The next morning I finished the sliced fruit, waited for my hostess to come by and take the empty bowl, then quietly headed back behind the buildings. Two fresh palm-leaf offerings sat at the same spots where the others had been the day before. These were filled with rice. Yet as I gazed at one of the offerings I noticed, with a start, that one of the kernels of rice was moving. Only when I knelt down to look more closely did I see a tiny line of black ants winding through the dirt to the palm leaf. Peering still closer, I saw that two ants had already climbed onto the offering and were struggling with the uppermost kernel of rice; as I watched, one of them dragged the kernel down and off the leaf, then set off with it back along the advancing line of ants. The second ant took another kernel and climbed down the mound of rice, dragging and pushing, and fell over the edge of the leaf, and then a third climbed onto the offering. The column of ants seemed to emerge from a thick clump of grass around a nearby palm tree. I walked over to the other offering and discovered another column of ants dragging away the rice kernels. This line emerged from the top of a little mound of dirt about fifteen feet away from the buildings. There was an offering on the ground by a corner of my building as well, and a nearly identical line of ants.

I walked back to my room chuckling to myself. The balian and his wife had gone to so much trouble to placate the household spirits with gifts, only to have them stolen by little six-legged thieves. What a waste! But then a strange thought dawned within me. What if the ants themselves were the "household spirits" to whom the offerings were being made?

The idea became less strange as I pondered the matter. The family compound, like most on this tropical island, had been constructed in the vicinity of several ant colonies. Since a great deal of cooking took place in the compound (which housed, in addition to the balian and his wife and children, various members of their extended family), and also the preparation of elaborate offerings of foodstuffs for various rituals and festivals, the grounds and buildings were vulnerable to infestations by the ant population. Such invasions could range from rare nuisances to a periodic or even constant siege. It became apparent that the daily palm-frond offerings served to preclude such an attack by the natural forces that surrounded (and underlay) the family's land. The daily gifts of rice kept the ant colonies occupied—and presumably, satisfied. Placed in regular, repeated locations at the corners of various structures around the compound, the offerings seemed to establish certain boundaries between the human and ant communities; by honoring this boundary with gifts, the humans apparently hoped to persuade the insects to respect the boundary and not enter the buildings.

Yet I remained puzzled by my hostess's assertion that these were gifts "for the spirits." To be sure there has always been some confusion between our Western notion of "spirit" (often defined in contrast to matter or "flesh") and the mysterious presences to which tribal and indigenous cultures pay so much attention. I have already alluded to the misunderstandings arising from the circumstance that many of the earliest Western students of these other customs were Christian missionaries all too ready to see ghosts and immaterial specters where the tribespeople were simply offering their respect to the local winds. While the notion of "spirit" has come to have, for us in the West, a primarily anthropomorphic or human association, my encounter with the ants was the first of many experiences suggesting to me that the "spirits" of an indigenous culture are primarily those modes of intelligence or awareness that do *not* possess a human form.

As humans we are well acquainted with the needs and capacities of the human body—we *live* our own bodies and so know from within the possibilities of our form. We cannot know, with the same familiarity and intimacy, the lived experience of a grass snake or a snapping turtle; we cannot readily experience the precise sensations of a hummingbird sipping nectar from a flower, or a rubber tree soaking up sunlight. Our experience may be a variant of these other modes of sensitivity, yet we cannot, as humans, experience entirely the living sensations of another form. We do not know with full clarity their desires or motivations—we cannot know, or can never be *sure* that we know, what they know. That the deer *does* experience sensations, that it carries knowledge of how to orient in the land, of where to find food and how to protect its young, that it knows well how to survive in the forest without the tools upon which we depend, is readily evident to our human senses. That the apple tree has the ability to create apples, or the yarrow plant the power to reduce a child's fever, is also evident. To humankind, these Others are purveyors of secrets, carriers of intelligence that we ourselves often need: it is these Others who can inform us of unseasonable changes in the weather, or warn us of imminent eruptions and earthquakes—who show us where we may find good berries to eat when we are lost, or the best route to follow back home. By watching them build their shelters and nests we glean clues regarding how to strengthen our own dwellings, and their deaths teach us of our own. We receive from them countless gifts of food, fuel, shelter, and clothing. Yet still they remain Other to us, inhabiting their own cultures and enacting their own rituals, never wholly fathomable. Finally, it is not only those entities acknowledged by Western civilization as "alive," not only the other animals or the plants that speak, as spirits, to the senses of an oral culture, but also the meandering river from which those animals drink, and the torrential monsoon rains, and the stone that fits neatly into the palm of the hand. The mountain, too, has its thoughts. The forest birds whirring and chattering as the sun slips below the horizon are vocal organs of the rain forest itself.

Bali, of course, is hardly an aboriginal culture—its temple architecture, irrigation systems, festivals, and crafts all bespeak the influence of various civilizations, most notably the

Hindu complex of India. In Bali, nevertheless, these influences are thoroughly intertwined with the indigenous animism of the Indonesian archipelago; the Hindu gods and goddesses have been appropriated, as it were, by the more volcanic spirits of the local terrain.

Yet the underlying animistic cultures of Indonesia, like those of many islands in the South Pacific, are steeped as well in beliefs often referred to by anthropologists as "ancestor-worship," and some may argue that the ritual reverence paid to one's long-dead human ancestors, and the assumption of their influence in present life, easily invalidates the assertion that the various "powers" or "spirits" that move throughout the discourse of these peoples are ultimately tied to *nonhuman* (but nonetheless sentient or intelligent) forces in the surrounding landscape.

This objection trades on certain notions fundamental to Christian civilization, such as the assumption that the "spirits" of dead persons necessarily retain their human form, and that they reside in a domain beyond the physical world. However, most indigenous tribal peoples have no such ready recourse to an immaterial realm outside earthly nature. For almost all oral cultures, the enveloping and sensuous earth remains the dwelling place of both the living and the dead. The "body"—whether human or otherwise—is not yet a mechanical object in such cultures, but a magical entity, the mind's own sensuous aspect, and at death the body's decomposition into soil, worms, and dust can only signify the gradual reintegration of one's elders and ancestors into the living landscape, from which all, too, are born. Each indigenous culture elaborates this recognition of metamorphosis in its own fashion, taking its clues from the natural environment in which it is embedded.

Often the invisible atmosphere that animates the visible world, the subtle presence that circulates both within us and around all things, retains within itself the breath of the dead person until the time when that breath will enter and animate another visible body—a bird, or a deer, or a field of wild grain. Some cultures may burn or "cremate" the body in order more completely to return the person, as smoke, to the swirling air, while that which departs as flame is offered to the sun and stars, and that which lingers as ash is fed to the dense earth. Still other cultures, like some in the Himalayas, may dismember the body, leaving parts in precise locations where they will likely be found by condors, or where they will be consumed by leopards or wolves, thus hastening the reincarnation of that person into a particular animal realm within the landscape. Such examples illustrate simply that death, in tribal cultures, initiates a metamorphosis wherein the person's presence does not "vanish" from the sensible world (where would it go?) but rather remains as an animating force within the vastness of the landscape, whether subtly, in the wind, or more visibly, in animal form, or even as the eruptive, ever to be appeased, wrath of the volcano. "Ancestor-worship" in its myriad forms, then, is ultimately another mode of attentiveness to nonhuman nature; it signifies not so much an awe or reverence of *human* powers, but rather a reverence for those forms that awareness takes when it is *not* in human form, when the familiar human embodiment dies and decays to become part of the encompassing cosmos.

This cycling of the human back into the larger world ensures that the other forms of life that we encounter, whether ants, or willow trees, or clouds, are never absolutely alien to ourselves. Despite their obvious differences in shape and ability and style of being, they remain distantly familiar, even familial. It is, paradoxically, this perceived kinship and consanguinity that renders the difference or otherness so eerily potent.

Several months after my arrival in Bali, I left the village where I was staying to visit one of the pre-Hindu sites on the island. I arrived on my bicycle early in the afternoon, after the bus carrying tourists from the coast had departed. A flight of steps took me down into a lush, emerald valley lined by cliffs and awash with the sound of the river and the sighing speech of the wind through high, unharvested grasses. I crossed a small bridge and stood in front of a great moss-covered complex of passageways, rooms, and courtyards carved by hand out of the black volcanic rock.

I noticed, at a distant bend in the canyon downstream, a further series of caves carved into the cliffs. These appeared more isolated and remote, unapproached by any footpath I could discern, and so I set out in their direction. After getting somewhat lost in the head-high grass and fording the river three times, I at last found myself beneath the caves. A short scramble up the rock wall brought me to the mouth of one of them, and I entered on my hands and knees.

It was a wide opening, maybe four feet high, and the interior receded only about five or six feet into the cliff. The floor and walls were covered with mosses, painting the cave with green patterns and softening the harshness of the rock; the place, despite its small size, or perhaps because of it, had an air of great friendliness. I climbed to two other caves, each about the same size, but felt drawn back to the first one, to sit cross-legged on the cushioning moss and gaze out across the canyon. It was quiet inside, a kind of intimate sanctuary. I began to explore the rich resonance of the enclosure, first just humming, then intoning a chant taught to me by a balian some days before. I was delighted by the overtones that the cave added to my voice and sat there singing for a long while. I did not notice the change in the wind outside, or the cloud-shadows darkening the valley until the rains broke, suddenly and with great force. The first storm of the monsoon!

I had experienced only slight rains on the island before then and was startled by the torrential downpour now sending stones tumbling along the cliffs, building puddles and then ponds in the landscape below, swelling the river. There could be no question of returning home—I would be unable to make my way back through the flood to the valley's entrance. And so, thankful for the shelter, I recrossed my legs to wait out the storm. Before long the rivulets falling along the cliff outside gathered themselves into streams, and two small waterfalls cascaded across the cave's mouth. Soon I was looking into a solid curtain of water—thin in some places, where the canyon's image flickered unsteadily, and thickly rushing in others. My senses were all but overcome by the wild beauty of the cascade and by the ferocious roar of sound, my body trembling inwardly at the weird sense of being sealed into my hiding place.

And then, in the midst of this tumult, I noticed a small, delicate activity just in front of me. Only an inch or two to my side of the torrent, a spider was climbing a thin thread stretched across the mouth of the cave. As I watched, it anchored another thread to the top of the opening, then slipped back along the first thread and joined the two at a point about midway between the roof and floor. I lost sight of the spider then. For a while it seemed to have vanished, thread and all, until my focus rediscovered it. Two more filaments now radiated from the center to the floor, and then another; soon the spider began to swing between these as on a circular trellis, trailing an ever-lengthening thread which it affixed to each radiating rung as it moved from one to the other, spiraling outward. Now and then it broke off its spiral dance and climbed to the roof or the floor to tug on the radii there, assuring the tautness of the threads, then crawled back to where it had left off. The spider seemed wholly undaunted by the tumult of waters spilling past. Whenever the web disappeared from my view, I waited to catch sight of the spinning arachnid, and then let its dancing form gradually draw the lineaments of the web back into visibility, tying my focus into each new knot of silk as it moved, weaving my gaze into the deepening pattern.

Abruptly, my vision snagged on a strange incongruity: another thread slanted across the web, neither radiating nor spiraling from the central juncture, violating the symmetry. As I followed it with my eyes, pondering its purpose in the overall pattern, I discovered that it was on a different plane from the rest of the web, for the web slipped out of focus when this new line became more clear. I soon saw that it led to its own center, about twelve inches to the right of the first, another nexus of forces from which several threads stretched to the floor and the ceiling. And then I saw that there was a different spider spinning this web, testing its tautness by dancing around it like the first, now setting the silken cross-weaves around the nodal point and winding outward. The two spiders spun independently of each other, but to my eyes they wove a single intersecting pattern. This widening of my gaze soon disclosed yet another spider spiraling in the cave's mouth, and suddenly I realized that there were *many* overlapping webs coming into being, radiating out at different rhythms from myriad centers poised—some higher, some lower, some minutely closer to my eyes and some farther away—between the stone above and below.

I sat mesmerized before this complexifying expanse of living patterns upon patterns— my gaze drawn like a breath into one converging group of lines, then breathed out into open space, then drawn down into another convergence. The curtain of water had become

David Abram

utterly silent. I tried at one point to hear it, but could not. My senses were entranced. I had the distinct impression that I was watching the universe being born, galaxy upon galaxy.

Night filled up the cave with darkness. The rain had not stopped. Yet strangely, I felt neither cold nor hungry, only remarkably peaceful and at home. Stretching out upon the moist, mossy floor near the back of the cave, I slept.

When I awoke the sun was staring into the canyon, the grasses below rippling with blue and green. I could see no trace of the webs, nor their weavers. Thinking that they were invisible to my eyes without the curtain of water behind them, I felt carefully with my hands around and through the mouth of the cave. But the webs were gone. I climbed down to the river and washed, then hiked across and out of the canyon to where my bicycle was drying in the sun and headed back to my own valley.

I have never, since that time, been able to encounter a spider without feeling a great strangeness and awe. To be sure, insects and spiders are not the only powers, or even central presences, within the Indonesian universe. But they were *my* introduction to the spirits, to the magic afoot in the landscape. It was from them that I first learned of the intelligence that lurks in nonhuman nature, the ability of an alien form of sentience to echo one's own—to instill in one a reverberation that temporarily shatters habitual ways of seeing and feeling, leaving one open to a world all alive, awake, and aware. It was from such small beings that my senses first learned of the countless worlds within worlds that spin in the depths of this world that we commonly inhabit, and it was from them that I learned my body could, with practice, enter sensorially into these dimensions. The precise, minuscule craft of the spiders had so honed and focused my awareness that the very web-work of the universe, of which my own flesh was a part, seemed to be being spun by their arcane art. I have already spoken of the ants, and of the fireflies, whose sensory likeness to the lights in the night sky had taught me of the impermanence of galaxies and the fickleness of gravity. The long and cyclical trance that we call malaria was also brought to me by insects, in this case mosquitoes, and I lived for three weeks in a feverish state of shivers, sweat, and visions.

I had rarely paid much attention to the natural world before, but my exposure to traditional magicians and seers was rendering me increasingly susceptible to the solicitations of nonhuman things. I began to see and to hear in a manner I never had before. When a magician spoke of a power or "presence" lingering in the corner of his house, I learned to notice the ray of sunlight that was pouring through a chink in the wall, illuminating a column of drifting dust, and to realize that that column of light was indeed a power, influencing the air currents by its warmth, even influencing the mood of the room. Although I had not consciously seen it before, it had already been structuring my experience. My ears began to attend in a new way to the songs of birds—no longer just a melodic background to human speech, but meaningful speech in its own right, responding to and commenting on events in the surrounding world. I became a student of subtle differences: the way a breeze may flutter a single leaf on a tree, leaving the others silent and unmoved (had not that leaf, then, been brushed by a magic?); or the way the intensity of the sun's heat expresses itself in the precise rhythm of the crickets. Walking along the dirt paths, I learned to slow my pace in order to feel the difference between one hill and the next, or to taste the presence of a particular field at a certain time of day when, as I had been told by a local *dukun*, the place had a special power and proffered unique gifts. It was a power communicated to my senses by the way the shadows of the trees fell at that hour, and by smells that only then lingered in the tops of the grasses without being wafted away by the wind, and other elements I could only isolate after many days of stopping and listening.

Gradually, other animals began to intercept me in my wanderings, as if some quality in my posture or the rhythm of my breathing had disarmed their wariness; I would find myself face to face with monkeys, and with large lizards that did not slither away when I spoke, but leaned forward in apparent curiosity. In rural Java I often noticed monkeys accompanying me in the branches overhead, and ravens walked toward me on the road, croaking. While at Pangandaran, a peninsula jutting out from the south coast of Java ("a place of many spirits," I was told by nearby fishermen), I stepped out from a clutch of trees and discovered I was looking into the face of one of the rare and beautiful bison that are found only on that island. Our eyes locked. When it snorted, I snorted back; when it shifted its shoulders, I shifted my stance; when I tossed my head, it tossed its own in reply. I found myself caught in a nonverbal conversation with this Other, a gestural duet with which my reflective awareness had very little to do. It was as if my body were suddenly being motivated by a wisdom older than my thinking mind, as though it were held and moved by a logos—deeper than words—spoken by the Other's body, the trees, the air, and the stony ground on which we stood.

I returned to North America excited by the new sensibilities that had stirred in me—my newfound awareness of a more-than-human world, of the great potency of the land, and particularly of the keen intelligence of other animals, large and small, whose lives and cultures interpenetrate our own. I startled neighbors by chattering with squirrels, who quickly climbed down the trunks of their trees and across the lawns to banter with me, and by gazing for hours on end at a heron fishing in a nearby estuary, or at gulls dropping clams on the rocks along the beach.

Yet, very gradually, I began to lose my sense of the animals' own awareness. The gulls' technique for breaking open the clams began to appear as a largely automatic behavior, and I could not easily feel the attention that they must bring to each new shell. Perhaps each shell was entirely the same as the last, and no spontaneous attention was necessary. . . .

I found myself now observing the heron from outside its world, noting with interest its careful, high-stepping walk and the sudden dart of its beak into the water, but no longer feeling its tensed yet poised alertness with my own muscles. And, strangely, the suburban squirrels no longer responded to my chittering calls. Although I wished to, I could not focus my awareness on engaging in their world as I had so easily done a few weeks earlier, for my attention was quickly deflected by internal verbal deliberations of one sort or another, by a conversation I now seemed to carry on entirely within myself. The squirrels had no part in this conversation.

It became increasingly apparent, from books and articles and discussions with various people, that other animals were not as awake and aware as I had assumed, that they lacked any genuine language and hence the possibility of real thought, and that even their seemingly spontaneous responses to the world around them were largely "programmed" behaviors, "coded" in the genetic material now being mapped by biologists. Indeed, the more I spoke *about* other animals, the less possible it became to speak *to* them. I slowly came to discern that there was no common ground between the unlimited human intellect and the limited sentience of other animals, no medium through which we and they might communicate and reciprocate one another.

As the sentient landscape gradually receded behind my more exclusively human concerns, threatening to become little more than an illusion or fantasy, I began to feel, particularly in my chest and abdomen, as though I were being cut off from vital sources of nourishment. I was indeed reacclimating to my own culture, becoming more attuned to its styles of discourse and interaction, yet my bodily senses seemed to be losing their edge, becoming less awake to certain patterns and changes. The thrumming of crickets, like the songs of the local blackbirds, readily faded from my awareness, and it was only by a great effort of will that I could bring them back into my perceptual field. The flights of sparrows and of dragonflies no longer carried my attention very long, if I noticed them at all. My skin quit registering the changes in the breeze, and smells seemed to have vanished from the world almost entirely. My nose woke up only once or twice a day, perhaps while cooking, or when taking out the garbage.

In Nepal, the air had been filled with smells—whether in the cities, where burning incense combined with the aromas of roasting meats and honeyed pastries and fruits for trade in the open market, and the stench of organic refuse rotting in the ravines, and sometimes of corpses being cremated by the river; or in the high mountains, where the wind carried the whiffs of countless wildflowers, and of the newly turned earth outside the villages, where the fragrant dung of the yaks was drying in round patties on the outer walls of the houses, to be used when dry as fuel for the household fires, and where smoke from those many home fires always mingled in the outside air. And sounds as well: the chants of aspiring monks and Buddhist adepts blended with the ringing of prayer bells on near and distant slopes, accompanied by the raucous croaks of ravens, and the sigh of the wind pouring over the passes, and the flapping of prayer flags, and the distant hush of the river cascading through the far-below gorge. There the air was a thick and richly textured presence, filled with invisible but nonetheless tactile, olfactory, and audible influences. In America, however, the air seemed thin and void of substance or influence. Here it was not a sensuous medium—the felt matrix of our breath and the breath of the other animals and plants and soils—but merely an absence, and indeed was commonly spoken of as empty space. I found myself lingering near wood-fires and even garbage dumps—much to the dismay of my friends—for only such an intensity of smells served to remind my body of its immersion in an enveloping medium, and with this experience came a host of body-memories from my sojourn among the shamans and village people of rural Asia.

Today, in the "developed world," many persons in search of spiritual meaning or self-understanding are enrolling for workshops in "shamanic" methods of personal discovery and revelation. Meanwhile some psychotherapists have begun to specialize in "shamanic healing techniques." "Shamanism" has thus come to denote an alternative form of therapy; the emphasis among these practitioners of popular Shamanism is on personal insight and curing. These are noble aims, to be sure. But they are secondary to, and derivative from, the primary role of the indigenous shaman, a role that cannot be fulfilled without long and sustained exposure to wild nature, its patterns and vicissitudes. Mimicking the indigenous shaman's curative methods without his intimate knowledge of the wider natural community cannot, if I am correct, do anything more than trade certain symptoms for others, or shift the locus of dis-ease from place to place within the human community. For the source of illness lies in the relation *between* the human culture and the natural landscape in which it is embedded. Western industrial society, of course, with its massive scale and hugely centralized economy, can hardly be seen in relation to any particular landscape or ecosystem; the more-than-human ecology with which it is directly engaged is the biosphere itself. Sadly, our society's relation to the living biosphere can in no way be considered a reciprocal or balanced one. With thousands of acres of nonregenerating forest disappearing every hour and hundreds of species becoming extinct each month as a result of our excesses, we can hardly be surprised by the amount of epidemic illness in our culture, from increasingly severe immune dysfunctions and cancers, to widespread psychological distress, depressions, and ever more frequent suicides, to the growing number of murders committed for no apparent reason by otherwise coherent individuals.

From an animistic perspective, the clearest source of all this distress, both physical and psychological, lies in the aforementioned violence needlessly perpetrated by our civilization upon the ecology of the planet; only by alleviating the latter will we be able to heal the former. This may sound at first like a simple statement of faith, yet it makes eminent and obvious sense as soon as we recognize our thorough dependence upon the countless other organisms with whom we have evolved. Caught up in a mass of abstractions, our attention hypnotized by a host of human-made technologies that only reflect us back upon ourselves, it is all too easy for us to forget our carnal inherence in a more-than-human matrix of sensations and sensibilities.

Our bodies have formed themselves in delicate reciprocity with the manifold textures, sounds, and shapes of an animate earth—our eyes have evolved in subtle interaction with other eyes, as our ears are attuned by their very structure to the howling of wolves and the honking of geese. To shut ourselves off from these other voices, to continue by our lifestyles to condemn these other sensibilities to the oblivion of extinction, is to rob our own senses of their integrity, and to rob our minds of their coherence. We are human only in contact and conviviality with what is not human. Only in reciprocity with what is Other will we begin to heal ourselves.

"INTO THE FUTURE"

Thomas Berry

Since the appearance of *Silent Spring* by Rachel Carson in 1962 we have been reflecting on the tragic consequences of the plundering industrial society that we have brought into existence during these past few centuries. That we should have caused such damage to the entire functioning of the planet Earth in all its major biosystems is obviously the consequence of a deep cultural pathology.

Just as clearly there is need for a deep cultural therapy if we are to proceed into the future with some assurance that we will not continue in this pathology or lapse into the same pathology at a later date. We still do not have such a critique of the past or a therapy for the present. Yet even without such evaluation of our present situation we must proceed with the task of creating a viable future for ourselves and for the entire planetary process.

The two things needed to guide our judgment and to sustain the psychic energies required for the task are a certain terror at what is happening at present, and a fascination with the future that is available to us if only we respond creatively to the urgencies of the present.

I am concerned in this chapter with the second of these requirements. I wish especially to outline the conditions for entering onto a future that will lead to that wonderful fulfillment for which the entire planet as well as ourselves seems to be destined.

The first condition for achieving this objective is to realize that the universe is a communion of subjects, not a collection of objects. The devastation of the planet can be seen as a direct consequence of a loss of this capacity for human presence to the nonhuman world. This reached its most decisive moment in the seventeenth-century proposal of René Descartes that the universe is composed simply of "mind and mechanism." In this single stroke he, in a sense, killed the planet and all its living creatures with the exception of the human.

The thousandfold voices of the natural world suddenly became inaudible to the human. The mountains and rivers and the wind and the sea all became mute insofar as humans were concerned. The forests were no longer the abode of an infinite number of spirit presences but were simply so many board feet of timber to be "harvested" as objects to be used for human benefit. Animals were no longer the companions of humans in the single community of existence. They were denied not only their inherent dignity, but even their rights to habitat.

As we recover our awareness of the universe as a communion of subjects a new interior experience awakens within the human. The barriers disappear. An enlargement of soul takes place. The excitement evoked by all natural phenomena is renewed. Dawn and sunset are once again transforming experiences as are all the sights and sounds and scents and tastes and the feel of the natural world about us, the surging sea, the sound of the wind, the brooding forests. All this could be continued in a never-ending listing of the experiences that take place constantly throughout the planet, experiences that have been lost to large segments of the human community in recent centuries—not because the phenomena do not surround us constantly, but that we have become autistic, as though large segments of the human mind have become paralyzed. It is no wonder that humans have devastated the planet so extensively. It was only a collection of objects to be used.

Associated with this attitude is the loss of realization that the planet Earth is a onetime endowment. It came into being at a moment that will never occur again. It was given a structure and a quantum of energy for its self-shaping processes whereby it could bring forth all those remarkable geological formations and all those magnificent modes of life expression that we see about us. The Earth was caught up in an inner dynamism that is overwhelming in its impact on human consciousness. These energies have been functioning throughout these past millennia with remarkable genius in a sequence of transformations on this planet that will never take place again. The quantum of energy needed has been expended. Species that we wantonly extinguish will never appear again. The quantum of energy involved in their historical existence has been expended.

There does exist at present a quantum of energy available for a creative movement from the terminal Cenozoic era to the emergent Ecozoic. Yet it will be available only for a brief period of time. Such transformation moments arise in times of crisis that need resolution immediately. So with the present the time for action is passing. The devastation increases. Yet the time is limited. The Great Work remains to be done. This is not a situation that can be remedied by trivial or painless means. A largeness of vision and a supreme dedication are needed.

Our only hope for such a renewal is our awakening to the realization that the Earth is primary and that humans are derivative. That this relation should be so obvious and yet so consistently violated is beyond all understanding. This primacy of the Earth community applies to every mode of human activity: economics, education, law, medicine, religion. The human is a subsystem of the Earth system. The primary concern in every phase of human activity must be to preserve the integrity of the Earth system. Only then can the subsystems function with any efficacy. Yet no phase of human activity is so directly violated as this relation of the human to the Earth.

In the realm of jurisprudence, the English Common Law tradition that has claimed such superiority in its conceptions of the human and the dignity of the human, has little sense of the larger governing principles of the universe or of the planet. This tradition lays great emphasis on the rights of humans. In this context the nonhuman world has become property to be used by the human. A governance and a jurisprudence founded in the supremacy of the already-existing Earth governance is needed. An interspecies jurisprudence is needed. The primary community is not the human community but the Earth community. The primary obligations are to the success of this larger community.

Especially in religion the human depends on the natural system. For it is the wonder and majesty of the universe that evokes the sense of the divine and the sensitivity to the sacred. For the universe is a mysterious reality. We can know only the marginal aspects of how the universe or the Earth functions. Once the divine is perceived through written Scriptures there is then a tendency to exclude the evidences of the natural world of things, for these, it is thought, do not communicate the sense of the sacred except in some minor way. Yet we can never replace our need for a resplendent natural world if we are to respond effectively to the exaltation of the divine or our sense of the sacred.

Since the discovery of the universe as an evolutionary process there is the need to establish a new sense of the revelatory experience. That this new mode of experiencing the universe carries with it a new modality in the manifestation of the ultimate mysteries of the universe implies that future generations will need to be religious within this context. Our traditional Scriptures will probably not be effective in awakening future generations to a sense of the sacred as they have done in past generations. This will involve a serious process of adaptation, a new awakening to the divine not only through the awesome qualities of the universe as experienced immediately, but also through the immense story of the universe and its long series of transformations.

We also need to establish rituals for celebrating these transformation moments that have enabled the universe and the planet Earth to develop over the past many years. This would involve celebrating the primordial moment of emergence of the universe and such other transformation moments as the supernova collapse of the first generation of stars whereby the ninety-some elements needed for life and consciousness came into existence. We should especially celebrate that star out of which our own solar system was born and the various life forms of Earth became possible.

The discovery of sexual reproduction upon which the evolutionary process depends so directly, the discovery of photosynthesis, of respiration, the emergence of life out of the sea and its venturing onto the land, the appearance of the first trees, the first flowering plants, the transition to the Cenozoic period, the emergence of the human—all these are sacred moments. To celebrate these occasions would renew our sense of the sacred character of the universe and of the planet Earth.

Another condition for entering a viable relationship of the human with the Earth community is a realization that the planet Earth will never again function in the future in the manner that it has functioned in the past. A decisive transformation has taken place, for whereas the human had nothing to say in the emergent period of the universe prior to the present, in the future the human will be involved in almost everything that happens. We have passed over a threshold. While we cannot make a blade of grass, there is liable not to be a blade of grass in the future unless it is accepted, protected, and fostered by the human. Sometimes, too, there is a healing that can be brought about by human assistance.

Just now our modern world with its scientific technologies, its industrial processes, and its commercial establishments functions with amazing arrogance in our human attitude toward the natural world. The assumption is that the human is the supreme reality and that every other being is available for exploitation in the service of the human. The supreme law of economics is to take as much as possible of the Earth's resources to be processed, passed through the consumer economy as quickly as possible, and then deposited as residue on the waste heap. The greater amount of natural resources consumed in this manner, the greater the Gross Domestic Product or the Gross Human Product, the more successful the human enterprise is thought to be, although the final consequence of such an economic program is to turn the entire planet into a wasteland. Any sense of the sacred, any restraints in favor of the inner coherence and resplendence of the natural world, these are thought of as the expression of an unendurable romanticism.

Yet the planet now exists in a more intricate relation with the human than ever before. The very devastation wrought by the human has brought about a new type of violence in human-Earth relationships. Yet this apparent control by the human does not imply that the human can, as it were, run the planet or bring the planet into any context that the human wishes. The human can bring about extinction on a broad scale, but it cannot bring about life through its own power. It can only assist in some limited way in evoking life through the processes inherent in the Earth itself.

The ultimate goal of any renewal process must be to establish a "mutually enhancing mode of human presence on the Earth." While this mutual enhancement can be achieved only within limits, since the human, as every other being, in some manner places stress upon the larger process, it is something that can make the gains and the losses more proportional and more acceptable within the larger context of the planetary community.

What can be hoped for is a sense of the human joining in the larger liturgy of the universe itself. The very cosmological patterns of universe-functioning that were established in much earlier times can be considered as a primordial liturgy. This liturgy inherent in the ancient mystique of the Earth and its functioning might be established once again— this time, however, not simply in the traditional sequence of seasonal renewal, but also in the sequence of irreversible transformations that can now be identified as the larger story of the planetary process.

This story of the universe now becomes the basic context for education. This comprehensive context includes all education, from the earliest period of schooling through to professional schools. The story of the universe expresses a functional cosmology that needs to be taught at every level of training. To be educated is to know the story and the human role in the story. Through this story we come to know the manner whereby we ourselves came into being and the role that we should be fulfilling in the story. Because our capacity to tell this story in its full dimensions in space and in its sequence of transformations in time is only recently attained, we are only now beginning to understand its significance.

Through this story we can now guide our way through this transition phase of our history, from the terminal Cenozoic into the emerging Ecozoic. This emergent phase of Earth history can be defined as that period when humans would be present to the Earth in a mutually enhancing manner. This story evokes not only the guidance but also the psychic energy needed to carry out the sequence of transformations that is now required of us as we move into the future.

Throughout its vast extent in space and its long sequence of transformations in time the universe constitutes a single, multiform, sequential, celebratory event. Every being in the universe is intimately present to and influencing every other being in the universe. Every being contributes to the magnificence of the whole. Because the universe is the only self-referent mode of being in the phenomenal world it constitutes the norm of all reality and value. The universe is the only text without context. Every particular mode of being is universe-referent and its meaning is established only within this comprehensive setting. This is the reason why this story of the universe, and especially of the planet Earth, is so all-important. Through our understanding of this story our own role in the story is revealed. In this revelation lies our way into the future.

Thomas Berry

"FAITH, POWER, AND ECOLOGY"

Joanna Macy

Yesterday morning at this time I was standing for about an hour in the sweet, gentle, English drizzle. I was in a large meadow with about forty men and women; three of them held toddlers. We stood in a circle and at the center of the circle were two ancient, sacred standing stones. We had come there at the close of a five-day workshop on ecology, and our band included activists from all over the island—social workers, civil servants, artisans, teachers, homemakers—drawn together by a common concern for the fate of our planet.

In the presence of those stones, thousands of years old, we seemed to find ourselves in two dimensions of time simultaneously. One was vast and immeasurable. As we tried to reach back to the ancient Earth wisdom of the culture that erected the stones, we sensed the long, long journey of the unfolding of life on this planet. At the same time, given the focus of the workshop, we were acutely aware of this particular historical moment when forces our culture has unleashed seem to be destroying our world.

Among us were Christians, Jews, Buddhists, Pagans. Yet, despite the differing belief systems to which we belonged, the prayers and affirmations that spontaneously arose in that circle expressed a common faith and fueled a common hope. They bespoke a shared commitment to engage in actions and changes in lifestyle on behalf of our Earth and its beings. They expressed a bonding to this Earth, where we go beyond feeling sorry for the Earth or scared for ourselves, to experience relationship—relationship that can be spiritually as well as physically sustaining, a relationship that can empower.

Fresh from that experience, it seems fitting to address the issue of faith and ecology. Faith is an elusive and questionable commodity in these days of a dying culture. Where do you find it? If you've lost a faith, can you invent one? Which faith to choose? Some of us have retained a faith in a just creator God or in a lawful, benevolent order to the universe. But some of us find it hard, even obscene, to believe in an abiding providence in a world of such absurdity as ours where, in the face of unimaginable suffering, most of our wealth and wits are devoted to preparing a final holocaust. And we don't need nuclear bombs for our holocaust, it is going on right now in the demolition of the great rainforests and in the toxic contamination of our seas, soil, and air.

Reprinted from *World as Lover, World as Self* by Joanna Macy (1991), Parallax Press, Berkeley, CA.

Faith, in a world like this? The very notion can appear distasteful, especially when we frequently see faith used as an excuse for denial and inaction. "God won't let it happen." Or even, as we hear in some circles today, "It may be God's will," a fearful assertion indeed when it refers to nuclear war itself, seen as the final just and holy battle to exterminate the wicked. The radical uncertainties of our time breed distortions of faith, where fundamentalist beliefs foster self-righteousness and deep divisions, turning patriotism into xenophobia, inciting fear and hatred of dissenters, and feeding the engines of war. If we are allergic to faith, it is with some reason.

Another option opens, however, that can lead to a more profound and authentic form of faith. We can turn from the search for personal salvation or some metaphysical haven and look instead to our actual experience. When we simply attend to what we see, feel, and know is happening to our world, we find authenticity. Going down into a darkness where there appears to be no faith, we can make three important discoveries. I see them as redeeming discoveries that can ground us in our ecology and serve as our faith; and I believe that our survival depends on our making them. These three are: (1) the discovery of what we know and feel, (2) the discovery of what we are, and (3) the discovery of what can happen through us or, as one might express it, grace.

DISCOVERING WHAT WE KNOW AND FEEL

To discover what we know and feel is not as easy as it sounds, because a great deal of effort in contemporary society is devoted to keeping us from being honest. Entire industries are focused on maintaining the illusion that we are happy, or on the verge of being happy as soon as we buy this toothpaste or that deodorant or that political candidate. It is not in the self-perceived interests of the state, the multinational corporations, or the media that serve them both, that we should stop and become aware of our profound anguish with the way things are.

None of us, in our hearts, is free of sorrow for the suffering of other beings. None of us is indifferent to the dangers that threaten our planet's people, or free of fear for the generations to come. Yet when we are enjoined to "keep smiling," "be sociable," and "keep a stiff upper lip," it is not easy to give credence to this anguish.

Suppression of our natural responses to actual or impending disaster is part of the disease of our time, as Robert Jay Lifton, the American psychiatrist who pioneered the study of the psychological effects of nuclear bombs, explains. The refusal to acknowledge or experience these responses produces a profound and dangerous splitting. It divorces our mental calculations from our intuitive, emotional, and biological imbeddedness in the matrix of life. That split allows us passively to acquiesce in the preparations for our own demise.

Joel Kovel, a psychiatrist teaching at Albert Einstein College, says that we are kept subservient and passive by "the state of nuclear terror." This terror is not the fear of nuclear weapons and other means of mass annihilation so much as our fear of experiencing the fear that we might break apart or get stuck in despair if we open our eyes to the dangers. So the messages we tend to hear or give are: "Don't talk to me about acid rain, or the arms race. There is nothing I can do about it. I have a family to support, a job to keep. If I were to take it all in and allow myself to think about it and to *feel* it, I wouldn't be able to function."

The first discovery, opening to what we know and feel, takes courage. Like Gandhi's *satyagraha*, it involves "truth-force." People are not going to find their truth-force or inner authority in listening to the experts, but in listening to themselves, for everyone in her or his way is an expert on what it is like to live on an endangered planet. To help this happen and counter habits of suppression, Interhelp, an international network, has evolved methods and workshops for people to come together to find their own inner authority. Without mincing words, without apology, embarrassment, or fear of causing distress, participants find they can simply tell the truth about their experience of this world. A boy talks about the dead fish in a stream he loves; a young couple wonders about the Strontium 90 in the bones of their children.

Justin Kenrick, an Interhelper in Great Britain, has said:

> We need permission in our minds and hearts and guts to accept that we are destroying the Earth and to feel the reality of who we are in that context; isolated, desperate, and powerless individuals, defeated by our old patterns of behavior before we have even begun to try to heal our lives and the Earth. Only then can we give ourselves permission to feel the power our culture denies us, to regain our intuitive sense of everything being in relation rather than in opposition, to regain our intuitive sense of the deep miraculous pattern to life that opens to us as we accept it.

When we come to the authority of what we know and feel, when we acknowledge our pain for the world, we remember the original meaning of *compassion*, "to suffer with." Suffering with our world, we are drawn now into the cauldron of compassion. It is there; it awaits us; and as Kenrick's words suggest, it can reconnect us with our power.

DISCOVERING WHAT WE ARE

Acknowledging the depths and reaches of our own inner experience, we come to the second discovery: the discovery of what we are. We are experiencers of compassion. Buddhism has a term for that kind of being—it is *bodhisattva*. The bodhisattva is the Buddhist model for heroic behavior. Knowing there is no such thing as private salvation, she or he does not hold aloof from this suffering world or try to escape from it. It is a question rather of returning again and again to work on behalf of all beings, because the bodhisattva knows there is no healing or transformation without connection.

The *sutras*, or scriptures, tell us that we are all bodhisattvas, and our fundamental inter-connections are portrayed in the beautiful image of the Jeweled Net of Indra. It is similar to the holographic model of the universe we find emerging from contemporary science. In the cosmic canopy of Indra's Net, each of us, each jewel at each node of the net, reflects all the others and reflects the others reflecting back. That is what we find when we listen to the sounds of the Earth crying within us—that the tears that arise are not ours alone; they are the tears of an Iraqi mother looking for her children in the rubble; they are the tears of a Navajo uranium miner learning that he is dying of lung cancer. We find we are interwoven threads in the intricate tapestry of life, its deep ecology.

What happens for us then is what every major religion has sought to offer—a shift in identification, a shift from the isolated "I" to a new, vaster sense of what we are. This is understandable not only as a spiritual experience, but also, in scientific terms, as an evolutionary development. As living forms evolve on this planet, we move not only in the direction of diversification, but toward integration as well. Indeed, these two movements complement and enhance each other. Open systems self-organize and integrate by virtue of their differentiation, and, vice-versa, they differentiate by virtue of their interactions. As we evolved we progressively shed our shells, our armor, our separate encasements; we grew soft, sensitive, vulnerable protuberances, like eyes, lips, and fingertips, to better connect and receive information, to better know and interweave our knowings. If we are all bodhisattvas, it is because that thrust to connect, that capacity to integrate with and through each other, is our true nature.

In his book *Ecology and Man*, Paul Shepard writes: "We are hidden from ourselves by patterns of perception. Our thought forms, our language, encourage us to see ourselves or a plant or an animal as an isolated sac, a thing, a contained self, whereas the epidermis of the skin is ecologically like a pond surface or a forest soil, not a shell so much as a delicate interpenetration." Paul Shepard is calling us to a faith in our very biology. He goes on to say, "Affirmation of its own organic essence will be the ultimate test of the human mind."

We begin to see that a shift of identification can release us not only from the prison cell of ego, but also from the tight compartment of a solely human perspective. As John Seed, Director of the Rainforest Information Center in Australia, points out, it takes us "beyond anthropocentrism." In his essay by that title, he says that anthropocentrism or human chauvinism is similar to sexism, but substitute "human race" for man and "all other species" for woman. And he says,

> When humans investigate and see through their layers of anthropocentric self-cherishing, a most profound change in consciousness begins to take place. Alienation subsides. The human is no longer an outsider apart. Your humanness is then recognized as being merely

the most recent stage of your existence; as you stop identifying exclusively with this chapter, you start to get in touch with yourself as vertebrate, as mammal, as species only recently emerged from the rainforest. As the fog of amnesia disperses, there is a transformation in your relationship to other species and in your commitment to them . . . The thousands of years of imagined separation are over and we can begin to recall our true nature; that is, the change is a spiritual one—thinking like a mountain, sometimes referred to as deep ecology.

As your memory improves . . . there is an identification with all life . . . Remember our childhood as rocks, as lava? Rocks contain the potentiality to weave themselves into such stuff as this. We are the rocks dancing.

BEING ACTED THROUGH

That leads us to the third discovery we can make in our ecological *Pilgrim's Progress:* the discovery of what can happen through us. If we are the rocks dancing, then that which evolved us from those rocks carries us forward now and sustains us in our work for the continuance of life.

When I admired a nurse for her strength and devotion in keeping long hours in the children's ward, she shrugged off my compliment as if it were entirely misplaced. "It's not *my* strength, you know. I get it from them," she said, nodding at the rows of cots and cribs. "They give me what I need to keep going." Whether tending a garden or cooking in a soup kitchen, there is the sense sometimes of being sustained by something beyond one's own individual power, a sense of being acted "through." It is close to the religious concept of grace, but distinct from the traditional Western understanding of grace, as it does not require belief in God or a supernatural agency. One simply finds oneself empowered to act on behalf of other beings—or on behalf of the larger whole—and the empowerment itself seems to come "through" that or those for whose sake one acts. This phenomenon, when approached from the perspective of ecology, can be understood as synergy. This is an important point because it leads us to reconceptualize our very notion of what power is.

From the ecological perspective, all open systems—be they cells or organisms, cedars or swamps—are seen to be self-organizing. They don't require any external or superior agency to regulate them, any more than your liver or your apple tree needs to be told how to function. In other words, order is implicit in life; it is integral to life processes. This contrasts with the hierarchical worldview our culture held for centuries, where mind is set above nature and where order is assumed to be something imposed from above on otherwise random, material stuff. We have tended to define power in the same way, seeing it as imposed from above. So we have equated power with domination, with one thing exerting its will over another. It becomes a zero-sum, or win-lose, game, where to be powerful means to resist the demands or influences of another, and strong defenses are necessary to maintain one's advantage.

In falling into this way of thinking, we lost sight of the fact that this is not the way nature works. Living systems evolve in complexity, flexibility, and intelligence through interaction with each other. These interactions require openness and vulnerability in order to process the flow-through of energy and information. They bring into play new responses and new possibilities not previously present, increasing the capacity to effect change. This interdependent release of fresh potential is called synergy. It is like grace, because it brings an increase of power beyond one's own capacity as a separate entity. I see the operation of this kind of grace or synergy everywhere I go. For example, I see it in the network of citizens that has sprung up along the tracks of the "white train" that carries the nuclear warheads from the Pantex plant in Amarillo, Texas, up to the Trident base in the northwest on Puget Sound and across the south to the Charleston Naval Base on the Atlantic. Sitting up late at night to watch the tracks they telephone to alert each other that the train is coming their way; then these ordinary citizens come out of their homes, to stand by the rail-road line and vigil with lighted candles or, on occasion, put their bodies on the tracks to stop the train. Even though this network is scattered across thousands of miles and relatively few of its members have met face to face, it calls itself now the Agape community; for these people have learned to feel each other's presence and support. And the tracks that bear the weapons for the ultimate war have become arteries interconnecting people and eliciting new dimensions of caring and courage.

I see this grace in the Sanctuary movement, where local churches and groups give protective asylum to refugees from the U.S.-supported violence in Central America. In January 1985, the FBI, in an effort to break the movement, which then included 105 centers, brought a number of its members to court and some were jailed. Although the local citizens who participated in decisions to grant sanctuary are largely law-abiding people—middle-aged, middle-class, respected and respectable—the FBI crackdown discouraged few of them. A year and a half later, the number of groups offering protection to Central American refugees, against the will of the Administration, had doubled.

The members of a small Quaker Meeting I know near Philadelphia hesitated to take this step, because they feared they might not be numerous enough or strong enough to provide the constant care and vigilance that is required when you adopt an illegal alien. But, inspired by similar actions elsewhere, they took the risk and granted sanctuary to a young Salvadoran woman. When I visited them a year later, Paz was still with them and the membership of the Meeting itself had become far larger and more active than ever before. By risking action together, action that made them more vulnerable, their power had increased.

There are countless such innovative grassroots actions; they do not make headlines, but taken all together, they amount to an unprecedented silent explosion of people who are quietly putting the interests of the planet ahead of their personal profit or pleasure. I see it in the growing number of citizens who are refusing to pay taxes for weapons of war; I see it in the thousands of Americans who have been paying their own way to the USSR, simply to connect with their Soviet counterparts so they might begin to know and comprehend each other first-hand. I see it in the bands of eco-warriors who risk their lives to protect marine mammals, and old-growth forests. I see it among the Vietnam veterans who fasted publicly to protest America's undeclared war on Nicaragua, and among the many other veterans across the United States who rallied to support them. As they do this, they expand our understanding of patriotism, demonstrating that love for one's country does not have to exclude the other beings of our planet.

These people show us what can happen through us when we break free of the old hierarchical notions of power. They show that grace happens when we act with others on behalf of our world.

ROOTS OF POWER

What can we do to nourish these efforts and strengthen the bodhisattva in ourselves? Two ways that I know are community and practice.

The liberation struggles in Latin America and the Philippines have demonstrated the efficacy of spiritually-based communities for nonviolent action. These tough networks of trust arise on the neighborhood level, as people strive together to understand, in their own terms and for their own situation, what they need to do to live without fear and injustice. These groups need be neither residential nor elite, just ordinary people meeting regularly in a discipline of honest searching and mutual commitment.

In our own society, too, such communities have been arising in the form of local support and action groups. Here neighbors or co-workers, parents or professionals organize and meet regularly to support each other in action—be it in responding to the poisons leaching from a nearby dump or to the need for a peace curriculum in the local school. Those of us who participate in such "base communities" know that they enhance both personal integrity and our belief in what is possible.

In addition to such external support, we need, in this time of great challenge and change, the internal support of personal practice. I mean practice in the venerable spiritual sense of fortifying the mind and schooling its attitudes. Because for generations we have been conditioned by the mechanistic, anthropocentric assumptions of our mainstream culture, intellectual assent to an ecological vision of life is not enough to change our perceptions and behaviors. To help us disidentify from narrow notions of the self and experience our interexistence with all beings in the web of life, we turn to regular personal practices that range from meditation to the recycling of our trash.

Spiritual exercises for cultivating reverence for life arise now out of many traditions and are welcomed by people regardless of their religious affiliation. I have found adaptations from Buddhist practices particularly helpful because they are grounded in the recognition of the dependent co-arising or deep ecology of all things. Similarly, Native American prayers and ritual forms, evoking our innate capacity to know and live our Earth, are increasingly adapted and included in gatherings for work and worship.

This is a prayer from the Laguna Pueblo people:

> I add my breath to your breath
> that our days may be long on the Earth,
> That the days of our people may be long,
> that we shall be as one person,
> that we may finish our road together.

from *THE OTHERS: HOW ANIMALS MADE US HUMAN*

Paul Shepard

We are space-needing, wild-country, Pleistocene beings, trapped in overdense numbers in devastated, simplified ecosystems. We project our problems onto mythic forms of barbarism. Whereas the sanctity of nonhuman life was a normal part of small-scale societies for thousands of years, the "world religions," with their messianic, human-centered, and otherworldly emphasis, trampled those traditions and now are beginning to recognize what they lost: sensitivity to human membership in natural communities and affirmation of and compliance with the biological framework of life. Greek ethics and biblical morality, organically alienist to begin with, cannot cope with our circumstances. Our ethics and morality deny the sacredness of the human connection with other life as it is played out in metabolic chains and the numinous presence of animals at the heart of religious experience. When we try to extend our ethics to that with which it is incompatible, we get pictorial and esthetic images of nature, the Renaissance spectator, museum patronage, the culture of abstract appearances and dissociation.

The recent history of kindness to animals is a vast self-reproach. It says that nature is full of innocent persecuted animals who would rather be friends with people, that we must adopt a "reverence for life" or an "ethic" of animal rights as we might put on a clean shirt. It patronizes life, poses the important question of our true relationship to nature as condescension, and confuses a sentimental fiction with civilized enlightenment.

Formal philosophy cannot contain the question because its original assumptions are estranged from nature: the view that a metaphysics of the earth and its life is a primitive error. The neoclassical, rational discourse, the watery stuff of empathy, and the "feeling" for the individual move us into metaphysics without polytheism. We are trapped in reason on the one hand and kindness on the other. Our environmental deprivations deny to much of modern experience and understanding the physical and allusive connections to the Others which are the visible expressions of an inner spiritual community and a larger cosmology.[1]

In the end, the abuse of animals will not be solved by ethics any more than by rebuke or exhortation. Neither logic nor charity can deal with what is, beyond pets and chicken

Reprinted from *The Others: How Animals Made Us Human* (Island Press, 1996).

factories, a mystery and an ecology: the ambiguity of life living on death, the spiritual nature of nonhuman life, traditions of human membership in natural communities embedded in place and ancestry. Earth history places us among the animals, as one of them, in food chains and other symbioses which we do not invent, but inherit, and which set our limitations among the Others.

The humane movement is an appropriate response to the abuses of domesticated animals, who need physical and legal protection. The pet is itself a singular redress to urban life and human crowding, a balm and true helper in the miseries of the multitude, but a monster in nature. The therapeutic beast and the urban society are made for each other. The escalation of pets to institutions such as hospitals, hospices, and prisons, like the formalization of humane concern for animals in statutes and laws, corresponds to the general drift of technological civilization in which the countermeasures against our loss of nature are found in industrialized therapy.

But the heart of animal life is gone from animals created in dependency and so emotionally appealing. We lose sight of their exclusion from the larger "nature." Wild animals have so receded from human experience that they seem as peripheral as sparrows and cockroaches or appear only in television, in art, or as captives—either in calendar art or in sensational, intimate views of the lives of eagles and dolphins as remote from our own experience as the landscapes of the moon.

James Rachels argues that what we need is "a philosophy that does not discriminate between different species, one that addresses each being on an individual basis."[2] The individualizing of our anguish over animals is reminiscent of the "person/planet" mesopia, with its lack of middle ground of species and communities. After all, how can a population or an ecosystem feel pain? Species are abstracts which you cannot touch or love. There is no place in "rights" for normal death, disease, or deprivation, only happy faces. The fundamentalists of interspecies sensibility hew to a literal text, to the physical problem of the helpless animal, seeing it like the heathen person, to be saved. "Human *kind?*" asks Cleveland Amory, and replies: there is no kindness in killing things.[3] His thesis cannot be reconciled with a world where all must die and all living is at the expense of others. It is a surreal view of "animals" which exist only as ideas and not in the wilderness; hence his feeling is directed to images that live "forever" like those on a Grecian urn.

At the heart of the ideal of animal protection is their "right to be," or their "right to be let be," to serve no human end. Its best expressions are magnificent pieces of rhetoric which perfectly express the detached ethos of the educated, urban mind. It seems to say: why shouldn't we all just leave animals alone (except perhaps for filming them or otherwise appreciating or studying them at a distance), just as the activist animal protectors in their homes, libraries, cafés, and theaters do? Why struggle with the problem of how to relate to

animals, especially when it is complicated with the protoplasmic pitfalls of disease, predation, all that ecological/evolutionary quagmire, and all those disturbing primal and ethnic
human precursors? Why work out relationships to animals in terms of that morass of prehistory and the demented (or fallen) creation so interwoven with death? In Cleveland
Amory's world our kindest act is avoidance, our deepest obligation protection at a distance, our best satisfaction a friendship like that of Petrarch for Laura, without response, a
comfortable, ecstatic remoteness, its recompense of the heart rather than the stomach. We
can stand back from it all and enjoy "nature" in art and literature and science, a subject
matter in a great museum refuge and art gallery. What a truly civilized idea! With the finality of disconnection.

In this way the ethics of "let be" deals with the enigmas and perennial inquiry, finalizing
the game by freezing nature in place and removing ourselves. But the true vocation of humankind, to puzzle out reciprocity, requires that we know, as the elders of a million years
past knew, that there is no "solution," but instead an ongoing participation. Bystanding is
an illusion. Willy-nilly, everybody plays. This play contains that most intimate aspect of the
mystery—our own identity—signified in finding ourselves in relationship to the Others.

A hideous overabundance of humans and our demands on energy and space diminish
the place for other species. The loss of wildness, extirpation of species, reductions of natural populations, extinctions, compression of habitat, and poisoning of life by air and
water are the tragic circumstances in which we see animal protectionists as indulging in a
kind of sentimental morality that is more important to them than the world of animals. As
Paul and Ann Ehrlich and Garrett Hardin have been telling us for thirty years, the ridiculous code of medicine that prolongs human life at any cost and advocates death control
without birth control has damaged life on earth far more than all the fox hunters and cos-
metic laboratories could ever do—perhaps beyond recovery—and leads us toward disasters that loom like monsters from hell.

Human political rights are meaningless as interspecies relationships. "Liberation"
means nothing to a calf elk about to be eaten by a wolf or a salmon about to be eaten by a
man. "Bonding" to animals is a willful, Disneyish dream. Most of the advocates of these
ideas have never watched wild animals closely and patiently, have little notion of their intelligence, otherness, or the complexity of their lives, cannot imagine combining holiness
as killing them or celebrating them by wearing their skins, do not recognize the flesh of
animals as a food sanctity, or perceive animals as a means of speculative thought, referen-
tial analogy, or immanent divinity.

NOTES

1. The carping against Greek rationality and philosophy in this chapter should be understood as aimed at formal philosophy on the one hand and the "philosophy" of zealots for animal rights on the other. Despite all those

academic philosophers who have projected domestication and "friendship" as a view of nature, there are some who see how shortsighted and artificial that "philosophy" is. Indeed, the discipline of philosophy has responded with more verve and openness to twentieth-century environmental issues than many other elements of the educated community.

2. James Rachels, "Created from Animals," in Bernard E. Rollin, ed., *The Unheeded Cry: Animal Consciousness, Animal Pain and Science* (Oxford: Oxford University Press, 1989).

3. Cleveland Amory, *Man Kind? Our Incredible War on Wildlife* (New York: Harper & Row, 1974).

Paul Shepard

Part VI

RELIGIOUS PRACTICE FOR A SACRED EARTH

In safety and in Bliss

May all creatures be of a blissful heart

Whatever breathing beings there may be

Frail or firm . . . long or small

Seen or unseen, dwelling far or near

Existing or yet seeking to exist

May all creatures be of a blissful heart.

—Sutta Nipata (Buddhist Scriptures)

Training began with children who were taught to sit still and enjoy it. They were taught to use their organs of smell, to look when there was apparently nothing to see, and to listen intently when all seemingly was quiet. A child that cannot sit still is a half-developed child.

—Standing Bear, Lakota Indian Chief

In order to serve God, one needs access to the enjoyment of the beauties of nature, such as the contemplation of flower-decorated meadows, majestic mountains, flowing rivers. For all these are essential to the spiritual development of even the holiest of people.

—Moses Maimonides

To Plant a tree is to say Yes to life:

It is to affirm our faith in the future.

To plant a tree is to acknowledge our debt to the past:

Seeds are not created out of nothing.

To plant a tree is a token of sorrow for past mistakes:

When we took life's gifts for granted.

—Reverend Francis Simons

I feed thee, Spirit of the Earth
Spirit of the Forest, of the Green Trees,
Spirit of the Forest,
Spirit of the Village Sites;
decree that the Paddy grow,
that the Fire devour.
Leading my younger brothers,
leading my elder brothers,
tomorrow, and the day after tomorrow, I will again act
in the same way.

—Prayer of the Mnong Gar, Vietnam

For many people, the heart of religious life resides not in abstract theology, but in rites and ceremonies. The repetitive nature of rituals can provide a comforting constancy in an often uncontrollable world. The symbolic material of candles or wine, special foods or familiar melodies may reach our emotional center in a way that little else does. If they have become authentic for us, religious rituals soothe our spirits or raise them to ecstasy, giving us a brief taste of the indwelling Spirit of God, Goddess, or Life.

What follows here is a brief sampling of religious practices that are designed to help us honor the earth and feel the depth and sacred character of our connection to it. The content of these practices once again expresses the twofold character now indelibly stamped on the nonhuman world. On the one hand, as *nature*, the nonhuman world has an integrity, beauty, and majesty that leads us to see it as a gift from God or as a Sacred Presence. On the other hand, as the *environment* we see something threatened and polluted by human action. We feel awe as we stand before nature, but anxiety and concern as we confront the environment.

Of the practices which follow, some are taken from or are adaptations of long-established religious forms. Thich Nhat Hanh's "Earth Gathas" are meant to bring mindfulness to our everyday transactions with nature. Ellen Bernstein and Dan Fink examine traditional Jewish prayers and concepts that directly bear on our attitudes towards nature, and provide a framework to study those materials. The Earth Day service from the National Council of Churches shows how prayers in a traditional setting can express environmental concerns. The meditations by John Seed, Pat Fleming and Joanna Macy reflect a deep ecological sensibility, while Marina Lachecki has reoriented a familiar Christian practice. Dee Smith offers something simple, new, and exhilarating. Finally, Black Elk's account of the Sun Dance should remind us that the spiritual practices of many indigenous peoples contain a long-established wealth of environmental wisdom.

"DANCE TO HEAL THE EARTH"

Dee Smith

Whenever you dance, wherever you dance, dance to heal the earth!

Dancing is power. Dancing is prayer. Some say that all is dance. Maybe. Now there's a big dance coming, a dance to heal the earth. If you're reading this, you're probably part of it. You take part whenever you do whatever you do to help heal the earth. When you recycle. When you choose to show love, to fight for justice, to bring healing, to bring out what is good in others. When you avoid cruelty and dishonesty and waste. When you are outraged. When you speak out. When you give. When you consider the generations to come. When you protest to the oppressors and encourage those who feel the cutting edge of injustice. And, of course, when you dance. There is a tree that all the prophets see, and whenever you let your love show, you make the flowers grow.

Soon this dance will be done in a big way, in the old way, on sacred ground. All living things will take part. If you want to, you can take part. No one is twisting your arm. You can stop any time you need to, and start up again whenever you're ready. If you've read this far, you probably know what I'm talking about. You've probably been doing it in one way or another for a good while. Soon will be the time to make no bones about it! Cut loose!

Anytime you dance, anywhere, whether at a party or in church, dance to heal the earth! Let your feet beat a healing rhythm into the earth. Let your feet beat a strengthening rhythm for those who struggle the hardest. Let your feet beat a life-giving rhythm for all peoples, regardless of race or national boundary, regardless of whether we're human or whether we're the trees, the air, the fish, the birds, the buffalo, the bear, the crow. We come out of hiding, we come back from the dead, and we dance, and our dance is a prayer, and our songs and our rhythms and our breath give life.

Is the music they're playing some mindless jingle? Never mind, as long as it's not bad music, and you can dance to the beat! Make your own words, and make the words a prayer. A prayer for the end of exploitation, a prayer for the end of lies, a prayer for healing, for justice, for life. Remember your prayer-song, feed it and let it get strong and pass it along. Dance and pray, whenever you dance, dance to heal the earth.

Have you seen anything? Wear it out! Make it so that all can see what you see! Take a white T-shirt and mark it with your dreams. Is there anything you'd like to tell the world?

Reprinted from www.indigenouspeople.net by permission of Glenn Welker. See ghwelker3@comcast.net.

Take your shirt and mark it with your song! This is the way it has been done, so you can do it too. Use any color except black (there are reasons for that that will become clearer later), and you'll probably find that a loose, pure cotton T is most comfortable for dancing in. Cos this is an actual dance, you dance hard, you sing and breathe hard and sweat. Wear it when you plan to go out dancing, to dance to heal the earth.

Some people do this dance while fasting, and dance for several days straight. But even a few minutes of dancing helps, and joins with all the other dancing going on, everywhere on Earth. Not everyone can fast these days. Besides, you never know when you're gonna dance, and you have to eat sometimes! But if you plan to dance, hold off eating till later, or just have a little. It's easier to dance if you don't have a hotdog weighing you down.

Some people say, do not do sacred things where people are drinking and partying. But all the universe is a sacred place. It really doesn't matter what others are doing, you can make a place sacred wherever you are, with your intention and your prayers. Some people use smoke to make a place sacred; a cigarette or incense stick will do fine. You can dance to heal the earth anywhere, even a party or a bar! The earth is everywhere, so you can dance anywhere to heal her. Only one thing. Please hold off drinking or using any other intoxicants till you're done. It works better that way.

The Lie has gone far enough. It spreads and makes everyone sick. Now is the time for this dance to begin. It, too, will spread, and it will bring healing to all. In the beginning, they say, God put a rainbow in the sky, to let us know that Spirit never forgets. Now is the time for us to put a rainbow across the earth, to let God know that we, too, remember.

Dance to heal the earth. Not just when you're dancing, but always. Live the dance, whenever you move, in all you do, dance to heal the earth.

Dee Smith

"EARTH GATHAS"

Thich Nhat Hanh

The green Earth   (first step of the day)
is a miracle!
Walking in full awareness,
the wondrous Dharmakaya is revealed.

Water flows from the high mountains.   (turning on water)
Water runs deep in the Earth.
Miraculously, water comes to us
and sustains all life.

Water flows over my hands.   (washing hands)
May I use them skillfully
to preserve our precious planet.

As I mindfully sweep the ground of enlightenment   (sweeping)
A tree of understanding springs from the Earth.

In this plate of food,   (eating)
I see the entire universe
supporting my existence.

The mind can go in a thousand directions.   (walking)
But on this beautiful path, I walk in peace.
With each step, a gentle wind.
With each step, a flower.

Earth brings us into life and nourishes us.   (gardening)
Countless as the grains of sand
in the River Ganges,
all births and deaths are present in each breath.

Water and sun green these plants.   (watering garden)
When the rain of compassion falls
even the desert becomes an immense, green ocean.

Garbage becomes rose.   (recycling)
Rose becomes compost—
Everything is in transformation.
Even permanence is impermanent.

Reprinted from *Dharma Gaia: A Harvest of Essays in Buddhism and Ecology* edited by Allan Hunt Badiner (1990), Parallax Press, Berkeley, CA, USA.

Dear plant, do not think you are alone.   (watering plants)
This stream of water comes from Earth and sky.
This water is the Earth.
We are together for countless lives.
I entrust myself to Buddha;   (planting trees)
Buddha entrusts himself to me.
I entrust myself to Earth;
Earth entrusts herself to me.

Thich Nhat Hanh

"BLESSINGS AND PRAISE"
and
"BAL TASHCHIT"

Ellen Bernstein and Dan Fink

"BLESSINGS AND PRAISE"

INTRODUCTION

Our busy lives, our need or desire to get ahead—all of our seemingly important obligations—often pull us away from life's simple daily miracles. Staying aware of the purpose and meaning of things, remembering their interconnections and knowing that all of our actions have consequences is not easy. Yet these may be our most important tasks in becoming shomrei adamah. If we do not remember who we are and what our place is, the human tendency to become masters and controllers of our universe can get the better of us.

It takes practice to learn to "see" and value all of life, just as it takes practice to become a good athlete, musician, artist, doctor or student. Judaism provides us with a multitude of practices to help us remember our place in the web of nature. Our rabbis understood the human condition and the tendency toward arrogance. They provided us with a wide range of practices to keep us on track, in harmony with God's creation. Reciting brachot (blessings) is one such practice. Brachot remind us that ultimately we humans are not the ones in charge. Brachot remind us to stop and pay attention to the world around us at times when we might otherwise take things for granted. In this way, brachot can train our eyes and our minds and enrich our lives.

Objectives

* Participants will understand where brachot and giving thanks fit into the Jewish way of life, and how they are basic to an ecological perspective.
* Participants will have an opportunity to express their thanks for an aspect of creation.

Reprinted from *Let the Earth Teach You Torah*, 1992, with permission of the author and Shomrei Adamah.

Materials and Preparation

- A loaf of bread or challah.
- Copies of Readings & Worksheets
- Paper and fine-point markers.

BLESSINGS AND PRAISE

OPENING

Invite participants to say the blessing over the bread with you. Break the bread and share it.

ברוך אתה ד׳ אלקינו מלך העולם המוציא לחם מן הארץ.

Baruch Atah Adonai Eloheynu Melech Ha-olam ha-mo-tzi lehem min ha-aretz.
Praise to You Adonai, our God and Universal Ruler, Who brings forth bread from the earth.

Discussion Questions

- What is the purpose of brachot?

  Brachot *are a Jewish way of telling us to slow down and pay attention—something special is happening that we don't want to miss. Brachot can help us to know our place in the universe and to know that God has given everything a purpose (whether or not we are aware of that purpose).*

  Brachot *are a momentary pause between the awareness of an act and the act itself. From a naturalist perspective, this pause may be considered unnatural; animals do not contemplate their food before eating. In this way brachot remind us of our humanity, and the distinctions between humans and the animal world.*

  Have a volunteer read the selection from *God in Search of Man* by Abraham Joshua Heschel (see Readings & Worksheets). Rabbi Abraham Joshua Heschel was a modern theologian and important Jewish thinker who taught at the Jewish Theological Seminary. He wrote numerous books and was renowned for his work in the civil rights movement.

- Have you ever looked at brachot in the same way that Heschel does?

- Do you agree with Heschel? Could you imagine any change in your life if you looked differently at brachot?

- According to the Talmud (Brachot 35), "Man may not take pleasure in [or derive benefit from] any worldly thing until he has recited a blessing over it. Anyone who takes pleasure [or derives benefit] from this world without making a blessing is guilty of misappropriating sacred property [a sin punishable by death]." What does this mean?

Everything in nature is a gift from God; it does not belong to us. If we use something of nature without thanking God, we are, in effect, stealing. Giving thanks is our way of recognizing the Creator who gave us the gift.

- Can you think of traditions similar to brachot in any other cultures or religions, in which giving back to the earth is considered of critical importance?

  Native American tradition: One always utters thanks when using anything from nature.

- Many people may have had the wonderful and important experience of noticing how magnificent or beautiful a tree is. Is there a difference between saying, "Oh wow, nice tree," and "Praise to You, God, who has created the trees"?

  Both are personal expressions that praise and honor the life of the tree. One uses the Jewish vehicle for praise and appreciation, but both exclamations may stem from the same intentions.

TEXT STUDY: THE BRACHOT

There is a whole set of brachot which are less familiar to many Jews. These brachot are recited when a person experiences various natural phenomena.

After the Bible was written, the early rabbis interpreted and expanded upon the biblical laws. Around 200 C.E., Rabbi Judah the Prince collected all the rabbis' discussions and interpretations of the Bible's laws and wrote them down in a book called the Mishnah.

It is in the Mishnah that we will find the roots of the brachot we say today. It is traditional for Jews to study the Mishnah in pairs called Hevrutot (sing. Hevrutah). Participants will study a selection from the first masechet (division): Brachot (Blessings), of the first seder (order): Zeraim (Seeds) 9:2.

Divide the group into Hevrutah pairs and hand out copies of the text and questions (see Readings & Worksheets). Allow ten minutes to study the texts and answer the questions. Regroup and discuss the texts, using the questions as a guide.

Points to Emphasize

By giving us these brachot to recite, the Mishnah is training us to appreciate the wonders of the daily world that have become commonplace to most of us.

Through the brachot, the Mishnah is teaching us of God's presence in nature—even in the frightening, powerful aspects of nature.

Many people feel closest to God outdoors; that is why we have a custom of putting windows in our synagogues. For some of us, praying indoors feels unnatural; we prefer the mountains for our temples.

Athletes, artists and musicians all exercise to improve their skills. Brachot are spiritual exercises that we can do to help us remember the source and the Eternal in everything. Reciting brachot can expand our appreciation and joy in life. With an expanded awareness of the inherent value of all life, can we still exploit the earth?

Your Own Brachot and Praises

The Jewish people did not stop composing brachot after the Mishnah was compiled. Like Rabbi Judah, many sages believed that some natural phenomena were special enough to merit a new, unique brachah (sing. for brachot).

Examples of these post-Mishnaic brachot include:

• The blessing over a rainbow, the sign of God's covenant with Noah:

ברוך אתה ד׳ אלקינו מלך העולם זוכר הברית ונאמן בבריתו וקים במאמרו.

Baruch Atah Adonai Eloheynu Melech ha-olam, zocher ha-brit v'neeman b'vreeto v'kayam b'mamaro.

Praise to You *Adonai*, our God and Universal Ruler, Who remembers the covenant and keeps its promise faithfully with all creation.

• The blessing over fruit trees in bloom in Spring (this may be recited only once a year):

ברוך אתה ד׳ אלקינו מלך העולם שלא חסר בעולמו דבר וברא בו בריות
טובות ואילנות טובים להנות בהם בני אדם.

Baruch Atah Adonai, Eloheynu Melech Ha-olam, she'lo chiser ba'olamo davar, oobarah bo briyot tovot v'eelanot tovim, l'hanot bahem b'nai adam.

Praise to You *Adonai*, our God and Universal Ruler, Who created a universe lacking in nothing, and who has fashioned goodly creatures and trees that give people pleasure.

Brachot are one way in which the Rabbis taught us to honor nature and God. Can you think of others?

The following story is told of Rabbi Nachman of Bratslav. He was raised in a city and never spent time in a natural setting until he was married (at age 14) and went to live with his wife in her village. Her village was in the midst of a beautiful countryside, and when he first got there, he couldn't believe how wonderful it felt to be in nature. He felt that outside, he could easily pray and talk to God. There was no one to bother him, and all the animals and plants helped his prayers reach heaven. He spent much time outdoors. When he became a rabbi, he told his congregants to spend one hour a day outdoors to commune with God. Have a volunteer recite Rabbi Nachman's prayer (see Readings & Worksheets).

Ask participants to also create their own *brachot and prayers*. Have them choose a part of nature for which they would like to compose a *brachah* or poem (for example: thunder, snowstorms, an eclipse, clouds, flowers, bird songs).

Ellen Bernstein and Dan Fink

If it is to be a *brachah*, it should begin with the words "Praise to You *Adonai*, our God and Universal Ruler." Tell the class to think about how the part of nature they have chosen makes them think and feel about God. The *brachah* can be simple ("Praise to You, *Adonai* . . . Who makes grasshoppers") or more elaborate ("Praise to You, Eternal . . . Who creates flying insects that sing in the summer night"). The *brachot* should say something about God's presence in nature. Encourage participants to use a name for God that speaks to them, like "Eternal" or "Source of Life," and so on.

Brachot Sheets

Hand out paper and fine-point markers. Have participants write their newly-created brachot and prayers along with some of the traditional *brachot* we have discussed. Encourage them to decorate their "*brachot* sheets" with drawings and designs.

[Note: According to some traditional Jewish legal teachings, it is no longer permissible to create our own brachot. If you take this stance, explore this and talk about the possible rationale for this position. Then, go ahead and have participants write on their sheets and illustrate them, using the traditional *brachot* only.]

Bringing It Home

Brachot help us see God as part of everything in the world. When we view nature as connected with God we are less likely to mistreat or destroy it. Rabbi Meir said that "it is a mitzvah (commandment) to recite 100 blessings every day" (Babylonian *Talmud, Menahot* 43b). Could this help you in your life today? Is it appropriate to expect people to do this? Would it make a difference in the world if people did this? Try to notice the number of times a day you feel appreciation for anything. How do you feel when you are appreciative? What does it feel like on a day when you forget to appreciate things? It takes work to be conscious of your world and to be appreciative of it. Try over the next week to bless things in whatever way is comfortable to you. Compare notes next time and see if the work pays off.

For Further Reading: Abraham Joshua Heschel, *God in Search of Man*.

BLESSINGS AND PRAISE

Opening: From Abraham Joshua Heschel, *God In Search Of Man*, pp. 48–51.

Reading

Three times a day we pray:

We Thank Thee . . .

For Thy miracles which are daily with us,
For thy continual marvels . . .

In the evening liturgy we recite the words of Job (9:10):

Who does great things past finding out,
Marvelous things without number.

Every evening we recite: "He creates light and makes the dark." Twice a day we say: "He is One." What is the meaning of such repetition? A scientific theory, once it is announced and accepted, does not have to be repeated twice a day. The insights of wonder must be constantly kept alive. Since there is a need for daily wonder, there is a need for daily worship.

The sense for the "miracles which are daily with us," the sense for the "continual marvels," is the source of prayer. There is no worship, no music, no love, if we take for granted the blessings or defeats of living. No routine of the social, physical, or physiological order must dull our sense of surprise at the fact that there is a social, a physical, or a physiological order. We are trained in maintaining our sense of wonder by uttering a prayer before the enjoyment of food. Each time we are about to drink a glass of water, we remind ourselves of the eternal mystery of creation, "Blessed be Thou . . . by Whose word all things come into being." A trivial act and a reference to the supreme miracle. Wishing to eat bread or fruit, to enjoy a pleasant fragrance or a cup of wine; on tasting fruit in season for the first time; on seeing a rainbow, or the ocean; on noticing trees when they blossom; on meeting a sage in Torah or in secular learning; on hearing good or bad tidings—we are taught to invoke His great name and our awareness of Him. Even on performing a physiological function we say "Blessed be Thou . . . who healest all flesh and *doest wonders.*"

This is one of the goals of the Jewish way of living: to experience commonplace deeds as spiritual adventures, to feel the hidden love and wisdom in all things.

> . . . The belief in "the hidden miracles is the basis for the entire Torah. A man has no share in the Torah, unless he believes that all things and all events in the life of the individual as well as in the life of society are miracles. There is no such thing as the natural course of events . . . " (Nachmanides).

BLESSINGS AND PRAISE

Text Study: The *Brachot. Mishnah Brachot* 9:2

Reading

A. Upon seeing shooting stars, earthquakes, lightning, thunder, and storms, one says:

ברוך אתה ד׳ אלקינו מלך העולם שכחו וגבורתו מלא עולם.

Baruch . . . she'kocho oog'voortoh maleh olam.

Praise to You . . . Whose strength and power fill the entire world.

B. Upon seeing mountains, valleys, oceans, rivers, and wilderness, one says:

ברוך אתה ד׳ אלקינו מלך העולם עשה בראשית.

Baruch . . . oseh breisheet.

Praise to You . . . making Creation work.

C. Rabbi Yehudah taught: One who sees the Great Sea (the Mediterranean) very rarely says:

ברוך אתה ד׳ אלקינו מלך העולם שעשה את הים הגדול.

Baruch . . . she'asah et ha-yam ha-gadol.

Praise to You . . . Who made the Great Sea.

D. Over rain and over good news, one says:

ברוך אתה ד׳ אלקינו מלך העולם הטוב והמטיב.

Baruch . . . ha-tov v'ha-mateev.

Praise to You . . . Who is Good and does Goodness.

BLESSINGS AND PRAISE

TEXT STUDY: *THE BRACHOT. MISHNAH BRACHOT* 9:2

Participant Worksheet

1. What do the items in section A have in common? What do the items in section B have in common? How do the items in section A differ from those in section B?

2. Are the blessings in sections A and B appropriate for the items over which they are said? What do the blessings make us think about in each case? Why do you think the Rabbis chose these blessings for these items?

3. What items could you add to the lists in sections A and B?

4. Even though we already have a blessing for oceans, in section C, Rabbi Judah assigns the Grent Sea its own *brachah*. Why do you think he does this? Are there any events or parts of nature that you believe deserve their own special blessing? Why?

5. Why do you think the blessing for rain is the same as the one for good news, and not the one for storms and thunder? This blessing would make a great deal of sense in a time of drought; should we still recite it in a time of flood?

6. Why do you think the *Mishnah* instructs someone who sees these things every day not to recite the blessing each time?

7. If we observed this tradition and recited blessings on a regular basis, how might it change the way we looked at the world around us?

8. Based on these blessings, the Rabbis seem to feel that when we look closely enough, every part of nature tells us something about God (examples: God's power, God's creative force). How might looking at nature in this way change the way we treat the natural world?

BLESSINGS AND PRAISE

Text Study: *The Brachot. Mishnah Brachot* 9:2

Leader Worksheet

1. What do the items in section A have in common? What do the items in section B have in common? How do the items in section A differ from those in section B?

   All the items in section A are powerful, even frightening or destructive events. They are not everyday occurrences. The items in section B are common but beautiful, natural features. These items are constant—so constant that we often take them for granted.

2. Are the blessings in sections A and B appropriate for the items over which they are said? What do the blessings make us think about in each case? Why do you think the Rabbis chose these blessings for these items?

   Yes. In the first case, the blessing speaks of God's power and in the second, the blessing speaks of evidence of God's amazing creativity. The first section's items are powerful and even frightening. They might seem to represent God's power. The second list of items might not seem special until we remember that God made them.

3. What items could you add to the lists in sections A and B?

   A: volcanic eruptions; tidal waves; an eclipse
   B: flowers; rocks; waterfalls

4. Even though we already have a blessing for oceans, in section C, Rabbi Judah assigns the Great Sea its own brachah. Why do you think he does this? Are there any events or parts of nature that you believe deserve their own special blessing? Why?

   The Mediterranean had a special importance and meaning in the life of the Jewish people; it is the largest body of water close to the land of Israel. In the ancient world, the Mediterranean helped to define the boundaries of the "known" world.

5. Why do you think the blessing for rain is the same as the one for good news, and not the one for storms and thunder? This blessing would make a great deal of sense in a time of drought; should we still recite it in a time of flood?

   As we all know (although we may not appreciate it all the time), rain is good news, providing sustenance for the crops, insuring that our tables will be full. What could be

better than the knowledge that we will be able to eat another meal, and will be able to ex-
perience another day!! In the ancient Middle East, as well as in many parts of the world
today, rain was unpredictable and often scarce. During a time of floods, we can pray for
gentle, nourishing rains instead of destructive torrents.

6. Why do you think the Mishnah instructs someone who sees these things every day not to recite the blessing each time?

    If one recited the same blessing every day, it could become rote and meaningless. Some-
    one who has never seen the mountains or ocean before will undoubtedly be impressed on
    first viewing them.

7. If we observed this tradition and recited blessings on a regular basis, how might it change the way we looked at the world around us?

    We may notice more, we may appreciate the beauties of nature more, we may be
    more careful about preserving the natural world, and we may feel closer to God more
    often.

8. Based on these blessings, the Rabbis seem to feel that when we look closely enough, every part of nature tells us something about God (examples: God's power, God's creative force). How might looking at nature in this way change the way we treat the natural world?

    We would see the world as holy (connected with God) and therefore treat it with more
    respect and concern.

BLESSINGS AND PRAISE

Your Own *Brachot* and Praises: Rabbi Nachman's Prayer

Reading

> Master of the Universe, grant me the ability to be alone:
> May it be my custom to go outdoors each day, among the trees and grasses, among all growing things, there to be alone and enter into prayer.
> There may I express all that is in my heart, talking with You, to Whom I belong.
> And may all grasses, trees and plants awake at my coming.
> Send the power of their life into my prayer, making whole my heart and my speech through the life and spirit of growing things.

"BAL TASHCHIT"

Introduction

Humans are guests on earth; God is our host. We are part of the web of life, and simultaneously, we have a unique task: the responsibility to preserve this beautiful gift of the earth for the next generation. This responsibility is a part of what it means to be human. For Jews, caring for the earth is our birthright and responsibility: we need only remember the most intimate relationship between *adam* (earthling) and *adamah* (earth).

The goal of this lesson is to demonstrate how a Jewish law, bal tashchit, "Do Not Destroy," is applicable to the contemporary environmental crisis.

Objectives

- Participants will be able to articulate the law of bal tashchit and its rabbinic genesis.
- Participants will examine their own behaviors in terms of bal tashchit, and will learn to decrease the waste in their lives.

Materials and Preparation

- Bring the following for the Opening exercise: Paper bag, a sandwich wrapped in plastic, soda can or foil, some prepackaged food like chips, juice pack and a sample of an unpackaged food like an apple.
- Each group member should bring in one item of what they normally consider garbage.
- Art supplies including glue, paints, glitter.
- Copies of Readings & Worksheets.
- Speak to your institution's administrators and ascertain whether your group may perform an environmental audit (see "Detective Work").

BAL TASHCHIT

OPENING

Our American society is the most wasteful society in the history of humanity. The value of the resources that we throw away is higher than the GNP (Gross National Product) of many other countries. In the average American's lifetime, he or she will throw out 45 tons of garbage. The problem of garbage is worsened by our inadequate means of disposal. Most landfills are filling up fast, and other means, such as incineration, are not considered environmentally sound. Waste reduction through the use of the three R's, Reduce waste, Reuse products and Recycle, is considered the intelligent way to approach the waste problem.

Take out a paper lunch bag filled with what would be a typical lunch and proceed to take out each item. The lunch should contain the following types of items:

Paper: the bag itself
Plastic: a sandwich wrapped in plastic

Ellen Bernstein and Dan Fink

Aluminum: soda can or foil

Packaged food: chips, juice pack

Unpackaged food: fruit

Take out each food item and the packaging associated with it.

Where does plastic come from, and where does it go after lunch is over? Repeat this question for each of the items in the lunch.

- Plastic: Every year 50 billion pounds of plastic are made in the United States (see "The Path of Plastic" in Readings & Worksheets).

- Aluminum: Every three months we throw away enough aluminum to replace all the commercial airplanes in the U.S.

- Paper: The paper equivalent of 500,000 trees is used every Sunday to print the Sunday paper in the U.S.

- Packaged food: Thirty-three percent of our garbage is just unnecessary packaging.

TEXT STUDY: THE LAW OF *BAL TASHCHIT*

There are two concerns about waste expressed in Deuteronomy. Ask volunteers to read the following passages:

> There will be an area beyond the military camp where you can relieve yourself. You will have a spade among your weapons; and after you have squatted, you will dig a hole and cover your excrement.
>
> —Deuteronomy 23:13–15

> When you lay siege and battle against a city for a long time in order to capture it, you must not destroy its trees, wielding an ax against them. You may eat of them, but you must not cut them down. Are the trees of the field human to withdraw before you into the besieged city? Only trees which you know do not yield food may be destroyed; you may cut them down for constructing siege works against the city that is waging war on you, until it has been captured.
>
> —Deuteronomy 20:19–20

Discussion Questions

- The first passage is rather explicit. Are you surprised to hear such things in the Bible? How does this law make you feel (do you find it repulsive, fascinating, etc.)?

Judaism is concerned with all aspects of life in this world. One of the beauties of the tradition is its attention to the small details we often take for granted.

- The second passage is more difficult. We will be studying this in detail. What does this law mean?

In wartime we may eat from fruit trees, but are forbidden to cut them down. This law is referred to as Bal Tashchit.

In general, fruit trees serve no other purpose but to bear fruit. Compare fruit trees to other trees: oak, maple, cedar. These trees are much larger, and are solid. They are excellent for building. They could serve well to construct the siege works. Fruit trees, on the other hand, are not useful for building. They serve primarily to bear fruit. Animals and humans can benefit from the fruit. The Torah is telling us we cannot cut down trees senselessly, simply for convenience, because we don't like them or because we want to harm the enemy. A scorched earth policy is forbidden according to the Bible. If not, it would be wasteful or destructive.

The Rabbis used many different interpretive tools in order to understand the Bible. One tool is called *kal v'homer* (literally, from hard to easy). *Kal v'homer* means that we infer from a difficult situation how to behave in an easier situation. In other words, if you find one law in a specific biblical context the rabbis can extend its application to other related situations. An example of this is reciting a blessing before eating. The only blessing that we are commanded to make is the blessing after eating. The Rabbis reasoned that if we are commanded to recite a blessing after eating, when our appetite is satiated, when we are tired and do not feel compelled to make a blessing, then there is all the more reason to say a blessing before we have eaten, when we are eager to eat and making a blessing would be a simple act.

Deuteronomy 20:19–20 was extended to other situations based on the law of *kal v'homer*. In this activity, we'll be thinking about how we can apply *kal v'homer* to *bal tashchit*.

Divide the group into pairs. Hand out the text and questions on *bal tashchit* (see Readings & Worksheets). Have participants answer the questions, using the text study sheet as a reference. Reconvene after ten minutes and discuss the material using the study questions as a guide.

[Note: Leader may use current and local environmental issues for a more up-to-date and inspiring discussion.]

GARBAGE ART

When you throw something away, where is "away"? *There is no such thing as "away." Garbage always goes somewhere.* The only way to deal with the problem of garbage is through the three R's. To demonstrate how we can reduce the amount of waste by reusing what would normally go into the waste stream, the class will make an art project out of the waste items they have brought in with them.

Ellen Bernstein and Dan Fink

What Do You Know About Waste?

Ask participants to take the "What Do You Know Quiz" (see Readings & Worksheets). Go over answer. Participants will be astonished at how much we ourselves and our country waste or unnecessarily destroy.

Detective Work: Conducting an Audit of Your School or Institution

Invite participants to be bal tashchit detectives and investigate where their institution wastes; submit suggestions to the administration to decrease waste. Begin this activity now. Participants will need to take on the responsibility to research more on their own. After hours or during lunch, participants could examine the trash generated in various offices and classrooms. Participants can give a booby prize to the greatest offenders, and an award to the most creative conserver.

Begin with a brainstorming session. Have a volunteer write on the blackboard, while participants offer suggestions of areas that use resources and produce waste. Ask for suggestions on how waste can be decreased in each area. If after brainstorming they have not come up with the following ideas, you can offer them.

- Do they recycle paper, plastics and metals? Check the packaging of the toilet paper and paper towels used. Is there a "recycled" label?

- Is recycled paper used for photocopying and office needs? Hold the paper up to the light; if it is recycled, there will probably be a watermark of the recycling sign.

- What is the volume of paper used for fliers and newsletters? Can it be consolidated? Are memos written on the backs of old letters?

- Does the institution use non-recyclable items? Can recyclables or reusables be substituted (for instance, cheap silverware instead of plastic throw-away eating utensils)? What is thrown away that can be reused or can be replaced with a recyclable alternative?

- What is the energy source of the institution? Are there alternatives? What is the usual heat setting? Are excess lights left on at night?

- How much energy is used? Can energy be reduced? What sort of light bulbs are used? How is the insulation?

- Is the institution making maximal use of its space? Are unused rooms heated? What happens in the space at night, and in the summer?

- What is the air conditioner's usual setting? Will a fan suffice? Are there trees planted around the facility that could cool the building, eliminating the need for air conditioning?

- Are carpooling, public transportation, or bike riding encouraged?

- Are cleaning supplies or lawn products toxic?

- What sort of toxics are thrown away? How are they disposed of?

- How much food is thrown away at events?

- Where does the waste water (dishwater) go?

At this point focus on a few of the items and come up with a plan on how the institution can follow *bal tashchit*.

When planning, be sure to:

- Choose a plan of action that the administration will allow

- Set a reasonable goal

- Determine how to measure waste

- Assign tasks to participants, and follow through with your plan!

BRINGING IT HOME

(This activity may be substituted for the audit if you feel it is more appropriate. Many of the same questions will apply.)

We must realize that we have the ability and power to make changes in the world. Good stewardship (caring for the earth) begins at home. Therefore the participants must look at their habits and the habits of their families to determine what needs to be changed. Spend a few minutes discussing participants' own personal habits in reference to bal tashchit. Discuss areas where they waste resources. Decide how they may be able to improve these behaviors and habits. Have participants perform a week-long project at home, recording everything that is thrown away or used up (such as gallons of gasoline for the cars, gallons of water for the lawn or garden, gallons of bathwater, gallons of toilet bowl water, gallons of dishwater). Encourage them to work out plans for following the commandment of bal tashchit at home.

For Further Reading: The Earthworks Group, *50 Simple Things You Can Do to Save the Earth.*

BAL TASHCHIT

OPENING: THE PATH OF PLASTIC

Reading

Fossil fuels are the remains of plants and animals (organic matter) that died millions of years ago. Over the millennia, layers upon layers of sediment were deposited, compressing the remains with their enormous weight. Under this pressure, heat was generated. This heat, along with chemical and bacterial activity, gradually reformed the organic matter into the compounds of hydrogen and carbon we know as petroleum (when distilled, petroleum produces oil).

In order to obtain petroleum, the land must be "cleared": stripped of all plants and guarded against the return of indigenous animals. The land is then graded—bulldozed to accommodate derricks. Often roads must be built to make the area accessible to heavy equipment and workers. Sometimes a larger area is cleared in order to establish nearby housing for the oil field workers.

After the oil is pumped and shipped to a factory, chemicals and heat are added to transform it into plastic. The heat causes the molecules in oil to move around rapidly, and the chemicals cause the carbon molecules to bond in various formations. The fraction of carbon molecules that bond determines whether the plastic is hard or soft.

BAL TASHCHIT

TEXT STUDY: THE LAW OF *BAL TASHCHIT*

Readings

> When in your war against a city you have to besiege it for a long time in order to capture it, you must not destroy its fruit trees, wielding an ax against them. You may eat of them, but you must not cut them down. Are the trees of the city human to withdraw from you into the besieged city? Only trees which you know do not yield food may be destroyed; you may cut them down for constructing siege works against the city that is waging war on you, until it has been captured.
>
> —Deuteronomy 20:19–20

> Whoever breaks vessels or rips up garments, destroys a building, stops up a fountain, or ruins food is guilty of violating the prohibition of bal tashchit.
>
> —Babylonian *Talmud Kiddushin* 32a

> It is forbidden to cut down fruit-bearing trees outside a [besieged] city, nor may a water channel be deflected from them so that they wither, as it is said: "You must not destroy its trees" [Deut. 20:19]. It [a fruit-bearing tree] may be cut down, however, if it causes damage to other trees or to a field belonging to another man or if its value for other purposes is greater [than that of the fruit it produces]. The law forbids only wanton destruction.
>
> —Maimonides, *Mishnah Torah*; Judges, Laws of Kings and Their Wars 6:8–10.

> . . . [D]estruction does not only mean making something purposelessly unfit for its designated use; it also means trying to attain a certain aim by making use of more things and more valuable things when fewer and less valuable ones would suffice; or if this aim is not really worth the means expended for its attainment. [For example] kindling something

which is still fit for other purposes for the sake of light; . . . wearing down something more than is necessary . . . consuming more than is necessary . . .

On the other hand, if destruction is necessary for a higher and more worthy aim, then it ceases to be destruction and itself becomes wise creating. [For example] cutting down a fruit tree which is doing harm to other more valuable plants, [and] burning a vessel when there is a scarcity of wood in order to protect one's weakened self from catching cold . . .

—Reprinted and adapted with permission of the publisher from Hirsch, Samson Raphael, *Horeb: A Philosophy of Jewish Laws and Observances*, translated from the German by I. Grunfeld, (New York: Soncino Press) 1962, 1968, 1972, 1981, pp. 280–281.

BAL TASHCHIT

Text Study: The Law of Bal Tashchit

Participant Worksheet

1. Read Deuteronomy 20:19–20 again. Using *kal v'homer* reasoning, how do you think the Rabbis may have extended this law?
2. What might have been the Rabbis' reason to extend this law?
3. What does a fruit tree symbolize? What is its importance?
4. Jews have invoked the principle of *bal tashchit* in all instances of wanton destruction. It is said that there was a Rabbi who used to cry whenever his students would pick a leaf off of a tree unnecessarily. But what happens when there is a more pressing human need at stake? What if you need to cut down a fruit tree because it is on the site that you have purchased to build a synagogue or a hospital?
5. Can you spray dandelions because you don't like them?
6. Can you weed your garden?

BAL TASHCHIT

Text Study: The Law of *Bal Tashchit*

Reader Worksheet

1. Read Deuteronomy 20:19–20 again. Using kal v'homer reasoning, how do you think the Rabbis may have extended this law?

   They extended the prohibition of cutting down trees in time of war (hard situation) to any unnecessary destruction of anything (easier situation). Specifically, the Rabbis said that "Whoever breaks vessels or rips up garments, destroys a building, stops up a fountain, or ruins foods is guilty of violating the prohibition of bal tashchit."

Ellen Bernstein and Dan Fink

2. What might have been the Rabbis' reason to extend this law?

If the destruction of fruit trees is prohibited in a time of war, when one would most likely destroy them (we are all familiar with the scorched earth policy of many armies: at wartime, opponents become demoralized through the total destruction of the environment), then it is certainly prohibited to cut fruit trees down in times of peace, when one is not likely to do so.

3. What does a fruit tree symbolize? What is its importance?

To the rabbinic mind, the fruit tree is a gift from God that is useful to humans. It has a purpose: to bear fruit that serves the rest of creation. A fruit tree should be used for the purpose of feeding people and other creatures. To use a fruit tree for any other purpose would be needless waste and destruction. Furthermore, the trees are harmless and vulnerable, and should be allowed to live in most situations.

4. Jews have invoked the principle of bal tashchit in all instances of wanton destruction. It is said that there was a Rabbi who used to cry whenever his students would pick a leaf off of a tree unnecessarily. But what happens when there is a more pressing human need at stake? What if you need to cut down a fruit tree because it is on the site that you have purchased to build a synagogue or a hospital?

Rabbis have often made the choice that is best for the community. If destruction is needed for a higher goal, then it ceases to be destruction; it is then "wise use." The challenge, then, is to determine what is the "common good."

5. Can you spray dandelions because you don't like them?

Not if it is purely for your convenience.

6. Can you weed your garden?

Yes, this insures the greater good of the garden; with fewer weeds, your vegetables will receive ample sunlight and nutrients, and will grow more successfully.

BAL TASHCHIT

WHAT DO YOU KNOW ABOUT WASTE?

Participant Worksheet

What Do You Know Quiz

1. What percentage of paper used yearly in the United States is used just for packaging?

a. 8%   b. 23%   c. 50%

2. If you are an average adult who weighs 150 pounds, how much garbage will you generate in your lifetime?

a. 1 ton (2,000 lbs.)   b. 10 tons (20,000 lbs.)   c. 45 tons (90,000 lbs.)

3. If all the aluminum thrown away in the U.S. were recycled, how long would it take to gather enough aluminum to rebuild all the commercial airliners in the U.S.?

a. 10 years   b. 2 years   c. 3 months

4. How much of your garbage is packaging that you throw out immediately?

a. 10%   b. 18%   c. 33%

5. The paper equivalent of how many trees is used each week to supply U.S. citizens with the Sunday newspaper?

a. 10,000 trees   b. 50,000 trees   c. 500,000 trees

6. What is the percentage of newspapers that are thrown away and not recycled?

a. 25%   b. 48%   c. 71%

7. Which of the following breaks down first in a landfill?

a. paper cup   b. plastic cup   c. aluminum can   d. none of the above

8. Which country uses half as many resources as we do in the U.S. to produce a single manufactured item?

a. Japan   b. Germany   c. Sweden   d. all of the above

BAL TASHCHIT

What Do You Know About Waste?

Reader Worksheet What Do You Know Quiz

1. What percentage of paper used yearly in the United States is used just for packaging?

a. 8%   b. 23%   c. 50%

2. If you are an average adult who weighs 150 pounds, how much garbage will you generate in your lifetime?

a. 1 ton (2,000 lbs.)   b. 10 tons (20,000 lbs.)   c. 45 tons (90,000 lbs.)

3. If all the aluminum thrown away in the U.S. were recycled, how long would it take to gather enough aluminum to rebuild all the commercial airliners in the U.S.?

a. 10 years   b. 2 years   c. 3 months

4. How much of your garbage is packaging that you throw out immediately?

a. 10%   b. 18%   c. 33%

5. The paper equivalent of how many trees is used each week to supply U.S. citizens with the Sunday newspaper?

a. 10,000 trees   b. 50,000 trees   c. 500,000 trees

6. What is the percentage of newspapers that are thrown away and not recycled?

a. 25%   b. 48%   c. 71%

7. Which of the following breaks down first in a landfill?

a. paper cup   b. plastic cup   c. aluminum can   d. none of the above

8. Which country uses half as many resources as we do in the U.S. to produce a single manufactured item?

a. Japan   b. Germany   c. Sweden   d. all of the above

Answer: 1.a, 2.c, 3.c, 4.c, 5.c, 6.c, 7.d (most landfill contents are "mummified" because there is no air to catalyze the breakdown), 8.d

Source of Information: *50 Simple Things You Can Do to Save the Earth*

"*WIWANYAG WACHIPI*: THE SUN DANCE"

Black Elk

The *wiwanyag wachipi* (dance looking at the sun) is one of our greatest rites and was first held many, many winters after our people received the sacred pipe from the White Buffalo Cow Woman. It is held each year during the Moon of Fattening (June) or the Moon of Cherries Blackening (July), always at the time when the moon is full, for the growing and dying of the moon reminds us of our ignorance which comes and goes; but when the moon is full it is as if the eternal light of the Great Spirit were upon the whole world. But now I will tell you how this holy rite first came to our people and how it was first made.

Our people were once camped in a good place, in a circle, of course, and the old men were sitting having a council, when they noticed that one of our men, Kablaya (Spread), had dropped his robe down around his waist, and was dancing there all alone with his hand raised towards heaven. The old men thought that perhaps he was crazy, so they sent someone to find out what was the matter; but this man who was sent suddenly dropped his robe down around his waist, too, and started dancing with Kablaya. The old men thought this very strange, and so they all went over to see what could be the matter. Kablaya then explained to them:

"Long ago *Wakan-Tanka* told us how to pray with the sacred pipe, but we have now become lax in our prayers, and our people are losing their strength. But I have just been shown, in a vision, a new way of prayer; in this manner *Wakan-Tanka* has sent aid to us."

When they heard this the old men all said, "*How!*" and seemed very pleased. They then had a conference and sent two men to the keeper of the sacred pipe, for he should give advice on all matters of this sort. The keeper told the men that this was certainly a very good thing, for "we were told that we would have seven ways of praying to *Wakan-Tanka*, and this must certainly be one of them, for Kablaya has been taught in a vision, and we were told in the beginning that we should receive our rites in this manner."

The two messengers brought this news back to the old men, who then asked Kablaya to instruct them in what they must do. Kablaya then spoke to the men, saying: "This is to be the sun dance; we cannot make it immediately but must wait four days, and during this time we shall prepare, as I have been instructed in my vision. This dance will be an offering of our bodies and souls to *Wakan-Tanka* and will be very *wakan*. All our old and holy men should gather; a large tipi should be built and sage should be placed all around inside it. You must have a good pipe, and also all the following equipment:

Ree twist tobacco	a tanned buffalo calf hide
bark of the red willow	rabbit skins
Sweet grass	eagle plumes
a bone knife	red earth paint
a flint axe	blue paint
buffalo tallow	rawhide
a buffalo skull	eagle tail feathers
a rawhide bag	whistles from the wing bones of the Spotted Eagle."

After the people had secured all these sacred things, Kablaya then asked all those who could sing to come to him that evening so that he could teach them the holy songs; he said that they should bring with them a large drum made from a buffalo hide, and they should have very stout drum sticks, covered at the end with buffalo hide, the hair side out.

Since the drum is often the only instrument used in our sacred rites, I should perhaps tell you here why it is especially sacred and important to us. It is because the round form of the drum represents the whole universe, and its steady strong beat is the pulse, the heart, throbbing at the center of the universe. It is as the voice of *Wakan-Tanka*, and this sound stirs us and helps us to understand the mystery and power of all things.

That evening the singers, four men and a women, came to Kablaya, who spoke to them in this manner: "O you, my relatives, for a very long time we have been sending our voices to Wakan-Tanka. This He has taught us to do. We have many ways of praying to Him, and through this sacred manner of living our generations have learned to walk the red path with firm steps. The sacred pipe is always at the center of the hoop of our nation, and with it the people have walked and will continue to walk in a holy manner.

"In this new rite which I have just received, one of the standing peoples has been chosen to be at our center; he is the wagachun (the rustling tree, or cottonwood); he will be our center and also the people, for the tree represents the way of the people. Does it not stretch from the earth here to heaven there?[1] This new way of sending our voices to *Wakan-Tanka* will be very powerful; its use will spread, and, at this time of year, every year, many people will pray to the Great Spirit. Before I teach you the holy songs, let us first offer the pipe to our Father and Grandfather, *Wakan-Tanka*."

"O Grandfather, Father, *Wakan-Tanka*, we are about to fulfill Thy will as You have taught us to do in my vision. This we know will be a very sacred way of sending our voices to You; through this, may our people receive wisdom; may it help us to walk the sacred path with all the Powers of the universe! Our prayer will really be the prayer of all things, for all are really one; all this I have seen in my vision. May the four Powers of the universe help us to do this rite correctly; O Great Spirit, have mercy upon us!"

The pipe was smoked by all, and then Kablaya began to teach the songs to the five people. Many other people had gathered around the singers, and to these Kablaya said that while they listen they should frequently cry "O Grandfather, *Wakan-Tanka*, I offer the pipe to You that my people may live!"

There were no words to the first song that Kablaya taught the singers; it was simply a chant, repeated four times, and the fast beat on the drum was used. The words to the second song were:

Wakan-Tanka, have mercy on us,
That our people may live!

And the third song was:

They say a herd of buffalo is coming;
It is here now!
Their blessing will come to us.
It is with us now!

The fourth song was a chant and had no words.

Then Kablaya taught the men who had brought their eagle-bone whistles how they should be used, and he also told the men what equipment they should prepare and explained the meaning of each ritual object.

"You should prepare a necklace of otter skin, and from it there should hang a circle with a cross in the center. At the four places where the cross meets the circle there should hang eagle feathers which represent the four Powers of the universe and the four ages. At the center of the circle you should tie a plume taken from the breast of the eagle, for this is the place which is nearest to the heart and center of the sacred bird. This plume will be for Wakan-Tanka, who dwells at the depths of the heavens, and who is the center of all things.

"You all have the eagle-bone whistles, and to the ends of each of these an eagle plume should be tied. When you blow the whistle always remember that it is the voice of the Spotted Eagle; our Grandfather, *Wakan-Tanka*, always hears this, for you see it is really His own voice.

"*A hanhepi wi* [night sun, or moon] should be cut from rawhide in the shape of a crescent, for the moon represents a person and, also, all things, for everything created waxes and wanes, lives and dies. You should also understand that the night represents ignorance, but it is the moon and the stars which bring the Light of *Wakan-Tanka* into this darkness. As you know the moon comes and goes, but anpetu wi, the sun, lives on forever; it is the source of light, and because of this it is like *Wakan-Tanka*.

"A five-pointed star should be cut from rawhide. This will be the sacred Morning Star who stands between the darkness and the light, and who represents knowledge.

"A round rawhide circle should be made to represent the sun, and this should be painted red; but at the center there should be a round circle of blue, for this innermost center represents *Wakan-Tanka* as our Grandfather. The light of this sun enlightens the entire universe; and as the flames of the sun come to us in the morning, so comes the grace of *Wakan-Tanka*, by which all creatures are enlightened. It is because of this that the four-leggeds and the wingeds always rejoice at the coming of the light. We can all see in the day, and this seeing is sacred for it represents the sight of that real world which we may have through the eye of the heart. When you wear this sacred sign in the dance, you should remember that you are bringing Light into the universe, and if you concentrate on these meanings you will gain great benefit.

"A round circle should be cut and painted red, and this will represent Earth. She is sacred, for upon Her we place our feet, and from Her we send our voices to *Wakan-Tanka*. She is a relative of ours, and this we should always remember when we call Her "Grandmother" or "Mother." When we pray we raise our hand to the heavens, and afterwards we touch the earth, for is not our Spirit from *Wakan-Tanka*, and are not our bodies from the earth? We are related to all things: the earth and the stars, everything, and with all these together we raise our hand to *Wakan-Tanka* and pray to Him alone.

"You should also cut from rawhide another round circle, and this should be painted blue for the heavens. When you dance you should raise your head and hand up to these heavens, looking at them, for if you do this your Grandfather will see you. It is He who owns everything; there is nothing which does not belong to Him, and thus it is to Him alone that you should pray.

"Finally, you should cut from rawhide the form of *tatanka*, the buffalo. He represents the people and the universe and should always be treated with respect, for was he not here before the two-legged peoples, and is he not generous in that he gives us our homes and our food? The buffalo is wise in many things, and, thus, we should learn from him and should always be as a relative with him.

"Each man should wear one of these sacred symbols on his chest, and he should realize their meanings as I have explained to you here. In this great rite you are to offer your body as a sacrifice in behalf of all the people, and through you the people will gain understanding and strength. Always be conscious of these things which I have told you today; it is all wakan!"

The next day it was necessary to locate the sacred rustling tree which was to stand at the center of the great lodge, and so Kablaya told his helper of the type of tree which he should find and mark with sage, that the war party will be able to locate it and bring it back to camp. Kablaya also instructed the helpers how they must mark out the ground where the sacred sun-dance lodge will be set up, around the holy tree, and how they should mark the doorway at the east with green branches.

The following day the scouts, who had been chosen by the spiritual leaders, went out and pretended to scout for the tree. When it was found they returned immediately to camp, and after circling sun-wise around the place where the lodge was to be, they all charged for the doorway trying to strike a coup on it. These scouts then took up a pipe, and, after offering it to the six directions, they swore that they would tell the truth. When this had been done, Kablaya spoke to the men in this manner:

"You have taken up the holy pipe, and so you must now tell us with truth all that you have seen. You know that running through the stem of the pipe there is a little hole leading straight to the center and heart of the pipe; let your minds be as straight as this Way. May your tongues not be forked. You have been sent out to find a tree that will be of great benefit to the people, so now tell us truthfully what you have found."

Kablaya then turned the pipe around four times, and pointed the stem towards the scout who was to give the report.

"I went over a hill, and there I saw many of the sacred standing peoples."

"In which direction were you facing, and what did you see beyond the first hill?"

"I was facing the west," the scout replied, "and then I went further and looked over a second hill and saw many more of the sacred standing people living there."

In this manner the scout was questioned four times, for as you know with our people all good things are done in fours; and then this is the manner in which we always question our scouts when we are on the warpath, for you see we are here regarding the tree as an enemy who is to be killed.

When the scouts had given their report, they all dressed as if they were going on the warpath; and then they left the camp as if to attack the enemy. Many other people followed behind the scouts. When they came to the chosen tree, they all gathered around it; then, last of all, Kablaya arrived with his pipe, which he held with its stem pointing towards the tree; he spoke in this manner:

"Of all the many standing peoples, you O rustling cottonwood have been chosen in a sacred manner; you are about to go to the center of the people's sacred hoop, and there you will represent the people and will help us to fulfill the will of Wakan-Tanka. You are a kind and good-looking tree; upon you the winged peoples have raised their families; from the tip of your lofty branches down to your roots, the winged and four-legged peoples have made their homes. When you stand at the center of the sacred hoop you will be the people, and you will be as the pipe, stretching from heaven to earth. The weak will lean upon you, and for all the people you will be a support. With the tips of your branches you hold the sacred red and blue days. You will stand where the four sacred paths cross—there you will be the center of the great Powers of the universe. May we two-leggeds always follow your sacred example, for we see that you are always looking upwards into the heavens. Soon, and with all the peoples of the world, you will stand at the center; for all beings and all things you will bring that which is good. Hechetu welo!"

Kablaya then offered his pipe to Heaven and Earth, and then with the stem he touched the tree on the west, north, east, and south sides; after this he lit and smoked the pipe.

I think it would be good to explain to you here why we consider the cottonwood tree to be so very sacred. I might mention first, that long ago it was the cottonwood who taught us how to make our tipis, for the leaf of the tree is an exact pattern of the tipi, and this we learned when some of our old men were watching little children making play houses from these leaves. This too is a good example of how much grown men may learn from very little children, for the hearts of little children are pure, and, therefore, the Great Spirit may show to them many things which older people miss. Another reason why we choose the cottonwood tree to be at the center of our lodge is that the Great Spirit has shown to us that, if you cut an upper limb of this tree crosswise, there you will see in the grain a perfect five pointed star, which, to us, represents the presence of the Great Spirit. Also perhaps you have noticed that even in the very lightest breeze you can hear the voice of the cottonwood tree; this we understand is its prayer to the Great Spirit,[2] for not only men, but all things and all beings pray to Him continually in differing ways.

The chiefs then did a little victory dance there around the tree, singing their chief's songs, and as they sang and danced they selected the man who was to have the honor of counting coup on the tree; he must always be a man of good character, who has shown himself brave and self-sacrificing on the warpath. Three other men were also chosen by the chiefs, and then each of these four men stood at one of the four sides of the tree—the leader at the west. This leader then told of his great deeds in war, and when he had finished the men cheered and the women gave the tremulo. The brave man then motioned with his axe three times towards the tree, and the fourth time he struck it. Then the other three men in turn told of their exploits in war, and when they finished they also struck the tree in the same manner, and at each blow all the people shouted "*hi! hey!*" When the tree was nearly ready to fall, the chiefs went around and selected a person with a quiet and holy nature, and this person gave the last blow to the tree; as it fell there was much cheering, and all the women gave the tremulo. Great care was taken that the tree did not touch the ground when it fell, and no one was permitted to step over it.

The tree was then carried by six men towards the camp, but before they reached camp they stopped four times, and after the last stop they all howled like coyotes—as do the warriors when returning from the warpath; then they all charged into camp and placed the sacred tree up upon poles—for it must not touch the ground—and pointed its base towards the hole which had already been prepared, and its tip faced towards the west. The lodge around the tree had not yet been set up, but all the poles had been prepared, and all the equipment for constructing the *Inipi* had been gathered.

The chief priest, Kablaya, and all those who were to take part in the dance, then went into a large tipi where they were to prepare themselves and receive instructions. The lodge was shut up very tightly, and leaves were even placed all around the base.

Kablaya, who was seated at the west, scraped a bare place on the ground in front of him, and here a coal was placed; as Kablaya burned sweet grass upon the coal, he said: "We burn this sacred herb for *Wakan-Tanka*, so that all the two-legged and winged peoples of the universe will be relatives and close to each other. Through this there shall be much happiness."

A small image of a drying rack was then made from two forked sticks and one straight one, and all were painted blue, for the drying rack represents heaven, and it is our prayer that the racks always be as full as heaven. The pipe was then taken up, and after being purified over the smoke, it was leaned against the rack, for in this way it represents our prayers and is the path leading from earth to heaven.

All the sacred things to be used in the dance were then purified over the smoke of the sweet grass: the hide figures; the sacred paints; the calf skin; and the buckskin bags; and the dancers, also, purified themselves. When this had been done, Kablaya took up his pipe, and, raising it to heaven, he prayed.

"O Grandfather, *Wakan-Tanka*, You are the maker of everything. You have always been and always will be. You have been kind to your people, for You have taught us a way of prayer with the pipe which You have given us; and now through a vision You have shown to me a sacred dance which I must teach to my people. Today we will do Thy will."

"As I stand upon this sacred earth, upon which generations of our people have stood, I send a voice to You by offering this pipe. Behold me, O *Wakan-Tanka*, for I represent all the people. Within this pipe I shall place the four Powers and all the wingeds of the universe; together with all these, who shall become one, I send a voice to You. Behold me! Enlighten my mind with Your never fading Light!"

"I offer this pipe to *Wakan-Tanka*, first through You O winged Power of the place where the sun goes down; there is a place for You in this pipe. Help us with those red and blue days which make the people holy!"

Kablaya then held up a pinch of tobacco, and after motioning with it to Heaven, Earth, and the four Powers, he placed it in the bowl of the pipe. Then after the following prayers, he placed pinches of tobacco in the pipe for each of the other directions.

"O winged Power of the place where *Waziah* lives, I am about to offer this pipe to Wakan-Tanka; help me with the two good red and blue days which You have—days which are purifying to the people and to the universe. There is a place for You in the pipe, and so help us!

"O You, Power there where the sun comes up; You who give knowledge and who guard the dawn of the day, help us with Your two red and blue days which give understanding and Light to the people. There is a place for You in this pipe which I am about to offer to Wakan-Tanka; help us!

"O You, most sacred Power at the place where we always face; You who are the source of life, and who guard the people and the coming generations, help us with Your two red and blue days! There is a place for You in the pipe.

"O You, Spotted Eagle of the heavens! we know that You have sharp eyes with which you see even the smallest object that moves on Grandmother Earth. O You, who are in the depths of the heavens, and who know everything, I am offering this pipe to *Wakan-Tanka*! Help us with Your two good red and blue days!

"O You, Grandmother Earth, who lie outstretched, supporting all things! upon You a two-legged is standing, offering a pipe to the Great Spirit. You are at the center of the two good red and blue days. There will be a place for You in the pipe and so help us!"

Kablaya then placed a small grain of tobacco in the pipe for each of the following birds: the kingbird; the robin; the lark, who sings during the two good days; the wood-pecker; the hawk, who makes life so difficult for the other winged peoples; the eagle hawk; the magpie, who knows everything; the blackbird; and many other wingeds. Now all objects of creation and the six directions of space have been placed within the bowl of the pipe. The pipe was sealed with tallow and was leaned against the little blue drying rack.

Kablaya then took up another pipe, filled it, and went to where the sacred tree was resting. A live coal was brought, and the tree and the hole were purified with the smoke from sweet grass.

"O *Wakan-Tanka*," Kablaya prayed as he held his pipe up with one hand, "behold this holy tree-person who will soon be placed in this hole. He will stand with the sacred pipe. I touch him with the sacred red earth paint from our Grandmother and also with the fat from the four-legged buffalo. By touching this tree-person with the red earth, we remember that the generations of all that move come from our Mother the Earth. With your help, O tree, I shall soon offer my body and soul to *Wakan-Tanka*, and in me I offer all my people and all the generations to come."

Kablaya then took the red paint, offered it to the six directions, and again spoke to the sacred tree: "O tree, you are about to stand up; be merciful to my people, that they may flourish under you."

Kablaya painted stripes of red on the west, north, east, and south sides of the tree, and then he touched a very little paint to the tip of the tree for the Great Spirit, and he also put some at the base of the tree for Mother Earth. Then Kablaya took up the skin of a buffalo calf, saying: "It is from this buffalo person that our people live; he gives to us our homes, our clothing, our food, everything we need. O buffalo calf, I now give to you a sacred place upon the tip of the tree. This tree will hold you in his hand and will raise you up to Wakan-Tanka. Behold what I am about to do! Through this, all things that move and fly upon the earth and in the heavens will be happy!"

Kablaya next held up a small cherry tree, and continued to pray: "Behold this, O Wakan-Tanka, for it is the tree of the people, which we pray will bear much fruit."

This little tree was then tied upon the sacred cottonwood, just below the buffalo hide, and with it there was tied a buckskin bag in which there was some fat.

Kablaya then took up the hide images of a buffalo and a man, and, offering them to the six directions, he prayed: "Behold this buffalo, O Grandfather, which You have given to us; he is the chief of all the four-leggeds upon our sacred Mother; from him the people live, and with him they walk the sacred path. Behold, too, this two-legged, who represents all the people. These are the two chiefs upon this great island; bestow upon them all the favors that they ask for, O *Wakan-Tanka*!"

These two images were then tied upon the tree, just underneath the place where the tree forks; after this Kablaya held up a bag of fat to be placed underneath the base of the tree, and he prayed in this manner:

"O Grandfather, *Wakan-Tanka*, behold this sacred fat, upon which this tree-person will stand; may the earth always be as fat and fruitful as this. O tree, this is a sacred day for you and for all our people; the earth within this hoop belongs to you, O tree, and it is here underneath you that I shall offer up my body and soul for the sake of the people. Here I shall stand, sending my voice to You, O Wakan-Tanka, as I offer the sacred pipe. All this may be difficult to do, yet for the good of the people it must be done. Help me, O Grandfather, and give to me courage and strength to stand the sufferings which I am about to undergo! O tree, you are now admitted to the sacred lodge!"

With much cheering and many shrill tremulos, the tree was raised, very slowly, for the men stopped four times before it was straight and dropped into the hole prepared for it. Now all the people—the two-leggeds, four-leggeds, and the wingeds of the air—were rejoicing, for they would all flourish under the protection of the tree. It helps us all to walk the sacred path; we can lean upon it, and it will always guide us and give us strength.

A little dance was held around the base of the tree, and then the surrounding lodge was made by putting upright, in a large circle, twenty-eight forked sticks, and from the fork of each stick a pole was placed which reached to the holy tree at the center.

I should explain to you here that in setting up the sun dance lodge, we are really making the universe in a likeness; for, you see, each of the posts around the lodge represents some particular object of creation, so that the whole circle is the entire creation, and the one tree at the center, upon which the twenty-eight poles rest, is *Wakan-Tanka*, who is the center of everything. Everything comes from Him, and sooner or later everything returns to Him. And I should also tell you why it is that we use twenty-eight poles. I have already explained why the numbers four and seven are sacred; then if you add four sevens you get twenty-eight. Also the moon lives twenty-eight days, and this is our month; each of these days of the month represents something sacred to us: two of the days represent the Great Spirit; two are for Mother Earth; four are for the four winds; one is for the Spotted Eagle; one for the sun; and one for the moon; one is for the Morning Star; and four for the four ages; seven are for our seven great rites; one is for the buffalo; one for the fire; one for the water; one for the rock and finally one is for the two-legged people. If you add all these days up you will see that they come to twenty-eight. You should also know that the buffalo has twenty-eight ribs, and that in our war bonnets we usually use twenty-eight feathers. You see, there is a significance for everything, and these are the things that are good for men to know, and to remember.[3]

NOTES

1. In the *Atharva Veda Samhita* of the Hindu scriptures, we find a description of the significance of their World Tree, which is quite identical to the symbolism of the tree for the Lakota: "The World Tree in which the trunk, which is also the sun pillar, sacrificial post, and axis mundi, rising from the altar at the navel of the earth, penetrates the world door and branches out above the root of the world (*A. V.* X. 7.3.); as the 'non-existent (unmanifested) branch that yonder kindreds know as the Supernal' (A. C. X. 7.21.)." (Translated by A. K. Coomaraswamy, "Svayamatrna: Janua Coeli," Zalmoxis.) For a full explanation of the symbolism of the tree, see René Guénon, *Le Symbolisme de la Croix*, Les Edition Vega (Paris, 1931); especially Chap. IX, "L'Arbre du Milieu."

2. An interesting parallel to this attitude towards trees is found in an Islamic source: "[Holy] men dance and wheel on the [spiritual] battlefield: From within them musicians strike the tambourine: at their ecstacy the seas burst into foam. You see it not, but for their ears the leaves too on the boughs are clapping hands . . . one must have the spiritual ear, not the ear of the body." (Jalaluddin Rumi, *The Mathnawi* [R. A. Nicholson translation, 8 vols., Cambridge University Press, Cambridge, 1926], III 9.)

3. Editor's note: For discussion of the number seven as sacred, please see *The Sacred Pipe: Black Elk's Account of the Seven Rites of the Oglala Sioux*, Joseph E. Brown, ed. (New York: Viking Penguin, 1971).

"WORSHIP RESOURCES, EARTH DAY SUNDAY"

National Council of Churches

EARTH DAY SUNDAY, FOURTH SUNDAY AFTER EASTER APRIL 21, 2002

The celebration of Earth Day provides a uniquely visible time for churches to draw attention to the Christian's call to care for all God's creation.

CALL TO WORSHIP   (Based on Hymn #555, "Forward Through the Ages")

Leader: Forward through the ages in an unbroken line, move the faithful spirits at the call divine.

People: We gather today in the presence of God and in communion with those who have gone before us and those who will come after.

Leader: On this Earth Sabbath, we open our minds to learn about ecological threats to the health of present and future generations and to the whole community of life.

People: We open our hearts to the message of hope that comes to us through Jesus Christ.

Leader: We reach out our hands to bring healing and change, for the sake of the children of the earth–past, present, and future.

People: And we raise our voices to join with the rest of creation in singing praise to God, whose steadfast love and faithfulness endures to all generations.

OPENING HYMN: #555 Forward Through the Ages

A LITANY OF CONFESSION AND GRACE

Reader 1: John Wesley said: Sin is the refusal to acknowledge our dependence on God for life and breath and all things.

Reader 2: God of life, we confess that we often forget that we are utterly dependent upon you and interdependent with the rest of your creation.

People: Forgive us, O God, and inspire us to change.

Reader 1: Jesus quoted the prophet Isaiah when he challenged the people, saying: This people's hearts have grown dull. They have eyes, but do not see; ears, but do not hear; hearts, but do not understand.

Reader 2: God of love, we confess that at times we would rather stay in denial than see, hear, and understand how our lifestyles affect our world.

People: Forgive us, O God, and inspire us to change.

Reader 1: The prophets Isaiah and Hosea said: The land lies polluted under its inhabitants. The beasts of the field, the birds of the air, even the fish of the sea are dying.

Reader 2: God of mercy, we confess that we are damaging the earth, the home that you have given us. We buy and use products that pollute our air, land, and water, harming wildlife and endangering human health.

People: Forgive us, O God, and inspire us to change.

Reader 1: Chief Seattle said: Whatever we do to the web of life we do to ourselves.

Reader 2: God of justice, we confess that we have not done enough to protect the web of life. We have failed to insist that our government set standards based on precaution. We allow companies to release dangerous toxins that destroy fragile ecosystems and harm human beings, especially those among us who are most vulnerable.

People: Forgive us, O God, and inspire us to change.

All: God of compassion, today we acknowledge our dependence upon you and our interconnectedness with the whole web of life. We open our eyes, ears, and hearts to the pain of the earth, that we may be open to your truth, see your way of hope, and walk with courage in your way.

Reader 1: So be it. You are beloved children of God, forgiven, renewed, and sent out into the world to work for healing and justice, hope and wholeness, in faithfulness to God.

HYMN: #140 Great Is Thy Faithfulness

PASTORAL PRAYER (from Genesis 9, Genesis 17, and Deuteronomy 30)

Gracious God, your amazing love extends through all time and space, to all parts of your creation, which you created and called good. You made a covenant with Noah and his family, putting a rainbow in the sky to symbolize your promise of love and blessing to every living creature, and to all successive generations. You made a covenant with Abraham and

Sarah, blessing them and their descendants throughout the generations. You made a covenant with Moses and the Israelite people to all generations, giving them the 10 commandments and challenging them to choose life. In Jesus, you invite us to enter into a new covenant, in communion with all who seek to be faithful to you. As people of faith, we are called into covenant. Your covenant of faithfulness and love extends to the whole creation. We pray for the healing of the earth, that present and future generations may enjoy the fruits of creation, and continue to glorify and praise you.

OFFERTORY PRAYER

Generous God, you have blessed us with the resources to share the good news of your love for all creation. We dedicate these gifts and pray that they may bring healing, wholeness, and hope to the world, that future generations may also know your graciousness and love. Amen.

RESPONSIVE BENEDICTION (Hebrews 12)

Leader: Certainly God is raising up people even today to bring us through this dark time.

People: Life-giving God, we offer ourselves in service to you, supported by a great cloud of witnesses who urge us on.

Leader: We are connected to other people of faith and conscience around the world who are working for a peaceful, just, and sustainable world.

People: This global community supports us—we support each other.

Leader: We are connected with those who have gone before us: the martyrs and heroes, all the ancestors who invested themselves for the sake of future generations, and we are connected with those who will come after us.

People: Our ancestors and descendents support us—we are their champions.

Leader: We are related to the earth and all its creatures in a web that cannot be broken without injury to all.

People: The earth and our fellow creatures support us—we are their advocates.

Leader: We are connected to Jesus Christ, who reveals God to us, sends us the Spirit, and sends us out in his name.

People:

Leader: Therefore, let us lay aside every weight and sin that clings so closely, and let us run with perseverance the race that is set before us, looking to Jesus, the pioneer and perfecter of our faith, resisting all powers that destroy, bringing healing and hope to the world.

People: O God, Creator, Redeemer, Sustainer, we offer our lives in service to you.

CLOSING HYMN: #581 Lord, Whose Love Through Humble Service

OTHER HYMNS FOR EARTH DAY: #126 Sing Praise to God Who Reigns Above, #311 Now the Green Blade Riseth, #92 For the Beauty of the Earth, and Hymns #145 to #152. All hymn numbers are from the United Methodist Hymnal (1989).

NOTES

The Earth Ministry web site www.earthministry.org/earthday.htm features many additional worship resources for use during Earth Day Sunday.

The Web of Creation site at http://www.webofcreation.org/ also has many resources for Earth Day Sunday.

"INVOCATION"

John Seed

We ask for the presence of the spirit of Gaia and pray that the breath of life continues to caress this planet home.

May we grow into true understanding—a deep understanding that inspires us to protect the tree on which we bloom, and the water, soil and atmosphere without which we have no existence.

May we turn inwards and stumble upon our true roots in the intertwining biology of this exquisite planet. May nourishment and power pulse through these roots, and fierce determination to continue the billion-year dance.

May love well up and burst forth from our hearts.

May there be a new dispensation of pure and powerful consciousness and the charter to witness and facilitate the healing of the tattered biosphere.

We ask for the presence of the spirit of Gaia to be with us here. To reveal to us all that we need to see, for our own highest good and for the highest good of all.

We call upon the spirit of evolution, the miraculous force that inspires rocks and dust to weave themselves into biology. You have stood by us for millions and billions of years—do not forsake us now. Empower us and awaken in us pure and dazzling creativity. You that can turn scales into feathers, seawater to blood, caterpillars to butterflies, metamorphose our species, awaken in us the powers that we need to survive the present crisis and evolve into more aeons of our solar journey.

Awaken in us a sense of who we truly are: tiny ephemeral blossoms on the Tree of Life. Make the purposes and destiny of that tree our own purpose and destiny.

Fill each of us with love for our true Self, which includes all of the creatures and plants and landscapes of the world. Fill us with a powerful urge for the well-being and continual unfolding of this Self.

May we speak in all human councils on behalf of the animals and plants and landscapes of the Earth.

May we shine with a pure inner passion that will spread rapidly through these leaden times.

May we all awaken to our true and only nature—none other than the nature of Gaia, this living planet Earth.

Reprinted from *Thinking Like A Mountain: Towards a Council of All Beings*, edited by John Seed, by permission of New Society Publishers.

We call upon the power which sustains the planets in their orbits, that wheels our Milky Way in its 200-million-year spiral, to imbue our personalities and our relationships with harmony, endurance and joy. Fill us with a sense of immense time so that our brief, flickering lives may truly reflect the work of vast ages past and also the millions of years of evolution whose potential lies in our trembling hands.

O stars, lend us your burning passion.

O silence, give weight to our voice.

We ask for the presence of the spirit of Gaia.

"GAIA MEDITATIONS"

John Seed and Joanna Macy

What are you? What am I? Intersecting cycles of water, earth, air and fire, that's what I am, that's what you are.

Water—blood, lymph, mucus, sweat, tears, inner oceans tugged by the moon, tides within and tides without. Streaming fluids floating our cells, washing and nourishing through endless riverways of gut and vein and capillary. Moisture pouring in and through and out of you, of me, in the vast poem of the hydrological cycle. You are that. I am that.

Earth—matter made from rock and soil. It too is pulled by the moon as the magma circulates through the planet heart and roots suck molecules into biology. Earth pours through us, replacing each cell in the body every seven years. Ashes to ashes, dust to dust, we ingest, incorporate and excrete the earth, are made from earth. I am that. You are that.

Air—the gaseous realm, the atmosphere, the planet's membrane. The inhale and the exhale. Breathing out carbon dioxide to the trees and breathing in their fresh exudations. Oxygen kissing each cell awake, atoms dancing in orderly metabolism, interpenetrating. That dance of the air cycle, breathing the universe in and out again, is what you are, is what I am.

Fire—Fire, from our sun that fuels all life, drawing up plants and raising the waters to the sky to fall again replenishing. The inner furnace of your metabolism burns with the fire of the Big Bang that first sent matter-energy spinning through space and time. And the same fire as the lightning that flashed into the primordial soup catalyzing the birth of organic life.

You were there, I was there, for each cell of our bodies is descended in an unbroken chain from that event. Through the desire of atom for molecule, of molecule for cell, of cell for organism. In that spawning of forms death was born, born simultaneously with sex, before we divided from the plant realm. So in our sexuality we can feel ancient stirrings that connect us with plant as well as animal life. We come from them in an unbroken chain—through fish learning to walk the land, feeling scales turning to wings, through the migrations in the ages of ice.

We have been but recently in human form. If Earth's whole history were compressed into twenty-four hours beginning at midnight, organic life would begin only at 5

Reprinted from *Thinking Like A Mountain: Towards a Council of All Beings*, edited by John Seed, by permission of New Society Publishers.

p.m. . . . mammals emerge at 11:30 . . . and from amongst them at only seconds to midnight, our species.

In our long planetary journey we have taken far more ancient forms than these we now wear. Some of these forms we remember in our mother's womb, wear vestigial tails and gills, grow fins for hands.

Countless times in that journey we died to old forms, let go of old ways, allowing new ones to emerge. But nothing is ever lost. Though forms pass, all returns. Each worn-out cell consumed, recycled . . . through mosses, leeches, birds of prey . . .

Think to your next death. Will your flesh and bones back into the cycle. Surrender. Love the plump worms you will become. Launder your weary being through the fountain of life.

Beholding you, I behold as well all the different creatures that compose you—the mitochondria in the cells, the intestinal bacteria, the life teeming on the surface of the skin. The great symbiosis that is you. The incredible coordination and cooperation of countless beings. You are that, too, just as your body is part of a much larger symbiosis, living in wider reciprocities. Be conscious of that give-and-take when you move among trees. Breathe your pure carbon dioxide to a leaf and sense it breathing fresh oxygen back to you.

Countless times in that journey we died to old forms, let go of old ways, allowing new ones to emerge. But nothing is ever lost. Though forms pass, all returns.

Remember again and again the old cycles of partnership. Draw on them in this time of trouble. By your very nature and the journey you have made, there is in you deep knowledge of belonging. Draw on it now in this time of fear. You have earth-bred wisdom of your interexistence with all that is. Take courage and power in it now, that we may help each other awaken in this time of peril.

"EVOLUTIONARY REMEMBERING"

John Seed and Pat Fleming

PART ONE: FROM THE BEGINNING OF THE UNIVERSE

Let us go back, way back before the birth of our planet Earth, back to the mystery of the universe coming into being. We go back 13,500 million years to a time of primordial silence . . . of emptiness . . . before the beginning of time . . . the very ground of all being . . . From this state of immense potential, an unimaginably powerful explosion takes place . . . energy travelling at the speed of light hurtles in all directions, creating direction, creating the universe. It is so hot in these first moments that no matter can exist, only pure energy in the form of light . . . thus time and space are born.

All that is now, every galaxy, star and planet, every particle existing comes into being at this great fiery birthing. Every particle which makes up you and me comes into being at this instant and has been circulating through countless forms ever since, born of this great cauldron of creativity. When we look at a candle flame or a star, we see the light of that fireball. Your metabolism burns with that very same fire now.

After one earth year, the universe has cooled down to some 13 billion degrees centigrade. It now occupies a sphere of perhaps 17 billion miles in diameter . . . This continues to expand and stream outward . . .

Some 300,000 years pass while space grows to about one billionth of its present volume and cools to a few thousand degrees—about as hot and bright as the visible surface of the sun. The electrons are now cool enough for the electric force to snare, cool enough for matter to take form.

Matter begins to assume its familiar atomic form for the first time. The first atoms are of hydrogen, then helium and then other gases.

These gases exist as huge swirling masses of super-hot cosmic clouds drawn together by the allure of gravity . . . these slowly condense into forms we know as galaxies and our own galaxy; the Milky Way dances among them. Purged of free electrons, the universe becomes highly transparent by its millionth birthday.

Reprinted from *Thinking Like A Mountain: Towards a Council of All Beings,* edited by John Seed, by permission of New Society Publishers.

Within the Milky Way, our sun was born about 5 billion years ago, near the edge of this galaxy while the cosmic dust and gas spinning around it crystalized into planets. The third planet from the sun, our own earth, came into being about 4½ billion years ago.

The ground then was rock and crystal beneath which burned tremendous fires. Heavier matter like iron sank to the center, the lighter elements floated to the surface forming a granite crust. Continuous volcanic activity brought up a rich supply of minerals, and lifted up chains of mountains.

Then, about 4 billion years ago, when the temperature fell below the boiling point of water, it began to rain. Hot rain slowly dissolved the rocks upon which it fell and the seas became a thin salty soup containing the basic ingredients necessary for life.

Finally, a bolt of lightning fertilized this molecular soup and an adventure into biology began. The first cell was born. You were there. I was there. For every cell in our bodies is descended in an unbroken chain from that event.

Through this cell, our common ancestor, we are related to every plant and animal on the earth.

PART TWO: MEDITATION ON THE EVOLUTION OF ORGANIC LIFE

Remember that cell awakening. BE that cell awakening (as indeed you are). We are all composed of that cell which grew, diversified, multiplied and evolved into all the biota of the earth.

What does it feel like to reproduce by dividing into two parts that were me and now we go our separate ways?

Now, some hundreds of millions of years have passed. First we were algae, the original green plants, then the first simple animals. The algae started to produce oxygen as a byproduct of photosynthesis and this over a billion years or so created a membrane of ozone, filtering out some of the fiercest solar rays.

Now I am a creature in the water. For 2½ billion years, simple forms of life washed back and forth in the ocean currents. Imagine them as I speak their names: coral, snails, squid, worms, insects, spiders. Imagine yourself as perhaps a simple worm or an early coral living in the warm sea. Feel your existence at this time for it remains within each of your cells, the memories of this period in your childhood.

Fish: This was followed by the evolution of fish and other animals with backbones. How does it feel to have a flexible backbone? . . . How do you move through the water as a fish?

Lying belly down, staying in one place, begin to experience gentle side-to-side rolling, with your head, torso and lower body moving all as one. How does the world look, feel . . . sound? Be aware of your backbone, your head and gills. What does it feel like to move through the ocean, to listen through the ocean?

Amphibian: Finally about 450 million years ago the first plants emerged from the water and began to turn the rock into soil, preparing the ground for animals to follow. The first animals to emerge from the seas were the amphibians . . . slowly use your forearms to drag your body along. Pull with your left and right together . . . as amphibians we are still very dependent on the water, especially for our reproductive cycle.

Reptile: It wasn't until the evolution of the reptilian amniotic egg that we were liberated from our dependence on water and able to move completely onto dry land . . . still crawling on your belly start to use legs coordinated with arms, alternating from one side to the other. Notice how our range of movement and perception changes . . . By 200 million years ago, we had successfully moved onto the land.

Early mammal: As mammals we became warm-blooded. Remember how as a reptile you used to have to wait, sluggish, for the sun to warm you? The sun now fuels your metabolism in a more complex way. What are the advantages of this?

Living in holes, alert, sense of smell, sampling molecules from the air. To breed before being consumed. All of us are descended from this pedigree for 4 billion years. At every step billions fell by the wayside but each of us was there. In this game, to throw tails once is to fall by the wayside, extinct, a ghost.

Imagine yourself as a lemur, or perhaps as a small cat . . . Notice how supple your spine feels . . . Now with your belly off the floor, begin crawling on your hands and knees. How does this new-found freedom feel? How does your head move?

Now our young need to be looked after until they can fend for themselves.

Early monkey: Begin moving on hands and feet with greater lightness, leaping and climbing. Discover more flexibility in movement of the spine, head and neck. Make sounds. Notice increasing playfulness and curiosity. We move through the trees, running along branches and swinging through them, our strong opposable thumbs giving us the grip we need. Our sensitive fingertips (with nails instead of claws) able to judge the ripeness of fruit or groom. Agile balance and keen vision develop. We eat food on the spot where we find it.

Great ape: Our body becomes heavier and stronger. We can squat erect but use knuckles to walk. Experiment with balancing. How does the world look and smell? Communication?

Ten million years ago a major climatic change began and the forests, home of the ape, began to retreat to the mountains and were replaced by woodland and open savannah.

Early human: It is here on the open savannah that we first learned to walk on two legs . . . standing on two feet with strong jaw thrust forward. How does it feel? Vulnerable but inventive and adaptable. Able to look up and easily see the sky. We postpone eating food until it can be brought back to camp and shared. We live in families, discover language, catch fire, make art, music, tools . . . the complexities and subtleties of cooperating successfully with others in a group involves the development of language, the telling of stories, the use of tools, the making of fires.

About 100,000 years ago during the warm interglacial period, a new hominid species emerged called Neanderthal. They bury their dead, sometimes with flint tools—many in a fetal position suggesting a return to the womb of Mother Earth for rebirth, often in graves lying on an east/west axis—on the path of the sun which is reborn every day—their practice of burying the dead shows a dramatic increase in human self-consciousness. Now physical evolution stands still and cultural evolution takes over.

Modern human: Developing farming, working on the land, in market places, moving to town—seeing houses, temples, skyscrapers, walking through busy streets, driving in cars, what do you see and hear and smell and feel? How does it feel to be dwelling more often in cities? How have you become more separate from the earth? Now you are pushing your way through a crowded street, you are in a hurry . . . everyone is in your way.

Future human: The possible human: to the extent that we can surrender our tiny self to our actual, biological being, we can then manifest the powerful erotic energy of evolution and then our personalities slowly come to partake of the nature of evolution, the nature of this planet home.

Sitting down quietly by yourself . . . in your mind's eye, open to any glimpses, images, forms that are waiting to emerge as future human life . . . potential in us that is waiting to awaken a larger ecological Self, living fully as part of nature expressing our full potential in whatever way may occur to us . . . form.

Now slowly come back and, opening your eyes, find a partner close by and sit with them. Taking turns speaking, going back over the stages you remember, describing in the first person what you experienced, what you noticed about each life form. Use the present tense—"I am a single cell and I notice . . . " You are now recounting your evolutionary journey, recounting how the cosmic journey has been for you so far.

"THE BLESSING OF THE WATER"

Marina Lachecki

May the blessings of the Jordan be upon this water.
May the blessings of the Jordan be upon this water.
May the blessings of the Jordan be upon this water.

Three times I dipped the processional cross in the winter waters of Lake Superior. A circle of college students, wrapped in scarves and bedecked with mittens and winter coats, kept the wind to our backs on this day observing the Epiphany. After I raised the cross the final time, I took a cedar branch and dipped it in the now blessed water of the largest freshwater lake in the world. I blessed the four corners of the earth, and then individually, each student. I invited them to dip their hands in this renewed water of the earth. Many drew the water to their lips, their eyes, their ears, and their noses.

In planning for this worship experience, I wanted to celebrate a ritual which spoke to the care of God's creation, a primary value at the institution which I serve as campus minister. Northland College is a liberal arts/environmental college in northern Wisconsin which is affiliated with the United Church of Christ. In my search, I discovered a number of religious customs and rituals from the early liturgical tradition of the church.

While Christians in the Western tradition celebrate the Epiphany as the visitation of the Magi, priestly scholars from Asia, churches in the Eastern tradition observe January 5 and 6 as the Blessing of the Waters. Their appointed readings for this day tell of the baptism of Jesus in the river Jordan. As His divinity was pronounced, there was a subsequent sanctification of the waters by His immersion in them.

St. John Chrysostom delivered a homily with this understanding in 387. "For this is the day on which He was baptized and sanctified the natures of the waters. Therefore also on this solemnity in the middle of the night all who are gathered, having drawn the water, set the liquid aside in their houses and preserve it throughout the year, for today the waters are sanctified."[1] By the 6th century in communities along the Mediterranean, Christians gathered at midnight for this ritual. After the water had been blessed, they would boat out to pan aromatic substances into the water. Afterwards, they drew the water in jars and urns to later use in blessing their homes and fields. In their understanding, the waters of the

Reprinted with permission of the author, Rev. Marina Lachecki, Pastor, St. John's United Church of Christ, Madeline Island.

earth were renewed in this blessing. Waters of the blessed rivers and seas were stirred by the winds and transported by the waves throughout the earth.

As centuries passed, the blessing of the waters turned away from flowing water, and became a ritual celebrated in the fountains in the atria of churches, and then with vessels small enough to be carried in procession from the rivers, lakes and seas which were then placed on the altars. On this winter day, we returned this ancient ritual to its place alongside the waters of the earth.

Prayers from several liturgies were used in re-creating this ritual. The students and I gathered outside the Religious Life Center, a residence for students who want to live in an intentional community focused on spiritual concerns. They are students who are struggling with faith questions, rediscovering their Christian or Jewish heritage, or finding a new way with Buddhism or American Indian spiritualities. We began with an invocation from a Milanese liturgy.

> Eternal God, you revealed yourself from heaven in the sound of thunder over the river Jordan in order to make known the Savior of the world and show yourself the God of Eternal Light. You opened the heavens, blessed the air, purified the water-springs, and pointed out your only Son by sending the Holy Spirit in the form of a dove.[2]

A student then read from Genesis. We listened to this ancient creation story and heard the rhythm of God's voice bringing forth life into the world and pronouncing what was created "good."

Following a processional cross, we journeyed the mile from the campus to the shores of Lake Superior. The mood was festive on this cold January day when students returned from their Christmas break. Friends were greeted and stories shared as we marched behind the cross. Along the way a few others were drawn into our procession and joined our ranks. At one point in our pilgrimage, we were stopped by a car of Ojibwe women who were also students on our campus. They asked us what we were doing. When I told them we were traveling to the lake to pray for the waters of the earth, they told me that they had a ceremony like that, too.

Upon our arrival, I led the students in an Orthodox litany:

> Today, the grace of the Spirit, in the likeness of a dove, comes down upon the waters; today, there shines the Sun that never sets, and the world is sparkling with the light of God; today, the moon is bright, together with the earth, in the glowing radiance of its beams; today the clouds from heaven shed upon us a shower of justice; today the whole universe is refreshed with mystical streams; today, we are delivered from the ancient mourning; today, the whole creation is brightened from on high . . .

Marina Lachecki   559

In reading this litany, I was awestruck at the appropriateness of these ancient words to the plight of our world in the 20th century.

As the prayers were concluded, the students began to chip a hole in the two-foot thick ice which covered the bay. The blue-green ice gave way to the sharp edge of an ice pick. No words were spoken during this time. We listened to the call of the wind, and were drawn back into the story of Jesus' baptism in the Jordan. For time stopped then as John anticipated the baptism of the son of God. Tiny ice fragments were taken from the deepening hole and piled inside this circle of students. We awaited the water breaking forth as the scripture from Isaiah foretells. And the water did indeed break forth in the dryness of the winter ice. The vacuum we had created when we chipped out this ice vase was swiftly filled. We cheered in celebration. A student then proclaimed the promised renewal of the earth in the words of the prophet Isaiah, the 35th chapter.

> ... for water gushes in the desert, streams in the wasteland, the scorched earth becomes a lake, the parched land springs of water ... and through it will run a highway undefiled which shall be called the Sacred Way. (Isaiah 35.6–8)

These words were familiar to the students who gathered on the shores of Lake Superior. They are proclaimed at each convocation and graduation at the college. It was a reading from the scripture the college adopted when it was founded in 1892.

A college freshman, new to the school that January, then took the Holy Book and read the story of Jesus' baptism from the gospel of Mark. As the processional cross was raised above the water, an Armenian litany was shared:

> Today the grace of the Holy Spirit descends upon the waters in the form of a dove.
> Today the waters of the Jordan are changed into a remedy by the presence of the Lord.
> Today sins are wiped away in the waters of the Jordan.
> Today paradise is opened to us, and the Sun of Justice shines.

And then I immersed the cross, symbolic of the baptismal immersion of Jesus and reminiscent of more ancient fertility rites of the Canaanite people, into the water.

> And may we who partake of it be cleansed and purified, blessed and sanctified, healed and made whole, so that we may be filled with the fullness of God who is all in all.

Our liturgy did not end with its ancient conclusion. In today's world, the cry of the earth called us to pray for its healing. I asked students to call to mind the places on this earth where the water needs to be healed: the places of pollution, of drought, and of degradation. As each student visualized a specific place, we prayed for its healing. We prayed for the spirit of renewal to wash over the face of the earth. We prayed for the people of the earth that they would recognize the sacred gift of the land which was created by the word of God. We prayed for teachers and healers to come forth with a prophetic voice. And then we paused in a sacred moment.

The winds at the end of a winter's day encircled us again. And we closed with these words:

> The voice of God cries upon the waters, saying, "O come and receive all the Spirit of wisdom, the Spirit of understanding, the Spirit of the fear of God."

We journeyed back to campus in a winter silence, mindful of the grace and hope of God for all of creation.

NOTES

1. *Origins of the Liturgical Year* by Thomas J. Talley. Pueblo Publishing Company, New York, 1986.

2. Liturgical prayers were found in *A Christmas Sourcebook,* edited by Mary Ann Simcoe, Liturgical Training Publications, 1984.

Part VII

ECOLOGY, RELIGION, AND SOCIETY

A disenchanted world is, at the same time, a world liable to control and manipulation. Any science that conceives of the world as being governed according to a universal theoretical plan that reduces its various riches to the drab application of general laws thereby becomes an instrument of domination. And man, a stranger to the world, sets himself up as its master.

—Ilya Prigogine and Isabelle Stengers

All the streams have dried up or become muddy. The fish we used to catch have disappeared. The water is not clear anymore. And the birds of paradise have also disappeared; they have flown away to other places.

—Moi Tribesman, Indonesia

We the indigenous Peoples of the world, united in this corner of our Mother the Earth in a great assembly of men of wisdom, declare to all nations:

We glory in our proud past:

when the earth was our nurturing mother,

when the night sky formed our common roof,

when Sun and Moon were our parents,

when all were brothers and sisters,

when our great civilization grew under the sun,

when our chiefs and elders were great leaders,

when justice ruled the Law and its execution.

—from the World Council
of Indigenous Peoples, 1977

As a child I understood how to give; I have forgotten this grace since I become civilized. I lived the natural life, whereas I now live the artificial. Any pretty pebble was valuable to me then; every growing tree an object of reverence. Now I worship with the white man before a painted landscape whose value is estimated in dollars! Thus the Indian is reconstructed, as the natural rocks are ground to powder and made into artificial blocks which may be built into the walls of modern society.

—Ohiyesa

The FBI says we are from a radical, secretive, loosely organized Animal Liberation Front. We are not radical, we choose to conserve life, not destroy it. We are not secretive, our voice has been heard since the harmonic balance of nature was first broken by human domination. Yes, we are the animal liberation front, but we are also the earth, air and water liberation front. We are one people. We are bound together by a 500 years resistance to ecological and cultural genocide. . . . Our beliefs are not the product of twentieth-century European philosophers. Our fight is the same fight as the Mohawk, Dine, Blackfoot, Lakota and Apache. . . . In Earth First! we see ourselves. In the American Indian Movement, we see ourselves. Red, brown, white, fur, feathers, and fins, we are all sisters and brothers. For a rebirth of the harmonious relationship with all life, let us no longer stand apart, but TOGETHER.

—Ron Coronado,

Animal Rights and Native American activist

There is a racial divide in the way the U.S. government cleans up toxic waste sites and punishes polluters. White communities see faster action, better results, and stiffer penalties than communities where blacks, Hispanics, and other minorities live. The unequal protection often occurs whether the community is wealthy or poor.

—*National Law Journal*

We are all victims. Not just blacks. Whites are in this thing, too. We're all victimized by a system that puts the dollar before everything else. That's the way it was in the old days when the dogs and whips were masters, and that's the way it is today when we got stuff in the water and air we can't even see that can kill us deader than we ever thought we could die.

—Amos Favorite,

resident of Louisiana's "Cancer Alley"

The passions we feel for the environment direct us to try to alter humanity's current mode of life. To paraphrase Marx: the point is not just to worship nature, but to save it! Furthermore, the religious vision of a sacred earth can be a powerful presence in the environmental movement; and the attempt to bring about social change can pose deeply troubling but also highly fruitful occasions for religious reflection.

Once we leave the temples and prayer circles, however, matters become infinitely more complex and difficult. To actually change social conduct towards nature involves changing our personal lives, to be sure, but also impels us to confront the entrenched interests of governments and corporations, and the dynamics of class, racial, national and gender inequality.

The essays in Part VII help reveal the details of that complexity, and also show that religious environmentalism is a powerful force in the global effort to resist the degradation of other species and the oppression of our own. To begin, essays by myself and Mark Wallace offer overviews of the particular contributions a religious sensibility can make to environmental politics and how the encounter with environmental politics has fundamentally transformed religion itself. Various public statements by religious organizations at the end of this part provide documentary evidence of the dramatic interpenetration of religion and environmental politics.

Accounts of "Green Sisters" (Sarah Taylor) and "Redwood Rabbis" (Seth Zuckerman) and a struggle for a sacred mountain (Evelyn Martin) describe the religious presence in different American contexts. Bruce Byers, by contrast, reflects on the power of traditional African concepts to protect areas threatened by development in Africa.

One of the most important issues raised by the last fifteen years of environmental politics has to do with "environmental racism"; that is, the way people of color face a disproportionate amount of pollution in their communities. The United Church of Christ was instrumental in bringing the issue forward, and Part VII contains a statement of principles from a summit organized by the church, as well as their accounts of a particular struggle in St. Louis. Jonna Higgins-Freese and Jeff Tomhave describe the impact of toxic material on Native Americans.

The general issue of globalization and the concrete resistance to it are the focus of the essays by B. D. Sharma and Mary John Mananzan. Sharma's 1992 address to the U.N. sponsored Earth Summit provides a deeply critical view of the "advanced" industrial nations from the perspective of the Third World, while Mananzan critiques the new "religion" of global power, money, and consumerism. Their analysis is given concrete expression in the Cochabamba "Declaration on Water," which was issued after the "privatization" of water in this Colombian city led to drastic price increases, demonstrations, and government repression.

Ernst Conradie (and his colleagues) and William Fisher examine the intersection of religion and politics in concrete environmental struggles in South Africa and India. An interview with Cesar Chavez reveals connections between Christian nonviolence and the struggle against chemical pesticides. In a poignant meditation, Melody Ermachild reflects on what it is like to try to live an ecologically responsible and spiritually aware life in the midst of urban poverty. Her essay reminds us that we must be wary of a "spiritual bypass" that will see God only in the pleasant.

The writings of Part VII leave off where the real work begins. If we are to save the earth and ourselves, religious ideals had better be translated into political action. It is to be hoped that such action will keep in mind both our collective human plight and our fundamental differences. *Everyone* is threatened by global warming and the hole in the ozone layer. By contrast, however, some people make a great deal of money selling pesticides, while others who work the fields die from exposure to them.

Yet we cannot let either the complications of political life or the virtually overwhelming scope of the task before us deflect our efforts. As bleak as the present is, it may yet be that the tide is turning. We cannot know now what the effects of today's acts will be. In that ignorance may be our greatest hope.

"SAVING THE WORLD: RELIGION AND POLITICS IN THE ENVIRONMENTAL MOVEMENT"

Roger S. Gottlieb

Christians are joining together to save the world's rainforests in Jesus' name.

—Target Earth[1]

"Bishops Say Dealing with Global Warming a Moral Imperative"

—Boston Globe, June 16, 2001

We must learn to . . . recognize the interconnectedness of all living creatures, and to respect the value of each thread in the vast web of life. This is a spiritual perspective, and it is the foundation of all Green politics.

—Petra Kelly, *Thinking Green*[2]

Two short stories:

March 25, 2000. Over 1,000 people crowded the halls of the urban campus of Boston's Northeastern University. This was, in terms reminiscent of the 1960s, a teach-in. It was called Biodevastation—in ironic parody of the simultaneous Boston gathering of high-tech entrepreneurs, scientists, and policy wonks of the genetic engineering industry. Public demonstrations and civil disobedience actions were planned for the next day. Calls would be made for an end to the commercialization of genetically engineered products, corporate control over food and health, and ownership of forms of life (patenting of seeds, and so on); and for tighter public regulations of potentially dangerous biotechnologies.[3]

As one of the day's many workshops, I had been asked to give a talk about the role of spirituality in environmental politics. Because the crowd seemed heavily political, I wasn't sure anyone would show up. Much to my gratified surprise, the medium-size lecture hall held a standing-room-only crowd, with bearded activists, student leaders, and passionate organizers sprawled on the floor and spilling out into the hallway. Although I would have liked to believe it was my vast fame that had brought folks to hear me, I was well aware that most of them didn't know me from Adam, but were drawn by the topic. Like me, they intuited that resistance to the interconnected issues of global environmental crisis, genetic engineering of organisms, and centralized international power of institutions like the World Bank and the International Monetary Fund necessitate a new spiritual and political vision. Concern for humanity's place in the cosmos will have to join resistance to the inequalities of race and class; a moral commitment to future generations of human beings will be matched by care for other species; a deep distrust in the wisdom of markets will be balanced by an emerging faith in ordinary people's knowledge of their own lands and lives.

March 1998. In my own community of Jamaica Plain, a racially and economically mixed section of Southwest Boston, people are banding together to protect our treasured Jamaica Pond: an actual lake—one and one-half miles around—within the city limits! The pond is bordered by a thin belt of trees and graced by seagulls, Canada geese, ducks, mysterious looking cormorants, snapping turtles, and imported swans. Its marvelously clear water attracts joggers, baby carriages, dog walkers, drummers on hot summer nights, old Chinese ladies doing Tai Chi, and couples of various sexual persuasions dreamily holding hands. On brilliant weekends in July or sweltering August afternoons, city-owned rowboats and sailboats allow the city dwellers to feel like they've gone away to their country estates.

When you stand at the little boathouse where popsicles and popcorn are sold, you can look across the water and see the sun set over wooded hills. These hills, which border the park but are not actually part of it, had been sold to a builder seeking to replace the old trees with luxury condos—so that proud owners can enjoy the vista of the pond while the rest of us can view the sun setting over expensive apartments. On the coldest night of the winter of 1998, 350 people jammed a local church to express their disagreement. After a variety of audience members spoke their piece, I approached the mike and said, quite gently, that I was going to use a word rarely heard in political circles but that I hoped people would understand. "The pond," I declared quietly, "is sacred space."

Although this was not a particularly religious crowd, a stunned silence soon gave way to a rising murmur of agreement that soon swept the room and culminated in sustained applause. In thirty years of university teaching and of public speaking in a wide variety of contexts, I had never sensed such an immediate, visceral, and heartfelt response. I had voiced my truth, and it seemed to serve virtually everyone in the room.

These two stories illustrate the theme of this chapter, that in the environmental movement there is a dramatic confirmation of the major ideas of this book. World-making politics and emancipatory religion have joined in environmental politics and ecological spirituality. Theology has been transformed by political awareness and action. And political ideology has transcended the constraints of individual rights and group self-interest. If the civil rights struggle shows religion transforming the world of politics and feminist theology demonstrates the political transformation of religion, then the environmental movement reveals the two working together in critically important ways, at times virtually fusing to form a historically unprecedented phenomenon.

Modern environmentalism has challenged and changed religion throughout the world. Awakened by environmental activists, religious institutions have been moved by the seriousness of pollution, climate change, endangered species issues, resource depletion, and overpopulation. Religious leaders, theologians, and local clergy have signed on to the recognition that the earth as a whole is in an unprecedented predicament. Even if this response is not uniform and absolute, it is still extremely widespread.

Using language that would not be out of place in a Greenpeace broadside, Rabbi Arthur Hertzberg, vice president of the World Jewish Congress, has warned: "Now when the whole world is in peril, when the environment is in danger of being poisoned, and various species, both plant and animal, are becoming extinct, it is our Jewish responsibility to put the defense of the whole of nature at the very center of our concern."[4] In 1990, Pope John Paul II spoke of the worldwide threat caused by "*a lack of due respect for nature* . . . the plundering of natural resources and . . . the widespread destruction of the environment."[5] The Dalai Lama, in his foreword to the first major anthology of writings on Buddhism and ecology, wrote: "The Earth, our Mother, is telling us to behave. All around, signs of nature's limitations abound. Moreover, the environmental crisis currently underway involves all of humanity, making national boundaries of secondary importance."[6]

Yet claims that we are in ecological hot water do not, in themselves, make for a particularly religious contribution to environmentalism. Part of what is so important about that contribution is that it brings to the context a new language, expressing a distinct point of view. For instance, Bartholomew I, ecumenical patriarch of the Eastern Orthodox Church's more than 100 million members, wrote in 1997:

> To commit a crime against the natural world is a sin. For humans to cause species to become extinct and to destroy the biological diversity of God's creation . . . to degrade the integrity of Earth by causing changes in its climate, by stripping the Earth of its natural forests . . . to contaminate the Earth's waters, its land, its air, and its life, with poisonous substances: these are sins.[7]

Conversely, as a Protestant theologian and environmental activist puts it: "The specter of ecocide raises the risk of deicide: to wreak environmental havoc on the earth is to run the risk that we will do irreparable, even fatal harm to the mystery we call God."[8]

A religious perspective applied to the earth, to a "nature" that because of human action has become the "environment," offers insights and prompts emotions that a purely secular story cannot. Spiritual language offers the environmental movement a means to express its passion, hope, and love, regardless of whether activists accept the explicit details of one theology or another. Instead of a large rock with vegetation growing on it, the world becomes "creation" or "the goddess." We experience the world as "holy"—and mean we believe in a God who created it, or that it is of "ultimate concern," or simply that it is heartbreakingly beautiful and infinitely worth cherishing and preserving. Commonplace processes—the co-evolution of a rain-forest plant with its pollinating insect partners, how wetlands clean water, the murmur of whale songs—become "daily miracles."

When religion engages in environmental concerns, the customary boundaries of "religious issues" in political life are decisively broken. Asserting that environmental degradation is not only a health danger, an economic catastrophe, or an aesthetic blight but also *sacrilegious, sinful,* and an *offense against God* catapults religions directly into questions of political power, social policy, and the overall direction of secular society. Religious organizations now take it as given that their voices deserve to be heard on issues such as energy, economic development, population, transportation, industrial production, and agriculture. These topics are, to put it mildly, a far cry from the usual public religious concern with abortion, school prayer, tax exemptions for churches, Holocaust memorials, national Christmas trees, or even pornography in the media.

For example, in March 2001, six senior Christian and Jewish religious leaders wrote to President George W. Bush asking for a meeting with him about his environmental policy, especially around issues of climate change. In a fascinating combination of scriptural references, quotes from the Environmental Protection Agency (EPA), and appeals to scientific expertise, representatives of conservative Judaism (the chancellor of its major rabbinical school), the head of the National Council of the Churches of Christ, and senior officers of the Presbyterian Church, the United Methodist Church, the Disciples of Christ, and the African Methodist Episcopal Church sought to use religious authority to influence national politics.

In another instance, we find that the World Council of Churches (WCC), an international Christian umbrella organization representing 340 churches in 122 countries, has tied its environmental concerns to a deep suspicion of globalization. In doing so, it has challenged the globe's dominant institutions, from the International Monetary Fund and the World Bank to corporations whose budgets are larger than most countries. Globalization is intimately linked to environmentalism because the new global institutions consistently preempt local efforts to control pollution or create sustainable economies. Their tribunals have ruled against clean air legislation in the United States, Canadian restrictions on toxic gasoline additives, attempts to protect marine mammals, European rejection of hormone-injected beef, and efforts to support indigenous, organic farmers rather than Chiquita bananas.[9]

Recent developments have reinforced our perception that issues of justice, peace and creation need to be seen together. One such development is globalization. Globalization impacts not only national and regional economies, causing ever-greater social and economic injustice. It also destroys relationships between individuals, groups, communities, nations, causing conflicts, wars and violence. And it affects the environment of our whole inhabited earth.[10]

The secular left, too, has begun to realize that religious organizations are part of the environmental movement. In the May 2001 issue of *The Nation*, environmentalist David Helvarg has listed actions by the National Council of Churches, the Evangelical Environmental Network, and the Jewish Council of Public Affairs in an article titled, "Bush Unites the Enviros."[11] Over the past several years, all of the major environmental magazines—including *Sierra, Audubon, Amicus Journal,* and *E Magazine*—have run features on the rise of religious environmentalism.[12] They have recognized that from the National Religious Partnership for the Environment, with constituent groups numbering 100 million Americans, to the New England Friends' recent collective commitment to "speak truth to power" in protecting human health and the environment, self-defined religious groups are now major players on the environmental stage.

On the religious side, the environmental crisis is seen by some thinkers as the critical test of their faith's contemporary relevance. As Catholic priest and cultural historian Thomas Berry, whose own attempt to offer a new understanding of humanity's place in the cosmos has been enormously influential, says: "The future of the Catholic church in America, in my view, will depend above all on its capacity to assume a religious responsibility for the fate of the earth."[13] Bearing this out, the web site of the Lutheran Church offers study material on "health and the environment." One situation offered for reflection asks what a "Christian response" would be to a family whose children are suffering from environmentally caused asthma and who cannot move because no one will buy their house, which is surrounded by polluting industries.[14] For Lutherans, in other words, the interlocking contexts of health, the economy, and pollution are now part of their ministry—as much as sexual ethics or the discipline of prayer.

These few instances of the extremely numerous meetings between religion and environmentalism further exemplify modern religion's political transformation. Historically, the dominant attitudes of religious leaders toward modern industrialism—that is, to the immediate source of the environmental crisis—was positive. Once it was clear that capitalism and democracy were here to stay, most churches saw increases in scientific knowledge and technical expertise as promising a better life. Provided that industrial workers achieved a reasonable standard of living, technology meant progress. Challenges to the modern economy came from poets like Blake and Wordsworth, anti-Communist Western Marxists like Max Horkheimer and Herbert Marcuse, philosophers like Martin Heidegger, and imaginative nature lovers like Thoreau and John Muir. As in the case of feminism, it was only after a political movement brought global ecological crisis to the fore of public discussion that religion jumped on board.[15] Yet jump on board it did, and with an energy and acumen that has, so far, outpaced corporations, organized labor, the academic community, and such professionals as doctors or lawyers.

Besides an acknowledgment of the severity of the crisis, new theologies have been devised in which the earth, or nature, or our fellow creatures are recognized as carrying a divine and sacred meaning. Such theologies are in stark contrast to what has been the dominant position of world religions, especially those of the West. Despite the presence of occasional dissenting voices, Western religions long stressed the gap between humans and the rest of creation, espousing ethical systems in which concern for the nonhuman was peripheral at best. Just as feminism has required a new valuation of women, so the ecological crisis has led to a new—or at least a revised—sense of our proper relationship to nature.

These new theologies sometimes originate in attempts to recover the few nature-respecting elements that can be found in tradition. Thus, Lynn White, whose 1967 essay criticizing the "anthropocentrism" (human-centeredness) of Western religions helped initiate a dialogue on the subject that continues to this day, did not suggest a total rejection of Christianity. Rather, he proposed St. Francis's love of animals and the whole of physical creation as an alternative to the reigning Christian attitudes.[16] Similarly, essayist and farmer Wendell Berry challenged dominant interpretations of the biblical passage often cited as divine justification for human dominion, God's command to Adam: "Go forth, subdue the earth, and master it" (Genesis 1:28). By stressing the importance of other passages of the Torah, especially Deuteronomy 8:10 ("Thou shalt bless the lord thy God for the good land which He has given you"), Berry teaches that biblical ethics requires us to live "knowingly, lovingly, skillfully, reverently" rather than "ignorantly, greedily, clumsily, destructively." In the first case, our use of Creation will be a "sacrament," in the latter, a "desecration."[17] Jewish writers have recovered biblical and Talmudic doctrines stressing the sinfulness of squandering resources (*bal tashchit* ["do not waste"]), holidays celebrating the birthday of the trees, and biblical restrictions on the exploitation of animals (if your ox is threshing your grain, you can't muzzle him, even if he ends up eating some of it!). These traditions are then applied to a host of contemporary ecological issues, such as recycling, carpooling, the disposal of toxics, the waste of food, factory farming, and the protection of old-growth forests.[18]

Buddhist teacher Thich Nhat Hanh has adapted the mindfulness practice of Buddhist *gathas* (short prayers or poems used to focus attention) to include ecological awareness. For instance, while planting trees, one may recite: "I entrust myself to Buddha;/Buddha entrusts himself to me./I entrust myself to Earth;/Earth entrusts herself to me."[19] The National Council of Churches offers the following prayer to be included in First Sunday after Easter as part of a service called "Witnessing to the Resurrection: Caring for God's Creation":

We pursue profits and pleasures that harm the land and pollute the waters.
We have squandered the earth's gifts on technologies of destruction.
The land mourns, and all who live in it languish; together with the wild animals and the birds of the air, even the fish of the sea are perishing.[20]

Or in the words of the general secretary of the United Methodist Church: "Our biblical tradition affirms that God calls people of faith to defend and protect all of God's creation, both human and non-human."[21]

Feminist versions of Christianity and Judaism may, in good conscience, focus their efforts on creating inclusive God language, getting women into positions of power in religious organizations, and criticizing the sexism of past doctrine. By contrast, the new theologies of nature necessarily involve their adherents in political life. Once religions assert that "ecology and justice, stewardship of creation and redemption are interdependent"[22] or that "[w]here human life and health are at stake, economic gain must not take precedence,"[23] they are—like it or not—headed for a confrontation with the dominant powers of economics and politics.

In this confrontation, religious discourse has and will continue to play a significant role. If this is not a universal religious response, it is an extremely widespread one. As one journalist puts it: "More and more it appears religion and ecology are walking hand-in-hand. The sermon titles are the Kyoto treaty on global warming and endangered species protection."[24] For example, there is the 1997–1999 campaign of the "Redwood Rabbis," a group of rabbis and lay Jewish environmental activists who struggled to protect an ancient redwood grove in Northern California. Working with the local Sierra Club, the group invoked biblical principles and contemporary ecological values to try to influence Charles Hurwitz, a visible leader of the Houston Jewish community and head of the corporation that was clear-cutting the site. The Redwood Rabbis received backing from the Coalition on the Environment and Jewish Life—which is itself supported by mainstream Jewish groups such as Hillel, Hadassa, and B'nai Brith—and engaged in civil disobedience by planting redwood seedlings in defiance of Hurwitz's orders.[25]

Buddhists in both the United States and Japan have actively resisted the storage and transportation of dangerous nuclear material, while in Germany, Buddhists have challenged both the ethics and the environmental consequences of factory farming.[26] Christian groups have formed coalitions to reduce global warming, have held religious services to celebrate lakes, and have authorized study groups to reduce the environmental impact of church buildings. National and international organizations have formed to radically transform theological education to take account of the environmental crisis.[27]

Roger S. Gottlieb

In these and thousands more examples, it is clear that to be ethical in relation to environmental issues is also to be political. The economy, the government, the military, health care, transportation, and just about everything else are called into question. Believers may still pray for a pure heart and train their awareness mindfully, but environmental problems simply cannot be solved though individual action. In just this way, environmental issues are a direct confirmation of the claims I made in Chapters 1 and 3 about how the modern world politicizes ethics. Through the work we do and the taxes we pay, what we buy and what we drive, our personal moral lives have a global meaning. When any serious religious group talks about the environment, it necessarily expresses support for certain concrete political policies: for instance, the need to monitor and restrict market forces, limit the prerogatives of corporations, make the government responsive to the interests of ecosystems and the socially powerless, limit military expenditures, and direct technology toward sustainability.

As they confront the environmental crisis, many religious groups throughout the world advocate not only the values of "ecotheology" but the pursuit of "ecojustice," i.e., the seamless blending of concern for earth's creation and human beings, the biotically marginalized and the socially powerless, endangered species and endangered human communities. This blending includes issues of class, race, gender, and indigenous rights, alongside more familiar concern with "nature." It requires—and is achieving—a comprehensive understanding of political life that joins religious visionaries with the most sophisticated and principled of secular political movements.

Consider the comprehensive notions of environmental racism and environmental justice, phrases that refer to the fact that racial minorities and the poor in the United States, just like indigenous peoples worldwide, are exposed to a great deal more pollution than are the racially and economically dominant groups. Lacking social power, their lives are held as less valuable; the environmental crisis is written on—and in—their bodies.[28] During the last thirty years, a comprehensive concern with environmental justice developed with the constant input of black religious social activists.[29] The historic 1987 report *Toxic Wastes and Race*, the first comprehensive account of environmental racism, was researched and written by the commission for racial justice of the United Church of Christ.[30] This report detailed the fundamental racial and class inequality in the siting and cleanup of hazardous wastes in the United States. Its lead investigator, Reverend Benjamin Chavis, was instrumental in connecting the civil rights, religious, and environmental communities of the South. Four years later, in 1991, the very first principle of the historic National People of Color Environmental Leadership Summit proclaimed that "environmental justice affirms the sacredness of mother Earth, ecological unity and the interdependence of all species, and the right to be free from ecological destruction."[31] A few years later, President Clinton ordered government agencies to take environmental justice issues into account in their programs.

Alongside racial and class issues, an ecojustice perspective focuses on the ways in which Western thought has historically equated women and nature and devalued both. The initial justification for this dual subordination was found in the claim that both lacked the holiness or closeness to God of men. Later, it was men's (self-proclaimed) rationality that was thought to justify masculine social privileges. In terms of concrete social policy, contemporary Western schemes of economic development for poor countries often have disastrous effects on Third World women, whose lives and livelihood are tied to their immediate surroundings. For example, in poorer countries men plant cash crops, but women plant subsistence crops. When export agriculture promoting a single agricultural commodity takes over, women in the local community are hurt more than men. Awareness of the combination of the cultural devaluation of women with their economic subordination helps create an "ecofeminism" that has powerful religious and political implications.[32]

The religious presence in environmental politics, like a good deal of the entire environmental movement, not only breaks barriers between religion and politics, theology, and social activism but also helps develop a world-making *political* agenda that may avoid being limited to one or another particular social group. Religions have a powerful contribution to make here. Insofar as they have a mandate, it is, after all, from God: a God who is not tied, one hopes, to the valid but inevitably partial concerns of one political group or another. Of course, in the past much of traditional religion was rabidly sectarian, racist, colonialist, or just downright nasty. But religions that have been deeply affected by the liberal and radical politics of the last two centuries have moved beyond those moral failings, or at least are trying to.

Ecojustice is, thus, a comprehensive political and spiritual vision. In the words of the Ecojustice Ministries, a Denver-based Protestant activist organization, part of that vision involves "Confronting Power Relationship":

> Faithful and ethical living is not confined to personal choices. Moses and the prophets all spoke to, and about, the power structures of their communities. Jesus and Paul dealt with the realities of political power. An eco-justice perspective recognizes that the power relationships of each situation must be analyzed and addressed. In our globalized economy, it is absurd to suggest that personal choices alone can address the crises we face. Various forms of power—economic, political, military, intellectual and personal—must be taken into account in the ways that we understand the world and live within it.
>
> Eco-justice is not one "issue" out of the many from which congregations can pick and choose: hunger, housing, guns, abortion, militarism, morality, globalization, families, wilderness, affirmative action, civil rights, economic justice, education, immigration, hunger, health care—and the list goes on and on. Rather, eco-justice is a theological perspective that shapes the way that we approach each of these issues.[33]

The religious participation in the environmental justice movement is not simply a matter of pious statements. There are many places where religious organizations play an active role in the movement itself. For instance, The White Violet Center for Eco-Justice of Indiana is staffed by Catholics and focuses on a range of justice and environmental issues, including wetlands preservation, organic agriculture, and preservation of endangered bird species. It "exists to foster a way of living that recognizes the interdependence of all creation" and "seeks to create systems that support justice and sustainability, locally and globally."[34]

The Social Action Office of Queensland, Australia, is also centered in the Catholic Church. It has an annual budget of $A160,000 and employs one full-time coordinator and four part-time employees. One of its main areas is "ecojustice," in the pursuit of which it prepared a detailed and technically sophisticated account of the human and environmental effects of a prospective development of the Brisbane harbor. It also encourages readers to boycott Exxon, and its web site provides links to both church statements on environmental issues and secular political groups like Greenpeace.[35]

When in 2001 a Boston coalition was formed to confront environmental justice issues in the local distribution of toxic materials, the Greater Boston Coalition on the Environment and Jewish Life played a critical role.[36] When the first resistance to dumping of PCBs in predominantly poor and black Warren County, North Carolina, got underway in 1982, it was the black religious community that took the lead. Worldwide, indigenous peoples resist environmentally destructive "development" of their land in part because they have religious bonds to the land that are essential to their culture and community.[37]

These examples are a tiny fraction of the whole picture. But the essential point is clear. It is simply no longer true of religions, as political radicals have been claiming for nearly two centuries: "They concentrate on the individual and not social institutions; they are unwilling to envision radical social changes; they cannot see the links among different moral and political concerns; they seek changes in attitudes or values rather than in basic social institutions; they are unwilling to learn from the insights of world-making political theory." Such criticisms may well continue to apply to some groups, but they have become completely inapplicable to others. The great divide between religion and progressive politics, weakened by Protestant abolitionism, the social teachings of the Catholic Church, and the social gospel of the late nineteenth century, cracked by Gandhi and King and the religious presence in the peace and anti-apartheid movements, has in the global environment movement finally been decisively overcome.

If religions have to some extent turned Green, Green politics are in some important ways religious. In the contemporary environmental movement, even those groups totally unconnected to religiously identified organizations are often practicing a new kind of politics, one in which a religious or spiritual sensibility is present. It is this simultaneous transformation of both religion and political activism that helps make environmental politics dramatically new and historically important.

The politics I have in mind here include but are not limited to government programs and laws. Politics, as political scientist Paul Wapner says, also "takes place in the home, office, and marketplace."[38] At one end of the spectrum of activities and concerns that make up Green politics, we find direct actions aimed at stopping some particular instance of "development" or some concrete industrial practice. When the women of India's Chipko movement physically encircle the trees of their beloved forest (which provides herbs, fodder for animals, and firewood) to prevent them from being chopped down, when Greenpeace plugs the outflow pipe of a chemical factory, when thousands protest "free trade" agreements that would cripple communities' rights to limit ecological degradation, environmental politics means putting your body on the line to protect both other species and human beings. At the other end of the spectrum, we find attempts to influence world culture through teaching, writing, films, Internet sites, poetry, and art. In between these two poles are a host of governmental and nongovernmental policies, institutions, and activities: from government regulation of pesticide use to the creation of wildlife refuges, from lobbying to protect wetlands to resisting environmental racism, from researching the duplicity of the chemical industry to organizing neighbors to clean up a local river. In this light, non-governmental organizations like transnational environmental groups "contribute to addressing global environmental problems by heightening world-wide concern for the environment. They persuade vast numbers of people to care about and take actions to protect the earth's ecosystems."[39]

What gives this wide spectrum of Green politics a religious or spiritual dimension? Well, in some cases this dimension will not be present. If we seek to preserve a forest so that we can hunt big game in it (one of the original motivations for wildlife preservation efforts)[40] or if our sole concern with pesticides is their effect on human health, then our approach to environmental issues is purely "instrumental." It is, we might say, simply a continuation of the "anthropocentric" attitudes that have marked Western culture for at least 3,000 years, attitudes resting on the belief that only human beings are morally valuable. In this form, caring for a river or an endangered species is little different from concern over auto safety or tennis elbow—valuable and important, to be sure, but not historically new or spiritually significant.

If however, we are at least partly motivated by "ecocentric" or biocentric values, if there is an element of "deep ecology" in our passion, if we see nature as a mother, a lover, or a partner, then the situation is different[41]—for then we are expressing a distinct vision of the value of our surroundings and a new and powerful sense of the meaning of human identity itself.[42] When environmental politics are motivated by a concern for life as a whole or ecosystems above and beyond the human, I believe, they are profoundly spiritual and, in a deep and general sense, *religious.*

Whether known as deep ecology, ecofeminism, bioregionalism, the land ethic, or simply the special place that some beach, forest, or mountain has in our hearts, this sensibility involves a passionate communion with the earth. What is "deep" about this perspective is the experience—and the conviction—that our surroundings are essential to who we are. And this is not just because they are useful, but because we are tied to them by invisible threads of inspiration, memory, esthetic delight, emotional connection, and simple wonder. Sky and earth, bird and fish, each leaf on each tree—without them, we could not be ourselves. As one of the architects of modern environmental politics, David Brower, wrote: "To me, God and Nature are synonymous."[43] Poisoning nature thus not only leads to the concrete suffering of soaring cancer rates and our children's asthma but creates the emotional and spiritual crisis comparable to what would happen if our families were murdered, our cathedrals bombed, or our holy books burned.

In contrast to the precisely formulated content of ecotheology, with its biblical references, new models of God, and creative applications of traditional concepts to environmental issues, some of the new environmental spirituality is diffuse and at times hard to capture. As Christopher Childs, longtime Greenpeace activist and spokesperson says, "[T]here is broad acceptance among Greenpeace staff that the work is quintessentially spiritual, though definitions of what is meant by the term vary."[44]

When this sensibility enters environmental politics, it takes a variety of forms. One element is the simple faith in the political power of a moral statement. For instance, the Quaker-inspired practice of "bearing witness" is "central to Greenpeace's well-publicized actions in the face of pollution or mammal killing."[45] The goal is to reveal the damaging actions to the world and to help encourage an alternative perception of reality that might lead to massive resistance or at least a shift in public sentiment. Similar elements can be found in Buddhist and feminist resistance to the production and transport of radioactive materials. In these settings ecoactivism calls on a quasi-religious sense of the ultimate imperative of moral action, a sense that hopes for victory but does not depend on it. As I indicated in Chapter 4, it is one of religion's gifts to assign to moral acts an abiding importance in and of themselves, an importance that can keep us going even when (as almost always seems the case in environmental politics) we have no certainty of getting the results we seek.

This spiritual vision of environmental politics also provides a crucial alternative to the destructive values of the global marketplace, values that privilege economic growth, rising exports, and individual autonomy above all else. The "religion" of modernity demands control over nature and a model of development that turns every meadow and village into the same old mall. Nature is thought of as a thing, an element to be used. Selfhood is defined by consumption, and there is a widespread attempt to broadcast excessive styles of consumption throughout the world.

Sulak Sivaraksa, Buddhist environmental activist from Thailand, writes that "Western consumerism is the dominant ethic in the world today . . . The new 'spiritual advisors' are from Harvard Business School, Fletcher School of Law and Diplomacy, and London

School of Economics. . . . The department stores have become our shrines, and they are constantly filled with people. For the young people, these stores have replaced the Buddhist temples."[46] The drive toward globalization, says a Third World Christian theologian, is often seen as a sort of new religion: "it has its God: profit and money. It has its high priests: GATT [General Agreement on Tariffs and Trade], WTO [World Trade Organization], IMF-WB. It has its doctrines and dogmas: import liberalization, deregulation . . . It has its temples: the super megamalls. It has its victims on the altar of sacrifice: the majority of the world—the excluded and marginalized poor."[47]

Referring to the conflict between native peoples and economic development over the proposed building of a massive, ecosystem-destroying and native-people-uprooting hydroelectric dam in James Bay, Ontario, David Kinsley argues:

> If hunting animals is a sacred occupation among the Mistassini Cree, building dams to harness power for electricity is equally sacred for many members of modern industrial society. . . . the conflict between the Cree and [Ontario political leader] Bourassa, then, is not so much a conflict between a religious view and a secular view as it is a conflict between two contrasting visions of the nature of human beings and human destiny, that is, two conflicting myths about the place of human beings in the natural order, two contrasting ecological visions.[48]

Charlene Spretnak describes the difference between these two visions: "Modern culture . . . is based on mechanistic analysis and control of human systems as well as Nature . . . nationalistic chauvinism, sterile secularism, and monoculture shaped by mass media. . . . Green values, by contrast, seek a path of 'ecological wisdom' and attempt to integrate freedom *and* tradition, the individual *and* the community, science *and* Nature, men *and* women."[49] To accomplish that goal, said leader of the German Green Party Petra Kelly, "We must learn to . . . recognize the interconnectedness of all living creatures, and to respect the value of each thread in the vast web of life. This is a spiritual perspective, and it is the foundation of all Green politics."[50] Or as Earth First! activist Mark Davis said, in explaining why he broke the law in trying to prevent the further expansion of a ski resort into mountains revered by the Hopi and Navajo, "[T]he bottom line is that those mountains are sacred, and that what has occurred there, despite our feeble efforts, is a terrible spiritual mistake."[51]

In fact, spiritual values in general and the value(s) of nature in particular give us a way out of the ecocidal cul-de-sac of the endless mall. They help us to develop an alternative sense of self that acknowledges dependence, mutuality, and happiness *without* requiring endless "development," soulless gadgetry, and the elimination of other life forms. This alternative allows the withdrawal of psychic energy from a cultural and economic system that threatens the earth and people alike. In the same vein, a spiritual relationship with the natural world allows us to orient political struggle in a direction not tied (or at least less tied) by psychic addiction to the very social system that destroys us. Greens have, some observers believe, "moved beyond materialist values while at the same time embracing some preindustrial values derived from indigenous non-European cultures. These value shifts have been tied to specific issues that are crucial for the Greens but often ignored by the Democratic Left."[52] The interface of spiritual and Green values has helped create the emerging discipline of "ecopsychology," which is oriented to understanding the psychic costs of our alienation from the rest of the earth, and the psychologically and spiritually healing experiences that come from lessening that alienation.[53]

Sociologist Manuel Castells describes a deep Green perspective as one in which

> The holistic notion of integration between humans and nature . . . does not refer to a naive worshipping of pristine natural landscapes, but to the fundamental consideration that the relevant unit of experience is not each individual, or for that matter, historically existing human communities. To merge ourselves with our cosmological self we need first to change the notion of time, to feel "glacial time" run through our lives, to sense the energy of stars flowing in our blood, and to assume the rivers of our thoughts endlessly merging in the boundless oceans of multiform living matter.[54]

Such a perspective, Castells believes, leads environmentalism to be in fundamental opposition to the dominant values of multinational corporate power, transnational economic institutions like the IMF and the World Bank, and placeless cultural and economic icons like MTV and Nike. When Green values inform the best of Green politics, "we are a long way from the instrumentalist perspective that has dominated the industrial era, in both its capitalist and statist [i.e., socialist] versions. And we are in direct contradiction with the dissolution of meaning in the flows of faceless power that constitute the network society."[55]

It is environmentalism, more than any other political setting, that unites the "cultural creatives" described in Chapter 2; the nonviolent spiritual resistance of the civil rights movement, feminist theology, and spirituality of Chapter 6, and in fact the comprehensive notion that religion has something specific and precious to add to political life. In environmentalism, liberal support for individual rights and the socialist concern with economic rationality can meet each other and join forces with the non-Western emphasis on community and responsibility.

Environmentalists can be dramatically different from each other. They include those who long nostalgically for a hunter-gatherer lifestyle, those who support Aldo Leopold's call for "an individual responsibility for the health of the land,"[56] as well as hard-headed city planners eager to replace cars with bikes, integrate communities with an ecofriendly Internet, and design apartment complexes with organic rooftop gardens. Yet the comprehensive values referred to by Spretnak, Kelly, and Castells resonate throughout much of the movement. These include a distrust of uncontrolled economic growth and thoughtless technological innovation, in combination with the belief that both the market and technology should serve collective rather than narrowly human interests. There is a corresponding belief that has clear spiritual overtones: the idea that human life has other purposes than the acquisition of power and wealth. It is stressed, rather, that we live for the development of wisdom, peacefulness, harmonious coexistence with the earth, and the quiet (itself a radical demand in these deafening times) enjoyment of life. Journalist Mark Dowie suggests that despite the enormous diversity of the environmental movement, a number of common principles can be found. Along with familiar political goals, these include an ethical and spiritual redefinition of human beings as part of nature and not its master or the only part that really matters.[57]

What applying these values would mean is often far from clear. Since the ecological crisis is a product of our entire civilization, broader in scope and more universally threatening than any other form of political injustice or collective irrationality, the transformation called for is correspondingly large. We might take as a hopeful example the enormous social success of Kerala, India's southernmost state, which has dramatically increased literacy and education, reduced infant mortality, raised life expectancy to nearly Western levels, improved women's social position, and cultivated a culture of intellectual and artistic engagement *without* high levels of industrialization or the raising of per capita income. We might consider Colombia's village of Gaviotas, where appropriate technology has led to a sustainable life in the midst of a formerly barren wasteland, sustainable crops help regenerate a rain forest, and children's swings power the water pumps.[58] We might notice how the citizens of Maine, who suffer each year through several weeks of highly annoying and virtually impossible-to-stop black flies, reject the use of potentially dangerous chemical pesticides, even if it will cost them tourist income. "If people can't live with the flies," some say, "they just shouldn't come here."[59]

We can see the new sensibility expressed in political campaigns aimed at inclusive goals of protecting endangered species, preserving the culture and ecosystems of indigenous peoples, and preventing industrial pollution. In one powerful example, international activity mobilized in response to the Narmada River Valley Project in India.[60] Called by critics the "world's greatest planned environmental disaster," the project envisaged thirty major, 135 medium, and 3,000 minor dams throughout Central India. If completed as planned, it would have displaced close to 400,000 people, destroyed wildlife habitat, and flooded some of the last remaining tropical forests in India. As early as 1977, local opposition formed when people realized that there was in fact no land available for the residents who were to be displaced—that they would simply join the tens of millions of other "refugees from development." During the next decade and a half, opposition grew and took a variety of forms: road blockades, hunger fasts, demonstrations at state capitals, and massive gatherings at sites that were to be flooded. A ring of international solidarity

Roger S. Gottlieb

formed. Japanese environmentalists persuaded their government not to advance money to it, while American activists pressured the World Bank. The San Francisco-based International Rivers Project organized financial and technical aid. In 1992, facing reports that the entire project was marked by fraud and incompetence, legislators in Finland, Sweden, and the United States asked the World Bank not to lend any more money. In this heartening case, the more familiar dimension of human rights mixed with concern for other species; citizens of different countries and continents gave time, energy, and money to support those of another. A vital mix of personal and group self-interest, abstract political principle, and transpersonal celebration of the earth took shape.

Such principles can be found anywhere environmental struggles emerge. In an attempt to protect their village from predatory commercial fishing, a Brazilian group stresses values connected to Catholic liberation theology: "group solidarity, the participation and inclusion of all in . . . group decisions and . . . a suspicion if not of material wealth itself at least a distrust of what wealth acquisition requires in terms of . . . oppressive and unjust structures."[61] In resistance to ecologically damaging mining and timber practices in India, local groups have combined concern for health, local communities, and the sacred status of forests or rivers.[62]

In all these struggles, environmentalism is not simply interest-group politics applied to forests and toxic incinerators. Rather, it is informed by a comprehensive vision of human identity and of how that identity is interrelated with the universe as a whole. This vision deserves to be considered, in the broadest sense, religious.

When the United Church of Christ talks about racism in citing toxic waste sites, when religious organizations instruct the president of the United States on global warming, when Buddhist monks protest globalization, they show how contemporary religious and spiritual voices have adopted some of the conceptual tools of progressive political theory. Broad orientations toward human identity (we are kin to the rain forest); or to moral values (we have obligations to other species and to humans injured by our industrial practices); or to the meaning of life or the cosmos (our task is to be part of life, we are to be loving stewards to the earth) have always been part of religion. However, when the critique of dams, the diagnosis of racism in the placing of Superfund sites, and analysis of the economic and human costs of globalization are added in, something new is afoot.

For example, consider the Dalai Lama's suggestion that "[w]hen we talk about preservation of the environment, it is related to many other things. Ultimately, the decision must come from the human heart. The key point is to have a genuine sense of universal responsibility, based on love and compassion, and clear awareness."[63] This statement correctly points out that each person who opposes the juggernaut of industrialism must make a personal commitment, with no guarantee of "success," to a daunting task. However, the statement ignores the fact that *personal* awareness, love, and compassion are extremely limited if they are not joined by an understanding of—and an attempt to change—our collective institutions. The Dalai Lama—exactly like the author of this book and, in all probability, the reader as well—plugs into the same electronic grid as everyone else, burns fossil fuels to fly from place to place, and employs the resources of our environmentally unsustainable society in his struggle to save some vestige of his people's national identity. His personal love and compassion, in short, do not keep him from contributing to the mess! Understanding the problems, criticizing them fully, and offering alternatives requires a "social" ecology whose nuts-and-bolts account of the economic and political sources of ecocrisis take its place alongside appeals to personal love, compassion, and awareness.

To take another example, one of the most ambitious descriptions of what an ecological society might look like, *For the Common Good: Redirecting the Economy Toward Community, the Environment and a Sustainable Future* is—significantly—the joint product of a Protestant theologian (John Cobb) and a professor of economics and former senior economist for the World Bank (Herman Daly). Daly and Cobb propose a rich combination of policy and value changes. They challenge existing economies of scale and current trade policies, suggest new ways to cultivate local communities, and redesign educational priorities. And they address the cosmic meaning of human existence and the ethical standards that should guide it. Similarly, when theologian Dorothy Soelle confronts the prospects of religion in the twenty-first century, she must diagnose the political ills of globalization along with the more familiar problems of Christian complacency or arrogance.[64]

What we are witnessing, then, is a double movement: the entry of spiritual values into world-making political perspectives and religion's assimilation of analytic tools for understanding the logic of ecological destruction. Here, despite the moral, political, and economic institutional failures of Communist nations, it is not hard to see how much of Marxist theory is in fact extremely useful. And despite the fact that many claim to have left Marxism in the dustbin of history, its general understanding of capitalism is widely used.

Marx's original theory correctly predicted much of the economic future of capitalism: the expansion and development of productive technology, the ascendancy of corporate power in politics and culture, the evolution of larger and more concentrated forms of wealth, and the worldwide spread of social relationships based on money. Since Marx, theorists under his influence have described an economy dominated by national and global megacorporations, the role of the government in organizing and stabilizing the economy, and the manner in which the international market economy leads to the internationalization of poverty and ecological destruction. We have not "outgrown" Marxist insights in our age of global capitalism, corporations larger than many nations, and frequently unrestrained state power in the service of big business.[65]

Roger S. Gottlieb

Let us examine, for example, the replacement of subsistence agriculture with large plantations producing a single crop for export. This pattern has been repeated countless times throughout Asia, Latin America, and Africa, almost always with disastrous results. Basic Marxist premises provide a straightforward explanation. Land oriented toward local production for use has been converted to production for profitable export. Because the land is no longer directly connected to a self-subsistent community, its distant owners have no compunctions about using techniques that degrade both land (now overburdened by unsustainable pesticides, chemical fertilizers, and water use) *and* the human community (now turned into poverty-stricken "masses," usually forced to join the unemployed in overburdened urban centers). If enough profits are made, it does not matter whether much is left of the land (or people) when the capital is transferred to some other investment. In this way international *trade* in sugar and bananas, coffee and cotton, degrades agricultural *communities and land* throughout the world. And the situation is only made worse when genetic engineering further reduces the diversity of seeds, farming techniques, and input from traditional farming communities.[66]

Another problem that can be easily understood in broadly Marxist terms concerns the way corporations can treat the pollution they cause as "external" to the cost of the commodities they sell.[67] Production, sale, and profits are typically the business of the company in question; cleanup and health costs are borne by society—and the ecosystem—as a whole. What looks like "freedom of the market" is really the privilege to acquire wealth while impoverishing the human (and nonhuman) community.

In cases such as these, abstractions about our "attitudes toward nature" may be relevant, but not nearly so much as is an understanding of the capitalist globalization of agriculture or the vital need for some collective control of productive life.

For a Marxist political orientation, the ultimate question is whether this control can be realized. Even though most religious environmentalists do not call for complete nationalization of the forces of production, the vast majority of them do demand serious social constraints on the productive activity of private corporations. This Marxian goal, though rarely acknowledged as such, is common to all but the most timid and conservative forms of religious environmentalism. In many other instances, more direct condemnations of the imperatives of capitalism are present.

What I have just described in reference to Marxism could be repeated in relation to religious environmentalists' use of a feminist critique of patriarchy, antiracism theory, and postcolonial perspectives on the pernicious effects of globalization. The United Church of Christ report, after all, was about a structural racism that had little or nothing to do with emotional racial antagonism, traditional segregation, or minorities refused jobs or mortgages. Religious voices concerned with environmental justice focus on contrasting real estate values, differences in the capacity of communities for self-defense, and lack of personal connections to motivate institutional concern.

Whether those who use such language to describe social problems needing religious attention are ministers, professors of political science, or paid organizers, the language itself is the stuff of progressive political theory and originates in secular political movements. Without these perspectives, the new values of environmental theology simply cannot comprehend the real world.

Just as the pressure of a historically unprecedented environmental crisis transforms traditional religion and nondenominational spirituality, so political theory has had to change as well. For a start, Western liberals and radicals, like their religious comrades, have had to question their own anthropocentric premises. Democratic theory, rooted in the notion of the autonomous, "rational" individual, has been extended to discussions of the rights of animals, trees, and ecosystems. Marxism, in many ways functioning under the same human-centered premises as liberalism, has similarly had to ask whether the liberation of the working class and the fulfillment of human goals were the sole purposes of political movements. All progressive political positions have been challenged to answer new questions about what they mean by happiness, freedom, justice, and human fulfillment. As Andrew McLaughlin has argued, and many Greens have agreed, the problem is not simply capitalism, but an "industrialism" that privileges human consumption, unchecked technological innovation, and a mindless popular culture over tradition, community, and ties to other species.[68] If traditional religion was not up to the demands of the environmental crisis, most world-making political theories weren't either. Just as the nonviolent activists of biodevastation were eager to think about the spiritual roots of their passion for the earth and my Jamaica Plain neighbors understood the pond as sacred, so it is that many hardheaded accounts of the death of forests or toxic air quality indicate a fundamental concern that is spiritual in terms of its transcendence of purely instrumental interest.

I've argued throughout this book that the religious spirit can add something to political life. In particular, we often find in world-making religious social activists certain values typically absent in the secular left. These values include compassion, empathy even for the guilty, self-awareness, and some reflective distance from the typical pursuit of status and power within the movement.

Such virtues are especially important for environmentalism. One reason this is true is that the universality and severity of the ecological crisis offer environmental activists an enormous range of potential allies. Harshness, unforgiving self-righteousness, and uncontrolled anger will alienate many who might join the cause. Self-destructive infighting, arrogance, aggression, name-calling, and factionalism can—once again—only lead to failure. These were, according to its most well-known leader, the source of the downfall of the once-powerful German Green Party.[69]

Roger S. Gottlieb

For environmental politics, simple pieties like those of Thich Nhat Hanh about how it is important to smile, breathe, and be pleasant to adversaries become critically important. The spiritually rooted practice of moral self-examination, the awareness of the near-universal tendency toward egotism (or "sin"), and the trust that others act badly only out of ignorance can lead spiritual social activists to a more human, inclusive, and ultimately successful politics. Often, environmental struggles involve fundamental shifts in community life: Jobs are at stake, freedom to use private property is curtailed, cultural values such as hunting are challenged. In the face of the inevitable emotional pain such struggles create, activists need all the resources of empathy and compassion that spiritual traditions—at their best—can offer.

Similarly, the environmentalists' concern for nature is a value that can provide the basis for a new kind of social solidarity. We might remember that whatever else divides us as human beings, we all need air and water; and virtually all of our hearts rejoice in the sounds of spring. These commonalities may save us when the divisions of race, class, gender, ethnicity, or sexuality leave us deeply suspicious of each other. Emphasizing what we share is a particular gift of spiritual social activists.[70] Such activists cultivate respect for each person's essential spiritual worth and not just condemnation of the "bad guys"; and this attitude is stressed as much within the movement as on the outside. As an example of detailed thought on this matter, consider the "Fourteen Precepts for the Order of Interbeing," which Thich Nhat Hanh wrote as a kind of guidebook for Buddhist social activists. These precepts stress humility, peacefulness, and integrity in the pursuit of political change. "Do not force others," one precept teaches, "to accept your views, whether by authority, threat, money, propaganda or even education. However, through compassionate dialogue, help others renounce fanaticism and narrowness."[71] Of course, one person's peaceful pursuit of ecological wisdom might be another's fanaticism. Guidelines of this kind cannot end all the tensions of political life. However, even a casual examination of the history of world-making political organizations reveals how much more successful political groups might have been if they had even been aware such principles existed! The environmental movement has had its share of bitterness, infighting, careerism, and energy wasted on internal hostility. We might remember how the career of David Brower, perhaps the single most important architect of modern activist environmentalism, was marked by situations of unnecessary conflict.[72]

Because activists are struggling against a system in which they themselves take part, spiritual values of humility and self-awareness seem particularly appropriate. In the more familiar contexts of racism or sexism, one can overcome prejudicial attitudes, refuse to support stereotyping or discrimination, and promote the interests of the oppressed group; and, in the case of men and feminism, a man can do his share of the housework and make respect for women a basic masculine virtue. However, when it comes to the environment, it is unlikely that we will stop using electricity, consuming food transported from thousands of miles away, or driving. To be sure, everyone is not equally responsible. Only a tiny percentage of us control energy policy, displace peasants to create pesticide-drenched export farming, or support political candidates who will lessen restrictions on automobile fuel efficiency. But we all consume the fruits of industrial civilization and contribute to the mess.

Also, environmental movements from developing nations, particularly those of Asia, offer an emphasis on collective well-being and communal values that is an important counterweight to the Western stress on individual rights. Having been catapulted into a global economy without the centuries-long development of extreme forms of individualism, Buddhist and indigenous groups can remind the rest of us that concern for the village, the tribe, the community, the clan, and the people are as essential to the creation of a just and rational social order as is the "individual." These are political concerns that focus on peoplehood, on shared culture, and on ties to a particular place rather than on issues of economic class or generalized race or ethnicity.[73]

Further, unlike movements keyed solely to economic gain or group interests, environmentalism must counter the reigning belief that the "good life" is defined by high consumption. It must propose alternative models of human goodness, fulfillment, and happiness.

Most secular political viewpoints have ignored this task. Liberalism, after all, was concerned with untrammeled personal freedom in social and economic life. Marxism sought to liberate exploited classes. Most of the dominant social movements of the last two centuries have focused on equal treatment for their constituents and raising standards of living. As products of the Enlightenment, they carried its strengths and its weaknesses.

Although certain elements of the 1960s counterculture and feminism did challenge some of modernity's basic principles, these elements have come to full flower in environmentalism—especially environmentalism that is infused with some spiritual values. These radically new perspectives ask: What is the ultimate worth of this construction project, these jobs, that commodity? Whose needs or wants deserve to be satisfied? Which desires are or are not healthy? Rational? Spiritually fulfilling? How might they be altered? If we truly suffer, as writers from David Abram to Stephanie Kaza have insisted, from a great loneliness for the "more-than-human," what do we need to change to encounter its mystery once again?[74] Asking these questions goes to the core of both our broad cultural values and our hard-edged institutions. They allow us to confront inner-city toxic incinerators and wildlife preservation, the commodification of agriculture and saving the redwoods. For example, deep ecology's emphasis on the value of the nonhuman offers a measure of and a limit to what we are seeking when we pursue an improved "standard of living." The notion of a "sustainable" form of life begins to condition what we are after, becoming an essential defining element along with "justice," "freedom," and even "community."

Roger S. Gottlieb

Buttressing these challenges to our way of life with a religious vocabulary gives us a leg to stand on when so much that is familiar is being criticized. Perhaps only the divine right of God is powerful enough to challenge what many take to be the divine right of the economy! As Max Oelschlaeger suggests:

> [R]eligious discourse, expressing itself in the democratic forum, offers the possibility of overcoming special interest politics—especially those which are narrowly economic—on environmental issues . . . Biblical language has been a vital part of our nation's public debate over the structure and texture of the good society. There is no reason that it cannot play a role in determining an environmental agenda.[75]

In this line of thought, there is a clear overlap between ecological activists and the religious traditions, for many elements of both share a love of simplicity, an appreciation for life, and a long-term, nonmonetary definition of "success."[76] As world-making movements, religion and politics now converge.

Finally, as I argued at the end of Chapter 4, religious traditions can offer social activists the practical techniques of moral and emotional self-transformation found in prayer, meditation, and ritual. Such resources are particularly needed in the environmental movement. The scope of the problem, the daunting resources of the adversary, the awareness of how much has been lost already—all these make ecological activism rife with grief, anger, and despair. Yet as the Dalai Lama said, when asked why he did not hate the Chinese for what they had done to Tibet, "They have taken so much else from me, I will not give them my peace of mind."[77] In fact, a spiritual perspective on our successes and failures can help sustain us in hard times. Prayers of thanksgiving, beseeching pleas to a Great Spirit (of whatever form) to help us along the way, rituals to mourn for the dead and take joy in what remains—all these are the common stuff of religion, easily adapted to the great task of coming to a sane and sustainable relation with the rest of the planet. As necessary counterbalances to a constant focus on rising cancer rates, clear-cut ancient forests, and extinguished species, rituals of celebration and joy allow activists to feel some happiness no matter what. Such rituals, however, do not come easily to most great traditions of social struggle. The lifestyle of secular radicalism rarely has a place for moments of silence, prayers for peace, candles lit in memory of the fallen, or—as Thich Nhat Hanh puts it— moments of delight in the trees that have not yet been stricken by acid rain.

We can now return to the question of religious pluralism, of how politically oriented religious groups can function in modern society without undermining the enlightenment values of religious freedom, free speech, and a reasonable separation of church and state.

Religious participation in environmental politics, it seems to me, has solved this problem: if not by addressing it theoretically then—more important—in practice. The common bond of love of the earth and the use of the vocabulary of divinity, sacredness, and ultimate concern far outweighs the names of gods, the holidays celebrated, or the precise form of prayer. In interfaith partnerships for environmental reform and programmatic statements, religious environmentalists have realized the goal I described in Chapter 2: to hold fast to ethics while allowing for a pluralism of metaphysics.

Consider, for example, these excerpts from a remarkable statement on global warming and climate change by the North Carolina Interfaith Coalition on Climate Change:

> As witnesses of the serious climate changes the earth is now undergoing, we leaders of North Carolina's *various spiritual traditions* join together to voice our concerns about the health of the planet we share with all species. We acknowledge the need to commit ourselves to a course of action that will help us recognize our part in the devastating effects on much of our planet brought about by increasingly severe weather events. We declare the necessity for North Carolina's *spiritual communities* to be leaders in *turning human activities in a new direction* for the well-being of the planet . . .
>
> We believe that global warming is a challenge to all people but particularly to the spiritual communities that recognize the *sacredness of preserving all eco-systems* that sustain life . . .
>
> Global warming *violates that sacredness*. Already we see people dying from extreme weather conditions exacerbated by climate change, including record-breaking storms, heat waves, floods, and droughts. The burdens of a degraded environment fall disproportionately upon the most vulnerable of the planet's people: *the poor, sick, elderly*, and those who will face still greater threats in future generations . . .
>
> We pledge ourselves to . . . organize our communities to meet with local and state political leaders, and members of Congress, to encourage their participation and support.[78]

The thirty-six signers listed on the group's web site include rabbis, Buddhist priests, Roman Catholic and Episcopal bishops, and ministers from the Lutheran, Unitarian Universalist, Quaker, Baptist, Methodist, and United Church of Christ denominations. If we examine the language of the document, we see what appears to be a self-conscious attempt to put in practice a conception of religious life that prizes finding common ground on which different groups can work together. The frequent use of the term "spiritual" signals an acceptance of the variety of paths to God; the acknowledgment of the sacredness of the earth announces an end to theological anthropocentrism; naming the special vulnerability of the poor opens the way for an account of irrational and unjust social institutions and for common work with secular liberal to leftist organizations. The challenge to existing political and economic arrangements is direct and serious.

In another example, we find that in 1986, the World Wide Fund for Nature celebrated its twenty-fifth anniversary by bringing together representatives of five major world religions to focus on how their respective faiths understood and could respond to the environmental crisis. Catholic priest Lanfranco Serrini declared: "We are convinced of the inestimable value of our respective traditions and what they can offer to re-establish ecological harmony; but, at the same time, *we are humble enough to desire to learn from each other*. The very richness of our diversity lends strength to our shared concern and responsibility for our planet earth."[79]

In these two illustrative cases, the Gordian knot of pluralism—how religions can coexist despite their different beliefs—is undone. And if that is undone, then our fear that any serious religion is necessarily fanatical and undemocratic should be similarly assuaged. Facing the enormous implications of the environmental crisis, believers have shown that they are capable of actively working with people whose theologies are different from their own. But that was always the key question: Could the faithful function respectfully with people who held contradictory beliefs? Contrary to the secular left's belief that religion is inherently antidemocratic, religious environmentalists have shown both a broad spiritual openness and a deep civic concern. More than this, surely, is not necessary. Religions become—like the AFL-CIO, the World Trade Organization, General Motors, and Ralph Nader's Green Party—one more group that seeks to realize its particular vision in social life. Each vision promotes certain values and institutions rather than others—whether those are the rights of private property, higher wages, the SUV, or sustainable agriculture. The demands of religion are no more irrational, partial, or exclusive than those of any other group in our uneasy democracy. That some leaders or groups are bigoted or tyrannical may be true, but which secular movement doesn't have its share of the same? Given this similarity, the task is to oppose bigotry and tyranny, and not world-making religion or politics.

Religions now enter the modern world as legitimate and authentic partners in the political drama of making—and remaking—the world. Further, their values now color the world's most important political movement. Surprisingly, as time progresses it is getting harder and harder to tell the two of them apart.

NOTES

1. A Christian organization devoted to "love our neighbors as ourselves and to care for the earth," at www.targetearth.org.

2. Petra Kelly, *Thinking Green: Essays on Feminism, Environmentalism, and Nonviolence* (Berkeley, CA: Parallax Press, 1964), p. 37.

3. See http://www.biodev.org/index2.htm.

4. In Libby Bassett, ed., *Earth and Faith: A Book of Reflection for Action* (New York: United National Environmental Programme, 2000), p. 11.

5. Pope John Paul II. "The Ecological Crisis: A Common Responsibility," in Roger S. Gottlieb, ed., *This Sacred Earth* (New York: Routledge, 1995), p. 230. Emphasis in original.

6. Foreword to Allan Hunt Badiner, ed., *Dharma Gaia: A Harvest of Essays in Buddhism and Ecology* (Berkeley, CA: Parallax Press, 1990).

7. Bassett, *Earth and Faith*, p. 52.

8. Mark Wallace, *Fragments of the Spirit* (New York: Continuum, 1996), p. 141.

9. The antiglobalization literature is now very large. For informative recent treatments, see Jerry Mander, "Economic Globalization and the Environment," *Tikkun* (September-October 2001); Mark Weisbrot, "Tricks of Free Trade," *Sierra* (September–October 2001); the International Foundation on Globalization, www.ifg.org; and Global Exchange, www.globalexchange.org.

10. See www.wcc-coe.org.

11. *Nation*, May 7, 2001.

12. For example, *Sierra* (November–December 1998).

13. Thomas Berry, "Ecology and the Future of Catholicism," in Albert P. LaChance and John E. Carroll, eds., *Embracing Earth: Catholic Approaches to Ecology* (Maryknoll, NY: Orbis Books, 1994), p. xi.

14. See www.elca.org.

15. A range of information and sources can be found in Gottlieb, *This Sacred Earth*.

16. Lynn White, "The Historical Roots of Our Ecological Crisis," *Science* 155 (3767), March 10, 1967.

17. Wendell Berry, *The Gift of Good Land* (San Francisco: North Point Press, 1981), pp. 317–318.

18. Ellen Bernstein and Dan Fink, *Let the Earth Teach You Torah* (Philadelphia: Shomrei Adama, 1992).

19. Quoted in Gottlieb, *This Sacred Earth*, p. 449.

20. National Council of Churches web site, www.nccusa.org.

21. See www.umc.org.

22. American Baptist Churches, "Creation and the Covenant of Caring," in Gottlieb, *This Sacred Earth*, p. 239.

23. "Safety and Health in Workplace and Community," United Methodist Book of Resolutions, 1996, www.umc.org.

24. Justin Torres, "Religion and Environmentalism: Match Made in Heaven?" January 19, 2000, www.cns.com.

25. Seth Zuckerman, "Redwood Rabbis," *Sierra Magazine* (November–December 1998).

26. For a range of political activities of Buddhists see Christopher S. Queen, ed., *Engaged Buddhism in the West* (Boston: Wisdom, 2000).

27. For example, Theological Education to Meet the Environmental Challenge, www.webofcreation.org, has organized dozens of major conferences and offers resources to seminaries, divinity schools, and so on.

28. Of the now enormous literature on environmental racism and environmental justice, one might start with Robert D. Bullard, *Unequal Protection: Environmental Protection and Communities of Color* (San Francisco: Sierra Club Books, 1994); and James Lester, David Allen, and Kelly Hill, *Environmental Injustice in the United States: Myths and Realities* (Boulder: Westview Press, 2001).

29. Deeohn Ferris and David Hahn-Baker, "Environmentalists and Environmental Justice Policy," in Bunyan Bryant, ed., *Environmental Justice: Issues, Policies, and Solutions* (Washington, DC: Island Press, 1995).

30. Commission for Racial Justice, *Toxic Wastes and Race in the United States* (New York: United Church of Christ, 1987).

31. Reprinted in Gottlieb, *This Sacred Earth*, p. 634.

32. See discussion in Peter Wenz, *Environmental Ethics Today* (New York: Oxford University Press, 2001), pp. 200–208. Also, Vandana Shiva, *The Violence of the Green Revolution* (Atlantic Highlands, NJ: Zed Books, 1991). For a useful overview of the by now large ecofeminist literature, see Victoria Dayton, "Ecofeminism," in Dale Jamieson, ed., *A Companion to Environmental Philosophy* (London: Blackwell, 2001).

33. See www.eco-justice.org.

34. See www.spsmw.org/ministries/wvc_html.

35. See www.sao.clrq.org.au.

36. Daniel Faber, director of the coalition, personal communication, September 2, 2001.

37. See essays in Barbara Rose Johnston, ed., *Who Pays the Price: The Sociocultural Context of Environmental Crisis* (Washington, DC: Island Press, 1994); and Aubrey Wallace, ed., *Eco-Heroes: Twelve Tales of Environmental Victory* (San Francisco: Mercury House, 1993).

38. Paul Wapner, *Environmental Activism and World Civic Politics* (Albany: State University of New York Press, 1996), p. 41.

39. Ibid., p. 42.

40. Raymond Bonner, *At the Hand of Man: Peril and Hope for Africa's Wildlife* (New York: Knopf, 1993).

41. Macy, *World as Lover, World as Self;* Carolyn Merchant, *Earthcare: Women and the Environment* (New York: Routledge, 1999); Riane Eisler, *The Chalice and the Blade: Our History, Our Future* (San Francisco: Harper and Row, 1988).

42. Of many sources, see George Sessions, ed., *Deep Ecology for the Twenty-First Century* (Boston: Shambala, 1994). For connections with traditional religions, see David Barnhill and Roger S. Gottlieb, eds., *Deep Ecology and World Religions: New Essays on Common Ground* (Albany: State University of New York Press, 2001).

43. David Brower, *Let the Mountains Talk, Let the Rivers Run* (New York: HarperCollins, 1995), p. 176.

44. Christopher Childs, *The Spirit's Terrain: Creativity, Activism, and Transformation* (Boston: Beacon Press, 1999) p. 50.

45. Wapner, *Environmental Activism*, p. 50.

46. Sulak Sivaraksa, "The Religion of Consumerism," in Kenneth Kraft and Stephanie Kaza, eds., *Dharma Rain: Sources of Buddhist Environmentalism* (Boston: Shambhala, 2000), pp. 178–179.

47. Mary John Mananzan, "Globalization and the Perennial Question of Justice," in Mary Hembrow Snyder, ed., *Spiritual Question for the Twenty-First Century* (Maryknoll, NY: Orbis Books, 2001), p. 157.

48. David Kinsley, *Ecology and Religion: Ecological Spirituality in Cross-Cultural Perspective* (Englewood Cliffs, NJ: Prentice-Hall, 1995).

49. Charlene Spretnak, "The Spiritual Dimension of Green Politics," in Gottlieb, *This Sacred Earth*, pp. 532–535.

50. Kelly, *Thinking Green*, p. 37.

51. Bron Taylor, "Earth First! From Primal Spirituality to Ecological Resistance," in Gottlieb, *This Sacred Earth*, pp. 545–546.

52. Daniel Neal Graham, "The Theory of a Transformational Political Movement: Green Political Theory," in Stephen Wolpert, Christ Slaton, and E. W. Schwerin, eds. *Transformational Politics: Theory, Study, and Practice* (Albany: State University of New York Press, 1998), p. 75.

53. Theodore Roszak, Mary E. Gomes, and Allen D. Kanner, eds., *Ecopsychology: Restoring the Earth, Healing the Mind* (San Francisco: Sierra Club Books, 1995).

54. Manuel Castells, *The Information Age*, vol. 2, *The Power of Identity*, pp. 125–126.

55. Ibid., p. 126.

56. Aldo Leopold, *A Sand County Almanac* (New York: Oxford University Press, 1949), p. 258.

57. Mark Dowie, *Losing Ground: American Environmentalism at the Close of the Twentieth Century* (Cambridge: MIT Press, 1996), p. 226.

58. See McKibben, *Hope, Human and Wild*; Alan Wiesman, *Gaviotas: A Village to Reinvent the World* (Chelsea, VT: Chelsea Green Publishing, 1998).

59. Sue Hubbell, *Broadsides from the Other Orders: A Book of Bugs* (New York: Random House, 1993), pp. 74–89.

60. See accounts of this in Bruce Rich, *Mortgaging the Earth*, pp. 251–253; and Madhava Gadgil and Ramachandra Guha, "Ecological Conflicts and the Environmental Movement in India," in Dharam Gahi, ed., *Development and Environment: Sustaining People and Nature* (Oxford and Cambridge: Blackwell, 1994).

61. Heidi Hadsell, "Profits, Parrots, Peons: Ethical Perplexities in the Amazon," in Bron Taylor, ed., *Ecological Resistance Movements: The Global Emergence of Radical and Popular Environmentalism* (Albany: State University of New York Press, 1995), p. 77.

62. Vikram K. Akula, "Grassroots Environmental Resistance in India," in Taylor, *Ecological Resistance Movements*.

63. Bassett, *Earth and Faith*, p. 144.

64. Dorothy Soelle, *The Silent Cry: Mysticism and Resistance* (Minneapolis: Fortress Press, 2001), especially pp. 191–207.

65. For an accessible survey of nineteenth- and twentieth-century Marxism, see Gottlieb, *Marxism 1844–1990*. For some recent Marxist work on ecological issues, see the journal *Capitalism, Nature, Socialism*; James O'Connor, *Natural Causes: Essays in Ecological Marxism* (New York: Guilford Press, 1997). And, for an area study, see Daniel Faber, *Environment Under Fire: Imperialism and the Ecological Crisis in Central America* (New York: Monthly Review Press, 1993).

66. Among many treatments of this theme, see Shiva, *Violence of the Green Revolution*; Tom Athanasiou, *Divided Planet: The Ecology of Rich and Poor* (Athens: University of Georgia Press, 1998); and the journal *Ecologist*.

67. See Mike Jacobs, *The Green Economy: Environment, Sustainable Development, and the Politics of the Future* (London: Pluto Press, 1993).

68. See Andrew McLaughlin, *Regarding Nature: Industrialism and Deep Ecology* (Albany: State University of New York Press, 1993); as well as the well-known Green self-description: "We're neither left nor right, but out in front."

69. Kelly, *Thinking Green*, p. 123.

70. For an inspiring account of individual leaders, see Catherine Ingram, *In the Footsteps of Gandhi: Conversations with Spiritual Social Activists* (Berkeley, CA: Parallax Press, 1990). For responses to current events, see publications such as *Fellowship Magazine, Tikkun*, and *Reconciliation*.

71. Thich Nhat Hanh, *Being Peace*, p. 91. See a commentary on these principles applied to environmental politics: Joan Halifax and Marty Peale, "Interbeing: Precepts and Practices of an Applied Ecology," in Darrell Posey, ed., *Cultural and Spiritual Values of Biodiversity* (London: United Nations Environment Programme, 1999), pp. 475–480.

72. See accounts in John McPhee, *Encounters with the Archdruid* (New York: Farrar, Straus, and Giroux, 1971); and David Brower, *For Earth's Sake: The Life and Times of David Brower* (Salt Lake City: Peregrine Smith Books, 1990).

73. For one brief but precise statement of these issues, see George Tinker, "The Full Circle of Liberation: An American Indian Theology of Place," in David G. Hallman, ed., *Ecotheology: Voices from South and North* (Maryknoll, NY: Orbis Books, 1994).

74. David Abram, *The Spell of the Sensuous: Language and Perception in a More Than Human World* (New York: Pantheon, 1997); Stephanie Kaza, *The Attentive Heart: Conversations with Trees* (New York: Fawcett Columbine, 1993).

75. Max Oelschlaeger, *Caring for Creation: An Ecumenical Approach to the Environmental Crisis* (New Haven: Yale University Press, 1994), pp. 57, 68.

76. Robert Paehlke, *Environmentalism and the Future of Progressive Politics* (New Haven: Yale University Press, 1988), p. 3.

77. I heard him say this during an interview on television, many years ago.

78. See www.webofcreation.org. Comparable groups exist in close to twenty other states.

79. Bassett, *Earth and Faith*, p. 8. My emphasis.

"ENVIRONMENTAL JUSTICE, NEOPRESERVATIONISM, AND SUSTAINABLE SPIRITUALITY"

Mark I. Wallace

Radical Green politics in America today is divided between two camps: antitoxics groups, organized against environmental hazards in economically distressed communities, and conservation activists and scientists, who work toward the restoration of biodiversity in wilderness areas. Both camps consist of grassroots organizations that emphasize all persons collective responsibility for healthy environments. Both camps, while generally not self-consciously Marxist or even New Leftist, recognize that the consumerist logic of the market-state—"grow or die"—will continue to result in the degradation of clean water and air, animal well-being, and human flourishing. As such, both camps are frontal challenges to the American liberal ideal that the pursuit of enlightened self-interest somehow guarantees that all members of the body politic will achieve a reasonable standard of living in relatively healthy home and work environments.

But the affinities between antitoxics and biodiversity activists are initially difficult to discern in the face of the deep disagreements between the two camps. The antitoxics movement has its origins in the plight of human communities—urban, suburban, and rural—precariously situated close to health hazards such as waste dumps, polluted water supplies, contaminated soil sites, and toxic storage plants. Antitoxics argue that large industrial polluters in collusion with local public officials look for economically distressed areas in which to build hazardous facilities that promise immediate economic gains for the area's inhabitants. In urban areas, more often than not, poor people of color are most directly impacted by these new economic initiatives; in many suburban and rural areas, low-income whites are often disproportionately affected by the use and abuse of their environment and its resources. "Numerous studies have found that those who live in close proximity to noxious facilities are disproportionately people of color or of low income, and race has been found to be the stronger indicator of the two."[1] The antitoxics movement, therefore, is primarily concerned with environmental justice for *disenfranchised persons* who have suffered from historic class and racial discrimination and now have been deprived of their right to live and work in safe and healthy environments.

The new preservationist movement focuses primarily on the exigency to restore ecological richness and vitality in under- and nondeveloped areas that have not been irredeemably damaged by the influx of human populations. Here the emphasis falls on rehabilitating wildlife and wilderness areas for the sake of biodiversity rather than on the promotion of justice as such for disadvantaged human communities that have suffered environmental degradation. Otherwise disparate groups and movements such as Greenpeace, the Sea Shepherd Society, Earth First!, and Deep Ecology are united by their vigorous bioregional attempts to recover the integrity of nonhuman species by preserving their habitats. One such movement, the Wildlands Project, states that its mission is "to help protect and restore the ecological richness and native biodiversity of North America through the establishment of a connected system of reserves."[2] From this perspective, the best way to address the degraded environments of impoverished human cities and towns is to do so indirectly through the promotion of wild spaces that ensure the welfare of *all* life, not just human life.

At first glance, then, the differences between the antitoxics and the new conservationists appear stark and irreconcilable: either the focus falls on enabling disenfranchised human communities to overcome historic economic and environmental degradation, or it is on protecting the ecosystemic integrity of all beings without assigning any special concern to the needs of human beings. The understandable but unfortunate continuation of this disagreement further fragments an already divided environmental movement.

In light of this division within contemporary Green populism, what role if any can an environmentally nuanced spirituality play in healing this breach? Can champions of wilderness preservation and antitoxics activists find common ground in a "sustainable spirituality," to use Charlene's Spretnak's felicitous phrase, that both seeks to protect nature for its own sake and fight social injustice?[3] I define *sustainable spirituality* as a nonsectarian spiritual vision concerning the deep interrelationships of all life-forms on the planet and the concomitant ethical ideal of preserving the integrity of these relationships through one's social and political praxis. While different historic religious traditions have articulated this vision in their own idiom—for example, the Jewish and Christian idea of the "Spirit" as binding all things to one another; or the Buddhist notion of "dependent origination," the belief that no entity, human or otherwise, is ontologically separate from any other entity—such a vision is not the province of any one tradition. On the contrary, sustainable spirituality is a generic sensibility available to all persons interested in crafting a holistic vision of life on the planet. This mode of spiritual awareness neither entails (nor precludes) belief in God (or the gods) nor subscription to any particular creed or ritual practice. Its roots are deep in the rich soil of various earth-friendly spiritualities. Sustainable spirituality offers its practitioners a powerfully useful root metaphor—the image of all life as organically interconnected—that can enable a fresh reappraisal of the debate between biocentric conservationists and advocates for environmental justice.

This essay is divided into three parts. Parts one and two use a case-study approach to explicate the agendas of antitoxics groups and contemporary conservation coalitions, respectively. Part three considers the role of sustainable spirituality in mediating the differences that now divide the two movements. In light of this mediation, I conclude with suggestions concerning the challenge of Green populism to the market mentality of the late capitalist West.

TOXIC SACRIFICE ZONES
AND THE QUEST FOR JUSTICE

Many local economies in urban and rural America today are dependent upon the production and management of toxic wastes. In economically distressed communities, the promise of a stabilized tax base, improved infrastructure, and jobs for underemployed residents is almost impossible to resist. The waste management industry offers an immediate quick fix to chronic poverty and instability in declining cities and neighborhoods that can no longer attract government and private investment. The price for allowing the storage and treatment of biohazardous materials in one's community may be long-term environmental problems. But people in the grip of poverty and joblessness have few options when their very survival, materially speaking, is contingent upon the construction of a trash incinerator or chemical dump in their neighborhood.

Corporate investors know a good thing when they see it. Waste management facilities cannot be sited where politically empowered middle- and upper-class residents will fight the establishment of such facilities through the courts. Close proximity to hazardous industries immediately depresses property values in residential areas where virtually no one wants to risk endangering his or her physical and economic well-being by allowing such a liability to be built in their own backyard. And in those rare instances where such facilities have come on line in high-income areas, the residents have the means and mobility to "'vote with their feet' and move away from a high risk place of residence."[4]

Recent popular movements of resistance to the expansion of the toxics industry into various communities—poor and middle class alike—is surprisingly resilient. The conflict at Love Canal, New York, in the 1970s is the best known example of a successful grassroots response to callous irresponsibility in the powerful waste industry. A citizens' movement led by Love Canal homeowner-activist Lois Gibbs protested Hooker Chemical's disposal of toxic chemicals into the ground on which homes and schools were later built. The Love Canal homeowners convincingly documented the deleterious health effects that had resulted from living in the middle of a chemical dump and persuaded officials to buy out and permanently relocate town residents.[5] Other local antitoxics campaigns of the 1980s and 1990s are also notable, if not always as successful: the protest against siting a PCB landfill in Warren County, North Carolina; the movement against building a waste incinerator by the Mothers of East Los Angeles; the campaign by Native American activists against building a waste-to-fertilizer plant on native lands in Vian, Oklahoma.[6]

The problems and prospects of antitoxics campaigns in blighted urban areas is graphically evident in the resistance to a series of waste management plants in Chester, Pennsylvania, a postindustrial city just west of Philadelphia. Chester is an impoverished, predominantly African-American community in an almost all-white suburb, Delaware County. Its median family income is 45 percent lower than the rest of Delaware County; its poverty rate is 25 percent, more than three times the rate in the rest of Delaware County; and its unemployment rate is 30 percent. Chester has the highest infant mortality rate and the highest percentage of low-weight births in the state.[7] Chester would appear to be the last place to build a constellation of hazardous facilities. Nevertheless, three waste and treatment plants recently have been built on a square-mile site surrounded by homes and parks in a low-income, African-American neighborhood in Chester. The facilities include the Westinghouse trash-to-steam incinerator, the Delcora sewage-treatment plant, and the Thermal Pure Systems medical-waste autoclave. A fourth waste processing plant devoted to treating PCB-contaminated soil has recently received a construction permit. The clustering of waste industries only a few yards from a large residential area has made worse the high rate of asthma and other respiratory and health problems in Chester; it has brought into the neighborhood an infestation of rodents, the omnipresence of five hundred trucks a day at all hours, soot and dust covering even the insides of people's homes, and waves of noxious odors that have made life unbearable.[8] In a landmark health study of the environmental degradation of Chester, the EPA found that lead poisoning is a significant health problem for the majority of Chester children; that toxic air emissions have raised the specter of cancer to two-and-a-half times greater than the average risk for area residents; and the fish in Chester waters are hopelessly contaminated with PCBs from current and previous industrial abuses.[9]

The EPA study has made public what many Chester residents have long known: the unequal dumping of municipal wastes in Chester has permanently undermined the health and well-being of its population. Chester is a stunning example of environmental racism: 100 percent of all municipal solid waste in Delaware County is burned at the Westinghouse incinerator; 90 percent of all sewage is treated at the Delcora plant; and close to a hundred tons of hospital waste per day from a half-dozen nearby states is sterilized at the Thermal Pure plant.[10] As Jerome Balter, a Philadelphia environmental lawyer puts it, "When Delaware County passes an act that says all of the waste has to come to the city of Chester, that *is* environmental racism."[11] Or as Peter Kostmayer, former congressman and head of the EPA's midatlantic region says, high levels of pollution in Chester would "not have happened if this were Bryn Mawr, Haverford or Swarthmore [nearby well-to-do white suburbs]. I think we have to face the fact that the reason this happened is because this city is largely—though not all—African American, and a large number of its residents are people of low income."[12] *Chester has become a "local sacrifice zone," where the disproportionate pollution from its waste-industrial complex is tolerated because of the promise of economic revitalization.*[13] But the promise of dozens of jobs and major funds for the immediate areas around the existing toxics industries have never materialized. Indeed, of the $20 million the Westinghouse incinerator pays to local governments in taxes, only $2 million goes to Chester while $18 million goes to Delaware County.[14]

Chester is Delaware County's sacrifice zone. The surrounding middle-class, white neighborhoods would never allow the systematic overexposure of their citizens to such a toxics complex. The health and economic impact of siting even one of the facilities now housed in Chester would likely be regarded as too high of a risk. But to build a cluster of such complexes in nearby Chester is another matter. Nevertheless, many in Chester have tried to fight back against this exercise in environmental apartheid. The Chester Residents Concerned for Quality Living, led by community activist (or as she prefers, "reactivist") Zulene Mayfield, has used nonviolent resistance tactics—mass protests, monitoring of emissions levels, protracted court actions, and so forth—to block the expansion of the complex. In opposition to granting a permit for operation for the fourth waste facility to be built in the area, the soil remediation plant, former Chester democratic mayor Barbara Bohannan-Sheppard concluded her remarks at a public hearing with the following:

> Chester should not and will not serve as a dumping ground. A dumping ground for what no other borough, no other township, or no other city will accept. Yes, Chester needs the taxes, Chester needs the jobs. But, Chester also needs to improve its image and not be a killing field.[15]

Hope is not lost in Chester. There is a growing awareness of the injustice being done to low-income, often minority communities that have suffered from the unequal distribution of environmental hazards in their neighborhoods. Bill Clinton recently signed an executive order mandating all federal agencies to ensure the equitable location of polluting industries across race and economic lines.[16] But the signs are not good that the Chester Residents organization can successfully combat the expansion of the waste industry in their area. Ms. Bohannan-Sheppard recently lost her reelection bid and was replaced by a proindustry mayor and city council. No major environmental organization has taken up the Chester cry against environmental racism as its own. And time is running out as the investors in the fourth envisioned waste plant are preparing to overcome the last legal hurdles to bringing the soil remediation firm on line.

What role if any can Green spirituality play in the struggle against environmental racism in areas like Chester, Pennsylvania? In response, it should first be noted that few

Mark I. Wallace

people see it as in their interests to express solidarity with disadvantaged communities that have suffered the brunt of unequal distribution of environmental risks. Many people have become inured to the gradual environmental degradation of their home and work environments and most likely consider the development of occasional toxic "sacrifice zones" and "killing fields" to be a tragic but necessary result of modern technological life and its attendant creature comforts. If everyone has the right to pursue his or her own material self-interests, and if some persons are better able to do this on the basis of their natural advantages because of family or national origin, socioeconomic class, and so forth, then it follows that some disadvantaged groups will be marginalized in the human struggle for increased wealth, security, and power. Green spirituality challenges this liberal assumption by affirming instead that all persons are fundamentally equal and that everyone has the right to family stability and meaningful work in a healthy environment regardless of one's racial, cultural, economic, or sexual identity. *Moreover, Green spirituality affirms the common interdependence of all persons with each other—indeed, of all species with each other—as we all struggle to protect the integrity of the life-web that holds together our planet home.* In religious terms, Green religion testifies to the bond of unity that unites all God's children together on a sacred earth. As the participants of the First National People of Color Environmental Leadership Summit put it: "Environmental justice affirms the sacredness of Mother Earth, ecological unity and the interdependence of all species, and the right to be free from ecological destruction."[17] Earth-centered religion values the interconnections between all members of the biosphere in contradistinction to the liberal ideal of maximizing self-interest.

I envision Green spirituality as a distillation of the earth-centered sensibilities within different world religions. It is not a reductionist syncretism of all global spiritualities into one totalizing perspective but rather a selective and self-conscious interpretation of many different religious traditions for the sake of renewing the earth and its inhabitants. The earth-centered mythologies of different world religions make up the content of sustainable spirituality. Depending upon one's religious and cultural background and interests, possible religious ideas, among many others, that could be candidates for inclusion in such a spiritual vision are the following: the Jewish narrative of a common creation story where all species possess inherent worth as the handiwork of the Creator;[18] the Christian idea of the Holy Spirit, the animating power of life in the universe who unifies and sustains all things;[19] the Chinese doctrine of *Ch'i*—the vital force within nature that dynamically integrates all forms of life into common flow patterns;[20] and the Amerindian and neopagan imagery of the earth as our Great Mother which entails the values of care and respect for the "body" of our common parent.[21] Alternately theistic and nontheistic, scriptural and preliterate, eastern and western, these earth-friendly religious traditions offer a body of rich stories and images for enabling the quest for environmental justice.[22]

As a Green hermeneutic of these traditions (and many others could be mentioned as well), sustainable spirituality is an exercise in rhetorical reason rather than a scientific enterprise in the narrow sense of that term. Its goal is to motivate all persons to live responsibly on the earth; its aim is not to prove through observation and experimentation that the doctrines and beliefs of green religious traditions are incorrigibly certain. The point of sustainable spirituality is not to demonstrate empirically that the world really *is* just as Green spirituality figures it to be (though there is compelling evidence to support the claim that the earth is an interconnected living organism, a claim consistent with the spiritual vision adumbrated here). Rather, the point is to imagine the world as a communitarian family of beings that mutually depend upon one another in order to liberate sisterly feelings for the many life-forms that populate the earth. Neither disinterested nor value free in orientation, Green spirituality does not claim to provide scientific or metaphysical descriptions of the physical world; instead, it offers spiritually nuanced refigurations of the world that can set free a primal sense of identification with all forms of life—to set free, as Jonathan Edwards wonderfully puts it, the union of heart with Being as such.[23]

In the struggle against environmental injustice, Green spirituality can serve an important role: the inculcation of a comprehensive world view concerning the underlying unity of all things that can sustain communities of resistance over the long haul. While this model cannot directly fund the material needs of antitoxics campaigns, it can fire the imagination and empower the will as members of embattled communities seek to end the inequitable dumping of hazards and toxins in their neighborhoods. The study and use of fact sheets and health reports alone is not enough to enable the struggle over the long term and in the face of overwhelming odds. By motivating all of the participants to better understand their interdependence on one another—to envision the common bond between rich and poor, city folk and suburbanites, anglos and people of color, humankind and otherkind—Green religion provides the attitudinal resources necessary for enduring commitments to combatting environmental racism and injustice.

DEEP ECOLOGY AND WILDERNESS ACTIVISM

Radical conservationism today is a practical application of the philosophy of Deep Ecology.[24] The goal of neopreservationism is to renew and reconnect endangered bioregions in order to promote ecological richness and diversity. The core insight of Deep Ecology—namely, that all living things are equal in value and possess the inherent right to grow and flourish—provides the underlying warrant for this goal. First formulated by Arne Naess in a 1973 article by that name, Deep Ecology articulates a spiritual vision of nature as a communal exercise in biotic interdependence, where each life-form is a bearer of equal and intrinsic worth.[25] The ethical corollary to this model centers on equal regard for all species populations. Insofar as all life-forms are codependent members of the biosphere, the hierarchical distinctions that prioritize the interests of humankind over otherkind are consistently effaced.

Since Naess's landmark article, current studies in biocentric moral philosophy stress an attitude of equal regard as the *summum bonum* of environmental ethics. Since all organisms, from single-celled bacteria to highly developed mammals, are coequal centers of biological activity, the maintenance of healthy environments in which the realization of a bio-community's life cycle can be sustained is the primary concern of a nature-based ethic. The moral rule that results from this premise is variously formulated as the "duty of noninterference," the "principle of minimum impact," or the "principle of nonmeddling."[26] This rule, then, entails a hands-off, live-and-let live behavioral norm that would encourage the practice of thoughtful noninterference in various biotic populations. In conflict situations where humans and other life-forms have competing claims to resources and habitats, the ethical goal would be to develop policies that register *no or as little human impact as possible* on the natural world. Practically, this would entail that in situations where nonessential human interests are furthered by the destruction of plants and animals (for example, in the case of the bulldozing of a coastal wetland in order to make room for a housing development), the decision should be to make little or no provision for such environmental impact. On the other hand, however, in situations where the essential integrity and well-being of a species population is at stake, human or nonhuman, more latitude could be given to measures that will benefit the needy population in spite of the negative effects on the populations not benefiting from the measures in question (for example, in cases where the study and use of some organic specimens are necessary for eradicating certain human diseases). Nevertheless, the same rule applies in both situations, namely, the path of minimum impact on other species.[27]

A minimal impact orientation rooted in Deep Ecology philosophy is the mainspring of neoconservationism. The work of Dave Foreman and others with Earth First! in the 1980s and the Wildlands Project in the 1990s represents the leading edge of this movement. Earth First! emerged out of the disillusionment with the protracted environmental policy debates of the 1970s. Wilderness Society staffer Dave Foreman and some of his colleagues broke with a number of the Group of Ten major environmental organizations and founded the direct-action wilderness defense movement Earth First! in the early 1980s.[28] Foremen and other Earth First!ers became well known for highly public, colorful acts of "monkey-wrenching" or "ecotage" in their efforts to undermine the industrial exploitation and destruction of unprotected wild habitats. Foreman and associates appropriated the sometimes gnomic ruminations of Deep Ecology and turned this philosophy into an ideological foundation for controversial, often illegal forays into saving wild places. Taking their cues from the Deep Ecology activism embodied in the novel *The Monkey Wrench*

Gang by Edward Abbey, Earth First! members style themselves as the final line of defense against a rapacious industrial machine hell-bent on destroying the last undeveloped areas in North America, with special emphasis on the vast frontiers of the American West. Earth First!'s vision of restoring a Green Wild West in the aftermath of a mass ecocide of biblical proportions—a sort of cowboy apocalypticism—is given voice in the figure of George Hayduke in Abbey's novel:

> When the cities are gone, he thought, and all the ruckus has died away, when sunflowers push up through the concrete and asphalt of the forgotten interstate freeways . . . when the glass-aluminum sky-scraper tombs of Phoenix Arizona barely show above the sand dunes, why then by God maybe free men and wild women on horses . . . can roam the sagebrush canyonlands in freedom . . . and dance all night to the music of fiddles! banjos! steel guitars! by the light of a reborn moon!—by God, yes![29]

Hayduke is an antindustrial saboteur who prophesies certain eschatological doom; his end-time fantasy provides the master metaphors for Earth First!'s extremist rhetoric. Through vandalizing logging vehicles, spiking trees targeted for logging, and generally playing havoc with wilderness development operations, Earth First! has emerged as the most charismatic, if not always most successful, activist organization for wilderness preservation in the wake of the Reaganesque market-oriented model of "wise use" environmentalism.

In the early 1990s Earth First! split into two factions. Dave Foreman organized the minority faction into a splinter organization that publishes the journal *Wild Earth* and advocates for the Wilderness Project, an ambitious network of activists and scientists working to establish a connected system of wilderness parks and preserves. This rump faction represents a significant change in philosophy and tactics from the larger Earth First! movement: wilderness *recovery* is now the watchword of the minority group instead of wilderness *defense,* and the angry monkeywrenching tactics of civil disobedience have been replaced by the moderate discourse of earth science and public policy studies. Instead of Hayduke-like apocalypticism, the Wilderness Project is seeking long-term solutions to declining biodiversity in wilderness areas; instead of the countercultural youthful hostility to mainstream bureaucratic environmentalism, the Wilderness Project is eager to make common cause with any prowilderness groups, from biocentric grassroots movements to the more conservative Group of Ten environmental organizations, including entities such as the Sierra Club and the World Wildlife Fund.

The central focus of the Wildlands Project is the enactment of a system of nature preserves for the sake of furthering biological growth and diversity. This system would consist of interconnected core reserves that would allow genetically diverse populations to cross-fertilize, evolve, and flourish.

Mark I. Wallace

> The mission of The Wildlands Project is to help protect and restore the ecological richness and native biodiversity of North America through the establishment of a connected system of reserves. . . . The environment of North America is at risk and an audacious plan is needed for its survival and recovery. Healing the land means reconnecting its parts so that vital flows can be renewed. . . . Our vision is continental: from Panama and the Caribbean to Alaska and Greenland, from the high peaks to the continental shelves, we seek to . . . restore evolutionary processes and biodiversity.[30]

While this mission statement may appear to hark back to turn-of-the-century conservationism, the goals of contemporary preservationism are different from the ideals of the national parks and related movements that have sought to set aside scenic places for the sake of human recreation and edification. *Today the concern is with the preservation of whole ecosystems in order to sustain the health of the planet in general rather than with the establishment of picturesque sites and outdoor zoos, so to speak, whose purpose is to refresh and uplift the human spirit.* What distinguishes neopreservationism from its conservationist precursors is its plea for the establishment of large nature preserves as nurseries for comprehensive biodiversity without which, its proponents argue, diverse life on the planet as we know it will be seriously eroded—if not extinguished altogether.

What is the relevance of sustainable spirituality to contemporary conservation efforts? Initially it seems that religion and conservationism have little in common. Indeed, one of the sources of disagreement that led to the split among Earth First!ers in the first place was the contention by Dave Foreman and his allies that the movement had been coopted by spiritually oriented, social justice types who were blunting the hard edge of the movement's originally uncompromising anti-industrial message.[31] Foreman's protestations to the contrary notwithstanding, both militant and bureaucratic forms of neoconservationism are deeply spiritual movements at their core. Let me explain. I have argued that grassroots nature activism represents the tactical edge of Deep Ecology philosophy. As such, the expansive vision of a transcontinental wilderness recovery strategy within neopreservationism is animated by a deeply felt spiritual awareness that all life, human and nonhuman, has intrinsic value and should not be subordinated to the growth needs of late capitalist societies. I label this intuitional perspective "spiritual" in this context because its exponents are committed to preserving the integrity of life as such as an ultimate value. Whatever may or may not be said about its scientific merits, Deep Ecology is a spiritual vision of the highest order concerning the organic wholeness and biotic equality of all life-forms on the planet; and insofar as contemporary conservationism is politically applied Deep Ecology, it is a bearer of Green spirituality to a culture that hungers for authentic religion in an age of corporate televangelism and reactionary fundamentalism.

In the same way, then, that Green religion can empower long-term antitoxics commitments in the face of powerful countervailing market forces, it can also engender a comprehensive, emotionally resonant world-view concerning the sacred, inviolable character of every biotic community. Thus the reason for recovering wilderness places is not for the sake of human flourishing—though human flourishing would be a direct consequence of such recovery work—but because all members of the life-web deserve to achieve their full biological potential as much as possible. In short, green spirituality helps to answer the "Why" question for conservationism, namely, Why care about wild places in the first place? The answer is because such places make up the fragile life-support systems that render the earth a teeming biosphere of interconnected living things. Wild places are the nurseries that make biodiversity possible. This understanding of the distinctive role of wilderness in evolutionary processes is both a scientific and spiritual insight: scientific, because it recognizes that wilderness is essential to maintaining diversity at all levels, and spiritual, because this recognition accords to wilderness the supreme value of being essential to the maintenance of life itself.

MEDIATING THE DEBATE, GREEN RELIGION, AND MARKET VALUES

To this point I have considered the antitoxics movement and conservationism as often opposing factions, albeit factions that share a comprehensive spiritual vision of restored nature. Yet it is the oppositional character of each movement in relation to the perceived concerns of the other group that is so striking and, at the same time, in dire need of mediation. On the one hand, antitoxics leaders like Lois Gibbs sometimes appear to see little relationship between combatting pollutants in the home and workplace and the mainstream environmental movement's interest in protecting plant and animal habitats: "Calling our movement an environmental movement would inhibit our organizing and undercut our claim that we are about protecting people, not birds and bees."[32] On the other hand, Dave Foreman sometimes strikes a misanthropic note in order to underscore the dissimilarities between wilderness protection and fighting against the social causes that force some human communities into toxic environments: "We aren't an environmental group. Environmental groups worry about health hazards to human beings, they worry about clean air and water for the benefit of people and ask us why we're so wrapped up in something as irrelevant and tangential and elitist as wilderness. . . . [But] wilderness is the essence of everything. It's the real world."[33] To put the differences between the two movements in the most extreme terms, the antitoxics are sometimes derided as anthropocentric and not truly biocentric while the neopreservationists are criticized as antihuman and ecofascist.

Mark I. Wallace

The claim has been made that "[a] balance *can* be struck between *preserving* the wild and *reorganizing* our transactions in cities, suburbs, and countryside."[34] But how can such a mediation between antitoxics and neopreservationists be possible if the one appears to prioritize the needs and interests of discrete human populations while the other appears to prioritize the needs and interests of the organic whole? My thesis is that Green spirituality has the resources for forging rapprochement between these two movements by articulating the operative worldview that is logically entailed by both forms of environmental populism. I am not arguing that this worldview is self-consciously understood as such by adherents of both movements, but that it is the mind-set that is implied by the commitment to the integrity and sanctity of life shared by both groups. This shared worldview is holistic in its vision of the biosphere, prophetic in its despair over the earth's declining biological carrying capacity, and interventionist in its struggle against global market forces that have degraded human and nonhuman environments alike. *"Wholeness" is the epithet for a life-centered spirituality adequate to the ecocrisis of our times.* The English word "whole" is a derivative of a constellation of old Teutonic and old English terms that signified well-being, health, and healing. Etymologically, the word "whole" stems from the Germanic *Heil*, which is associated with vitality, integrity, strength, soundness, and completeness. Likewise, the English word "holy"—derived from *heilig* (a cognate of *Heil*)—historically also had the meanings of well-being and integrity in addition to its denotation as consecrated and set-apart. Wholeness, the whole, and the holy, then, are terms that have historically cross-pollinated one another. To uphold, therefore, the integrity of the *whole* is to experience the *holy* or sacred through living a life of personal and communal *healing* and *well-being*.[35]

My suggestion is that sustainable religion enables a mediation between antitoxics and conservationists by explicating the common spiritual-holistic philosophy that is implied by the beliefs and actions characteristic of both movements. It is important, however, to nuance my claim about the joint status of this implied mind-set so that adherents in both groups can recognize their own orientation in what I am labeling a common worldview. At its core this worldview stresses unity and interdependence, but it also carries different valences of meaning for each group: for antitoxics the commitment to ecological unity can still emphasize attention to human needs in systemically unjust situations; for conservationists, the inherent equality between humans and nonhumans means that the question of human welfare is generally subordinated to, or at best addressed indirectly by, the task of preserving the integrity of whole bioregions. Both groups stress biotic interdependence, but for antitoxics this stress need not include the espousal of biotic equality in the Deep Ecology sense. My point is that rapprochement between the two movements need not entail agreement on all issues, including the question of biotic equality. As long as members of both organizations can recognize their tacitly held (if not always explicitly articulated) commitment to the unity and integrity of all living things, then the ground has been laid for mediating the oppositional stances the two groups sometimes take in relation to the interests of the other group. If, therefore, this common ground can be secured—that is, a unitary vision of all organisms and entities as interdependent, if not always coequal members of an organic whole—then the response to the question whether environmental justice or wilderness recovery should be one's primary focus is a response that is tactical, strategic, and contextual—not deep-down philosophical. The problem, then, is not one of disagreement over the fundamental orientation needed to combat further ecocide but over the political focus and practical measures necessary for enacting this core vision of sustainable ecocommunities, human and nonhuman alike.

For those who suffer from the daily onslaught of toxins in the homes and places where people work and play, it is understandable why such communities seek first and foremost to liberate themselves from the killing fields of America's waste industries. To force such communities into the false choice of unsafe livelihoods or chronic unemployment is an unconscionable Catch-22 that results from aggressive industry efforts to dump toxins into neighborhoods that can least afford to house such hazards. Under these conditions it makes tactical sense for antitoxics groups first to labor against the unequal distribution of waste products in degraded human ecosystems close to home before turning to the equally important task of combatting the despoliation of wildland ecosystems in more remote locales. I am suggesting that this decision should be understood in strategic terms. It is not that antitoxics activists do not appreciate the basic connection between human health and the welfare of the biosphere—indeed, as I have argued here, the implied commitment to holism on the part of antitoxics necessitates just such an understanding, at least tacitly—but rather that the direct threat of killer toxins in their immediate neighborhoods should propel antitoxics to organize against these threats first and foremost.

By the same token, the imminent decline and eventual extinction of numerous species and habitats across North America—from large predators and shorebird populations to native forests and tallgrass prairies—understandably shoulders conservationists with a heavy burden for the long-term health and biodiversity of the continent. This burden should not and need not be regarded in opposition to the similar but distinct environmental burden of antitoxics; rather it is one among many counter-points to the expansive medley of approaches one can take to restoring the harmony among all living things. For embattled citizens of toxic neighborhoods who are fighting the daily struggle for their very survival, it makes sense for such persons to take up the antitoxics cause as their own; by the same token, for individuals and communities whose survival needs are not as immediately critical, it is equally understandable why such persons privilege the reclamation and rehabilitation of nonhuman nature and only consider the needs of human populations in relation to sustaining the health of the wider biosphere. In spite of these differences, I believe the bedrock commitment to the integrity and inviolability of life as such among antitoxic and biodiversity activists is the common spiritual vision that sustains both movements. While this common vision leads to different strategic interventions on behalf of healing the Earth, the reverence for life at the foundation of each group needs to be recalled amid the welter of the claims and counterclaims advanced by defenders and detractors of both movements.

The debate between antitoxics and conservationists may appear initially irresolvable. But when one considers the lived context of the environmental crisis as understood by the different disputants in the debate—for example, the daily stream of pollutants into minority urban neighborhoods, on the one hand, or the ongoing attenuation of biodiversity in wild habitats, on the other—then the debate becomes one over which tactics and strategies are effective in which particular circumstances and not over which moral claimant is right or wrong. *One's social location—urban/rural, rich/poor, black/white, and so forth—largely determines the appropriate response to the ecorisis.* "Nature" is not the special preserve of wilderness activists alone; nature is the lived environment common to humankind and otherkind alike wherever both kinds live and work and love and eat. Nature is the lead-filled air breathed in by schoolchildren in toxic urban killing fields; nature is the pristine landscapes and watersheds that still survive in rural parks and wildlands. Whether antitoxics or neopreservationist in orientation, how one responds to the challenges presented by nature in its myriad forms is shaped by the particular places one inhabits. Thus the environmental orientations of both groups—groups whose core philosophy is similar but whose organizational approaches are often different—are equally legitimate and equally dependent upon the social, economic, and ethnic locatedness of the different participants in the common struggle for ecological wholeness and balance.

Finally, it is important to note that sustainable spirituality is not only valuable as a means of forging a common link among radical Green activists who are alternately justice oriented and biodiversity centered, respectively. In turn, it shines a bright spotlight on the exploitative growth philosophy of market individualism that has led to the environmental squalor that characterizes our own time. Even as sustainable spirituality hopes to mediate the dispute between both forms of Green populism by specifying the animating worldview behind each movement, it also seeks to arbitrate this understandable but unnecessary dispute by identifying expansionist market forces as the real culprit in creating both human sacrifice zones and depleted wilderness areas. When everything is a potential commodity for buying and selling—including whole neighborhoods like Chester, Pennsylvania, or America's current and prospective wilderness reserves, as envisioned by the Wilderness Project—human poverty and biological poverty are the inevitable result. *When every organism or entity becomes commodified or thingified, then life and world lose their sacred character and become objects to be bought and sold.* When all life-forms, human and nonhuman, only have meaning as "products" or "resources" to enable the growth of the market state, the prospects for environmental sanity are meager indeed.

Economic competition breeds more competition, market growth breeds more growth, and the needs and values of fragile human and wilderness ecosystems have little hope for survival against these withering assaults. Growth-obsessed market liberalism driven by the "mindless 'laws' of supply and demand, grow or die, eat or be eaten" tears apart the social and ecological fabric that supports life in urban slums and rural bioregions alike.[36] Sustainable spirituality reminds both the advocates of environmental justice and wilderness protection that they share a core vision of healthy and diverse communities living together on a Green planet. This visionary role is the priestly function of sustainable spirituality: to inculcate in all who struggle for a Green future a common worldview and ethic that can sustain the combatants over the long term. But sustainable spirituality performs a prophetic role as well. It decries the rapacious power of the market to undermine our collective ability to grasp the inherent value and worth of Life itself wherever it is found in the biotic communities that make up our planet home. This unitive vision of a Green sacred Earth has the potential to renew and sustain antitoxics campaigners and neopreservationist activists alike in the long struggle against the regnancy of market liberalism—a regnancy that must be overcome if the prospects for life on the planet in the twenty-first century are to improve.

NOTES

1. Bob Edwards, "With Liberty and Environmental Justice for All: The Emergence and Challenge of Grassroots Environmentalism in the United States," in Bron Raymond Taylor, ed., *Ecological Resistance Movements: The Global Emergence of Radical and Popular Environmentalism*, ed. (Albany: SUNY Press, 1995), p. 37.

2. "The Wildlands Project Mission Statement," *Wild Earth* 5 (Winter 1995/96): inside front cover, n.a.

3. See this discussion in Charlene Spretnak, *The Spiritual Dimensions of Green Politics* (Santa Fe: Bear, 1986), pp. 25–53; cf. Catherine L. Albanese, *Nature Religion in America: From the Algonkian Indians to the New Age* (Chicago: University of Chicago Press, 1990), pp. 171–78.

4. Edwards, "With Liberty and Environmental Justice for All," p. 37.

5. See Robert Gottlieb, *Forcing the Spring: The Transformation of the American Environmental Movement* (Washington, DC: Island Press, 1993), pp. 184–91.

6. See Carolyn Merchant, *Radical Ecology: The Search for a Livable World* (New York: Routledge, 1992), pp. 162–67.

7. I have drawn this information from "Chester Decides It's Tired of Being a Wasteland," *Philadelphia Inquirer*, July 26, 1994; and Chester Residents Concerned for Quality Living, "Environmental Justice Fact Sheet" and "Pollution and Industry in Chester's 'West End,'" pamphlets. I am grateful to Swarthmore College students Laird Hedlund and Ryan Peterson for making available to me their expertise and research concerning the Chester waste facilities.

Mark I. Wallace

8. Maryanne Voller, "Everyone Has Got to Breathe," *Audubon*, March–April 1995.

9. Editorial, "Chester a Proving Ground," *Delaware County Daily Times*, December 8, 1994; and "EPA Cites Lead in City Kids, Bad Fish," *Delaware County Daily Times*, December 2, 1994.

10. Maryanne Voller, "Everyone Has Got to Breathe," *Audubon*, March–April 1995; and Chester Residents Concerned for Quality Living, "Environmental Justice Fact Sheet," pamphlet.

11. "——," *Delaware County Times*, 1 August 1995.

12. Howard Goodman, "Politically Incorrect," *Philadelphia Inquirer Magazine*, February 11, 1996.

13. The phrase belongs to Merchant, *Radical Ecology*, p. 163.

14. Chester Residents Concerned for Quality Living, "Pollution and Industry in Chester's 'West End,'" pamphlet.

15. Barbara Bohannan-Sheppard, "Remarks," Department of Environmental Resources Public Hearing, 17 February 1994, transcript.

16. Bill Clinton, Executive Order Number 12898, February 1995; cf. Gretchen Leslie and Colleen Casper, "Environmental Equity: An Issue for the 90s?" *Environmental Insight*, 1995.

17. The First National People of Color Environmental Leadership Summit, "Principles of Environmental Justice," in Roger S. Gottlieb, ed., *This Sacred Earth: Religion, Nature, Environment* (New York: Routledge, 1996), p. 634.

18. See, for example, Arthur Green, "God, World, Person: A Jewish Theology of Creation, Part I," *The Melton Journal* 24 (Spring 1991): 4–7.

19. On this point see my *Fragments of the Spirit: Nature, Violence, and the Renewal of Creation* (New York: Continuum, 1996), pp. 133–70.

20. See Tu Wei-ming, "The Continuity of Being: Chinese Visions of Nature," in *Nature in Asian Traditions of Thought: Essays in Environmental Philosophy* (Albany: SUNY Press, 1989), pp. 67–78.

21. On Native American traditions see John A. Grim, "Native North American Worldviews and Ecology," in *Worldviews and Ecology*, eds. Mary Evelyn Tucker and John Grim, pp. 41–54; on neopagan resources see Margot Adler, *Drawing Down the Moon: Witches, Druids, Goddess-Worshippers, and Other Pagans in America Today*, rev. ed. (Boston: Beacon Press, 1986), pp. 372–421.

22. For a collection of source material and analysis on Green religion, see Gottlieb, *This Sacred Earth*; for general analysis also cf. David Kinsley, *Ecology and Religion: Ecological Spirituality in Cross-Cultural Perspective* (Englewood Cliffs, NJ: Prentice Hall, 1995); and Tucker and Grim, *Worldviews and Ecology*.

23. On Edwards's spirituality see Jonathan Edwards, *The Nature of True Virtue* (Ann Arbor: University of Michigan Press, 1960), pp. 1–26; cf. William A. Clebsch, *American Religious Thought: A History* (Chicago: University of Chicago Press, 1973), pp. 11–56.

24. I say radical conservationism in order to distinguish this movement from the reformist orientation of mainstream conservationism. The radicals seek to preserve maximum biological diversity in wilderness areas as their goal, while the reformists emphasize responsible development and resource management as their goals. Groups such as Earth First!, Greenpeace, and the European Greens belong in the radical grouping, while entities within the Group of Ten environmental organizations (for example, the National Audubon Society and the National Wildlife Federation) can be grouped under the reformist label. For the differences here see Merchant, *Radical Ecology*, pp. 157–82.

25. See Arne Naess, "The Shallow and the Deep, Long-Range Ecology Movement," *Inquiry* 16 (1973): 95–100.

26. The articulation of this rule is quoted from Paul W. Taylor, *Respect for Nature: A Theory of Environmental Ethics* (Princeton: Princeton University Press, 1986), p. 174; Bill Devall and George Sessions, *Deep Ecology: Living As If Nature Matered* (Salt Lake City: Peregrine Smith Books, 1985), p. 68; and Tom Regan, "The Nature and Possibility of an Environmental Ethic," *Environmental Ethics* 3 (1981): 31–32.

27.   In the vein of the noninterference maxim, Taylor provides a helpful list of five principles—self-defense, proportionality, minimum wrong, distributive justice, and restitutive justice—for resolving conflicting "claims" between human and nonhuman populations. He also provides a number of case-studies illustrating the relevance of these principles to different hypothetical conflict scenarios. See Taylor, *Respect for Nature*, pp. 256–313.

28.   On the history of Earth First! see Dave Foreman, *Confessions of an Eco-Warrior* (New York: Harmony Books, 1990), Christopher Manes, *Green Rage: Radical Environmentalism and the Unmaking of Civilization* (Boston: Little, Brown, and Company, 1990); and Bron Raymond Taylor, "Earth First! And Global Narratives of Popular Ecological Resistance," in *Ecological Resistance Movements: The Global Emergence of Radical and Popular Environmentalism* (Albany: SUNY Press, 1995), pp. 11–34.

29.   Edward Abbey, *The Monkey Wrench Gang* (New York: Avon Books, 1975), pp. 100–101.

30.   "The Wildlands Project Mission Statement," *Wild Earth* 5 (Winter 1995/96). inside front cover, n.a.

31.   On this point see Bron Taylor, "The Religion and Politics of Earth First!" *The Ecologist* 21 (November/December 1991): 258–66.

32.   Gottlieb, *Forcing the Spring*, p. 318.

33.   Ibid., p. 197.

34.   Roger S. Gottlieb, "Spiritual Deep Ecology and the Left: An Attempt at Reconciliation," in Gottlieb, *This Sacred Earth*, 529; cf. a similar attempt to resolve the conflicts between Deep Ecology-inspired wilderness advocates and environmental justice proponents in Michael E. Zimmerman, "The Threat of Ecofascism," in this volume.

35.   Definitions and etymologies for these terms are drawn from *The Oxford English Dictionary* (New York: Oxford University Press, 1971).

36.   The quotation is from Murray Bookchin, "What is Social Ecology?" in Michael E. Zimmerman, ed., *Environmental Philosophy: From Animal Rights to Radical Ecology* (Englewood Cliffs, NJ: Prentice-Hall, 1993), p. 368. Much of my thinking about the relationship between environmental degradation and market liberalism has been inspired by the writings of social ecologists Bookchin, Janet Biehl, and John Clark. For a thoughtful counterpoint to this approach cf. the argument for a modified "social liberalism" in Avner de-Shalit, "Is Liberalism Environment-Friendly?" in this volume.

"REINHABITING RELIGION: GREEN SISTERS, ECOLOGICAL RENEWAL, AND THE BIOGEOGRAPHY OF RELIGIOUS LANDSCAPE"

Sarah McFarland Taylor

In the midst of the public turmoil generated by the widely publicized abuses of power within the Roman Catholic male hierarchy, women religious in North America are quietly, steadfastly dedicating themselves to "healing and restoring Earth's life support systems."[1] There is a growing movement on this continent (and abroad) of what are now being popularly called "green nuns," "green sisters," or even "eco-nuns."[2] Catholic religious sisters are building new "earth ministries" and are reinhabiting their traditional community lands in "greener" (that is, more ecologically conscious) ways.[3] Some sisters are sod-busting the neatly manicured lawns surrounding their motherhouses to create community-supported organic gardens where they engage in "sacred agriculture." Others are building alternative housing structures from renewable materials, using straw bale, rammed earth, and cobbing materials instead of forest products. They are building composting toilets, heating their buildings with solar panels, cooking with solar ovens, and opting for new "hybrid" vehicles when replacing older cars. They are putting their community lands into land trusts and creating wildlife sanctuaries on their properties. They are disrupting shareholder meetings of corporate polluters, contesting the construction of garbage incinerators, and combating suburban sprawl. They are developing "green" liturgies that honor the whole life community, and they are adopting environmentally sustainable lifestyles both as daily spiritual practice and as a model to others.

In 1993, Sister Mary Southard, C.S.J., and a handful of women religious concerned about ecological devastation to the planet founded a loose, decentralized network called "Sisters of Earth."[4] Sisters of Earth co-founders stress the "informal nature" of the network and their aim to provide support and informational resources for ecologically concerned sisters (and some lay women) "without becoming yet another centralized hierarchical institution."[5] There is no headquarters for Sisters of Earth, no president, and no central

Printed with permission from the author.

leader. Although there is a rotating conference planning committee, this committee issues no policy statements and does not require that members adhere to any tenets. Using an image of which philosopher Gilles Deleuze would most certainly approve, Sisters of Earth often invoke the metaphor of "rhizomes" to describe the decentralized and nonhierarchical quality of their work on behalf of the earth.[6] Their biennial conferences serve, in particular, as gathering sites for sisters involved in many different forms of earth activism—organic farming, land trusts, antitoxics work, eco-justice, farmland renewal, food safety, heritage seed conservation, earth literacy education, ecospirituality, and so forth.

It is important to note that not all "green sisters" are members of Sisters of Earth, but many of them are, and the network itself is one of the more visible manifestations of the larger movement of ecologically active religious sisters.[7] In Lora Ann Quinonez and Mary Daniel Turner's history *The Transformation of American Catholic Sisters* (1992), they point to ample survey research demonstrating that ideologically American sisters are by no means a monolithic group.[8] Likewise, green sisters are not a monolithic group—some are feminist and some are not, some are vegetarian and some are not, some are politically conservative and others are not—and that diversity is honored while still recognizing what Dominican Sister Mary Ellen Leciejewski calls "common ground."[9] In her video documentary of the same name, Leciejewski shows that, across diverse communities of women religious, there is a recognition that the earth is in trouble, and that there are ways that sisters can work together to answer this call, whether by "greening" existing institutions or by "planting" new ecological centers and organic gardens that minister to local needs.

A GREEN BLADE RISING

During my eight years researching green sisters and composing a contemporary history of this movement, I have seen emerging a radically different picture of contemporary women religious from those portrayed in other recent studies. Lucy Kaylin's *For the Love of God* (2000), for example, opens with a scene of an aging motherhouse of feeble nuns, many of whom are confined to the infirmary or who suffer from Alzheimer's disease. Kaylin depicts a very real and depressing scene of atrophy and decay, where sisters dial up Mass on their closed-circuit television sets because they are too frail to leave their rooms.[10] In remarkable contrast, I have been privy to a world of athletic, Levi-clad, sun-tanned nuns out digging vegetable beds, pruning fruit trees, building "eco-villages," launching clean-water campaigns, and celebrating planetary seasons and cycles. These are not the nuns of the "doom and gloom" reports on dying religious communities.[11] Undeniably, many communities of Catholic sisters have been devastated by a lack of new vocations in recent decades, but in the process of finding new ways to "reinhabit" their community lands, sisters are also creating more sustainable ways to "reinhabit" the spiritual landscapes of Catholic tradition and vowed religious life. For centuries, women religious have periodically created movements to reinvent and reinvigorate religious life; the culture of green sisters is arguably one of these movements.[12] Leciejewski, also the Ecology Program Coordinator for Catholic Healthcare West, observes:

> Earth ministry has changed the way I think, the way I love, the way I live. I've been blessed with a lot of energy, but this has tapped a reservoir of energy that baffles me. This call beckons me to grow, search, forgive, let go, accept, appreciate, question assumptions I grew up with regarding my place in the world and my connection to all creation. I have experienced a profound calling that I dare not ignore and for which I am grateful.[13]

Leciejewski's level of energy, like that of sisters across the spectrum of this movement, is palpable and bespeaks a strong sense of spiritual renewal and reinvigorated mission, a green blade rising amidst what other authors have characterized as the post-Vatican Council II rubble.[14] Carole Rossi, a Dominican sister and a co-founder of Crystal Spring Earth Literacy Center in Massachusetts, echoes the energizing effect this movement has had in the lives of women religious.

> I think it's amazing the way this consciousness has *bubbled* across women's religious congregations . . . I mean, I think this is at a time when it seems most of us would be sort of pulling in, you know, pulling the shades down and closing the back door and saying, "Well, it's all over." But there are people who are moving ahead and willing to say, "This is something important. This is what we've given our lives to." I think that's pretty intriguing.[15]

Not only is it intriguing; ultimately, *how* green sisters "reinhabit" both their communal lands and the spiritual landscape of religious life provides powerful insight into religion and culture themselves as organic and dynamic processes at work in the American landscape.

STAYING AT HOME AND DIGGING IN

"Reinhabiting" the land is a theme that pervades the earth ministries and community-supported farms initiated by green sisters. It is a term that is used by bioregionalist environmental philosophers to signify a process of relearning how to "live in place."[16] That is, instead of abandoning and "moving on" from a certain geographic region, no matter how damaged that place has become, one instead makes the conscious decision to *stay in place*, to repair the damage that has been caused there, and to devise ways to make that place habitable in a way that is more ecologically sustainable. "Reinhabitation" is thus about staying home and "digging in" where you are; it is the antithesis of using up local resources and then moving on to colonize anew.[17]

At Genesis Farm, an earth literacy center founded in 1980 by Dominican Sister Miriam MacGillis in western New Jersey, workshops and program curricula reflect *bioregional* themes with titles such as "To Know the Place for the First Time," "Coming Home to a New Cosmology," and "Reinhabiting Our Own Backyard."[18] MacGillis has also written about her process of "reinhabiting" the land of Genesis Farm, which is described in the farm's mission statement specifically as "a learning center for *re-inhabiting* the earth."[19] MacGillis's earth literacy students learn bioregional approaches to economics, food and agriculture, community, health, education, art, and spiritual practice—all framed within the context of a sacred pilgrimage "home," in which students work on becoming, as Wes Jackson says, "truly native to a place."[20] This language of "reinhabiting" is echoed in the variety of newsletters and programming at other earth ministries planted by green sisters in the last two decades—from Green Mountain Monastery in Vermont, to Michaela Farm in Indiana, Santuario Sisterfarm in Texas, and Eartheart in California.[21] For green sisters who have chosen to stay within their religious tradition and within a vowed religious life ("digging in" where they are), finding more life-giving or ecologically sustainable ways to "live in place" has become an especially meaningful challenge.

"Reinhabiting" has emerged (in the terms of anthropologist Clifford Geertz) as a "powerful and pervasive" embedded concept within the movement, although it is by no means the only one.[22] Healing metaphors and agricultural metaphors (planting seeds, cultivating, and harvesting) are also prevalent in the literature, narratives, and liturgies of green sisters, as are the philosophies of self-described "geologian" Thomas Berry, which I deal with elsewhere.[23] For the purposes of the present article, however, I will focus on this notion of "reinhabiting"—"staying at home" yet transforming the ways in which one lives at home.

To do this, I will explore three specific "regions of reinhabitation," looking at the ways that women religious innovate and negotiate new and "greener" ways to live "in place"—within both their religious tradition and the actual lands they inhabit. Sisters' activities and cultural productions in each of these regions provide us particularly rich insight into the workings of religion and culture. The data point to religion and culture as mutually shaping and mutually absorbing processes of exchange. As Susan Mizruchi has said, contrary to many of our inherited models of both, religion and culture are "amoebas rather than clams."[24] I further argue that, as scholars of religion increasingly begin to understand themselves as "biogeographers" of the religious landscape, this living model of religion becomes increasingly pronounced.

REGIONS OF REINHABITATION

REINHABITING COMMUNITY LANDS: CENTERS, SANCTUARIES, ORGANIC GARDENS

Historically, when orphanages were needed in North America, religious sisters' communities built orphanages. When hospitals were needed, sisters built hospitals and staffed them.

When schools were needed, sisters built schools and taught in them. When peace and social justice concerns intensified, especially in the context of the Vietnam War, the civil rights movement, the violence in Central and South America, and the widening economic disparities between wealthier countries and the world's poor, sisters formed ministries to respond, including commissions on peace and justice that took sisters' lobbying efforts to Congress and to the United Nations.[25] Today, sisters are hearing and answering a call from the earth, and it is to these needs that they are directing their efforts. Founding numerous ecological learning centers, community-supported farms, and other earth ministries on their lands has been one such response. Data from personal interviews and field research over a series of years and, more recently, from 65 electronic interviews of religious sisters conducted in the winter and spring of 2002, indicate that at least thirty of these centers and ministries are now active in North America.[26] Although Dominicans, Franciscans, Sisters of St. Joseph, and Sisters of Loretto represented the highest percentages of involvement in earth ministries, Sisters of Notre Dame, Sisters of Charity, Sisters of the Humility of Mary, Medical Mission Sisters, and a wide variety of others were also involved in ecological centers, community gardens, or other earth ministries. At a variety of locations, such as Genesis Farm in New Jersey, EarthLinks in Colorado, and Eartheart in California, founders and staff are intercongregational, combining participation and sometimes support from multiple Catholic women's religious communities. Although the bulk of these ministries are located either in the Midwest or on the East Coast, every region of the United States is represented, as are some parts of Canada.[27]

At the time of their founding, many religious community properties were of course purposefully located "away from the world," often in rural areas, in order to create barriers between sisters and secular influences.[28] Traditionally, Christian monasticism has been associated with liminality and withdrawal to "empty landscapes."[29] In the twentieth century, especially after the Second Vatican Council in the mid-1960s, much of this marginality shifted for women's religious communities, which now observe a more open form of life and model of "engagement" in the world, particularly concerning the plight of the poor. After decades of selling off rural land holdings to channel resources toward the needs of urban populations, green sisters are now working to take what is left of community lands and put them into trusts that will prevent the land from being sold for future development. Genesis Farm's Miriam MacGillis has been particularly active in counseling religious communities on ways to preserve their farmland and open space. Dominican Sister Chris Loughlin, a co-founder of Crystal Spring Earth Literacy Center in Massachusetts, also educates congregations about land trusts and serves as a steering committee member of "Who Shall Inherit the Land?," a task force Loughlin describes as "a grassroots effort of Dominicans to create a new vision for the sacred lands held in common." Of the large push to sell off community lands, Loughlin says, "Thank goodness that there were some sisters who had the vision to fight against that."[30] MacGillis, Loughlin, and other sisters are now seeking ways to conserve and sustainably *reinhabit* communal land that has been considered to be extraneous or a financial burden.

Although once located at "the margins," sisters' communities that are still surrounded by considerable undeveloped land have ironically become some of the last outposts of open space amid rapidly encroaching suburban sprawl. At Crystal Spring, the surrounding area has become increasingly suburbanized and continues in this trend. Crown Point, a 130-acre property in Ohio that the Sisters of St. Dominic converted into an ecology learning center and community-supported organic farm thirteen years ago, is faced with increasing road congestion and nearby developments. On my visit to Michaela Farm in Indiana, Franciscan Sister Claire Whalen pointed out to me the housing development occupying the slope just south of the farm. That land had once belonged to her community but was sold off to developers a few decades ago. Now new development is on its way. Michaela Farm is still in a fairly rural area, but sisters there (as in many other communities) are feeling the pressures of suburban encroachment and the loss of farmland. When I first drove out to Genesis Farm back in 1994, the area in western New Jersey surrounding the farm was unquestionably rural; locals boasted to me how, until recently, the town had more cows than people. Since then, a string of upscale "McMansions" have been constructed, devouring open space and farmland. In response to the region's continually shrinking wildlife habitat, MacGillis and staff have marked out a section of the farm to be set aside where humans are specifically asked not to go. Thus, part of the process of reinhabiting Genesis Farm has been about setting limits and boundaries on human habitat.

When Santuario Sisterfarm's co-founders Dominican Sister Carol Coston and Elise Garcia introduced me to the land they now caretake in the Texas hill country, they also made sure to point out the area of the farm that is respectfully off limits to humans. As I interviewed Coston and Garcia, they grieved over the rapid expansion of megastore malls, sprawling housing developments, and costly golf courses into this fragile hill-country habitat. For Garcia, the ultimate insult has been the bulldozing of open space to make way for long-term storage facilities. "We have so much junk," she remarks incredulously, "we can't even keep it all in our houses. We need to take up more and more land just to store our *stuff* some place."[31] Located in the "borderlands" of the U.S. and Mexico, Santuario Sisterfarm provides safe haven for the "cultivation of diversity"—both biodiversity and cultural diversity. This focus on the "cultivation of diversity" is at the heart of the three major efforts the community is currently undertaking, which include a heritage ("GMO-free") seed-saving project among collaborating communities of women religious, a women's press, and what Coston and Garcia term an "eco-ethno-spiritual journey with Latinas from the Borderlands."[32]

Once again, a common pattern across the earth ministries that sisters have planted in North America is that, for the most part, these centers and projects are rooted in the philosophies of Thomas Berry. At Santuario Sisterfarm, however, we see an interesting contrast to this more general pattern. Although co-founders Coston and Garcia have incorporated some themes and perspectives from Berry, they have drawn their inspiration for Sisterfarm primarily from women writers, philosophers, and theologians of diverse ethnic backgrounds—women such as Indian physicist Vandana Shiva and Brazilian ecofeminist theologian Ivone Gebara.[33] In discussing the motivation for creating Sisterfarm's programs in biotic, ethnic, and cultural diversity, Coston and Garcia specifically cite a passage from Shiva's work in which she writes: "An intolerance of diversity is the biggest threat to peace in our times; conversely, the cultivation of diversity is the most significant contribution to peace—peace with nature and between diverse peoples."[34] In their daily spiritual practice, in their organic garden, in their natural foods kitchen, in their partnership with local Latina women, and in their planning decisions for Sisterfarm, Coston and Garcia consciously embody this diversity.

In reinhabiting the ecological, cultural, and religious landscape on a variety of levels, the community at Sisterfarm also provides a model illustration of what the sociologist Wade Clark Roof has identified as key developments in religion and culture. In mapping the "terrain" of American religion, Roof has observed that "the images and symbols of religion have undergone a quiet transformation. Popular discourses about 'religion' and 'spirituality,' about the 'self' and 'experience,' about 'god' and 'faith' all point to subtle—but crucially important—shifts in the meaning of religious life."[35] Roof has spoken about the creation of new "religious borderlands"—the expanding areas where the edges of multiple cultures, ethnicities, religious signs and symbols all meet together and defy the rigid categorizations of the past.[36] Arguably, the "greening" of religion (that is, the integration of religion, ecological consciousness, and green culture) has become one of these borderland areas where subtle but significant symbolic shifts are taking place.

As green sisters bring concerns about ecological sustainability to the forefront of their communities, they also invoke the history of motherhouses and monasteries that were once totally self-sufficient: in some cases, growing or raising all their own food up until the 1960s. Going back to their records and studying how their own religious communities managed to live almost totally within the resources of the local bioregion, sisters now explore possible ways to restore this kind of proto-environmentally friendly lifestyle. The Franciscan sisters at Michaela Farm are engaged in reforestation and prairie restoration and are host to a community-supported organic garden (CSG) that provides local, chemical-free produce to families in their area. Genesis Farm also has a thriving CSG that is able to provide about 200 area families with organic produce 52 weeks out of the year. The Dominican Sisters of Sinsinawa, Wisconsin (the community that hosted the 1998 Sisters of Earth conference), have returned to many of the basic, sensible (pre-bovine growth hormone [BGH], pre-antibiotics) dairying methods that once sustained their community. By selling shares to area families who agree to invest in their organic dairy, the Sinsinawa sisters are able to keep their farmlands profitable while inhabiting them in a more ecologically sustainable way. Like the sisters at Michaela Farm, they are also engaged in reinhabitation through prairie restoration.

In planting their organic gardens on the landscape, and in some places tearing up thirsty and chemically dependent lawns to do so, green sisters have also reinhabited conventional approaches to agriculture, embracing instead principles of "biomimicry."[37] That is, they follow as closely as possible the way nature grows food, and then they adapt their agricultural practices to those models. Instead of planting vast fields with a single crop such as wheat or corn (an industrial agricultural technique referred to as "monoculture"), sisters intensely interplant a variety of species, combining flowers, vegetables, and fruit trees, specifically matching up species that "like" to grow together in nature (carrots and tomatoes, pumpkins and beans, etc.).[38] Sisters explain that industrial monoculture strips the land of its mineral resources by imposing one crop over a vast area.[39] *Pluraculture*, on the other hand, consciously mimics nature's own ways of keeping the soil healthy and vital by encouraging diversity.[40] Not insignificantly, sisters' "spiritual landscapes" are similarly characterized by pluraculture, as they cultivate diverse and ecumenical expressions of an earth-mindful spirituality.

REINHABITING RELIGIOUS LIFE: IT ISN'T EASY BEING GREEN

For a growing number of religious sisters, adopting more ecologically sustainable practices and lifeways (eating organically, seasonally, and from within the bioregion; using renewable energy technologies; and building and inhabiting alternative eco-design structures, such as strawbale houses) has come to constitute a new kind of spiritual discipline and daily mindful practice. Green sisters also ascribe new meaning to their vows of poverty, chastity, and obedience through the practice of a nonmaterialistic lifestyle that uses few of earth's resources, remains chaste from consumerist desires, and observes a nonprocreative lifestyle— one that helps to mitigate human population stress on ecosystems. Sisters of Earth organizer Toni Nash, C.S.J., has spoken extensively to religious communities about the broader context for the vows within the larger earth story and its implications for their renewed understanding.[41] Miriam MacGillis's audiotape program "Re-visioning the Vowed Life," which also offers creative ways to understand the vows in more ecologically meaningful contexts, has become a staple resource within the movement.

For more than a decade, Sister of Charity Maureen Wild has been putting "greener" perspectives on religious life into practice on the grassroots level. In her profession of vows in 1990, she spoke the following:

I profess a life commitment to poverty / by striving to become more and more creatively simple in my living; / learning to live appropriately within the limitations / of the earth-life process. / I profess a life commitment to chastity / acknowledging the sacredness of my own relational, sexual being / and desiring to relate to all of life as sacred. / I profess a life commitment to obedience / by listening to the needs of life within and around me / and responding with my gifts.[42]

Wild, a native of Canada and a former director of Genesis Farm, is now working to found an earth ministry in British Columbia. In the selection above, she conserves the traditional form of the profession of vows but "reinhabits" that form in innovative ways that extend her commitment to the whole earth community. As she directs her vows to the "Loving Mystery of Life . . . whose presence pervades the natural world / in the grandeur of the universe / and the splendid modes of earth's expression," Wild finds new and "sustainable" ways to live *within* the vows.

Ecologically sustainable living, from diet and dress to modes of shelter and even cleaning products and composting toilets, has also become part of a new and "greener" context for the vowed life. Sister of Loretto Elaine Prevallet makes the case that, for sisters,

practical disciplines such as recycling, being sparing in our use of water or paper or electricity, being attentive to choices we make in our buildings and our purchases (how things are packaged, whether or not they are "environmentally friendly"), eating low on the food chain—these need to be recognized as spiritual practices.[43]

Indeed, 95 percent of electronically interviewed sisters identified such things as conserving water, paper, and electricity with spiritual practice. Sisters who did not explicitly identify them as such instead spoke of them as practices in "daily mindfulness." Sister Gail Worcelo, co-founder of the Sisters of the Green Mountain Monastery in Vermont, was one of these sisters; indeed, I observed one of these mindful practices when I visited the mountain monastery.[44] Each time the sisters needed to drive somewhere unreachable on foot or by bicycle, they paused before actually starting their vehicle to ring a meditation chime on the dashboard. Then they sat quietly in meditation for a full minute as they acknowledged the earth's resources they were about to consume and the impact of burning fossil fuel on creation.

In addition to her role in the creation of "Sisters of Earth," Mary Southard has also co-founded Spiritearth, an ecospirituality center in the Hudson River Valley of New York, and has helped to initiate and form Allium, another ecospirituality center based in her congregation in La Grange, Illinois.[45] Southard identifies daily activities like starting the car, turning on the faucet, and turning on a light—or even daily practices such as yoga and other types of embodied awareness—as both spiritual practices and "bells of mindfulness" that she says help her to remember "the reality beneath the surface." Such practices, adds Southard, "can call us to 'remember' the presence of the Holy, in whom we live and move and have our being!"[46]

The foodways of green sisters who adopt organic vegetarian diets or who commit to eating "low on the food chain" also reflect a kind of reinhabiting and reinventing of pre-Vatican Council II restrictions on Friday meat consumption and, in some ways, even the convent culture of fasting and abstinence.[47] But whereas the monastic tradition of meager meals and abstinence from meat fostered, as Patricia Curran writes, "detachment from things of this world," green sisters' foodways reflect a conscious sacred engagement with the natural world.[48] Instead of being associated with penance or mortification of the flesh, vegetarian diets are connected to both ethical choice and mindful practice, inspired by a desire to live "lightly" upon creation. Sixty-four percent of the 65 sisters with whom I conducted electronic interviews responded either that they are mostly, almost always, or always vegetarian.[49] Eighty-one percent responded that they eat organic food mostly or all the time.[50] Sisters whom I interviewed also spoke of communion with the earth through the act of eating, and of how the act of eating transmits into the body the intent with which food has been grown and the spirit with which the land has been tended. Food produced in accordance with a kind of mindful cultivation that respects the earth becomes, in turn, part of a miraculous transformation of the earth's divine fruits into spiritual deed and prayer, giving a new and "greener" spin to the meanings of communion, transubstantiation, and Eucharist.[51] At Genesis Farm, Miriam MacGillis speaks of "food as sacrament," and of each meal as entering into communion with the whole of the life community.[52] Contaminating and poisoning creation with toxic chemicals and creating "frankenfoods" through biotech genetic manipulation are frequently characterized by sisters in terms of desecration. "I hope that all food might be presented to us without being genetically or chemically damaged," says Sister Marilyn Rudy of Eartheart in California. "Food is holy. Let us eat as a spiritual experience."[53] Through organic farming, land restoration projects, and mindful foodways, green sisters seek to heal what self-described "geologian" Thomas Berry has identified as the "profound earth autism" that in modernity has separated humans from the primary source of revelation: not the Bible, but the earth.[54]

Similarly, all of the green sisters I interviewed have, in some way, "reinhabited" the traditional habit or religious garment, making a commitment either to exchange or to buy used and recycled clothes or, when affordable, consciously to support sustainable agriculture by wearing organically produced clothing. Having mostly set aside traditional garments in the 1960s and 1970s to adopt the dress of the day, green sisters in their clothing choices reflect yet another area of daily earth mindfulness. Sisters have also begun to cultivate a series of "green habits," such as mixing their own nontoxic cleaning supplies and conserving energy by minimizing use of television sets and other electronics from their lives.[55] In a number of ministries, sisters have succeeded in their commitment to construct on their lands straw-bale hermitages that avoid forest-based products for construction and that can be heated and powered by solar means. In giving a tour of one of Genesis Farm's straw-bale hermitages, Miriam MacGillis advised: "We need to look to the earth to see how it shelters and provides, in order to see how humans should shelter and provide. The earth's ways are our models."[56] This kind of "eco-design" housing is yet another way to reinhabit both the physical landscape and the landscape of religious life.[57] Sister Gail Worcelo envisions the Green Mountain Monastery in Vermont eventually taking the form of an "eco-village" incorporating tree-free straw-bale construction, renewable energy sources, composting toilets, and other low-impact features geared toward "living lightly" on the earth.[58] All of this is to be combined with an earth-aware daily practice in which community members observe the monastic prayers at dawn and dusk, and participate in contemplative labor such as organic farming.[59]

In other words, *it isn't easy being green.* Indeed, in many ways, *reinhabiting* the vowed life in "green" terms generates just the kind of "costly religious investment" that Roger Finke and Rodney Stark, in their market-based model, link to statistics of higher levels of religious commitment and satisfaction. In the daily rigors of ecologically sustainable living, there is a way in which the green sisters movement ironically taps into the renewal of interest in traditional forms of religious life and worship that have fueled new conservative movements such as those featured by Mary Jo Weaver and R. Scott Appleby.[60] Statistically, we know that conservative women's congregations are currently attracting the most vocations. The author and religious sister Mary Jo Leddy responds to this trend in *Reweaving Religious Life* (1991), questioning "pluralism without purpose" and lobbying for not "throwing the baby out with the bathwater" when effecting reform in religious life. She makes the case for "loosening the bonds of liberalism" over religious life, arguing that having all community members "comfortable" with the tenets of religious life is not the same as having them challenged.[61] Leddy finds something distinctly satisfying about the difficulty of sacrificing individual commitments in the service of common commitments. Interestingly, by observing a challenging daily ecological practice in purposeful service to the whole earth community, green sisters creatively reclaim some of the traditional elements that have made conservative religious communities so attractive in recent years, yet they do so in nontraditional ways.

And yet, words like "strictness" or "costliness" are somewhat misleading when used to describe sisters' ecologically mindful living because these terms are usually associated with withdrawal from the world and a denial or rejection of its pleasures. Although such things as growing or purchasing organic vegetarian food or organically grown clothing may indeed be more "costly," and although substituting biking and walking for car trips may entail more challenge and inconvenience, the organic food may also be tastier, the clothing more comfortable, and the walks meditative and therefore more deeply enjoyable. Living "simply" (conserving electricity and natural resources, cleaning with home-mixed non-toxic products, eschewing microwaves in favor of slow-cooked meals) may be more challenging, especially in the midst of a fast-paced consumer-driven culture, but it also may be a more luxurious and sensuous pace of life that makes challenge very satisfying for reasons that have little to do with self-denial. In effect, greening the vows and the practice of every-day life cultivates challenge and strictness, but it also fuses discipline with the pleasure of enjoying the earth's fruits at a more human pace.

REINHABITING "PUBLIC AND PRIVATE PRAYER"

Bioregionalist Michael McGinnis writes that community and "a sense of place" are restored through direct human participation with nature; he points out that "this is achieved through cultural mimesis—in the form of dance, art, poetry, theater, and ritual."[62] The "Earth Meditation Trail" at Genesis Farm is an example of direct, prayerful human participation in nature. The trail takes the form of a kind of "Stations of the Earth," punctuated by a series of prayer stations in which the pilgrim contemplates her relationship to the earth. Each person who travels the trail does so holding a stone throughout the path, infusing that stone with her prayers for the earth as she journeys along what is symbolically cast as the "path of life, death, and renewal." At the end of the trail, the traveler uses pastels to transpose a symbol of her prayers or of her unique gift or commitment to the earth onto her stone. The trail culminates in the "Gift Station" or "Heart Station," an enormous collective cairn of individual devotions to creation, where each pilgrim contributes her stone. One of the most striking aspects of the Earth Meditation Trail is the way it reflects a conservation of the Christian framework of "walking the stations" or "the way," employing various representations of pilgrimage, labyrinth walking, devotional para-liturgy, and connections to a "sacramental world," and yet these forms are reinhabited and infused with content related to cultural, spiritual, and ecological renewal. The stations themselves symbolically suggest the "*earth's* passion" and renewal, providing not only space to celebrate the life community but space also for *confession, communion,* and *atonement* for sins perpetrated against the planet.

Earth Literacy students at Genesis Farm have further opportunity for meditation when they begin each morning with a body prayer to the four directions of the earth, using tai-ch'i-like movements that honor and greet the directions, embracing and releasing their energy into the day. In addition to these forms of private prayer, those participating in the farm's "Exploring the Sacred Universe" programs have an opportunity to experience collectively the "Cosmic Walk." Innovated by Miriam MacGillis, the Cosmic Walk is a ritual walk back through time to the "flaring forth of the universe." Inspired by

Thomas Berry's notion of the sacred "Universe Story," MacGillis created the walk as a way for participants to connect spiritually to "deep time," coming to know the universe's story as their own human story.[63] Sister Gail Worcelo says of her first ritual Cosmic Walk: "My experience was one of having an understanding of the Universe Story drop from my head into my body! The experience was one of knowing the Story to be in me—in my cells, bones, body—literally star stuff!"[64]

At many of the ecological centers, organic gardens, and other earth ministries, sisters now integrate "earth feast days" into their liturgical calendar. Allium Eco-Spirituality Center in Illinois, for instance, sponsors seasonal Equinox and Solstice prayers and rituals that include symbols of the four elements (earth, air, wind, and fire) as well as time for reflection, walking meditation, pilgrimage, dancing, music, and drumming. These "green" liturgies have become such an integral part of Allium co-founder Mary Southard's life that she remarks, "I can't imagine not doing it anymore. I find myself experiencing the changes and rhythms of the seasons in connection with the rest of the earth community—migrations, sounds, sights, dynamics, temperatures, stories, etc. I feel a part of all of these."[65] Once again, expressions of public and private prayer are diverse within the movement, so some sisters prefer to integrate earth liturgies into saint's days, Ash Wednesday, Christmas, or Holy Week. Still others I interviewed adopted both approaches.

With the growth and development of the green sisters movement in the past two decades has also come the creation of a variety of prayer-focusing tools such as "earth prayer beads" and "Universe Story" beads. Although not a replacement for the Rosary, the earth prayer beads co-conceived by Green Mountain Monastery sisters Gail Worcelo and Bernadette Bostwick have a devotional quality to them, are worn as bracelets around the wrist, and are used to pray for the needs of the planet. A suggested prayer included in the beads' handmade pouch invokes the elements that make up the earth as a way of addressing the Divine: "Fire of Love, purify my heart / Burning Bush, consume me / Living Waters, wash over me / Deep Well, draw me to you . . . " Universe Story beads are held in the hand and used to remember the major events in the "epic of evolution." The first bead is the "big bang" or "flaring forth," and each bead after that is decorated to symbolize a "one-time event" in the universe story, such as the spinning off of galaxies, the cooling of the earth, or the migration of life from the oceans onto the land. The beads are used as both a storytelling device and as a meditation tool to reconnect prayerfully with the sacred and revelatory dimensions of the evolutionary cosmogony.

Ultimately, in reinhabiting traditions of public and private prayer, green sisters retain mystical traditions of Christianity that are powerful and resonant for their lives. Preserving familiar forms of liturgy, prayer, and religious life, sisters renew the content of these forms in greener and (admittedly, to some) unorthodox ways. As a young nun in 1976 grappling with that period's renewal movement in religious life, Patricia Lucas wrote in her diary, "God, when Mother Loretta Theresa reads this she is going to think I flipped, but somehow I have to make her realize that we must be women of vision, not clinging to the old, beautiful ways of the past but rather seeking the precarious new and frightening path that will lead us into the 21st century."[66] Now, in the 21st century, green sisters seem to be doing both, innovating new paths while also conserving the ways of the past.

CONCLUSIONS: RELIGIONISTS AS BIOGEOGRAPHERS

Looking at the bioregionalist concept of "reinhabiting" on a multiplicity of religious, cultural, and geographical levels within the lives of green sisters not only provides valuable insight into a new religious movement; it also raises compelling questions about the various ways we think about religion. For instance, one of the qualifications ascribed to notions of bioregionalism from a geographer's viewpoint is the recognition that the entire concept of a "bioregion" per se is in part a function of culture; its borders and boundaries are mutable, permeable, and widely open to interpretation. There are no definitive, objective lines to point to and say, "That is in one bioregion" and "That is in another." Definitions that conceive of bioregions as fixed entities or static bounded areas simply do not work, and bioregionalists such as Peter Berg and Raymond Dasmann are quick to recognize that the bioregion is not an objective "natural entity" but a thoroughly human (and thus protean) construct. This process of geographic boundary negotiation parallels debates in religious studies that address the failings of static theoretical models of religion.[67] Synthesizing the work of Jonathan Z. Smith and a cadre of other scholars who have taken the "cultural turn" in the study of religion, Susan Mizruchi writes: "Religions are, by definition, 'polythetic' as opposed to 'monothetic': they are amoebas not clams, which is to say that their survival depends on their capacity for transformation and incorporation, to borrow, influence, and be influenced, to maintain coherence in the face of diversity and crisis."[68]

Yet empirically, the observer knows that forest is not marshland, and marshland is not mountains, mountains are not seashore, and seashore is not desert. Berg and Dasmann point out that "the realities of the bioregion are obvious in a gross sense. Nobody would confuse the Mojave Desert with the fertile valley of central California."[69] There are, however, as Berg and Dasmann remind us, "many *intergradations*" between regions. "The chaparral-covered foothills of southern California are not markedly distinct from those of the coastal ranges of northern California. But the attitudes of people and the centers to which they relate (e.g., San Francisco versus Los Angeles) are different, and these can lead to different approaches to living on the land."[70] Berg and Dasmann further point out that historical attitudes about place, even as flora and fauna change and shift over time, still influence how a region comes to be inhabited and reinhabited over time. Bioregions, as with "regions of religion," clearly have some distinguishing features—Buddhism is not Christianity—though the boundaries of what does or does not "belong" to a "region" shift in

Sarah McFarland Taylor

accordance with a living religious landscape and its inhabitants. That is, what biogeographers call "intergradations" from one region to the next are fundamentally fluid, complex, overlapping, and dependent on the perceptions of those who, as Berg says, live "in-place."

In the "intergradations" of Catholic vowed religious life and the culture of American environmentalism, green sisters in effect embody resistance toward and creative affirmation of both tradition and change, reconciling the inherent conflicts between institutional convention and grassroots community adaptation. Martin Heidegger speaks of *inhabitation* in terms of "*der Aufenthalt bei den Dingen*," literally "staying with things."[71] In practicing *reinhabitation*, sisters are indeed staying with things, yet dwelling quite differently, self-reflexively considering what it means truly to dwell.[72] Based upon my study of this movement, I would further suggest that by becoming *biogeographers* of the religious landscape, we as scholars begin to reinhabit the "back yard" of religious studies, retaining aspects of our theoretical and methodological legacy while innovating approaches and analytical lenses more representative of the living, changing, organic nature of our subject of inquiry.

NOTES

1. This phrase comes from the announcement for the conference theme ("Healing as a Planetary Agenda") for the Fifth International Conference of Sisters of Earth (2002), an informal network of Roman Catholic religious sisters based mostly in the United States and Canada.

2. In the course of conducting electronic interviews with 65 North American Roman Catholic sisters, I also corresponded with "green nuns" or "green sisters" in Australia, Ireland, the Philippines, the Netherlands, Peru, and Africa. The term "nun" itself is technically (and by canon law) used to refer to monastics. Most of the "nuns" featured in this article are religious sisters living in "open," not monastic, communities. However, in common parlance used by both women religious and North Americans in general, "nun" is also used more generally to mean women who are vowed members of Roman Catholic religious congregations. In this work, the terms "sisters" and "nuns" are used interchangeably and reflect their common usage.

3. It should be noted that the use of the word "green" (with lowercase "g") to identify environmentally activist nuns is not meant to connect them to the political movement in North America and abroad known as the Greens. Some "green sisters" very well may have affiliations and sympathies with the Green Party, but the term "green" is not used in this sense. It is used as shorthand, much as it is by Jhan Hochman (1998) or Laurence Coupe (2000), to indicate sensibilities or cultural productions shaped by an ecological consciousness and earth-referent perspective.

4. Interview by author with Mary Southard, La Grange, Illinois, December 13, 2001. Note that in subsequent exchanges Southard qualified my use of the word "founded" with more organic language, providing the following clarification: "It was more like noticing a seed, and planting it, and seeing it grow." (Personal communication with author, 18 July 2002.) Other "planters" of Sisters of Earth include Sister Evelyn Sommers (also a member of Southard's community), and sisters Toni Nash and Mary Lou Dolan—two sisters with whom Southard collaborated in 1993 while at Spiritearth, an ecospiritual center located along the Hudson River in New York.

5. Toni Nash, Sisters of Earth co-founder and organizer, in a phone conversation with the author, 30 November 2001.

6. In the small-group discussion portion of the 1998 Sisters of Earth conference, for instance, conference co-organizer Mary Lou Dolan offered the following question for consideration: *Is it time for rhizomes to rise?* Here,

Dolan employed the French philosopher Gilles Deleuze's image of the rhizome as a metaphor for the Sisters of Earth movement, following her reading of a discussion of Deleuze in an interview with deep ecologist Delores La Chapelle. See Deleuze and Guttari 1987, and interview with Dolores LaChapelle and Julien Puzey in Jensen 1995, pp. 244–47.

7. Manville 2000, pp. A1 and A12; Jones 1999, p. 13.

8. Quinonez and Turner 1992, p. x.

9. Evidence of this diversity was visible in the course of my field work and also reflected in the responses to the small section of standardized questions on my electronic interviews, but I am also indebted to my phone conversations with Toni Nash, in which Nash expressed concern over monolithic portrayals of the movement by some researchers. For a nuanced discussion of the "common ground" between ecologically minded sisters, see Leciejewski 1995.

10. Kaylin 2000, pp. 1–11.

11. See, for example, Wittberg 1994, Ebaugh 1993, and Nygren and Ukretis 1993. For an exception to more pessimistic analyses of the future of Roman Catholic religious orders, see Johnson 1998.

12. McNamara 1996, especially pp. 324–84, 489–525.

13. Mary Ellen Leciejewski, electronic interview, 22 March 2002.

14. Finke and Iannaccone 1993, pp. 27–39; Finke and Stark 1992; Iannaccone 1991.

15. Carole Rossi, interview with author, Plainville, Massachusetts, 29 June 1997.

16. Berg and Dasmann 1978.

17. For further discussion of this, see Andruss et al. 1990; Jackson 1994; Snyder 1995, pp. 183–192; and Tall 1993, p. 93.

18. Miriam MacGillis has written and lectured extensively on this topic. See MacGillis 1985, pp. 10–13; and MacGillis 1987, 1990, 1999.

19. Crystal Spring Earth Literacy Center in Massachusetts also specifically describes itself as a learning center for "reinhabiting the earth." For an extended description, see <http:/www.naisp.net/users/cryspr>.

20. Jackson 1993, pp. 87–103.

21. Note that these are just a few of the 30-plus earth ministries and ecological centers that have been planted by religious sisters on the North American landscape in the last two decades. This is only meant to demonstrate the geographical breadth of the movement. Additional lists can be found in the National Catholic Rural Life Conference publication *Religious Congregations on the Land: The Practical Links Between Community, Sustainable Land Use, and Spiritual Charism* (Des Moines, Iowa: National Catholic Rural Life Conference, 1996); and in my forthcoming book from Harvard University Press on "green sisters."

22. Geertz 1973, p. 90.

23. This includes a series of presentations delivered at the annual meetings of the American Academy of Religion, San Francisco, California, in 1997 ("Green Catholics and Grassroots Religion: Centers for Negotiation and Change"); Orlando, Florida, in 1998 ("Rooting Religion in the Land"); and Boston, Massachusetts, in 1999 ("Culture as Cultivation: Green Nuns, Sacred Agriculture, Seed Saving, and Spiritual Biodiversity"). There is also significant space dedicated to Berry's influence on this movement in my forthcoming book.

24. Mizruchi 2000, p. ix.

25. See Coburn and Smith 1999, especially chapters 5 and 7; and Quinonez and Turner 1992, pp. 126–130. See Leciejewski 1995 for cross-community examples of this and also the history of the founding of "Network," the National Catholic Social Justice Lobby, at <http:/www.networklobby.org>.

26. The 65 sisters were identified and interviewed because of their involvement with earth ministries in North America. These electronic interviews supplemented in-person interviews and field visits. The pool of those interviewed contains both "green sisters" who are affiliated with Sisters of Earth and those who are not, but all are actively working specifically with environmental concerns. Except for a short demographic and lifestyle section, the questions themselves were open-ended and intended to stimulate conversation and to allow room for personal expression. The intent was not to generate a strict sociological survey.

27. Four of the sisters with whom I conducted electronic interviews were Canadian citizens residing in Canada. One of the factors that has contributed to high representation of sisters' earth ministries in the Midwest region of the United States is that this region is where many religious communities still own substantial farmland.

28. Quinonez and Turner 1992, p. 66.

29. See Sheldrake 2001, especially chapter 4 on "The Practice of Place: Monasteries and Utopias," p. 91.

30. Chris Loughlin, interview with author, Plainville, Massachusetts, 29 June 1997.

31. Carol Coston and Elise Garcia, interview with author, Welfare, Texas, 4 March 2002.

32. Personal communication with author, 24 July 2002.

33. See, for example, Shiva 1997 and Gebara 1999.

34. Shiva 1997, p. 119.

35. Roof 1999, p. 4.

36. Roof 1998, pp. 1–14.

37. Benyus 1997.

38. For a classic discussion of the tensions between monoculture and pluraculture, see Shiva 1991. Riotte 1975 provides a good resource on "companion planting."

39. Genesis Farm's *Community-Supported Garden Handbook* provides particularly detailed explanations of the benefits of pluracultural approaches over monocultural approaches.

40. Bill Mollison's work on "Permaculture" has also been quite influential within the green sisters movement. Ecological learning centers such as Genesis Farm's have offered courses on Mollison's perspectives, many of which are grounded in a basic "Permaculture ethic" that champions "polyculture" over "monoculture." See, for example, Mollison 1991.

41. Nash 1998.

42. Maureen Wild, electronic interview, 10 April 2002.

43. Prevallet 1995, p. 39. The Loretto Community has been particularly active in environment issues. On 26 July 1994, the community's General Assembly adopted a statement of commitment that speaks both to the reinhabiting framework and to the influence of Thomas Berry and the story of the universe. The statement reads, in part: "Aware of the immanence of God in all creation, we, the Loretto Community, with joy commit ourselves to deepen our study of the Universe." Other women's communities either have already adopted or are in the process of adopting similar statements.

44. Gail Worcelo, electronic interview with author, 23 January 2002.

45. In 1990, Southard co-founded Spiritearth with John Surette, a Jesuit from the New England Province.

46. Mary Southard, electronic interview with author, 4 March 2002.

47. Curran 1989.

48. Ibid., pp. 52–59.

49. In July 2002, a Time/CNN poll reported that 4 percent of Americans considered themselves to be vegetarian (see Corliss 2002). Previously, a Gallup Poll in 1991 found that, although less than 1 percent of the U.S. popula-

tion were technically vegetarian (abstained from consuming meat, fish, or fowl), 20 percent were "semi-vegetarians." That is to say, these are people who primarily abstained from eating flesh but occasionally "lapsed" and consumed fish or fowl. For further statistics on vegetarian numbers, see Freeman 1997.

50. Many of these sisters who were not vegetarian or striving to be "mostly vegetarian" noted that they do make a point of consuming free-range and/or organic meat and fowl when available and affordable.

51. MacGillis 1993.

52. Ibid.

53. Marilyn Rudy, electronic interview with author, March 22 2002.

54. Berry and Clarke 1995, p. 20.

55. Once again, in the interview responses, sisters connected these "habits" to "mindful practice" or "spiritual practice."

56. Field journal, Genesis Farm, 22 August 1995.

57. Ecological designers Sim Van der Ryn and Stuart Cowan further explain that, in construction design, "a building should itself become, in Gregory Bateson's words, a 'pattern that connects' us to the change and flow of climate, season, sun, and shadow, constantly tuning our awareness of the natural cycles that support all life. A wall should be not a static, two-dimensional architectural element but a living skin that adapts to differences in temperature and light" (Van der Ryn and Cowan 1996, p. 162).

58. As of my field trip to the monastery in July 2002, the community was completely "off the grid" of electrical, water, and telephone services and planned to stay that way by installing renewable energy technologies.

59. Gail Worcelo, speech to the August 2000 Sisters of Earth Conference, Santa Barbara, California.

60. Weaver and Appleby 1995, especially William Dinges's, " 'We Are What You Were': Roman Catholic Traditionalism in America," pp. 241–269.

61. Leddy 1991, p. 147.

62. McGinnis 1999, p. 219.

63. For further description of the "Universe Story," see Swimme and Berry 1992.

64. Gail Worcelo, electronic interview with author, January 23 2002.

65. Mary Southard, electronic interview with author, 4 March 2002.

66. Patricia Lucas, "Diary of Change," in Ware 1985, p. 178.

67. See both Orsi 1997 and Hervieu-Léger 1997. Timothy Fitzgerald, as well, comments that religious studies has "institutionalized 'religion' in a way which does not reflect the actual research that many of us are doing." See Fitzgerald 1997, pp. 96–97; Roof and McFarland Taylor 1995; Smith 1998.

68. Mizruchi 2001, p. x.

69. Berg and Dasmann 1978, p. 218.

70. Ibid.

71. See Foltz 1995, p. 15. In discussing environmental ethics, Foltz cites Martin Heidegger's *Being and Time* (1966), arguing that, for Heidegger, *inhabitation* means fundamentally "being-in-the-world," not the way in which a chair is simply in a room but in the ways in which the chair is related to the room. Our inhabitation of the world, says Foltz, is constituted by our involvement with it. Foltz also says Heidegger's use of inhabitation involves the ingredient of care—that *dwelling*, in its essence, involves both relationship to place and caring. Heidegger's work, according to Foltz, communicates "the primacy of the poetic in the task of learning to inhabit the earth rightly."

72. Any conscious connection between Heidegger's term and Berg's term is likely inadvertent. Peter Berg is generally credited with having first coined this term (before Snyder 1977), and when I spoke with Berg by telephone in the spring of 1999 at the Planet Drum Foundation in San Francisco, Berg remarked that although he had read Heidegger, he was not consciously thinking about Heidegger's "inhabitation" when he first began theorizing "reinhabitation."

REFERENCES

Andruss, Van, et al., eds. 1990. *Home: A Bioregional Reader.* Philadelphia: New Society Publishers.

Benyus, Janine. 1997. *Biomimicry: Innovation Inspired by Nature.* New York: William Morrow and Company.

Berg, Peter and Raymond Dasmann. 1978. "Reinhabiting California." In Peter Berg, ed., *Reinhabiting a Separate Country: A Bioregional Anthology of Northern California.* San Francisco: Planet Drum Books, 217–220.

Berry, Thomas and Thomas Clarke. 1995. *Befriending the Earth: A Theology of Reconciliation Between Humans and the Earth.* Mystic, CT: Twenty-Third Publications.

Berry, Thomas and Brian Swimme. 1992. *The Universe Story.* San Francisco: Harper San Francisco.

Berry, Wendell. 1996. *The Unsettling of America: Culture and Agriculture.* San Francisco: Sierra Club Books, Third edition.

Coburn, Carol and Martha Smith. 1999. *Spirited Lives: How Nuns Shaped Catholic Culture and American Life, 1836–1920.* Chapel Hill: University of North Carolina Press.

Corliss, Richard. 2002. "Should We All Be Vegetarians?" *Time* 15 July 2002.

Coupe, Laurence. 2000. *The Green Studies Reader: From Romanticism to Ecocriticism.* New York: Routledge.

Curran, Patricia. 1989. *Grace Before Meals: Food Ritual and Body Discipline in Convent Culture.* Chicago: University of Illinois Press.

Deleuze, Gilles and Félix Guttari. 1987. *A Thousand Plateaus: Capitalism and Schizophrenia.* Translated by Brian Massumi, Minneapolis: University of Minnesota Press.

Ebaugh, Helen Rose Fuchs. 1993. *Women in the Vanishing Cloister.* New Brunswick, NJ: Rutgers University Press.

Finke, Roger and Laurence Iannaccone. 1993. "Supply-side Explanations for Religious Change." In Wade Clark Roof, ed., "Religion in the Nineties." *Annals of the American Academy of Political and Social Science* 527 (May):27–39.

Finke, Roger and Rodney Stark. 1992. *The Churching of America, 1776–1990.* New Brunswick, NJ: Rutgers University Press.

Fitzgerald, Timothy. 1997. "A Critique of 'Religion' as a Cross-Cultural Category." *Method and Theory in the Study of Religion* 9, 2: 96–110.

Foltz, Bruce. 1995. *Inhabiting the Earth: Heidegger, Environmental Ethics, and the Metaphysics of Nature.* Atlantic Highlands, NJ: Humanities Press.

Freeman, Jeanie. 1997. "How Many Adult Vegetarians Are There?" *Vegetarian Journal* 16, 5 (Sept/Oct): 23.

Gebara, Ivone. 1999. *Longing for Running Water: Ecofeminism and Liberation.* Minneapolis, MN: Fortress Books.

Geertz, Clifford. 1973. *The Interpretation of Cultures.* New York: Basic Books.

Heidegger, Martin. 1962. *Being and Time.* Translated by John Macquarri and Edward Robinson, New York: Harper & Row.

Hervieu-Léger, Daniele. 1997. "What Scripture Tells Me: Spontaneity and Regulation Within the Catholic Charismatic Renewal." In David Hall, ed., *Lived Religion in America.* Princeton, NJ: Princeton University Press, 22–40.

Hochman, Jhan. 1998. *Green Cultural Studies.* Moscow, ID: University of Idaho Press.

Iannaccone, Laurence. 1989. "Why Strict Churches Are Strong." Paper presented at the annual meeting of the Society for the Scientific Study of Religion, Salt Lake City, Utah.

_____. 1991. "The Consequences of Religious Market Regulation: Adam Smith and the Economics of Religion." *Rationality and Society* 3: 156–177.

Jackson, Wes. 1993. *Becoming Native to This Place.* Louisville: Western Kentucky Press.

Jensen, Derrick. 1995. *Listening to the Land: Conversations About Nature, Culture, and Eros.* San Francisco: Sierra Club Books.

Johnson, Mary. 1998. "The Reweaving of Catholic Spiritual and Institutional Life." *Annals of the American Academy* 558 (July):135–143.

Jones, Arthur. 1999. "Eco-Spirituality: Care for the Earth a Growing Mandate for Women Religious." *National Catholic Reporter* (30 July): 13.

Kaylin, Lucy. 2000. *For the Love of God: The Faith and Future of the American Nun.* New York, Harper Collins.

Leciejewski, Mary Ellen. 1995. *Common Ground: Women Religious Healing the Earth.* Master's Thesis [Video-recording]. University of Illinois, Springfield, IL.

Leddy, Mary Jo. 1991. *Reweaving Religious Life: Beyond the Liberal Model.* Mystic, CT: Twenty-Third Publications.

Lucas, Patricia. 1985. "Diary of Change." In Ann Patrick Ware, ed. *Midwives of the Future: American Sisters Tell Their Story.* Kansas City, MO: Leaven Press.

MacGillis, Miriam. 1985. "Reinhabiting Genesis Farm: A Center for Bioregional and World Order Education." *Breakthrough* (Spring/Summer): 10–13.

_____. 1987. *Re-inhabiting Our Backyard.* [Audiocassettes] Sonoma, CA: Global Perspectives.

_____. 1990. *To Know the Place For the First Time.* [Audiocassette] Sonoma, CA: Global Perspectives.

_____ . 1993. "Food as Sacrament." In Fritz Hull, ed., *Earth and Spirit: The Spiritual Dimension of the Environmental Crisis.* New York: Continuum Press, 159–164. Perspectives.

_____. 1999. *Coming Home to a New Cosmology.* [Audiocassettes] Sonoma, CA: Global Perspectives.

Manville, Rhonda Parks. 2000. "Heaven and Earth: A Growing Number of Religious Women Feel They Have Been Called On to Help Protect the Environment." *Santa Barbara News Press* (4 September): A1, A12.

McGinnis, Michael Vincent. 1999. "Re-wilding Imagination: Mimesis and Ecological Restoration." *Ecological Restoration* 17, 4 (Winter): 219–40.

McGuire, Meredith. 1997. *Religion: The Social Context.* New York: Wadsworth Publishing.

McNamara, Jo Ann Kay. 1996. *Sisters in Arms: Catholic Nuns Through Two Millennia.* Cambridge: Harvard University Press.

Mizruchi, Susan. 2001. *Religion and Cultural Studies.* Princeton, NJ: Princeton University Press.

Mollison, William. 1991. *Introduction to Permaculture.* Tyalgum, Australia: Tagari Publications.

Mumford, Lewis. 1961. *The City in History: Its Origins, Its Transformations, and Its Purpose.* New York: Harcourt, Brace, and World.

Nash, Toni. 1998. "What Are the Implications of Our Commitment for the People of God?: Notes For a Talk on the New Cosmology and Religious Vows." [Lecture Transcript] Los Angeles, California, 11 October.

National Catholic Rural Life Conference. 1996. *Religious Congregations on the Land: The Practical Links Between Community, Sustainable Land Use, and Spiritual Charism.* Des Moines, IA: National Catholic Rural Life Conference.

Nygren, David and Miriam Ukretis. 1993. *The Future of Religious Orders in the United States.* Westport, CT: Praeger Press.

Orsi, Robert. 1996. *Thank You, St. Jude.* New Haven: Yale University Press.

_____. 1997. "Everyday Miracles: The Study of Lived Religion." In David Hall, ed., *Lived Religion in America.* Princeton, NJ: Princeton University Press, 3–21.

Prevallet, Elaine. 1995. *A Wisdom for Life: A Series of Presentations on Earth Spirituality Presented at a Conference Sponsored by the Loretto Earth Network.* Nerinx, KY: Loretto Earth Network.

Quinonez, Lora Ann and Mary Daniel Turner. 1992. *The Transformation of American Catholic Sisters.* Philadelphia, PA: Temple University Press, p. x.

Riotte, Louise. 1975. *Carrots Love Tomatoes.* Pownal, VT: Storey Books.

Roof, Wade Clark and Sarah McFarland Taylor. 1995. "The Force of Emotion: James's Reorientation of Religion and the Contemporary Rediscovery of the Body, Spirituality, and the 'Feeling Self.'" In Donald Capps and Janet Jacobs, eds., *The Struggle for Life: A Companion Volume to William James's 'The Varieties of Religious Experience.'* West Lafayette, IN: Society for the Scientific Study of Religion Monograph Series, no. 7: 197–208.

Roof, Wade Clark. 1999. *The Spiritual Marketplace.* Princeton, NJ: Princeton University Press.

_____. 1998. "Religious Borderlands: Challenge for Future Study." *Journal for the Scientific Study of Religion* 37, 1 (March): 1–14.

Sasillo, Robert. 1992. "Lewis Mumford and the Organicist Concept in Social Thought." *Journal of the History of Ideas* 53, 1 (January/March): 91–116.

Sheldrake, Philip. 2001. *Spaces of the Sacred.* Baltimore: Johns Hopkins University Press.

Shiva, Vandana. 1997. *Biopiracy.* Boston: South End Press.

_____. 1991. *The Violence of the Green Revolution.* London: Zed Books.

Smith, Jonathan Z. 1998. "Religion, Religions, Religious." In Mark Taylor, ed., *Critical Terms for Religious Studies.* Chicago: University of Chicago Press, 269–284.

Snyder, Gary. 1977. "Re-Inhabitation." In *The Old Ways.* San Francisco: City Lights Books.

Tall, Deborah. 1993. *From Where We Stand: Recovering a Sense of Place.* Baltimore: Johns Hopkins University Press.

Van der Ryn, Sim and Stuart Cowan. 1996. *Ecological Design.* Washington, D.C.: Island Press.

Ware, Ann Patrick. 1985. *Midwives of the Future: American Sisters Tell Their Story.* Kansas City, MO: Leaven Press.

Weaver, Mary Jo and R. Scott Appleby. 1995. *Being Right: Conservative Catholics in America.* Bloomington, IN: Indiana University Press.

Wittberg, Patricia. 1994. *The Rise and Fall of Catholic Religious Orders.* Albany: State of New York University Press.

"INTERVIEW WITH CESAR CHAVEZ"

Catherine Ingram

When Cesar Chavez was thirteen years old, he participated in his first field strike near El Centro, California. His father, Librado, had organized the hundred men who would also participate. They had made their demands to the farm manager clear: they wanted a minimum wage of fifty cents per hour, overtime pay after eight hours of work, no child labor, and separate toilets for men and women. They also wanted free drinking water while picking in the fields, instead of being charged a nickel per ladle. It was dangerous to even approach the farm manager with such demands, and when they did, the manager accused Librado Chavez of being a communist. He also warned the men that the company had ways of dealing with troublemakers.

The grapes hung full on the vines, beckoning to be picked immediately or they would rot. The strikers formed a picket line in front of the vineyard's main gate. On the other side of the entry way, state troopers, labor contractors, and farm supervisors waited forebodingly, periodically glancing down the road.

Suddenly roaring trucks descended on the vineyard amidst clouds of dust. More than a hundred braceros, Mexican peasants, arrived to work the fields. They and the families they had left behind in Mexico were desperately poor and hungry. The braceros were willing to do the lowliest jobs for long hours with little pay. Librado Chavez pleaded with them in Spanish not to cross the picket lines, but although the braceros understood the plight of the grape-pickers, their own needs came first and they sadly crossed the lines.

The following day, it was the striker families' turn to face hunger. Labor contractors refused to hire anyone who had participated in the strike, and the Chavez family was forced to move on—to another field in another town, to another shack that would become home for a picking season.

In that time, there were few precedents for a successful strike by farmworkers. The National Labor Relations Act which Congress had passed in 1935 insured the right to organize of almost every labor group in the country, and it required that industry bargain with organized labor "in good faith." Agriculture was an exception. No protection under the law existed at that time for farm workers; a union was unthinkable. Many years and a "mighty hard road"

Reprinted from *In the Footsteps of Gandhi: Conversations with Spiritual Social Activists*, by Catherine Ingram (1990), Parallax Press, Berkeley, CA.

later, Cesar Chavez would become the first man in the history of the United States to organize a successful union for farmworkers.

INTERVIEW WITH CESAR CHAVEZ
APRIL 22, 1989 KEENE, CALIFORNIA

Catherine Ingram: Do you see any similarities between the civil rights struggle in India and the struggle of the farmworkers? For instance, Gandhi struggled to eliminate the caste system, and, in a way, we experience a modern caste system here with the poor minorities of color.

Cesar Chavez: Oh, there are a lot of similarities. Gandhi was dealing with the powerless and the poor and the ones who were discriminated against, and we have that now—the poor, and the people who are discriminated against. We have classism, racism. Gandhi was also working against a foreign domination, and this is similar to our situation in that agribusiness is really like a foreign domination. They don't live here.

CI: They don't?

CC: The multi-nationals, more and more, are being controlled by foreigners—Japanese, Germans. People don't realize what Japan owns here—they own subsidiaries of subsidiaries, a lot of California. They own a great deal of the wine country.

The other similarity is that people Gandhi dealt with tended to be religious, and the people we deal with tend to be religious as well.

CI: What aspects of Catholicism inspire you in your work, and what aspects have inspired the people you work with? Are there particular teachings that you focus on?

CC: Well, Christ's teachings. The Sermon on the Mount is the most inspiring, and that was one of Gandhi's inspirations also. The message of Christ is all about love, all about loving—not only God, but also one another. I think that's the point.

CI: The teachings of love.

CC: Yes, but what love is, that is to be interpreted. In our work, you know, love is really sacrifice. It's actually not vocal. Although it can be enunciated, it has to be practiced. You need both.

I think part of Gandhi's greatness was that he didn't want to be a servant, he wanted to be of service. It's very easy to be a servant, but very difficult to be of service. When you are of service, you're there whether you like it or not, whether it's Sunday, Monday, or a holiday. You're there whenever you are needed.

CI: I know that a lot of your current work has to do with raising people's awareness about the use of chemicals and pesticides on our food. What is happening to the farm workers who are exposed to these chemicals, and what is happening to the people who are eating the food on which they are sprayed?

CC: Our struggle with pesticides goes back more than thirty years. We raised this issue a long time ago, because we were the victims. In fact, right after the Second World War, I was a victim of pesticide poisoning. I knew very little about it at the time and it took me a few years to learn more. But when most of the people were worried about how thick the eggshells were on the birds, we were talking about human beings—about workers and then about consumers. For many years people would laugh at us, or they would ignore us, or they would just stare at us as if we were crazy. But today, everybody knows about pesticides.

We've been raising this issue a long time. In fact, we were successful in banning the use of DDT about nineteen years ago. We got it banned on grapes, but they came back with other poisons. Those were the ones that Rachel Carson wrote about in *Silent Spring*.

You know, either we ban these poisons and get rid of them, or they will get rid of us. These are deadly, deadly agents. They are organophosphates, nerve gas poisons. That's how they kill the insects; they affect their nervous systems. And so, too, they affect our nervous systems. Pesticides have killed a great number of workers and incapacitated many others; they have wrecked the health of the workers, their families, their children. See, now these pesticides are everywhere—in the water, in the soil, in the atmosphere, every place. And what we've learned is that body weight is a kind of buffer, and the more weight you have the more you can buffer; the less you weigh, the more you are at risk. So it is children who are suffering the cancers and the birth defects. The number of miscarriages of women working with grapes is very high. We now see lots of cancer and lots of birth defects—terrible, terrible examples of birth defects—children born without arms or legs.[1] Oh, it's just horrible. We did a video about this, "The Wrath of Grapes."[2] It is just incredible what is happening. We've been campaigning to the point where we now have our workers pretty aware of it, and I think we've played a major role in the awareness of the issue all over the country, all over the world.

CI: I think your fast of last year raised awareness on this issue.[3]

CC: It did a lot. The fast is a great communicator. Like Gandhi, because we don't have the economic or political force, we have to appeal to the moral force, and the boycott is the best instrument. Gandhi said that boycotts were the most near-perfect instrument for social change.

CI: People's pocketbooks often awaken their conscience.

CC: And beyond that, it really is a moral force. Gandhi worked this out for all of us, because it's the moral force that compels, and then it translates into economic pressure. It starts from a moral stance, but it takes time.

CI: When you do these fasts, what gives you inner strength?

CC: That's a good question. I really don't know. Sometimes I fast for only one or two or three days and have a difficult time. In fact, I tried to fast two days ago and I couldn't do it. I'm trying again today, and it's very difficult. Then at other times, it just happens.

Catherine Ingram

CI: Do you think it has to do with the issue you're fasting for or the amount of support you have around you?

CC: I don't know. I've never been able to tell except that, well, Gandhi spoke about the door, or the window, the light. I can't really talk about those things, but sometimes it is *comparatively* easier than at other times. There is . . . there is a force there. I don't quite know what it is.

CI: For a long time your family has had to sacrifice with you for the cause. They've had to watch you go without food, they've seen you be put in prison. There were times when you were so poor you couldn't buy food for them. And when your children were growing up there were many times when you had to leave at crucial moments. I read in your book *La Causa* that even on the day of your daughter's wedding, you had to leave after just one dance with the bride in order to negotiate a contract. This is similar to Gandhi's situation as well. A lot of times his own family had to be relegated to a lesser priority.

CC: Oh, with him it was pretty bad. But I've been very lucky in that I've been able to keep the support of my family. You don't have to be present to spend time with them when you engage in the same struggle, because you are together when you engage in the same project. I think the strength in our family comes because it's always been directed away from ourselves.

When I was growing up, my dad and my mother instilled in us a really strong awareness of doing something for other people. It was preached, and it was practiced by them. We grew up in that way. We thought nothing of doing for other people, and we also saw the great advantages of doing things for others. The great payback comes in feeling good about helping people, and we understood that from the time we were very small. I don't think I have done this as much as my mother did, and I don't think I preached it as much. I think I acted on it quite a bit though, and so my kids—most of them—picked it up, the idea of helping, putting others first. If you do for somebody else, it's really doing for yourself. You can't explain it, but you understand it through doing it and once we experience it, it becomes a lot easier. I think this is what has happened in my home.

Now, with my mother it was planned. For instance, when we were growing up we were very poor, and yet my mother would send my brother and me—we were just small boys—to look for hobos or for people who were hungry and bring them home to eat with us, even though we had barely enough food for our own family. Those are very strong impressions, lasting impressions, to see people willing to do that. I often think that the reason that I discovered and became interested in Gandhi was because of my mother. I was predisposed because of the training at home. Anyway, my kids, most of them, have picked up some of this. Some of them are working with us here, but even those who are not working with us are committed to the ideals of being of service and helping people.

CI: It's been passed down in your family.

CC: Yes, even to the grandchildren. What happens is that they see it in the home. It's like anything else; if they see dope or drink at home, they do that. If they see making money, they do that.

CI: What changes have you seen for the farm workers in all these years?

CC: [Laughing] Our work is like two steps forward, and one and nine-tenths back. We've been able to accomplish quite a bit in terms of increasing society's awareness. We made the plight of the farmworkers a household word throughout North America. We have developed a broad understanding of the problem and a network of support. Some polls show that as much as eighty percent of the public know about the work we do. That's the biggest thing we have accomplished. And as a result of that, a limited number of workers now have traditional union benefits—better wages and so forth—but not a lot of the workers. We still face a day to day battle.

It has taken most unions between thirty and fifty years to get established. We're pioneers in this field, so it's going to be awhile before we really get established. Once we break that barrier, I think it will go very fast. But it's been back and forth and up and down—a long, long struggle.

We've been subjected to so much hardship, legal maneuvering, you name it.

CI: Yes, there's that 1987 lawsuit of $1.7 million, in which a vegetable grower claims that a farmworker strike cost him the loss of a harvest. I don't understand how you can be sued for that. Isn't potential loss the leverage for any strike?

CC: Yes. The claim against us is illegal. That law is unconstitutional. We continually have to challenge the unconstitutionality of such claims. That was the reason for my second major fast back in 1972, a twenty-five day fast, and that was a hard one. I ended it and they took me to the hospital; my vital signs were down. I was in bad shape. Only twenty-five days, but it was hard. We saw even back then that we couldn't get the legislation we needed on this.

Now with the most recent case, it has gone back to the state courts from the Supreme Court to see how they would interpret it. Unlucky for us, it was interpreted with a $5.6 million judgment against us.

Well, the bond itself is $5.6 million to appeal. We don't have $5.6 million. You've got to put up at least the exact amount of money that the judgment is for. So we recently went to court and got a judge in Yuma, Arizona, to set the bond at $250,000, and then the growers appealed too. Oh they drain you. They use the courts.

CI: In other words, even though the growers know that eventually they may lose the case, they can just wipe you out in the meantime with expensive legal tactics.

CC: Yes. Our system is not as democratic as people think. It's not as free as people think. We're quick to make judgments about other countries, but we're pretty bad ourselves. For eight years under Reagan, we were harassed with federal investigations here. It was so bad that we even assigned a room for the investigators. In fact, the last group that was here said, "We've looked at these books three times!" And they left.

See, if they find that I've taken one penny, I can be thrown out of the union. And they've done that to a lot of union leaders. They can't believe that I don't take pay, or that I don't have an expense account. I have to sit here and tell them how I live. If I go somewhere, I don't stay in hotels, I don't buy my food. People give it to me. That's how I do it, so what do I need money for? The investigators at first didn't want to believe that, but finally we convinced them. Well, they laid off of that, but it's always something else. We've been harassed up and down by the authorities.

Our power is with the people. That's where our power is. People—all shapes, all colors, all sizes, all religions. We have people who are very conservative who support what we do, people who are even anti-union. See, everybody interprets our work in a different way. Some people interpret us as a union, some people interpret our work as an ethnic issue, some people interpret our work as peace, some people see it as a religious movement. So we can appeal to broad sectors because of these different interpretations.

CI: How do you organize nonviolently around the issue of pesticides? It's an unseen enemy. I suppose you can say that the effects are seen, but the actual substance is unseen.

CC: It is immediately unseen, though in the long term, it is seen. But it's a lot harder to make people aware, because for the consumer, if you eat this grape, it won't harm you now, but it may harm you ten, fifteen years down the line. But you take the same grapes that may harm you in five, ten, or fifteen years, and you see that they are harming people instantly—you see what the pesticides are doing to the workforce and their children. You carry the message by showing the impact on the people in the front lines.

CI: So the workers are the front lines, and in their exposure and subsequent harm from the pesticides, they represent what is to come for the consumers down the line.

CC: Right, the workers get it instantly, but the consumer is going to be affected later on, because it's cumulative. Now people know this, but for years and years we were just the laughingstock when we spoke of this. Or we would hear things like, "Without pesticides, we'd starve." Well, they didn't have pesticides many years ago, and if people starved, they starved for other reasons. The thing is that about twenty years ago, about twenty percent of the crops of the world were lost to pests and today it's twenty-seven percent with jillions of more pesticides.

CI: The pests get more immune.[4]

CC: Yes. And then they need to use much more poison to kill them. Take, for example, the deadly nerve gas, parathion. Twenty years ago they were using about two pounds per acre. Today they are using up to six pounds per acre.

CI: I have a feeling that we are going to see a lot more immune-deficiency problems in our lives because we're being saturated with these poisons. What must the soil be like after all this spraying?

CC: The soil is becoming like a piece of plastic; you just stick plants there and you grow them artificially.

CI: Who or what would you say is the biggest enemy of the farmworkers?

CC: The biggest enemy is the system. Agriculture has changed from the time that our founding fathers laid out the foundation for our country. But the perception about ownership of land hasn't changed. There is something peculiar the world over about owning land. Land gives you power beyond its wealth, beyond liquid cash. Land has a powerful, powerful influence on people. You're dealing with landowners who literally own where you live, where you walk, and where you breathe. That power is awesome. And power tends to corrupt, and the system gets corrupted.

Agribusiness in California has developed on cheap labor—and not by accident; it's been planned. To maintain cheap labor the growers have worked out a horrible system of surplus labor—a surplus labor pool that they are experts at maintaining. Experts! See, agribusiness controls immigration policy, and it has for years. So much so that not long ago the Immigration and Naturalization Service was part of the Department of Agriculture. They control it.

CI: Do they turn a blind eye and let people get in illegally?

CC: That too. But they also set the immigration policy and control how it will be carried out and how it will be interpreted. They have tremendous influence.

CI: How does that work to benefit the growers?

CC: Let me give you an example. The beginning of agribusiness, the way we know it now, started back in the late 1800s. Curiously enough, unlike most systems, the workers were here before the jobs were. See, all the railroads, like the one running right by here, were built by the Chinese. And after the railroads were built, there were thousands of Chinese without work. So the early entrepreneurs, that's what they were in agriculture, came and saw this tremendous amount of labor, and that's why they developed labor-intensive crops in California, unlike in the Midwest and other places. It was because the labor was here. Other places had the climate and the water, but here they had a tremendous surplus of labor. So that was the beginning. It was in that system the labor contractor system started. And as in all systems, they polished it, they honed it, and now it's . . .

CI: . . . big business. I never realized that California produced so much of our food because of the surplus labor rather than the actual soil, climate, and water.

CC: Oh yes. There are other parts of the world that have the same or an even better climate than we have, although California has about fourteen climatic regions.

Then, too, everything is interwoven with agribusiness, so when you take on the growers you're also taking on the large insurance companies who also happen to be owners of land, and you're taking on the large banks, and the railroads, and the pesticide and fertilizer companies. Talk about a power base against you. That's why legislatively and politically there's no way we can do anything. They've got it clamped.

That's what Gandhi realized and why he went over to the boycott.

CI: I still don't understand exactly what agribusiness does in manipulating immigration policy to create a surplus labor pool.

CC: Well, what agribusiness does is often outside the law. They would recruit in, say China, and then they'd send recruitment teams into Japan (the Japanese didn't last too long, they had different ideas and they came with their families—the only other immigrants who came with families were the Mexicans). Then after that they sent recruits to India, and then they tried the Philippines. After the revolution in Mexico, people came. And then during the Dust Bowl, they went to Mexico and recruited for the Dust Bowl and then there was the Brassario program during World War II.[5] Now they're recruiting in Mexico, Asia, Africa, Honduras, Nicaragua, El Salvador, Guatemala. This is all recruitment for agribusiness, and that's how they do it.

CI: So they bring in all of these foreigners and it's to their advantage that the people remain illegal.

CC: Oh yes, because they exploit them and the illegals can do nothing about it. They cannot make a move. They have to accept whatever they are given. It's terrible.

CI: In your life, in your work, and in all that you have struggled for, is there something you could say about how life is?

CC: Well, not really. Life is so many things. But we're here playing the record every night and finding out every day whether we did what we're supposed to do. The message was clear from Christ, Gandhi, all the good people who said exactly what has to be done. So every night you've got to think, "What did I do today?"

Life is very complicated. But we try to keep it simple. Get the work done. We're essentially activists. We have our precepts and our principles, and then we act.

I was never for writing on nonviolence. What can you add? It's all been written. In the very early days, we gave the impression that nonviolence was sort of saintly, like saints who go around lightly stepping on eggshells. But now over the years we see nonviolence is not that. It is not that.

So we don't write about nonviolence, we don't preach it. We never talk about nonviolence to the workers unless there's a need to talk about nonviolence. In other words, if we're negotiating a contract, I'm not going to talk about nonviolence, but if we're in a picket line I'm going to talk about nonviolence. Because if you talk too much about it, it becomes . . .

CI: . . . less authentic.

CC: Yes, exactly. And we were very worried about that. Now we have legions of people who are nonviolent out there, the workers. But in the early days it was very hard. Now people know how to act, what to do. And not because we have said to do this. We haven't had one hour of teaching; it's all been by example.

We want to be men and women of the world. We want to work. We just want to do things nonviolently.

CI: How did you first come into contact with Gandhi's ideas?

CC: Oh, it was very interesting. As I recall, I was eleven or twelve years old, and I went to a movie. In those days, in between movies they had newsreels, and in one of the newsreels there was a report on Gandhi. It said that this half-naked man without a gun had conquered the might of the British empire, or something to that effect. It really impressed me because I couldn't conceive of how that had happened without guns. Even though I had never heard the name of Gandhi before, the next day I went to my teacher and asked her if she knew anything about him. She said, "No, but I have a friend who knows quite a bit about him." Then she gave me the name of her friend, a construction worker who was studying Gandhi. He gave me a little book on Gandhi. As I grew up, I started learning more, and ever since then, I have made a life project of reading about Gandhi and his message.

CI: What about Gandhi's life and message has most influenced you?

CC: His activism. He was a saint *of the world*. He did things, he accomplished things. Many of us can be so holy, you know, but we don't get very much done except satisfying our own personal needs. But Gandhi did what he did for the whole world. Not only did he talk about nonviolence, he showed how nonviolence works for justice and liberation.

CI: In your own life and work, have you experienced any new thoughts or new ways of seeing how nonviolent strategy works?

CC: No. It was all done by Christ and Gandhi and St. Francis of Assisi and Dr. King. They did it all. We don't have to think about new ideas; we just have to implement what they said, just get the work done. Gandhi offered everything there is in his message.

As I said, what I like about Gandhi is that he was a doer. He did things. He had thoughts *and* actions. Also he did a lot that he is not recognized for but which also has a lot of meaning. You know, he organized quite a few unions—there's nothing much written about this—but even today those unions are active. My biggest disappointment with the movie *Gandhi* was that it mentioned nothing whatsoever about the unions that he built. He organized the clothing workers, as you know, in Ahmedabad. In fact, I had a chance to meet one of the people from that union.

Gandhi was also a fantastic fundraiser. He raised millions of rupees, and he had a huge network of social services. He had probably the largest circulation of any newspaper in the history of the world. Even though there were only one or two thousand copies printed in the original, everybody reprinted it. So the message for me is that of his nonviolence and the fact that he was a doer. He made things happen.

CI: Does the fact that he was successful influence you in your appreciation of him? A lot of people attempt to do similar things, but for whatever reasons—their time in history, or circumstances beyond their control—they're not successful.

CC: No, what influences me is not whether or not they're successful, it's that they don't give up. I lose faith in someone who doesn't continue a project, who starts something and then leaves it. The world is full of us quitters. Even if Gandhi had not liberated India, he stayed with the project all his life. And that is my great attraction. He just didn't give up.

NOTES

1. For example, in the town of McFarland in the California Central Valley which is a crop-growing area regularly sprayed with pesticides, childhood cancers are eight times the normal level. Dr. Marion Moses, a leading medical researcher among farmworkers, cites cancer cases as the "hardest data," and she says that she has "soft data" on stillbirths and miscarriages. However, Dr. Moses suggests caution in concluding culpability and feels that lengthier studies are needed. She also adds that while body fat can more safely harbor chemicals than lean tissue, weight loss or expended energy poses a danger as the chemicals are released.

2. According to the United Farm Workers Union, fifty-four percent of table grapes tested by the government contain pesticide residues, but the government does not test for forty-four percent of the poisons used on grapes.

3. In 1987 Cesar Chavez fasted for thirty-six days on water only to "identify himself with the many farmworker families who suffer from the scourge of pesticide poisonings."

4. According to Professor George Georgehiou of the Department of Entomology, University of California, the number of species of insects resistant to pesticides increased from 224 in 1970 to 447 in 1984.

5. The program was implemented to recruit Mexican farmworkers who, after working the fields, were then sent back to Mexico

"REDWOOD RABBIS"

Seth Zuckerman

It was a ritual at once traditional and radical that drew 250 people to an ancient redwood grove ten miles from Northern California's Headwaters Forest on a stormy January day in 1997. Between rain squalls they were celebrating Tu B'shevat, the Jewish New Year of the Trees. But this ceremony was not just about spiritual connection with the plant kingdom, and included more than the usual ritual meal of fruits, nuts, and wine. The forestry chair of the local Sierra Club chapter gave an overview of the threat posed to the old-growth redwood forests by the Houston-based Maxxam Corporation. Another worshipper chanted the haunting Kaddish, or mourner's prayer, in memory of creatures displaced or killed by logging.

Most radical of all, the ceremony set the stage for an act of civil disobedience: the planting of redwood seedlings on an eroding stream bank on Maxxam property to symbolize hope for the restoration of land already clearcut and creeks stripped of their tree cover. Maxxam had refused permission to plant, but the worshippers vowed they would break the law and trespass, seedlings and shovels in hand.

The religious action was part of a larger campaign to invoke Jewish traditions in defense of Headwaters Forest, the largest tract of unprotected ancient redwoods in the world, acquired by Maxxam in a hostile takeover of Pacific Lumber Company in 1986. Because Maxxam CEO Charles Hurwitz is a leading member of Houston's Jewish community, organizers have been seeking to appeal to him by contrasting his actions with Jewish teaching. They're also working to build a strong Jewish constituency for the protection of old-growth redwoods and other ecosystems, a campaign that's part of a nationwide interfaith effort to apply spiritual principles in environmental battles.

Such applications are hardly new—the Book of Deuteronomy, for example, prohibited the Israelites from destroying the fruit trees of cities they besieged. Activists tapped this tradition in 1995 by sending a letter to Hurwitz just before Yom Kippur, the Day of Atonement, when observant Jews reflect on their actions of the preceding year. A small congregation in northwestern California, B'nai Ha-Aretz (Children of the Earth), wrote to Maxxam's CEO urging him to repent his destruction of the forest. The lead author, student rabbi Naomi Steinberg, explains: "Repentance isn't a private, ascetic process. Judaism is a very communal religion, and part of our duty as Jews is to help each other to repent."

Reprinted with the author's permission from the November/December 1998 issue of *Sierra*, "The Magazine of the Sierra Club."

The invocation of Jewish values may have touched a nerve at the top of Maxxam. At an interfaith press conference on Headwaters in the spring of 1996 in nearby Eureka, Rabbi Lester Scharnberg wondered aloud whether "perhaps Mr. Hurwitz has forgotten the faith of his ancestors." Scharnberg's remarks, carried on the wire services and picked up by the Houston press, drew a stinging phone call from Hurwitz's rabbi, Samuel Karff, who disputed whether this member of his congregation deserved rebuke. Karff defended Hurwitz as a charitable man; the Hurwitz family has donated heavily to Karff's Temple Beth Israel, and the synagogue's school is housed in the Hurwitz Building. Despite their disagreement, Karff arranged for Scharnberg to speak with Hurwitz directly.

In the 45-minute conversation that ensued, Hurwitz was taken aback to find a rabbi on the other side of the Headwaters battle, recalls Scharnberg. "He didn't know me, but he has an image of what a rabbi is," Scharnberg says, "and he expressed surprise that I was aligned with 'conga drums, dreadlocks, tie-dye, and hippie radicals who threaten to kill, maim,' and so forth. I said, 'I'm not aligning myself with people who kill, but I am an environmentalist.'"

Scharnberg didn't have an opportunity to confront Hurwitz again until the May 1998 Maxxam stockholders meeting, armed with a proxy signed over to him by another Headwaters activist. Christian and secular speakers addressed issues of science, economics, and corporate responsibility, and left religion up to Scharnberg. That was probably a wise call given that the roster of Maxxam's officers and board members has a substantial Jewish representation.

Scharnberg asked the board if Maxxam had considered moral questions in the course of its operations, and if not, how the firm could hope to act ethically. The very question provoked a firestorm of response that continued after the 90-minute official meeting. "The directors of Maxxam were outraged that we should introduce religion into this board meeting," Scharnberg says. In fact, when the rabbi tried to talk with Hurwitz afterward, the CEO directed him to board member Ezra Levin, who began debating Scharnberg in a conversation peppered with Hebrew and Aramaic. "I finally said, 'You and I could go on all day like this. You quote your Talmud passage and I quote mine. Both of us know there's no environmental mandate there. But nowhere in the entire Torah does it forbid rape, and that doesn't make it right. There's nothing in there that forbids slavery, and that doesn't make it right either.'"

Hurwitz, Levin, and Scharnberg left the Houston hotel in a theological stalemate, but the case is being pressed in many other forums. Last summer, the Coalition on the Environment and Jewish Life—which claims such prominent member groups as Hadassah, Hillel, B'nai Brith, and the American Jewish Congress—called for stronger habitat protections in Headwaters and in all remaining old-growth redwood groves. Several other major Jewish organizations have adopted or are considering similar resolutions. And on Hurwitz's home turf, a group of Houston Jews rented the Jewish Community Center for another ecologically oriented Tu B'shevat. Maxxam reps called officials at the center alleging that the ritual would be "political" and that "activists would be stapling themselves to trees," says organizer Annette Lamoreaux. But the event went on without incident.

Back in the redwoods in January 1997, a caravan of 100 worshippers—some wearing talliths, or fringed prayer shawls, as Jews have for thousands of years—hiked onto the timber firm's property and planted two dozen redwood seedlings along a barren stream bank. Some used shovels, some trowels, some their bare hands. Longtime Earth First! activist Darryl Cherney described it as a miracle. "At a place where demonstrators before have been met with billy clubs, nightsticks, and arrests, we are now walking freely," he said. "It reminds me of the parting of the Red Sea."

Nearly two years have passed and student rabbi Steinberg—who lives just a few miles away—hasn't revisited the site. "I'd rather remember the trees beautifully planted than to see that Pacific Lumber has pulled them up or that the whole bank has fallen away," she says.

At presstime, the fate of Headwaters Forest was hinging on Governor Pete Wilson's approval of controversial plans for Maxxam to sell 9,500 acres of key old growth to the public while agreeing not to log ten other old-growth groves for the next 50 years. Maxxam stands to gain $480 million from the sale and would be allowed to log on most of its remaining 200,000 acres. The proposed safeguards for coho salmon in this huge remaining tract, though improved over earlier drafts, are still inadequate, says the Sierra Club.

Steinberg reminds activists to look at the big picture. "If you approach a campaign like this as spiritual work, the moments along the way can be transformative to you as an individual soul." It's that transformation of souls that will determine whether "the forest trees shout for joy," as the Psalmist sang.

"OF TELESCOPES, SQUIRRELS, AND PRAYERS: THE MT. GRAHAM CONTROVERSY"

Evelyn Martin

If you want to travel from Mexico to Canada, but have only half a day to spend, try visiting Mt. Graham, 75 miles (120km) north-east of Tucson. This 'sky island' hosts the visitor to five of American's seven biological zones. Ascending from the Lower Sonoran desert to the Hudsonian spruce-fir forest, the mountain is home to 18 plant and animal species found nowhere else. But as you near the 10,720-foot (3,267-metre) summit, you will be in a battle zone between heaven and earth.

Fanning the flames of controversy is the University of Arizona's plan to build the Mt. Graham International Observatory. The kind of research to be carried out on the mountain is the stuff of which scientific dreams are made: studies of the early universe and galaxy formation from up to 10 billion years ago, star and planet formation in the Milky Way and other galaxies, and the search for other planetary systems. These studies would be conducted in collaboration with the Vatican Observatory and other international partners.

The university has telescopes on mountains such as Kitt Peak near Tucson. But explosive population growth has created 'light pollution', and the new wave of advanced telescopes requires higher altitudes than are found at existing sites. To house its own new telescopes, the university originally surveyed 280 potential sites in the United States. Of three astronomically-preferred locations, Mt. Graham alone was not in a designated wilderness or national monument.

However, an analysis by two scientists at the National Optical Astronomical Observatories indicated that Mt. Graham's 'merit ranking' was only 38 out of 57 sites reviewed. But Peter Strittmatter, Director of the university's Steward Observatory, praises the site's excellence: 'Mt. Graham is expected to at least match the best image sharpness demonstrated anywhere in the continental U.S. People around here are all dreaming of the day it will open'. But others are dreaming of the day the telescopes will be torn down.

Reprinted from *Cultural and Spiritual Values of Biodiversity*, United Nations Environment Programme (2000). Used by permission of United Nations Environment Programme.

The Mt. Graham red squirrel (*Tamiasciurus hudsonicus grahamensis*) is an endangered subspecies whose only earthly habitat is the summit area of Mt. Graham. Genetically isolated within its sky island, it faces a precarious future as a result of the previous logging of some of its habitat. The mammal is one of 25 currently-recognized subspecies of red squirrel in North America. Listed as an endangered species in 1987, the average estimate of its population declined to a low of 123 in 1989, but rose steadily to a high of 377 in spring 1992, before dropping to 332 in the fall.

What has so vehemently fuelled environmentalists' concerns is the way that Congress went about approving the observatory. Prior to the issuance of the Forest Service's final environmental impact statement, and based on a biological opinion of the U.S. Fish and Wildlife Service, Congress attached a rider to the 1988 Arizona-Idaho Conservation Act (AICA). The rider stated that provisions of the Endangered Species Act and the National Environmental Policy Act shall be deemed satisfied with respect to the observatory.

Mark Hughes, staff attorney for the Sierra Club Legal Defense Fund, comments, 'AICA was completely irresponsible, a perversion of the system.' In 1990, observatory opponents forced Congress to hold oversight hearings. The two Fish and Wildlife Service biologists who had written the biological opinion testified that they had been ordered, against their professional judgement, to conclude that the observatory would not harm the squirrel. And their regional director was caught explaining to Congress that he had allowed non-biological information—that is, the prestige and importance of the observatory—to affect the finding, contrary to provisions of the Endangered Species Act.

For three years, the Sierra Club Legal Defense Fund has lost most of its court challenges because of judicial support of AICA. Two remaining counts concern what Hughes calls the university's scientifically-indefensible monitoring of the red squirrel. According to Steve Emerine, Associate Director of the university's public information office, the university has, during the first three years, spent double the required minimum of $100,000 per year on monitoring. 'The most recent squirrel numbers show that the observatory is not having a negative effect,' notes Emerine. 'Although the fall 1992 numbers were down somewhat from the earlier numbers, the recent estimate is still about double that of 1989.' But Hughes claims that every party *except* the university agrees that clearing part of the habitat harms the squirrels.

Adding fuel to the controversy over Mt. Graham is the fact that the mountain is sacred to the San Carlos Apache Indians. *Dzil nchaa si an*, or Big-Seated Mountain as traditional Apaches call it, is home to the *ga'an* spirit dancers. The Apaches want their prayers to flow unimpeded from the summit.

Beginning at least in the 1600s, several Apache tribes lived and travelled in the area around Mt. Graham. During the so-called Indian Wars in the mid-to-late 1800s, the mountain variously provided sanctuary to the Apaches and served as a summer recuperation area for ailing U.S. soldiers and their families. Reflecting Apache territorial patterns, the original San Carlos Apache Reservation encompassed *Dzil nchaa si an*. But, as happened so often, the U.S. subsequently decided it wanted the land—the mountain for logging, and the adjacent Gila River valley for mining and agriculture. In 1873, the Apaches lost their mountain.

Ola Cassadore Davis, a San Carlos Apache, has matched the astronomers' figurative dreams of scientific inquiry with her own literal dream of saving the sacred mountain. Thus was formed the Apache Survival Coalition, with Davis as chairperson.

Dzil nchaa si an is 'of vital importance for maintaining the integrity' of cultural traditions, according to a 1990 resolution passed unanimously by the San Carlos Tribal Council. Elders, as well as medicine men and women, use the mountain for religious activities. The *ga'an* spirit dancers teach the medicine people how to heal the sick through song and prayer, and how to apply special herbs and plants found only on *Dzil nchaa si an*. In addition, the mountain contains ancient religious shrines and burial grounds.

What is difficult for outsiders to appreciate, though, is that the entire mountain, not just a given site, is considered sacred. 'It's the mountain that gives life, sustains life,' emphasizes coalition vice-chairman Ernest Victor, Jr. 'If God created what is on the earth, holy places, it is wrong for man to desecrate them.' The Apaches accept for now the mountain's other uses. What makes the observatory different, claims Victor, is that 'nature will reclaim the other uses. The communications towers have only a small amount of cement, and the tree roots will go through the pavement. But the concrete of the telescopes will be there for centuries—it will be scarred for centuries.'

Coming under special attack by the coalition is the Vatican, for two reasons. The first is the irony by which the Vatican is building its telescope, when Pope John Paul II visited the south-west in 1986 and urged American Indians to be bold and fight for their land rights. The second is the affront to traditional religious interests that the Apaches perceive in the Vatican's official statement. Reverend George Coyne, Director of the Vatican Observatory, writes, 'We are not convinced . . . that Mt. Graham possesses a sacred character which precludes responsible and legitimate use of the land . . . there is to the best of our knowledge no religious or cultural significance to the specific observatory site.'

Exacerbating the Apaches' uphill fight is the fact that they themselves did not take their plight public until 1989, in part because Native Americans are extremely reluctant to openly discuss sacred matters. Although Forest Service records show numerous notifications, starting in 1985, about the environmental reviews, San Carlos tribal records do not indicate that the notifications were received. Yet, according to the Forest Service's Abbott, 'It's hard for me to imagine that anyone was not aware of the proposed observatory.' In 1987, a group called the Friends of Mt. Graham did send the Forest Service a letter indicating that traditional Apaches used the mountain for ceremonial purposes.

The coalition's lawsuit against the Forest Service cites provisions of the American Indian Religious Freedom Act (AIRFA), the National Environmental Policy Act, the National Historic Preservation Act, the National Forest Management Act, and the First and Third Amendments of the U.S. Constitution. The gist of the lawsuit concerns the broad element of religious freedom, and the technical element of the requisite cultural surveys. However, the toothlessness of AIRFA has already resulted in the U.S. Supreme Court placing strict interpretations on religious freedom, including access to sacred sites. An archaeological survey was conducted for the Forest Service by the university, but critics emphasize that this survey is insufficient and misses the point, especially in the case of Apaches, who do not leave physical evidence of their shrines.

University spokesman Emerine hopes that some access solution can be found. To the coalition, the issue is not access, which already exists, but respect for the mountain. For, as Apache Burnette Rope stresses, 'If the spirits leave, we don't know where they'll go.' Adds Victor, 'It's very hard to say what will happen.'

At the heart of the controversy is the failure of America to come to grips with broad issues of land ethics. Aldo Leopold urged us to become plain members and citizens of the land community, rather than conquerors of it. The Vatican Observatory was established in part to acknowledge the centuries-old criticism of the Holy See forcing Galileo to deny that the sun, not the earth, was the centre of the solar system. Now, the debate is increasingly about whether humans are at the centre of the earth community, or are one among many at the centre.

The Mt. Graham controversy presently pits astronomers who revere the skies through technology against a small mammal with a cloudy future, and against Apaches who engage the heavens with only their eyes and hearts. Mainstream society locks away its equivalent of sacred lands in wilderness designations. But until our land ethic also embraces whole ecosystems, sacred Indian lands, and other areas that are the foundation of both our physical and spiritual existences, controversies like Mt. Graham will continue to be addressed in less than comprehensive fashion.

"MHONDORO: SPIRIT LIONS AND SACRED FORESTS"

Bruce Byers

"We will advance deep into the undergrowth of mythology and ritual, of symbolism and belief."

—David Lan, *Guns and Rain:*
Guerillas and Spirit Mediums in Zimbabwe

Following a narrow track we pushed in through the thornthicket. Huge baobabs, as big as the round thatch and mud huts clustered under them, rose from the heavily gullied land, their smooth trunks shining silver and pink in the hot noon sun. Using aerial photos as a map, Nick Dunne and I were trying to get to a point on the east bank of the Musengezi River at the northern end of the largest remaining fragment of forest in this part of northern Zimbabwe.

Finally we reached the top of the riverbank, parked the Toyota Land Cruiser on a steep incline, and put a couple of rocks under the wheels to keep it from rolling. We were about to eat lunch when a man in a torn khaki shirt and dirty blue shorts appeared, coming up from his small, handwatered vegetable garden by the river, which was heavily fenced with brushwood against cattle and goats. He was curious and friendly, especially after we shared one of our warm beers with him. His name was Jeremiah Manhango, and his English was not bad. Jeremiah warned us immediately not go into the thick forest just south of here:

"If you do you can get lost. A lot of rain may come and fall on you, even now, in the dry season. Or you can get eaten by a lion. There is a big white snake in there. It doesn't bite you, but if you see it, you'll go mad!"

This forest was one of three places sacred to Mbuya Nehanda, an important ancestral spirit of this part of the Zambezi Valley, Jeremiah told us. This area is the home of the Korekore people, a subgroup of Zimbabwe's largest ethnic group, the Shona. As is true in many central African cultures, belief in ancestral spirits and their power to influence everyday life is a central tenet of Shona religion. Jeremiah had moved here with his family from central Zimbabwe in 1971, as a boy of fifteen. Even though he was an immigrant, and not a Korekore, he was still a Shona, and he respected the sacred places of the local people, he said.

Reprinted by permission from the author, from *Camas*, Fall 2002.

I was here in the Muzarabani District with Nick Dunne, a young white Zimbabwean who grew up on a citrus farm in the south, near Beitbridge. Trained as a botanist, he now worked for the Zambezi Society, an environmental organization based in Harare. "Zam-Soc," as its members often call it, promotes the conservation of nature and biological diversity throughout the Zambezi River Basin.

Here in the communal lands of Muzarabani, ZamSoc was interested in some remaining patches of a unique type of dry tropical forest. Most of the trees found in these forests lose their leaves during the dry season that lasts from May through November. At ground level is a thicket understory, dominated by an acacia that grows in a viney tangle and has wicked, backward-curving thorns.

This type of dry, thicket forest is rare, found only along a few rivers flowing into the Zambezi from the south, especially along the Musengezi River. The forests have an unusually large number of trees and woody climbing vines, which botanists call lianas, and many plants that are unusual or rare in Zimbabwe grow in them. What Nick was most excited about, however, was that here, species common in several different types of forests and woodlands were all growing together in one place. He had the idea that this was some kind of relict community of plants, left over from the last Ice Age when the climate was wetter here. In fact, he liked to call these forests "witness stands," and argued that if they are protected, they could be helpful in understanding long-term climate change in this part of Africa.

The Zambezi Society was also interested in conserving these forest patches because of evidence that they are important in maintaining elephant movements in this part of the Zambezi Valley. Elephants move through these forests as they travel between the Mvuradonha Mountains and the Zambezi River to the north, and they sometimes linger here, especially during the dry season when wild *musawu* fruit are ripe. In 1998 a group of about ten bulls spent three months hanging around in several forest patches near where we had met Jeremiah.

We knew from aerial photographs taken between 1960 and 1993 that these forests once covered more than twice as much area as they do now. In the last forty years some forest patches have been completely cleared. Others have been reduced in size as villages and fields eat into their edges. Once-continuous forests have been fragmented into several smaller patches in some cases.

Because of their botanical uniqueness, their role as elephant habitat, and the threat of further forest loss, the Muzarabani forests had a high priority for conservation, according to the Zambezi Society. About a year earlier, Nick had approached the Muzarabani District Council and explained its interest in conserving the remaining patches of forest along the Musengezi. The District Council members said they were interested, but not much had happened, and ZamSoc wanted to move the process forward.

To do so, we needed more information. What did local people think of these forests? What would it take to keep the rest of them from being cut down? When we met Jeremiah Manhango we were just beginning to talk to local residents, traditional religious and political leaders, and modern political leaders who lived near the forests. We had a lot of questions, a lot to learn. Nick's view of the value of these forests—that of a modern, educated, white scientist—was very different than Jeremiah's view, and I wondered whether these two views could ever come together for the common purpose of conservation.

I guess the real reason I was poking around in these thickets was to explore some thorny issues in my professional field. I had come to the University of Zimbabwe for a year as a Fulbright Scholar, both to teach and do research. Because I'm an ecologist by training, most people assumed I saw things the way Nick Dunne and other conservation biologists do. But in fact I was fed up with the arguments I'd heard so often from my colleagues at home: that conservation means putting fences around natural areas and keeping people out, or that people should care about "biodiversity" because all species, no matter how tiny or seemingly useless, have "intrinsic value." Here in Zimbabwe those arguments seemed naive and completely impractical.

On the other hand, I was skeptical about the mainstream view in wildlife conservation circles in Zimbabwe, which was that unless poor rural Zimbabweans saw cash flowing into their pockets from natural resources, they would have no incentive to conserve them. The assumption was that economics was the only thing that could influence people's behavior toward nature. But if local people really considered these forests sacred, and protected them because of that belief, it meant that money isn't everything, even to poor people. It suggested that traditional religious beliefs might still be a powerful motivating force for conservation.

We drove west from Muzarabani the next morning along the base of the Escarpment. This is spectacular country. The Zambezi Escarpment is the southernmost section of the Great Rift Valley of Africa, and here the Rift rises like a rampart from the flat floor of the Zambezi Valley to the high plateau of central Zimbabwe, a jumbled wall of cliffs and hills a kilometer high. Massive tectonic forces involved in the breakup of the ancient supercontinent of Gondwanaland are recorded in the rocks, and the movement of crustal plates is still ripping the continent apart here. If the Great Rift were a giant serpent lying stretched across eastern Africa, with its tail dipping into the Red Sea at Djibouti, the Mvuradonha Mountains that brooded above us now would be its head, its eyes those cliffs on the side of Banerembezi, the highest peak, staring down on the forests of Muzarabani.

For the first few kilometers north of the Musengezi River men were working on the road, getting it ready for asphalt, and it was all torn up. After that it was good, smooth gravel. We crossed the Kadzi River into Guruve District, and soon reached Mahuwe, a busy hub of dusty shops and people waiting for buses to take them either north—deeper into the Valley, and the past—or south—up the Escarpment toward Harare, and the modern world.

Nick and I were looking for Phanuel Rupiya, a farmer and district councilor from Mahuwe. Rupiya's house was just off the road about a kilometer north of town. No one was at home in the cluster of round, mud-plastered, thatched huts that Rupiya calls home. A young mother in a compound nearby pointed us into the cotton and maizefields, where she said Rupiya's wife was working. We walked along a path for fifteen minutes or so, until we heard voices. It was Mrs. Rupiya, picking cotton with a friend. But no, she had not seen her husband for a couple of days. He went off toward Mushumbi Pools to evaluate some projects—maybe for NORAD, the Norwegian Development Agency, she thought. He might be back tomorrow, but she didn't know for sure.

So we walked back to the Land Cruiser, parked in the shade of a scraggly *musawu* tree loaded with green fruit, and spread out our 1:250,000 scale topographic map on the hood. We had hoped to get Rupiya's help in pinpointing the sacred sites he had been learning about. Now it looked like we needed to lay Plan B. Just then a huge truck loaded with baled cotton groaned up the dusty road from the direction of Mushumbi Pools, bound for the climb up the Escarpment to Guruve and beyond. It slowed in front of Rupiya's road, and a couple of men jumped down with their dufflebags. We continued to look at the map. As the men walking toward us got closer we recognized one of them as Phanuel Rupiya from his unique newsboy-style cap, made of leather that once was rust-colored, but was now dark from sweat and dirt. We had found Rupiya after all. The other man was Rupiya's friend Everson Tauro. Tauro, shorter and heavier than the lanky Rupiya, wore a thin mustache and goatee.

Rupiya invited us to talk in the shade by his round mud and thatch house. The door was locked, and his wife, still in the cottonfield, apparently had the key with her, so he climbed in the open window and handed out a folding metal table and five tiny wooden chairs, the size they use in kindergarten classrooms in the U.S., painted bright orange. We sat in the tiny chairs, spread out the topo again, and started to mark sacred sites on the map. Rupiya had been doing simple anthropological fieldwork in the Muzarabani Communal Lands, getting a few dollars a month from the Zambezi Society. He would put his bicycle on a local bus, take the bus to the area where he wanted to work, and then pedal around talking to people about sacred places nearby.

"Different types of sacred sites exist," Rupiya explained. "Places where traditional beer is brewed during the *huruwa* ceremony, usually under big, old fig trees, are considered sacred. There are sacred forests. And certain rivers or mountain ranges, such as the Mvuradonha Mountains, may be sacred too."

Sacred pools are another type of sacred site. These can be pools in rivers, or springs, or in some cases the shallow seasonal ponds that form during the rainy season. Rupiya had heard about a sacred pool in the Musengezi River, called Ngwandongwondo Pool, which local people said had been disturbed by a recent immigrant to the area.

"That man put poison in Ngwandongwando Pool to catch fish. The poison killed a python that was living in the pool, protecting it. Now the Musengezi River has changed its course and the pool is drying up."

Some tree species are sacred, including baobab, tamarind, fig, and *marula*.

"If you use the wood from a sacred tree for building a house, or for firewood, in that house you will always see snakes," Tauro explained.

"What about animals?" I asked. "Are there sacred animals?"

"The spirit mediums say the animals belong to them. They have a special name, *vakaranga*, for all sorts of sacred animals—elephants, snakes, kudus, and especially lions. When our chiefs die, their spirits come back in the form of lions, and watch over us—we call them *mhondoro*. They make sure we are respecting the land. The spirit mediums say the forests and thickets are sacred because they keep their *vakaranga* there."

I suddenly realized, listening to Tauro, that these forests may be as much a cultural phenomenon as an ecological one—that, in fact, an interaction between ecology and traditional religion may explain why the forests exist along the Musengezi. The old alluvial soils found along the Musengezi created the conditions required for this type of forest to develop. Because of the forests, wild animals are found here—the sacred animals in which the spirits of the ancestors dwell. Because of the animals, the forests are sacred. And because they are sacred they have not been cleared, at least not completely, not yet.

As a general rule, Rupiya said, sacred things are life sustaining. "They provide food, fruit, or water, for example. The concept of sacredness is closely linked with rain, and the fertility of the land." In our Western worldview we think of "spiritual" and "material" things as very different in kind. To a Shona farmer, that distinction doesn't really exist. Religion is a very practical thing. People must respect nature for a very practical reason: their lives depend on it. It is good to respect sacred places not because of some abstract religiosity, but because people need food, and crops need rain, and only happy ancestors will send good rains.

Tauro and Rupiya talked about spirit mediums, people who can be possessed by the spirits of the royal ancestors, and who can communicate the wishes of those *mhondoro* to people alive today. Today no one is possessed by the spirit of Nehanda, who was a powerful and beloved queen of this part of the Zambezi Valley. Today, without a medium, Mbuya Nehanda is silent.

"There is a woman from the Mt. Darwin area now living along the base of the Escarpment east of Muzarabani. She claims to be possessed by the spirit of Grandmother Nehanda," Rupiya said. To prove she is really possessed by Nehanda's spirit, a claimant must pass a test: she must swim in Nehanda's Pool in the Musengezi River, a sacred pool full of crocodiles.

"If she doesn't get eaten, she must be the real Mbuya Nehanda. We had arranged for a test recently, but she did not turn up. So now we are quite inquisitive whether she is the genuine one." There is another woman from Hurungwe who also claims to be possessed by Mbuya Nehanda, but so far she also has refused to take the crocodile test.

"Chidyamauyu, a famous spirit medium from Muzarabani, and a personal friend of President Mugabe because of his contribution to the Liberation War, went to see the President in Harare to ask the government to recognize the woman from Mt. Darwin as the real Nehanda," Tauro said. "But until she enters Nehanda's Pool, no one will believe she is genuine—even if President Mugabe himself says she is!"

"People now may be becoming too modern, they may not believe this, but the spirits are still strong," said Tauro. To emphasize this point, he told us that not long ago a lion killed more than twenty people in the Omay communal lands, not far from Muzarabani. This lion killed its victims around sundown, and with deliberate irony local people named it *Maskwera sei*—*maskwera sei* is a Shona greeting, used in the late afternoon, which means roughly, "how was your day?"

When a lion does something unusual, there is always a question of whether it is a normal lion or a spirit lion, a *mhondoro*. In the Shona language a biological lion is called *shumba*. A *mhondoro* is something altogether different. *Mhondoro* often become active, and disturbed, when something in the relationship between the people and the land is not right. They may show their displeasure by killing those who have not behaved properly and respectfully.

Local people in Omay suspected that *Maskwera sei* was a *mhondoro*, not a mere *shumba*. They could find something in the behavior of each victim that seemed to explain why each might have been killed. Perhaps one of them cut a tree without permission from the chief, another collected water from a sacred pool using a metal container, while another neglected to share meat with his relatives. The Department of National Parks and Wildlife Management sent a team of rangers to Omay to track the lion and kill it as a "problem animal." Local people refused to help them find *Maskwera sei*, an ancestor, *mhondoro*.

Electrical transmission lines finally reached Muzarabani last year. Before that a few people in town had electric lights powered by a big diesel generator, but there was no industry to speak of. Now power flows from Kariba Dam, upstream on the Zambezi, and a new gin for processing cotton has been built in town, its corrugated metal sides a shining symbol of progress. Now that Muzarabani is on the national grid, a local politician is talking about setting up a sawmill in the area. A sign in front of the new gin says: "Bring your cotton to us. Build a better life for your children." People want progress, a better life.

Still, when the new gin was built, construction workers carefully avoided a big old baobab that is still standing inside the high chain link fence around the factory. If the tree had been cut, according to Chidyamauyu, the local spirit medium, the spirits that inhabited it might have caused problems for the gin or its workers. So it was spared.

Cotton cultivation is expanding rapidly in Muzarabani. For the small farmers here, cotton is the main cash crop, from which they earn roughly half of their annual income of a few hundred dollars a year. The *mopane* woodlands in the area have been extensively cleared, because the heavy soils on which they grow are good for cotton. Cotton also grows well on the alluvial soils where the dry forests are found, and those soils are sandier and easier to plow with oxen than the *mopane* soils. If they weren't sacred, the forests would have been long gone.

Nick and I left Phanuel Rupiya and Everson Tauro sitting in the shade, and drove east along the Escarpment, back to Muzarabani. Now penciled on our topographic map were two dozen sacred sites that Rupiya had identified. We wanted to visit some of those if we could, but that required the permission of the ritual assistant of the local spirit medium, called a *mutape*, who keeps his eye on sacred sites and makes sure they are respected. At Muzarabani we turned north toward Kapembere village, where Rupiya said we'd be likely to find the *mutape*, Mr. Chipendo, "boozing it up" at the village bottle store.

When we reached the Kapembere shops we found that Rupiya was right. Mutape Chipendo was there, drinking beer with the district councilor from Kapembere, Crispen Honde. We explained what we wanted, and they quickly drained their beers and jumped in the back seat of the Land Cruiser. We drove a few kilometers back down the road toward Muzarabani.

Just off the road to the west was the Rukonde Forest, the largest fragment of this type of forest remaining in Zimbabwe. At its widest point Rukonde is about two kilometers across, and extends along the Musengezi River for about five kilometers. We had met Jeremiah Manhango at its northern edge yesterday, and now we parked by a cluster of huts west of the road that belonged to Jeremiah and his kin. The village occupied an alcove cut into the wall of trees, and the forest that used to stand here had metamorphosed into wooden structures—corrals for goats and cattle, racks for drying maize, chicken coops, and the huts themselves.

We walked a couple of dozen meters and stopped at the edge of a gully. On the other side stood the forest. A few candelabra euphorbias, which looked something like giant cactus, rose above an impenetrable maze of thorny vines, and above them stood the trees, forming a tangled canopy of branches over our heads. Councilor Honde said that the *mhondoro*, like to rest under euphorbias during the heat of the day. My neck prickled involuntarily and I scanned the tangle of undergrowth, but if *Maskwera sei* was crouching there now, watching us, I couldn't see him.

Mutape Chipendo searched for a certain plant, picked some leaves, and rubbed them in his hands with a scrubbing motion. The crushed leaves had a faint, acrid smell. A small flock of grey louries flew from tree to tree calling, a slow, sad call that sounded like "go-away, go-away, go-away." We squatted and clapped in a steady, slow rhythm while the *mutape*, Mr. Chipendo, began a chantlike beseeching of the spirits of the place. This went on for what seemed like a long time, but it may only have been a minute or so. When the chanting stopped, we continued to clap until Chipendo stood up abruptly. The spirits apparently knew we were here, and it was safe now to talk.

"A big snake guards this forest," Honde began. "The snake is seen maybe once a year and is so big that when it crosses the road along the edge of the forest, even the buses stop."

"A python?" I asked. African rock pythons are the biggest snakes in Africa, up to six meters long.

"No, it's not a python—it's much bigger than that! As big as that tree," Honde said, pointing to a tree a foot in diameter. "People are afraid of the big snake."

"No one is supposed to settle to the west of the road between Muzarabani and Kapembere, in the edge of Rukonde Forest, because of its sacredness," Honde said, and in the old days no one would have done so. Many houses now lie to the west of the road—the village of the Manhangos.

"The chief has asked these people to move, and even asked the District Administrator to make them pay a fine," Honde said. "They haven't, but the D.A. won't make them pay, and the chief won't evict them. It's a big problem."

We left Rukonde and drove north, with Chipendo and Honde directing from the back seat. When the track we were following dead-ended in a cotton field we got out and walked toward a circle of trees surrounding Chikampo Pool, another sacred site on Rupiya's map. The pool was shallow, about an acre in size, and a well-worn path crossed its edge. A group of women and girls appeared, walking home from the fields. One pushed a wheelbarrow overloaded with three bags of newly picked cotton.

The water of Chickampo Pool is used to brew ceremonial beer for the *huruwa* ceremony, a rainmaking ceremony that comes at the end of the seven-month dry season, in October or November. The purpose of *huruwa* is to enlist the help of ancestral spirits in bringing good rains. In the past, when traditional rules were followed, the pool held clean water throughout the dry season, Honde said. To protect the water, certain things are not allowed. Washing with soap is taboo, for example, and only traditional wooden or gourd containers—nothing metal—can be used for collecting water, for fear of scaring or poisoning the spirits of the pool. No livestock are supposed to drink here, only wild animals, some of which may be *mhondoro* or other ancestral spirits. Traditional rules strictly forbid wheeled vehicles near the pool.

"People are no longer respecting this place," Chipendo complained. "They should not be pushing a wheelbarrow through here! This wouldn't have happened in the old days!" Hoofprints indicated that lots of cattle and goats had been here to drink.

"This is the Number One Sacred Spot in the area," Honde said, "even more sacred than the Rukonde Forest!" I didn't ask why, but guessed it had something to do with the role of the pool in the *huruwa* ceremony, and of that ceremony in keeping the ancestors happy and bringing rain to the living.

A rising tide of immigration and settlement makes it difficult to maintain respect for these sacred places. Only about a fifth of the inhabitants of the area now are long-time residents, the rest are recent immigrants. In the past decade small-scale cotton cultivation has expanded rapidly, pulling land-hungry immigrants from the high plateau of Zimbabwe, where cotton doesn't grow. The new gin will only increase the pull.

"New immigrants don't know the sacred places here, and even if they know, they don't respect them," Honde said. "The ancestral spirits here aren't *their* ancestors."

"What would be the solution?" I asked.

"Put a fence around this place!" the councilor said.

"Really?" I asked, taken aback to hear him propose a technical solution to what I thought of as a social, not a technical, problem. I had once heard a traditional leader speak against fencing sacred sites, saying "Spirits don't want areas to be fenced. They don't like metal, they don't like wire." But Honde said at least a fence would keep the livestock out, and it would indicate that this was a sacred place.

We walked slowly back to the Land Cruiser, and I wondered what would happen to this pool, these forests, to the elephants, lions, and other wild animals who still live here, among these villages and their fields of maize and cotton. What are the prospects for the future? Can these people really preserve their traditional beliefs in the face of the rapid cultural change that is happening here? And if they do, will the belief that certain forests or pools are sacred really protect them in the face of technological and economic changes that are coming? I didn't know for sure what would happen, but I did know that many people still hold strongly to the traditional beliefs, and that those beliefs *had* conserved these forests until now. And I suspected that the Shona worldview I was learning about could help build a bridge to a new view, a practical conservation ethic locally-grown from ancient roots.

The bare branches of the big trees around the pool shone in the late afternoon sun, wound with lianas thick as giant snakes. A two-wheeled wooden cart came down the track toward us, pulled by a pair of trotting donkeys. An empty metal oildrum bounced on the cart.

"*Maskwera seï?!*" The driver greeted us with a big smile—"How was your day?"

Obviously his day had satisfied him so far. He was driving his cart to the sacred pool to fill his drum with water.

"SEEKING ECO-JUSTICE IN THE SOUTH AFRICAN CONTEXT"

Ernst Conradie, Charity Majiza, Jim Cochrane, Welile T. Sigabi, Victor Molobi, and David Field

We begin in Cape Town, where, some three and a half centuries ago, the Dutch East India Company established the first European settlement on this part of the African continent. Our route takes us on a mental tour of four specific places, each of which symbolizes something important about our reality, and the meaning and scope of eco-justice in our context.

Our tour commences at the statue of Cecil John Rhodes, the grand imperial agent who sought British rule "from Cape to Cairo." The statue stands in the former gardens of the Dutch East India Company. Rhodes is raising his arm, eyes staring North with an intensity that projects him as the great visionary anxious to bring the blessings of British rule to the entire African continent. The inscription at the foot of the statue reads: "This is our hinterland." Rhodes is also reputed to have said: "I am of the opinion that we are truly the best race in the world and that the more of our world we inhabit, the better it is for mankind." Underlying this statement are three fundamental ideological assumptions: (1) that unlimited space and scope for colonial and imperial expansion is accorded to the members of an allegedly superior race; (2) that the rights of indigenous peoples in the different countries have to give way and be subordinated to interests and potential of this allegedly superior race; and (3) that the natural resources of the continent and the cheap labor of its people are available to foreign colonial powers and immigrant settler communities for the implementation of this vision.

Our second stop is the national parliamentary building. This was the symbol of colonialism and apartheid. Here the dispossession of land was legalized, apartheid was institutionalized, and resistance against apartheid was criminalized. This same parliament—reborn, now belonging to all South African citizens, and remarkably open to the public—has become a symbol of the new democratic political order. A corner has been turned, though the road ahead remains long.

Next we board the ferry to Robben Island, seven miles off the mainland in Table Bay. From here one may stare back at the city, at the parliamentary complex, at the gardens where Rhodes looks stonily ahead. This island, since early colonial rule, has been a symbol of dehumanization, exclusion, and repression. It stands for the attempt to break the spirit of resistance against colonial domination. For a while it was a leper colony, and then once more it became the prison that held those who challenged the dominating powers. But it broke fewer spirits than anticipated. Known during the years of struggle against apartheid as "the university," because of the unceasing, often surreptitious debate and self-run education programs of its prisoners, Robben Island became a powerhouse of the liberation struggle and a potent symbol of the strength of the human spirit.

From Robben Island, looking across the bay, we see Table Mountain, our fourth stop. Other monuments are all overshadowed by the majestic bulk and presence of this mountain, sacred to our Khoi ancestors and to many others who still live under its shadow. Walk reverently up the mountain and you will be struck by the incredible variety of vegetation and the beauty of the coastline and of the mountain itself.

Once at the top we are able to look over the Cape metropolitan area—if the layer of urban smog permits—to see the city center and its industries, the affluent northern and southwestern suburbs and the vast areas of the Cape Flats, where millions of impoverished people live in squalid houses, shacks, and on rubbish dumps. We look down upon a sea of contradictory representations in geography and architecture: They represent injustice and the struggle for justice, poverty and the struggle for well-being, dehumanization and the search for a fuller human being, degradation and the desire for a clean and whole environment.

These four stops on our mental journey capture the ambiguities, the fragility, the pain of a context within which any attempt to tackle issues on eco-justice must be placed. They also point to vistas that are inhabited by hope and energy, faith and commitment. It is this paradox of actuality and possibility that defines our response to the challenges presented to local communities, and the ecclesial community in particular, by the vision of an ecumenical Earth.

FROM POLITICAL TO ECONOMIC LIBERATION

The past decades in the history of South Africa have been dominated by the struggle for political liberation. During the past twenty-five years liberation theology has spelled out the gospel in the context of the suffering of marginalized people. It addressed the cries of the victims of discrimination, humiliation, land dispossession, forced removals, oppression tyranny, torture, rape. It insisted that God is to be encountered among the victims of injustice. The scope of a concern for liberation from political oppression now has to be extended—not only to economic liberation but also to the liberation of the earth and all its creatures.

E. Conradie, C. Majiza, J. Cochrane, W. T. Sigabi, V. Molobi, and D. Field

Since the miracle of a peaceful transition to democracy in 1994, the focus of the public debate in South Africa has indeed shifted, at least to some extent, from political liberation to economic liberation. This is born from the realization that justice is still to come.[1] Even more acutely, it arises from the cries of the poor, the hungry, the homeless, the sick, the abused, the unemployed, the aged, the illiterate. In that respect South Africa is a low-income, highly indebted, developing country with insufficient resources to deal with its problems and needs and considerable vulnerability to international markets and financial speculation. In the struggle for economic and social justice, the issues of poverty, employment, education, housing, health services, crime and AIDS demand our attention and consume our energy. The combination of these factors has led to a marginalization of a concern for the environment.

The environment as such means quite different things to different people, reflecting different social locations and cultural experiences within our complex and fractured society. Some think that "the environment" refers to nature conservation. Others experience it in the form of air and water pollution that affects their daily lives and health. Some focus on the proper management of natural resources under their control. Others are concerned with inadequate health and safety standards in the working environment. Some think about it only when there is news about an environmental catastrophe. Yet others are anxious about somewhat remote global issues, such as the melting of the ice caps, which may have great consequence, but which are difficult to locate clearly within our own context.

An Emerging Environmental Awareness

Despite the marginalization of the environment as a focus of concern, there is an emerging awareness that care for economic and social justice cannot be separated from the environment. This emerging awareness has two important aspects.[2]

On the one hand, there is a broad recognition that human well-being is dependent on the well-being of the land. Most informed people, including a great many South Africans of all kinds, are well aware that the destruction of a healthy environment will necessarily affect human dignity. We are rooted in the soil of Africa, our "mother." This is the home (*oikos, ikhaya*) where we belong.[3] The notion that we have to care for the earth so that the earth can care for us is integral to traditional African wisdom. The mindful husbanding of land and cattle that was part of traditional practices has not entirely disappeared, notwithstanding a century of industrialization, modernization, and urbanization. This is true even for those in urban areas who no longer have cattle and land, but whose vision of well-being draws on traditions of the past.

On the other hand, there is a realization that the problems poor people experience on a daily basis are essentially environmental problems. This has both urban and rural dimensions. People living in urban townships are often the victims of environmental degradation caused elsewhere—by nearby industries, for example.[4] Townships were often located precisely on environmentally degraded land that was therefore not in demand. We may list the following as some of the typical health hazards of township life:

- air pollution—either through nearby industries or through the use of braziers and coal stoves (even in electrified houses);

- pollution of water supplies by broken sewerage pipes, stagnant pools, or people doing their washing next to water taps to avoid walking characteristically long distances to reach a decent washing place, if one exists at all;

- the visual ugliness of pollution, leading to a lack of basic human dignity;

- typically very high population densities—a localized form of over-population;

- inadequate sanitation;

- a high incidence of contagious diseases;

- regular floods or landslides;

- a lack of basic infrastructure;

- cutting of trees for firewood in the neighborhood, where any are left; and

- the struggle for political control over ever scarcer resources.

In rural areas, the scarcity of clean drinking water and firewood, which has serious human and economic consequences, is an environmental problem at its very roots. Deportation or removals under apartheid forced many South Africans to live in overcrowded conditions on land unable to support them effectively, resulting in extreme poverty. This process has reinforced environmental degradation: through overgrazing, soil erosion, and the exhaustion or depletion of water supplies. Many people have resorted to poaching and forms of deforestation as a survival strategy. These forms of environmental degradation are seldom deliberate but an increasing number of humans in a limited area inevitably exacts an environmental toll. This environmental damage increases poverty, leading to a vicious circle in which people are damaging the very fabric on which they depend for their survival.

Women and children often bear the brunt of coping with these environmental problems. As soil deteriorates, women have to work longer hours in backbreaking toil to harvest food from barren soil. Children suffer most, from diseases like diarrhea owing to a lack of drinkable water and inadequate sanitation. In deforested rural communities, girls and women expend increasing energy and time to collect firewood. Women are often forced to work in environmentally hazardous conditions for low wages. Women receive fewer financial rewards, work more hours, have less access to education, do more of the household caretaking, and have to bear and provide for their children. Typically, mothers sleep last and rise first.[5]

The middle-class and elite members of South African society enjoy First World standards of water, energy, sanitation, health care, and education.[6] Their lives display the con-

E. Conradie, C. Majiza, J. Cochrane, W. T. Sigabi, V. Molobi, and D. Field

sumerism and wastefulness that is characteristic of most of the First World with its devastating effect on the earth. Inadequate environmental legislation does little to mitigate this impact at this point in our history.

The Social Location of the Struggle for Eco-Justice

From this analysis it becomes more than clear that to address poverty is to address this range of environmental hazards: The quest for economic justice is a quest for environmental justice. The struggle for eco-justice has to challenge the abuse of power that results in a situation where poor people suffer the effects of environmental damage caused by the greed of others.

In South Africa, this vision for eco-justice is beginning to emerge in the context of civil society. It is the focus of the Environmental Justice Networking Forum, a loose alliance of more than five hundred nonprofit, community-based, and nongovernmental organizations. This vision suggests that the environment has to be "marginal" in a second important sense of the word: The struggle for eco-justice has to affect the lives of those on the economic periphery of society. Indeed, we may go further and say that the extent to which the struggle for eco-justice effectively addresses this reality is, in important respects, the measure of its purpose and value.[7] This is possible only if the struggle for eco-justice can be rooted practically in local black communities under black leadership among the poor and deprived. Unless this is achieved, we will be falling far short of what is required in South Africa.

Furthermore, it is crucial to recognize that poverty is also a strongly gendered reality, that women generally bear the bulk of the burdens of poverty, and that effective development work must take much more seriously the constraints upon and potentials of women in this context. One may say, therefore, that eco-justice needs to take root not only among black communities under black leadership, but also among black women under the leadership of black women.

The capacity to deal with environmental dimensions of poverty rests as much on the people themselves as it does on structural and systemic interventions by government or other external agencies. The emphasis on the role of local marginalized communities has to be understood within the context of the tendency (in South Africa and elsewhere) in state organs, in government, and in business toward macro-solutions and "expert"-driven policy processes on the one hand, and a consonant downgrading of, if not hostility toward, micro-initiatives on the part of ordinary citizens on the other. A strong sense of participatory democracy accompanied the initial transition in South Africa, carried on the back of about fifteen years of struggle deeply rooted in "illegal" civic associations, youth groups, women's organizations, street committees, and a host of other forms of civil society. This has begun to dissipate in the face of policy processes, which all too frequently seem not to prize local initiatives and policy interventions very highly. Eco-justice will be achieved only through particular ways of conceiving democracy and particular kinds of democratic practice.

It is therefore clear that any adequate discussion of eco-justice must be grounded in the context of the challenge of poverty and a vision of democracy if it is to have an impact on South African society.

POLICY IMPLICATIONS

A moral vision for eco-justice clearly has to be effective in marginalized communities. If it is to be sustained, however, it must also be expressed in the form of public policy, accompanied by appropriate budgetary allocations to enable policy to be carried out. The need for a policy framework is in part met, in the first instance, through a section of the new South African constitution. Clause 24 of the Bill of Rights states that everyone has the right (1) to an environment that is not harmful to his or her health or well-being; and (2) to have the environment protected, for the benefit of present and future generations, through reasonable legislative measures that (a) prevent pollution and ecological degradation, (b) promote conservation, and (c) secure ecologically sustainable development and use of natural resources while promoting justifiable economic and social development.[8]

Implementation of this constitutional goal involves confronting the central dilemma of the struggle for eco-justice in South Africa: How are we to promote desperately needed social and economic development without compromising ecological integrity? Current economic and political dynamics in South Africa indicate that this will prove to be an excruciatingly complex task.

Given the resources of the state and of markets in a "globalizing" framework, which has a direct, heavy, and frequently negative effect on emerging economies such as South Africa, citizen-oriented programs, actions, and agencies may well be swamped. It is imperative, therefore, that all available positive resources be harnessed in synergy with each other—an appropriate vision for the ecologically minded person. It is here that the churches have a significant role to play as they seek to bear witness to God's commitment to the earth and to act as a voice for the voiceless. This is particularly important in rural areas, where churches are often the only (or the chief) organ of civil society and the clergyperson may be one of the few members of the community with a tertiary education and access to needed resources (human, organizational, informational, and material resources).

The real question is whether churches and Christian agencies can meet such a challenge, recognizing the interlinked character of justice and ecology in the context of poverty. They are, in fact, severely pressured at the moment, with depleted resources, massive new demands for which we have no deep thinking or adequate practice, a sense of loss

E. Conradie, C. Majiza, J. Cochrane, W. T. Sigabi, V. Molobi, and D. Field

of identity and purpose in the absence of a clear common enemy, and a secular polity environment that tends to push them to focus on narrow moral concerns or to drift into privatized religious practices.

AN ECUMENICAL CONTRIBUTION

The Christian faith has to do with an awareness of a calling. This, however, differs fundamentally from the nationalistic visions of Western states and empires:

- God calls people from the ranks of those who are enslaved and considered outcasts.

- God liberates God's people, not for dominating other people, but in order to become a blessing to humankind.

- God wants God's people to serve God's purpose to recover creation from the forces of destruction that have been unleashed by humanity's refusal to act as responsible stewards of creation.

- Through the Holy Spirit the crucified and risen Christ is present in the midst of the fellowship of believers and shares in the suffering not only of humans but also of the whole creation. At the same time the Spirit empowers believers to contribute to the liberation of creation.

The churches played a crucial role throughout the years of struggle against apartheid in seeking to address the dispossession of land and other resources. This activity set a precedent for a continued activism to promote the restoration and healing of the land. The churches supported the resistance of communities threatened by dispossession of their land by the apartheid regime. A particular case is the Mogopa community. In cooperation with other organizations, the South African Council of Churches (SACC) succeeded through its ecumenical links in raising such an outcry that the apartheid regime had to refrain in the time that followed from using bulldozers to remove people from their land.

The ecumenically based Covenant Program did a lot to strengthen communities affected by removal measures, by conducting ecumenical worship services, and by linking them with Christian groups in other countries who pray for them. These international ecumenical groups then lobbied their own governments demanding that they intervene.

In 1984 the SACC sent an ecumenical delegation to partner churches to challenge them to draw the attention of their governments to the forced removal policy of the South African government. It also drew the attention of member churches to the challenge they face as owners of land in a country in which the majority of people have been dispossessed of their land. Church leaders were asked to commit themselves to promoting measures that aim at responsible use of the land, which would restore it to its fullness.

After the transition to democracy, churches are faced with the task of raising awareness in the South African public of the obligation to redistribute land and resources, and to heal the land. Even if land is restored to its original owners the question has to be solved as to how it can be used to the benefit of all the stakeholders concerned. Could it be that people in this region—which is considered to be the cradle of humankind—have been endowed with special possibilities to contribute to the rehumanization of humankind and the liberation of creation? This remains an ambiguous question with a fragile footing. It is likely to be answered in the positive only if a far greater level of engagement with the issues of eco-justice follows, based on practical foundations and with material consequences through an integrated, holistic vision of an ecumenical Earth.

ECO-JUSTICE: BLIND SPOT OR NEW VISION?

In 1991 Jacklyn Cock, a South African sociologist, published a report titled, "Towards the Greening of the Church in South Africa."[9] In this report she investigated the environmental awareness of church leaders and official church publications, and resolutions on the environment. She concluded that there is a "blind spot" and a "deep silence" within Christian churches in South Africa on environmental issues.

The reasons given (and defended!) by her informants for the silence of the church on environmental issues tend to confirm the earlier suspicions of Lynn White that Christianity bears a huge burden of guilt for the environmental crisis.[10] These reasons include the following: a preoccupation with human salvation, the doctrine of divine transcendence, the emphasis of the Judeo-Christian tradition on human domination over nature, the dismissal of environmental issues as "new age" concerns, and even the perception that the ecological crisis confirms apocalyptic prophecies in the Bible. By contrast, Cock's interviews with environmental activists in South Africa revealed a striking absence of any religious affiliation!

Since 1991 this discouraging state of affairs has improved somewhat. This is evident from the following five indicators:

- Several Christian communities are beginning to respond to environmental concerns in their local contexts (some case studies are mentioned below).

- Some Christian denominations as well as the South African Council of Churches have recently passed resolutions on the environment, symbolically indicating an awareness of the need to attend to environmental degradation.

- An acknowledgement of environmental agendas is beginning to creep into the dominant discourse and rhetoric of theologians, church leaders, and Christian communities. Still, such discourse is characterized predominantly by notions of conservation and stewardship and not by a concern for eco-justice.

- Several recent theological conferences have specifically addressed environmental issues.[11]

E. Conradie, C. Majiza, J. Cochrane, W. T. Sigabi, V. Molobi, and D. Field

- A growing number of academic articles on Christianity and the environment are being published in theological journals in South Africa.[12]

Despite these indicators, it has to be acknowledged that the church is not (yet) an important role player toward eco-justice in South Africa and that some degree of resistance against environmental agendas remains prevalent. Nevertheless, the potential of local Christian communities to make a significant contribution toward eco-justice should not be underestimated. There are three important sociological reasons for this.[13]

1. According to several important studies, the church is one organization in South Africa that can make a real difference. Local Christian communities enjoy the trust of people at a grassroots level beyond any political party, labor union, or community organization, and, taken together, Christian churches form the largest, most influential, and most active organized civil body in the country with a demographic reach second to none.
2. The church is a unique source of moral leadership. It has often provided people with moral vision and courage who have played a vital role in the country's well-being (for example, people such as Desmond Tutu, Beyers Naude, and Frank Chikane, to name but some of the more prominent figures who have provided a rich legacy of engaged Christianity).
3. The biblical roots of the church and the history of Christianity are full of examples that can be retrieved to support the kind of ecological vision required today to face the ecological crisis.

Churches can respond to the challenge of eco-justice at several levels. Through preaching and teaching, Christian churches can encourage their individual members to make a difference where they live and where they work. Further, and perhaps most important, they can set in place concrete examples of ecologically sensitive communities. This may be done through Christian worship, Christian education, the formation of people of moral vision and character, the creation of a climate in which children can learn to appreciate and love creation, and through sustainable and creative practices on the land and property owned by the church. In these ways Christian communities may become a sign of hope for the world (see the case studies and reflection below).

The churches may also encourage members to cooperate with and support numerous other organizations concerned with the environment (among them, numerous examples of projects initiated by Christians). In this respect, it will not be helpful, nor is it necessary, for Christian churches to duplicate the work of other environmental organizations. Churches should, instead, support the work of these organizations as much as possible, establish the necessary channels and networks of communication, and encourage their members to participate in the work of these organizations. While Christians may ultimately have a distinct ecological vision, they could share the "penultimate" goals of many other environmental activists.

In the past church organizations often felt the need to establish schools, hospitals, centers for the disabled and elderly people, and agricultural projects, wherever such projects were necessary. More recently, several examples of environmental projects initiated by Christian communities have emerged throughout South Africa. They represent a range of theological and practical approaches to engagement by Christians, illustrating:

- prophetic annunciation and denunciation, the verbal addressing of pressing eco-justice issues of a particular context;

- didactic action aimed at educating congregations and the broader society;

- transformative action challenging ecological degradation and building healthy, eco-just community;

- restorative action directed at healing the earth, including efforts to clean up pollution, to remove alien vegetation, and to establish recycling programs; and

- enhancement programs aimed at enabling the earth to be fruitful in a sustainable manner.

CHRISTIAN PROJECTS FOR ECO-JUSTICE

The Khanya Programme is a ministry designed by the Methodist Church of Southern Africa for rural people. This model is "culture-creation-and-people-friendly" and can be pictured as a ship's wheel. The hub of the wheel represents revitalized worship. Emanating from this hub are five spokes representing development programs: permaculture design, livestock distribution, "serv-fari" adventures, appropriate housing, and micro-industries. This model is already assisting the church to steer a new approach in rural ministry. It uses available church land for the benefit of the poor by way of empowering people to overcome unemployment and hunger. It empowers rural communities to prepare for their own future.

The Hub—Revitalized Worship. The concentration here is upon: blessing of the seeds, firstfruits ceremonies, harvest festivals, combined worship with animals, land produce, and people.

In the blessing of the seeds, people are reminded of the time for planting and about our responsibility for our own food production. They take part in this ceremony by bringing their seeds and by reading a pledge that commits them to planting and caring for their gardens. For the firstfruits ceremonies, they offer thanks for God's act of leading our

E. Conradie, C. Majiza, J. Cochrane, W. T. Sigabi, V. Molobi, and D. Field

country away from apartheid while marking our responsibility to shape our country and our future (Deut 26:1–11).

During the harvest festivals people are encouraged to celebrate God's provisions and to commit ourselves again to making use of our gardens. The final liturgical activity consists of combined worship with animals, land produce, and people with the goal of linking worship of God with the lives of the rural people, their animals, and gardens. An integrated worship center is in the pipeline, planned to be a triple, concentric, connected structure with an altar at the center. The first circle is the church for the people; the second is the *kraal* for animals; and the third circle consists of gardens. The idea is to link worship with animals and the garden produce that we live upon. Through these worship ceremonies and festivals, the word of God is linked to the daily lives and experiences of the rural people.

The Five Spokes. (1) Permaculture design: In Genesis 41 we are told that Joseph encouraged the Pharaoh to fend off the pending famine in Egypt by constructing granaries. Through permaculture design, rural people are taught to combat hunger and poverty by planting vegetable- and fruit-producing "garden granaries" around their homes. Permaculture design teaches a sustainable way of integrated food production that cares for God's creation. It also encourages those who are involved in it to teach others design skills. According to Australian specialist Bill Mollison, "Permaculture is a system by which we can exist on earth by using energy that is naturally in flux and relatively harmless and by using food and natural resources that are abundant in such a way that we don't continually destroy life on earth."

(2) Livestock distribution: The Khanya Programme provides poor people with domesticated animals and training in animal care. This is done through close working with Heifer Project South Africa. These animals benefit their owners in a number of ways, providing manure for vegetable gardens and food for their tables. Recipients of animals pledge to "pass on the gift" by giving the first female offspring to another family with no animals.

(3) Serv-fari adventures: Combining the challenge of Christian service with the excitement of an African safari, the serv-fari program offers visitors a rare experience. They work at one of the Methodist Mission Stations in the Eastern Cape while being able to experience the beauty of Africa at nearby game reserves. They also work with the local people at their home places and thus gain firsthand information about and experience of their culture.

(4) Appropriate housing: The Khanya program seeks to equip the people to build affordable yet attractive and durable houses of mud bricks. (Housing is one of the major problems of a liberated South Africa.)

(5) Micro-industries: With the assistance of KSM Milling, rural people are taught baking skills and how to run a micro-bakery. Ovens are made from recycled 40-gallon steel

drums that are provided at cost. Ongoing customer service is also provided. Fresh bread is baked and sold from these micro-bakeries daily. Both operators and the community living nearby benefit from this project.

The Faith and Earthkeeping Project was founded in 1995, functions under the auspices of the World Wide Fund for Nature–South Africa, and is managed as a project within the Research Institute for Theology and Religion at the University of South Africa. Three staff members run the project. The principal aim of the project is to help raise consciousness of, empower, and support communities and individuals at a grassroots level to create and implement their own activities and policies for local, regional, and national environmental protection, conservation, and sustainable resource use, with a view to help improve their quality of life. This is done through the promotion of a religious engagement in ecological and development issues.

Three specific objectives follow from this, that is, research, consciousness raising, and mobilization. Research is primarily done with regard to what has been published locally and abroad in the fields of environmental philosophy, theology, and ethics, in order to promote an understanding of local and global environmental problems and the role that religious practices have played in this regard. It also investigates the role that religious communities can play in creating a lifestyle compatible with the ecological realities of the world in which we live, and it produces relevant educational material for schools, colleges, universities, and at a grassroots community level. Courses in religion and ecology are already offered in various institutions and at a grassroots level to equip and enable people to participate in environmental action.

Conscientiousness raising is a process that aims to develop an awareness of environmental problems and associated threats to local communities. It nurtures a sense of responsibility and urgency with respect to these problems and strengthens social values existing within local communities toward environmental stewardship. It is accomplished through presentations, workshops, projects in communities, discussion groups, retreats, tours, conferences, articles, lectures, the publication of a quarterly newsletter, and a series of degree, certificate, and personal development courses.

Wherever a particular need is identified, the Faith and Earthkeeping Project aims to mobilize people in those communities through their networks to address that specific need in an environmentally sensitive way. Local environmental conditions and priorities are at all times taken into consideration in the planning of projects. The aim is to achieve site-specific conservation objectives and projects. This leads to various kinds of initiatives, for example, tree planting, preservation of water resources, veld management and land use, cleanup operations, urban greening and agriculture, nurseries, and recycling projects.

Overall, this work in seven of the nine provinces in South Africa covers multidimensional urban projects, rural sustainable agriculture projects, and semi-urban agriculture and greening projects.

Abalimi Bezekhaya ("Planters of the Home") is an organization that promotes an urban agriculture and greening program. Its aim is to provide opportunities for the poor, especially women, in the townships of the Cape Flats, to support each other, to grow food for themselves and their families, and to gain self-respect by creating home food security. Low-cost resources and skills training are the means by which this support is offered. More than ten thousand people are already involved as small-scale vegetable farmers in this project. Abalimi Bezekhaya is a non-denominational organization, independently managed and funded, but affiliated with Catholic Welfare and Development.

The associated Cape Flats Tree Project promotes the greening of local neighborhoods, schools, and public parks. It establishes well-maintained models to inspire others to follow. By establishing these models, a greater environmental awareness and understanding of biological organic methods for the healing of both the earth and her people is encouraged.

The Struggle against Toxic Waste Near Philadelphia. In August 1994, a large waste-disposal company explored the possibility of a hazardous-waste dump ("gifgat" or "poison hole") two kilometers from the small rural town of Philadelphia, near Cape Town. The company offered a huge amount to an absentee farmer in the area for a suitable piece of land and promised employment for many workers. The farming community was soon up in arms about the dangers of highly toxic waste infiltrating the groundwater system of the area. One semi-employed farm worker responded to the offer of a well-paying job: "No, not if it will bring death to my children."

The local Dutch Reformed congregation facilitated a series of meetings, and a long and intricate battle ensued. The Department of Environmental Affairs, legal experts, environmental monitoring groups, and the local newspapers soon became involved in the process. The company used everything in its considerable power to enforce its plans—from bribery to clandestine scare tactics. After numerous meetings, telephone calls, peacemaking efforts, and prayers, the owner of the land unexpectedly withdrew his offer to sell the property. David had managed to deter the mighty Goliath.

"Wikkel, Woeker, Werk" Recycling Project. A congregation of the Gereformeerde Kerk in Alberton-West started in 1991 with a project to collect iron, tin, aluminum, glass, paper, and plastics for reuse and recycling. Enormous quantities of material have been collected since then. In this way the congregation helped to clean the environment, manage waste, give young and old in the congregation a sense of purpose, and encourage a spirit of community and cooperation, and this also helped to earn a considerable income for the congregation. It also published two booklets providing advice to other congregations on how to manage such a project.

The Diocese of Umzimvubu in the rural region of the Eastern Cape faces numerous environmental challenges. Many of these are a legacy of the homeland system. The Anglican Diocese of Umzimvubu, under the leadership of Bishop Geoff Davies, has attempted to address some of these issues as well as to raise the church's consciousness of environmental issues. This work is symbolized in the development of the Glenthorn Training Centre outside Kokstad. The Glenthorn farm, the residence of the Bishop of Umzimvubu, is in the process of being transformed. Efforts are being made to reverse the ecological degradation that has taken place. Part of the estate is being set aside and developed as a nature reserve. A training center has been set up where various conferences and training courses are held within the context of an awareness of the goodness of God's creation.

The work of the diocese is not confined to Glenthorn. The diocese appointed an agricultural officer, Bob Thelin, to teach and equip farmers within the diocese to engage in sustainable agriculture. It is envisaged that this project will not only contribute to providing food for many poverty stricken families but will also counter the effects of the ecological degradation of the past. The diocese also acted as a voice for the community in recent debates concerning the development of a toll road and holiday resorts along the Wild Coast. While the project was abandoned for financial reasons, Bishop Davies had become a spokesperson for the opposition to the development because of its environmentally destructive character and its failure to empower and develop the local communities.

A few examples from our Southern African Neighbors of church-based environmental projects were collected during a tour of the region in 1997. They are representative but not in any way comprehensive.

Tree-Planting Eucharists in Zimbabwe, initiated by African Instituted Churches in Zimbabwe, have become quite famous throughout the world. Since the formation in 1988 of ZIRRCON (Zimbabwe Institute of Religious Research and Ecological Conservation), churches in the country have been challenged on the basis of their Christian faith to engage in tree-planting activities. In 1991 the Association of African Earthkeeping Churches

E. Conradie, C. Majiza, J. Cochrane, W. T. Sigabi, V. Molobi, and D. Field

(AAEC) was established. These organizations promote massive programs for afforestation, wildlife conservation, and the protection of water resources. Several nurseries have been established from where trees are planted for fuel-wood, for nutrition (fruit trees), for commercial use and building operations (for example, blue gums), to protect and clothe the soil, and to provide for future generations (for example, red mahogany).

Tree-planting ceremonies are often linked to eucharistic services. These innovative liturgies are introduced to integrate environmental ethics and church praxis. In this way Christians are "proclaiming a widening message of salvation which encompasses all of creation, and in their services of worship they are dancing out a new rhythm which, in its footwork, spells hope for the ravaged earth" (Inus Daneel).

The Heritage of the Mission in Zambia. Since the 1890s mission stations have been built all over Zambia by the Catholic Church, the London Missionary Society, and the Dutch Reformed Church, often owing to requests from the local (Angoni) chiefs. The early missionaries set an example of enhancing the fertility of the land with their water projects, the planting of numerous fruit trees, and various small-scale agricultural projects. These examples still encourage people in local villages to plant and protect trees, to care for the environment, and to create a source of nutritional food in the process.

Projects for Sustainable Agriculture in Zambia. The Christian Council of Zambia is involved in numerous development projects all over Zambia. In some respects, it seems to provide infrastructure and training where the government is unable to fulfill its responsibility. One of these projects is based on a hundred-acre farm in Lusaka West that serves as a model and training center for sustainable agriculture. On this farm a system of rainwater harvesting and the building of small water tanks or wells has been developed. Other activities include fish farming, tree planting, the use of indigenous plants for fertilization and pesticides, etc. This project serves as an example to the government and local villages of what can be done regarding food security and sustainable farming with limited resources.

In Madzimoyo, the Reformed Church in Zambia has established a Church Lay Training Center. The emphasis of this center has shifted from a predominant emphasis on spiritual training to a more holistic approach. One of the projects is a demonstration plant to offer a model of sustainable agriculture to local farmers, to provide for basic nutritional needs (also for the training center), and to earn some additional income through selling the surplus produce. This project encourages the use of natural forms of fertilization and pesticides. This is not only more environmentally sustainable but also reduces expenditure and financial risks.

A Center for Appropriate Technology at Mindolo. The Mindolo Ecumenical Foundation is located at Kitwe, in the Cobberbelt region in Zambia. It provides training programs emphasizing self-employment to students from all over Africa. This includes a Center for Appropriate Technology (with an emphasis on carpentry and metalwork), a Pottery School, and a Small Holdings Farm. The emphasis in these courses falls on community-based self-employment that would be sustainable within a rural context. This requires less sophisticated forms of technology that would not be expensive to acquire or maintain. The farming project enables the Mindolo community to feed itself. In these ways a self-sustaining use of water, energy, and food is encouraged.

Animal Orphanage at Mua in Malawi. Deforestation has taken place on an enormous scale in Malawi. One of the consequences of this process is that the natural habitat of a large number of animals has been destroyed. At the Catholic mission at Mua, near Lake Malawi, an animal orphanage has been started to provide shelter for a wide variety of these homeless animals. This has helped local parishioners to develop a relationship with these animals instead of viewing them only as a source of meat.

Mua is perhaps best known for the Kungoni Arts and Crafts Center, which was developed there under the leadership of the local priest, Father Boucher. This center explores the relationship between Christian symbols and traditional symbols in the Chewa, Yao, and Kungoni cultures. The creation stories in these cultures are told through art in order to draw attention to the intrinsic link between culture and the environment and the threat of human insensitivity to the preservation of natural resources.

ECCLESIOLOGICAL REFLECTIONS

The case studies discussed above remind us that people and earth are thoroughly interrelated, either thriving or being oppressed together. The cases also suggest fresh ways in which a new vision of the church can be concretized within an African context. They help us to visualize what it means for the church to be the eschatological new creation amid the brokenness of the present creation.[14]

In the biblical image of the church as the "first fruits" of the new creation, it is portrayed as the first installment of the renewal of creation. In the exuberant harvest celebrations of numerous sustainable agriculture projects this image receives a new context. The firstfruits of the vegetable gardens are presented before God in gratitude for the harvest

E. Conradie, C. Majiza, J. Cochrane, W. T. Sigabi, V. Molobi, and D. Field

and for a new avenue toward self-sustenance and human dignity. The church thus becomes the firstfruits (and vegetables!) of the new creation.

To identify the church as the firstfruits of the new creation is to confess not only that the redemption that has begun with the church will extend to the entire earth, but also that through the church the earth will be sanctified and cleansed.[15] It is the presence of the Spirit that constitutes the church as the firstfruits of the new creation. "The Spirit is the pledge and guarantee, the 'down payment' of the coming redemption, which is designed to reach the whole creation."[16] The Spirit empowers and equips the church to engage in a praxis of transformation as it looks forward in hope to the redemption of all things. Thus when churches and other Christian groups become involved in the struggle for eco-justice, as is seen in the case studies that have been presented, they are giving expression to the nature of the church as the firstfruits of the new creation.

In 1 Cor. 15:20 Christ is described as the firstborn of a new dispensation. This image may be extrapolated to the church as the body of Christ and the firstborn of the new creation. The image of the firstborn has a rich heritage in the Bible. All believers participate as newborn people in a new creation. Those who have received a cow or a goat through the Khanya program—and thus a new livelihood for themselves—pledge to give the first female offspring to someone else in need. In this way concrete and visible signs of the new creation are established on Earth.

The eschatological vision of Isaiah 11 projects peace between God and animals, and not only between human beings and God. In the envisaged sanctuary of the Khanya program (where a *kraal* for animals forms one of the three circles in the building structure) something of this harmonious coexistence between God, humanity, and the animals becomes visible and concrete. The animals may also come into God's presence.

A further image of some potential is that of the church as a tree of life. Tree planting is a crucial aspect in the work of AZTREC (Association of Zimbabwean Traditional Ecologists), Abalimi Bezekhaya, and numerous others. Especially in rural areas this is a crucial form of earthkeeping in light of the problems of deforestation and the daily task of collecting ever more scarce firewood. In biblical imagery, trees are a symbol of the good life that God intended for creation in the beginning (the tree of life). The tree of life also appears as an eschatological symbol in the last chapter of Revelation, where it bears fruit twelve months of the year and where leaves of the tree bring healing for the nations. This rich imagery is concretized in the praxis of tree-planting eucharists. The church is a tree-planting community and therefore functions as a "tree" (source) of life for the whole creation.

There are numerous other eschatological symbols for the church that may be explored in a similar way (for example, the church as the communion of the saints, the river of life, a banquet for the poor, etc.). The direction is clear. The earthkeeping practices of these

African case studies help to concretize and renew the meaning of these eschatological symbols for the church. They provide an example of what the church as an agent of new creation could look like in the midst of the injustice, deprivation, and degradation of the world in which it is situated.

This notion of the church may be developed further on the basis of the Pauline motif of the church-as-community as the temple or dwelling place of the Spirit (1 Cor. 6:19, Eph. 2:21). Its potential contribution can be seen in the way in which the motif of the temple or sanctuary is used in the Old Testament to integrate issues of worship, ecological fertility, and social justice. A few examples will demonstrate this point.

The church as the sanctuary of the Spirit is the sign and foretaste of the eschatological dwelling of God with creation. It should thus become the place where the people of God experience the presence of God, which transforms them into a community in fellowship with God and in harmony with the rest of creation. This in turn ought to transform their social life and through them bring renewal to creation. Thus when the Khanya Programme and the African Initiated Churches place communal worship at the center of a praxis that fans out to serve the poor and bring healing to the earth, they are giving expression to church as the sanctuary or dwelling place of the Spirit.

A few further aspects emerging from these case studies may be noted: first, the importance of a worshiping community. The model provided by the Khanya Programme and the tree-planting eucharists of the African Initiated Churches in Zimbabwe are particularly suggestive with regard to the centrality of revitalized worship. In both cases responses to issues of eco-justice are integrated into a renewal of worship and thus into the heart of the life of the church. This renewed worship becomes the center and dynamo for the praxis of eco-justice. The exclusive focus on God and God's transcendence in worship functions as a critique of other absolutes and illuminates the contrast to the brokenness, suffering, and degradation in the context surrounding the worshiping community. It also inspires them to engage in small but meaningful actions toward a transformation of these realities.

The church celebrates God's presence in the midst of creation and together with the rest of nature. It therefore examines ways in which the whole of creation can be included in worship, in anticipation of the eschatological worship of "every creature in heaven and on earth and under the earth and in the sea and all that is in them" (Rev. 5:13). This will only take place as the Word is proclaimed in such a way that the people of God are brought into a new awareness of their identity as the community of the new creation."[17]

The worshiping community, however, is also quite specifically an African community. Important aspects of inculturation are evident in our case studies, which are rooted, in various ways, in the African context. Some draw on symbols and ideas from traditional African culture and religion. They are all shaped by the particularities of the sociohistori-

E. Conradie, C. Majiza, J. Cochrane, W. T. Sigabi, V. Molobi, and D. Field

cal context of Africa, particularly South Africa. They are responses to the socioecological realities of Africa. In some cases it is traditional African ideas of a community that includes creation—of worship as a channel of blessing to the earth, and of a religion affecting the whole of life that have pointed to biblical themes neglected in Western theology.

It would be wrong to idealize Africa or the traditional African world-view. They are ambiguous and at times problematic, but they do provide a challenge to the church in the rest of the world to develop contextual responses to the eco-justice crisis, rooted in the biblical witness that challenges the dominant trends in society and the church.

Our case studies also speak of a church that is a community providing a new alternative, embodying something of the new creation as an alternative community whose life and praxis are a sign of the ultimate eschatological community of the new creation. It should thus be a community in which the fractures and divisions of human society are overcome and the relationship between humanity and the rest of creation is healed. This reality is only partially accomplished, because Christians live within a wide variety of intersecting communities that influence and shape their identity and thus the life and praxis of the church.

Finally, we may also speak of the church in these contexts as a penultimate community. It emphasizes both the reality of the transformation that has taken place and the incompleteness of the transformation. The church is a pilgrim community moving toward the new creation, but it is still characterized by much of the brokenness of the old creation. It lives in hope of new creation.

NOTES

1. Justice, sociologically seen, may also be understood as the outcome of the way in which we regulate our lives together in society, through constitutions, agreements, contracts, regulations, and laws. Jürgen Habermas's view comes closest to this definition; compare Jürgen Habermas, *The Theory of Communicative Action*, vol. 1, *Reason and the Rationalization of Society*, trans. Thomas McCarthy (Boston: Beacon Press, 1984).

2. For more information on South African environmentalism and church-based responses, see *A Rainbow over the Land: A South African Guide on the Church and Environmental Justice* (Cape Town: Western Cape Provincial Council of Churches, 2000).

3. *Ikhaya* is an Nguni word whose nuances and depth of meaning are not dissimilar to that of the Greek *oikos*. For a great many black South Africans who experienced, directly or indirectly, the effects of the massive forced migratory labor system that was part of South Africa's history for so many decades (going back to the early part of the century), the issue of a "home place" is profoundly deep. It is also profoundly ecological.

4. As in the internationally publicized case against Thor Chemicals in Kwa-Zulu Natal for mercury poisoning, a case that not only brought to light the hazards to which the factory workers were exposed, but provided evidence of mercury solution run-offs into the dam that serves some hundreds of thousands of black South Africans in a poor, shack settlement area, Inanda.

5. The best analysis of these effects of poverty and their impact on human beings in South Africa remains that of Francis Wilson and Mamphela Ramphele, *Uprooting Poverty: The South African Challenge: Report for the Sec-*

ond Carnegie Inquiry into Poverty and Development in Southern Africa (Cape Town: David Philip, 1989). They focus in particular on fire, water, and earth as key touchstones for measuring poverty.

6. The Gini Coefficient, which measures levels of inequality in a society, shows this contradiction starkly. South Africa, with Brazil, consistently has the highest Gini Coefficient in the world, that is, the greatest inequality among income earners, among economies where data allows adequate measurement.

7. We do not mean that this criterion exhausts the meaning of "eco-justice." Yet it remains crucial, not only in the context of poor or developing countries such as South Africa, but also globally.

8. The Constitution of the Republic of South Africa, 1996 as adopted on May 8, 1996 and amended on October 11, 1996 by the Constitutional Assembly, chapter 2, clause 24.

9. See J. Cock, "Towards the Greening of the Church in South Africa: Some Problems and Possibilities." GEM Discussion document (Johannesburg: Group for Environmental Monitoring, 1991), 1–21. See also J. Cock, "Towards the Greening of the Church in South Africa: Some problems and possibilities," *Missionalia* 20:3 (1992), 174–85.

10. Lynn White, "The Historical Roots of our Ecological Crisis," *Science* 155, 1203–07.

11. Important recent academic conferences include: a 1987 symposium of the Institute for Theological Research (UNISA) called "Are We Killing God's Earth?" the 1991 annual meeting of the Missiological Society of South Africa on "Mission and Ecology," the 1991 annual meeting of the Theological Society of South Africa on JPIC; workshops in January 1997 on "Church and Environment" at the University of Cape Town; and the 1997 meeting of the Theological Society of South Africa on creation theology.

12. For references to most of these, see Ernst Conradie, *Christian Theology and Ecology: An Indexed Bibliography* (Bellville: University of the Western Cape, 1998).

13. See J. Cock, "Towards the Greening of the Church in South Africa: Some Problems and Possibilities," *Missionalia* 20:3 (1992), 174–85; and "The Gold Fields Faith and Earthkeeping Project: A Theological and Ethical Discussion," in *Questions about Life and Morality: Christian Ethics in South Africa Today*, Louise Kretzschmar and Len Hulley, eds. (Pretoria: J.L. van Schaik, 1998).

14. Khanya Programme Newsletter 5:1, 4, Winter 1997. More information is available at www.sa-eastcape.co.za/khanya/.

15. See also Ernst Conradie, *Hope for the Earth: Vistas on a New Century* (Bellville: University of the Western Cape, 2000), chapter 20.

16. Paul S. Minear, *Images of the Church in the New Testament* (Philadelphia: Westminster Press, 1960), proposed that the image of the firstfruits draws together a number of convictions; the following are suggestive for our discussion: (1) God's lordship over all being, (2) the dedication to God of agricultural produce, (3) the appearance and presentation of the first fruit as a pledge of the coming harvest, and (4) the power of the first to sanctify and to cleanse what is to follow.

17. Ibid., 112.

E. Conradie, C. Majiza, J. Cochrane, W. T. Sigabi, V. Molobi, and D. Field

"ON SUSTAINABILITY"

B. D. Sharma

Dhorkatta, Bastar, Madhya Pradesh, India—May 1, 1992. Honorable Members of the Earth Summit, Rio, Brazil: We, the residents of this small village republic, deep in the luxuriant subtropical forests of the Indian sub-continent, wish to invite the attention of your august assembly to some vital issues concerning "the future viability and integrity of the Earth as a hospitable home of human and other forms of life," the main theme of your deliberations at Rio. Before we begin, however, we profoundly compliment you on your bold initiative in holding the Earth Summit. At this end of the globe, in our small forest habitats, we too share your fears for Spaceship Earth.

You should know that in our villages we have stopped, totally, the commercial exploitation of our forests. The government of our country, of course, may not appreciate the spirit behind our decision. They have, in fact, taken it to be defiance of the law. For the forests formally belong to the state. We are, accordingly, treated as intruders in our own abodes where we have been living through the ages. Consequently, according to the law, we cannot even dig for roots and tubers, pluck fruits, or even breathe freely the nectar of earth. We cannot pick bamboo to cover our huts, or cut a pole to mend our plough. "That will destroy the forests," they say. And when magnificent tall trees of all varieties are mercilessly felled and carted away, leaving the earth naked and bare, we are told that is scientific management. That such acts are performed in the service of the nation. The little sparrow and owl meanwhile desperately flutter about searching for a place to perch. But even the hollow trunks of dried trees have not been spared!

This perception of national economy which the state today represents is not the perception of the people for whom forest, land, and water together comprise a primary life-support system. The legal fiction of the state's suzerainty over natural resources was created during the colonial era and has been continued and even reinforced after independence, in the name of development. This is not acceptable to us. It is a denial of the very right to life with dignity—the essence of a free democratic society. We are confident that this perception of ours is shared by the people similarly placed across the globe.

We, therefore, respectfully submit that the honorable representatives of governments at the Earth Summit are not competent to speak for the disinherited among us. Your perceptions and therefore your stand will be that of estate managers keen to exploit resources

Reprinted from *Sanctuary Magazine*, Bombay, India.

on the lines already set by the North. In the past this has invariably implied deprivation of the masses to benefit small elite groups. Frankly, we fear that even though the honorable representatives of Non-Government Organizations (NGOs)—notable exceptions apart— may differ in their views with the state, they are, by and large, bound to share such common basic frameworks as are necessary for their acceptance as partners in the negotiating process. It will not surprise us, therefore, if deliberations at the Summit turn out to be partial. In which case the conclusions will almost certainly be one-sided. This fear is amply borne out in the way the agenda has been framed and also by the Prepcon discussions.

The rich countries are justifiably keen that natural tropical forests be preserved. We too feel the same way, but for different reasons. You require "sinks" for the carbon dioxide emitted by your automobiles which are vital for your "civilization on wheels." We hear about a queer proposal for the declaration of our forests as "global commons." Forests as wilderness would be ideal for this purpose, though you would not mind enjoying usufructory rights. But our paddy fields will be out of place, for they produce CO_2 and thus compete with your cars for that sink. So your basic position as far as we can see is identical to that of our governments. In both cases the people themselves are dispensable. In truth, the two are virtually one as the modern sector of our country, for all practical purposes, is a mere extension of the Western economic system. Of late, in fact, even the thin veneer of national identity has been blown away by the gusty winds of globalization. Discussions at the Summit are bound to be in the nature of bouts for booty rather than for responsible handling of a sacred trust of humankind—generation after generation. But this can be avoided. Please give what follows a patient and considered hearing.

Friends, we are surprised at the casual and parochial vein in which grave issues concerning the survival of life itself have been taken up. If you fail, nothing will remain. If nothing remains, what will be there to share and fight about? But this is the way of all estate managers. They must assume they are always right. Our own experience, a very bitter one, bears this out. In the name of preservation of forests, for instance, our ancestors were mercilessly driven out. And what followed in the name of scientific management was catastrophic. Luxuriant natural forests which sustained us were replaced by teak, which does not even provide us shade in summer. Then came eucalyptus under which not even grass can grow! After that, it was the turn of vast plantations of pine, which would burn like a torch in high summer. But each of these decisions was proclaimed as *the* right way. And to question such projects was blasphemous. Tragically for us, the estate-managers never recognized that the true worth of the magnificent sal, *Shorea robusta*, was far, far greater than the cash recovered from a dead log. The sal is *Kalpavriksha*, the tree that fulfills all desires. Once sal vanished from our forests the struggle of forest dwellers became reduced to physical survival—the evening meal. You see the irony. You worry about how your cars and air-conditioners can continue to operate for a hundred, or a thousand years. Our concern is the next meal that has to be procured at any cost. How can these two perceptions ever meet unless *you* see things from our end of the world and set your own perspectives in order. Friends, can you really not see how far such trivial priorities as air-conditioning and aerosol, with all they represent, have pushed the earth? Yet, you continue to talk about business as usual, of development through your lens, fueled by the same ecological system which has pushed us to the brink of an ecological abyss. Worse, you pose poverty as the worst pollutant and dedicate most of your agenda to eradicating this "environmental hazard."

On the face of it your endeavor might well sound laudable, but consider the hackneyed prescriptions you have chosen to tackle poverty—management of capital, technology, and resource flows. There are two reasons why this framework does not sit well with us. Nor, incidentally, can it help you in the long run. Let's first take the economic frame. Be clear that the phenomenon you are talking about has little to do with poverty. The issue is one of deprivation and denial. You seem ignorant of the fact that we have been robbed of not only our resources, but the great wealth of our life-sustaining skills acquired over millennia. Seen from your horizon, ordinary people are ignorant. Even despised.

Why are we despised? Because we live closer to nature, we do not don many clothes, nor do we have much use for your kind of energy options. We are, therefore, "poor" in your book. And since you, with missionary zeal, wish to "eradicate poverty" we must be enabled to acquire more commodities, consume more. Is this not why the czars of your ecological system incessantly bombard us with visuals of the glittering life? Making our simple ways look ridiculous by contrast to your own may well whip up new demands and expand your markets, but can you seriously suggest this to be the way to eradicate poverty? Such approaches have been directly responsible for the phenomenal inequality we see around us today. These are also the very reasons that the ecology of vast portions of the globe has been so terribly fractured. Yet, the estate managers of the world continue to wrangle for inflated entitlements and deflated obligations, indulging in reckless brinkmanship in dealing with the commons.

This, friends, is the law of the market. Little wonder that the focus of the Earth Summit has already shifted from land, water, and air, to the illogical issue of money! This drift, to our minds, is contemptible.

Those who have crossed the Rubicon of consumerism must point out at this stage that the Summit debate seems poised to miss the main point. You are no doubt talking about the quality of life, but *within* the consumerist paradigm of development and bounded inescapably by an economic framework. Other aspects of life have not even been brought up. We do not blame you for this lapse, for as leaders of the "modern" economic world, you have no experience of the "real life." In a bid to make the system produce more, for that is what decides its competitiveness in the market and its ranking in the world, all that is human is squeezed out, bit by tiny bit. Human concerns and relationships are dispensable, or at best market-convertible. Rushing to the faraway home to be by the side of an ailing mother, leaving the working machine unattended, is not rational. "Do not get emotional, you are not a doctor, send money instead," counsels the manager, worried by the high incidence of absenteeism in his production unit. To us this is the advice of an eccentric. To you it is the cold logic of your economic system. The machine *must* be used round the clock or else you lose your competitive edge. And people? They are but extensions of the machine! For them, even sleeping at night represents lost opportunities! But you have designed ways for the rattled living robot to enjoy "perfect equanimity." A variety of vintage spirits, or still more modern aids such as heroin, cocaine, and LSD are on hand. At the end of the day, the market determines the cost of life and living.

Look again at your world. The community has already been sacrificed on the altar of productivity. The family now is the last impediment in the way of achieving "perfect rationality" and highest levels of productivity. But even here solutions were at hand. Within the family you dispensed with the burden of dead wood by packing your elders, where necessary, to senior citizen's homes. Now only the nucleus of husband-wife remains, at best. But this too appears to be haunted. Why should a man and a woman remain tied by emotional bonds for life? They too must subjugate themselves to the dictates of the economic system, each one serving the system at points most suited to it. Thus, marriage must break. Living together is good enough for sex. And sex, of course, can be rationally negotiated in a free market. The recent trend towards cynicism about motherhood and about women having eternally to carry the cross of procreation is really the culmination of the challenge of reason against human emotion. Such are the compulsions of perfectly rational beings.

Can you recognize the ugly, twisted logic of your economic system? Perhaps it is too much to ask. For you are clearly dazzled by its benign aura. You have surrounded yourselves and studded your abodes with all sorts of gadgets—surrogates for human concerns, relationships, and emotions. Even your moments of leisure, acquired at heavy financial costs, are determined once again by the market. You are no longer able even to laugh and dream unaided! Having lobotomized the soul from your neighborhoods you now take refuge in the mirage of telecommunications and rapid transport to create the illusion of "one earth."

But let us, for the moment, set aside human concerns and relations. Instead, let us consider the implications of this market-substitution which the economic system is coercing the rest of us to emulate as a lifestyle model. Given the proclamations of your scientists and even some of your world leaders, you obviously admit that we are poised on the brink— even before one in five people (who command four-fifths of the earth's resources) have been able to attain the desired standard of life. How much further must we continue to tread the same lethal path before the final collapse? This is the question the Earth Summit must ponder. Can you really not see the catastrophe you have set into motion? Having "coopted" your own elite, you state that poverty alleviation is now your objective. This is the mirage we are condemned to chasing in vain, endlessly. Meanwhile you content yourself in tinkering with buttons, watching us follow in your footsteps even as a void engulfs us and our communities and families shatter. The writing is on the wall. The omnipotent, omnipresent market is turning living, breathing men and women into commodities-in-trade.

Honorable members of the Summit: it is in the face of this deluge that we earnestly call upon you to put your agenda, indeed your houses, in order. The development and associated lifestyles you chase are a hallucination. There is nothing sustainable about your ambitions. Your blueprint of sustainability will not even nourish a tiny section of humankind. Ironically, even as the bulk of humanity suffers hitherto unthinkable indignities and hardships, even the few who do manage to monopolize resources will be condemned to a veritable hell, as they stand bereft of the small innocent pleasures of life, the security and the warmth of their community, and the assurance of a family bond.

The basic question then, even before those who represent privileged groups at the Summit, is how long and how far can you afford to ignore and barter away the human face of existence. Such basic human values cannot be taught through lectures and books, nor can they be nurtured in formal systems which at best treat them as naive and irrelevant aspirations. Such values can only be imbibed in human institutions—small face-to-face communities and families where they are assiduously practiced and lovingly cultivated. We must caution you that this great heritage of mankind can be lost to posterity even if one generation trips and thus causes the chain to be broken. Are we prepared for that cataclysm?

Time is of the essence, friends. We, the disinherited of the earth, particularly in India, wish to make our position clear. The tide of "development" which started rising with the industrial revolution and gained huge momentum during the colonial phase of human history, has now run its full course. The allocation of benefits and costs of this development have been oppressively unfair and iniquitous. The more profitable and amenable activities at every stage have been reserved for themselves by the captains of development—the *Brahmins* (the highest caste) of the new order. The drudgery and the sloth was passed over to the *shudras* (outcasts) comprising the rest. Thus, the creation of a Third World was a precondition of your model. And a Fourth World is in the making, now that the Third World countries have accepted your prescription for their economies. This is the cold logic that must sit in the many minds that deliberate ways and means to save the world. The tide, thus, has reached the furthest shore and has begun to turn menacingly inward. The machine must now feed on itself.

We in Dhorkatta, Bastar, Madhya Pradesh, India are a fragment of this newly created Fourth World. As a logical unfolding of your paradigm, the modern economy of our country, a mere extension of the Western system, has misappropriated our resources. On the principle that you cannot make an omelet without cracking an egg, our little world

B. D. Sharma   685

must disintegrate. It cannot be allowed, of course, to stake any claim to the fruit enjoyed by the estate managers. We either get absorbed in the more powerful system, to the extent possible, or get exhumed and expelled. This logic, if accepted, will not remain circumscribed to one area like ours. It will inform all the disinherited of the Third World and also the deprived of the First and the Second Worlds. The prevailing conditions in the erstwhile Eastern Block and among the non-white minorities in the U.S. and Europe are clear pointers in this direction.

We cannot possibly accept these inevitable consequences of your paradigm as our ordained fate. We do not believe in any iron laws of history, or of economics—free, planned, or mixed in any hue. Man is the maker of history and can chart his own path. Accordingly, after careful consideration, we have rejected outright your paradigm, and its associated lifestyle. It is not only socially unjust, but ecologically unsustainable, besides being devoid of human concerns.

A new paradigm—ecologically viable, socially equitable, and rich in human content—is the historical need of our time. You, at the Summit, have missed the human element totally and considered the social issue only superficially. The outcome of your deliberations will therefore be biased and slanted—perversions which we will have to carefully guard ourselves against. In rejecting your paradigm and raising these issues about the Summit, we are not alone. We echo the deepest feelings of ordinary people across the globe. In doing so, we unwittingly accept a historic role for ourselves, which so far you have refused even to consider. But we are, for all the reasons enumerated above, perhaps better placed in this regard, for we in our system still rank human concerns high. As you can see we have questioned and rejected some of the most fundamental elements of your paradigm. The quality of life cannot be measured by how much we consume or how much energy we utilize. It must, instead, be defined in terms of personal accomplishment of individuals, and the richness of interpersonal relationships within the family and community. A precondition naturally is the fulfillment of basic physical needs for a reasonable living. Accepting this should be the first decisive step towards dismantling the unbearable burden created in the name of so-called development at the cost of earth's fragile ecology. Obviously, human concerns and relationships are non-negotiable. The scope of market, on the other hand, must be circumscribed to the bare minimum. Some areas of life such as enjoyment of leisure must be out of bounds for market, in the interest of a sane society recreating conditions for absorbing dialogue and spontaneous laughter.

Contrary to what the ignorant believe of us, we heartily celebrate advances in science and the expanding horizons of man's universe. But we reject technological regimes built up with an eye on centralization of economic and political power. Technology in such hands has "deskilled" humans and pushed us from the center to the periphery of the stage. While drudgery can and should be erased through harnessing of technology, it must be remembered that honest physical labor is an essential condition of human life and happiness. In this scheme of things production must be non-centralized in units of human dimension, keeping the master-labor relations to the minimum and slashing heavily on trade, advertisements, and transport. These are the devices of distribution wielded by the haves, whose burden our earth can no longer carry. These are clearly wasteful luxuries created as a sequel to a massive usurpation spree. We reject the production system which has depleted even our non-renewable capital resource-base (subsoil water) for frivolous, temporary gains. By casting this heavy burden on ecology such resources have been rendered out of the reach of ordinary people, forever. Thus, not only do we reject the perceptions and the paradigm, but also the legal framework of the estate-managers which seeks to legitimatize wanton destruction of natural resources and prey even on tomorrow's children of nature.

It should be clear that we are not for the negation of life and progress. What we insist on is that development must have a human face, or else it is tantamount to destruction. Towards this end we wish to announce that a beginning has already been made here in our small corner of the globe. We are clear about our goals, our rights, and our responsibilities. We are establishing village republics (*Nate-na-raj*) in the true spirit of democracy, equity, and fraternity following Gandhian tenets to the extent possible. Our village-republics are not islands in the wilderness, but they encompass even the smallest amongst the ever-expanding circles of the human canvass. We believe that life and vivacity in its totality can be perceived, experienced, and realized only in the microcosms of community and family. It is the community and community alone—not the formal state—which can save the earth for humankind and other forms of life.

So, friends, we have taken upon ourselves a great challenge, with humility yet fully cognizant of the historic role we are playing in one of the most bewildering eras of history. We do not await the advent of a messiah or the conclusion of a revolution—white or red—to move ahead and achieve our goal. The radical structural change associated with the formation of village-republics is a concomitant of the people's struggle. A corollary objective is to assert their will and right of self-governance in the short run and work for a new world order based on equity, fraternity, and democratic values in the long run.

We may, of course, appear momentarily to be moving against the current of history. But that is what it is. We have made a conscious choice that way. But it should be noted, and noted well, that the tide has changed its course. We, therefore, call upon the nations of the world to acknowledge this change, break from the past, and chart out a new path at the Summit for the establishment of a more humane, sustainable, and equitable world.

"GLOBALIZATION AND THE PERENNIAL QUESTION OF JUSTICE"

Mary John Mananzan

INTRODUCTION

After reflecting on the question posed by the editor of this *Festschrift*, "What is the most important spiritual question of our time?" I have come to the conclusion that it still is the question of justice. I also find it fitting to write on this topic because this *Festschrift* is in honor of a woman passionately committed to justice. For a long time justice has been the preoccupation of the church and yet it is as urgent now as ever before. In our times this question of justice is, for me, tied up with a global phenomenon—globalization. In this essay I propose to clarify this elusive term, discuss its impact on the peoples of the third world, especially Asia, particularly the Philippines. I would then make some theological and ethical conclusions and see its impact on one's spirituality.

WHAT IS GLOBALIZATION?

It is very necessary to say exactly what we mean by the word "globalization," because so many things are meant by it. It can mean the worldwide development of technology that makes the world into the so-called global village. As such, we have nothing against this development. Some people will take it to mean the networking going on internationally in all fields, and if this is all that is meant, we also have nothing against it, because true international solidarity cannot but be positive. I would like to define it, however, in the context in which it arose—in its economic *Sitz im Leben*. In the '60s and '70s activists (including me) went into the streets to denounce "foreign control of the economy," "economic imperialism," and so on. Today, these words have become unpopular and yet the reality they describe is still very much with us but decked with the euphemistic word "globalization." So generically, globalization means the integration of the economies of the world into the liberal market economy of the West controlled by the G8. Here are some of its main features:

Reprinted with permission from *Spiritual Questions for the Twenty-First Century: Essays in Honor of Joan D. Chittister*, Mary Hembrow Snyder, ed. (Orbis Books, 2001).

1. *Borderless economy.* It advocates the elimination of protective tariffs and gives free play to the market.

2. *Import liberalization.* This is a corollary of the borderless economy. Goods from all other countries can enter our country. This may seduce us as consumers to think that it is good because then we have many choices and the competition can bring down the prices. But this will also kill local industries, and when they are killed we will be dependent for our basic needs on other countries and this certainly will not ensure, for example, food security. This is not sustainable consumption.

3. *Free play of the market.* This advocates less control from the state and making the market forces the main criteria of activities. This will make profit and market demand the supreme values. Everything else will be sacrificed to these—consumers, labor, and so on. This does away with social and ethical concerns.

4. *Privatization.* All productive enterprises will be put into private hands, and in our case, mostly foreign hands. This effectively entrenches the foreign control of our economy (Calabarzone controlled by Taiwanese, Lotto by Malaysians, textiles by Germans, and so on). This will also put basic services, such as energy, into private hands, whose motive is profit. Therefore, subsidies will have to be taken away and prices of basic services will soar.

5. *Financial capitalism.* Today, there is actually not much productivity going on in our country. What is going on is financial speculation. So even production is done not to serve needs but for speculation. The only two productions happening are textiles and electronics, but these depend upon imports for 80 percent of their components.

The result of this is an export-oriented, import-dependent, foreign-investment-controlled, and debt-ridden economy.

THE IMPACT OF GLOBALIZATION ON PEOPLES

Globalization is not a new phenomenon. As mentioned above, it is the euphemistic term for that we have fought against for many years: the foreign control of our economy—in short, economic imperialism. But the new word is seductive because it promises so many things that would make a heaven on earth. And yet, when we look at the actual consequences of globalization, it is just the opposite.

Consider the crisis we are suffering in Asia. Barely five years ago Asian countries were supposed to be "tigers" and "cubs." Now, no Asian country, not even Japan, is spared a currency crisis, stock market crisis, food crisis, energy crisis, employment crisis, and so on.

Janet Bruin aptly observes,

Instead of spreading wealth around, "globalization" and current macro-economic policies in both North and South are concentrating wealth in fewer hands. Unemployment and the number of people living in poverty are increasing in many countries. Workers are being forced into low paying jobs and women are being forced into unsafe workplaces, into the unprotected informal economy where social security and other benefits do not apply, or into prostitution. Children are forced to leave school for work in carpet factories, farms or in the streets to help support their families, and people are forced to leave their countries in search of paid labor elsewhere, provoking an international backlash against immigrants as economic and security threats. Both migration and anti-immigrant xenophobia are expected to intensify as population pressures, unemployment, and economic disparities between countries become ever more acute.[1]

This has lately been confirmed by the United Nations Development Program (UNDP), which has come up with a comprehensive report involving many countries of the third world, pointing to one uncontested fact: globalization has widened the gap between the rich and the poor.[2]

In the Philippines and in Asia conversion of fertile lands into golf courses and industrial complexes has reduced the land available for the cultivation of staple food. Some cultivated lands are reserved for cash crops like asparagus and cut flowers. This not only reduces lands available for cultivation of staple food for local consumption, but also causes adverse effects on soil fertility because of the massive use of fertilizers and pesticides. The Philippines now imports rice, whereas it provided that staple sufficiently for itself in the past. Lack of subsidy and technological help to farmers renders agriculture a nonsustainable activity and reduces farmers to amassing continuous debt. The proliferation of prawn farms and fishing pens for growing prawns and fish for export has allotted marine resources, which form part of the peoples' daily fare, to the export business.

Deregulation of the oil companies has caused them to raise the price of oil arbitrarily and, in a domino effect, that of all basic commodities. All this, plus the recent devaluation of the Philippine peso, has caused housewives to stretch their marketing money to the breaking point. Import liberalization tries to convince the consumer that this would mean more choices and cheaper prices in competition. But this eventually destroys local industries and local businesses, leading to the loss of food security because the consumers become dependent on foreign producers. The Chernobyl incident underlined the dependence of a lot of countries with regard to dairy products.

The Center for Women Resources study on the General Agreement of Tariffs and Trade (GATT) concludes,

> As our economy is oriented more and more towards producing "cash crops" and depending more and more on imports for basic staples such as rice and corn, sources of our daily food consumption become unstable, putting the very survival of the Filipinos at stake.[3]

So are we saying that no one is benefiting from globalization? Of course not! But the question is, Who benefits from it? The upper 2 percent who have capital. Maybe it trickles down to the 10 percent who are used in the management of the enterprises. And basic sectors are not only excluded from the gains of the economic activities going under globalization, but are also negatively affected by it. Homes of urban poor were violently demolished during the last Asia-Pacific Economic Cooperation (APEC) meeting hosted by the Philippines. Due to land conversions, thousands of Filipino farmers have been dispersed and have lost the lands they till. Indigenous people are suffering the loss of their ancestral lands due to mining. Further, the strip mining has polluted their rivers and seas, depriving them of still another source of living. Workers who are supposed to be the main beneficiaries of industrialization are now suffering the loss of job security because of contractual labor practices. And in all these sectors, women are the most adversely affected because of the feminization of poverty.

Globalization has no respect for the uniqueness of peoples' culture. It has successfully "macdonalized" or "cocalized" the world. Urban youth culture is a monoculture of discos, malls, and jeans. Indigenous culture is exploited and bastardized for tourists. So the effect of globalization is not only on our economic life but also on our culture. It also has political implications because the decision makers of international agencies like the IMF-WB, WTO, and GATT are not elected by people, yet their decisions adversely affect the lives of so many. Nicanor Perlas writes, "The posture of GATT is totalitarian and radically arrayed against any notion of sovereignty and self-determination."[4]

THEOLOGICAL AND ETHICAL REFLECTIONS

When one looks at the effects of globalization on the majority of excluded peoples, one can conclude that it has unleashed forces of death. Pope John Paul II writes in *Solicitudo Rei Socialis*,

> In today's world, including the world of economics, the prevailing picture is one destined to lead us more quickly toward death rather than one of concern for true development which would lead all toward a "more human world" as envisaged by the encyclical *Populorum Progressio*.[5]

The Ecumenical Association of Third World Theologians (EATWOT) has drawn this same conclusion. Thus, it has made globalization its main concern in its last general assembly in December 1996 in Tagaytay, Philippines, with its theme "Search for a New Just World Order: Challenges to Theology." Moreover, it has adopted as its theological theme for the next five years, "Towards a Fullness of Life: Theology in the Context of Globalization."

In all the national, continental, and intercontinental meetings of EATWOT the members are urged to continue the theological reflection begun in the general assembly. In some theological reflections EATWOT members see globalization as a sort of "new religion." It has its God: profit and money. It has its high priests: GATT, WTO, IMF-WB. It has its doctrines and dogmas: import liberalization, deregulation, and so on. It has its temples: the super megamalls. It has its victims on the altar of sacrifice: the majority of the world—the excluded and marginalized poor.

In the face of globalization EATWOT sees the need for a prophetic theology

> that will critique prince and priest, market and mammon, multinationals and war merchants and all hegemony and all plunder of the poor. It will call into question the silence of religions and churches as children die of hunger in Iraq, in Orissa, due to imperialist policies of superpowers or local magnates. It will call into question the centuries old oppression of women at home and in society. And it will seek to serve people's dreams and struggles for a beautiful tomorrow.[6]

The values of globalization are also ethically questionable. Its foremost value of profit and market is definitely an example of "serving mammon." It has commodified people, treating workers as merely factors in production. This is shown by its policies of "flexibilization of labor" and "labor-only contracting." Women and children are likewise commodities to be used in child labor or in sex trafficking. Its practice of cutthroat competition, which even prevents governments from protecting their fledgling industries, is an economic survival of the fittest. This leads to the economic dictatorship of the rich and powerful, who become even richer and more powerful. For globalization, people such as the urban poor, who do not have capital or skills to be in the playing field, are totally expendable. Globalization promotes consumerism by its aggressive advertising techniques and by luring consumers with megamalls and supermarkets. It convinces people that their wants are needs and that they have the right to buy anything as long as they can afford it. This leads to surplus production, which has not only depleted our irreplaceable natural resources, but also has caused ecological disasters such as deforestation, pollution, thinning of the ozone layer, global warming, and, with these, the consequent "natural" calamities.

One ethically questionable issue that is connected with globalization is biotechnology or genetic engineering. Nicanor Perlas describes it this way:

> This science and technology package is based on the belief that there is nothing sacred in life, that life is simply a bunch of chemicals (DNA and related compounds) and their interactions and that all traits—from chemical properties, outer appearance, and behaviour—can be understood and reconstructed on the basis of studies of the DNA and its manipulation. Human beings could now play God, disassembling, decoding, recombining all life forms on the planet.[7]

At present, tens of thousands of genetic experimentations are going on. Life forms have been patented, animals have been cloned, and both open the ominous possibility of cloning human beings. With GATT, activities of biopirates have been legitimized. Multinational companies go all over the world collecting precious plants and animal species, interfere with their genetic makeup, and patent them to the detriment of the peoples who had been using these for centuries for their livelihood. For the sake of profit, seeds are tampered with so that they cannot reproduce, forcing farmers to buy more seeds. Furthermore, science and technology are producing food products that are harmful, such as irradiated food, pesticide-laden products, and biotech food. Indeed, never before has the assault to life been as massive as in our times. Economics cannot continue to be immune from moral and ethical scrutiny. The tremendous injustice, exclusion of peoples, and assault to life resulting from globalization must be morally judged and condemned. The opposite values of sharing, service, compassion, equity, interdependence, and solidarity must be reemphasized.

SPIRITUALITY FOR OUR TIMES

In order to face the challenges of today, we need to develop a spirituality attuned to our times. There are several characteristics of this spirituality.

1. It is a *prophetic spirituality*. It is a spirituality that is convinced of the good news it has to announce and has the courage to denounce what it considers as the bad news. There are many people who are more convinced that God wants us to suffer than that God wants us to be happy. We somehow have to convey to people that God wants them to be truly happy in an integral way, meaning body and soul. When we see obstacles to this integral salvation of peoples, we must not hesitate to take a stand, even if this would mean risks or inconveniences for us. In other words, it is a committed spirituality. In our times it is a commitment to economic justice, gender and racial equality, and ecological activism.

2. It is an *integral spirituality*. Just as we proclaim an integral salvation, we also have to develop an integral spirituality that transcends dichotomies such as body-soul, sacred-profane, contemplation-action, heaven-earth, and so on. We need to integrate our relationships with God, with ourselves, with others, and with the planet. It is inclusive and resists exclusion of peoples for any reason, be it class, race, gender, or any other.

3. It is a spirituality that is characterized by *simplicity of lifestyle*. In contrast to consumerism, it strives to do without superfluities, mindful that the earth's resources are limited and that these have to be shared by all.

4. It is an *empowering spirituality*. It is self-affirming, aware, and grateful for God's gifts to us giving us a healthy self-esteem. It is also mutually empowering, affirming other people and facilitating their blossoming.

5. It is a *healing spirituality*. It is a process of healing one's own wounds and using one's own experiences to heal others.

6. It is a *contemplative spirituality*. It emphasizes moments of reflection, meditation, and contemplation—being present to the Presence, a constant awareness of the absolute within us, who is the inexhaustible source of joy, love, and energy and makes us committed but carefree.

7. It is an *Easter spirituality*. It is a spirituality that transcends Good Friday, that is infected with the fearless joy of Easter. It resists the forces of death and promotes the enhancement of life. It feasts more than it fasts. It is not so much control as surrender. It is not cold asceticism but a celebration of life.

CONCLUSION

The need is urgent to restore justice and harmony in human relationships at all levels and the relationship of human beings to the whole of creation. The continuing resistance of peoples' organizations against the forces of death in our society is a sign of hope. Christians have options. They can be obstacles to these efforts, bystanders, and let history move without them. Or, they can accompany the struggling peoples on their journey to the new Jerusalem, and together with them build a new heaven and a new earth.

NOTES

1. Janet Bruin, *Root Causes of the Global Crisis* (Manila: Institute of Political Economy, 1996), 11.

2. *Human Development Report* (New York and Oxford: Oxford University Press.

3. "The GATT," in *Piglas Diwa* (Manila: Center for Women Resources, 1995), 8.

4. Nicanor Perlas, *Elite Globalization and the Attack on Christianity* (Quezon City, Philippines: Center for Alternative Development Initiatives, 1998), 44.

5. Pope John Paul II, *Solicitudo Rei Socialis* (Rome: Vatican Press, 1987), 40.

6. K. C. Abraham, ed., *Search for a New Just World Order: Challenges to Theology* (Bangalore, India: Voices Publication of EATWOT), 207.

7. Perlas, *Elite Globalization*, 31.

Mary John Mananzan

"SACRED RIVERS, SACRED DAMS: COMPETING VISIONS OF SOCIAL JUSTICE AND SUSTAINABLE DEVELOPMENT ALONG THE NARMADA"

William F. Fisher

In the interactions among religion, ecology, and politics, politics usually prevails. This paper explores the evocations of varying visions of the Narmada River by those involved in the struggle over the damming of the Narmada River. Visions of the Narmada as goddess, homeland, or development resource punctuate the debate over the Narmada and often stand in for more complex and conflicting moral arguments about social justice and sustainable development. Through the cryptic use of symbols and simplified dichotomies, developmental, environmental, and moral concerns become politicized and fundamental differences obscured. The concern here is with where, how, and why key symbols of cultural and religious values enter into development discourse and what happens when they do.

This discussion takes heed of and evolves through the consideration of two related aspects of the Narmada debate. The first is that the Narmada controversy involves a highly complex set of issues and a multiplicity of stakeholders (including residents of the Narmada valley, residents in the command area, Gujarat development planners and politicians, various antidam activists in India, and "northern" environmentalists). Two issues here are pertinent: first, that these different stakeholders often have widely divergent perceptions of development, "facts," problems and solutions, and costs and benefits; and, second, that not all stakeholders are equally tolerant of other perspectives.

The second consideration is the degree to which these divergent positions, values, and beliefs are simplified, dichotomized, misrepresented, or otherwise obscured in the struggle over Narmada. This emerges and becomes manifest in a variety of ways. One of the most important is through the use of the same rhetoric and claims to some of the same power-

Reprinted from *Hinduism and Ecology: The Intersection of Earth, Sky, and Water*, ed. Christopher Key Chapple and Mary Evelyn Tucker (Cambridge, Mass.: Center for the Study of World Religions, Harvard Divinity School, 2000), pp. 401–421, reprinted by permission. Copyright © The President and Fellows of Harvard College, 2000.

ful symbols, a process which serves to obscure a fundamental clash of worldviews. These clashing worldviews each derive from a different set of assumptions about the good life and the relationship of humans to nature. Insofar as the appropriateness of a solution depends in large part on how a problem is defined, the power to shape the definition of the problem—as one of poverty, or as a shortage of resources, or as the need to maximize resource use for modern development—offers the opportunity to designate and describe appropriate "solutions." Sorting out the differing worldviews enmeshed in shared rhetoric and symbols reveals and illustrates the often inconspicuous but nevertheless treacherous power of rhetoric. Development actions and language have a complex relationship as multiple stakeholders jockeying for political advantage constantly recast and redescribe ends and means in response to critical feedback from a range of different influential audiences. In development debates, just as in others, language has the potential either to open up possibilities of thought or to obscure, either to clarify or to gloss over fundamental differences, either to generate new concepts or to coopt ideas and values (and thereby either transform or defang them).

The creative use of language is particularly apparent in highly emotional and deeply politicized debates like that over the damming of the Narmada. Rivers evoke deep and yet varying responses from different constituencies. As in this case, they may be valued as living goddesses, protected as complex habitats, or coveted as a store of resources for the vast quantity of "wasted" water running untapped to the sea. In the Narmada case, these contrasting visions serve a range of conflicting moral arguments for social justice and sustainable development. But not all of these visions have received equal attention in the public debates about Narmada. Least heard are the views and values of local people resident along the stretch of the Narmada valley destined to be inundated by the waters of the Sardar Sarovar reservoir. Instead, idealized versions of *âdivâsi* and tribal beliefs can be found appropriated into both development and environmentalist positions.

BACKGROUND: WHAT'S AT STAKE?

Narmada has become a familiar case to those concerned with either environmental or South Asia issues.[1] The damming of the Narmada River in western India is an issue where the perceived conflicts between economic development and environmental protection have become the battleground of other conflicts over human rights, decision-making processes, and development objectives. By articulating issues that have a significance far beyond the particular details of the Sardar Sarovar Project, a domestic construction project along a remote sector of an Indian river has become a highly emotional symbol at the center of an international controversy.

William F. Fisher

Tapping the resources of the Narmada, the largest westward flowing river in India, and one of the most sacred rivers in India, has been the dream of political leaders and development planners for decades. The Narmada River, 1,312 kilometers in length, rises in the state of Madhya Pradesh in central India and passes through the states of Maharashtra and Gujarat on its way to the Gulf of Khambhat. The Narmada drainage basin covers 98,796 square kilometers, with an estimated population of 22 million people. Exploiting the water resources of the river is complicated by the fact that 90 percent of the Narmada's flow occurs during the three months of monsoon rains, from June through September. The river is the subject of the largest river development scheme in the world that would include, if it were to be completed, 30 major, 135 medium, and about 3,000 minor dam projects in the Narmada River valley.[2]

The terminal dam of this project, Sardar Sarovar, stands almost complete. It includes a dam, a riverbed powerhouse and transmission lines, a main canal, a canal powerhouse, and a 75,000-kilometers-long irrigation network which will occupy 80,000 hectares of land. The water is to be collected in a storage reservoir which will resemble a narrow lake extending more than 200 kilometers upstream. At its full reservoir level of 455 feet, the reservoir will submerge 37,000 hectares of land and will adversely affect at least 100,000 people in 245 villages. A larger number of farmers, as many as 140,000, will lose land to the canal and irrigation systems.

Financing to initiate the current project was secured in 1985 when the World Bank entered into credit and loan agreements with the government of India, providing US$ 450 million for the construction of the dam. Construction began in earnest in 1987. Its supporters claim that it is the only viable means of delivering critically needed irrigation water to drought-prone areas of northwestern Gujarat and Rajasthan and electrical power and drinking water to thousands of other rural and urban communities in Gujarat.

From the beginning, the project has been the subject of local, national, and international opposition that has criticized it on environmental, technical, and humanitarian grounds.[3] Critics of the project cite its potentially negative environmental and social impacts, particularly the relocation of tens of thousands of people, the majority of them members of lower socioeconomic communities. In the past decade, social action groups representing rural communities along the Narmada and independent nongovernmental organizations have lobbied prime ministers of India, chief ministers of the Indian states of Gujarat, Maharashtra, and Madhya Pradesh, state and national bureaucrats, the Japanese government, the World Bank, and governments funding the Bank.[4]

On 14 March 1991, in response to growing criticism of the project and under pressure from the global campaign of international NGOs against the project, the president of the World Bank commissioned an unprecedented independent review of the Sardar Sarovar

Project. The review of environmental impacts and resettlement and rehabilitation began in September 1991. Its final report, submitted in June 1992, was very critical of the World Bank's involvement in the project. It stated:

> We think the Sardar Sarovar Projects as they stand are flawed, that resettlement and rehabilitation of all those displaced by the Projects is not possible under prevailing circumstances, and that the environmental impacts of the Projects have not been properly considered or adequately addressed. Moreover, we believe that the Bank shares responsibility with the borrower for the situation that has developed.[5]

World Bank funding of the project ended in March 1993, but the government continued to build the dam and opponents continued to oppose their efforts. As of late 1998, despite lawsuits, coordinated lobbying, an unprecedented independent review of a World Bank project, the Indian rejection of World Bank funding for the project, a negative review by an Indian review team, and a high-profile protest movement characterized by marches, rallies, and hunger strikes, "Narmada" remained an unfinished story, its outcome not yet resolved. When World Bank funding for the project ceased in March 1993, the government of Gujarat proceeded with the project on its own while the opposition pursued its case through the courts. The project continues to be controversial: the dam is near completion but approval to proceed remains stalled in the Supreme Court. The government of Gujarat remains determined to complete the dam as planned and the activists remain just as determined to prevent it.[6]

The Significance of Narmada

There is not one but many Narmada stories. One of the striking aspects of the local, national, and global debates over Narmada is the array of actors with different objectives who nevertheless defend their positions in the same terms, a phenomenon made possible when these terms—like "sustainable development"—are conceptually flexible and vague. While the range of actors and issues involved in the Narmada controversy are remarkably diverse, both those resisting and those defending the Sardar Sarovar Project use the same moral vocabulary of social justice, the same economic rhetoric of sustainable development, and similar evocations of the legacy of Gandhi.

Narmada has captured the imagination of many actors on many stages: depending on the audience, the name evokes the hopeful image of an exploitable and renewable natural resource, refers to a homeland in the river valley, stands for the river itself as a powerful religious symbol, or denotes a historic religious pilgrimage route. Both in India and in the international arena, Narmada has become a symbol for the struggle for local autonomy against forced displacement associated with state-directed and internationally funded development. The struggle over Narmada provides a poignant example of how local people are caught between the threat of destruction of their way of life and the promises of development, while government agencies, NGOs, activists, and academics step forth to speak for them. In this process, idealized, sanitized, or simplified versions of local beliefs are appropriated into developmentalist, Gandhian, and social ecological positions.

The Narmada controversy has had significant ramifications far beyond the river valley. An internal review of the World Bank's performance in the Narmada case is partly responsible for structural changes within the Bank;[7] the transnational alliances of NGOs supporting the Narmada Bachao Andolan (Save the Narmada Movement) helped establish more permanent linkages among dam-affected peoples all over the world and led to the first international meeting of peoples affected by large dams in Curitiba, Brazil, in 1997;[8] and the lessons of Narmada were a primary motivation for the formation in 1998 of a world commission on large dams sponsored by the World Bank and the International Union for the Conservation of Nature and Natural Resources (IUCN).[9]

Deploying Gandhi

Religion creeps into the Narmada issue in many ways, not least because the Narmada is, for Hindus, one of the most sacred rivers in India: its banks are lined with numerous sacred monuments and sites and it is the subject of circumambulation by devout pilgrims. Religious identity is also invoked by the Morse report,[10] in its defense of the indigenous identity of many people affected by the Sardar Sarovar Project, and by critics of the report, who contest the characterization of project-affected people as indigenous and tribal people, arguing instead that they are "backward Hindus."[11]

Even more striking in the Narmada issue, perhaps, is the omnipresence of Gandhi. No matter where one turns in the Narmada issue, one encounters the icon of Mahatma Gandhi: from the nonviolent strategies of the Narmada Bachao Andolan, which opposes the dam as an example of "destructive development"; to the Gandhian groups working to assure adequate resettlement rights for the "oustees"; to the Gandhian groups now working in the command area of the project, who long ago took seriously Gandhi's admonition to settle in remote villages and who now look to the promised irrigation water from the Narmada as a boon that would help further their work to improve the lives of poor Gujarati villagers; to the large statue of Gandhi not far from the massive block building which serves as headquarters to the Sardar Sarovar Narmada Nigam in Gandhinagar.

The image or icon of Gandhi is evoked in the Narmada debate for numerous reasons—and there are variations in the degree to which it is underscored by the evoker—but it is used most frequently to assert a link between one's own actions, on one hand, and the goals of social justice and the needs of the poor and marginalized groups, on the other.

Gandhi as an icon for those concerned with the poor and with traditional values contrasts most clearly with the forward-looking, development-oriented industrialization legacy of Nehru.[12] While the contrasts and contradictions between the visions of these two men are sharp, and in many ways represent two opposed views of modernity (one predicated upon industrialization and the other opposed to industrialization),[13] in the Narmada case, many dam proponents argue that they have made a successful and progressive merger of Nehru's modernist vision with a Gandhian concern for the poor. It was Nehru who laid the cornerstone for a dam on the Narmada in 1961, but, ironically, references to Gandhi's concern for the poor are now used to justify it. Dam opponents, on their part, characterize the dominant Nehruvian development vision as one which results in worsening conditions for the poorest of the poor and most marginalized elements of society, and one which results from a decision-making process that fails to consult with the poor and thus fails to take seriously their needs and concerns.

The omnipresence of Gandhi as a legitimizing symbol to both dam builders and dam opponents can be a bit disorienting to everyone. One day in November 1991, as I was conducting interviews in an office of the headquarters of the Sardar Sarovar Narmada Nigam, the Gujarat institution responsible for building the dam and canal system, official after official came by to volunteer their genuine concern for the poor and cited as part of their credentials that in their own way they were followers of Gandhi.[14] In justifying their current activities in the Nigam, these officials made attempts to reconcile their Nehruvian visions of a modernized India with the views of Gandhi, while at the same time dismissing the dam opponents as misguided antidevelopment, antinationalist neo-Luddites. Echoing a widely held view, one official told me that, "the Narmada Project holds all the hopes for the future of Gujarat." Another insisted that "the project is necessary for the poor farmers of northern Gujarat." And as one of my visitors put it, "the masks must be removed from the environmentalists, exposing them as antidevelopment agitators."[15]

"Baba Amte," Nigam officials told me repeatedly, referring to the famed Gandhian activist who resettled along the Narmada to show his support for the opponents of the Narmada development projects, "has been misled by his supporters."[16] Each of them was convinced that the SSP was a project which offered real hope for the alleviation of drought in northern Gujarat and one that had been unfairly mischaracterized and victimized by the protesters.

Later that same day, accompanied by Amar Gargesh, who was at that time in charge of public displays supporting the dam, I left the massive Narmada building in Gandhinagar and headed toward the city of Ahmedabad. Outside, we found ourselves again in the presence of Gandhi in the form of the prominent statue celebrating Gandhi and his spinning wheel that seems to stand guard in the city of his name outside the modernist building that houses the staff responsible for building a major nature-altering technological project.

William F. Fisher

At the museum in Ahmedabad, Amar and I toured the Nigam's display extolling the technological wonders of the dam and the features of the canal system. The display revealed enthusiasm, even if a bit uninspired, and featured confident assertions like those which are displayed on the billboards that line the road to Kevadia and the dam site:

"Backbone of the western Indian economy."

"The only remedy against recurring drought."

"A planned ecological harmony among men, water, and vegetation."

"A ray of hope to thirty million people."

Though time was short, the engineer and the museum curator were insistent that I visit the permanent exhibit next door which traces the life of the Indian independence movement and, particularly, the roles played in it by Gujarat's native sons. Throughout this tour, my hosts pointed out, in hushand tones of reverence, the hardships suffered by these men, their remarkable determination and dedication to their cause, and their willingness to go to prison for their principles. In front of a picture of Gandhi and Sardar Patel emerging from prison, Amar took a long pause, following which, in a low voice, almost to himself, as if the thought were occurring to him for the first time, he said quietly and respectfully, "they [Gandhi and Patel] were just like the [Narmada Bachao] Andolan" [the antidam activists].

COMPETING VISIONS: WORSHIPING A GODDESS OR TAMING NATURE

While dam advocates and opponents are generally sincere in their advocacy of sustainable development and social justice, and in their evocation of Gandhi, what they mean by the use of these terms and symbols differs profoundly. Sharing the same rhetoric to describe very different goals and means disguises fundamental philosophical differences, maintains confusion in the debate about development, and makes it more difficult to mount an effective challenge to the dominant development paradigm. Underlying the conflicting arguments are visions of the Narmada as goddess, homeland, or development resource. These contrasting visions serve a range of positions on social justice and sustainable development.

For millions of people in India, "Narmada Mai is a goddess." This is one of the most dramatic and long-standing visions of the river. Along its banks are thousands of temples dedicated to Ganga and Siva, and each year thousands of pilgrims throng to these and other sacred places. The *parikrama*, or pilgrimage, involves the circumambulation of the river from its source at the spring on the Amarkantak plateau to the mouth of the river and back again along the opposite bank. The *parikrama basis* (lit., dwellers on the circuit) carry no money or extra clothing and accept food along their journey.

Along their journey these pilgrims pass through a valley which serves as homeland for hundreds of thousands of people. For these residents, too, the river, like many aspects of their environment, is sacred. It is a timeless environment of which they are an integral part and which is consequently to be treated with respect and reverence.

Contrasted with these views of the timeless sacredness of the Narmada geography, the focus on the Narmada as a resource which might supply irrigation water for up to one hundred years seems a narrow, temporal concern. The vision of the relationship between human and nature implied by this view is also dramatically different. The Sardar Sarovar Dam is a vivid example of modernist convictions that one can obtain mastery over nature, and that the failure to do so will mean ruin. It derives from the conviction that as humans we can and must make our own destiny, that human history has been a history of progress, and that we can find technological solutions to all the problems we encounter. It reflects Descartes's conviction that the general good of all humankind could be pursued by the attainment of knowledge that is useful in life so as to make ourselves "the masters and possessors of nature."[18] This perspective on development defines and responds to two aspects of nature. Nature is seen as threatening and dangerous—in need of containment— while, simultaneously, it is viewed as a stockroom of resources for technological advancement. For development planners, both aspects present problems requiring technical solutions. The diverting of the Narmada waters to drought-prone areas of northern Gujarat is promoted as an appropriate technical response to both of these aspects of nature, diverting the "wasted" water of the Narmada to prevent the continued disasters caused by drought.[19]

From this perspective, it is less the river that is sacred than the dam. Hailed as "the lifeline of Gujarat," the dam and its complex canal system become an embodiment of Nehru's modernist vision that high dams would become "the secular temples of modern India."[20] This emergence of the dam as a sacred icon of modernization has the unfortunate consequence of presenting the dam as an end rather than a means of development. And the devotees of this temple of modernization have demonstrated an ardent commitment to their shrine that will not permit them to step back to reconsider its efficacy. The focus remains fixed on completing the dam and refusing to consider the possibility of other creative solutions to the initial problem.

With this unquestioning commitment, the chief minister of Gujarat in 1991 insisted that: "1) a review of the Sardar Sarovar Project will not be accepted under any circumstances; 2) the work will not be stopped for even one day; 3) and the height of the dam will not be lowered by even one inch." While the government has been forced to accept a review (indeed, more than one review), and the work has stopped, the devotion to the dam has not lessened. Six years later, in 1997, another chief minister of Gujarat fervently insisted that he was still committed to the dam, a commitment driven by his concern for "the weaker and downtrodden segments of society," and the chief minister linked his efforts to a concern for "the Adivasis, Harijans, Dalits, and other Backward classes and Scheduled Tribes."[21]

William F. Fisher

The view of progress and modernization from which projects like Sardar Sarovar emerge has been expressed by Vidyut Joshi:

> we have welcomed change in the name of progress, development or modernization. This being so, why should anyone oppose when tribal culture changes? A culture based on lower level of technology and quality of life is bound to give way to a culture with a superior technology and higher quality of life. This is what we call "development." What has happened to us is bound to happen to them because we both are parts of the same society.[22]

This view allows no room for the tolerance of different ways of life and different relationships with the environment, especially where conflict over resources is at issue. Instead, it makes clear the conviction that dominant elements of society are justified and even duty-bound to force the change of marginal populations. Of course, despite Joshi's generous and inclusive use of the first personal plural, the oustees of the Sardar Sarovar Project cannot look forward to the same life that Joshi enjoys.

Three practical consequences that emerge from the attempt to conquer nature are apparent in the Narmada case. One is the transfer or redistribution of resources from low-resource-use populations to high-resource-use populations—a transfer that is done without the consent of the low-use group and justified in terms of both human need and progress. Resources perceived as unused or wasted are taken as part of the manifest destiny of high-use portions of the population. Second, this diversion of natural resources is done in such a way that it entails further alteration and domination of nature. Third, the process allows and even requires that governments consolidate their control over both resources and people.

Drowning Voices

While the Narmada conflict may be a vivid illustration of a paradigm shift in process, a working-out through conflict and struggle of the nature of social justice and sustainable environmental use that concerns communities all over the world, the completion of this paradigm shift is not assured.[23] Nor does the process itself ensure that either the environment or justice will be served. Meanwhile, in many ways, the process itself continues to do violence to the views and lives of local people in the Narmada valley.

Despite the wide array of actors with a stake in the Narmada controversy, the struggle is often oversimplified as a battle between two ardently held positions pitting the people of the Narmada valley against a large development apparatus. The oversimplified division of actors into developers and resisters emerges from the dominant rhetorical exchanges of the controversy between developmentalists and environmentalists, and it imbues the struggle over Narmada with a compelling black-and-white character that allows it to resonate far beyond the valley. Ironically, while everyone steps up to talk about and talk for the local people of the Narmada valley, both the views and values of those in the Narmada valley and the values of groups in the command area of Gujarat are appropriated and oversimplified by this dominant contestation.

It is important to highlight what happens in the politicization of religion and the environment in the Narmada conflict and the violence done to local lives and views. As the struggle between dam builders and dam opponents evolves from a struggle over a specific dam to a clash about the process of development—a clash in which the dam builders and opponents each harden their points of view, and a contestation in which a sacred dam is made to confront a sacred river—the voices of the local people are at risk of being drowned out, their views and lives reduced through overgeneralization to simplistic caricatures.

CRITIQUING DEVELOPMENT

From the massive block building in Gandhinagar with its fleet of chauffeured Ambassador cars, through the network of comfortable Nigam guest houses with their plentiful buffets, one travels a long way to the spare, narrow, cramped third-floor room in Baroda that served as the base for the activists of the Narmada Bachao Andolan. Here, while the terms of sustainable development and social justice and the evocation of Gandhi are familiar, the meanings are profoundly different. For the activists, the dam, far from being sacred, is a sacrilege. The Sardar Sarovar Project is just one more of too many projects said to be in the "national interest," but which in fact undermine the ability of the rural poor to control and use local resources. The positions of environmentalists and activists opposing the Sardar Sarovar Dam are ideologically heterogenous and include a number of hybrid positions blended from Gandhian, Marxist, and "indigenous knowledge" positions.[24] In the view of some of these activists, the struggle of the inhabitants of the Narmada is a living example of a true environmental movement, a challenge by communities who worship nature and use it sustainably.[25] Some activists would go so far as to claim that the beliefs and practices of these local communities contain an implicit critique of development and an alternative vision of the relationship between humans and nature.[26]

This is an attractive and compelling point of view, and use of this compelling image was extremely effective in rallying support against the dam, but there are other stakeholders in the Narmada conflict whose voices are not widely heard and whose views are often over-simplified in the conflict.

RESPECTING NATURE

The journey from Baroda to the villages of the submergence area, while physically more difficult, doesn't seem as far, conceptually, as that from the Nigam headquarters to Baroda.

William F. Fisher

There, six months after my tour of the museum in Ahmedabad, I sat outside one warm evening listening to talk about gods and nature; people spoke about their way of life, their relationship to the earth, the forests, and the river. At first encounter, one is struck by the tranquility of life and the respectful attitude toward nature. Here, the environment is not merely a stockroom of resources, but a living landscape where the natural and the supernatural are intricately intertwined. Spiritual power which resides within trees, rocks, or hills is perceived as intervening actively in people's lives. Virtually all of them emphasized their ties to ancestral land, to the river, to the goddess Narmada, and to the local spiritual world: "our gods cannot move from this place," one said to me; "how can we move without them?"

Are the cultural and economic histories and conditions of the people living in these different landscapes distinct? The answer to that question is essentially political. Identifying or labeling this local set of practices as "Hindu" or "indigenous" does it a great injustice and misrepresents the specificity of local life. Dam proponents have argued that the potential "oustees" of the submergence area are simply "backward Hindus" and do not have a proper "indigenous" tradition. Activists have been careful to counter this image and to emphasize so-called tribal characteristics of their social practices. A great deal is at stake in the way valley residents are represented. Scheduled Tribes and Castes are of course entitled to concessions from the central government.[27] "Indigenous and tribal" people are covered by World Bank and other international guidelines that require the expenditure of additional caution and money when their way of life is disrupted by development projects.[28]

The hybrid culture characteristic of the valley residents does not fit easily with bureaucratic and academic needs for sharply distinct categories. Active within the daily social lives of valley inhabitants is a multicultural panoply of Hindu and local gods and spirits.[29] In conversations with me, the inhabitants did not repudiate Hinduism. Indeed, aspects of it are obviously part of their life: there are Hindu as well as local specific deities and shrines. Calling them either Hindu or non Hindu would seem inappropriate and irrelevant, were it not for the political ramifications of these labels.

Material life in the valley is also closely tied to the forests. Homes are built of local materials, and even in so-called degraded forests the inhabitants gather useful fruits and medicines. The environment is vibrant with life: trees and rocks become shrines and the river is seen as the source and support of spiritual life. In this context, what can the dam symbolize but the end of that life?

But these observations too easily slip into an idealized view of what is in fact a complex and messy relationship with a difficult, degraded environment. While it is difficult to desegregate the environment from cosmology, cultural and spiritual values, human life, and identity, it is important to examine this complex relationship closely. Most simply, nature, like gods, may be both threatening and protecting and, like gods, may require propitiation.

But nature, like gods, then, can also be trusted to care for itself, to rejuvenate itself when abused and overexploited—an attitude that shares less with the advocates of sustainable development and more than we might want to acknowledge with the development planners of the Sardar Sarovar Dam.

While society in the Narmada valley is respectful of nature, it is not necessarily one still in harmony with it. There is little point in idealizing life in the remote and difficult terrain of the valley. It is a life neither as harmonized with nature as sometimes presented in the West nor as riven with poverty as portrayed by the Nigam. But understanding it as it is, with all of its wisdom or tribulations, is often overwhelmed by the need for immediate political activism.

Even before the difficulties created by the scheme to dam the Narmada, life in the valley was hard and the relationship with the environment was a complex and ambiguous one. That realization must accompany the criticism of simplistic technological solutions which are offered to ease life for some (while in fact making life more difficult for others).

Writing about similar groups elsewhere in India, Christoph von Fürer-Haimendorf asked that we consider how it came about that populations which were self-sufficient for centuries now need to be protected, aided, or rescued by the government.[30] From his own observations, he asserted that these populations enjoyed well-balanced ecologies only one or two generations ago and had a quality of life superior in many ways to that of large sections of the Indian rural population—with adequate food, nonexploitative social structures, and freedom from indebtedness.[31] Contemporary problems, he argued, do not stem from within these societies but derive from the loss of land and resources.

When so much is at stake, when people are faced with displacement from their homeland and the disruption or termination of their way of life, it may become politically expedient in the defense of that way of life to misrepresent it and to emphasize, even exaggerate, the harmony of their relationship with their environment. It is also tempting to find in local practices all that is missing in development ideologies and practices, to find and use indigenous ideas to add legitimacy to our own ecological revisionist views. What is at stake is the idea of different kinds of society, but, inspired by political necessity and ideological hopefulness, the conflict becomes simplified into a view of two contesting views of nature and the environment.

CONCLUSION

It has been widely recognized in recent development literature that while the impacts of environment and development policy choices are often experienced most acutely at the local level, local communities often have little voice in the policy-making process. As a consequence, when they are able to make themselves heard at all, it is often in resistance to policies already decided elsewhere and implemented locally. In the Narmada case, too, people in the submergence area had no voice in the policy-making process, despite World Bank guidelines that project-affected and relocated people should be the first beneficiaries of a development project.

Environmental and human rights are varyingly described in the back and forth between Sardar Sarovar opponents and proponents. In these debates the right to water is opposed to the right to a low-energy use, low impact way of life; the right to development benefits is opposed to the right to participate in the decision-making processes that determine the reassignment of natural resources; and the development of a high-technology distribution of diverted water resources to (perhaps) needy segments of the population is opposed to the understudied, undervalued damage that will be done to an existing ecology. All of these concerns are framed within and subsumed under the terms sustainable development and social justice.

In the Narmada controversy we find every reference to Gandhi except, perhaps, his devotion to truth. By that comment I mean to strike a cautionary note about the power of rhetoric. Rhetoric is not an irrelevant and easily dismissed by-product of the development process. It may have the power to open up new possibilities, but it may also mystify what is actually happening. Rhetoric mystifies when it suggests consensus where there is none, directs attention away from conflict, and obscures relationships of inequality and power. Rhetoric does all of these things in the Narmada conflict.

The academic practice of solving problems by coining new terms is unlikely to cease anytime soon, but we need to direct our attention to the ease with which these new terms are easily hijacked by policy makers to conduct business as usual. It is so easy to embrace the rhetoric of sustainability and social justice and then to use these terms to defend essentially unchanged actions directed toward essentially unchanged ends. If, in the interactions among religion, ecology, and politics, politics usually prevails, we must resist premature celebrations of changes in rhetoric that are unaccompanied by changes in practice. Dominant discourses—be they developmentalist or environmentalist—have the power to absorb, coopt, and alter the way the views and values of local people are represented. The Narmada controversy is not just a simple disagreement about whether this dam is or is not a viable project. It strikes right to the heart of the philosophical, political, and moral debates about contemporary development efforts. What is called for, then, is not simply a more informed mechanism for deciding the costs and benefits of building the dam, but both a more fundamental transformation of the way development decisions are made and a reexamination of the measures by which difficult development trade-offs should be weighed.

It is clear that within this debate some points of view get more hearing than others. A great deal of violence has been done to the people of the Narmada valley—the great bulk of it by those who wish to flood the valley and uproot their communities, but some by those who misrepresent them in order to save them. In the immediacy of struggles, many "truths" are politicized and many nuances are unfortunately, but perhaps inevitably, overlooked. It is a conflict which, in part, pits those who can afford the luxury of further abusing the environment in order to exploit it against those who can afford the luxury of protecting it, while those who have no choice but to come to terms with life in a difficult environment must struggle on.

NOTES

1. Narmada has become almost a cottage industry for journalists and a fertile topic for academics. It has been the subject of numerous books, several international conferences, at least three documentary films, a PBS radio special, and hundreds of magazine articles, Of the books published, see Y. K. Alagh, R. D. Desai, G. S. Guha, and S. P. Kashyap, *Economic Dimensions of the Sardar Sarovar Project* (New Delhi: Har-Anand Publications, 1995); Amita Baviskar, *In the Belly of the River: Tribal Conflicts over Development in the Narmada Valley* (Delhi: Oxford University Press, 1995); *The Dam and the Nation: Displacement and Resettlement in the Narmada Valley*, ed. Iean Drèze, Meera Samson, and Satyajit Singh (Delhi: Oxford University Press, 1997), *Toward Sustainable Development? Struggling over India's Narmada River*, ed. William F. Fisher (Armonk, N.Y., M. E. Sharpe, 1995); Yidyet Joshi, *Rehabilitation: A Promise to Keep: A Case of the SSP* (Ahmedabad: The Tax Publications, 1991); and Vijay Paranjpye, *High Dams on the Narmada*, Studies in Ecology and Sustainable Development, no. 3 (New Delhi: Indian National Trust for Art and Cultural Heritage, 1990).

2. For sources on the Sardar Sarovar Project, see Alagh et al., *Economic Dimensions of the Sardar Sarovar Project*; Y. K. Alagh and D. T. Buch, "The Sardar Sarovar Project and Sustainable Development," in *Toward Sustainable Development?* ed. Fisher, Thomas A. Blinkhorn and William T. Smith, "India's Narmada: River of Hope," in *Toward Sustainable Development?* ed. Fisher; *The Dam and the Nation*, ed. Drèze, Samson, and Singh; Government of Gujarat, "Comment on the Report of the Independent Review Mission on Sardar Sarovar Project," draft (Gandhinagar, 1992); Bradford Morse and Thomas Berger, *Sardar Sarovar: The Report of the Independent Review* (Ottawa: Resource Futures International, 1992); Paranjpye, *High Dams on the Narmada*; C. C. Patel, "The Sardar Sarovar Project: A Victim of Time," in *Toward Sustainable Development?* ed. Fisher; and World Bank, Staff Appraisal Report: India, Narmada River Development—Gujarat. Supplementary Data Volume (1985).

3. See, for example, Asia Watch, "Before the Deluge: Human Rights Abuses at India's Narmada Dam" (1992); Shripad Dharmadhikary, "Hydropower at Sardar Sarovar: Is it Necessary, Justified, and Affordable?" in *Toward Sustainable Development?* ed. Fisher; William F. Fisher, "Development and Resistance in the Narmada Valley," in *Toward Sustainable Development?* ed. Fisher; Lawyers Committee for Human Rights, "Unacceptable Means: India's Sardar Sarovar Project and Violations of Human Rights," October 1992 through February 1993; *Lokayan, Bulletin*, Special Issue on Dams on the River Narmada, 9, no. 4/5 (1991); Kalpavriksh, *Narmada: A Campaign Newsletter* (New Delhi), no. 5 (1990); Morse and Berger, *Sardar Sarovar*; Anil Patel, "What Do the Narmada Valley Tribals Want?" in *Toward Sustainable Development?* ed. Fisher; Medha Patkar, "The Strength of a People's Movement," in *Indigenous Vision: Peoples of India Attitudes to the Environment*, ed. Geeti Sen (New Delhi: Sage Publications, 1992); Medha Patkar, "The Struggle for Participation and Justice: A Historical Narrative," in *Toward Sustainable Development?* ed. Fisher; Rahul N. Ram, "Benefits of the Sardar Sarovar Project: Are the Claims Reliable?" in *Toward Sustainable Development?* ed. Fisher; Ashvin A. Shah, "A Technical Overview of the Flawed Sardar Sarovar Project and a Project and a Proposal for a Sustainable Alternative," in *Toward Sustainable*

Development? ed. Fisher; and Lori Udall, "The International Narmada Campaign: A Case of Sustained Advocacy," in *Toward Sustainable Development?* ed. Fisher.

4. Opposition to the project has a long complex history. See Gail Omvedt, *Reinventing Revolution: New Social Movements and the Socialist Tradition in India* (Armonk, N.Y.: M. E. Sharpe, 1993); Anil Patel, "What Do the Narmada Valley Tribals Want?"; Patkar, "The Struggle for Participation and Justice: A Historical Narrative"; and Udall, "The International Narmada Campaign."

5. Morse and Berger, *Sardar Sarovar*, xii.

6. For the moment attention has shifted elsewhere, including upstream to another proposed dam site along the Narmada. See, for example, Narmada Bachao Andolan, "Narmada NAPM Tour," electronic release, 7 March 1996; Narmada Bachao Andolan, "Update," electronic release, 20 February 1998; National Front for Tribal Self Rule, "A Major Victory," press release, 5 March 1996; International Rivers Network, "World Commission on Dams Launched," press release, 16 February 1998; and the Declaration in Support of the Struggle for the Promised Suspension of Construction on the Maheshwar Dam."

7. See the discussion in Robert Wade, "Greening the Bank: The Struggle over the Environment: 1970–1995," in *The World Bank: Its First Half Century*, ed. Devesh Kapur, John P. Lewis, and Richard Webb (Washington, D.C.: Brookings Institution, 1997).

8. See First International Meeting of People Affected by Large Dams, Declaration of Curitiba, Brazil, 14 March 1997.

9. International Rivers Network, "Independent Commission to Review World's Dams," *World Rivers Review* 12, no. 3 (June 1997); and Patrick McCully, with assistance from Peter Brosshard and Shripad Dharmadhikary, "An NGO Report on the April 1997 World Bank-IUCN Dams Workshop and on the Proposal for an Independent International Dam Review Commission," 4 May 1997.

10. Bradford Morse and Thomas Berger, *Sardar Sarovar: The Report of the Independent Review* (Ottawa: Resource Futures International, 1992).

11. Government of Gujarat, "Comment on the Report of the Independent Review Mission on Sardar Sarovar Project."

12. Gandhi's own words on this subject make this contrast clear. In 1928 Gandhi said: "God forbid that India should ever take to industrialization after the manner of the West. . . . If an entire nation of 300 million took to similar economic exploitation [as that of England], it would strip the world bare like locusts." Mohandas Gandhi, *Collected Work of Mahatma Gandhi*, vol. 38 (Delhi: Publications Division, Ministry of Information, Government of India, 1958), 243–44.

13. One might also compare Sir Mokshagundam Visvesvarayya's exhortation, "industrialize or perish," and Gandhi's response, "industrialize and perish" (cited in Sunil Khilnani, *The Idea of India* [New York: Farrar, Straus Giroux, 1998], 73).

14. Nigam officials often talked to me about their commitment to uplifting the lives of Scheduled Tribes and Castes. Most were sincerely convinced that current resettlement efforts would achieve this upliftment. Some officials were unable to restrain their frustration with the reluctance of project-affected people to agree to resettlement and expressed annoyance with valley inhabitants who were holding up the completion of the dam. One, frustrated with the slow rate at which inhabitants of the valley had accepted resettlement, suggested that "they will move quickly enough when the waters of the reservoir rise and they are forced to climb to higher ground like monkeys" (personal communication, 12 January 1992).

15. These are but a few representative comments of many made to me by dam planners that echoed these sentiments. In conversations with me, Nigam officials seemed determined not to give in to Malthusian pessimism, or to let the activists cancel their hopes for the future.

16.   Baba Amte moved to the banks of the Narmada to show his support for the inhabitants of the valley. In 1990 he accepted the Templeton Prize for Progress in Religion, saying, in part:

> How long are we to watch passively as all that is our common heritage is destroyed and lost forever in the name of 'development'? Today I have become part of the battle to save the Narmada, one of the most sacred rivers in India, from massive dams which would destroy a whole way of life that depends on the river and its life-sustaining water. The battle is not for the Narmada alone, it has an even larger meaning. The battle is for the whole earth, to stop the immorality of destructive 'development' and replace it with a new vision, a new way of human living.
>
> We must seek a path of greater kindness, tolerance and respect for all forms of life; a way of living founded on compassion, which seeks sufficiency for all rather than superfluity for some. *Real* development is natural . . . this, the way of nature, is the only basis for real development; it is our solemn responsibility to preserve and enrich our natural heritage for the sake of children yet to be born. Cited in Geoffrey Waring Maw, *Narmada: The Life of a River*, ed. Marjorie Sykes (Hoshangabad, 1991), 82.

17.   For a discussion of the sacredness of the Narmada, see Chris Deegan, "The Narmada in Myth and History," in *Toward Sustainable Development?* ed. Fisher. See also Maw, *Narmada: The Life of a River*.

18.   René Descartes, *Discourse on Method and the Meditations*, trans. F.E. Sutcliffe (Hammondsworth: Penguin, 1971), 78.

19.   C. C. Patel, "The Sardar Sarovar Project"; and Alagh et al., *Economic Dimensions of the Sardar Sarovar Project*.

20.   Nehru also observed in 1954, at the site of a high dam: "As I walked round the site I thought that these days the biggest temple and mosque and gurdwara is the place where man works for the good of mankind. Which place can be greater than this, this Bhakra-Nangal?" (Jawaharlal Nehru, *Jawaharlal Nehru's Speeches*, vol. 3, *March 1953–August 1957* (New Delhi: Publications Division, Ministry of Information and Broadcasting, 1958), 3. The deification of Gandhi in the pantheon of nationalism and the designation of high dams as the temples of modern India seem peculiarly discordant.

21.   This later claim serves as the basis for the rather astonishing insistence of the dam proponents that the Sardar Sarovar Project is an example of sustainable development. The dam builders insist that sustainable development is compatible with large-scale, ambitious, centrally controlled schemes that are capable of mitigating the effects of natural catastrophes and meeting the increased needs of a growing economy for food, water, and energy.

22.   Joshi, *Rehabilitation: A Promise to Keep*, 68.

23.   William F. Fisher, "Full of Sound and Fury? Struggling Toward Sustainable Development," in *Toward Sustainable Development?* ed. Fisher.

24.   Ramachandra Guha has identified three distinct strains (crusading Gandhian, appropriate technology, and ecological Marxism) that he believes contribute to contemporary environmental positions within India: see Ramachandra Guha, "Ideological Trends in Indian Environmentalism," *Economic and Political Weekly* 23 (988): 29, and "The Environmentalism of the Poor," in *Between Resistance and Revolution: Cultural Politics and Social Protest*, ed. Richard G. Fox and Orin Starn (New Brunswick, N.J.: Rutgers University Press, 1997). The Narmada controversy also awkwardly encompasses the environmentalism of the poor as well as the various ideological environmentalisms of Indian intellectuals and northern NGOs.

25.   I base this summary on extensive conversations with Narmada Bachao Andolan activists as well as on their own publications.

26.   See, for example, Sen, *Indigenous Vision*, and Pramod Parajuli, "Power and Knowledge in Development Discourse: New Social Movements and the State in India," *International Social Science Journal* 127 (1991): 173–90. Baviskar (*In the Belly of the River*, 47) summarizes the position this way: "The collective resistance of indigenous

people is not a rearguard action—'the dying wail of a class about to drop down the trapdoor of history'—but a potent challenge which strikes at the very heart of the process of development."

27.   Article 46 of the Indian constitution reads: "The State shall promote with special care the education and economic interests of the weaker sections of the people, and, in particular, of the Scheduled Castes and Scheduled Tribes, and shall protect them from social injustice and all forms of exploitation."

28.   See, for instance, the International Labor Organization Convention no. 107 and the 1987 statement of the World Commission on Environment and Development, both cited in Independent Commission on International Humanitarian Issues, *Indigenous Peoples: A Global Quest for Justice* (London and Atlantic Highlands, N.J.: Zed Books, 1987), and World Bank, Operational Directive 4.01 (1991).

29.   For a detailed discussion of the Bhilala community of the Narmada valley, see Amita Baviskar's excellent book, *In the Belly of the River*, particularly chapter 7.

30.   Christoph von Fürer-Haimendorf, *Tribes of India: The Struggle for Survival* (Berkeley and Los Angeles: University of California Press, 1982), and *Tribal Populations and Cultures of the Indian Subcontinent* (Leiden: E. J. Brill, 1985).

31.   Fürer-Haimendorf, *Tribal Populations and Cultures of the Indian Subcontinent*, 170.

"STATEMENTS BY UNITED CHURCH OF CHRIST ON ENVIRONMENTAL RACISM IN ST. LOUIS"

United Church of Christ

JUSTICE AND PEACE: ENVIRONMENTAL JUSTICE

Justice and Witness Ministries board members witness in opposition to a U.S. Army plan to incinerate tons of neutralized nerve gas near East St. Louis, Illinois.

Members of the UCC's Justice and Witness Ministries board of directors held a public witness on April 20, 2002 outside of Onyx Environmental Services, a company near East St. Louis, Illinois that is planning to incinerate tons of neutralized nerve gas for the United States Army. East St. Louis is already one of the most contaminated cities in the country. Below are press statements made by Dr. Bernice Powell Jackson, Executive Minister, and the Rev. Henry T. Simmons, Board Chairperson.

Bernice Powell Jackson
Executive Minister, Justice and Witness Ministries
April 20, 2002

Fifteen years ago, on the eve of Earth Day 1987, the United Church of Christ's Commission for Racial Justice published a landmark report, Toxic Wastes and Race.

For the first time in history, Toxic Waste and Race conclusively documented the disproportionate burden that African American, Latino, Native American, and Asian American communities bear as the "dumping grounds" for our nation's waste and pollution.

Toxic Waste and Race led to the coining of the term "environmental racism" and helped to jump start the environmental justice movement.

One of the people of color communities cited in this report for having an unusually high number of toxic waste dumps was East St. Louis, Illinois. Yet, even though 15 years

Reprinted from www.ucc.org.

have now passed, we must speak the truth once again that for many communities—like East St. Louis—the more things change, the more they remain the same.

It is commendable that the U.S. Environmental Protection Agency has created an Office of Environmental Justice—and foundations like Ford, Beldon and Turner have funded grassroots efforts to educate communities and lawmakers about the need to create healthy and sustainable communities. But still the sad truth remains: The more things change, the more they remain the same.

Fifteen years later, East St. Louis, Illinois—one of the most contaminated communities in America—is being targeted once again as a potential site for disposal of toxic substances. The United States Army—and Onyx Environmental Services—currently have plans to incinerate "neutralized nerve gas" in the facility located behind us. Still . . . many important questions remain unanswered.

- Why was the East St. Louis area selected given the disproportionate exposure of its residents to over 20 years of toxic waste dumping?

- Did the East St. Louis area's high asthma rate among its children factor into Onyx's decision? Or was that fact even considered at all?

- Were all segments of the community—especially those most likely to be affected—involved in the decisionmaking process?

- Can the burden of disposing potentially toxic wastes be shared equally among all communities and not borne by the most vulnerable members of our society?

Today, on the eve of Earth Day 2002, the United Church of Christ is still asking the questions that remain unanswered for the people of East St. Louis.

Justice and Witness Ministries, a covenanted ministry of the United Church of Christ, is issuing a call to action.

We call on elected officials, the press, the medical community, industrial leaders, environmentalists, the Illinois and Missouri departments of health and environmental protection, the religious community, and the general public in and around East St. Louis—and St. Louis—to raise the real question, which is this:

Should East St. Louis continue to bear an unfair burden for our nation's waste?

Until this question is finally heard and rightly answered, the voices of God's people—and the cry for justice—will not and cannot be silenced.

The Rev. Henry Simmons
Board Chair, Justice and Witness Ministries
April 20, 2002

In the first pages of the Bible, in the book of Genesis, we learn that God created the heavens and the earth and charged humankind with responsibility for its care and protection.

In a story found soon thereafter—the one about Cain and Abel—we discover clearly that, no matter how much we might prefer otherwise, we truly are our brothers' and sisters' keepers.

To love God is to love God's creation and to love God's people. This is a fundamental and essential truth that runs throughout the sacred stories of our faith. As Christians, we are called to invest ourselves in the work of justice, and by so doing, we are witnesses to Jesus Christ's continual redeeming presence in the world.

Therefore, it is out of our deep concern for God's Earth and for the well-being of all who inhabit it, that we gather here as a people of faith from all across this nation to stand in solidarity with the community of East St. Louis, Illinois.

We come here as multi-racial and multi-cultural witnesses to the disproportionate burden that continues to be placed upon the people who live in East St. Louis and surrounding communities. We come here to shed light on long-term health consequences associated with toxic waste, and we come here to say enough is enough.

We are here to name the sin of environmental racism—just as we did 15 years ago—and to renew our call for real and lasting environmental justice in order that the burden of toxic waste will be shared by all—and not just some.

As members of the United Church of Christ, we are proud of our church's legacy that helped build the environmental justice movement. We are proud that, in 1987, we concretely documented the connections between toxic waste and race.

We are proud that, in 1991, the United Church of Christ hosted the first Environmental Justice People of Color Summit, and we are proud that—throughout the years—our commitment has been to work with grassroots folks, in order to help them claim their own power to overcome environmental injustice and racism.

Do not misunderstand us . . . We are not opposed to the elimination of chemical weapons. In fact, we applaud the United States and 59 other nations for entering into the 1997 Chemical Weapons Convention Treaty. As a just-peace church and as a people committed to overcoming violence, we support any effort designed to reduce our collective reliance on weapons of destruction.

BUT . . . we do insist—with renewed dedication—that this major undertaking not be borne solely by people of color . . . or by people in poverty. The people of East St. Louis have endured far more pollution and toxic waste than their fair share. It is now someone else's turn.

This is the moment of new opportunity. We stand before you as people of the Spirit committed to a new era of bold environmental justice advocacy.

However, we not only rededicate ourselves to this important work, but we call upon you to do the same. On this eve of Earth Day Sunday, we ask you to recommit yourself to justice for all of God's creation.

So this year, on Earth Day, we ask that you do more than pick up trash or plant a tree, but together let us raise our voices for environmental justice. This Earth Day, let us demand justice from our politicians and government leaders, from Congress, from President Bush, and from the Secretary of the Army. Tell them to STOP the raping and exploitation of East St. Louis. Tell them that we will not tolerate any more disproportionate burdens . . . starting at this very moment . . . here in East St. Louis.

"RACE, SACRIFICE, AND NATIVE LANDS"

Jonna Higgins-Freese and Jeff Tomhave

Across the United States, non-native peoples' interest in shamanic and indigenous based spiritual practices is strong, as can be seen by the large number of sweat lodges, drum circles, dream catchers, references to quotes from Chief Seattle—even the fact that shamanism is the theme for this issue of *EarthLight*.

This interest in native eco-spiritual practices contrasts sharply with the actual state of the environment in native communities. For example, the most polluted site under the Environmental Protection Agency's (EPA) Superfund program is at Tar Creek, Oklahoma. Toxic contamination from lead and zinc mines at Tar Creek has had significant impact on seven Indian tribes and three states. Acid mine drainage and wind-blown dust have poisoned many of the tribes' sacred and ceremonial sites. The dust blows off the mine tailing piles, which stand like gray mountains hundreds of feet high above the flat plains. The underground mine system reaches into the aquifer, leaching heavy metals, and depositing them to the surface water of Tar Creek.

Tar Creek is only one example of how places and communities have been "sacrificed" for the American way of life. This sacrifice has been recognized by the U.S. government in a National Academy of Sciences study, which concluded that some areas of the country could be used for national priorities irrespective of the resulting permanent environmental damage. Such places are designated "National Sacrifice Areas."

Many of these areas are on native land and are open to resource extraction and defense activities. The Four Corners area of the Navajo Nation and the Black Hills of South Dakota, sacred to the Lakota Nations, have been officially designated as "national sacrifice areas." Seventy-five percent of the U.S. national uranium reserve is on Indian land under the control of the major oil companies. In fact, most of the armaments and munitions that supplied American forces in both World Wars and Korea came out of the Tar Creek mine fields.

In secular terms, a sacrifice occurs when a person or group gives up something in order to achieve another, greater good. In this context, it is important to ask what "greater

---

Reprinted with permission from *Earthlight* (Summer 2002).

good" is being aimed for—and to note that no one should have the ability to give up another person's land or health for any reason.

A closer look at the western religious origins of the term is even more disturbing. The "sacrificial lamb" or "scapegoat" is symbolically understood to take on the weight of the community's sins, and is then either exiled from the community or killed as an act of atonement. In that sense, the designation of many Indian lands as National Sacrifice Areas is a disturbingly accurate recognition of present reality.

Native communities are the scapegoats for Western consumer culture, bearing the burdens of the sins of the community. Indian communities have hosted toxic waste, a by-product of white middle class consumer lifestyles, without ever having benefited from those lifestyles. Government officials and community leaders have even claimed that native communities are good hosts for such toxic materials precisely because of their concern for the Earth. This is not a problem of politicians far away, but of the way white privilege still provides benefits—including the leisure to study shamanic practices.

Given the history of exploiting the natural resources of native communities, it is important to be careful that native spiritual traditions are not appropriated and used in the same way. Any ecospiritual tradition that draws upon shamanic or indigenous practices must be careful not to become yet another way that native traditions are used to the detriment of the Earth and native people.

The first step is to overcome any tendency to romanticize native cultures or to see them as "spiritual resources" rather than complex, vibrant, living traditions within communities that have suffered grave abuse. As George Tinker has written, "Euro-Americans and their elected officials seem to engage in a behavior pattern well-known in alcohol and drug addiction therapies: denial. Too many churches and too many politicians have lived out such a denial, as if such eco-devastation and national injustice and immorality cannot possibly affect them, living in the protected comfort zones of American society. [In this context], it becomes all too easy to think of Indian reservations as 'National Sacrifice Areas.'"[1]

The truth of Tinker's analysis was demonstrated recently when one of the co-writers of this piece, Jonna Higgins-Freese, led an ecotheology training for a group of Episcopal priests who have been designated as leaders within their communities. When they were shown a video about the environmental and health effects of the acid mine drainage at Tar Creek, one of them commented, "Well, this is interesting, but I wonder if it's really effective to play the 'race card'—is there a reason to make this into a race issue? Won't people be put off by thinking of environmental problems in racial terms? And what's the link to religion and spirituality?"

This is a clear example of denial, of the conviction that as long as we don't use racial epithets or specifically and consciously set out to harm people of a particular race, the actual harmful outcome is irrelevant. It demonstrates a cultural conviction that as long as we don't talk about the racial dimensions of environmental problems, they won't exist. And it demonstrates the all-too-common belief that spiritual practice is individual and other-worldly—that it is separate from real communities, present realities, and the mess of politics.

What, then, are our responsibilities if we want to turn to shamanic ecospiritual practices as a resource? The first step is to overcome our denial and squarely face the truth of the way native people and people of color have been sacrificed and made scapegoats for the toxic by-products of the American consumerist lifestyle. Across the U.S., race is the determining factor for a number of environmental quality indicators.

Once called environmental racism, "environmental justice" is typically perceived to be an urban issue, and for good reason. In 1987 the United Church of Christ's Commission for Racial Justice issued the landmark study "Toxic Wastes and Race in the United States." The study found race to be the single most important factor (more important than income, home ownership, property value, etc.) in the location of abandoned toxic waste sites.

The study also found that:

1. Sixty percent of African Americans live in communities with one or more abandoned toxic waste sites.
2. Three of the five largest commercial hazardous waste landfills are located in predominantly African American or Latino communities and account for 40 percent of the nation's total estimated landfill capacity.
3. African Americans are heavily overrepresented in the population of cities with the largest number of abandoned waste sites.

In 1998, a cursory EPA survey of tribal lands found over 180 off-reservation air pollution sources, scores of federally built schools and houses with lead paint and asbestos, and over 1,000 leaking underground storage tanks impacting the health and environment of Indian tribes. Smokestack dioxins impact the tribes of the Northeast and Great Lakes. Military dumpsites dot the landscape surrounding Alaska Native villages. Bombing ranges continually threaten western tribes.

Until recently, there has not been empirical data documenting the various environmental threats which impact Indian communities and tribal peoples. However, Jeff Tomhave, the other co-writer of this piece, is currently shepherding a three-year research project unprecedented in its scope. The project marks the first time ever that tribes are being asked to supply information as to what they know or suspect to be hazardous waste contamination from manufacturing, municipal landfills, mining, and defense and energy activities on or near their land (see www.taswer.org/ for more information on the tribal hazardous contamination study).

Nationally, only about 44 percent of African Americans own their homes compared to over two-thirds of the nation as a whole. Homeowners are the strongest advocates of the "not in my backyard" positions taken against locally unwanted land uses such as the construction of garbage dumps, landfills, incinerators, sewer treatment plants, recycling centers, prisons, drug treatment units, and public housing projects. Generally, affluent white communities have greater access than communities of color when it comes to influencing land use and environmental decision making. The ability of individual families to escape a health-threatening physical environment is directly related to affluence.

For tribal communities, home ownership is a foreign concept. Tribes don't actually own their land; the federal government does. Without land as collateral, private lending doesn't extend to tribal communities. The idea that tribal people could mount a public campaign against an unwanted land use is next to impossible. The idea that tribal people would move, even if they could, away from the last remnant of their land is similarly improbable.

However, simple awareness of the problem is not enough. As George Tinker says, "we need to move beyond the mere naming of ecological devastations that are affecting Indian peoples and other indigenous and poor peoples today. . . . Changing individual patterns of behavior has failed us as a strategy. We need more holistic and systemic solutions" (Tinker, page 166).

Any eco-spiritual tradition that draws upon native traditions or shamanic practices should properly include justice and alliance-building as central elements of the spiritual practice. Many people have a deep love for Native cultures and a sense that the history of their treatment in the U.S. is shameful and wrong. We must move beyond guilt to practical action—to become allies with Native people as they work for justice.

One way to engage in such action is to support tribal organizations that engage in work to protect the health and environment of Indian communities. Effective Self Determination Solutions (ESDS) is one such organization. ESDS is based on the age-old knowledge that the best form of charity is to help people help themselves. ESDS deploys multi-disciplinary teams (law, science, health, finance, and media) to work with individual tribes at a time until the tribe's specific environmental problem is solved. These individual tribes benefit because they attain the skills, experience, and resources necessary to protect their own health and environment in a culturally appropriate way that benefits tribal and non-tribal people alike.

Many native spiritual practices include the recognition that every place on Earth is sacred. Our spiritual practices—including work for environmental justice—must also be locally based.

We can begin with examining our daily lives and noticing the connections between what happens here and what happens far away. For example, the proposed permanent nuclear waste storage site at Yucca Mountain has recently been in the news; the site is near the

Western Shoshone tribe, and they are concerned about its potential health impacts. All of us use electricity; some portion of it likely comes from nuclear power plants. From an ecospiritual perspective, we must actively support and promote alternatives to nuclear power, including energy conservation and renewable energy.

Finally, any healthy ecospiritual practice should include engagement with these issues in our own communities. Look around at the people who live in your community. Find out what issues are of concern to them and ask whether there is an environmental link—are there unusual rates of asthma or other illnesses? Is the problem simply that there is inadequate health care, so that it is impossible to know if disproportionate health problems exist? Are there brownfields or abandoned toxic waste sites near these communities? If so, ask yourself what you can do to be an ally to these communities as they address the problem. To do so should be as central to our ecospiritual practice as drumming or attending sweat lodges.

NOTES

1.   George E. Tinker, "An American Indian Theological Response to Ecojustice," in Jace Weaver, ed., *Defending Mother Earth: Native American Perspectives on Environmental Justice*, Orbis: Maryknoll, 1996, 166–167.

Jonna Higgins-Freese and Jeff Tomhave

"THE COCHABAMBA DECLARATION ON WATER: GLOBALIZATION, PRIVATIZATION, AND THE SEARCH FOR ALTERNATIVES"

Coordinadora de Defensa del Agua y de la Vida (Coalition in Defense of Water and Life)

On December 8, 2000 several hundred people gathered in Cochabamba, Bolivia for a seminar on the global pressure to turn water over to private water corporations. For many of those who attended it was the first time they had come together since the mass uprising at the beginning of the year when the people of Cochabamba took back their water from the private water company. Also in attendance was an international delegation of water activists. The result of that meeting was the following declaration that captures the essence of their struggle and the struggle of more and more communities around the world. If you agree please sign on below. This declaration is a rallying call to join the struggle to protect the planet and human rights.

DECLARATION

We, citizens of Bolivia, Canada, United States, India, Brazil:

Farmers, workers, indigenous people, students, professionals, environmentalists, educators, non-governmental organizations, retired people, gather together today in solidarity to combine forces in the defense of the vital right to water.

Here, in this city which has been an inspiration to the world for its retaking of that right through civil action, courage and sacrifice standing as heroes and heroines against corporate, institutional and governmental abuse, and trade agreements which destroy that right, in use of our freedom and dignity, we declare the following:

"The Cochabamba Declaration," drafted and signed by participants in the international seminar on Water: Globalization, Privatization, and the Search for Alternatives, convened by the Coordinadora de Defensa del Agua y de la Vida (Coalition in Defense of Water and Life), Cochabamba, Bolivia, 8 December 2000.

For the right to life, for the respect of nature and the uses and traditions of our ancestors and our peoples, for all time the following shall be declared as inviolable rights with regard to the uses of water given us by the earth:

1. Water belongs to the earth and all species and is sacred to life, therefore, the world's water must be conserved, reclaimed and protected for all future generations and its natural patterns respected.

2. Water is a fundamental human right and a public trust to be guarded by all levels of government, therefore, it should not be commodified, privatized or traded for commercial purposes. These rights must be enshrined at all levels of government. In particular, an international treaty must ensure these principles are noncontrovertible.

3. Water is best protected by local communities and citizens who must be respected as equal partners with governments in the protection and regulation of water. Peoples of the earth are the only vehicle to promote democracy and save water.

"STREET TREES"

Melody Ermachild Chavis

I was drawn to my upstairs bedroom window by shouting in the street. The shouter was a middle-aged black man in shabby pants, and he strode, fast, right down the middle of the street. Storming across the intersection, the man beat the air with his fists and shouted into the sky. "Somalia!" he cried. "Somalia!"

Ours is a neighborhood where poverty and addiction have made misery for years, and this was when airlifts of food to the Horn of Africa were all over the nightly news. "I know what you mean," I thought. "Why there? Why feed them but not you?"

Then he walked up to the newly planted tree under my window, grabbed its skinny trunk with both hands, yanked it over sideways, and cracked it in half on his knee. He threw the tree's leafy top onto the sidewalk and stomped off, cursing. I pressed my palms to the glass as he disappeared up the sidewalk.

The tree was just a baby, one of the donated saplings our neighborhood association planted with help from the children on our block. Men from the public-works department had come and cut squares in the sidewalk for us, reaming out holes with a machine that looked like a big screw. The kids planted the trees, proudly wielding shovels, loving their hands in the dirt.

I had made name tags for each tree, with a poem printed on each one, and we asked the kids to give each tree a name. "Hi, my name's *Greenie*, I'm new and neat, just like the children on our street." If we made the trees seem more like people, I thought, the kids would let them live.

Both trees and people around here are at risk of dying young. After our neighborhood was flooded with crack cocaine and cheap, strong alcohol, things got very rough. In the last five years, 16 people have been murdered in our small police beat. Most of them were young black men, and most of them died on the sidewalks, where the trees witness everything: the children, the squealing tires and gunshots, the blood and sirens.

My neighbors and I did all we could think of to turn things around, including planting the trees.

But the dealers still hovered on the corners and the young trees had a hard time. Idle kids swung on them like playground poles, and peeled off strips of bark with their nervous little fingers.

Reprinted with permission of the author from *Sierra: The Magazine of the Sierra Club*, July/August, 1994.

One of the saplings planted in front of my house had fallen victim to a car, and now the other one had been murdered by a man mad about Somalia.

Discouraged, I let the holes in the cement choke with crabgrass. In the center of each square, a pathetic stick of dead trunk stuck up.

When things are bad, I stand in my kitchen window and look into my own garden, a paradise completely hidden from the street outside. For 15 years I've labored and rested in my garden, where roses clamber on bamboo trellises. There are red raspberries and rhubarb. Lemon, apricot, apple, and fig trees are sheltered by young redwoods and firs that hide the apartment house next door. I planted the apricot tree 13 years ago when it was a bare stick as tall as myself. Now I mark the seasons with its changes. In early spring the apricot blooms white, tinged with pink, and feeds the bees. When our chimney fell in the earthquake, I used the bricks to build a low circular wall I call my medicine wheel. Inside it I grow sage, lavender, rosemary, and oregano. A stone Buddha sits under fringed Tibetan prayer flags, contemplating a red rock.

Not far from my house is a place I'm convinced is a sacred site. Within one block are a large African-American Christian church, a Black Muslim community center, and a Hindu ashram. Someone put a Buddha in a vacant lot near there, too, and people built a shrine around it. All this is close to the place where the Ohlone people once had a village.

I dream of those who lived here before me—an Ohlone woman, members of the Peralta family whose hacienda this was, and a Japanese-American farmer who had a truck garden here until he lost it when he was interned during World War II.

I often feel I'm gardening with my dear old next-door neighbor Mrs. Wright. An African-American woman from Arkansas, Mrs. Wright came to work in the shipyards during the war. When she bought the house next door this was the only neighborhood in town where black people were allowed to live. She was foster mother to many children, and she was sadly disapproving of the young people who used drugs when that started. Mrs. Wright farmed every inch of her lot, and had it all in food, mainly greens, like collards and kale. She gave most of the food away.

Her life exemplified the adage, "We come from the earth, we return to the earth, and in between we garden." I miss her still, although she died six years ago, in her 70s, after living here nearly 50 years. I was almost glad she didn't live to see the night a young man was shot to death right in front of our houses.

A map of the neighborhood 15 years ago, when my family came, would show community places that are gone now: bank, pharmacy, hardware and small, black-owned corner stores. There are a lot of vacancies now, jobs are gone, and people travel to malls to shop. Many families run out of food the last days of the month.

Melody Ermachild Chavis

On my map I can plot some of what killed this community's safety: the too-many liquor outlets—nine within four blocks of my house; the drug dealers who came with crack about 1985. Clustered near the drugs and alcohol are the 16 murder sites: the 15 men, the one woman.

"I want to get away from all this," I think often. But *really* getting away would mean selling our home and leaving, and so far, my husband and I have been unwilling to give up, either on our neighbors or on our hopes for helping make things better.

But we do get away, to the mountains. We've been walking the John Muir Trail in sections the last few summers. I've never liked the way it feels good to go to the mountains and bad to come home. That's like only enjoying the weekends of your whole life.

According to my mail, "Nature" is the wilderness, which I'm supposed to save. And I want to. But right here and now, if I go outside to pick up trash, I might have to fish a used syringe out of my hedge. That's saving nature too. The hard task is loving the earth, all of it.

The notes I stick on my refrigerator door remind me of the unity and sacredness of life. There's a quote from Martin Luther King, Jr. on "the inescapable network of mutuality." I know I can't take a vacation from any part of this world.

Still, the habit of my mind is dual. This I hate: (the littered sidewalk); this I love: (the alpine meadow). I could get into my car and drive to that meadow. But when I drive back, the sidewalk will still be dirty. Or, I could stay here, pick up a broom, and walk out my front door.

The sidewalk yields clues that people have passed this way, like trail markers in the mountains: candy wrappers the kids have dropped on their way back from the store; malt liquor cans and fortified-wine bottles inside brown bags. Sometimes there are clothes, or shoes, or car parts. I tackle it all in thick orange rubber gloves, wielding my broom and dustpan, dragging my garbage can along with me. I recycle what I can. "This is *all* sacred," I tell myself. "All of it."

There are bigger waste problems. But when I think about the ozone hole, I find that it helps me to clean up. Thinking globally without acting locally can spin me down into despair.

Or into anger. I know that other people somewhere else made decisions that turned our neighborhood, once a good place, into a bad one. Like the alcohol-industry executives who decided to aim expensive ad campaigns at African-American teens. I know decisions happen that way to the old-growth forests, too.

I went to a lecture at the Zen Center not far from my house, to hear the head gardener there. She talked about what is to be learned from gingko trees. I've always liked their fan-shaped leaves, bright gold in the fall, but I hadn't known they were ancient, evolved thousands of years ago. They exist nowhere in the wild, she said, but were fostered by monks in gardens in China and Japan. Somehow, gingkos have adapted so that they thrive in cities, in polluted air. They remind me of the kids around here, full of life in spite of everything. I've seen teenage boys from my block, the kind called "at risk," "inner city," sometimes even "thugs," on a field trip to an organic farm, patting seedlings into the earth like tender young fathers putting babies to bed.

The day after the lecture, I went to the nursery, ready to try planting trees again in the holes in the sidewalk. Now in front of my house are two tiny gingkos, each inside a fortified cage of four strong metal posts and thick wire mesh. To weed them, I kneel on the sidewalk and reach in, trying not to scratch my wrist on the wire.

Kneeling there, I accept on faith that this little tree will do its best to grow according to its own plan. I also believe that every person wants a better life.

One evening last summer I lay flat out in a hot spring in the broad valley on the east side of the Sierra. I imagined one of the little street gingkos growing upright from my left palm. Out of my right palm, an ancient bristlecone pine of the White Mountains. This is how the trees live on the earth, as out of one body. They are not separate. The roots of the city tree and the summit tree pass through my heart and tangle.

"STATEMENT ON GLOBAL WARMING AND CLIMATE CHANGE BY NORTH CAROLINA'S RELIGIOUS AND SPIRITUAL LEADERS"

Interfaith Global Climate Change Campaign, North Carolina Chapter

Signed by religious leaders of Judaism, Protestantism (Unitarian, Lutheran, Baptist, Episcopal, Presbyterian, Methodist), Catholicism, and Buddhism

As witnesses of the serious climate changes the earth is now undergoing, we leaders of North Carolina's various spiritual traditions join together to voice our concerns about the health of the planet we share with all species. We acknowledge the need to commit ourselves to a course of action that will help us recognize our part in the devastating effects on much of our planet brought about by increasingly severe weather events. We declare the necessity for North Carolina's spiritual communities to be leaders in turning human activities in a new direction for the well being of the planet.

Scientific evidence indicates that greenhouse gases are linked to global warming or climate change, which threatens the health of the entire planet and all its inhabitants. We believe that global warming is a challenge to all people but particularly to the spiritual communities that recognize the sacredness of preserving all eco-systems that sustain life.

Global warming violates that sacredness. It leads to species extinction, destruction of habitat for all species, melting ice caps, and rising sea levels. It disrupts our supplies of food and water. Already we see people dying from extreme weather conditions exacerbated by climate change, including record-breaking storms, heat waves, floods, and droughts. The burdens of a degraded environment fall disproportionately upon the most vulnerable of the planet's people: the poor, sick, elderly, and those who will face still greater threats in future generations.

In response to the global warming crisis, we join with you in establishing the North Carolina Interfaith Climate Change Campaign. We commit our spiritual community to join with others to address this serious issue in the following ways:

Reprinted by permission from *Climate Connection*: North Carolina Interfaith Ecojustice Network.

- Attend with awe, humility, and gratitude to the spiritual beauty in nature as well as in scripture.

- Pray for the wisdom to address global warming as a violation of the integrity of the earth.

- Distribute educational materials, offer presentations, and convene study groups to help our communities understand the negative impact on the earth of some personal behaviors and lifestyles, and take action to conserve energy and reduce waste and use of fossil fuels.

- Share our perspectives on global warming with representatives of key sectors in our business, agricultural, and environmental organizations, seeking ways to work together for the common good.

- Encourage others in North Carolina communities to act on their responsibility to care for the earth.

- Organize our communities to meet with local and state political leaders, and members of Congress, to encourage their participation and support.

- Declare our support for U.S. Senate ratification of the Kyoto Protocol, thereby join in the international effort to address the threat of climate change.

Let us now "join together as many and diverse expressions of one loving mystery: for the healing of the earth and the renewal of all life" (UN Environmental Sabbath Program).

"PRINCIPLES OF ENVIRONMENTAL JUSTICE"

The First National People of Color Environmental Leadership Summit

PREAMBLE

We the people of color, gathered together at this multinational People of Color Environmental Leadership Summit, to begin to build a national and international movement of all peoples of color to fight the destruction and taking of our lands and communities, do hereby re-establish our spiritual interdependence to the sacredness of our Mother Earth; to respect and celebrate each of our cultures, languages and beliefs about the natural world and our roles in healing ourselves; to insure environmental justice; to promote economic alternatives which would contribute to the development of environmentally safe livelihoods; and to secure our political, economic and cultural liberation that has been denied for over 500 years of colonization and oppression, resulting in the poisoning of our communities and land and the genocide of our peoples, do affirm and adopt these Principles of Environmental Justice:

1. Environmental justice affirms the sacredness of Mother Earth, ecological unity and the interdependence of all species, and the right to be free from ecological destruction.
2. Environmental justice demands that public policy be based on mutual respect and justice for all peoples, free from any form of discrimination or bias.
3. Environmental justice mandates the right to ethical, balanced and responsible uses of land and renewable resources in the interest of a sustainable planet for humans and other living things.
4. Environmental justice calls for universal protection from nuclear testing, extraction, production and disposal of toxic/hazardous wastes and poisons and nuclear testing that threaten the fundamental right to clean air, land, water, and food.
5. Environmental justice affirms the fundamental right to political, economic, cultural and environmental self-determination of all peoples.

From the First National People of Color Environmental Leadership Summit, June 1991.

6. Environmental justice demands the cessation of the production of all toxins, hazardous wastes, and radioactive materials, and that all past and current producers be held strictly accountable to the people for detoxification and the containment at the point of production.

7. Environmental justice demands the right to participate as equal partners at every level of decision-making including needs assessment, planning, implementation, enforcement and evaluation.

8. Environmental justice affirms the right of all workers to a safe and healthy work environment, without being forced to choose between an unsafe livelihood and unemployment. It also affirms the right of those who work at home to be free from environmental hazards.

9. Environmental justice protects the right of victims of environmental injustice to receive full compensation and reparations for damages as well as quality health care.

10. Environmental justice considers governmental acts of environmental injustice a violation of international law, the Universal Declaration On Human Rights, and the United Nations Convention on Genocide.

11. Environmental justice must recognize a special legal and natural relationship of Native Peoples to the U.S. government through treaties, agreements, compacts, and covenants affirming sovereignty and self-determination.

12. Environmental justice affirms the need for urban and rural ecological policies to clean up and rebuild our cities and rural areas in balance with nature, honoring the cultural integrity of all our communities, and providing fair access for all to the full range of resources.

13. Environmental justice calls for the strict enforcement of principles of informed consent, and a halt to the testing of experimental reproductive and medical procedures and vaccinations on people of color.

14. Environmental justice opposes the destructive operations of multinational corporations.

15. Environmental justice opposes military occupation, repression and exploitation of lands, peoples and cultures, and other life forms.

16. Environmental justice calls for the education of present and future generations which emphasizes social and environmental issues, based on our experience and an appreciation of our diverse cultural perspectives.

17. Environmental justice requires that we, as individuals, make personal and consumer choices to consume as little of Mother Earth's resources and to produce as little waste as possible; and make the conscious decision to challenge and reprioritize our lifestyles to insure the health of the natural world for present and future generations.

—Adopted, 27 October 1991

"STATEMENT BY RELIGIOUS LEADERS AT THE SUMMIT ON ENVIRONMENT"

In June 1991, the following statement was issued by the heads of many religious denominations and faith groups reflecting the growing consensus about the importance of environmental issues in North American religious life. They call upon people of faith to offer their wisdom, courage, creativity, and hope to efforts to preserve and safeguard the Earth.

On a spring evening and the following day in New York City, we representatives of the religious community in the United States of America gathered to deliberate and plan action in response to the crisis of the Earth's environment.

Deep impulses brought us together. Almost daily, we note mounting evidence of environmental destruction and ever-increasing peril to life, whole species, whole ecosystems. Many people, and particularly the young, want to know where we stand and what we intend to do. And, finally, it is what God made and beheld as good that is under assault. The future of this gift so freely given is in our hands, and we must maintain it as we have received it. This is an inescapably religious challenge. We feel a profound and urgent call to respond with all we have, all we are and all we believe.

We chose to meet, these two days, in the company of people from diverse traditions and disciplines. No one perspective alone is equal to the crisis we face—spiritual and moral, economic and cultural, institutional and personal. For our part, we were grateful to strengthen a collaboration with distinguished scientists and to take stock of their testimony on problems besetting planetary ecology. As people of faith, we were also moved by the support for our work from distinguished public policy leaders.

What we heard left us more troubled than ever. Global warming, generated mainly by the burning of fossil fuels and deforestation, is widely predicted to increase temperatures worldwide, changing climate patterns, increasing drought in many areas, threatening agriculture, wildlife, the integrity of natural ecosystems and creating millions of environmental refugees. Depletion of the ozone shield, caused by human-made chemical agents such as chlorofluoro-carbons, lets in deadly ultraviolet radiation from the Sun, with predicted consequences that include skin cancer, cataracts, damage to the human immune system, and destruction of the primary photosynthetic producers at the base of the food chain on which other life depends. Our expanding technological civilization is destroying an acre and a half of forest every second. The accelerating loss of species of plants, animals and microorganisms which threaten the irreversible loss of up to a fifth of the total number within the next 30 years, is not only morally reprehensible but is increasingly limiting the prospects for sustainable productivity. No effort, however heroic, to deal with these global conditions and the interrelated issues of social justice can succeed unless we address the increasing population of the Earth—especially the billion poorest people who have every right to expect a decent standard of living. So too, we must find ways to reduce the disproportionate consumption of natural resources by affluent industrial societies like ours.

Much would tempt us to deny or push aside this global environmental crisis and refuse even to consider the fundamental changes of human behavior required to address it. But we religious leaders accept a prophetic responsibility to make known the full dimensions of this challenge, and what is required to address it, to the many millions we reach, teach and counsel.

We intend to be informed participants in discussions of these issues and to contribute our views on the moral and ethical imperative for developing national and international policy responses. But we declare here and now that steps must be taken toward: accelerated phase-out of ozone-depleting chemicals; much more efficient use of fossil fuels and the development of a non-fossil fuel economy; preservation of tropical forests and other measures to protect continued biological diversity; and concerted efforts to slow the dramatic and dangerous growth in world population through empowering both women and men, encouraging economic self-sufficiency, and making family education programs available to all who may consider them on a strictly voluntary basis.

We believe a consensus now exists, at the highest level of leadership across a significant spectrum of religious traditions, that the cause of environmental integrity and justice must occupy a position of utmost priority for people of faith. Response to this issue can and must cross traditional religious and political lines. It has the potential to unify and renew religious life.

We pledge to take the initiative in interpreting and communicating theological foundations for the stewardship of Creation in which we find the principles for environmental actions. Here our seminaries have a critical role to play. So too, there is a call for moral transformation, as we recognize that the roots of environmental destruction lie in human pride, greed and selfishness, as well as the appeal of the short-term over the long-term.

We reaffirm here, in the strongest possible terms, the indivisibility of social justice and ecological integrity. An equitable international economic order is essential for preserving the global environment. Economic equity, racial justice, gender equality and environmental well-being are interconnected and all are essential to peace. To help ensure these, we pledge to mobilize public opinion and to appeal to elected officials and leaders in the private sector. In our congregations and corporate life, we will encourage and seek to exemplify habits of sound and sustainable householding—in land use, investment decisions, energy conservation, purchasing of products and waste disposal.

Commitments to these areas of action we pledged to one another solemnly and in a spirit of mutual accountability. We dare not let our resolve falter. We will continue to work together, add to our numbers, and deepen our collaboration with the worlds of science and government. We also agreed this day to the following initiatives:

1. We will widely distribute this declaration within the religious community and beyond. We have established a continuing mechanism to coordinate ongoing activities among us, working intimately with existing program and staff resources in the religious world. We will reach out to other leaders across the broadest possible spectrum of religious life. We will help organize other such gatherings as ours within individual faith groups, in interfaith and interdisciplinary formats, and at international, national, and regional levels.

2. We religious leaders and members of the scientific community will call together a Washington, D.C., convocation and meet with members of the Executive and Congressional branches to express our support for bold steps on behalf of environmental integrity and justice. There too we will consider ways to facilitate legislative testimony by religious leaders and response to local environmental action alerts.

3. We will witness firsthand and call public attention to the effect of environmental degradation on vulnerable peoples and ecosystems.

4. We will call a meeting of seminary deans and faculty to review and initiate curriculum development and promote bibliographies emphasizing stewardship of Creation. We will seek ways to establish internships for seminarians in organizations working on the environment and for young scientists in the study of social ethics.

5. We will prepare educational materials for congregations, provide technical support for religious publishers already producing such materials, and share sermonical and liturgical materials about ecology.

6. We will establish an instrument to help place stories on environment in faith group and denominational newsletters and help assure coverage of the religious community's environmental activities in the secular press.

7. We will urge compliance with the Valdez Principles and preach and promote corporate responsibility.

8. We will encourage establishment of one model environmentally sound and sustainable facility within each faith group and denomination. We will provide materials for environmental audits and facilitate bulk purchasing of environmentally sound products.

It has taken the religious community, as others, much time and reflection to start to comprehend the full scale and nature of this crisis and even to glimpse what it will require of us. We must pray ceaselessly for wisdom, courage, and creativity. Most importantly, we are people of faith and hope. These qualities are what we may most uniquely have to offer to this effort. We pledge to the children of the world and, in the words of the Iroquois, "to the seventh generation," that we will take full measure of what this moment in history requires of us. In this challenge may lie the opportunity for people of faith to affirm and enact, at a scale such as never before, what it truly means to be religious. And so we have begun, believing there can be no turning back.

June 3, 1991, New York City

Signers:

Bishop Vinton R. Anderson, President, World Council of Churches; Rabbi Marc. D. Angel, President, Rabbinical Council of America; The Most Reverend Edmond L. Browning, Presiding Bishop and Primate of the Episcopal Church; Reverend Joan Brown Campbell, General Secretary, National Council of Churches of Christ; The Reverend Herbert W. Chilstrom, Bishop, Evangelical Lutheran Church in America; Father Drew Christiansen, S.J., Director, Office of International Justice and Peace, United States Catholic Conference; Ms. Beverly Davison, President, American Baptist Churches; Reverend Dr. Milton B. Efthimiou, Director of Church and Society, Greek Orthodox Archdiocese of North and South America; Bishop William B. Friend, Chairman of the Committee for Science and Human Values, National Conference of Catholic Bishops; Dr. Alfred Gottschalk, President, Hebrew Union College-Jewish Institute of Religion; Dr. Arthur Green, President, Reconstructionist Rabbinical College; His Eminence Archbishop Iakovos, Primate, Greek Orthodox Archdiocese of North and South America; The Very Reverend Leonid Kishkovsky, President, National Council of Churches of Christ; Chief Oren Lyons, Chief of the Turtle Clan of the Onondaga Nation; Dr. David McKenna, President, Asbury Theological Seminary; The Very Reverend James Parks Morton, Dean, Cathedral of St. John the Divine; Dr. W. Franklyn Richardson, General Secretary, National Baptist Convention; Dr. Patricia J. Rumer, General Director, Church Women United; Dr. James R. Scales, President Emeritus, Wake Forest University; Dr. Ismar Schorsch, Chancellor, Jewish Theological Seminary; Dr. Robert Schuller, Pastor, the Crystal Cathedral; Dr. Robert Seiple, President, World Vision U.S.A.; Bishop Melvin Talbert, Secretary of the Council of Bishops, United Methodist Church; Dr. Foy Valentine, Former Executive Director, Christian Life Commission, Southern Baptist Convention.

"DECLARATION OF THE 'MISSION TO WASHINGTON'"

Joint Appeal by Religion and Science for the Environment

Despite many philosophical differences, the 150 religious heads and scientists who gathered for the Mission to Washington in May of 1992 reached out to one another across historic antagonisms. Together they issued a declaration dedicating themselves to undertake bold action to cherish and protect the environment and affirmed a deep sense of common purpose.

We are people of faith and of science who, for centuries, often have traveled different roads. In a time of environmental crisis, we find these roads converging. As this meeting symbolizes, our two ancient, sometimes antagonistic, traditions now reach out to one another in a common endeavor to preserve the home we share.

We humans are endowed with self-awareness, intelligence and compassion. At our best, we cherish and seek to protect all life and the treasures of the natural world. But we are now tampering with the climate. We are thinning the ozone layer and creating holes in it. We are poisoning the air, the land and the water. We are destroying the forests, grasslands and other ecosystems. We are causing the extinction of species at a pace not seen since the end of the age of the dinosaurs. As a result, many scientific projections suggest a legacy for our children and grandchildren of compromised immune systems, increased infectious disease and cancer rates, destroyed plants and consequent disruption of the food chain, agriculture damaged from drought and ultraviolet light, accelerated destruction of forests and species and vastly increased numbers of environmental refugees. Many perils may be still undiscovered. The burdens, as usual, will fall most cruelly upon the shoulders of the poorest among us, especially upon children. But no one will be unaffected. At the same time, the human community grows by a quarter of a million people every day, mostly in the poorest nations and communities. That this crisis was brought about in part through inadvertence does not excuse us. Many nations are responsible. The magnitude of this crisis means that it cannot be resolved unless many nations work together. We must now join forces to that end.

Our own country is the leading polluter on Earth, generating more greenhouse gases, especially CO_2, than any other country. Not by word alone but by binding action, our nation has an inescapable moral duty to lead the way to genuinely effective solutions. We signers of this declaration—leaders in religion and science—call upon our government to change national policy so that the United States will begin to ease, not continue to increase, the burdens on our biosphere and their effect upon the planet's people.

We believe that science and religion, working together, have an essential contribution to make toward any significant mitigation and resolution of the world environmental crisis. What good are the most fervent moral imperatives if we do not understand the dangers and how to avoid them? What good is all the data in the world without a steadfast moral compass? Many of the consequences of our present assault on the environment, even if halted today, will take decades and centuries to play themselves out. How will our children and grandchildren judge our stewardship of the Earth? What will they think of us? Do we not have a solemn obligation to leave them a better world and to ensure the integrity of nature itself? Insofar as our peril arises from a neglect of moral values, human pride, arrogance, inattention, greed, improvidence, and a penchant for the short-term over the long, religion has an essential role to play. Insofar as our peril arises from our ignorance of the intricate interconnectedness of nature, science has an essential role to play.

Differences of perspective remain among us. We do not have to agree on how the natural world was made to be willing to work together to preserve it. On that paramount objective we affirm a deep sense of common cause.

Commitment to environmental integrity and justice, across a broad spectrum and at the highest level of leadership, continues to grow in the United States religious community as an issue of utmost priority—significantly as a result of fruitful conversations with the scientific community. We believe that the dimensions of this crisis are still not sufficiently taken to heart by our leaders, institutions and industries. We accept our responsibility to help make known to the millions we serve and teach the nature and consequences of the environmental crisis, and what is required to overcome it. We believe that our current economic behavior and policies emphasize short-term individual material goals at the expense of the common good and of future generations. When we consider the long-term as well as the short-term costs, it seems clear that addressing this problem now rather than later makes economic as well as moral sense. We impoverish our own children and grandchildren by insisting that they deal with dangers that we could have averted at far less cost in resources and human suffering.

We reaffirm here, in the strongest possible terms, the indivisibility of social justice and the preservation of the environment. We also affirm and support the indigenous peoples in the protection and integrity of their cultures and lands. We believe the wealthy nations of the North, which have historically exploited the natural and human resources of the Southern nations, have a moral obligation to make available additional financial resources and appropriate technology to strengthen their capacity for their own development. We believe the poor and vulnerable workers in our own land should not be asked to bear disproportionate burdens. And we must end the dumping of toxic waste materials disproportionately in communities of low income and of people of color. We recognize that there is a vital connection between peacemaking and protecting our environment. Collectively, the nations of the world spend one trillion dollars a year on military programs. If even a modest portion of this money were spent on environmental programs and sustainable economic development, we could take a major step toward environmental security.

We commit ourselves to work together for a United States that will lead the world in the efficient use of fossil fuels, in devising and utilizing renewable sources of energy, in phasing out all significant ozone-depleting chemicals, in halting deforestation and slowing the decline in species diversity, in planting forests and restoring other habitats and in realizing worldwide social justice. We believe there is a need for concerted efforts to stabilize world population by humane, responsible and voluntary means consistent with our differing values. For these, and other reasons, we believe that special attention must be paid to education and to enhancing the roles and the status of women.

Despite the seriousness of this crisis, we are hopeful. We humans, in spite of our faults, can be intelligent, resourceful, compassionate, prudent and imaginative. We have access to great reservoirs of moral and spiritual courage. Deep within us stirs a commitment to the health, safety and future of our children. Understanding that the world does not belong to any one nation or generation, and sharing a spirit of utmost urgency, we dedicate ourselves to undertake bold action to cherish and protect the environment of our planetary home.

Washington, D.C.

May 12, 1992

"CATHOLIC SOCIAL TEACHING AND ENVIRONMENTAL ETHICS"

United States Catholic Conference

The tradition of Catholic social teaching offers a developing and distinctive perspective on environmental issues. We believe that the following themes drawn from this tradition are integral dimensions of ecological responsibility:

- God-centered and sacramental view of the universe, which grounds human accountability for the fate of the earth;

- consistent respect for human life, which extends to respect for all creation;

- world view affirming the ethical significance of global interdependence and the common good;

- an ethics of solidarity promoting cooperation and a just structure of sharing in the world community;

- an understanding of the universal purpose of created things, which requires equitable use of the earth's resources;

- an option for the poor, which gives passion to the quest for an equitable and sustainable world;

- a conception of authentic development, which offers a direction for progress that respects human dignity and the limits of material growth.

Although Catholic social teaching does not offer a complete environmental ethic, we are confident that this developing tradition can serve as the basis for Catholic engagement and dialogue with science, the environmental movement, and other communities of faith and good will.

A. SACRAMENTAL UNIVERSE

The whole universe is God's dwelling. Earth, a very small, uniquely blessed corner of that universe, gifted with unique natural blessings, is humanity's home, and humans are never

---

so much at home as when God dwells with them. In the beginning, the first man and woman walked with God in the cool of the day. Throughout history, people have continued to meet the Creator on mountaintops, in vast deserts, and alongside waterfalls and gently flowing springs. In storms and earthquakes, they found expressions of divine power. In the cycle of the seasons and the courses of the stars, they have discerned signs of God's fidelity and wisdom. We still share, though dimly, in that sense of God's presence in nature. But as heirs and victims of the industrial revolution, students of science and the beneficiaries of technology, urban-dwellers and jet-commuters, twentieth-century Americans have also grown estranged from the natural scale and rhythms of life on earth.

For many people, the environmental movement has reawakened appreciation of the truth that, through the created gifts of nature, men and women encounter their Creator. The Christian vision of a sacramental universe—a world that discloses the Creator's presence by visible and tangible signs—can contribute to making the earth a home for the human family once again. Pope John Paul II has called for Christians to respect and protect the environment, so that through nature people can "contemplate the mystery of the greatness and love of God."

Reverence for the Creator present and active in nature, moreover, may serve as ground for environmental responsibility. For the very plants and animals, mountains and oceans, which in their loveliness and sublimity lift our minds to God, by their fragility and perishing likewise cry out, "We have not made ourselves." God brings them into being and sustains them in existence. It is to the Creator of the universe, then, that we are accountable for what we do or fail to do to preserve and care for the earth and all its creatures. For "[t]he Lord's are the earth and its fullness; the world and those who dwell in it" (Ps 24:1). Dwelling in the presence of God, we begin to experience ourselves as part of creation, as stewards within it, not separate from it. As faithful stewards, fullness of life comes from living responsibly within God's creation.

Stewardship implies that we must both care for creation according to standards that are not of our own making and at the same time be resourceful in finding ways to make the earth flourish. It is a difficult balance, requiring both a sense of limits and a spirit of experimentation. Even as we rejoice in earth's goodness and in the beauty of nature, stewardship places upon us responsibility for the well-being of all God's creatures.

B. RESPECT FOR LIFE

Respect for nature and respect for human life are inextricably related. "Respect for life, and above all for the dignity of the human person," Pope John Paul II has written, extends also to the rest of creation (*The Ecological Crisis: A Common Responsibility* [=EC], no. 7).

Other species, ecosystems, and even distinctive landscapes give glory to God. The covenant given to Noah was a promise to all the earth.

> See, I am establishing my covenant with you and your descendants after you and with every living creature that was with you: all the birds, and the various tame and wild animals that were with you and came out of the ark. (Gn 9:9–10)

The diversity of life manifests God's glory. Every creature shares a bit of the divine beauty. Because the divine goodness could not be represented by one creature alone, Aquinas tells us, God "produced many and diverse creatures, so that what was wanting to one in representation of the divine goodness might be supplied by another . . . hence the whole universe together participates in the divine goodness more perfectly, and represents it better than any single creature whatever" (*Summa Theologiae*, Prima Pars, question 48, ad 2). The wonderful variety of the natural world is, therefore, part of the divine plan and, as such, invites our respect. Accordingly, it is appropriate that we treat other creatures and the natural world not just as means to human fulfillment but also as God's creatures, possessing an independent value, worthy of our respect and care.

By preserving natural environments, by protecting endangered species, by laboring to make human environments compatible with local ecology, by employing appropriate technology, and by carefully evaluating technological innovations as we adopt them, we exhibit respect for creation and reverence for the Creator.

C. THE PLANETARY COMMON GOOD

In 1963, Pope John XXIII, in the letter *Pacem in Terris*, emphasized the world's growing interdependence. He saw problems emerging, which the traditional political mechanisms could no longer address, and he extended the traditional principle of the common good from the nation-state to the world community. Ecological concern has now heightened our awareness of just how interdependent our world is. Some of the gravest environmental problems are clearly global. In this shrinking world, everyone is affected and everyone is responsible, although those most responsible are often the least affected. The universal common good can serve as a foundation for a global environmental ethic.

In many of his statements, Pope John Paul II has recognized the need for such an ethic. For example, in *The Ecological Crisis: A Common Responsibility*, his 1990 World Day of Peace Message, he wrote,

> Today the ecological crisis has assumed such proportions as to be the responsibility of everyone. . . . [I]ts various aspects demonstrate the need for concerted efforts aimed at es-

tablishing the duties and obligations that belong to individuals, peoples, States and the international community. (no. 15)

Governments have particular responsibility in this area. In *Centesimus Annus*, the pope insists that the state has the task of providing "for the defense and preservation of common good such as the natural and human environments, which cannot be safeguarded simply by market forces" (no. 40).

D. A NEW SOLIDARITY

In the Catholic tradition, the universal common good is specified by the duty of solidarity, "a firm and preserving determination to commit oneself to the common good," a willingness "to 'lose oneself' for the sake of the other[s] instead of exploiting [them]" (Pope John Paul II, *Sollicitudo Rei Socialis* [=SRS], no. 38). In the face of "the structures of sin," moreover, solidarity requires sacrifices of our own self-interest for the good of others and of the earth we share. Solidarity places special obligations upon the industrial democracies, including the United States. "The ecological crisis," Pope John Paul II has written, "reveals the urgent moral need for a new solidarity, especially in relations between the developing nations and those that are highly industrialized" (EC, no. 10). Only with equitable and sustainable development can poor nations curb continuing environmental degradation and avoid the destructive effects of the kind of overdevelopment that has used natural resources irresponsibly.

E. UNIVERSAL PURPOSE OF CREATED THINGS

God has given the fruit of the earth to sustain the entire human family "without excluding or favoring anyone." Human work has enhanced the productive capacity of the earth and in our time is as Pope John Paul II has said, "increasingly important as the productive factor both of non-material and of material wealth" (CA, no. 31). But a great many people, in the Third World as well as in our own inner cities and rural areas, are still deprived of the means of livelihood. In moving toward an environmentally sustainable economy, we are obligated to work for a just economic system which equitably shares the bounty of the earth and of human enterprise with all peoples. Created things belong not to the few, but to the entire human family.

F. OPTION FOR THE POOR

The ecological problem is intimately connected to justice for the poor. "The goods of the earth, which in the divine plan should be a common patrimony," Pope John Paul II has reminded us, "often risk becoming the monopoly of a few who often spoil it and, sometimes, destroy it, thereby creating a loss for all humanity" (October 25, 1991 Address at Conference Marking the Presentation of the Second Edition of the St. Francis "Canticle of the Creatures" International Award for the Environment).

The poor of the earth offer a special test of our solidarity. The painful adjustments we have to undertake in our own economies for the sake of the environment must not diminish our sensitivity to the needs of the poor at home and abroad. The option for the poor embedded in the Gospel and the Church's teaching makes us aware that the poor suffer most directly from environmental decline and have the least access to relief from their suffering. Indigenous peoples die with their forests and grasslands. In Bhopal and Chernobyl, it was the urban poor and working people who suffered the most immediate and intense contamination. Nature will truly enjoy its second spring only when humanity has compassion for its own weakest members.

A related and vital concern is the Church's constant commitment to the dignity of work and the rights of workers. Environmental progress cannot come at the expense of workers and their rights. Solutions must be found that do not force us to choose between a decent environment and a decent life for workers.

We recognize the potential conflicts in this area and will work for greater understanding, communication, and common ground between workers and environmentalists. Clearly, workers cannot be asked to make sacrifices to improve the environment without concrete support from the broader community. Where jobs are lost, society must help in the process of economic conversion, so that not only the earth but also workers and their families are protected.

G. AUTHENTIC DEVELOPMENT

Unrestrained economic development is not the answer to improving the lives of the poor. Catholic social teaching has never accepted material growth as a model of development. A "mere accumulation of goods and services, even for the benefit of the majority," as Pope John Paul II has said, "is not enough for the realization of human happiness" (SRS, no. 28). He has also warned that in a desire "to have and to enjoy rather than to be and to grow," humanity "consumes the resources of the earth, subjecting it without restraint . . . as if it did not have its own requisites and God-given purposes."

Authentic development supports moderation and even austerity in the use of material resources. It also encourages a balanced view of human progress consistent with respect for nature. Furthermore, it invites the development of alternative visions of the good society and the use of economic models with richer standards of well-being than material productivity alone. Authentic development also requires affluent nations to seek ways to reduce and restructure their overconsumption of natural resources. Finally, authentic development also entails encouraging the proper use of both agricultural and industrial technologies, so that development does not merely mean technological advancement for its own sake but rather that technology benefits people and enhances the land.

H. CONSUMPTION AND POPULATION

In public discussions, two areas are particularly cited as requiring greater care and judgment on the part of human beings. The first is consumption of resources. The second is growth in world population. Regrettably, advantaged groups often seem more intent on curbing Third World births than on restraining the even more voracious consumerism of the developed world. We believe this compounds injustice and increases disrespect for the life of the weakest among us. For example, it is not so much population growth, but the desperate efforts of debtor countries to pay their foreign debt by exporting products to affluent industrial countries that drives poor peasants off their land and up eroding hillsides, where in the effort to survive, they also destroy the environment.

Consumption in developed nations remains the single greatest source of global environmental destruction. A child born in the United States, for example, puts a far heavier burden on the world's resources than one born in a poor developing country. By one estimate, each American uses twenty-eight times the energy of a person living in a developing country. Advanced societies, and our own in particular, have barely begun to make efforts at reducing their consumption of resources and the enormous waste and pollution that result from it. We in the developed world, therefore, are obligated to address our own wasteful and destructive use of resources as a matter of top priority.

The key factor, though not the only one, in dealing with population problems is sustainable social and economic development. Technological fixes do not really work. Only when an economy distributes resources so as to allow the poor an equitable stake in society and some hope for the future do couples see responsible parenthood as good for their families. In particular, prenatal care; education; good nutrition; and health care for women, children, and families promise to improve family welfare and contribute to stabilizing population. Supporting such equitable social development, moreover, may well be the best contribution affluent societies, like the United States, can make to relieving ecological pressures in low developed nations. At the same time, it must be acknowledged that rapid population growth presents special problems and challenges that must be addressed in order to avoid damage done to the environment and to social development. In the words of Pope Paul VI, "it is not to be denied that accelerated demographic increases too frequently add difficulties to plan for development because the population is increased more rapidly than available resources. . . . " (*Populorum Progressio*, no. 37). In *Sollicitudo Rei Socialis*, Pope John Paul II has likewise noted, "One cannot deny the existence, especially in the southern hemisphere, of a demographic problem which creates difficulties for development" (no. 25). He has gone on to make connections among population size, development, and the environment. There is "a greater realization of the limits of available resources," he commented, "and of the need to respect the integrity and the cycles of nature and to take them into account when planning for development . . . " (no. 26). Even though it is possible to feed a growing population, the ecological costs of doing so ought to be taken into account. To eliminate hunger from the planet, the world community needs to reform the institutional and political structures that restrict the access of people to food.

Thus, the Church addresses population issues in the context of its teaching on human life, of just development, of care for the environment, and of respect for the freedom of married couples to decide voluntarily on the number and spacing of births. In keeping with these values, and out of respect for cultural norms, it continues to oppose coercive methods of population control and programs that bias decisions through incentives or disincentives. Respect for nature ought to encourage policies that promote natural family planning and true responsible parenthood rather than coercive population control programs or incentives for birth control that violate cultural and religious norms and Catholic teaching.

Finally, we are charged with restoring the integrity of all creation. We must care for all God's creatures, especially the most vulnerable. How, then, can we protect endangered species and at the same time be callous to the unborn, the elderly, or disabled persons? Is not abortion also a sin against creation? If we turn our backs on our own unborn children, can we truly expect that nature will receive respectful treatment at our hands? The care of the earth will not be advanced by the destruction of human life at any stage of development. As Pope John Paul II has said, "protecting the environment is first of all the right to live and the protection of life" (October 16, 1991 Homily at Quiaba, Mato Grosso, Brazil).

I. A WEB OF LIFE

These themes drawn from Catholic social teaching are linked to our efforts to share this teaching in other contexts, especially in our pastoral letters on peace and economic justice and in our statements on food and agriculture. Clearly, war represents a serious threat to the environment, as the darkened skies and oil soaked beaches of Kuwait clearly remind us. The pursuit of peace—lasting peace based on justice—ought to be an environmental priority because the earth itself bears the wounds and scars of war. Likewise, our efforts to defend the dignity and rights of the poor and of workers, to use the strength of our market economy to meet basic human needs, and to press for greater national and global economic justice are clearly linked to efforts to preserve and sustain the earth. These are not distinct and separate issues but complementary challenges. We need to help build bridges among the peace, justice, and environmental agendas and constituencies.

SUGGESTIONS FOR FURTHER READING

Achtemeier, Elizabeth. *Nature, God and Pulpit.* Grand Rapids, Mich.: Eerdmans, 1992.

Adams, Carol, ed. *Ecofeminism and the Sacred.* New York: Crossroad Press, 1993.

Agwan, A. R. *The Environmental Concern of Islam.* New Delhi: Institute of Objective Studies, 1992.

Ahmad, Akhtaruddin. *Islam and the Environmental Crisis.* London: Ta-Ha Publishers, 1998.

Albanese, Catherine L. *Nature Religion in America: From the Algonkian Indians to the New Age.* Chicago: University of Chicago Press, 1990.

Allen, Paula Gunn. *The Sacred Hoop: Recovering the Feminine in the American Indian Tradition.* Boston: Beacon, 1986.

Alpert, Rebecca T., and Arthur Waskow. "Toward an Ethical Kashrut." *Reconstructionist* 52, no. 5 (1987): 9–13.

Ames, Roger T. "Taoism and the Nature of Nature." *Environmental Ethics* 8 (1986): 317–50.

Anderson, E. N. *Ecologies of the Heart.* New York: Oxford University Press, 1996.

Anderson, Robert S., and Walter Huber. *The Hour of the Fox: Tropical Forest, the World Bank, and Indigenous People in Central India.* Seattle: University of Washington Press, 1988.

Andrews, Valerie. *A Passion for this Earth.* San Francisco: Harper, 1990.

Apffel-Marglin, Frédérique, and Stephen Marglin, eds. *Decolonizing Knowledge.* Oxford: Oxford University Press, 1994.

Austin, Richard Cartwright. *Baptized into Wilderness: A Christian Perspective on John Muir.* Atlanta: J. Knox Press, 1987.

Ba Kader, Abou Bakr Ahmed. *Environmental Protection in Islam.* Washington, D.C.: Island Press, 1995.

Badiner, Allan, ed. *Dharma Gaia: A Harvest of Essays in Buddhism and Ecology.* Berkeley: Parallax Press, 1990.

Baker-Fletcher, Karen. *Sisters of Dust, Sisters of Spirit: Womanist Wordings on God and Creation.* Minneapolis: Fortress, 1998.

Banuri, Tariq, and Frédérique Apffel-Marglin, eds. *Who Will Save the Forests?* London: Zed, 1993.

Banwari. *Pancavati: Indian Approaches to Environment.* Translated by Asha Vohra. Delhi: Shri Vinayak Publications, 1992.

Bari, Judi. "We All Live Here: An Interview with Judi Bari." By Susan Moon. *Turning Wheel,* Spring 1994, 16–19.

Barnhill, David Landes, and Roger S. Gottlieb, eds. *Deep Ecology and World Religions.* Albany: SUNY Press, 2000.

Basney, Lionel. *An Earth-Careful Way of Life: Christian Stewardship and the Environmental Crisis.* Downers Grove, Ill: InterVarsity Press, 1994.

Bergant, Dianne. *The Earth Is the Lord's: The Bible, Ecology, and Worship.* Collegeville, Minn.: Liturgical Press, 1998.

Berger, Pamela. *The Goddess Obscured: The Transformation of the Grain Protectress from Goddess to Saint.* Boston: Beacon, 1985.

Berman, Morris. *The Reenchantment of the World.* New York: Bantam, 1984.

Bernstein, Ellen, ed. *Ecology and the Jewish Spirit: Where Nature and the Sacred Meet.* Woodstock, Vt.: Jewish Lights, 1998.

Berry, Thomas. *The Dream of the Earth.* San Francisco: Sierra Club Books, 1988.

Berry, Thomas, and Thomas Clarke. *Befriending the Earth: A Theology of Reconciliation between Humans and the Earth.* Edited by Stephen Dunn and Anne Lonergan. Mystic, Conn.: Twenty-Third Publications, 1991.

Berry, Thomas, and Brian Swimme. *The Universe Story: From the Primordial Flaring Forth to the Ecozoic Era—A Celebration of the Unfolding of the Cosmos.* San Francisco: HarperCollins,1992.

Bierhorst, John. *The Way of the Earth: Native America and the Environment.* New York: William Morrow, 1994.

Birch, Charles, and John B. Cobb, Jr. *The Liberation of Life: From the Cell to the Community.* Cambridge, Mass: Cambridge University Press, 1981.

Birch, Charles, William Eakin, and Jay B. McDaniel. *Liberating Life: Contemporary Approaches to Ecological Theology.* Maryknoll, N.Y.: Orbis Books, 1990.

Black, Alison Harley. *Man and Nature in the Philosophical Thought of Wang Fu-chih.* Seattle: University of Washington Press, 1989.

Black Elk. *The Sacred Pipe: Black Elk's Account of the Seven Rites of the Oglala Sioux.* Recorded and edited by Joseph Epes Brown. Norman: University of Oklahoma Press, 1953.

Boff, Leonardo. *Cry of the Earth, Cry of the Poor.* Translated by Philip Berryman. Maryknoll, N.Y.: Orbis, 1997.

Boff, Leonardo. *Ecology and Liberation: A New Paradigm.* Translated by John Cumming. Maryknoll, N.Y.: Orbis, 1995.

Bowman, Douglas C. *Beyond the Modern Mind: The Spiritual and Ethical Challenge of the Environmental Crisis.* New York: Pilgrim Press, 1990.

Bradley, Ian C. *God is Green: Ecology for Christians.* New York: Doubleday, 1992.

Braidotti, Rosa, Ewa Charkiewicz, Sabine Hausler, and Sakia Wiernga. *Women, the Environment, and Sustainable Development: Toward a Theoretical Synthesis.* London: Zed, 1994.

Brown, Joseph Epes. *The Spiritual Legacy of the American Indian.* New York: Crossroads, 1982.

Brush, Stephen, and Doreen Stabinsky, eds. *Valuing Local Knowledge: Indigenous People and Intellectual Property Rights.* Washington, D.C.: Island Press, 1996.

Bullard, Robert D., ed. *Unequal Protection: Environmental Justice and Communities of Color.* San Francisco: Sierra Club Books, 1994.

Calderazzo, John. "Meditation in a Thai Forest." *Audubon,* January-February 1991, 84–91.

Callicott, J. Baird, and Roger T. Ames, eds. *Nature in Asian Traditions of Thought: Essays in Environmental Philosophy.* Albany: State University of New York Press, 1989.

Callicott, J. Baird. *Earth's Insights: A Multicultural Survey of Ecological Ethics from the Mediterranean Basin to the Australian Outback.* Berkeley: University of California Press, 1994.

Canan, Ibrahim. *Environmental Ethics in the Light of the Hadiths.* Istanbul: New Asia Press, 1995. (In Turkish.)

Canan, Janine, ed. *She Rises Like the Sun: Invocations of the Goddess by Contemporary American Women Poets.* Freedom, Calif.: Crossing Press, 1989.

Carmody, John. *Ecology and Religion: Toward a New Christian Theology of Nature.* New York: Paulist Press, 1983.

Carpenter, James A. *Nature and Grace: Toward an Integral Perspective.* New York: Crossroads Press, 1988.

Carroll, John E., Paul Brockelman, and Mary Westfall, eds. *The Greening of Faith: God, the Environment, and the Good Life.* Hanover, N.H.: University Press of New England, 1997.

Carroll, John E., and Albert LaChance, eds. *Embracing Earth: Catholic Approaches to Ecology*. Maryknoll, N.Y.: Orbis, 1994.

Chapple, Christopher Key. *Nonviolence to Animals, Earth, and Self in Asian Traditions*. Albany: State University of New York Press, 1993.

Chapple, Christopher Key, and Mary Evelyn Tucker, eds. *Hinduism and Ecology: The Intersection of Earth, Sky, and Water*. Cambridge, Mass.: Harvard University Center for the Study of World Religions/Harvard University Press, 2000.

Cheng Chung-Ying. "On the Environmental Ethics of the *Tao* and the *Ch'i*." *Environmental Ethics* 8 (1986): 351–70.

Chung Hyun Kyung. "Welcome the Spirit; Hear Her Cries: The Holy Spirit, Creation, and the Culture of Life." *Christianity and Crisis* 51 (15 July 1991): 220–23.

Clark, J. Michael. *Beyond Our Ghettos: Gay Theology in Ecological Perspective*. Cleveland, Ohio: Pilgrim Press, 1993.

Clarkson, Linda, Vern Morrissette, and Gabriel Regallet. *Our Responsibility to the Seventh Generation: Indigenous Peoples and Sustainable Development*. Winnipeg: International Institute for Sustainable Development, 1992.

Clinebell, Howard J. *Ecotherapy: Healing Ourselves, Healing the Earth*. Philadelphia: Fortress, 1996.

Coalition on the Environment and Jewish Life (COEJL). *Caring for the Cycle of Life: Creating Environmentally Sound Life-Cycle Celebrations*. New York: Coalition on the Environment and Jewish Life, 1999.

Cobb, John B., Jr. *Sustainability: Economics, Ecology, and Justice*. Maryknoll, N.Y.: Orbis, 1992.

Cobb, John B., Jr. *The Earthist Challenge to Economism: A Theological Critique of the World Bank*. New York: St. Martin's Press, 1999.

Cobb, John B., Jr., and Herman E. Daly. *For the Common Good: Redirecting the Economy toward Community, the Environment, and a Sustainable Future*. Boston: Beacon, 1989.

Coward, Harold, ed. *Visions of a New Earth: Religious Perspectives on Population, Consumption, and Ecology*. Albany: State University of New York Press, 2000.

Daly, Herman E., and John B. Cobb, Jr. *For the Common Good: Redirecting the Economy toward Community, the Environment, and A Sustainable Future*. 2d ed., updated and expanded. Boston: Beacon, 1994.

Damad, Mostafa Mohaghegh. "A Discourse on Nature and Environment from an Islamic Perspective." Tehran: Department of the Environment, 2001 http://www.ir-doe.org/hamaiesh/pub2.htm (cited 24 August 2001).

Dankelman, Irene, and John Davidson. *Women and Environment in the Third World*. London: Earthscan, 1988.

Davies, Shann, ed. *Tree of Life: Buddhism and the Protection of Nature*. Hong Kong: Buddhist Perception of Nature Project, 1987.

De Vos, Peter, et al. *Earthkeeping in the Nineties: Stewardship of Creation*. Grand Rapids, Mich.: Eerdmans, 1991.

De Witt, Calvin B. *The Environment and the Christian: What Does the New Testament Say About the Environment?* Grand Rapids, Mich.: Baker Book House, 1991.

De-Shalit, Avner. "From the Political to the Objective: The Dialectics of Zionism and the Environment." *Environmental Politics* 4, no. 1 (1995): 70–87.

Devall, Bill, and George Sessions. *Deep Ecology: Living as if Nature Mattered*. Salt Lake City: Peregrine Smith Books, 1985.

Diamond, Irene, and Gloria Feman Orenstein, eds. *Reweaving the World: The Emergence of Ecofeminism*. San Francisco: Sierra Club Books, 1990.

Dunn, Stephen, and Anne Lonergan, eds. *Befriending the Earth: A Theology of Reconciliation between Humans and the Earth.* Mystic, Conn.: Twenty-third Publications, 1991.

Durning, Alan. *Guardians of the Land: Indigenous Peoples and the Health of the Earth.* Washington, D.C.: Worldwatch, 1993.

Dwivedi, O. P. "Environmental Protection in the Hindu Tradition." In *Ethical Perspectives on Environmental Issues in India,* ed. George A. James, 161–88. New Delhi: A. P. H., 1999.

Dwivedi, O. P., ed. *World Religions and the Environment.* New Delhi: Gilanjal, 1989.

Edwards, Denis. *Jesus the Wisdom of God: An Ecological Theology.* Maryknoll, N.Y.: Orbis, 1995.

Eisler, Riane Tennenhaus. *The Chalice and the Blade: Our History, Our Future.* San Francisco: Harper & Row, 1987.

Elder, John, and Hertha Wong, eds. *Family of the Earth and Sky: Indigenous Tales of Nature from Around the World.* Boston: Beacon, 1994.

Elvin, Mark, and Liu Ts'ui-Jung, eds. *Sediments of Time: Environment and Society in Chinese History.* Cambridge: Cambridge University Press, 1998.

Engel, J. Ronald, and Joan Gibb Engel, eds. *Ethics of Environment and Development: Global Challenge, International Response.* Tucson: University of Arizona Press, 1990.

Engel, J. Ronald, Peter Bakken, and Joan Gibb Engel. *Ecology, Justice, and Christian Faith: A Guide to the Literature, 1960–1993.* Westport, Calif.: Greenwood, 1994.

Foltz, Richard. *Green Muslims: Environmentalism in the Contemporary Islamic World.* Albany: State University of New York Press, 2003.

Fowler, Robert Booth. *The Greening of Protestant Thought.* Chapel Hill, N.C.: University of North Carolina Press, 1995.

Gilkey, Langdon Brown. *Nature, Reality, and the Sacred: the Nexus of Science and Religion.* Minneapolis: Fortress Press, 1993.

Gimbutas, Marija. *The Gods and Goddesses of Old Europe, 7000 to 3500 B.C.: Myths, Legends, and Cult Images.* Berkeley, Calif.: University of California Press, 1974.

Girardot, Norman J., James Miller, and Liu Xiaogan, eds. *Daoism and Ecology: Ways Within A Cosmic Landscape.* Cambridge, Mass.: Harvard University Center for the Study of World Religions/Harvard University Press, 2001.

Goldsmith, Edward. *The Way: An Ecological World-view.* Boston: Shambhala, 1993.

Gottlieb, Roger S. *Joining Hands: Politics and Religion Together for Social Change,* Cambridge, Mass.: Westview, 2002.

Gottlieb, Roger S. *A Spirituality of Resistance: Finding a Peaceful Heart and Protecting the Earth.* New York: Crossroads, 1999.

Gottlieb, Roger S. "Deep Ecology and the Left: An Effort at Reconciliation," and "Reply to Critics." *Capitalism, Nature, Socialism* 6, no. 3 (1995): 1–20, 40–4.

Granberg-Michaelson, Wesley. *Redeeming the Creation: the Rio Earth Summit: Challenges for the Churches.* Geneva: WCC Publications, 1992.

Griffin, David Ray, ed. *The Reenchantment of Science: Postmodern Proposals.* Albany: State University of New York Press, 1988.

Griffin, David Ray. *God and Religion in the Postmodern World.* Albany: State University of New York Press, 1989.

Griffin, Susan. *Made from This Earth.* New York: Harper & Row, 1982.

Grim, John A., ed. *Indigenous Traditions and Ecology: The Interbeing of Cosmology and Community.* Cambridge, Mass.: Harvard University Center for the Study of World Religions/Harvard University Press, 2001.

Grinde, Donald A., Jr., and Bruce E. Johansen. *Ecocide of Native America: Environmental Destruction of Indian Lands and Peoples.* Santa Fe, N.M.: Clear Light, 1995.

Grumbine, Edward. *Ghost Bears: Exploring the Biodiversity Crisis.* Washington, D.C.: Island Press, 1992.

Guha, Ramachandra. *The Unquiet Woods: Ecological Change and Peasant Resistance in the Himalaya.* Berkeley: University of California Press, 1989.

Gustafson, James M. *A Sense of the Divine: The Natural Environment from a Theocentric Perspective.* Cleveland, Ohio: Pilgrim Press, 1994.

Habel, Norman C. *The Land is Mine: Six Biblical Land Ideologies.* Minneapolis: Fortress, 1995.

Haleem, Harfiya Abdel, ed. *Islam and the Environment.* London: Ta-Ha Publishers, 1998.

Hall, Douglas John. *Imaging God: Dominion as Stewardship.* Grand Rapids, Mich.: Eerdmans.

Hargrove, Eugene C., ed. *Religion and Environmental Crisis.* Athens: University of Georgia Press, 1986.

Harrison, Paul. *The Greening of Africa.* London: Penguin, 1987.

Hendry, George S. *Theology of Nature.* Philadelphia: Westminster, 1980.

Hessel, Dieter T. *After Nature's Revolt: Eco-justice and Theology.* Minneapolis: Fortress, 1992.

Hessel, Dieter T. and Rosemary Radford Ruether, eds. *Christianity and Ecology: Seeking the Well-being of Earth and Humans.* Cambridge, Mass.: Harvard University Center for the Study of World Religions/Harvard University Press, 2000.

Hill, Brennan R. *Christian Faith and the Environment: Making Vital Connections.* Maryknoll, N.Y.: Orbis, 1998.

Hoogstraten, Hans-Dirk Van. *Deep Economy: Caring for Ecology, Humanity, and Theology.* Atlantic Highlands, N.J.: Humanities Press, 1997.

Hughes, J. Donald. *American Indian Ecology.* El Paso: Texas Western Press, 1983.

Hull, Fritz, ed. *Earth and Spirit: The Spiritual Dimension of the Environmental Crisis.* New York: Crossroads, 1993.

Inter Press Service. *Story Earth: Native Voices on the Environment.* San Francisco: Mercury House, 1993.

International Union for the Conservation of Nature (IUCN-Pakistan. *The Pakistan National Conservation Strategy.* Karachi: IUCN, 1992.

Ip Po-Keung. "Taoism and the Foundation of Environmental Ethics." *Environmental Ethics* 8 (1986): 335–43.

Izzi Deen, Mawil Y. *The Environmental Dimensions of Islam.* Cambridge: Lutterworth, 2000.

Jackson, Wes. *New Roots for Agriculture.* Lincoln: University of Nebraska Press, 1985.

Johnson, Elizabeth A. *Women, Earth and Creator Spirit.* New York: Paulist Press, 1993.

Jones, Ken. *Beyond Optimism: A Buddhist Political Ecology.* Oxford: Jon Carpenter, 1993.

Jung, Shannon. *We are Home: A Spirituality of the Environment.* New York: Paulist Press, 1993.

Kalechofsky, Roberta, ed. *Rabbis and Vegetarianism: An Evolving Tradition.* Marblehead, Mass.: Micah, 1995.

Katz, Eric. "Nature's Healing Power, the Holocaust, and the Environmental Crisis." *Judaism* 46, no. 1 (1997): 79–89.

Kaza, Stephanie, and Kenneth Kraft, eds. *Dharma Rain: Sources of Buddhist Environmentalism.* Boston: Shambhala, 2000.

Khalid, Fazlun, and Joanne O'Brien, eds. *Islam and Ecology.* New York: Cassell, 1992.

Khoshoo, T. N. "Gandhian Environmentalism." In *Ethical Perspectives on Environmental Issues in India,* ed. George A. James, 241–82. New Delhi: A. P. H., 1999.

King, Paul G., and David O. Woodyard. *Liberating Nature.* Cleveland, Ohio: Pilgrim Press, 1999.

Kinsley, David R. *Ecology and Religion: Ecological Spirituality in Cross-Cultural Perspective.* Englewood Cliffs, N.J.: Prentice-Hall, 1995.

Lane, Belden C. *The Solace of Fierce Landscapes: Exploring Desert and Mountain Spirituality.* New York: Oxford University Press, 1998.

Linzey, Andrew, and Dorothy Yamamoto, eds. *Animals on the Agenda: Questions about Animals for Theology and Ethics.* Urbana: University of Illinois Press, 1998.

Linzey, Andrew, and Tom Regan, eds. *Animals and Christianity: A Book of Readings.* New York: Crossroad, 1988.

Lovelock, James. *The Ages of Gaia: A Biography of Our Living Earth.* New York: Norton, 1988.

Macy, Joanna. *World as Lover, World as Self.* Berkeley, Calif.: Parallax, 1991.

Macy, Joanna, and Molly Young Brown. *Coming Back to Life: Practices to Reconnect Our Lives, Our World.* Gabriola Island, B.C.: New Society Publishers, 1998.

Maguire, Daniel C., and Larry L. Rasmussen. *Ethics for a Small Planet: New Horizons on Population, Consumption, and Ecology.* SUNY Series in Religious Studies. Albany: State University of New York Press, 1998.

Major, John S. *Heaven and Earth in Early Han Thought.* Albany: State University of New York Press, 1993.

Mander, Jerry. *In the Absence of the Sacred: The Failure of Technology and the Survival of the Indian Nations.* San Francisco: Sierra Club Books, 1991.

Maybury-Lewis, David. *Indigenous Peoples, Ethnic Groups, and the State.* Boston: Allyn and Bacon, 1997.

McDaniel, Jay B. *With Roots and Wings: Christianity in an Age of Ecology and Dialogue.* Maryknoll, N.Y.: Orbis, 1995.

McFague, Sallie. *Models of God: Theology for an Ecological, Nuclear Age.* Philadelphia: Fortress, 1987.

McGaa, Ed (Eagle Man). *Mother Earth Spirituality: Native American Paths to Healing Ourselves and Our World.* Toronto: Harper, 1990.

McKibben, Bill. *The Comforting Whirlwind: God, Job, and the Scale of Creation.* Grand Rapids, Mich.: Eerdmans, 1994.

McLuhan, T. C. *The Way of the Earth: Encounters with Nature in Ancient and Contemporary Thought.* New York: Simon and Schuster, 1994.

Mick, Lawrence E. *Liturgy and Ecology.* Collegeville, Minn.: Liturgical Press, 1997.

Moltmann, Jürgen. *God in Creation: A New Theology of Creation.* New York: Harper and Row, 1985.

Monet, Don, and Skanu'u (Ardythe Wilson). *Colonialism on Trial: Indigenous Land Rights and the Gitksan and Wet'suwet'en Sovereignty Case.* Philadelphia: New Society, 1992.

Muir, John. A *Thousand-Mile Walk to the Gulf.* Boston: Houghton Mifflin, 1916.

Murphy, Charles M. *At Home on Earth: Foundations for a Catholic Ethic of the Environment.* New York: Crossroads, 1989.

Narayan, Vasudha. "One Tree is Equal to Ten Sons: Hindu Responses to the Problems of Ecology, Population, and Consumption." *Journal of the American Academy of Religion* 65, no. 2 (January 1997): 291–332.

Nash, James A. *Loving Nature: Ecological Integrity and Christian Responsibility.* Nashville, Tenn.: Abingdon, 1991.

Nash, Roderick. *The Rights of Nature: A History of Environmental Philosophy.* Madison: University of Wisconsin Press, 1989.

Nasr, Seyyed Hossein. *Religion and the Order of Nature*. New York: Oxford University Press, 1996.

Neihardt, John G. *Black Elk Speaks: Being the Life Story of a Holy Man of the Oglala Sioux*. New York: Washington Square, 1972.

Nelson, Lance, ed. *Purifying the Earthly Body of God: Religion and Ecology in Hindu India*. Albany: State University of New York Press, 1998.

Nelson, Richard K. *Make Prayers to the Raven: A Koyukon View of the Northern Forest*. Chicago: University of Chicago Press, 1983.

Nollman, Jim. *Spiritual Ecology: A Guide to Reconnecting with Nature*. New York: Bantam, 1990.

Northcott, Michael S. *The Environment and Christian Ethics*. Cambridge: Cambridge University Press, 1996.

Oelschlaeger, Max. *Caring for Creation: An Ecumenical Approach to the Environmental Crisis*. New Haven: Yale University Press, 1994.

Palmer, Martin. "Saving China's Holy Mountains." *People and the Planet* 5, no. 1 (1996). http://www.oneworld.org/patp/vol5/feature.html

Peet, Richard, and Michael Watts. *Liberation Ecologies: Environment, Development, Social Movements*. New York: Routledge, 1996.

Plant, Judith, ed. *Healing the Wounds: The Promise of Ecofeminism*. Philadelphia: New Society, 1989.

Pope John Paul II. *Peace with God the Creator, Peace with All of Creation*. Vatican City: Libretto Editrice Vaticana, 1990.

Robb, Carol S., and Carl Casebolt. *Covenant for a New Creation: Ethics, Religion, and Public Policy*. Maryknoll, N.Y.: Orbis, 1991.

Roberts, Elizabeth, and Elias Amidon. *Earth Prayers from Around the World: 365 Prayers, Poems, and Invocations for Honoring the Earth*. San Francisco: HarperSanFrancisco, 1991.

Rockefeller, Steven C., and John C. Elder. *Spirit and Nature: Why the Environment is a Religious Issue*. Boston: Beacon, 1992.

Roszak, Theodore. *The Voice of the Earth: An Exploration of Ecopsychology*. New York: Simon and Schuster/Touchstone, 1992.

Ruether, Rosemary Radford. *Gaia and God: An Ecofeminist Theology of Earth Healing*. San Francisco: Harper, 1994.

Ruether, Rosemary Radford, ed. *Women Healing Earth: Third World Women on Ecology, Feminism, and Religion*. Maryknoll, N.Y.: Orbis, 1996.

Sandell, Klas, ed. *Buddhist Perspectives on the Ecocrisis*. Sri Lanka: Buddhist Publication Society, 1987.

Sardar, Ziauddin, ed. *An Early Crescent: The Future of Knowledge and the Environment in Islam*. London: Mansell, 1989.

Sasso, Sandy Eisenberg. *A Prayer for the Earth: The Story of Naamah, Noah's Wife*. Woodstock, Vt.: Jewish Lights, 1996.

Scharper, Stephen B., and Hilary Cunningham. *The Green Bible*. Maryknoll, N.Y.: Orbis, 1993.

Schumacher, E. F. *Small Is Beautiful*. New York: Harper and Row, 1973.

Shiva, Vandana. *Staying Alive: Women, Ecology and Development*. London: Zed, 1988.

Snyder, Gary. *Good. Wild. Sacred*. New York: Pantheon, 1984.

Sorrell, Roger. *St. Francis of Assisi and Nature: Tradition and Innovation in Western Christian Attitudes toward the Environment*. Oxford: Oxford University Press, 1988.

Spretnak, Charlene. *States of Grace: The Recovery of Meaning in the Postmodern Age.* San Francisco: Harper, 1991.

Spring, David, and Ellen Spring, eds. *Ecology and Religion in History.* New York: Harper Torchbooks, 1995.

Starhawk. *Dreaming the Dark.* Boston: Beacon, 1982.

Styles, John. *The Animal Creation: Its Claims on Our Humanity Stated and Enforced.* London: T. Ward, 1839. Reprint, Lewiston, N.Y.: E. Mellen, 1997.

Swan, James A. *Sacred Places in Nature.* Santa Fe, N.M.: Bear, 1990.

Taylor, Bron, *Ecological Resistance Movements.* Albany: SUNY Press, 1997.

Titmuss, Christopher. *The Green Buddha.* Devon, U.K.: Insights, 1995.

Tucker, Mary Evelyn, and John Berthrong, eds. *Confucianism and Ecology: The Interrelation of Heaven, Earth, and Humans.* Cambridge, Mass.: Harvard University Center for the Study of World Religions/Harvard University Press, 1998.

Tucker, Mary Evelyn, and John Grim, eds. *Worldviews and Ecology.* Maryknoll, N.Y.: Orbis, 1994.

Vecsey, Christopher, and Robert W. Venables, eds. *American Indian Environments: Ecological Issues in Native American History.* Syracuse, N.Y.: Syracuse University Press, 1992.

Ward, Churchill. *Struggle for Land: Indigenous Resistance to Genocide, Ecocide, and Expropriation in Contemporary North America.* Monroe, Me.: Common Courage, 1993.

Waskow, Arthur, ed. *Torah of the Earth.* Jewish Lights, 2000.

Wersal, Lisa. "Islam and Environmental Ethics: Tradition Responds to Contemporary Challenges." *Zygon* 30 (1995): 451–59.

Whitney, Elspeth, and Lynn White. "Ecotheology and History." *Environmental Ethics* 15 (Summer 1993): 151–69.

Wright, Nancy G., and Donald Kill. *Ecological Healing: A Christian Vision.* Maryknoll, N.Y.: Orbis, 1993.

Yaffe, Martin D. *Judaism and Environmental Ethics.* Lexington, 2001.

WEBSITES ON RELIGION AND THE ENVIRONMENT

The Internet is an invaluable resource for both research and action. A few clicks of the mouse will take you to statements by major religions and religious figures, whole essays and even books, comprehensive bibliographies, direct action campaigns, and accounts of political struggles throughout the world. Here are a few choice sites, which contain links to hundreds more. A large range of connections is also available through the websites of major environmental organizations and almost all of the major religious denominations.

1. Harvard Forum on Religion and Ecology: academic resources relating to all of world religions. http://www.environment.harvard.edu/religion

2. Encyclopedia of Religion and Nature: comprehensive connections to scholarship and research. http://www.religionandnature.com

3. National Religious Partnership on the Environment: action and local congregations oriented group with connections to American religions. www.nrpe.org/

4. The Indigenous Environmental Network: contains an enormous range of links to organizations, projects, and writings of indigenous peoples. http://www.ienearth.org/

5. The entire text of the enormous United Nations sponsored volume *Cultural and Spiritual Values of Biodiversity*. http://www.unep.org/Biodiversity/

6. Web of Creation: Institutional, educational and political connections largely oriented to American Christianity. www.webofcreation.org

7. Alliance for Religion and Conservation joined with the Worldwide Fund for Nature, an English partnership. http://www.wwf.org.uk

8. Cultural Survival, an organization dedicated to preserving native peoples throughout the world. http://www.culturalsurvival.org/newpage/index.cfm

9. Envirolink, connections on all issues of environmental concern: http://www.envirolink.org/

10. Planet Ark and the Environmental News Network, environmental news services: http://www.planetark.org/envpicstory.cfm/newsid/17550; http://www.enn.com/index.asp

ENVIRONMENTAL ORGANIZATIONS

AFRICAN AMERICAN ENVIRONMENTALIST ASSOCIATION
9903 Caltor Lane
Ft. Washington, MD 20744
AfricanAmericanEnvironmentalist@msn.com; http://communities.msn.com/AAEA

CENTER FOR HEALTH, ENVIRONMENT AND JUSTICE
P.O. Box 6806
Falls Church, VA 22040
703-237-2249
chej@chej.org; http://www.chej.org/

COALITION ON THE ENVIRONMENT AND JEWISH LIFE (COEJL)
443 Park Avenue South, 11th Floor
New York, NY 10016
212-684-6950, ext. 210
www.coejl.org

ENVIRONMENTAL DEFENSE
257 Park Avenue South
New York, NY 10010
212-505-2100; 212-505-2375
members@environmentaldefense.org
http://www.environmentaldefense.org

ENVIRONMENTAL JUSTICE RESOURCE CENTER AT CLARK ATLANTA UNIVERSITY
223 James P. Brawley Drive
Atlanta, GA 30314
404-880-6911
EJRC@CAU.edu; http://www.ejrc.cau.edu/

FRIENDS OF THE EARTH INTERNATIONAL
P.O. Box 19199
1000 GD
Amsterdam, Netherlands
31–20–6221369
foei@foei.org; http://www.foei.org

Greenpeace USA
1436 U St. NW
Washington, DC 20009
202-462-1777

The Greens/Green Party USA
POB 100
Blodgett Mills, NY 13738
607-756-4211
gpusa@igc.apc.org; http://www.greens.org/

National Audubon Society
700 Broadway
New York, NY 10003–9501
212-979-3000
http://www.audubon.org/

Natural Resources Defense Council
40 West 20th St.
New York, NY 110011
212/727–2700; nrdcinfo@nrdc.org; http://www.nrdc.org/

Sierra Club
730 Polk St.
San Francisco, CA 94109
415/776–2211
information@sierraclub.org; http://www.sierraclub.org/

ABOUT THE CONTRIBUTORS

Matsuo Basho (1644–1694) is known as the first great poet in the history of Japanese haikai and haiku.

David Barnhill is director of environmental studies at University of Wisconsin/Oshkosh and editor of *At Home on the Earth* and *Deep Ecology and World Religions*.

William Hazlitt wrote essays in the early 19th-century on literature, politics, and social life.

Henry David Thoreau, preeminent American 19th century naturalist and moral voice, is the author of *Walden* and "On Civil Disobedience."

Ralph Waldo Emerson was one of the most important essayists and public intellectuals of 19th-century America.

John Muir was a conservationist and writer who worked to save the Yosemite Valley in California.

Aldo Leopold was a conservationist, forester, writer, and teacher; organizer of the first designated wilderness area in the U.S.; and an intellectual inspiration of modern environmental ethics.

Luther Standing Bear was chief of the Oglala Lakota nation from 1905 to 1939. He wrote a classic account of Native American life, *Land of the Spotted Eagle*.

Robert Finch is an internationally known nature writer. His books include *Common Ground*, *Outlands*, and *The Norton Book of Nature Writing*.

Linda Hogan is a poet, essayist, and novelist whose books include *Solar Storms* and *Mean Spirit*.

Fanetorens (Ray Fadden) was a long-time teacher in Native American schools.

Joseph L. Henderson is an analytical psychologist and member of the C. G. Jung Institute of San Francisco.

Maud Oakes was an anthropologist and artist, author of *The Two Crosses of Todos Santos*.

Robert Pogue Harrison teaches literature at Stanford University and is the author of *The Body of Beatrice*.

Lao Tzu (6th cent. BCE) was a Chinese philosopher and spiritual teacher.

Louis Ginzberg was a leading Talmudic scholar of the early 20th century, and the author of the multivolume *The Legends of the Jews.*

Daniel Swartz is a rabbi and past Director of Congregational Relations for the Religious Action Center of Reform Judaism in Washington, D.C. He is currently Executive Director of the Children's Environmental Health Network.

Anna Peterson teaches environmental studies and religion at the University of Florida. She has written *Martyrdom and the Politics of Religion* and *Being Human: Ethics, Environment, and Our Place in the World.*

Michael Kioni Dudley teaches philosophy at Chaminade University in Hawaii and is a leading scholar of Hawaiian environmental thought. He wrote *Hawaiian Nation: Man, Gods, and Nature.*

Chatsumarn Kabilsingh is the chief Thai scholar of the Buddhist Perception of Nature project and teaches at Thammasat University in Bangkok. She has written *Study of Buddhist Nuns: Monastic Rules* and translated the *Lotus Sutra* into Thai.

Leslie E. Sponsel, professor of anthropology at University of Hawaii, has written widely on ecology, culture, and spiritual life, and edited *Endangered Peoples of Southeast and East Asia: Struggles to Survive and Thrive.*

Poranee Natadecha-Sponsel is assistant professor of religion at Chaminade University of Hawaii.

O. P. Dwivedi is professor of political studies at the University of Guelph, Canada, and has served as World Health Organization consultant to the Indian government. He is the coauthor of *Hindu Religion and the Environmental Crisis.*

Mawil Y. Izzi Deen (Samarrai) teaches at King Abdul Aziz University, Jeddah, Saudi Arabia, and is co-author of *Islamic Principles of the Conservation of the Natural Environment.*

Richard B. Peterson teaches environmental studies at the University of New England and wrote *Conversations in the Rainforest: Culture, Values, and the Environment in Central Africa.*

Stan McKay, a Cree, served as moderator for the United Church of Canada and directed the Dr. Jessie Saultreax Resource Centre, a training center for Native ministries.

Patrick Segundad is a member of the Kadazan community of Malaysia.

Lea Bill-Rippling Water Woman is a Native American activist and healer.

Lynn White was a medieval historian who taught at Princeton, Stanford, and University of California at Los Angeles.

Pope John Paul II is the leader of the Roman Catholic Church.

American Baptist Churches USA can be reached at http://www.abc-usa.org/.

Evangelical Lutheran Church in America can be reached at http://www.elca.org/.

Evangelical Environmental Network can be reached at http://www.creationcare.org.

Ecumenical Patriarch Bartholomew is the formal leader of Eastern Orthodox Christianity.

John F. Haught is a Catholic scholar who has written *The Cosmic Adventure* and *Minding the Time*.

John B. Cobb, Jr., professor emeritus at Claremont, has pioneered the field of ecotheology. His books include *Reclaiming the Church*, *Transforming Christianity and the World*, and *Postmodernism and Public Policy*.

Sallie McFague is professor of theology at Vanderbilt Divinity School. Her books include *Models of God* and *Metaphorical Theology*.

Arthur Waskow is director of the Philadelphia-based Shalom Center, an international network that brings Jewish thought and action to bear on protecting and healing the earth. He wrote *Seasons of Our Joy* and *Down to Earth Judaism*.

Theodore Walker, Jr., teaches ethics at Perkins School of Theology, Southern Methodist University, and is the author of *Empower the People: Social Ethics for the African-American Church*.

Nawal H. Ammar is associate dean of Kent State University, and widely published on women's rights, Islam, Middle Eastern politics, and ecology.

Christopher Key Chapple, professor of theology at Loyola Marymount University in Los Angeles, wrote *Of Karma and Creativity* and *Nonviolence to Animals, Earth, and Self in Asian Traditions*.

Tu Weiming, professor of Chinese history and philosophy at Harvard University, is the author of *NeoConfucian Thought in Action*, and *Way, Learning and Politics*.

Stephanie Kaza, professor of environmental studies at the University of Vermont, is the author of *The Attentive Heart: Conversations with Trees*, and co-editor of *Dharma Rain*.

Gary A. Kowalski has served as a Unitarian minister and has written widely on behalf of animal rights.

Andrew Linzey teaches theology and animal rights at Oxford University. His books include *Animal Rights*, *Christianity and the Rights of Animals*, and *Political Theory and Animal Rights*.

Roger S. Gottlieb, professor of philosophy of Worcester Polytechnic Institute, has written *A Spirituality of Resistance, Joining Hands: Politics and Religion Together for Social Change,* and edited *Liberating Faith: Religious Voices for Peace, Justice and Ecological Wisdom.*

Rosemary Radford Ruether has been a leading voice in feminist religious theory for two decades. Her earlier books include *Sexism and God-Talk* and *Women-Church.*

Ivone Gebara, one of Latin America's leading theologians, is a Brazilian Sister of Our Lady. She has written *Mary: Mother of God, Mother of the Poor,* and *Trinity.*

Shamara Shantu Riley is a political activist and scholar.

Karen Baker-Fletcher teaches at Southern Methodist University and has written *Sisters of Dust, Sisters of Spirit: A Creation-Centered Womanist Spirituality.*

Irene Diamond teaches political science at University of Oregon and has written *Fertile Ground* and co-edited the groundbreaking *Reweaving the World: The Emergence of Ecofeminism.*

David Seidenberg is an ordained rabbi and a peace and justice activist in the Seattle area.

Riane Eisler is a scholar, futurist, and activist, and is co-director of the Center for Partnership Studies in Pacific Grove, California. Her books include *Sacred Pleasure: Sex, Myth and the Politics of the Body.*

Brooke Medicine Eagle was brought up on the Crow Reservation in Montana and combines training in the Northern Plains Indian medicine path and Western ways of healing. She is the author of *Buffalo Woman Comes Singing* and *The Last Ghost Dance.*

Vandana Shiva, a leading critic of globalization and genetic engineering, directs the Research Foundation for Science, Technology, and Natural Resource (Dehradun, India) and is the author of *Staying Alive* and *Monocultures of the Mind.*

Edna St. Vincent Millay was a major American poet.

David Abram is a philosopher, writer, naturalist, and sleight-of-hand magician. He wrote *The Spell of the Sensuous: Language and Perception in a More-than-Human World.*

Thomas Berry is a widely read ecotheologian, founder of the Riverdale Center for Earth Studies in New York, author of *The Dream of the Earth,* and co-author of *The Universe Story.*

Joanna Macy teaches at the California Institute of Integral Studies and leads workshops worldwide on peace and environmental issues. Her books include *Despair and Personal Power in the Nuclear Age* and *Coming Back to Life.*

Paul Shepard taught human ecology at the Claremont Colleges. His groundbreaking works include *Nature and Madness* and *The Tender Carnivore and the Sacred Game*.

Dee Smith is a Native American writer and activist.

Thich Nhat Hanh chaired the Vietnamese Buddhist Peace delegation in Paris during the Vietnam War. The author of numerous books, including *Being Peace* and *The Miracle of Mindfulness,* he heads a spiritual community in southern France and has been a leading voice in socially engaged Buddhism.

Ellen Bernstein was the founder and director of Shomrei Adamah (Guardians of the Earth) and edited *Ecology and the Jewish Spirit*.

Dan Fink is a rabbi and leading Jewish environmental educator. He co-authored *Judaism and Ecology*.

Black Elk was a spiritual leader of the Oglala Sioux.

National Council of Churches can be reached at www.ncc-usa.org.

John Seed is director of the Rainforest Information Centre, Australia, and has worked to protect rainforests throughout the world.

Pat Fleming has worked as a psychologist, social worker, and teacher in the areas of peace, environment, and feminist politics.

Marina Lachecki is an environmental educator living in Wisconsin, whose books include *Teaching Kids To Love the Earth* and *More Teaching Kids To Love the Earth*.

Mark I. Wallace teaches religion at Swarthmore College and wrote *Fragments of the Spirit: Nature, Violence and the Renewal of Creation*.

Sarah McFarland Taylor teaches religious studies at Northwestern University and is the author of the forthcoming *Green Sisters: Answering the Call of the Earth*.

Catherine Ingram's journalism focuses on mediation and psychology, and their links with social activism, particularly in the areas of human rights and refugees.

Seth Zuckerman is a writer and journalist whose work focuses on the rainforest region of the Pacific Coast from the redwood groves of northern California to the shores of south coastal Alaska.

Evelyn Martin has served as a fellow at the Center for Respect for Life and the Environment, Washington, D.C.

Bruce Byers is a biologist and sustainability consultant. He is writing a book about his work in Africa.

Ernst Conradie teaches Christian studies at the University of the Western Cape, South Africa, and has written *Hope for the Earth: Vistas on a New Century*.

Charity Majiza is General Secretary of the South African Council of Churches, Johannesburg.

Jim Cochrane is Director of the Research Institute on Christianity in South Africa and Professor of Religious Studies, University of Cape Town, Rondebosch.

Welile T. Sigabi is Director of the Moiplaas Methodist Training Centre in South Africa.

Victor Molobi is a member of the Faith and Earthkeeping Project, Research Institute of Theology and Religion, University of South Africa.

David Field teaches Christian Ethics and theology at Africa University, Mutare, Zimbabwe, and coordinates the Research Institute on Christianity in South Africa's Ecological Project.

B. D. Sharma is a leading Indian thinker in the area of sustainable development, and an activist in defense of the rights of indigenous peoples. He edited *Indian Wildlife* and *Himalaya*.

Mary John Mananzan is a missionary Benedictine sister and President of St. Scholastica's College, Manila. She has written *Challenges to the Inner Room*, and *Woman Question in the Philippines*.

William F. Fisher teaches anthropology and social studies at Clark University. He wrote *Fluid Boundaries: Forming and Transforming Identity in Central Nepal* and edited *Towards Sustainable Development?*

The United Church of Christ can be reached at http://www.ucc.org/justice/environment. htm.

Jonna Higgins-Freese is Environmental Outreach Coordinator at Prairiewoods Franciscan Spirituality Center in Hiawatha, Iowa, and a fellow of the Environmental Leadership Program.

Jeff Tomhave is an enrolled member of the Three Affiliated Tribes in North Dakota and the founder of Effective Self Determination Solutions, an organization that trains Native American people to be their own advocates; and a fellow of the Environmental Leadership Program.

Coordinadora de Defensa del Agua y de la Vida (Coalition in Defense of Water and Life) originated in response to the destructive privatization of water resources in the city of Cochabamba, Bolivia.

Melody Ermachild Chavis is a writer and activist whose books include *Altars in the Street.*

North Carolina Chapter of the Interfaith Global Climate Change Campaign can be reached via Sister Evelyn Mattern, North Carolina Council of Churches, 1307 Glenwood Ave., Suite 162, Raleigh, NC 27605; 919-828-6501, email: EMattern@nccouncilofchurches.org.

The First National People of Color Environmental Leadership Summit was a historic 1991 meeting of more than 1,000 national and international environmental activists in Washington, D.C. It helped create the environmental justice movement.

The Summit on Environment was a 1991 meeting involving the heads of many religious denominations and faith groups.

Joint Appeal by Religion and Science for the Environment was issued by 150 religious leaders and scientists who gathered for the Mission to Washington in May 1992.

United States Catholic Conference can be reached at http://www.usccb.org/.